THE RICHARD DYER READER

THE RICHARD DYER READER

Edited by
Glyn Davis and Jaap Kooijman

THE BRITISH FILM INSTITUTE
Bloomsbury Publishing Plc
50 Bedford Square, London, WC1B 3DP, UK
1385 Broadway, New York, NY 10018, USA
29 Earlsfort Terrace, Dublin 2, Ireland

BLOOMSBURY is a trademark of Bloomsbury Publishing Plc

First published in Great Britain 2023 by Bloomsbury
on behalf of the
British Film Institute
21 Stephen Street, London W1T 1LN
www.bfi.org.uk

The BFI is the lead organisation for film in the UK and the distributor of Lottery funds for film. Our mission is to ensure that film is central to our cultural life, in particular by supporting and nurturing the next generation of filmmakers and audiences. We serve a public role which covers the cultural, creative and economic aspects of film in the UK.

Copyright © Richard Dyer, Glyn Davis and Jaap Kooijman, 2023

Richard Dyer, Glyn Davis and Jaap Kooijman have asserted their right under the Copyright, Design and Patents Act, 1988, to be identified as authors of this work.

Cover design by Louise Dugdale
Cover image: *On the Town* (1949), Mary Evans/AF Archive

All rights reserved. No part of this publication may be reproduced or transmitted in any form or by any means, electronic or mechanical, including photocopying, recording, or any information storage or retrieval system, without prior permission in writing from the publishers.

Bloomsbury Publishing Plc does not have any control over, or responsibility for, any third-party websites referred to or in this book. All internet addresses given in this book were correct at the time of going to press. The author and publisher regret any inconvenience caused if addresses have changed or sites have ceased to exist, but can accept no responsibility for any such changes.

A catalogue record for this book is available from the British Library.
A catalog record for this book is available from the Library of Congress.

ISBN: HB: 978-1-8390-2317-0
       PB: 978-1-8390-2316-3
       ePDF: 978-1-8390-2319-4
       eBook: 978-1-8390-2318-7

Designed and project managed by Ketchup/Tom Cabot
Printed and bound in India

To find out more about our authors and books visit www.bloomsbury.com and sign up for our newsletters.

Contents

Introduction
Glyn Davis and Jaap Kooijman ... 1

SECTION 1: *A STAR IS BORN*
and other essays on stardom and image ... 17

1. *A Star is Born* and the construction of authenticity (1981) ... 25
2. The meaning of Tom Jones (1971) ... 37
3. Gene Kelly (1972) ... 47
4. Jane Fonda (1979) ... 51
5. The way she is (1981) ... 55
6. Diana Ross (1982) ... 58
7. Never too thin (1993) ... 62
8. Charles Hawtrey (1994) ... 65
9. Between parturition and manufacture (2018) ... 72

SECTION 2: IN DEFENCE OF DISCO
and other essays on entertainment and ideology ... 79

10. In defence of disco (1979) ... 87
11. Views of *Nationwide* go wide (1980) ... 97
12. *Coronation Street* (1981) ... 99
13. Tea and cocoa tele (1982) ... 105
14. Bad for a laugh (1982) ... 107
15. Taking popular television seriously (1985) ... 110
16. The colour of entertainment (1995) ... 116
17. *Jurassic World* and procreation anxiety (2015) ... 125

SECTION 3: GETTING OVER THE RAINBOW
and other essays on gay liberation — **133**

18	Getting over the rainbow: identity and pleasure in gay cultural politics (1981)	141
19	Notes on gays and class (1976)	154
20	Pasolini and homosexuality (1977)	158
21	*Taxi zum Klo* (1982)	166
22	Vito Russo, *The Celluloid Closet: Homosexuality in the Movies* (1983)	169
23	Rock: the last guy you'd have figured? (1985)	178
24	Nice young men who sell antiques: gay men in heritage cinema (2001)	188
25	The idea of a gay icon (2009)	196

SECTION 4: WHITE
and other essays on representation and visibility — **209**

26	White (1988)	216
27	Jean-Jacques Rousseau and the right to love oneself (1968)	240
28	The role of stereotypes (1979)	244
29	Of rage and despair (1981)	251
30	Don't look now: the instabilities of the male pin-up (1982)	254
31	Heterosexuality (1997)	267
32	Is the camera racist? (1997)	279
33	White enough (2013)	282
34	The president's hair (2018)	293

SECTION 5: COMING TO TERMS
and other essays on bodies and affect — **297**

35	Male gay porn: coming to terms (1985)	304
36	*Scorpio Rising* (1981)	316
37	Why dance? (1981)	320
38	Old briefs for new (1989)	328
39	Dracula and desire (1993)	332
40	Idol thoughts: orgasm and self-reflexivity in gay pornography (1994)	340
41	ACTION! (1994)	354
42	The same over and over (2015)	360
43	Fond of little tunes: the sissiness of music in *Rope* and *Tea and Sympathy* (2023)	370

SECTION 6: THE PERSISTENCE OF TEXTUAL ANALYSIS
and other essays on form and meaning   **393**

44   The persistence of textual analysis (2023)   400
45   The television situation (1973)   412
46   *The Towering Inferno* (1975)   423
47   Notes on textual analysis (1981)   429
48   The space of happiness in the musical (1998)   436
49   Sound in *Seven* (1999)   448
50   The talented Mr Rota (2004)   455
51   *Far from Heaven* (2007)   462
52   Going Italian (2011)   470
53   Eisenstein's penis (2023)   476

SECTION 7: MASCULINITY IS SO *BORING*
and other conversations with Richard Dyer   **483**

54   Masculinity is so *boring* (1985)
     (with Joe McElhaney)   490
55   To be reel (1997)
     (with Matthew Rettenmund)   508
56   Pleasure | obvious | queer (2016)
     (with Catherine Grant and Jaap Kooijman)   516
57   Writing out of love or politics (2023)
     (with Glyn Davis and Jaap Kooijman)   527

Index   **541**

Richard Dyer holding a portrait of the German director Wieland Speck; photographed by Erwin Olaf at the 1986 International Gay and Lesbian Film Festival in Amsterdam. (Courtesy of Studio Erwin Olaf and Collection IAV-Atria)

INTRODUCTION TO
THE RICHARD DYER READER

Glyn Davis and Jaap Kooijman

In December 1986, Richard Dyer was arrested. He was attempting to get back into the United Kingdom after attending the International Gay and Lesbian Film Festival in Amsterdam. Dyer had been an invited speaker at the event, where he had given talks on Judy Garland and Rock Hudson, on underground cinema, and on pornography. The last of these was based on his essay 'Coming to terms' (see Section 5), and he had taken some pornographic materials with him to use as illustration. Returning from Amsterdam, he was stopped and searched for drugs; the customs officers found the porn. Dyer cooperatively admitted to having more such materials at home, which led to the officers searching Dyer's entire house. They confiscated all of his videos and a number of pornographic magazines; he was formally arrested on a charge of importing obscene materials. As he told Simon Shepherd and Mick Wallis the following year:

> I did eventually get everything back (apart from the tape I'd 'imported') after a lawyer had written to say they had no right to take it. I won on the grounds that the material had been legally obtained in Britain. I didn't fight to get the remaining tape back, partly because it's so easy to replace, but also because I couldn't be sure of the political support I would get, since the Left and feminists are divided on the issue.[1]

Dyer candidly relates this anecdote in a manner that combines the personal, the political, and the academic. Having delivered a public but scholarly talk on pornography, he subsequently found himself subject to personal and invasive scrutiny for owning copies of the material he had discussed; whilst under threat of legal action, he remained sensitive to wider debates and attitudes towards porn from various political groups.

---

1. Richard Dyer, 'A conversation on pornography', in Simon Shepherd and Mick Wallis (eds.), *Coming on Strong: Gay Politics and Culture*, London: Unwin Hyman, 1989, pp. 211–212.

The personal, the political, and the academic regularly combine in Dyer's writings and talks, sometimes in unexpected admixtures, always in ways that provide insight. *The Richard Dyer Reader* attempts to pay attention to all three facets, in isolation and in combination, by providing a substantive introduction to his output over a span of more than five decades. The direct title of the Reader recognises that these elements combine in one person and their work. The synthesis of these three distinct factors was acknowledged in an epistolary essay by Amy Villarejo, in which she articulated the multiple voices of Dyer's writing – its scholarly sources and inspirations; its queer sex-positive politics; and its democratic, reader-friendly accessibility:

> From Raymond Williams, Richard derives big-picture clarity about the role of culture and thought. From queer experience, or what he charmingly describes as the multiple experiences of queeritude, he offers a keen sense of the performative nature of identity [...], never diminishing the presence and pleasures of hanky-panky and eroticism, and never abandoning the complexity and delights of queer style. From a commitment to liveliness and readability, Richard delivers a prose that balances, entices, and specifies, all the while seeking to discover, with humility and wit [...], what matters and how.[2]

Dyer has used this composite voice and worldview to forge and present vital, groundbreaking contributions to a number of fields: cultural studies, film and television studies, lesbian and gay studies, whiteness studies. In the 1970s and 1980s, as he established his career and profile, he made key contributions to – and thus helped to shape – all of these nascent disciplines. He often did this in contrast to emerging orthodoxies. For instance, as Andy Medhurst has noted, Dyer's writing did not square with the dominant tone and approach of the then-leading academic film journal *Screen*: 'He liked Hollywood, he told jokes, he blasphemously neglected *La Grande Syntagmatique* in favour of Lana Turner's frocks.'[3] And yet Dyer's work has been published in an extraordinarily diverse array of publications (including *Screen*): radical pamphlets, newspapers and magazines, educational resources, festival programmes, conference proceedings, academic journals and edited collections… This Reader samples from across these many types of material, mingling canonical with lesser-known pieces of work, sustained explorations of topics with shorter interventions.

Born in Leeds in 1945 but raised in Beckenham (now part of Greater London), Dyer was sent away to boarding school where he was, as he told Dario Llinares, 'a lower-middle-class boy in a second-rate upper-class school.'[4] His experiences at

---

2. Amy Villarejo, 'The Gay and the Rad', *Cinema Journal* 57:2 (Winter 2018), p. 162.
3. Andy Medhurst, 'Queer feelings [review of *Only Entertainment*]', *Sight and Sound* 3:3 (March 1993), p. 35.
4. Dario Llinares and Neil Fox, The Cinematologists podcast, 'Episode 43: Professor Richard Dyer', 6 April 2017, http://www.cinematologists.com/podcastarchive/2017/4/6/episode-43-professor-richard-dyer

the school fostered a sense of class awareness that would subsequently permeate his writing. In 1968, Dyer graduated from the University of St Andrews with an MA in French; the earliest essay to feature in *The Richard Dyer Reader*, on Jean-Jacques Rousseau (see Section 4), was published while he was still a student. Following graduation, he spent a year exploring different opportunities. During the summer of 1968, Dyer lived in Paris where he was employed as an English teacher at a mental health institution. Back in the UK, he worked in theatre, first as the assistant to Laverne Meyer of the Northern Dance Theatre in Manchester, then to Julian Oldfield, the director of the newly-opened Gateway Theatre in Chester. When asked to direct Noël Coward's *South Sea Bubble*, a play he found too reactionary, Dyer left to live in London, where he worked at the gay coffee bar As You Like It on Monmouth Street. The bar was across the street from the Soul City record store, where Dyer could find the latest soul and Motown releases.[5]

During this peripatetic year, Dyer was awarded a grant to study for his PhD at the University of Birmingham's Centre for Contemporary Cultural Studies (CCCS).[6] Although he initially planned to write about gay literature, Dyer shifted his focus to popular forms of entertainment. The impact of the CCCS on Dyer's subsequent thought and writing is substantive; he forged lasting allegiances and friendships with his thesis supervisor Stuart Hall and fellow students including Rosalind Brunt. The students at the Centre undertook 'collective work' together; in 1969–70, this involved reading texts on structuralism (Dyer wrote a paper on Saussure) and a sustained cross-media study of the Western (Dyer wrote about *Once Upon a Time in the West*); in 1970–71, it involved working through a substantial body of theoretical material for consideration for a *Reader in Cultural Studies* (Dyer authored a piece on Sartre's 'Problem of method'); in 1971–72, the focus was on Karl Marx's work. Dyer contributed an essay on singer Tom Jones to the first issue of the CCCS journal, *Working Papers in Cultural Studies* (included in this Reader in abridged form; see Section 1). He completed his thesis promptly; as Rosalind Brunt remembered, 'Someone like Richard Dyer had the discipline to go away and complete his PhD in three years. But that was very unusual – there was always the pull of the collective work.'[7]

---

5. Some of the biographical details in this chapter are taken from different interviews with Richard Dyer, including: Kieran Connell, 'Transcript: CCCS interview Richard Dyer,' 12 August 2013; Jaime Valentine, interview with Richard Dyer for *OurStory Scotland*, 16 April 2014; Barbara Klinger, 'Fieldnotes: Richard Dyer interviewed by Barbara Klinger', Society for Cinema and Media Studies, 13 April 2015, https://vimeo.com/145394630.
6. On the CCCS, see: Kieran Connell and Matthew Hilton, 'The working practices of Birmingham's Centre for Contemporary Cultural Studies,' *Social History* 40:3 (2015), pp. 287–311.
7. Christopher Pawling and Rosalind Brunt, 'Christopher Pawling and Rosalind Brunt Interview', *Cultural Studies* 27:5 (2013), p. 708.

CCCS meeting, circa 1971. Top: Alan Shuttleworth, Stuart Hall, Richard Hoggart. Bottom: Rachel Powell, Richard Dyer, Anne Patchett. (Courtesy of Trevor Millum)

Dyer was approached by Fontana to turn his PhD into a 'reader-friendly' book. The manuscript he produced – called *That's Entertainment!* – included (amongst other topics) explorations of the idea of entertainment, escape and escapism, and the pervasiveness of conservative ideologies. One chapter had the tantalising title 'Motown, Martini and Massacres: The Boundaries of Entertainment'. However, the manuscript was rejected by the publisher, and Dyer shelved it. As he told us in a recent interview (see Section 7), 'they said, "Oh, it's too popular, it's not academic enough." […] I should have tried somewhere else, but I didn't.' Related material did make it into Dyer's first monograph, on *Light Entertainment*, published by the British Film Institute (BFI) in 1973. This short book marked the beginning of a long-standing relationship with the BFI and its associated cinema, the National Film Theatre (NFT; renamed BFI Southbank in 2007), and in particular with the BFI's education department. In 1974, Dyer was awarded one of three BFI-funded three-year lectureships at universities

INTRODUCTION

CCCS meeting, circa 1971; Alan Shuttleworth, Richard Dyer, Anne Patchett, and unidentified person. (Courtesy of Trevor Millum and Cadbury Research Library: Special Collections, University of Birmingham, USS138)

in England; he was appointed to a position at Keele University, where his time was divided equally between teaching American Studies and adult education classes.[8] (The other two lectureships were awarded to Robin Wood and Peter Wollen, for positions at the University of Warwick and the University of Essex, respectively.) In 1977, Dyer programmed the groundbreaking 'Images of Homosexuality' season of films for the NFT, also editing the short book, *Gays and Film*, that accompanied the season (he worked on other seasons for the cinema, including a survey of Jacqueline Audry's films co-curated with Elaine Burrows). Reviewing 'Images of Homosexuality' in the short-lived journal *Gay Left*, the filmmakers Paul Hallam and Ron Peck called it 'a pioneering season that introduced a lot of scarcely-known films and reintroduced others that were out of circulation.'[9] In the late 1970s and early 1980s, Dyer attended BFI summer schools; he contributed to the production of educational materials for

---

8. For detail on Dyer's time at Keele, see Richard Dyer, 'Film Studies at Keele', *Screen Education* 19 (Summer 1976), pp. 54–57.
9. Paul Hallam and Ron Peck, 'Images of Homosexuality: Notes on the National Film Theatre Season of Gay Films, July 1977', *Gay Left* 5 (Winter 1977), p. 20.

teachers, college tutors, and university lecturers – including teaching packs on stars, and on the dumb blonde stereotype. The BFI has published a significant number of Dyer's books: *Light Entertainment*, *Stars* (1979), the co-authored *Coronation Street* (1981), *Heavenly Bodies* (1986), three BFI Classics (1993; 1999; 2002), *Nino Rota* (2010), and *Lethal Repetition* (2015). This Reader swiftly – and appropriately – found a home at BFI publishing.

During the years of his studies at the CCCS and working at Keele, Dyer was resident in Birmingham; he would return there in the late 1970s, after a brief period of living in London, when he was appointed to a position at the University of Warwick. In Birmingham, Dyer became involved with gay liberation activism. He was a member of the Gay Action Group; amongst other activities, they leafleted screenings of *Sunday, Bloody Sunday*, provoking audiences to reflect critically on their responses to the film. Dyer was involved in co-authoring a gay sex education pamphlet (*Growing Up Homosexual*), and in outreach work with colleges. He wrote a critique of *The Killing of Sister George* for *Gladrag*, the newsletter of the Birmingham Gay Liberation Front. Dyer joined the Gay Left Collective in the second half of the 1970s, and wrote several pieces for their journal; through the Collective he met Ron Peck, who auditioned Dyer for the lead role in his film *Nighthawks* (about a gay teacher in London who spends his evenings cruising bars and clubs). Dyer was offered the role, but couldn't take it up.[10] His gay-affirmative activism included a body-positive dimension: he took part in nude photoshoots for the British magazine *Jeremy* and the Canadian *Attitude + Plus*. Over the decades, he has contributed essays to various gay/queer periodicals: the British *Playguy*, *The Body Politic*, *Attitude*.

Across the 1970s, Dyer's politics – feminist, Marxist, anti-racist – solidified. At the CCCS, he first encountered feminist thought; as he told Stefanie Leinfellner in 2018, he 'felt an immediate affinity for it and an immediate feeling of its importance', and took away an understanding that '[e]verything I do must be informed by the issues raised by feminism.'[11] His engagement with Marxism and socialist politics – fomented at St Andrews, stoked at the CCCS – became a lifelong preoccupation and influence. The Gay Left Collective was a socialist group; the first issue of its journal opened with a group statement that highlighted its aims 'to contribute towards a Marxist analysis of homosexual oppression', and 'to encourage in the gay movement an understanding of the links between the struggle against sexual oppression and the struggle for

---

[10]. See: Glyn Davis, '"A panorama of gay life": *Nighthawks* and British queer cinema of the 1970s', in Ron Gregg and Amy Villarejo (eds), *The Oxford Handbook of Queer Cinema*, New York: Oxford University Press, pp. 435-456.

[11]. Stefanie Leinfellner, '"I cannot imagine a world in which gender makes no difference" - Richard Dyer im Gesprach', *Journal Netzwerk Frauen- und Geschlechterforschung NRW* 43 (2018), p. 61.

INTRODUCTION

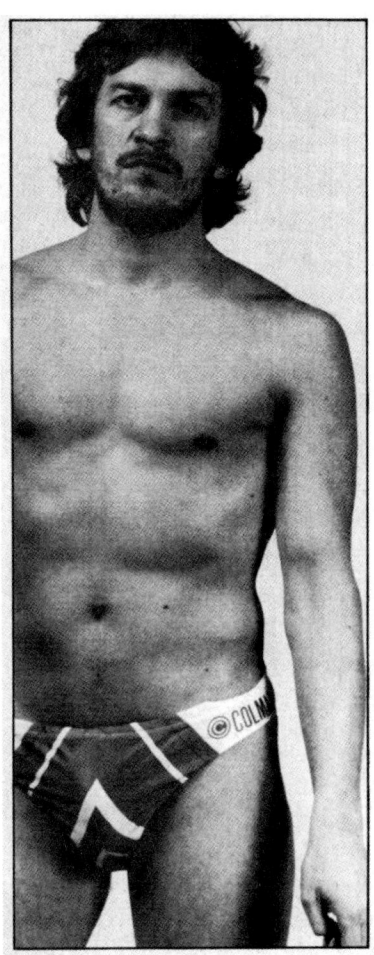 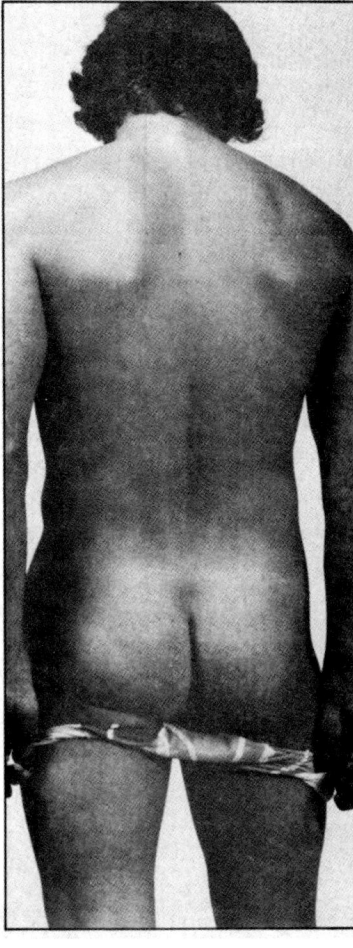

'Richard' posing in the Montreal-based gay journal *Attitude + Plus*, 1981. (Courtesy of Thomas Waugh)

socialism.'[12] Dyer's commitment to a Marxist politics led to him writing regular columns for the communist fortnightly *Comment* in the early 1980s, and for *Marxism Today* in the late 1980s and early 1990s – though it is worth noting that those columns were often on aspects of mass or popular culture that he deemed worthy of scrutiny, such as David Attenborough's natural history television series *Life on Earth* or the American sitcom *Soap*.[13]

Dyer regularly, in his writings, tells revealing personal anecdotes, which he then uses as a springboard for engaging in theoretical analysis. In 'Straight acting', for instance,

---

12. The Gay Left Collective, 'Collective statement', *Gay Left* 1 (Autumn 1975), p. 1.
13. Richard Dyer, 'Look at life the BBC way', *Comment* 18:10 (10 May 1980), p. 144; 'Soaping away the illusions', *Comment* 18:12 (7 June 1980), p. 192.

published in *Marxism Today* in 1990, Dyer reveals that he 'once had a relationship with a married man', and that when 'it came to an end, he said the reason was that he'd discovered that people he knew, knew about us and he couldn't stand the thought of being known to be homosexual.' Dyer uses this experience to highlight how heterosexuality 'as a social reality seems to be invisible to those who benefit from it.' He proposes ways 'to make heterosexuality strange', and thus expose its constructedness – not because he wants to get his own back on his ex-lover, but because 'the centrality of heterosexuality as a reference point and assumption remains secure.'[14] For Dyer, the personal encounter or experience always has the potential to lead to political insight. To give a further example, he lived in New York for most of 1981 and discovered there quite a different gay scene than the one in Birmingham; he regularly went dancing in the now legendary disco club the Paradise Garage. As he told Tim Lawrence in 2005: 'Obviously there were lots of white people at the Garage, but nonetheless one felt one was going to a Black-defined space. That made me reflect much more upon the fact that I was white.'[15] Although, as he has suggested elsewhere, Dyer 'was always interested in Black culture, I mean, that had always been a very important reference point for me', his experiences in New York led to a heightened awareness of whiteness that subsequently became a major thematic strand within his writing.[16]

Personal passions became topics worthy of study and discussion. Throughout his life and career, Dyer has been aware of the importance of dress. At Keele University, he had a penchant for wearing, as he told Matthew Rettenmund, 'pretty little women's jumpers' (see Section 7). Dyer was informed by a head of department that he dressed too much like a student, which could have been code for telling him that his dress was too flamboyant, too feminine, too queer. In 1992, the actor and comedian Lenny Henry received an honorary degree from the University of Warwick; Dyer (who was wearing an Italian designer suit) was introduced to him as 'the best dressed man in the university', to which Henry (wearing a blue pinstripe suit) replied, 'Not today!' The relationship between queerness and sartorial style has surfaced occasionally in Dyer's writings. In 'Fashioning change' (1994), for instance, published in a collection of essays marking the 25th anniversary of Stonewall, he related an anecdote about attending a job interview, and attempting to choose a tie: 'How ironic should it be, how over the top should I go to signal that I know that ties are just a piece of manly frippery; how far back from over the top should I withdraw in order not to appear to be sending the panel up? On such precipices of decision is gay style lived.'[17] A sensitivity to the

---

14. Richard Dyer, 'Straight acting', *Marxism Today* (August 1990), p. 24.
15. Tim Lawrence, 'In defence of disco (again)', *New Formations* 58 (Summer 2006), p. 133.
16. Kieran Connell, 'Transcript: CCCS interview Richard Dyer,' 12 August 2013, p. 2.
17. Richard Dyer, 'Fashioning change: Gay men's style,' in Emma Healey and Angela Mason (eds), *Stonewall 25: The Making of the Lesbian and Gay Community in Britain*, London: Virago, 1994, pp. 179-180. The essay

nuances of fashion coding is peppered throughout his analyses of individual films; for example, in 'Seen to be believed' (1983), Dyer draws attention to 'the tactility of the sweater, the pretty patterning of the scarf, the carefully adjusted set of the collar' of a character in *La dolce vita*.[18]

As already noted, Dyer's first teaching position was at Keele. He briefly taught at Bulmershe College (now part of the University of Reading), before taking up a position at the University of Warwick; much later, he moved to King's College London, and was awarded an Honorary Professorship position at the University of St Andrews. Across the decades, he has held Visiting Professorship positions at a number of international locations, including New York, Philadelphia, Stockholm, and Bergamo. And yet he has always sustained an interest in reaching audiences beyond higher education, an investment in the value of critical thought for the general public fostered, partly, by Richard Hoggart's influence on the workings and objectives of the CCCS. Keele provided Dyer with sustained experiences of teaching beyond the standard classroom. As he told Barbara Klinger, 'I learnt a lot from doing adult education […] I feel everyone ought to do that kind of education, it's really good training in thinking about teaching, and thinking about making ideas accessible and so on.'[19] Dyer had had some previous minor experience of teaching courses to broader demographics, through work at the film society in Birmingham (he delivered a course, amongst other topics, on Polish cinema); in the late 1970s and early 1980s, he helped to programme seasons of films at the Birmingham Arts Lab, writing screening notes and delivering accompanying talks and discussions. Through the BFI's educational activities – summer schools, conferences, assembly of teaching packs on particular topics – he contributed to evolving debates about the best ways to teach film, television, and cultural studies. In recent decades, reaching yet another public demographic, he has recorded a DVD/Blu-ray commentary (on *Seven*) and several 'bonus feature' interviews (for films including *Walk on the Wild Side*, *The Possessed*, and *The Iguana with the Tongue of Fire*).

Dyer's monographs and collections – *Stars* (1979), *Heavenly Bodies* (1986), *Now You See It* (1990), *Only Entertainment* (1992), *The Matter of Images* (1993), *White* (1997), *The Culture of Queers* (2002), *Pastiche* (2007), *In the Space of a Song* (2012), *Nino Rota* (2010), and *Lethal Repetition* (2015) – are, obviously, central to his status as a film studies scholar. Several of these titles have been reissued with supplemental essays by other scholars (Paul McDonald for *Stars*; Julianne Pidduck for *Now You See It*; Maxime Cervulle for *White*). The second editions of *Now You See It* (2003), *Only Entertainment* (2002), and

---

was retitled as 'Dressing the part' for its inclusion in Richard Dyer, *The Culture of Queers*, London and New York: Routledge, 2002, pp. 63–69.

18. Richard Dyer, 'Seen to be believed: some problems in the representation of gay people as typical', *Studies in Visual Communication* 9:2 (1983), p. 4.

19. Klinger, op. cit.

Richard Dyer's column in *Comment*, 16 May 1981.

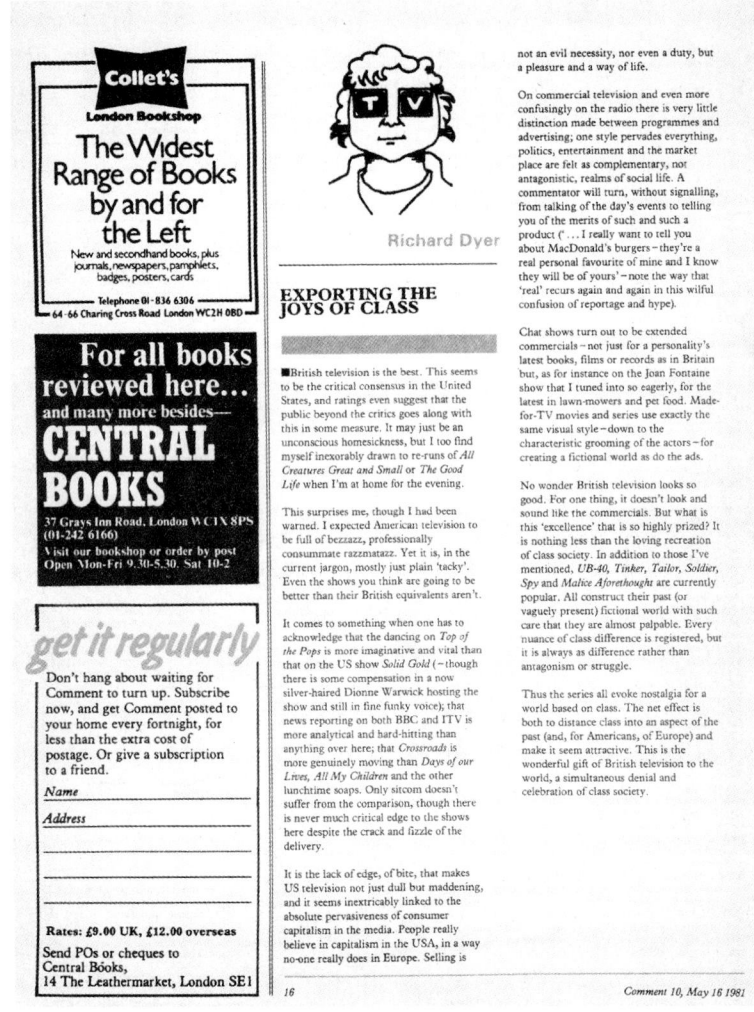

The Matter of Images (2002) had their content rejigged or expanded by Dyer. Individual books, or essays in collections, have become canonical texts, in the sense that they have helped to define academic debate, are widely cited, and/or are included in the syllabi of university courses. *Stars* and *White*, for instance, are amongst the founding texts of star studies and whiteness studies; essays such as 'Entertainment and utopia' (1977) and 'Homosexuality and film noir' (1977) continue to be widely taught and referenced.[20] The contents of this Reader could easily have been compiled from Dyer essays that

---

20. Richard Dyer, 'Entertainment and utopia', *Movie* 24 (Spring 1977), pp. 2–13; 'Homosexuality and film noir', *Jump Cut* 16 (1977), pp. 18–21.

can be considered as canonical – a book of 'Richard Dyer's Greatest Hits'. Instead, we have selected five canonical essays and one lecture ('The persistence of textual analysis', appearing in print for the first time) as a key text of each section, around which we have thematically compiled essays that may be less well known, less often anthologised, or less easily accessible. A seventh section includes four interviews with Dyer that provide additional context and insight on his career and work, including a new conversation with us that was conducted in 2021. Short introductions to each section outline ways to think through and across Dyer's writing career, highlighting connections between the texts selected and Dyer's wider oeuvre.

Although we do not claim that the selection is representative of Dyer's work, we have attempted to present a wide range of topics from across the different decades and from multiple sources of publication. Undoubtedly, the selection also reflects our personal preferences and our own subject positions as white European openly gay cismen, coming of age during the 1970s and 1980s. We have excluded writings that seem less relevant today than when they were published, such as Dyer's essay on Dame Edna Everage, or his piece on 'Yuppie culture'.[21] Other essays have been included precisely because they have retained their relevance. The 1981 essay on Lady Diana and Prince Charles 'Of rage and despair' (see Section 5), for instance, continues to have bite due to ongoing discussions about the place and status of the monarchy in British cultural life (a topic, incidentally, that Dyer suggested as a possible collective research focus for the CCCS in 1971, but which was not taken up).[22]

'In defence of disco' – the key text of Section 2 – is also a pertinent example, its relevance repeatedly refreshed. The essay was originally published in *Gay Left* in 1979 and subsequently appeared in Dyer's essay collection *Only Entertainment*. It has been anthologized in several readers, including *On Record* (1990), *Out in Culture* (1995), *The Faber Book of Pop* (1995), *Electronica, Dance and Club Music* (2012), and *Black Box* (2015).[23] Its 25th anniversary of publication was commemorated with an essay in the *European Journal of Cultural Studies* in 2005, and a special section in *New Formations* in 2006, the latter including essays by Jeremy Gilbert and Tim Lawrence as well as a reprint of

---

21. Richard Dyer, 'The Dame and the Knight', *Comment* 20:5 (6 March 1982), p. 16; 'Yuppie culture', *Marxism Today* (October 1985), pp. 47–48.

22. Richard Dyer, 'Some nasty remarks and some constructive ones', unpublished CCCS memo, 23 March 1971, Cadbury Research Library, Special Collections, University of Birmingham, Stuart Laing Papers, USS98.

23. Simon Frith and Andrew Goodwin (eds), *On Record: Rock, Pop and the Written Word*, London: Routledge, 1990; Corey K. Creekmur and Alexander Doty (eds), *Out in Culture: Gay, Lesbian and Queer Essays on Popular Culture*, London: Cassell, 1995; Hanif Kureishi and Jon Savage (eds), *The Faber Book of Pop*, London and Boston, MA: Faber and Faber, 1995; Mark J. Butler (ed.), *Electronica, Dance and Culture*, London and New York: Routledge, 2012; The Black Box Collective (eds), *Black Box: A Record of the Catastrophe, Volume One*, Oakland: PM Press, 2015.

the original essay.[24] In spring 2021, a Spanish translation was published in the Chilean journal *Resonancias*. The introductory article by translator Amparo Lasén not only traces the essay's history but also notes how it has attained a new significance during the COVID-19 crisis.[25] 'It is amazing how much [the disco essay] has been taken up and reprinted and endlessly quoted and referred to,' Dyer told Simon Dickel in 2022. 'I think I wrote it in a weekend. It wasn't deeply researched, and it didn't need to be.'[26]

Due to space restrictions, and a desire to include less well-known materials, it has been necessary to 'kill some darlings': we have excluded a number of essays that readers will probably have expected to be included in this Reader, most notably 'Entertainment and utopia' and 'Homosexuality and film noir', but also 'Lana: four films of Lana Turner' (1977), 'Believing in fairies: the author and the homosexual' (1991), and 'Is *Car Wash* a musical?' (1993).[27] We would have loved to include Dyer's extensive analysis of Genet's *Un Chant d'Amour* from *Now You See It* – an exemplary piece of historical and textual analysis – but sacrificed this for shorter pieces, less well-known but equally rich and deserving: a review of *The Towering Inferno* from *Movie* (Section 6), programme notes on Jane Fonda (Section 1) and dance films (Section 5) from Birmingham Arts Lab film programmes, a review of *Scorpio Rising* (Section 5) that offers a take on the film distinct from that included in *Now You See It*.

Three new pieces of writing are included in *The Richard Dyer Reader*: 'Fond of little tunes' (Section 5), 'Eisenstein's penis' (Section 6), and 'The persistence of textual analysis' (Section 6). A new edit of a chapter from *Lethal Repetition* ('The same over and over', Section 5) was produced by Dyer specifically for this collection. As we finalise this Reader, Dyer continues to author and publish new work; substantial essays on silence and noise in *La Captive* and on marginality in *La dolce vita* appeared in 2021.[28]

---

[24]. Jaap Kooijman, 'Turn the beat around: Richard Dyer's 'In defence of disco' revisited,' *European Journal of Cultural Studies* 8:2 (2005), pp. 257-266; Jeremy Gilbert, 'In defence of "In defense of disco"' and 'Dyer and Deleuze: Post-structuralist cultural criticism,' *New Formations* 58 (Summer 2006), pp. 99-100, 109-127; Tim Lawrence, 'In defence of disco (again),' *New Formations* 58 (Summer 2006), pp. 128-146.

[25]. Amparo Lasén, 'Invitación a la lectura y propuesta investigadora de la defensa de la música disco de Richard Dyer', *Resonancias* 25:48 (2021), pp. 157-165.

[26]. Simon Dickel, unpublished interview with Richard Dyer, 4 February 2022.

[27]. Richard Dyer, 'Lana: Four films of Lana Turner', *Movie* 25 (Winter 1977-1978), pp. 30-52; 'Believing in fairies: The author and the homosexual', in Diana Fuss (ed.), *Inside/Out: Lesbian Theories, Gay Theories*, New York and London: Routledge, 1991, pp. 185-202; 'Is *Car Wash* a musical?', in Manthia Diawara (ed.), *Black American Cinema*, New York and London: Routledge, 1993, pp. 93-106. (It is worth noting that the book's content page lists the essay as 'Is *Car Wash* a Black musical?').

[28]. Richard Dyer, 'Making sense of noise and silence in *La Captive*,' in Carlo Cenciarelli (ed.), *The Oxford Handbook of Cinematic Listening*, New York: Oxford University Press, 2021, pp. 241-251; 'On marginality: *La dolce vita*'s homosexuals,' in Ron Gregg and Amy Villarejo (eds), *The Oxford Handbook of Queer Cinema*, New York: Oxford University Press, pp. 308-327.

Online banner announcing the SCMS event honouring Richard Dyer. (Courtesy of SCMS)

Although now an Emeritus Professor, Dyer remains widely engaged with contemporary film and television. In the second edition of his short book on *Brief Encounter*, for instance, he offered a nuanced comparison of David Lean's 1945 film with the HBO series *Looking* (2014–2016):

> *Brief Encounter* and *Looking* are utterly of their time and place, the one so English and provincial, the other so San Francisco and now, *Brief Encounter*'s characters so indirect and its feelings so wholehearted, *Looking* so upfront and in your face and yet so self-conscious about emotional expression. The fact that they nonetheless play to the same affective concerns does not mean that nothing has changed in seventy years, but it does mean that emotional dedication and sexual jealousy are very deeply embedded in the societies we live in and so, when done right, continue to engage, fascinate and move us.[29]

Dyer's work has always been informed by a remarkably thorough knowledge of cultural history, and marked by his ability to make surprising connections between materials and arguments. In her introduction to a dossier of essays in *Cinema Journal* that emerged from the 'Richard Dyer in the House of Cinema' event at the Society for Cinema and Media Studies (SCMS) conference in Atlanta in 2016, Lisa Henderson

---

29. Richard Dyer, *Brief Encounter*, London: BFI/Palgrave, 2015, p. 9.

highlighted Dyer's skills, writing that his 'openness, grace, and sometimes daunting honesty are well matched to his capacity for scholarly labour, for conversation, for film going, watching, hearing, teaching, and especially writing.'[30]

All essays in the Reader have been edited to conform to a consistent style in referencing, punctuation, and spelling (UK English). We have 'silently' corrected obvious typos and innocent mistakes: for instance, the Diana Ross song is called 'Upside Down' not 'Inside Out' ('Diana Ross', Section 1); Jane Fonda's second husband was Tom Hayden not Tom Hagen (the latter is a fictional character who appears in *The Godfather*; 'Jane Fonda', Section 1). If a reprinted version of an essay differs from the original one, we have used the original. To give just one example, in the original version of 'Rock: the last guy you'd have figured?' (Section 3), published in the Canadian journal *The Body Politic* in December 1985, Dyer writes about Hudson's 'gayness', whereas in the expanded version, included in *The Culture of Queers* (2002), he uses 'homosexuality' instead; the later version features a discussion of the film *Seconds* which did not appear in the original, and therefore does not appear here. Although certain uses of language may now seem somewhat dated or potentially offensive – a 1985 use of the word 'spastic' ('Masculinity is so *boring*', Section 7), or some 1997 comments on trans identities ('Heterosexuality', Section 4) – we have decided not to update or edit these, leaving them intact as markers of their time.

We first raised the prospect of assembling a Reader of his work with Dyer late in 2019. He responded enthusiastically, flattered by the project, happy to be a 'silent partner' in its assembly. (The only essay he requested we include was 'The colour of entertainment' – see Section 2). Throughout the work on the Reader, Dyer has provided resources, drawn our attention to rare and lesser-known texts, fact-checked, and assisted with rights approvals. Like so many other academic books of the last two to three years, the labour involved in putting this collection together has taken place almost entirely online during the COVID-19 pandemic. We first discussed the project with Dyer in person, in a hotel lobby in London, in December 2019; this introduction was completed in person, in a hotel lobby in Bucharest, in June 2022. In between, the volume has been assembled almost entirely online. Individual archives and libraries to which we needed access were often closed or operating with severely restricted protocols; a new interview with Dyer (see Section 7) had to take place on Skype, rather than in person. Despite the barriers erected by the pandemic, however, the assembly of this book has provided regular, warm reminders of the pleasures of collaborative and collegiate scholarly projects, and of the high esteem in which Richard and his work are held in countries across the world. Friends, allies, and colleagues have been vocal in their enthusiasm for the project, and provided us with copies of materials from their

---

30. Lisa Henderson, 'Introduction: There is something about Richard Dyer', *Cinema Journal* 57:2 (2018), p. 150.

own collections or institutions that we could not source due to lockdowns. In particular, we would like to thank the following for their assistance: José Arroyo, Emilia Beatriz at Collective Text, Rosalind Brunt, Gloria Chalmers, Lucy Fife Donaldson, Jonathan Flatley, Catherine Grant, Ann Gray, Amy Holdsworth, Chris Holmlund, Daniel Humphrey, Joe McElhaney, Paula Massood, Mandy Merck, Trevor Millum, Erwin Olaf, Francesco Pitassio, Matthew Rettenmund, Ian Sanderson, Eliza Steinbock, Juan Antonio Suárez, Rob Verhorst, Thomas Waugh, and Pamela Wojcik, as well as the archivists at the University of St Andrews, the Cadbury Research Library of the University of Birmingham, the EYE Film Museum in Amsterdam, the Amsterdam Atria Institute on Gender Equality and Women's History, the Amsterdam IHLIA Institute of LGBTI Heritage, the International Institute of Social History in Amsterdam, and the National Library of Scotland. We are immeasurably grateful to Rebecca Barden, Tom Cabot, Sophia Contento, and Veidehi Hans, who have helped us in manifold ways throughout the assembly of this volume. Finally, we thank our respective partners, Iain Barbour and Jeroen van Ingen, for their extraordinary patience, love, and support.

This book is dedicated to Richard and Giorgio.

SECTION 1

A STAR IS BORN

and other essays on stardom and image

Barbra Streisand and Judy Garland performing on *The Judy Garland Show*, October 1963. (Archive Photos/Getty Images)

'Most people who like cinema, like stars, but those who teach cinema are seldom willing to take this liking, which they themselves share, seriously. But stars need to be studied, and can be studied.'[1] In the four-page article 'Studying the stars', published in *Screen Education Notes* in 1973, Richard Dyer presented an early exploration into his theory of stardom, which he would further develop in the two complementary monographs *Stars* (1979) and *Heavenly Bodies* (1986). Without denying their individual agency, Dyer perceives stars neither as 'real people' nor as merely commodities of the entertainment industry, but as cultural signs that can be analysed as mediated 'total star texts' consisting of the star's onscreen performances as well as promotional materials, interviews, critical reception, gossip in the tabloid press, and fan cultures. Most importantly, Dyer argues that stars express the often-contradictory ideological values of living as an individual in a capitalist society, functioning as 'embodiments of the social categories in which people are placed and through which they have to make sense of their lives, and indeed through which we make our lives'.[2]

While his work on stardom is usually associated with film stars, Dyer's first case study was of the Welsh singer Tom Jones, which he wrote whilst a graduate student at the Centre for Contemporary Cultural Studies and which was published in the first issue of the CCCS's journal *Working Papers in Cultural Studies*. In 'The meaning of Tom Jones' (1971, included here in an abridged version), Dyer analyses the Tom Jones star image, and its phallic masculinity in particular, as part of the popular *This Is Tom Jones* television show, already showcasing a queer wittiness in academic writing that was atypical and undoubtedly daring for its time: 'Tom Jones has a penis and one does not forget it, but he has the personality to back it up.' (Five decades later, Dyer would recall how Stuart Hall was 'elated' by this sentence).[3]

In his 1972 PhD dissertation 'Social Values of Entertainment and Show Business', Dyer discussed specific Hollywood musical stars, such as Julie Andrews, Fred Astaire, Doris Day, Judy Garland, Gene Kelly (included in this section), and Barbra Streisand. Building on Edgar Morin's *Les Stars* (1957) and Orrin E. Klapp's *Heroes, Villains, and Fools* (1962), Dyer introduced the seemingly paradoxical notion of the star being 'just like you and me' and simultaneously gifted with 'innate talent' and 'professionalism'.

---

1. Richard Dyer, 'Studying the Stars', *Screen Education Notes* 7 (Summer 1973), p. 17.
2. Richard Dyer, *Heavenly Bodies: Film Stars and Society*, London: BFI/Macmillan, 1987, p. 18.
3. Richard Dyer, e-mail to the editors, 14 September 2021.

As he wrote:

> The belief that stars simply are by birth more gifted than others, that some definite quality and talent shines through whatever a star does, is an important aspect of the star syndrome. At first sight it may seem to contradict the suggestion that stars are just like you and me, and in some cases – Streisand's for instance – it does. More often however it works with the sense of ordinariness in important ways. Firstly, it justifies the fact that a star has become famous: it holds at bay any resentment that someone ordinary has got to the top. Secondly, publicity stresses that despite the exceptional talent, the star is still in every other way just like you or me. Ordinariness is thus coupled with genius, and the notion that genius requires a special temperament is discounted with confidence.[4]

Here Dyer highlights the contradiction that would later become known in media studies as the 'ordinary/extraordinary paradox,' often associated with John Ellis's writing of a decade later.[5] But while Ellis argues that the contradiction cannot be resolved, leaving the star image 'incoherent' and 'incomplete', Dyer shows how the star's extraordinariness and ordinariness work together to enable stars to become exemplary embodiments of individualism within capitalism, to which audiences can relate in both admiration and recognition.

Throughout the 1970s, Richard Dyer's writing on stardom was often connected to the work of the educational department of the British Film Institute. Dyer developed packages of annotated film extracts and teaching manuals for courses at schools and universities, including *The Dumb Blonde Stereotype* (1979), *Teachers' Study Guide 1: The Stars* (1979), and *Marilyn Monroe: Star Dossier One* (1980). The latter contains a 33-page essay in which Dyer discusses not only the Marilyn Monroe star image during the period when she was alive (as he would also do in *Heavenly Bodies*), but also its posthumous prominence in popular culture. The dossier includes ten facsimile reproductions of newspaper clippings about Monroe and 44 slides of film stills and other Monroe-related images, such as the cover of Donna Summer's *Four Seasons of Love* album (1976), featuring the disco singer mimicking Monroe's famous *The Seven Year Itch* pose, which 'illustrates the continued currency of the image,' as well as raising questions about 'the fact that a Black woman can take the pose.'[6] Obviously, the packages only included selective samples of what constitutes a total star text, but they did enable the study of stars beyond the onscreen performance. Eventually, as Dyer

---

4. Richard Dyer, 'Social Values of Entertainment and Show Business,' unpublished PhD dissertation, Centre for Contemporary Cultural Studies, University of Birmingham, October 1972, p. 304.
5. John Ellis, *Visible Fictions: Cinema; Television; Video*, London: Routledge & Regan Paul, 1982, pp. 91–108.
6. Richard Dyer, *Marilyn Monroe: Star Dossier One*, London: British Film Institute Education, 1980, p. 37.

Star Dossier One with Marilyn Monroe and Donna Summer on the cover, 1980. (Courtesy of Jaap Kooijman)

would later recall, the teaching material on stars 'just got out of control and it clearly had to be a book,' thus leading to the writing of *Stars*.[7]

Stars was primarily a theoretical and methodological study guide, but also featured an extensive case study of Jane Fonda. In this section, we have included a shorter profile that Dyer wrote for the Jane Fonda film season he organised at the Birmingham Arts Lab in 1979. At the time of its publication, *Stars* received much praise. 'In its clarity and cogency it should have a decisive influence on all subsequent thinking about the implications of the star phenomenon,' wrote Robin Wood.[8] Yet there was also criticism, most notably by Pam Cook and Barry King, who both suggested that by

---

7. Barbara Klinger, 'Fieldnotes: Richard Dyer interviewed by Barbara Klinger', Society for Cinema and Media Studies, 13 April 2015, https://vimeo.com/145394630.

8. Robin Wood, 'The Dyer's Hand: Stars and Gays,' *Film Comment* 16:1 (1980), p. 72.

perceiving stars merely as cultural signs open to (often subjective) interpretation, Dyer not only ignored their agency, but also downplayed the role of the entertainment industry in the ideological meaning-making process.[9] In the supplementary chapter to the 1998 edition of *Stars*, Paul McDonald too argued for placing star studies more firmly within a historical and industrial context.[10]

The key text of this section is '*A Star Is Born* and the construction of authenticity', written for a weekend workshop on stardom organised by Christine Gledhill, held in January 1982. Dyer's essay was published in *Star Signs* (1982), a record of the workshop's proceedings, as well as the collection *Stardom: Industry of Desire* (1991), both edited by Gledhill – though the latter did not include the afterword in which Dyer presented his preliminary ideas regarding what would become the 'Judy Garland and Gay Men' chapter in *Heavenly Bodies*. Dyer delivered his workshop paper alongside contributions by John Ellis ('Star/Industry/Image') and Pam Cook ('Stars and politics'), using Judy Garland in the 1954 version of *A Star Is Born* as a case study to show how star images construct a sense of authenticity (stars are *born*), without denying that stars are also products of the entertainment industry (stars are *made*). That stars are 'manufactured and promoted' is widely recognised, Dyer writes, adding: 'Yet in the very same breath as audiences and producers alike acknowledge stars as hype, they are declaring this or that star as the genuine article. Just as the media are construed as the very antithesis of sincerity and authenticity, they are the source for the presentation of the epitome of those qualities, the true star.'

Around this time, Dyer also wrote essays on specific stars, such as 'The way she is' (1981) on Barbra Streisand for *The Movie* and 'Diana Ross' (1982) for *Marxism Today*, both included in this section. Previously, in his PhD dissertation, Dyer had suggested that it is difficult to see Streisand as someone 'like you or me' (or 'to believe she is even remotely nice'), a position he explored further a decade later.[11] Arguing that 'star images involve a great deal of rehearsal and manufacture, but few are experienced in that way,' Dyer perceived Streisand as an exception because of her overt professionalism. As he puts it, 'Her mannered portrayals draw attention to her performance as such. Her image tells the truth about the star phenomenon, namely, that all stars are performances.' Dyer's essay on Diana Ross, written after seeing her live in concert, focuses on how her 'unreal' performance celebrates that she, as a Black female star, is 'allowed' to be successful in mainstream culture: 'The sheer ecstasy of the whole

---

9. Pam Cook, 'Star Signs,' *Screen* 20:3-4 (1979), pp. 80-88; Pam Cook, '[Review of] *Stars*,' *Women's Studies International Quarterly* 3 (1980), pp. 123-125; Barry King, 'The star and the commodity: Notes towards a theory of stardom,' *Cultural Studies* 1:2 (1987), pp. 145-161.
10. Paul McDonald, 'Reconceptualising stardom,' in Richard Dyer, *Stars*, new edition, London: BFI/Palgrave Macmillan, 1998, pp. 175-200.
11. Dyer, 'Social Values of Entertainment and Show Business,' op. cit., p. 330.

Diana Ross thing is an outrageous revelling in what success could feel like, but not how to achieve it.'[12]

Dyer's most extensive discussion of specific stars can be found in his second monograph on stardom, *Heavenly Bodies* (a synonym of 'stars', of course), in which he presents three case studies of stars who each 'in some measure revolted against the lack of control they felt they had' within the capitalist Hollywood system.[13] The first two chapters, on Marilyn Monroe and Paul Robeson respectively, explore how both star images function within ideologies of gender and sexuality (femininity and masculinity) and race (whiteness and Blackness) during the times when their films were released. The third chapter focuses on how a specific subcultural group – white urban gay men – has appropriated the star image of Judy Garland, both during and after her life. In his review of *Heavenly Bodies*, Simon Watney deemed the Garland chapter 'the most successful' and praised the 'charm and openness' of Dyer's writing, yet he would have preferred 'a much more expansive and substantial book about Judy Garland, with room to explore the pressing question of how and why different audiences identify so intensely with different stars.'[14]

Although he told Matthew Rettenmund in 1997 (see Section 7 of this Reader) that he had stopped writing about stars ('I'm loyal to Judy'), Richard Dyer has occasionally discussed specific star images. Included in this section are essays about Audrey Hepburn's 'imperfections' that made her 'perfect', published in *Sight and Sound* (1993), and about Charles Hawtrey and the 'unambiguous ambiguity' of his sexuality, published in the first issue of the gay glossy magazine *Attitude* (1994). He has also written about Elizabeth Taylor for an exhibition at London's National Portrait Gallery (2000), about Lena Horne for a German academic journal (2010), and about Bette Davis on the occasion of the thirtieth anniversary of her death in 2019 ('Davis was doing performativity before Judith Butler was born').[15] The 2012 Arrow Blu-ray release of the 1950 Hollywood film *Born Yesterday*, starring Judy Holliday, includes the 25-minute featurette 'Blonde Ambition' in which Dyer not only discusses how Holliday added complexity to the dumb blonde stereotype, but also places her in a longer tradition of New York Jewish humour.

---

12. Dyer's 'Diana Ross' forms the basis of the audiovisual essay 'Success: Richard Dyer on Diana Ross [and Beyond]' by Jaap Kooijman, published in *[in]Transition: Journal of Videographic Film & Moving Image Studies* 2:4 (2016), http://mediacommons.org/intransition/success.

13. Dyer, *Heavenly Bodies*, op. cit., p. 6.

14. Simon Watney, 'Stellar Studies', *Screen* 28:3 (1987), pp. 111, 113.

15. Richard Dyer, 'First a star: Elizabeth Taylor,' in *Only Entertainment*, second edition, London and New York: Routledge, 2002, pp. 112–117; Richard Dyer, 'Singing Prettily: Lena Horne in Hollywood,' *Zeitschrift für Medien- und Kulturforschung*, 2010:2 (2010), pp. 11–25; Richard Dyer, short statement for 'The Bette Davis Testimonials,' 20 August 2019, published on Martin Shingler's website: http://www.martinshingler.co.uk/?p=856.

Dyer returned to *A Star Is Born* with his essay on the 2018 version of the film, published in the *Los Angeles Review of Books*. The film's star Lady Gaga is placed by Dyer in the tradition of David Bowie and Madonna as 'a hero of inauthenticity,' based on the self-reflexive theatricality of her star image that seems at odds with both Judy Garland's authenticity in the 1954 version as well as the 'premeditated quality of [Barbra] Streisand's performance style' in the 1976 version. Yet, as Dyer reminds us in the final paragraph of *Stars*, when analysing and demystifying star images we should not ignore their affective qualities of beauty and pleasure, how they make us *feel* – the way Marilyn Monroe makes him catch his breath, or Montgomery Clift makes him sigh. As Dyer concludes, 'while I accept utterly that beauty and pleasure are culturally and historically specific, and in no way escape ideology, nonetheless they are beauty and pleasure and I want to hang on to them in some form or another.'[16]

---

16. Dyer, *Stars*, London: British Film Institute, 1979, p. 185.

1 *A STAR IS BORN* AND THE CONSTRUCTION OF AUTHENTICITY (1981)

This paper deals with a narrow – but crucial – aspect of the film *A Star Is Born*, namely, the notion and construction of 'authenticity'. The processes of authentication discussed are the guarantee of both star 'quality' in general and of the particular image of the star concerned. At the weekend I will sketch in two elements not really discussed here – the components of Judy Garland's star image and her importance as a subcultural icon for gay men.

It is easy enough to outline the components of Judy Garland's star image in terms of social meanings. I only have to refer the stages in her career to three different stereotypes – the all-American small town girl-next-door; the personification of showbiz good humour and bezazz; the neurotic woman – for you to pick up on the social resonances of her image. If we wanted to understand the specificity of the image and account for its particular appeal and purchase, we could look closer at the precise inflection her image gives to those stereotypes, their place in the wider cultural discourses of the period, and the different concerns of the different known Garland audiences. We could begin to see why people paid to go and see her, and to differentiate between the various meanings that could be found in her image.

Yet none of this quite seems to deliver an understanding of the most common-sensical notions attached to the words 'star' and 'charisma' – notions like magic, power, fascination, and also authority, importance and aura. Part of the answer lies in the precise, and differentiated relation between the values perceived to be embodied by the star and the perceived status of those values (especially if they are felt to be under threat or in crisis, or to be challenging received values, or else to be values that are a key to understanding and coping with contemporary life). But I also want to suggest that all of this depends on the degree to which stars are accepted as truly being what they appear to be.

(There is a whole other way of relating to stars, a way that is essentially deconstructive, that refuses the guarantee that appearances are not deceiving. The most widespread, habitual form of such deconstructive reading practice is camp. Garland's relation to this, a phenomenon deeply rooted in male gay culture, is particularly paradoxical, considering that she is, and precisely in her authenticity, a key icon of traditional gay male culture.)

There is a whole litany in the fan literature surrounding stars in which certain adjectives endlessly recur – sincere, immediate, spontaneous, real, direct, genuine and so on. All of these words can be seen as relating to a general notion of 'authenticity'. It is these qualities that we demand of a star if we accept her or him in the spirit in which she or he is offered. Outside of a camp appreciation, it is the star's really seeming to be what s/he is supposed to be that secures his/her star status, 'star quality' or charisma. Authenticity is both a quality necessary to the star phenomenon to make it work, and also the quality that guarantees the authenticity of the other particular values a star embodies (such as girl-next-door-ness, etc.). It is this effect of authenticating authenticity that gives the star charisma, and that I want to look at here.

But first we need to consider the peculiarity that authenticity should be so crucial a notion in the whole phenomenon. The vocabulary of immediacy, sincerity, believability and so on is so familiar – since we also use it of people we encounter in life – that its particularity may not necessarily strike us. Yet it seems clear that it is a vocabulary of little more than two or three hundred years' existence (or rather, this way of using these words is only that old, the words themselves being much older). The peculiarity of this use of these words is their application to individual persons as the criteria for the truth or validity of social affairs. To put it another way, the truth of social affairs has become rooted not in general criteria governing social behaviour itself but in the performers themselves and, at the same time, the criteria governing performance have shifted from whether the performance is well done to whether it is truthful, that is, true to the 'true' personality of the performer. (I mean performer here in both its theatrical and its sociological usages.) Even truth is a peculiar criterion – we no longer ask if someone performs well or according to certain moral precepts but whether what they perform is truthful, with the referent of truthfulness not being falsifiable statements but the person's 'person'.

This development, charted by Richard Sennett in his book *The Fall of Public Man*, is essential to the development of humanism and individualism. All the major discourses of contemporary Western society address themselves to people as individuals, as free and separate human beings who are, in their separateness, the source of all social arrangements. Once individuals, in this sense, become the pivot of the whole ensemble of discourses that make sense of society, it is not surprising that it comes to matter very much whether those individuals are indeed functioning as they appear to be. If the individual is the guarantor of the social order, then he or she must be worthy of that role. Hence – to take one striking example – the enormous moral fervour surrounding lying; taken by the West as an absolute moral wrong, its acceptance as morally useful in many societies baffles us. We are hardly able to think another's statements without first determining whether the person really does mean what s/he says (and not whether it is right, or expedient, or formally correct, or kind).

Yet just at the point that this way of ordering and understanding human discourse and intercourse establishes itself as the fundament of human affairs, the possibility, and then probability, that what people say is *not* what they mean becomes even more clear, and disturbing. The major trends within Western culture that are hailed as intellectual revolutions have all done their bit to dislodge the security with which the individual holds her/his place as the guarantor of discourse. Marxism (at any rate in its most widely understood form) proposes that the political activity of society, in the form of freely operating spokespeople freely elected by freely constituted (i.e. 'individual') electors, is not the real politics of society at all, which on the contrary resides in the invisible operation and structures of the means and forces of production and reproduction. The behaviourisms propose that what we appear to do freely for reasons of which we are conscious we actually do for reasons that are barely available to consciousness at all, drives and instincts. Psychoanalysis equally proposes that consciousness is not really consciousness at all, but a surface masking the workings of that consciousness below consciousness that we choose to call unconscious. And some forms of linguistics, and aesthetic modernisms associated with them, insist that we do not speak language but that it speaks us, that the individual, far from being the guarantor of discourse, is in fact the product of it. I have sketched in these discourses at the level of their theoretical articulation, but they inform all levels of discourse, to varying degrees and in varying forms. Everyone is familiar with the notions that what we do, say, think and feel, and what happens in the world, are not due to us as we know ourselves but to economic forces, instincts, unconscious motivations, habits and patterns of speech. Two historical developments have further endangered the notion of the individual – the development of the mass media (and in particular advertising, both in itself and as an economic concomitant of commercial radio, television and journalism) and the rise of totalitarianisms (Nazism, Stalinism, etc.). The reigning concept behind both of these is that of 'manipulation', of the handling of human discourse and intercourse such as to yield vast profits and despotic power, on the one hand, and a docile populace on the other. (This is not the place to enter into discussion of the validity and notions of mass culture, totalitarianism and manipulation, though we should recognise how deeply problematic they are; what is at issue here is their widespread currency as indicators of the characteristic form of social relations in the 'developed' countries.)

Much of the internal intellectual history of Marxism, behaviourism, psychoanalysis, linguistics and modernism has been the attempt to reconcile their paradigms with those of humanism. I do not propose to go into that here. What is particularly fascinating about the mass media and totalitarianism is that, even as they are being identified as destroying the individual, they are also largely in the business of prompting the individual and the claims of humanism. To get back to stars, no aspect of the media can be more obviously attended by hype than the production of stars; there is nothing sophisticated about knowing they are manufactured and promoted, it is a sense that is common. Even the media knows it, as films like *A Star Is Born* show. Yet in the very same breath as audiences and producers alike acknowledge stars as hype, they are declaring this or that star as the genuine article. Just as the media are construed as the very antithesis of sincerity and authenticity, they are the source for the presentation of the epitome of those qualities, the true star.

How does the star image pull this off? How is the image authenticated as something more – truer, more real – than an image? In part, the star phenomenon is defined by an inbuilt means of authentication. Stars appear before us in media texts – films, advertisements, gossip columns, television interviews and so on – but unlike other forms of representation stars do not only exist in media texts. To say that stars exist outside of the media texts in real life would be misleading, but stars are carried in the person of people who do go on living away from their appearances in the media, and the point is that we know this. When he got home John Wayne may have become Marion Morrison again, but there was a real human being with a continuous existence, that is, who existed in between all the times he was 'being' John Wayne. But there is no way in which Elizabeth Bennett can leave the pages of *Pride and Prejudice* (except to be referred to in other media texts, in parodies, speculative continuations of the story, adaptations, etc.). In the first place then the question of the star's authenticity can be referred back to her/his existence in the real world.

This referral-back is tied up with the fact that stars exist in photographic media. Stars are a particular instance of the supposed special relation between a photograph and its referent. A photograph is always a photograph *of* something or somebody who had to have been there in order for the photograph to be taken. In the light of my remarks above, it is symptomatic that one of the best-known saws about photography is that 'the camera never lies'. The spread of photography as a casual practice has no doubt severely dented the confidence with which the camera's truth is believed: few people are the naive realists that theory belabours to refute. Yet the residual sense of the subject or person having-been-there remains powerful. Joan Crawford is not just a representation done in paint or writing – she is carried in the person née Lucille LeSueur who went before the cameras to be taken for us.

And if the existential bond (the indexicality, in C.S. Peirce's terminology) between Crawford and Crawford/LeSueur in the movie or pin-up is perceived to be distorted (de-authenticated) by the manipulation of the film-making or photographic process (glamour lighting, clever editing and so on), then we can always go and get photos of her doing the chores at home and cuddling baby Christina. And if we think those are a put-up job, then we might get a candid camera shot of her without make-up, or uncover a snapshot of her scowling at Christina. And so on in an infinite regress by means of which one more authentic image displaces another. But then they are all part of the star image, each one anchoring the whole thing in an essential, uncovered authenticity, which can then be read back into the performances, the roles, the pin-ups.

There is no need for what-is-uncovered to corroborate the particular character traits incarnated at the most obvious and familiar level of the star's image. In the development of the star phenomenon in Hollywood the attempt to make the different levels mutually reinforcing was certainly strenuously made – until the manipulations of that became so widely known that sources not apparently identified with Hollywood became the privileged access to the star's 'real' personality. Hence the growth of scandal magazines, unauthorised biographies, candid camera photo-journalism and so on.

The growth of this aspect of the total star text (i.e. as read across all her/his different media manifestations) draws on one possible way of taking the implications of Marxism, linguistics and, most explicitly, psychoanalysis and behaviourism. These displace the individual as the guarantor of discourse, but they do posit – or can be read as positing – a 'real' that is beneath or behind the surface represented by 'the individual' as a discursive category. Indeed, many of the claims of these theoretical discourses on our attention has been in their assertion of revealing a, or the, truth behind appearances, stripping away the veil of bourgeois categories or civilised (repressed) behaviours. The basic paradigm is just this – that what is behind or below the surface is, unquestionably and virtually by definition, the truth. Thus features of stars which tell us that the star is *not* like he or she appears to be on screen serve to reinforce the authenticity of the star image as a whole. And, very often, films made subsequent to a particular exposé will incorporate the truth revealed by the exposé as part of the authentication of the star in her/his next film.

At this point the authentication afforded by the ambivalent star-as-image: star-as-real-person nexus resembles nothing so much as a hall of mirrors. Not every case is so complicated. Many star images were authenticated by showing that the star really was like he or she was on the screen. In other cases, the off-screen reputation is either suppressed (as in the endless word of mouth about which indelibly heterosexual love gods and goddesses were in reality gay) or just does not get widely incorporated into the image's popular currency (e.g. every interview and biography assures us that James Cagney is of a gentle and kindly disposition, but it seems to have no impact on his image). But the full complexity of the potential inter-relations is illustrated by the career of Judy Garland. For instance, at the end of her career *I Could Go On Singing*, by drawing on all the publicity surrounding her Problems, offers itself as a guaranteed authentic portrait, and retrospectively, with the knowledge of her experiences as a child and adolescent at MGM, the films of the '40s can be re-read for signs of disturbance and neurosis. Thus there is a constant play of authenticating levels in the process of reading the image at different points in time. *A Star Is Born* is probably most complex in this regard, since it clearly reworks the MGM Garland image (in notions of innate talent, in various details of dress and performance recalling the innocent girl-next-door of the early films, and in the films-within-the-film which, as Wade Jennings points out, resemble nothing so much as the kind of big-production number MGM put Garland into in the '40s. Yet it seems also to incorporate into it oblique reference to the difficult years immediately preceding it (e.g. as Jennings suggests, in transferring the Garland career to the Mason character) and can also be read, particularly in terms of Garland's performance style, for signs (not hard to find) of what we are pleased to label neurosis.

So far all I have said is still rooted in the basic fact of the star phenomenon, that star images are carried in the person of real people. But it is also clear that this is unstable. Corroboration that a star is really like s/he appears to be *may* work, but may be read as further manipulation; showing that the star is not really like s/he appears to be *may* itself be taken up into the image, its further construction and re-reading, but it could shatter the illusion altogether. There is more to authentication – there is a rhetoric of authenticity. This too has its own in-built instability – yesterday's markers of sincerity and authenticity are today's signs of hype and artifice. Nevertheless it is a powerful rhetoric so long as it is not perceived as a rhetoric.

I am not concerned here to try to establish the particular codes of authenticity that were current at given points in time. What interests me here are the reigning notions that inform the shifting rhetorical strategies. Authenticity is established or constructed in media texts by the use of markers that indicate lack of control, lack of premeditation and privacy. These return us to notions of the truth being behind or beneath the surface. The surface is organised and under control, it is worked out in advance, it is public. In terms of performance this would mean that every detail is marked as deliberate and calculated; in terms of narrative it would mean that all the actions that really matter are set in the public domain. This kind of performance and this kind of narrative are, needless to say, just what we don't get when authenticity is at stake.

Much of the effort of a film must be the deployment of markers of authenticity to buoy up the unstable authenticity of the star; and this becomes still more so when the film is about the phenomenon of stardom. Few treatments of stardom are in fact as naive as the title *A Star Is Born* suggests. The Cukor-Garland film repeatedly indicates that stars are made by elaborate processes of production and manufacture; the extended 'Born in a Trunk' number is about the fact that being born in a trunk is not being born a star. Yet while it is acknowledging the constructedness of stars, it is also wishing to assert that stars are real, that this star, anyhow (whether we're thinking of her as Esther Blodgett, Vicki Lester or Judy Garland) is authentic. The whole film shifts between acknowledging manufacture as the rule and asserting the authenticity of this particular case.

The crucial moment of this assertion of authenticity is the 'The Man That Got Away' number. We must be convinced by this number that Esther really has 'star quality'; if this does not convince us, everything that follows suggests that her rise to stardom is just hype.

It may establish authenticity just by being Garland's big solo – it may be enough that it is Garland. Done in one long take, it may be accepted as capturing the continuousness of her performance which we may already think of as 'authentic' (– the Bazinian notion of the realism of the long take may be pertinent here). But the number is too crucial to the film to rest on that.

The number is located (by what is in fact a false point-of-view proceeding) as seen by James Mason (Norman Maine) and followed by his declaration that she has that 'little something extra' that is star quality. He looks at and appraises her, sober (for the first time so far in the film) and without lust (his usual mode of looking, as the previous scene establishes) – his judgement is signalled as unfuddled and disinterested, therefore more authoritative. He is himself a star, as well as a more fully established character in the film than is Esther/Garland at this point. For these reasons, he may be taken as the voice of truth. If he says she's a star, then she is. Still – this is not sure. He is hardly what we would call a reliable witness on the strength of what we've seen so far.

The film has to marshal markers of authenticity. *Lack of control*: several of Garland's gestures and facial (particularly mouth) expressions are redundant in terms of directly expressing or underlining the words or musical phrases of the song: such gestures are habitually read as neurotic (I'm sorry to keep using this word so lightly, but equally endlessly putting inverted commas around it is tedious – I intend neurosis as a socially constructed category) and her off-screen image by 1956 would have made such a reading easy. (For example – she brushes a lock of hair off her forehead after bringing her hand to her throat on the words, "No more that all time thrill"; but her hair is cropped, there is no lock on it; it is redundant as a practical gesture, but indecipherable as an expressive one, except as a gesture that can be taken to 'betray' neurosis.) *Unpremeditated*: other gestures, together with the opening "doo doo" and the raised eyebrow on the final piano phrase followed by a satisfied laugh, seem to be called forth by the music, to be improvised. She and the other musicians have already been described as jazz musicians, thus linking them to a music tradition that is assumed to be based on unpremeditated musical expressivity (– it is assumed that improvisations in jazz just happen, immediate and spontaneous, unrehearsed); and behind that, there is the link with Black culture, which has always functioned as a marker of authenticity and naturalness in white discourses. *Private*: she and the band do not know that they are being observed, that they are on. The dark lighting and the close grouping that the moving camera continually reframes both connote intimacy, not public performance. In all these ways, the number is overdetermined in terms of authenticity.

No number, no scene in a film, can guarantee that it will be read in the way it intends or 'prefers'. The reframing camera which keeps Esther/Garland in the centre *may* remind us that this is a performance for us; that Garland knows we are looking even if Esther doesn't know that Norman is. It is only a step from this to reminding ourselves that this could well be the twentieth take, which scotches the notions of unpremeditated, unrehearsed performance. And so on. But this is to deconstruct the film in the process of viewing, to see the markers of authenticity as markers. It is to go against the grain of the number, and the film.

One of the curious things about this number is that the song does not refer to anything that has happened so far in the film, and it seems to stretch a point to suggest that it refers forward to Norman's suicide. One could see it as referring to Garland's life, her previous marriages and affairs; and this is the resonance the song acquired as she used it in subsequent concert appearances. Yet this was never so insistent a part of her neurotic image as the legacy, in the form of pills and alcohol, of her years as a child star in Hollywood. The authenticity the number is after really has nothing to do with what Esther/Garland is singing about — it is the authenticity of her capacity to sing that is at stake. We must know that her star quality has nothing to do with recording techniques (even though what we are watching is perforce a recording...), with mechanical reproduction, but is grounded in her own immediate (= not controlled), spontaneous (= unpremeditated) and essential (= a private) self. That guarantees that her stardom is not a con, because an authenticated individual is acting as the guarantor of the truth of the discourse of her stardom. By not having a direct emotional referent, the number reinforces the authenticity of the star quality that can *then* legitimate the authenticity of whatever particular emotions Esther/Vicky will be called upon to express. In this way, the number is an especially interesting indicator of the processes of the authentication of star quality.

Afterword: On Judy Garland
At the session based around my paper at the 'Star Signs' Workshop, I omitted ways one might begin thinking about the relationship between the image of Judy Garland and a specific audience, namely gay men in the urban gay male subculture. At present my interest in this is at the level of a project for investigation, it is not yet the result of sustained work on the question. What follows are hypotheses towards work in progress. This is not the usual academic disclaimer, but a real signal to you of how very speculative these remarks are.

I am interested in Judy Garland more because I am interested in (male) gay culture than because I am interested in stars. However, the relationship between Garland and male gay culture does seem to me a particularly good example of the relationship between a media text (Garland) and the discourse of a particular cultural grouping, which enables us, in principle, to examine concretely the way that an audience can read a text. What is offered here, speculative as it is, is work that attempts to deal with the questions of the polysemy of media texts and the question of differentiated (but not purely individualised) readings that recent media theory has been concerned with.

Judy Garland has been a key icon in urban male gay culture. I could almost say that I learnt to be gay by learning how to love Judy Garland. Talking about her records, raving about her films, gossiping about her doings – these were (and to a certain extent, surprisingly, still are) a way of getting into the swing of being gay, the entrée to gay discourse. I've put this personally, but it is clear from even the cursory analysis of gay publications that I have made that this was a common, defining experience.

Why did the Garland image occupy this crucial place in the discourse? She was not the only star in the discourse, of course – the roll call of these stars is a well-known litany: Mae West, Joan Crawford, Bette Davis, Shirley Bassey, Diana Ross, Grace Jones, to name but a few. What must first strike an outsider is the fact that these are all women stars. Why did gay male culture so get off on women stars?

An immediate answer is that the culture required stars that express sexual desire for men. In the period we're talking about (and still, really) male stars could not express that desire. It is no accident that the stars concerned are associated either with popular song (especially ballads) and women's melodramas, the two forms that could signify, through the female singer or protagonist, desire for men. (I'll leave aside here the interesting fact that the most recent stars have been Black, except to mention that this must have something to do with the emergence in the sixties and seventies of a sense among gay men of being a minority that could be compared – rightly or wrongly – with ethnic minorities. The other major contemporary star in the gay male pantheon is Barbra Streisand, who is big on ethnicity too.)

It could have happened that the gay subculture would have fastened on to that other, more covert form of desire for men that has been discerned (mainly, it must be said, by straight critics) in buddy relationships in the western and other genres. If one can imagine such genres existing in classical Greek society, then perhaps something like them (though they'd have to be very different in many ways) would have been significant for contemporary gay male culture. Classical Greek society constructed same-sex physical intercourse within dominant definitions of masculinity, and very much at the expense of women. (This is also true of certain aspects of the current male gay culture, though it should be stressed that the differences between Hellenic and Greenwich Village homosexuality are far greater than their one similarity of

Judy Garland in *A Star Is Born*, 1954. (BFI National Archive)

being defined within rather than against 'masculinity'). However the traditional urban male gay subculture of the West in the twentieth century was not constructed within masculinity but rather over against it.

I don't want to get into the complex arguments here around the very notion of homosexuality. Suffice it to say that while same-sex sexual practice is universal, a category of persons labelled 'homosexuals' is a modern invention. As a category of the regime of sexuality it attempted to define same-sex sexuality as characteristic of a certain type of person and – and this is what is important here – as in some sense deviating from/transgressive of not just normal, that is hetero-sexuality, but also of gender roles too. In the category of homosexuality, we see vividly illustrated the conflation of sexuality and gender so characteristic of our age.

In terms of identifying with stars or screen characters then, the one position that gay men could not occupy (*as* gay men) was that of the heterosexual male star/hero, since he could not express desire for other men, not so much because that was not heterosexual as because it was not masculine. But we could identify with (heterosexual) women stars and characters because they could express that desire. (It should also be added that since homosexuality is forced on gay culture as a sexual category, so gay male culture very much knows itself as sexual – it does not recognise itself in buddy relations precisely because they hide, it is argued, rather than foreground sexuality.)

It is not *any* female star who becomes a figure in male gay subcultural discourse. Just as male homosexuality is a category defined outside of masculinity, so also it is not simply a 'feminine' position. Rather it has been defined as neither masculine or feminine (no matter how much male/female role playing it is credited with), a sexualised 'condition' outside of, or rather, in between, gender. Gay people have then been tempted by and drawn to notions of a sexual/gendered in-betweenism, to androgyny.

Garland's image is easily read in terms of androgyny. Even though sold by MGM as the ultimate in female normalcy, the girl-next-door, her roles and playing in her early films have tensions within them that could be read androgynistically. She is a girl-next-door, a stereotype instantly evoking associations of meekness, sweetness, subordination and so on, who is yet spunky, with a loud, belting singing voice. The films often – usually – set up her character over against a glamour girl type, thus foregrounding (or rather enabling us to foreground) the question of the relationship between competing female role stereotypes (virgin and vamp, for starters) and between gender and sexual stereotypes. *Meet Me in St. Louis* is particularly self-conscious in its play with these various elements (e.g. Esther initiates her relationship with boy-next-door John even while constructing herself as an object of gaze – sitting on the porch, standing on the stairs with the lights dimmed; their first love scene founders on his mumbled line, as they part, "You've got a good grip for a girl"). So, even in the MGM films, in the studio whose films are at least easily co-opted for a Comolli/Narboni category 'e' reading, Garland's image can be read through the discourse of androgyny. Later films exploit it far more directly, yielding those sequences that have been so re-worked in gay imagery – the 'Get Happy' number from *Summer Stock* and the 'Somewhere There's a Someone' from *A Star Is Born*, both with Garland dressed in man's clothing except for her legs in black tights. This was a look increasingly used for the stage shows, and the cropped hair style begun around the time of *A Star Is Born* is a further aspect of this.

Garland is then an example of a star who expresses desire for men in an androgynous mode – or, to make sure the operation I'm involved in here is clear, her image easily allowed itself to be read like this. In this respect she is like a number of other women stars; but she also relates to two further aspects of gay male subcultural discourse.

Firstly, to camp. This form of wit is a way of making fun of and protecting oneself against straight society. I don't propose to go into the arguments about it here. It is enough to say that Garland's act made much use of it. A camp appreciation of

Garland is not one at her expense (as it is of, say, John Wayne or Joan Crawford) but rather is an enjoyment of her being camp about other things, and including about what she's been made to do. This element comes out in wisecracks and the humorous delivery of a line – *The Pirate* makes the most sustained use of this of any of her films. Perhaps the classic Garland camp line is her reply to a woman who came up to her after a stage show and said, 'Never forget the rainbow, Judy, never forget the rainbow'; Garland replied, 'How can I forget the rainbow? I've got rainbows up my arse.'

To androgyny and camp – both ways of exploiting the space of the social category 'homosexual' – a third element must be added that is more negative. The category homosexual is not a neutral one – it is intended to define a pathology, a sickness. If the gay subculture internalised the idea of homosexuals as a discrete category of in-betweeners, then it is not surprising that it should in part internalise the definition of the category's sickness. Self-hatred, a belief in one's pathos, also marks gay male culture, and for this the later image of Judy Garland provided vivid imagery. Precisely because she could be our (androgynous, camp) star, her failures, her chaotic life, her problems with her appearances, her men, her career could also be used as an expression of what a mess gay men thought they were. There are two aspects to this – a deeply self-oppressive identification with her God-awfulness, but also an admiration for her ability to keep going in the face of it, to be brave and strong under the burden of her/our life. All of this applies far more to her stage and television work, and her image in publicity, though the few later films from *A Star Is Born* on also use it, particularly *I Could Go On Singing*.

All of this needs further research. The analysis of urban male gay culture has only just begun, and it needs to be put together with a detailed consideration of the textual possibilities of the Garland image. In particular, it is clear that Garland's place in gay cultural discourse is overdetermined – I need to get the complexity of the determinations clearer, to begin to see the contradictions and the different ways of inhabiting homosexuality that what I've said above tends to elide. All I have been suggesting is a way of beginning to think about these questions.

Originally published in Christine Gledhill (ed.), *Star Signs: Papers from a Weekend Workshop*, London: BFI, 1982, pp. 13–22.

2 THE MEANING OF TOM JONES (1971)

This is a study of the public personality of Tom Jones, the most highly paid British entertainer in history. It takes this image as a significant complex of meaning and subjects it to an immanent analysis of its aesthetic and moral values. It is concerned with the determinant meaning of the image rather than with the particular meaning or significance the image may assume in a given situation. It seeks to define and understand what objectively the value dimensions of the image are, rather than to understand its subjective meaning to audience, manager or star. Even beyond the errors of naivety of 'effects' research, a great deal of contemporary research is focussed, in principle if not in practice, on the meaning of the phenomenon in question to the actors. The present research is based on the belief that this meaning-to-actor can only be comprehended within an understanding as precise as possible, of what the phenomenon is.

THE SHOW

The following analysis is structured on the basis of the ATV Network production *This Is Tom Jones*. There are several reasons for this.

First, the analysis had to be of performance, since this is our primary definition of what Jones is. Second, television performances are the only kind available over a sufficiently wide area to make debate possible. That is to say that findings are needed upon which disagreements can be made, and this is only possible when the researcher deals with material that others can scrutinise; otherwise he will produce only journalistic assertion. Third, the television programme is much richer in evidence and semiological reference than other performance forms (cabaret, night club, variety one-night stand). Much of contemporary light entertainment on television consists of programmes built around a single performer and designed to present him or her not simply as a performer but as a personality. This it does by employing a variety of artistic devices to present a selection of facets which it is felt go to make up the public personality of the performer. Thus a television show will be particularly helpful to us when we are attempting to examine this public personality.

Like many weekly television shows, *This Is Tom Jones* has a regular structure or formula. The following treatment is essentially of this, rather than of any particular show.

THE SHOW: OPENING

The show opens with the camera trained on a microphone on a stand. A voice announces 'This is Tom Jones' and a hand grabs the mike. The camera tracks back to show Jones singing 'It's Not Unusual'. This opening, song and production, set off a train of associations that in effect set the tone for the whole show.

The song
'It's Not Unusual' was Tom Jones' first record to become a big hit, climbing in a very short time to number one in the Hit Parade. Jones as a public personality began here. It is important to dwell on this moment of public celebration, because it is here that so many of the elements which go to make up the image were first stated, and with a powerful impact. These images would both carry Jones, colouring his every performance or appearance in the press, and have to be carried by him, something he would have to live up to and bear out.

The song in itself, if one thinks of it apart from Jones' performance of it, is not unlike a type of song particularly popular in that year, 1965. This was a type composed principally by Burt Bacharach and Tony Hatch, and characterised by unusual 'sophisticated' harmonics and difficult and surprising rhythms and leaps in the tune's line. The words were also rather unusual, dealing with topics other than love and loss of love, or rather dealing with them distinctively – using urban or realistic images to express feelings – loss expressed by 'there's always something there to remind me', or the injunction to the beloved to 'walk on by' 'if you see me walking down the street', or the advice to the lonely to go 'downtown'. All this was supported by a luxuriant kind of orchestration which finally linked the songs to an older ballad tradition, different both to the frankly romantic ballads that put even comedians like Ken Dodd into the hit parade and to the beat, post rock 'n' roll numbers that were also popular. It was the sophisticated music of the same middle class urban society that had applauded Cole Porter and Jerome Kern.

That is the song, thought of apart from Jones' performance of it. For when Jones took it, provided a simple up-tempo backing for it and sang it in his own distinctive manner, it no longer belonged to this genre of popular music. That is, its connection with this genre was readily discernible (note the quirky rhythms at the end of each phrase, the double negative and use of 'wo-wo' in the words) but it clearly also expressed a whole different approach to music – bluesy, aggressive, with a heavy beat. Jones thus introduced a new music (and hence new values) to the hit parade whilst still relating to a widely acceptable idiom.

What was the difference? First, Jones was a man, and most of these songs had been sung by women (the song had itself been intended for Dusty Springfield). Not only this, he was very much a man, compared to the androgynous type that was then becoming popular. On the other hand, the masculinity was of a recognisable type – it did not have the strangeness, the shockingness, the hipness of a Mick Jagger. The masculinity was in the build, in the face, in the voice. On television he appeared in a string shirt of the kind Cliff Richard wore in 'Summer Holiday'; on Richard it had been coyly sexy, on Jones it was really provocative.

This masculine sexiness, surprising in the context of that song and that sort of pop singer, has remained the essential defining characteristic of Tom Jones, and we shall return to it repeatedly as we get nearer to understanding precisely what image of sexuality is involved. Newspapers were quick to pick it up at the time of the success of 'It's Not Unusual'. He was compared to P. J. Proby, at the time making headlines by splitting his velvet trousers on stage, but Jones had none of the campness and baroque which Proby introduced in his act. Nor was he like Billy Fury, who had seemed to be performing elaborate masturbatory rites with the microphone when he was on stage. Questioned about his sexiness, Jones would always say that he was merely 'presenting the number' – it was the emotion he felt at the time, and since he was a living man, this (of course) had a sexual dimension to it.

The production

The production of the opening number in *This Is Tom Jones* is also important. The microphone seems to be waiting for the star, and this is emphasised by the delay in its being used, the camera's concentration on it and the announcement over. The notion of the star will be considered at the end of this paper, but here it is important to consider the image of stardom which is part of Jones' public personality. Jones is defined by his masculine values, by his performing ability (which the microphone heralds) but also by his ontological status as a star, or a superstar. That is he is not just a sexy man who sings well, but a different order of being.

This kind of imagery is well expressed in two booklets, *Tom Jones*[1] and *This is Tom Jones*.[2] In both these the life of Jones is covered in a few pages and the rest is devoted to a celebration of what it is like to be a star. Two elements are particularly emphasised. The first is Tom's admission into a kind of mutual admiration society of stars. Such 'unquestionable' greats as Frank Sinatra and Betty Grable seek fleeting contact with Tom, whilst both booklets devote considerable space to a visit Elvis Presley and his wife paid Tom while he was touring the States. The Purnell booklet emphasises

---

1. *Tom Jones*, a Purnell TV Special, London: BBC Publications Ltd., 1969.
2. *This is Tom Jones*, A Daily Mirror Special, London: Hamlyn, 1969.

Tom Jones performing on *This Is Tom Jones*, September 1969. (ABC Photo Archives/Disney General Entertainment Content via Getty Images)

Tom's own admiration for Elvis as a teenager and continues: 'The great moment came and suddenly Tom was standing face to face with the man who has remained the true superstar of the last decade, carrying fans who had cheered him when they were sixteen, and who had now married and turned twenty-six or more, with him.' This extraordinarily loose sentence gives no specific idea of the kind of stardom Elvis embodies, but rather evokes a world of adulation, where existence is defined by the fact of being adulated. A second emphasis is Tom's possession of a Rolls Royce. A picture of him standing by it is captioned 'The symbol of success – showbiz style … a gleaming Rolls-Royce'. This is from the Purnell booklet; the *Daily Mirror* goes one better: 'Not one Rolls-Royce in the garage, but two. That's the ultimate symbol of success for Tom' and another picture shows him seated in one of them, a cut-glass decanter and glass in hand with the caption: 'Just testing the luxury of his new Rolls

Royce with a quick snifter from the concealed bar at the back'. The Rolls Royce is of course almost of itself suggestive of a different world of being – luxuriant, smoothness, wealth. Anyone who is at home in a Rolls Royce seems almost a different order of person. Or if that is felt to be going too far, the Purnell description makes a similar point rather more crudely: 'Outside the house a gleaming car sits waiting, the light catching on the highly polished surface as though ready for instant flight. It is a Rolls Royce and it shrieks expense'. The Purnell booklet has a section entitled 'A Day in the life of a Star'. Even the title seems to be suggesting that Tom is defined by being a star, rather than by more specific qualities. The article which follows shows Tom rising very late, driving to a club to rehearse, taking a sauna, giving a performance and going back to bed. This is spun out, but more time is spent discussing what Tom's manager Gordon Mills does or says or the progress of the car through various streets to various clubs than in anything Tom does. Apart from signing autographs and the fifty minutes of 'a-tomic Tom', he does nothing but be. His car is chauffeur-driven, his decisions are made for him, even his body is 'stretched, pulled and rolled into shape' by someone else. A superstar precisely does not do anything but just is.

These two booklets and the rest of Jones' publicity gives substance and detail to the resonances set up by the actual production of the opening number. This interplay of production and promotion is what together constitutes the image of Tom Jones.

Another aspect of production in the opening number of *This Is Tom Jones* is the phallic significance of the microphone. One could argue that all microphones are, but in this instance the observation fits well with the imagery of Jones. There is something about the way his hand grabs the mike which immediately makes of the mike a live thing. Moreover, the camera's concentration on it gives it a kind of vital, even autonomous quality. One might even speak of totems.

It is evident that in discussing Tom Jones one must at some point or other mention his penis. The idea that male performers are sex symbols is hardly original. Hortense Powdermaker, in her extremely unreliable book *Hollywood the Dream Factory* reports that young male leads were commonly referred to on the film lot as the Penis. However, in the case of Tom Jones it is not just symbolic, it's the penis itself. A series of articles in the *Daily Sketch* in the beginning of November 1969 referred repeatedly to Tom's tight trousers, always managing to imply that they revealed the shape of his penis. Letters from female viewers were quoted: one woman asked whether Tom padded his crutch, to which Tom replied 'There's nothing false about me but my nose'. Certainly, the trousers are cut in a revealing fashion, although not as revealing as the *Daily Sketch* made out, and in several of the photographs in the *Daily Mirror* booklet the lighting and angle show clearly a bulge at the crutch. Moreover, Tom's movements are either a thrusting forward of the groin or else, especially and increasingly, as the series has proceeded, a gyrating of the hips. He doesn't dance properly nor does he use his arms expressively. Of course, one can overplay this kind of observation and certainly Tom's sexuality cannot be reduced to a bulge in his pants. The point is that, with Tom Jones as compared to a sexy singer like Engelbert Humperdinck, the precise physical meaning of sexuality is not glossed over by a wash of sultry looks. Tom Jones has a penis and one does not forget it, but he has the personality to back it up.

The opening sequence of the Tom Jones TV show then gives us Tom the singer and record maker, Tom the superstar, Tom the penis and Tom of 'It's Not Unusual', a jumping off point for a complex series of understandings about what Tom is.

THE SHOW: REGULAR FEATURES

Apart from the guest spots, Tom does four other spots in his show, most of which emphasise aspects that have already emerged in the discussion of the show so far.

First, there is an up-tempo routine with the dancers. The dancing is frantic, and Tom stands in the middle moving but hardly dancing. Of particular interest are the sets and costumes for this sequence. In the first show, the routine took place before a huge blown-up photograph of Tom wearing a black leather outfit. The second show had him again in black leather, but had the dancers in weird lurex costumes, with bras for the girls and singlets for the boys, and a set that looked like a highly glamourised factory – the whole tone was industrial and dynamic. On 14th December 1969, Tom wore for this spot white trousers and Western jacket (see below), the dancers wore 'wet look' jumpsuits (trendy styling in a modern artificial fabric), the setting was back projection of circles and the camera work added to the hectic and gyrating effect. Another show had Tom and the dancers in Karate clothes, with the boys and the girls alternately defeating each other in bouts of very swiftly moving Karate. What these numbers do is project the *dynamic* aspect of Tom's image and the *aggressiveness*, which comes from the machine age, the Western or newly discovered forms (on a mass scale) of Japanese violence. (In fact, these sequences, often inventively conceived, tend to drown Tom – the dancing and design are so much more dynamic and professional than he is.) Then there is his country-and-western spot, when he sings accompanied by a guitarist called Big Jim Sullivan. On one occasion Tom introduced this spot by saying that it was one of his favourite kinds of music and that he felt so at home in it. Compared to the kind of music broadcast on 'Country meets Folk' on Radio One, Jones' country and western seems far more powerful and more in a tradition of industrial balladeering than the folksy flavour of most of what passes for country and western. Certainly with the Western gear and the heavy presence of Big Jim Sullivan it suggests a world of virility – the hard West.

Another regular spot for Jones in the shows is the moment when he sings a sentimental ballad. After 'It's Not Unusual' Tom's hits were in fact far more of the type associated with Engelbert Humperdinck or Ken Dodd – 'Delilah', 'Green Green Grass of Home', and 'Without Love'. They are characterised by big, soaring and easily memorised melodies, broadly sentimental lyrics and heavily romantic orchestration, closer to Rachmaninov than to Bacharach's Mahler. Undoubtedly it is these that have earned him his strong following amongst older women. What they contribute to the Jones image is an enlargement of the area of 'soul', a kind of bastard spiritualisation of it. In a sense, this is another kind of respectability, taking up the banal reassurances of popular romantic ballads but I think it works more especially as an apparent enrichment (but in my view actual impoverishment) of the total sexual field we have already picked out. It has the bigness of manly emotion; if it is sentimental, it is generously so and in an uncomplicated way. It is usually shot in a part of the set that looks like a rather plush and anonymous hotel lounge or first class passenger airport lounge, and often benefits from imaginative fluid camerawork; Tom does not sing to a camera but is caught singing wrapped in emotion.

THE SHOW: CLOSING SEQUENCE

Finally there is the closing sequence of the show. This begins like the opening sequence, with a close up of a microphone and the voice over 'This is Tom Jones' but when the camera swings back it is to see Tom entering a large arena lit from below (that is, a glass floor with underfloor lighting), surrounded on three sides by 'stalls' of women and backed on the fourth by a large orchestra and chorus (The Mike Sammes Singers). He does three numbers, a fast one to open and close, and a slow one in the middle. At the end of the first number he undoes his bow tie (he is wearing a dinner jacket) and mops his brow. At points during the songs he goes up to the front rows of women, shakes hands with some and sometimes kisses a few. They in turn shriek and hold out their hands and bodies to him. This sequence has a live feel to it, almost like an outside broadcast and one half fears and hopes that at any moment the women will drag Tom down among them. By this point, he has everything working for him – the publicity and promotion, the big sound of band and orchestra, the big (working-class) body (penis) bursting out of the dinner jacket (upper class/superstar class), the kinds of song referring back to specific aspects (virility, romance) of his image. Moreover, for viewers, as opposed to those actually in the audience, it is a sight of a celebration of all these things – it is sex symbol and superstar in action, validated by the screams of the audience.

We have been concerned above all with facets and features, with elements of meaning and aesthetic qualities. Of course, Jones is not a jumble or even an ordered collection of ideas or features. He is a human being and it is important to remember this. What gives any symbolic cluster its force in the world of entertainers is the fact that the actual physiognomy and existential reality of the cluster is unique and assured by the uniqueness of the individual human being. This is not a declaration of faith, but a simple observation of fact. Generalised values are here embodied in a particular person, and the fact that that person is particular acts as a 'guarantee' that the generalised values hold, have meaning. Jones does not simply symbolise or represent sexuality for instance: the fact that he exists means, or can be felt to mean, that this sexuality itself exists.

THE NOTION OF STARDOM

A star is someone in the world of entertainment who has charisma. He or she has that aura, that special magic, that star quality and excitement … clichés for the phenomenon are not hard to find – understanding is rather more difficult. Charisma has been defined as 'an *extraordinary* quality of a person, regardless of whether this quality is actual, alleged, or presumed.'[3] The qualification is important, since it raises the question of whether, in the present instance, a star really is extraordinary or not. Audiences and professional entertainers alike seem to need to believe that the charisma is real, an inborn 'something extra', but modern thought on charisma has tended to underplay this and stress the importance of social context. E.A. Shils writes: 'The charismatic quality of an individual as perceived by others or himself, lies in what is thought to be his connection with (including possession by or embodiment of) some *very central* feature of man's existence and the cosmos in which he lives. The centrality, coupled with intensity, makes it extraordinary'.[4]

There are two ways of understanding this in terms of how individuals come to have this particular role in society. On the one hand, the charismatic figures can be seen as simply a passive recipient of various social tendencies, someone who happened to be around when these tendencies were coming together. Clearly it is difficult – but not impossible – to hold such a view and in certain cases it may be singularly appropriate. The present Royal Family for instance may be said to have charisma, but it would be hard to think this an extraordinary quality they possess; infinitely passive they were born in the right place to embody certain central tendencies of our society. On the other hand, the charismatic individual may be seen as one more than usually responsive to the mood and tendencies of his society and able to act in such a way as to play an especially appropriate, and hence charismatic, role in it. The example of Napoleon may be relevant; one could argue that the condition of French society at the time made dictatorship by that kind of man possible and meaningful to the people, and that in addition Napoleon, being the kind of person he was, was able to

---

3. Max Weber, *Essays in Sociology*, translated and edited by H. H. Gerth and C. Wright Mills, New York: Oxford University Press, 1946, p. 295.
4. Edward Shils, 'Charisma, Order, and Status', *American Sociological Review* 30:2 (April 1965), p. 201.

understand the situation in terms of his won charismatic role in it. This ability to, as it were, 'seize the time', need not be deliberate or even conscious; in political history it does always seem to have been so (Louis XIV, Cromwell, Lenin, Churchill, Mao Tse-Tung …), but if we turn to the field of professional entertainers it seems less likely. Thus the apparent need of the American public for prematurely avuncular singers in the mid-twentieth century was surely not realised by Bing Crosby when he assumed this role and gave to it his own particular blandness and humour. He was neither passively in the right place, since the mass media industry is not highly structured in quite the same decisive way as the English class system, nor inexplicably charismatic, an extraordinary individual overwhelming all by his personality. The charisma came from both the appropriateness and the individuality of Crosby.

In any event, whether or not you believe in the reality of the charismatic figure's extraordinary qualities is ultimately a matter of choice that does not affect the analysis. That is to say that if one takes the line that the figure *does* possess these qualities, then one is still bound to show why these qualities should work at this time, which means examining the social context. My own bias, for what it is worth, is not to believe in the qualities themselves but to believe in the capacity of certain people to embody, sustain and effectively create these qualities. A star is someone who always manages to live up to his charismatic image. It may be that Tom Jones' meteoric rise in the USA, and the present falling-off of interest there is due to his inability to live up, over a sustained period, to his image.

Having said this, I do not see a simple way of showing the centrality of the values Jones expresses to our society. For one thing, whilst they certainly are central, I don't believe that one could show that there was a 'need' for Tom Jones. If he had not happened, there is no reason to suppose that he would have to have been invented. Peter Jones' image, in his recent biography of Tom Jones, of a nation crying out for masculinity in an entertainment industry swamped by effeminacy doesn't really seem adequate, although clearly this is part of the explanation. (But it doesn't explain why effeminacy should have got so far in the pop world). Jones does represent forcefully traditional images and values of the working-class male, which may be said to be under threat from the seductions of affluence and hooliganism – but paradoxically Jones catches the violence of the latter and the respectability and materialism of the former. Again, Jones' appeal to middle-aged women is suggestive, when one considers their role in the old working-class street culture, now diminishing, and their vulnerability to advertisers of consumer goods and labour-saving devices (which are associated too with respectability and knowing one's place). Jones, by suggesting the old values of pride in class and toughness and yet by being affluent and respectable, may be providing a set of values comparable to the aggression-without-bite that has made *The Sun* so successful. These are of course only hypotheses, but it is perhaps in providing such hypotheses that the real usefulness of the analysis of the mass media lies. Rather than seeking to explain why Tom Jones is popular, in itself rather a trivial question, one is saying, given that Tom Jones is popular, and with these people, what does this tell us about the kind of society we live in. Given that he is like *this* what can we suppose (and set up for further research) about contemporary culture and consciousness? It is reasonable after all to want art to tell us about life, and not parasitically to call on life to tell us about art.

Original (longer) version published in *Working Papers in Cultural Studies*, Birmingham: Centre for Contemporary Cultural Studies, Vol. 1 (1971), pp. 53–64.

3   GENE KELLY (1972)

Gene Kelly is good-looking, with a broad white smile and a muscular body. He is, in John Russell Taylor's words, 'the open, confident, brash … straightforward American male.'[1] His energy and his virility register in his dancing style, but his personality does not go uncriticised in the films and this gives him a certain vulnerability.

Kelly's style is, like most film dancers, a hybrid. Chiefly he draws on tap, folk and modern dance – social dances are conspicuously absent from his range. The styles are predominantly masculine – few women have mastered tap, American folk styles are actually limited to male expression, and modern dance, although many of its pioneers have been women, is especially associated with virile, aggressive, impressively physical performance. Kelly himself has admitted that Martha Graham was the biggest choreographic influence on him,[2] and although it may not be directly observable in the overall style, nonetheless it is recognizable in the tautness of the limbs, the development of dance to express lonely or neurotic states, and in a liking in solo numbers for oppositional asymmetrical shapes. The modern dance approach gives the dancing a strength and physical presence, a sense of effort and strain, which express masculine activity and power, and Kelly's own body, with big thighs and shaped torso, is a paradigm of muscular virility.

The masculinity of the dancing is complemented by the vehicles. Kelly always plays an all-American type – vaudeville performer (*For Me and My Gal*), ex-G.I., but very much seen as having once been a G.I. (*American in Paris*, *It's Always Fair Weather*) and particularly as a sailor (*Anchors Aweigh*, *On the Town*, *The Magic Lamp*). He has on occasion been quite fierce about masculinity and dancing, regretting "the paucity of men entering the dance field, for a reason no-one wants to talk about – the feeling that the field is dominated by homosexuals. … Dancing is a form of athletics, and I'd like to see it attract strong young men who can experience the value and the sheer

---

1. John Russell Taylor, *The Hollywood Musical*, London: Secker & Warburg, 1971, p. 60.
2. Albert Johnson, 'The tenth muse in San Francisco', a report of a lecture given by Gene Kelly, in *Sight and Sound* 26:1 (Summer 1956), p. 48.

Publicity shot of Gene Kelly, circa 1942. (Hulton Archive/Getty Images)

joy of it."[3] Yet his masculinity does not go unchallenged – it is often presented as being rather too overweening, self-satisfied, arrogant and insensitive. In *For Me and My Gal* (his first film after making a success on Broadway as the archetypal heel, Pal Joey) he played a coward and a boaster, in *The Pirate* he is a show-off, in *Singin' in the Rain* he is a very conceited film star, in *Les Girls* he thinks he is capable of winning any girl he chooses. Male pride is shown as being both splendid and foolish, and the girls he woos are always quick to mock him. Yet underneath it all, he is sensitive, and the mocking, while he recognises its aptness, upsets him – this is particularly clear in the scene in *On the Town*, where he finally meets up with 'Miss Turnstiles' (Vera-Ellen) and by bragging immediately puts her off him; it is only when he sheepishly admits how

---

3. Quoted in Marshall Stearns and Jean Stearns, *Jazz Dance*, New York: Macmillan, 1968, p. 355.

boastful and vain he has been, that she melts and agrees to go out with him. In this way honour is vindicated – the man gets the girl, the woman is not fooled by the boy. (His non-musical roles have exploited this ambiguity still further).

The image of American manhood that Gene Kelly embodies is complex, making appeals to both men and women in the audience. The strength shows in the dancing – but so does the tendency to show off. At best, this leads to an exuberant expression of self-satisfaction – the song 'I Like Myself' sung and danced on roller skates (*It's Always Fair Weather*) or the 'Nina' number from *The Pirate*, described by Michael Burrows as 'sheer athletic gymnastic display – full of zest, and alive with all the throbbing intensity, the sheer exuberance at Gene Kelly's happy command.'[4] But it also leads to a striving for effect, a desire to be more 'meaningful' and 'serious' and 'artistically important'. Where he has a hand in the choreography or direction himself, he tends to depart from the life-assertive, optimistic, entertaining modes of dance expression endemic to the musical and develop (with Martha Graham not far behind) dance as a means of expressing conflict, anxiety, stress, mood – the 'alter ego' number in *Cover Girl*, or the long dream sequences typical of his major MGM musicals, where in a melancholy mood he looks back over his life (*The Pirate*) or recent events (*On the Town, An American in Paris*). Much of the criticism that has been levelled at Kelly for these sequences has been made from the position of the high art critics, deprecating the aspirations of a popular artist. Thus David Vaughan writes of Kelly's bad tendency as '…a conscious striving after art, that results inevitably (in a mass entertainment medium) in the production of *kitsch*.'[5] It is not because he is working in a mass medium that Kelly's serious numbers seem odd and unsatisfactory (a view, incidentally, which is not anyway universally shared), but because they occur in the context of the musical genre. Where usually the number is an *escape* or *release* from problems or neurosis, in Kelly's serious numbers it is an intensification of the unhappy situation of feeling. Sometimes in the course of it, happy moments are joyously recalled, and sometimes at the end the process of going over things in his mind has lightened his mood; but at other times he ends up as dejected as he started.

Virtuosity and artistic seriousness can be interpreted as part of male pretentions, and they are also quite clearly aspects of being a splendid performer. What makes Kelly odd, and despite his enormous influence on the musical it may account for a feeling that he is perhaps not quite a star in the way that Crosby and Astaire are (i.e. embodiments of central value complexes), is that his initial image of the all-American male – broad grin, open personality, tough body – gradually becomes much less endearing as his roles tend to stress his weaknesses and his dancing tends to look

---

4. Michael Burrows, *Gene Kelly – Versatility Personified*, St. Austell: Primestyle, 1972, p. 11.
5. David Vaughan, 'After the Ball', *Sight and Sound* 26:2 (Autumn 1956), p. 90.

pretentious. This almost undermines the initial impact, so that [despite] the admiration he calls forth, his charismatic following is limited. He is a splendid performer, more versatile than Fred Astaire, 'deeper' than any other musical star – but precisely those qualities make us suspect his boy-next-door image, and our suspicions are reinforced by his roles. In the end he is not so much like you and me as we'd like.

Extract from Richard Dyer, 'Social Values of Entertainment and Show Business,' unpublished PhD thesis, Centre for Contemporary Cultural Studies, University of Birmingham, October 1972, pp. 325–8.

4   JANE FONDA (1979)

Few star images can have developed with such startling shifts of gear as that of Jane Fonda. If one divides her career up into three periods, it is hard to believe they all refer to the same star – an early period in which she was promoted as the all-American daughter of all-American Henry Fonda; a middle period in France, in the thrall of sexpot-maker Roger Vadim; the latest period, in which she is primarily associated with various kinds of radical politics. Yet to see her image in terms of these switches from all-American girl to sexpot to radical is also an oversimplification. In the early period, even while pin-ups, interviews and her first film, *Tall Story* (1960) were pushing her all-Americanness, she was playing characters in films who were primarily defined in terms of their sexuality – a sassy prostitute in *Walk on the Wild Side* (1962), a 'frigid' widow in *The Chapman Report* (1962). While being, in Sheilah Graham's words, 'the American girl gone to sex' in the French period, she also made a fun western, *Cat Ballou* (1965), and a straightforward Broadway Neil Simon comedy, *Barefoot in the Park* (1967). Even in recent years, the emphasis on political activism has not put a stop to a dwelling on her sexiness in publicity and many of the movies, to her continued appearance in light comedies such as *Fun with Dick and Jane* (1977), nor to the appropriateness of casting her in such all-American genres as the Western, *Comes A Horseman* (1979).

Here then is an image which brings into play three aspects of human life – Americanness, sexuality and radical politics – that the movies (and to a large extent our habits of thought) generally treat as separate, watertight compartments. At one point in the career one aspect is highlighted, at another another – yet all three are there to some degree all the way through. Plus a fourth that I won't go into here – the general acknowledgement of her capacities as an actor. The question is, how does it all hang together?

A preliminary question might seem to be – does it hang together at all? Do people just take the bits they want from the Fonda image and ignore the rest? Can a male chauvinist take an uncomplicated pleasure in her sexual objectification and someone into radical politics or accomplished acting not notice that the sexual objectification is there at all? In part this must certainly be the case, but what makes Fonda especially interesting is the way that each aspect of her image can also be read in terms of the others. What this means is that, on the one hand, the rather 'un-American' (and the McCarthyite flavour is intended) qualities of sexuality and radical politics are rendered acceptably American through her embodiment of them, and this might be deemed the progressive aspect of her image. On the other hand, the radical positions and causes she espouses are always in danger of being collapsed back into a trivialising emphasis on sexiness or that solvent of discontent, American normalcy. And these may be the fatal limitations of her image.

Let me illustrate this by tracing the relations of one aspect of the image – sexuality – to the other two. That she is deemed sexy is a constant of all the material one can read on her, be it publicity, reviews, ads or the films themselves. From her early promotion as a pin-up/starlet to the more recent up-market features on 'Fonda at Forty' in the colour magazines, there is no let-up in this emphasis, although clearly it was the French period that most relentlessly foregrounded it. As in the other periods, it is right to point to the objectification that this entailed – Fonda cannot magically escape the patriarchal construction of woman as object, and especially not under the tutelage of that Svengali of the sex object, Roger Vadim, the man who invented Brigitte Bardot. Yet one has to remember that at the time, Vadim-Bardot and all that it represented was seen by many people as a progressive image of women and sexuality. Simone de Beauvoir had written a pamphlet in praise of Bardot; Fonda spoke in interviews of Vadim "letting me be myself". The Vadim woman was held to be happily and self-directingly sexual; her sexuality was for her own enjoyment, not only men's. To us now, Bardot's adolescent capriciousness and the rather dated kinkiness of Fonda's work with Vadim such as *Barbarella* (1968) may appear the very antithesis of a liberated sexuality, but one has to remember what went before it, and especially in the case of Fonda. Her pre-French roles were highly sexual alright, but divided between the antiseptic cheerleader sex-appeal of *Tall Story* and the early pin-ups and the neurotic sexuality of her portrayals in *Walk on the Wild Side* and *The Chapman Report*. In the light of these two alternatives for female sexuality in the Hollywood of the Fifties, Vadim could be taken as liberating, and perhaps especially so with Fonda and her all-American associations. Thus enjoyment of sexuality was represented as a possibility for an American woman, without the childishness of Bardot (far more a throwback to Clara Bow), while Vadim's obsessions with bondage and fetishism seemed mere fun acted by healthy, sensible, resourceful, American Jane.

The problem in discussing this is not to overstate the case in either direction – not seeing at all the relatively progressive aspect of the French period, not recognising how it remained caught within patriarchal imagery. Both things are characteristic of the image at this point. It's important to hold on to the former emphasis for a moment, because it leads us to an understanding of the problems of the later, 'political' period.

Jane Fonda on the cover of *Birmingham Arts Lab* film programme, December 1979. (The Internet Archive)

The vague idea of sexual freedom, especially for women, espoused by Vadim-Fonda feeds into one understanding of the notion of 'liberation' in the women's movement in the early seventies. Fonda's relationship with feminism has always been oblique. She conformed to the media image of a feminist for a time, with her jeans, cropped hair and loose T-shirts; you *could* interpret *Klute* (the prostitute as the honest embodiment of women's social situation), *Julia* (female bonding) and both *Coming Home* and *The China Syndrome* (the politicisation of a woman) in feminist terms. Yet she has never directly promoted feminist issues nor been clearly identified with the women's movement. In a sense, this distance from feminism per se has paradoxically allowed her to be identified, at the level of *imagery*, with 'women's lib', as the media call it. It's the sexual connection – one way that the media could accommodate the new feminism was in terms of sexual permissiveness, women demanding the right of access to the *Playboy* lifestyle. Fonda, 'liberated' by Vadim, could appear to make the transition to the newly sexual woman – honestly hooking in *Klute*, talking openly about screwing in *Tout Va Bien*, discovering orgasm in *Coming Home*. I don't say this is how the 'real' Jane Fonda relates to feminism, nor the only way in which her image can be read in relation to it, but the sexual element is one of the ways that eases the passage of a certain sort of feminist feeling to her films.

But it's what gets left out in the process, the price paid for the *mass* media presence of a limited feminism, that is crucial. On the one hand, the political demands of feminism are absent – Fonda is seen campaigning for Vietnam, for Californian grape-pickers, for nuclear disarmament but not for women's rights. Moreover, she does this – that is, she is presented as doing this – under the sway of men, usually Tom Hayden, her husband (it's he who's running for office, not she). The films compound this – Lillian in *Julia* leans on wise old Dashiell, even though the film is supposed to be about the impact of Julia on her; in *The China Syndrome* the Fonda character has to learn politics from the two male leads, and she is similarly caught between two men in an age-old romantic opposition in *Coming Home*. On the other hand, the importance of lesbianism in the sexual-political programme of contemporary feminism is conspicuously absent in the Fonda image. Hideously stereotyped in the fun film *Barbarella*, it is hysterically avoided in *Julia*, a film crying out for some treatment of it.

One could put all this positively – and certainly, it would be wrong to be simplistically for or against Jane Fonda on ideological grounds. One could say that what Fonda's image does is make feminism a possible presence on the screens of the world, precisely by showing that women can participate meaningfully in radical politics and that feminism is relevant to heterosexual women (as the media have tended to assure us it isn't). Or you could say that sexual politics – the real demands of seventies feminism – is what has had to be sacrificed in order to accommodate the other radical aspects of Fonda's image.

It is in this ambiguity that much of the fascination of Fonda's image lies. She embodies in an exemplary fashion that critical conundrum of radical political culture – in order to make political headway, one has to reach a mass audience; but in order to reach a mass audience, one has to work within the largely reactionary constraints and traditions of mass popular culture. How does one pick one's way through this dilemma? Does Jane Fonda's image teach us any lessons in this regard?

Originally published in *Birmingham Arts Lab* programme (December 1979 – February 1980), pp. 27–8.

5 THE WAY SHE IS (1981)

Barbra Streisand has been a recording star for nearly twenty years, and a film star for almost as long. She has found fame as an intimate cabaret singer, as a player in both stage and film musicals, as a comedienne and as a recording artiste, and her name alone can virtually guarantee a film's success.

Streisand is admired profusely. She has influenced a whole generation of white women singers and is still the only 'bankable' contemporary female star. Her original treatment of songs, her impeccable comic timing, her range of talents – these are all soon acknowledged and are what make her a star. And yet it is curiously hard to find people who actually like her work and her star persona. Her talent, though, is extraordinary – but not limitless. She can't dance much, and as a singer is much better as a dramatic interpreter of a song than when trying to swing. Her sense of rhythm is not great – the slow opening bars of her recording 'Enough Is Enough' with Donna Summer suit her pure expressive vocal sound beautifully, but once the number rolls into disco, Summer triumphs. It is not yet clear whether Streisand can sustain a full-blooded tragic role without using singing – films like *Up the Sandbox* (1972) and *The Way We Were* (1973) are closer to the, perfectly legitimate, emotional range of soap opera rather than tragedy. But this is only to suggest limitations to a formidable talent. No-one can build a song vocally with such dramatic intensity *and* shading as she does in, say, 'People', 'The Way We Were' or 'What Did I Have That I Don't Have?'. Her comic timing never misses, her facial expressions are as varied as they are unusual, she wears clothes beautifully, gives every line of dialogue a wealth of meaning. And yet, perhaps somehow this is all too perfect, not in the way Fred Astaire's dancing is, or Ella Fitzgerald's singing, but in its calculation. It is like a finely honed and detailed surface that is, all the same, only a surface. That phrasing, that timing, those expressions, one can somehow hear and see them being produced. It is hard to experience it as a direct emanation of personality and feeling.

What's more, it is all there, all the time, the audience's attention is constantly grabbed. It is almost impossible to concentrate on someone else speaking on screen because of Streisand's display of brilliantly modulated reactions. Most of her leading men – Omar Sharif in *Funny Girl* (1968), Robert Redford in *The Way We Were*, James

Barbra Streisand in *A Star Is Born*, 1976.
(John Springer Collection/CORBIS/Corbis via Getty Images)

Caan in *Funny Lady* (1975), Kris Kristofferson in *A Star ls Born* (1976) – are laid-back to the point of being catatonic set beside Streisand, and few of her films have given other women any space. Though William Wyler, the director of her first film *Funny Girl*, seems to have kept her insistent display of talent at least somewhat subservient to the needs of the film, no director since has done so.

It is this sense of the constant assertion of a peerless surface talent that constitutes the core of Streisand's star appeal. It is an uncomfortable appeal. Unlike other stars, her image does not allow the viewer to sink back into the fiction that they are in unmediated contact with a real personality when watching the star. All star images involve a great deal of rehearsal and manufacture, but few are experienced in that way. Even though stars are constructed personalities like characters in fiction, the fact that these characters are always played by the same flesh-and-blood person makes it seem as if they are not just images but real people. Streisand is an exception to this rule. Her mannered portrayals draw attention to her performance as such. Her image tells the truth about the star phenomenon, namely, that all stars are performances. But this is a truth that is not really wanted – it is far preferable to believe the illusion that heart-to-heart contact has been made with the star.

Streisand not only disrupts the comfort of the illusion of the star-audience relationship, she is also assertive and thereby breaks another set of rules, those of femininity. There have always been strong independent women stars – Crawford, Davis, Hepburn, Stanwyck are the classics – but they seldom challenged male egos and were usually put into plots where at the end of the day they had to climb down and sink into the arms of the leading man. Streisand is not like this. Her insistent presence obliterates the male stars' egos; and the plots of her films either show her winning on her own terms as she does in *What's Up Doc?* (1972), or ending defiant in *Funny Girl*, plucky in *The Way We Were* or triumphant in *A Star Is Born* if she loses her man.

This assertiveness has other dimensions. She must be the first big star since Jolson who has used Jewishness not just for laughs, but for emotion and glamour as well. She represents too a modern rags-to-riches story, one of the few contemporary stars who has had to claw her way up from the bottom, with none of the child-of-the-famous advantages of the Fonda, Redgrave and Minnelli daughters – she was born in Brooklyn in 1942, and began her career by singing in nightclubs in Greenwich Village. This assertiveness has links with changing female roles, but feminism has only marginally informed her work. Her star predecessors are Jolson and Cagney, American individualism writ large – and perhaps that notion was always at the bottom meant for men. Feminism has challenged the very notion of individualism and not just its applicability. Streisand shows that individualism, as the assertion of a manufactured self, is possible for a woman – but how much is she liked for it?

Originally published in *The Movie*, no.75 (1981), pp. 1494–5.

6   DIANA ROSS (1982)

More and more, Diana Ross's concerts and albums are not a showcase for singing. There is plenty of performance, plenty of production, she is still good value – but singing is only one of the ingredients, and not necessarily the most impressive. Concerts and albums – she seems to have abandoned her film career – are now ecstatic celebrations of the myth and magic of Diana Ross.

Her voice of course is still at the heart of things. The qualities of the voice are both what made her a star, gave her that particular quality that caught on, and what made her a 'cross-over' figure, appealing equally to Black and white audiences. It combines opposite vocal textures that are also the different textures of the traditions of Black and white popular song. It has the fragile, cut-glass sweetness of soprano singers like Deanna Durbin or Moira Anderson, but also the funkiness of other Motown singers, Mary Wells or Gladys Knight. It has the vocal 'purity' of white song, but is also capable of all the 'dirty' notes as well, all the notes which the straitjacket of the whole tonal system has outlawed as flirty. Being a combination of textures, a cross-over sound, she doesn't exploit these vocal traditions to the full. She never has the coloratura precision and brilliance of the sopranos, and doesn't explore the expressive range of blues and soul – she never rasps and growls like Millie Jackson, never takes Billie Holiday's rhythmic risks, never evokes the gospel of Aretha Franklin. But her voice has other qualities that also fix her star image.

It is an almost unreal voice. The opening of 'Remember Me' – "Bye baby, see you around" – is ethereal, coming from nowhere, the echo chamber enhancing just that funky purity I've tried to describe. You can't quite believe anyone could sing like that. Donna Summer's early albums may have something of it, but cruder, more obviously sexual. The unreality of the voice is part of the magic of the act, one that is always reinforced by production. The album covers nearly always use soft focus, deliberate blurring, often with coloured smoke to enhance the effect; she is not photographed in any kind of concrete space, let alone any particular place; the clothes are in no way the clothes anyone would wear about the place. The shows often start with a series of such albums' cover images of her flashed up on a curtain; one of these freezes, and Ross walks out of it in the same costume as in the photograph. With her voice, her whole act is unreal, a fantasy.

The 'unreal' Diana Ross performing in Rotterdam, the Netherlands, June 1982. (Courtesy of photographer Rob Verhorst)

The other important quality of the voice is its 'femininity'. I don't mean femaleness — there is nothing intrinsically female about a high, delicate, but funky voice; but sex roles insist that there is something feminine about a vocal style that involves a range of devices such as: wordless cooing (the opening of 'Baby Love'), kittenish yelps (the climax of 'Ain't No Mountain High Enough'), supplicant whispers (the bridge passages of 'Touch Me in the Morning'), fragile screams of delight (throughout the concerts). And it is these feminine, and basically non-singing, qualities that have become so important as her career has developed.

The concerts, in particular, often have rather little in the way of sustained singing. What we get are endless reminders of past hits, snatches of 'Where Did Our Love Go?', 'I'm Still Waiting', 'Upside Down', which evoke different moments in her career, but which are not fully sung through or reworked musically. Like the albums, much of the musical element is Diana cooing and yelping to consummately orchestrated disco.

Her voice is often swallowed up in the strings and saxes, and then also in the fabulous costume changes and overwhelming lighting effects. Those bits of songs, those reminders of Diana Ross as a Supreme, Diana Ross in *Lady Sings the Blues*, Diana Ross as 'The Boss', are all swept up in a generalised celebration of Ross, star.

But then just what is Diana Ross, what is being celebrated? Above all, she is a success. She is the only female Black star whose name can be mentioned in the same breath as Frank Sinatra or Barbra Streisand — whose albums are always top best sellers, who is considered a big enough star to play at the top night clubs in Las Vegas and Atlantic City, who is, in other words, a one-hundred-per-cent certifiable star, with all the guaranteed profitability that implies. Billie Holiday, Ella Fitzgerald, Lena Horne, Donna Summer — none have quite made it so unarguably (whatever dispute there may be about their relative talents). Diana Ross is the epitome of something more characteristic of progressive directions in the USA than in Europe. She has been carried along on a tide of Black and feminist agitation and unrest that has not wanted to change society but to buy into, on fully equal terms, the goodies that white, male society already enjoys. Success has always been presented as one of the mainstream American goals of life — but the successful were not just any old Americans, but white male Americans. But just because success was presented as a general human goal, other — Black, female — people could demand that they be a part of it. Diana Ross is one of the most spectacular examples of someone who has been allowed to be a success, and not just in the marginalised spaces always permitted Black artistes — the obscurity of jazz ('the devil's music'), the supporting, servant roles in films, the chorus parts and speciality acts inserted into shows — but in the real mainstream of American popular entertainment.

At one level, we (Europeans) underestimate the force and importance of this form of social change. We fail to see the degree to which the USA is a more open society than any Western European country, that Black people and women can get on to an extent unimaginable over here. And if, with our excellent political hats on, our misgivings are based on our realising that such successes are still founded upon a system that must perpetuate inequality and oppression, I also detect a certain world-weary distaste for material pleasure, for commerce, for the paltriness of glamour and glitter, feelings that we inherit from an essentially aristocratic sensibility.

But of course we are right to be uneasy. Recent surveys show that the situation of Black people as a whole in the USA has got worse in the past ten years, not better, despite some spectacular cosmetic jobs of promotion. Ross epitomises a success that is still out of reach of most Black people or women (or indeed of working-class white men). But isn't that part of her act, too?

The sheer ecstasy of the whole Diana Ross thing is an outrageous revelling in what success could feel like, but not how to achieve it. The sexual imagery of the songs is often that of 'surrender' (evoked equally for men and women), and that is also what the experience of success is in the Ross shows – giving yourself up to the intoxication of worldly acclaim, of sensuous delight, of luxuriating passivity. These are real material pleasures, there is nothing wrong or strange in wanting them, but aren't they so excessively realised in the Diana Ross show that you can't believe in them as other than a gorgeous fantasy? The unreality of the voice, the insubstantial shimmer of the costumes, the fantastic orchestration – did anyone ever believe this was anything but a dream of how life could be more beautiful, not how it really was?

One of the high points in the show is the 'Reach Out and Touch' number. Diana goes into the audience and clasps hands with them, and then gets them all holding hands with whoever they are sitting next to, as she speaks, sings, coos, "Reach out and touch, somebody's hand, Make this world a better place, If you can." Surely no-one ever believed that's all you had to do, or that Diana was really going to lead us into a better world. But for a moment the ecstasy of success is linked to the joy of community, of feeling yourself part of a huge group of people bent on goodwill. We get to experience what a good feeling that is, even when we know we are only in the theatre experiencing it fleetingly.

I don't say listening to Diana Ross and reaching out and touching at her shows would make anyone join a movement to change the world; but at least it vividly expresses the pleasures of a better world. That goes along with the competitiveness of the success motif and the passivity of the femininity motif – no pleasures in this world are ideologically unalloyed. But with Diana, why not enjoy the best and forget the rest? There's nothing else quite like her around.

Originally published in *Marxism Today*, June 1982, pp. 36–7.

7 NEVER TOO THIN (1993)

Nothing is more entrancing, and nothing is harder to describe than the texture of a voice. Audrey Hepburn's was fresh, sweet and airy, but with soft, low vowels, other rather twangy ones and 's' sounds in danger of becoming a shade too sibilant. The accent too was a fascinating, ungraspable combination of the pure and the impure; she spoke in perfect BBC English, yet you just knew this was someone not born to it – there was such an indefinable, barely perceptible carefulness about it. As with her voice, so with her looks. She was exquisite, an ideal – yet her eyes and mouth were too big, her neck already betrayed veins and scrawniness by the time of *Breakfast at Tiffany's* and she was so bonily thin that she looked like she might snap in half if she didn't look out. Billy Wilder, who directed her in *Sabrina Fair* and *Love in the Afternoon*, spoke of 'that curious, ugly face of the dame'. Buddy Ebsen, playing her still besotted ex-husband in *Breakfast at Tiffany's*, tells George Peppard to make sure she eats, almost shuddering as he walks away, muttering, 'So skinny'. Her voice and her looks embody everything about her appeal – she is a catalogue of imperfections and yet she is perfect.

It is this that makes it possible to identify with her, even as she does what we never could. We all know only too well our imperfections. How wonderful to dream that, like Audrey, we could be the centre of attention, a touchstone of style and beauty, while still carrying those imperfections forward with us, somehow alchemically blending them into the dazzle of gorgeousness. So often in her career, in roles and in moments, that voice and those looks were held up as the last word in loveliness. She was a princess in her first Hollywood movie, *Roman Holiday*, and one of the classic literary heroines, Natasha, in *War and Peace*. In the '60s she was the ideal vehicle for the fashionable fashions of Givenchy. Her first appearance at the ball in *My Fair Lady*, where Eliza's credibility as a lady is put to the test, is breathtaking, shimmering and poised, instantly laying all doubts as to credibility aside. And the climax of the fashion shoot in *Funny Face*, rightly chosen by Paramount as a keynote illustration for their Hepburn special edition video box set, has her throwing her arms in the air, smiling hugely, walking confidently towards photographer Fred Astaire, and crying "Take the picture! Take the picture!" in an ecstasy of pleasure in being looked at. Who would not take pleasure in

A STAR IS BORN

Publicity shot of Audrey
Hepburn, mid 1950s.
(Getty Images)

it if they looked like Audrey? But, like her, most of us do have this and that too big, too small, too odd. You couldn't resent her and you could even imagine being her.

There is always a downside to such a phenomenon. Standards of beauty inevitably exclude the majority, and 'democratic' beauty such as Hepburn's may only induce a sense of misfortune or even failure in some in the audience. Her looks – so perfect for the ballerina she trained to be and which her fondness for ballerina slippers continually reminded us of – must have fed the anorexic imagination, which takes to lethal extremes the twentieth-century fashion dictum that 'one can never be too thin'. When she became a Goodwill Ambassador for UNICEF in 1988, she spoke of her experience of hunger as a child in occupied Holland, but this was never part of her image as a star. She just was perfectly – ridiculously, nearly gawkily – thin, but not from exercise or deliberate starvation. When in *Sabrina Fair* she tells Humphrey Bogart how hungry she is, not having eaten all day, it is quite startling. Audrey Hepburn eating? I really can't recall ever having seen her chomping away in any film – but then seeing women eating in movies is itself a rarity. Audrey does partake – is even perhaps the apotheosis – of this feminine syndrome, that denies appetite and elevates dangerous slenderness above all other physical attributes. Yet the sense of her being too thin, with consequent exaggeration of her eyes and mouth, suggested at least as much that she was gorgeous *despite* being so skinny.

Her imperfections, not least her skin and bones appearance, are transmuted into her perfection, and many of her roles are actually about this, about the transformation of an ugly duckling into a swan. She came to prominence not through her British film roles (mainly a case of blink and you'll miss her), but through her Broadway appearance as Gigi, an archetypal gawky-adolescent-transformed-into-stunning-woman plot that is also the basis of *Sabrina Fair*, *Funny Face* and *My Fair Lady*. As already described in the other two, *Sabrina Fair* has its moment of revelation as the camera tracks up Audrey in an Edith Head designed pencil skirted black suit, vindicating Audrey's voice over that she has become "the most sophisticated woman" and bringing William Holden's dashing car to a screeching halt (close-ups on tyres and all). Even when the whole story is not about such transformations, the idea may be implicit. *Roman Holiday* puts a spin on it by having her a rich and beautiful young woman who nonetheless needs to escape from the confines of her regal duties in order to be able to blossom. Transformation is also the basis of the story uncovered by the revelations of *Breakfast at Tiffany's*. In a way, this film turns the motif on its head. *Sabrina Fair* and the rest are about successful transformations, whereas Holly Golightly's is at best precarious. This is partly because her charmless wackiness is so unconvincingly expressed, but mainly because the movement of the film is towards despair, to her terrible admission that she does not believe in the part she has created for herself and for which she lives, and to a happy ending with a never more adorable George Peppard that is none the less set in the pouring rain down a back alley.

Paramount have chosen for their box set four of the films [*Breakfast at Tiffany's*, *Funny Face*, *Roman Holiday*, and *Sabrina Fair*] that most develop this dimension of her image. Yet I have always found her most genuinely loveable — she is one of the few stars whose death I really felt like a personal loss — in roles where this sense of the awkwardness of her perfection was a grace note rather than the subject of the film. As a nun unsure of her vocation in *The Nun's Story*, as a woman of mixed race (caucasian and Native American) in *The Unforgiven*, as a heterosexual woman more committed to her lesbian friend than her fiancé in *The Children's Hour*, there's a delicacy and warmth rarely conveyed in the portrayal of outsiders in Hollywood. Perhaps as a half-Irish, half-Dutch woman, brought up in Britain and making films in the USA, there was something especially suggestive for her about these roles. She's a displaced person, and yet suffers no anguish from this. Just as her voice and looks transformed imperfections into perfection, so in these roles she suggested what it might be like to be a serene misfit.

Originally published in *Sight and Sound* 3:12 (December 1993), p. 59.

8 CHARLES HAWTREY (1994)

The Wild West. A posse rides up to a redskin camp and asks for Chief Big Heap. The braves point to a wigwam. From within there is the sound of a toilet flushing, and out comes a thin, bespectacled figure who greets the posse, in a voice at once lascivious and ladylike, with "Oh, hello". It is Charles Hawtrey and this is *Carry On Cowboy*.

Hawtrey appeared in twenty-three of the thirty *Carry On* films and always he introduced himself with this drawling, suggestive yet refined "Hello". He did not give a fig for the circumstances or the appropriateness of this greeting. He was sometimes cast as a weed or even a fairy, but just as often as a rampant heterosexual or macho man. It didn't matter. He didn't change his style or manner one iota.

He was already a well-established character actor before the *Carry Ons* started. He began in 1930 at the age of sixteen and was not much out of work on stage and screen from then on. He was the kind of person you became familiar with in British films, though you might not be able to name them – people like Richard Wattis and Joan Hickson, who were like loveable but odd and sometimes difficult distant relations. But Hawtrey remained very much a bit player. It was only with *Carry On Sergeant* in 1958 that he really found the 'character' that was to make him not only recognisable but also a name.

It wasn't intended that *Sergeant* would be the first of a series, yet with Kenneth Williams, Kenneth Connor and Hattie Jacques, as well as Hawtrey on the team, the mould was cast. The series ran more or less annually until 1978 and Hawtrey was in the best of them – as an unsuitable recruit in *Sergeant*, a 'special constable' in *Constable*, secret agent 000 in *Spying*, Mark Anthony's father-in-law in *Cleo*, the chief in *Cowboy*, a lavatory attendant in *Screaming*, the Duc de Pommfrit in the Scarlet Pimpernel spoof *Don't Lose Your Head*, private Widdle of the Indian Army in *Up the Khyber* and the great Tonka, leader of an otherwise all-female tribe in *Up the Jungle*. In nearly all the parts he is miscast; in all of them he is wonderful.

He is always 'on'. Quite often he isn't given much to do other than to stand around, but he is perpetually animated. His eyes dart bird-like behind his wire-rimmed glasses, he nods at everything people say, looks delighted or crestfallen – no actor ever gave better value on the reaction front. He really enters into the spirit and the fun of it.

Charles Hawtrey in *Carry On Cowboy*, 1965. (BFI National Archive)

His laughter is infectious. For someone with such a high-pitched voice, his laugh was quite fruity, and it often gave the impression of being spontaneous and unrestrained. At the start of *Don't Lose Your Head*, he is an aristocrat about to be guillotined. He is quite unconcerned, however, lying in place, his neck in the blade shaft, reading a book and roaring with laughter. The book? Something by the Marquis de Sade. "Priceless!" quips Hawtrey and goes on laughing while the executioner gets ready.

He is a perpetual delight, but was he gay? The words Catholic and Pope may spring to mind, yet the films are oddly ambiguous – he is both 'obvious' and yet not explicit. Even in his private life, though his sexuality is hardly in doubt, he was not what we would now call 'out'. It was hardly a shock horror revelation when he was discovered to have, in the touching vocabulary of the tabloids, a twenty-year-old lad staying with him the night his house burned down in 1984, but hard gossip has not found its way into print. He certainly had a background in queer sensibility before the *Carry Ons*. He was in something called *Bluebell in Fairyland* in 1925, sang the surely

A STAR IS BORN

inappropriate 'A Country Life for Me!' at the Italia Conti school in 1925, played one of the lost boys in a production of *Peter Pan* and, most imaginable of all, was a male 'wilting lily' and a female secret agent in 1930s revues.

The films sometimes come on quite strong about his sexuality. In *Spying*, he is asked why he was given the odd number 000, when all the other spies have been given a final digit greater than zero. He recalls that the people assigning the numbers looked at him and said "oh-oh" (as in, "What have we got here?") and then "oh" (dragged out, as in "dear me!"). It's clear here that everyone has his number. Similarly in *Screaming* he's a gents' lavatory attendant; when cute Jim Dale and Harry Corbett go visiting, their efforts at making eye contact with him look like cottaging; when he proudly declares "I live in a man's world", the real meaning of the butch phrase is evident.

Yet just as often he is either asexual or even explicitly heterosexual. The very title of *Carry On Camping* leads one to expect the Hawtrey character to be, well, camp, but he's introduced in a camping equipment shop trying out a tent by strenuously

Charles Hawtrey and unidentifiable opponent in *Carry On Regardless*, 1960. (BFI National Archive)

snogging in it with a girlfriend. In *Henry*, he is a positively randy lord, who is bedding Henry VIII's present wife (Joan Sims) while the King (Sid James) is getting off with a cheeky chambermaid (Barbara Windsor). As always, in terms of being gay, he both obviously 'is' and isn't.

What is wonderful is the way that, whatever the part, he just doesn't even try to be butch. Delicious ambiguities ensue. In *Regardless* he has to act as a second for a boxing match, which involves him rubbing down the boxer, played by the forgotten but gorgeous Joe Robinson. When the boxer starts to whinge because he's been hit, which is after all the point of boxing, Hawtrey accuses his opponent of being a bully, then steps into the ring himself to defend Joe's honour. There's not a breath of suggestion that Charlie and Joe might be sexually interested in each other or that Hawtrey's character is anything other than straight. Yet the moment you put Hawtrey in the part, the rubbing down and sympathising with a muscleman's sissy behaviour take on a whole new complexion.

One of the effects of all this is to send up traditional masculinity. In *Sergeant*, he is one of a group of National Service recruits, compulsorily called-up to enlist in the army. Like several of the others, who include Bob Monkhouse as well as Kenneths Connor and Williams, the army needs to make a man of him. They fail, but mainly because he so wants to please that he exaggerates what they want to the point of hysteria. Asked to stand stiff and straight on parade, he does so so rigidly that he topples over. Required to bayonet a hanging dummy, he goes to it with a will, and is so carried away with the viciousness of it all that it is only with difficulty that he is persuaded to stop. By acting so exactly as the army requires, he ends up showing how utterly ridiculous normal masculinity is.

This mockery of masculinity is all the more fascinating in the context of films that often seem like hymns to sexism. The men are good-natured slobs who want nothing other than to have it away; the women, unless they are Barbara Windsor, are harridans intent on seeing that neither they themselves nor anyone else has any fun. This can be engaging – Sidney James and Barbara Windsor have a relish for the vulgar that is positively life-enhancing – but it can be dreary, in the remorseless sexism of men who fancy themselves, like Monkhouse in *Sergeant* or Leslie Phillips in *Nurse*, *Teacher* and *Constable*, and in the terrible misuse of talents like Joan Sims and June Whitfield. It's in this context that Hawtrey is such a tonic. He just sails plain through the unremitting heterosexual sexism, making straight masculinity look absurd and so making it look much more delightful to be a queen.

The unambiguous ambiguity of Hawtrey's sexuality works well in both upping the already obsessive innuendo stakes of the *Carry On* films and in undermining any vestiges of commitment to masculine values. But as a gay icon or role model? I have always loved him, yet he does embody one of the things that the Gay Liberation

Charles Hawtrey, circa 1965. (Larry Ellis Collection/Getty Images)

movement tended to disapprove of – the stereotype of the effeminate gay man. And no doubt much of the straight laughter at him is oppressive laughter. He confirms that gay men are ineffectual, trivial and, worst of all, like women. Yet for all the hatred that is expressed through the stereotype, it is also the case that Hawtrey was much loved – and anyway, I'll take the comparison with women as a compliment, thank you. Besides, who cares what people think? The most attractive thing about the turn to 'queer' in recent years is that it implies a rejection of worrying about what people will think. In his way, Charlie was like that too. What I relish most about him is his utter disregard for what anyone else may think. He just gets on with being himself.

The definitive example is in the second *Carry On* film, *Nurse*. He plays a patient who likes nothing better than to listen to the radio. His favoured listening? He likes classical music, a bit iffy still in 1959, and plays along with it, miming the piano part in concertos with such unguarded ecstasy that he flings himself out of bed. He also loves *Woman's Hour* (what sensible person does not?) and simply has to take the earphones off to share recipes with his uninterested fellow patients. Most of all he adores *Mrs Dale's Diary*, the long-established radio soap of the time. At one point he is sobbing

Grandmama would be so proud: Kenneth Williams and Charles Hawtrey in *Carry On Constable*, 1960. (BFI National Archive)

uncontrollably and a nurse rushes up concerned, but one of the others tell her not to worry – it's just Charlie listening to *Mrs Dale*. He is not quite defiantly queer; he just loves what he loves.

This reaches its peak in *Constable*, which has more, and the best, of Hawtrey than any of the others. His first appearance is unforgettable. There is squabbling among the constables at a local police station and in comes Charlie in his police uniform, a huge bunch of flowers in one hand and a bird in a cage in the other. "Hello!", he greets everyone and carries on as if it was entirely natural for policemen to come to work with flowers and a budgie.

Later he is teamed with Kenneth Williams. It is lovely to see these two queens together, but it also reveals the difference between them. What made Williams so funny in *Carry Ons* were his self-importance, extravagant delivery and general snottiness.

There was certainly a great sense of fun, but he had none of Hawtrey's unconcerned delight. Williams' humour was obsessed with other people, with his superiority to them, with what they may think; Hawtrey was oblivious to them, though generous and friendly. Here in *Constable*, he and Williams have to stake out a department store where there has been a rash of shoplifting. Williams has the idea for them both to drag up, so as to pass unnoticed among the women shoppers. Both get dressed in smart but not glamorous clothes. From the way Hawtrey primps in front of the mirror, it's obvious he wants to look nice. His delight in the whole business is expressed in a classic comic line: "You know I haven't done this since I was in the army – at a camp concert." The intended punch line is the play on 'camp', but audiences are usually falling about before this, at the idea that where a man would naturally remember dressing as a woman is, of course, in the army.

Even funnier to me, though, is a line that comes a little later. They decide what names to give each other. Williams says he'll be Agatha, his grandmother's name. He's in full drag and Hawtrey looks at him, and with a lump in his throat, says, "If grandmama could see you now, she'd be so proud". How wonderful to be able to think that a grandmother would take pride in a grandson dressed in women's clothes and obviously loving it. None but Charles Hawtrey could suggest such an innocent, unaggressive and unforced delight in transgression.

Originally published in *Attitude*, no.1 (May 1994), pp. 126–9.

9 BETWEEN PARTURITION AND MANUFACTURE (2018)

Stefani Germanotta is a hero of inauthenticity – a star of both invention, giving herself a stage name, Lady Gaga, that would never pass for a birth name, and reinvention, working her way through pop music genres and a succession of outlandish looks that refuse a fixed point of identity. She seems in line of succession to Cindy Sherman, David Bowie, and Madonna, with no doubt Joan Riviere and Judith Butler already mobilised in her name in many an academic quarter. Yet *A Star Is Born* is a property that wants to affirm authenticity.

There are more versions of it than the four films called *A Star Is Born* (from 1937, 1954, 1976, and 2018) and a radio version of the same name. The main elements are already in play in *What Price Hollywood?* (1932): the older alcoholic man whose career is on the skids, the younger female star, the fall of one against the rise of the other, ending in the man's suicide. The only major change in the transition from *What Price Hollywood?* to *A Star Is Born* is the addition of sexual relationship or marriage between the two. *What Price Hollywood?* is itself a reworking of elements from the novel *The Skyrocket* (1925), made into a (now lost) film the following year: the rise and fall motif, the ingénue, the enabling man of power, the conflict (for the woman) between career and marriage. Between the 1976 and 2018 Hollywood versions, there were two Indian films to hit each of these plot points: 2013's *Aashiqui 2 (Romance 2)* in Hindi and 2014's *Nee Jathaga Nenundali (I Want to Be Your Companion)* in Telugu. The gay porn film *The Light from the Second Story Window* (1973) is sometimes referred to as a version, and there are very many films called things like *A Porn Star is Born*.

All versions in various ways worry away at the ambiguity in the most familiar title. What does it mean to say a star is 'born'? The only time any of the films use the phrase is in the 1937 version, when Norman, the man who has discovered and championed Esther, says it to her after the premiere of her first film (where she now has her star name, Vicki). This is a straightforward colloquial usage, suggesting the way something may seem to suddenly appear. However, it leaves open the question of whether a star is someone indeed born with an innate star quality or whether stardom is something

Lady Gaga arrives for the premiere of *A Star Is Born* at the Venice Film Festival, August 2018. (Filippo Monteforte/ AFP via Getty Images)

manufactured, a manipulation, an illusion. All versions want to hold on to some sense of the former, but they differ in the degree to which they see it as something that breaks through industrial cultural production uncontaminated and authentic. *The Skyrocket* unequivocally acknowledges that Sharon, a nothing special young woman outside the spotlight, comes to fascinating life before the camera, but it also emphasises the role of the man, the director William Dvorak, in moulding this creation: she may have no talent as an actress but "he could always trick her before the camera for the things he needed". In the following versions, the idea of manipulation is played down. While there are scenes of the man Max (again a director) coaching the woman Mary in *What Price Hollywood?*, there is also a sequence in which, after a disastrous first shoot, she practises by herself all night so that the next day she delivers a mesmerising performance in a tiny role. Certainly, when it comes to the rushes, it is clear that Mary is aided by editing and lighting, but still, it is she who glows.

Mary's overnight labour on her performance suggests that her stardom is not (like Sharon's) just a happy accident of presence before the camera. However, like Sharon and Esther in the 1937 *Star*, there is also a sense that all she wants to be is 'a star'. None of them talk about acting. *What Price Hollywood?* has Mary dressing herself from the fan magazines and putting her own face in place of Garbo's in a double spread with Clark Gable, and the 1937 *Star* opens with Esther coming home dreamily after seeing a Norman Maine movie and avidly reading the fan magazines; they all just want to be 'in pictures'. There's none of this in the 1954 and subsequent versions. Of course Esther (1954, 1976), Aarohi (*Aashiqui 2*), and Lady Gaga's Ally (2018) want success, but there is also a sense of their sheer love of performing – they're longtime professionals who have finally gotten noticed. In each case, a sequence shows them singing in an unprestigious locale, establishing their exceptional, but as yet undiscovered, talent and quality. The starmakers are now actors or singers, who can open doors for their discovery but are not in a position to shape them. The film and music industry are seen as obstructive to varying degrees, but this is just what the star has to break through: authenticity will out.

The move away from an awareness of the manipulation, or at the least the role of others and technology, in the production of stars toward a wholehearted embrace of a notion of transparent star quality is aided by the role of men and Black people. One of the things that most struck me about the new *A Star Is Born* was how very male it is. There are fleeting glimpses of comedienne Luenell, singers Brandi Carlile and Halsey, an engaging but brief appearance by Rebecca Field as Gail, an aide to the man here, Jackson Maine, and his childhood friend Noodles has a wife (Drena De Niro), but the only sustained representations of the female, apart from Ally, are the drag queens in the bar where Jackson first sees Ally. With these, the film plays on the paradox of a swaggering, often muscly masculinity being adorned with sequins, lip gloss, and baroque hand gestures, the male beneath the feminine accoutrements emphasised by having Ally perform there, an assertion of a non-paradoxical alignment of body and adornment. She sings 'La Vie en Rose', a song made famous by the *ne plus ultra* of raw expressivity, Édith Piaf, but covered more recently by another pop performance artist, Grace Jones. The song positions Ally between the performativity that has made Gaga famous and the expressive self that the film wants us to credit her with. It also completes the salute to the queer culture that Gaga has allied herself with – a tribute that began in the film with Ally singing a snatch of the verse to 'Somewhere Over the Rainbow'; now the film, Ally, and perhaps Gaga can move on. When Ally makes forays into the kind of glam femme artifice that made Gaga famous, Jackson is contemptuous and the film shoots from behind television cameras and cuts away as soon as it decently can. By the end of the film, she has left queerdom behind.

Not only does this *A Star Is Born* sideline women (despite its central star and protagonist), it is also bursting with masculine maleness. The film opens with Jackson Maine in concert, his country rock among the most virile of authenticity musical genres (and the band used in the film is named Promise of the Real). Neither he nor Ally has mothers anymore. She has a father who hangs out with his taxi driver chums (all men), plays opera, and venerates Frank Sinatra. It's a cheerful background and we learn no more, and she seems to have no women friends or colleagues. Jackson, who has the fuller backstory and attendant occasions for melodrama, with a brother-manager old enough to be his father, anguishes over the destruction of his drunken father's grave and hard-drinking, hard-driving habits. The screen treatment of Ally's performances cuts back to him – his pleasure, his drunkenness – and her final affirmative performance, for the first time giving herself a surname, his, with a song he wrote that declares she'll never love again.

Earlier versions of the story have also had few women in them other than the star who is born. It is the incandescence of the star who played each one that distracted attention away from the lack of other women. There is even something of a progression through the various versions, as men gradually eclipse women. This may have something to do with the decreasing involvement of women in their making. Adela Rogers St. Johns, a successful journalist well connected to Hollywood, wrote *The Skyrocket* and the original story for *What Price Hollywood?* Dorothy Parker contributed to the script of the 1937 *Star* and Joan Didion to the 1976. Judy Garland was the driving force behind the radio version, although she had to wait until she left MGM and married Sid Luft to get the 1954 film made. Barbra Streisand was an even more decisive driving force behind the 1976 version.

The Skyrocket has a best friend, helpful wardrobe and make-up artist, rival and supportive stars and ex-stars, all women. While Max in *What Price Hollywood?* is a magnetic male figure (whose lack of apparent sexual interest in Mary, together with prissy mannerisms, might suggest him as queer), the film keeps Mary centre screen. And though much of the drama focuses on both her gratitude toward and need to get away from Max, there is also a well- (some say too well-) developed plot concerning her marriage to a playboy. In the 1937 *Star*, Esther's parents and brother make fun of her fandom, but it is her grandmother, a pioneer woman who compares Hollywood to the frontier, who understands Esther's aspirations, lends her the money to go to Hollywood, and then, at the end of the film, after Norman's suicide, persuades her to go back to work.

In the 1954 *Star*, attention is more or less equal between the man and the woman, but later versions build on the melodrama of his troubles, providing him with more screen time and backstory. One index of this is the presentation of his death. Norman Maine in 1937 and 1954 wades into the sea and drowns off screen, as if easefully swallowed by the watery element; John in 1976 kills himself in a car crash and Rahul in *Aashiqui 2* throws himself off a bridge, both in drawn-out dramatic sequences; in 2018, more discreetly but horribly, Jackson hangs himself.

It might be objected that the films do no more than reflect the fact that most of the powerful roles in Hollywood and the music industry have been occupied by men. Occasionally there does seem to be an awareness of this. In the 1937 *Star*, men discuss what name to give Esther, in front of her but without consulting her, and others worry over the qualities of her face. The latter idea is developed in the 1954 version, where three make-up men stand around Esther on the morning of her screen test, wondering what to do with her unsatisfactory face. The composition features mirrors within mirrors that Esther has, as it were, to peer round as the men discuss the problem, herself unable to get a word in edgeways. The men produce her as a pink amalgamation of a number of other stars, unrecognisable to Norman when he comes to pick her up. Yet such perceptive moments are rare and nowhere to be found in the later versions.

Men change women's names in more than one way. The studios make Esther Blodgett 'Vicki Lester' in 1937 and 1954, while bridegrooms make Mary Evans 'Mrs. Lonny Borden' in *What Price Hollywood?*, Esther/Vicki 'Mrs. Albert Henkel' in 1937, and 'Mrs. Ernest Gubbins' in 1954 (Norman Maine's birth name respectively in the two films). The films play on the tensions between these names. Being treated as Mr. Evans or Mr. Lester is wounding. After Norman's suicide, Esther/Vicki makes her first public appearance proudly announcing she is 'Mrs. Norman Maine', effectively subsuming her identity in both that of her husband and the film industry that gave him his name. In 1976, Esther refuses to have her name, Hoffman, changed, a gesture as much to do with not eclipsing a Jewish identity as female autonomy, but she does, after John's suicide, announce herself as 'Esther Hoffman Howard', a common gesture that nonetheless parades a woman's connection to a man in a context where the man rather seldom does the same vice versa. In 2018, Ally has a surname for the first time in the film, when, after Jackson's suicide, she is announced as 'Ally Maine'. Only in *Aashiqui 2* does the question of the woman's name not come up, neither from the studios nor from Rahul, since they do not marry.

In *What Price Hollywood?* Mary has a Black maid, Bonita (Louise Beavers, who had played the Black support for a white career woman in the 1934 *Imitation of Life*), whom she treats casually even as Bonita attends to Mary's material and cosmetic needs. In 1954, Black dancers are briefly seen, leaping with tambourines or performing a crooked walk, in the 'Swanee' routine in the 'Born in a Trunk' number, a routine celebrating, in time-honoured fashion, a Southern white homeland with marginalised and merry Blacks. Later, in 'Lose That Long Face', a number cut from the original release, Esther is dressed like a street urchin and dances between two Black kids. In 1976, Esther is first encountered as lead singer between two Black women in a trio called the Oreos, a naming decision which I won't even begin to try to unpack; the first word of their number is 'black' (sung only by Esther/Streisand, with a near-Afro hairdo alongside her African-American back-ups' relaxed styling). In 2018, Jackson's school friend Noodles (yes, well) is Black, and it is he and his Black wife who encourage Jackson and Ally to marry and in the former's local Black church. This shift from servant to terpsichorean and musical support to emotional, even spiritual validation suggests that in telling this story it is hard quite to let go of, or exactly to acknowledge, the role of African Americans in securing the material, rhythmic, and affective authenticity of white Americans. Perhaps Esther's grandmother in the 1937 *Star* is not all wrong when she compares Hollywood to the frontier.

Nearly all versions of the story have the moment in which the man sees the woman in performance for the first time. It's the moment when the man – and we – must be convinced the woman is the real deal, has "that little something extra," as Norman says in 1954. From 1954 on, that moment is a song, and in all cases they do not perform their own material and what they sing has nothing to do with what is happening in the story at that point. 'The Man that Got Away', the big torch song hit of the 1954 version, has no relation that we know of with Esther's past and everything to do with her skill and pleasure in singing, signalled by this emotionally desperate number ending with her smiling and laughing with her fellow musicians. Later, Esther, in deep despair at Norman's self-destructive drinking, pours out her sorrows to the studio boss, but in between takes of the upbeat 'Lose That Long Face' that is the antithesis of what she is feeling.

The following *Stars* close that gap between self and performance. This is partly signalled extra-textually: it is widely known that Streisand part-composed the songs she sings in 1976 and that Gaga was even more involved in the composition of the 2018 songs. Their characters in each film also write, to varying extents, the songs they sing. This conflates tropes from the musical biopic – where the song expresses the person's inner self and also what they are feeling at the moment of composing and/or performing – with the mythos of the singer-songwriter. (The cover of Carole King's LP *Tapestry* is prominent on Ally's bedroom wall.) Potentially, then, the *Star Is Born* template, and the ambiguity of that title, lends itself to exploration of the strange tension between self and performance in cultural production since romanticism, and even more so in conditions of industrial, capital-intensive and now digital production. However, in different ways, both the premeditated quality of Streisand's performance style, evident in every spontaneous wisecrack and affective grimace, and Gaga's chameleonic theatricality sit uneasily with this.

In *Aashiqui 2*, the song at the moment of discovery is by Rahul and he later tells Aarohi that she sang it better than he has and that he "never felt any of my songs like this." As she sings it she looks at a large portrait on the wall of Lata Mangeshkar, uncontested as the greatest playback singer in Hindi cinema; Rahul notices this and later tells Aarohi it was this that made him realise that she, Aarohi, wanted to be a singer. In fact, Shraddha Kapoor, who plays Aarohi, is sung for by three different singers: within the fiction of the film, the voice belongs to her and makes her special enough to be considered alongside Lata, but, to a culturally incompetent viewer at any rate, there is something giddying when in the film we see Aarohi/Kapoor recording a soundtrack to be dubbed for another actress when the voice we hear is anyway not Kapoor's. At this moment, *Aashiqui 2* seems to register the problematic of self and performance.

In the 1954 *Star*, we see the end of the screening of Vicki's first film. 'Swanee' comes to a climax and theatre curtains close on it; the lead singer steps through the curtains, thanks the audience for the applause, and then, in the 'Born in a Trunk' number, tells her life story, illustrated by danced and sung moments culminating in the just seen 'Swanee' number, which then, as the curtains close, dissolves back to the singer bringing the song to an end. But who is this and whose story? Vicki, who has only recently been invented by the studio? The character she plays in the film, about whom we know nothing? Esther? Judy Garland? A change of framing near the beginning of the sequence shifts it from being something more evidently a film within a film to something apparently taking place in a theatre and addressed to – whom? The theatre audience? The audience in the film (including Esther) watching the film? Us? These ambiguities are in part a result of the whole piece being added under a different director after the film had supposedly been completed, but it also catches the shifting ontological levels of stardom – real person, star image, character – that run through both this film and the whole star phenomenon. Lady Gaga would seem to be the perfect performer to play more fully on such complexities, but it is not the road that the film, or she, has chosen to go down. Rather than a celebration of female image-manufacture, we have the fantasy of male parturition and the lure of authenticity. A film for our times.

Originally published in *Los Angeles Review of Books*, 5 November 2018.

SECTION 2

IN DEFENCE OF DISCO

and other essays on entertainment and ideology

The 'Queen of Disco' Donna Summer, 1978. (Michael Ochs Archives/Getty Images)

At a 1972 symposium on 'Libraries and Leisure' organised for librarians and arts administrators, Richard Dyer spoke about the importance of entertainment. Since most people, he said, had 'boring, dreary, repetitive, uncreative, tiring and often dirty jobs' (and he was referring here to both paid employment and unpaid domestic work), entertainment provided a much-needed utopian escape, consisting of 'strong and unambiguous feeling, a world of abundance, of energy, a world of transparent relationships and a world of community.' Therefore, entertainment should not be left to 'commercial concerns alone', but be recognised as 'a distinctive, vital and authentic part of our culture' – a public good. 'Isn't there here the risk that life will be seen as entertainment?' an audience member asked him during the Q&A, to which Dyer replied: 'I think it would be wonderful if life were seen as entertainment.'[1]

Entertainment is a central topic in Dyer's work, starting with his PhD dissertation on the Hollywood musical, 'Social Values of Entertainment and Show Business' (1972), the opening sentence of which reads: 'The concept of entertainment is ubiquitous, unanswerable and unexamined.'[2] He would continue to examine the concept throughout his career, most notably in the short monograph on television *Light Entertainment* (1973), the canonical 'Entertainment and utopia' (1977, originally published in *Movie* and often reprinted), and the edited volume *Only Entertainment* (1992, second edition 2002). Whether writing about musicals, soap operas, Hollywood blockbusters, or disco, Dyer always takes entertainment seriously on its own terms, exploring how entertainment can make someone experience what a better world would feel like. As he writes in the introduction to the second edition of *Only Entertainment*: 'The task is to identify the ideological implications – good and bad – of entertainment qualities themselves, rather than seeking to uncover hidden ideological meanings behind and separable from the façade of entertainment.'[3] While ideological criticism in media and cultural studies tends to treat entertainment merely as a bearer of ideology, Dyer first wants to know what makes entertainment entertaining and then why and how that matters socially and politically.

---

1. Richard Dyer, 'The Rights of Entertainment,' in David Gerard (ed.), *Libraries and Leisure: A Topical Symposium of Views from Administrators and Practitioners of the Arts*, London: Diploma Press, 1975, pp. 39, 53.
2. Richard Dyer, 'Social Values of Entertainment and Show Business,' PhD dissertation, Centre for Contemporary Cultural Studies, University of Birmingham, October 1972, p. 1.
3. Richard Dyer, *Only Entertainment*, second edition, London and New York: Routledge, 2002, p. 2.

Richard Dyer (in white shirt) dancing at the Eagle and Tun, Birmingham, circa 1975. (Courtesy of Ian Sanderson)

Taking entertainment (or popular culture in general) seriously as a topic of academic research was not as widely accepted during the 1970s and 1980s as it is today. Richard Dyer and his colleagues at the Centre for Contemporary Cultural Studies often needed to defend their objects of study to those on the culturally conservative right who frowned upon their banality, or to those on the politically progressive left who condemned their capitalist and commercial character. After Dyer had published his essay 'In defence of disco' (1979) in the socialist journal *Gay Left*, the next issue included a letter to the editors from a reader who called the essay 'the most boring and lengthy piece of theoreticist self-justification that I've read for a long time,' and wondered why Dyer had not written about more subversive music, such as punk and reggae: 'And with these two progressive cultures around, Richard Dyer is into disco! A gay socialist is defending sexist, capitalist music!'[4] Yet Dyer did not defend disco to

---

4. John Munford, 'Lost in the music?', *Gay Left* 9 (Winter 1979), p. 39.

deny its capitalist character or to justify his own personal 'wrong' taste, but instead genuinely wanted to understand how such a commercial culture could be so exciting and liberating, in particular to gay men like himself. 'I had the feeling that the kind of music that I liked was constantly being disparaged,' he later recalled. 'It was just felt [that disco] was commercial, capitalist music of a cheap and glittery kind, rather than something that was real and throbbing and sexual.'[5]

'Entertainment and utopia' (not included in this Reader) and 'In defence of disco' present a similar argument about how a capitalist cultural form does not necessarily reproduce a capitalist ideology, but rather gives people – viewers of musicals and dancers to disco – the possibility of having their experience of living within a capitalist culture validated, or even more, offers them a utopian sensibility of what an escape from such a life could *feel* like, 'the sense that things could be better, that something other than what is can be imagined and maybe realised.'[6] Here a connection can be made to what has come to be known as affect theory in media studies. In reference to 'Entertainment and utopia', Anu Koivunen describes Dyer's utopian sensibility as 'a conceptualization of a horizon of experience, expectations, and desires rooted in the contemporary moment,' which 'provided an alternative to the language of psychoanalysis in understanding pleasure.'[7] Jeremy Gilbert too finds such a connection, as he perceives 'In defence of disco' as 'a remarkably prescient and concise statement of a theoretical and political position [...] which puts an analysis of the corporeal at the centre of experience without collapsing into aestheticism or romanticism.'[8] Dyer then has made crucial interventions into our understandings of the ways in which popular culture has affective dimensions and resonances, making him, in the words of Koivunen, a theorist of feeling.

Less well known than the two essays mentioned in the paragraph above is Dyer's work on television and entertainment. During the 1970s and 1980s, Dyer published quite extensively on this topic, including the aforementioned *Light Entertainment*, 'Soap opera and women' (1977, with Terry Lovell and Jean McCrindle),[9] the edited volume *Coronation Street* (1981), and 'Taking popular television seriously' (1985). Moreover, between 1980 and 1982, he wrote a column about popular media for the communist

---

5. Quoted in Tim Lawrence, 'In Defence of Disco (Again),' *New Formations* 58 (Summer 2006), p. 132.

6. Richard Dyer, 'Entertainment and utopia', *Movie* 24 (Spring 1977), p. 3.

7. Anu Koivunen, 'Theorist of feeling,' *Cinema Journal* 57:2 (Winter 2018), p. 164.

8. Jeremy Gilbert, 'In defence of "In defense of disco",' *New Formations* 58 (Summer 2006), p. 99.

9. Richard Dyer, Terry Lovell and Jean McCrindle, 'Soap opera and women', originally published in *Edinburgh International Television Festival 1977: Official Programme*, London: Broadcast, 1977, reprinted in Ann Gray and Jim McGuigan (eds), *Studying Culture: An Introductory Reader*, London: Edward Arnold, 1993, pp. 35-41.

fortnightly *Comment* (alternating contributions with Rosalind Brunt and Ian Connell). A recurring reference in his essays on television is Richard Hoggart's *The Uses of Literacy* (1957), which Dyer uses to emphasise the way popular culture can validate working-class everyday life and give voice to strong female characters. Another key intellectual source is Stuart Hall and Paddy Whannel's *The Popular Arts* (1964), although Dyer only realised this while writing the introduction to the 2018 edition of the book: 'Much of what I have written – on entertainment, musicals, stars, thrills – is all there in embryo and yet I must have so imbibed it and made it mine that I nowhere formally registered the fact.'[10]

Stuart Hall's writing also resonates throughout Dyer's 'Taking popular television seriously' (1985), which was one of three 'critical perspectives' presented at the 1983 Television and Schooling Conference, organised by the British Film Institute and the University of London Institute of Education. The conference was a response to the 1983 report *Popular TV & Schoolchildren* produced by the UK Department of Education and Skills (DES) and brought together broadcasters, policymakers, educators, and scholars. In his contribution, Dyer aims to extend the report's definitions of entertainment and representation, the former seen as trivial, the latter as serious. As he writes:

> Some argue that 'this' is a representation of 'that', but it is 'only entertainment' and therefore of no consequence. Alternatively, more perniciously, entertainment is seen to allow the representation to do its work under cover of the pleasure of the programme. We need to get beyond the assumptions contained in such views, to discuss with students the extent to which they feel that the fact that something is entertainment has written off the way it represents the world, and the extent to which they use the entertainment qualities of the programme to defend themselves against its representational concerns.

Instead of seeing them in opposition, Dyer argues that entertainment and representation should be considered together to discuss how television presents 'reality' and how audiences can relate to such a worldview. Similarly, in his column 'Tea and cocoa tele' (1982), Dyer gives the advice to the 'left cultural worker' who wants to make socialist and feminist television for the then soon-to-be launched Channel 4 to include entertainment – 'awareness of the rhythms of everyday life, of the legitimate desire to relax, of wanting to see things sparkle a bit' – in their programmes. If not, 'they may find many people turning off. Then the powers that be can say, there, we told you so, the people don't want socialist, feminist culture.'

---

10. Richard Dyer, 'Introduction to the 2018 Edition,' in Stuart Hall and Paddy Whannel, *The Popular Arts*, Durham and London: Duke University Press, 2018, p. xxii.

In his later essays on entertainment, Dyer discusses the limitations of the utopian sensibility. In 'The colour of entertainment' (1995), for instance, he returns to the classic Hollywood musical, including the 'Main Street' number in *On the Town* which presents the imaginary pleasures of small-town America. Then Dyer poses a rhetorical question:

> But down how many main streets in how many small US towns can we imagine a Black couple strolling with such unwary joy? This is not to demand that the musical be realistic, but rather to suggest how even the utopian imagination has its boundaries of plausibility. 'Main Street' works because it feels physically right to imagine whites – but only whites – so at ease in the heartland of the United States.

His essay was criticised by Stephen Bourne for 'underestimating those glorious moments' of Black musical performers, to which Dyer replied that he was sorry for 'not adequately convey[ing] my enthusiasm for Lena Horne,' but that was not the point he was attempting to make: 'I was trying to face up to the ethnic specificity and limitations of one of my favourite entertainments, the classic Hollywood musical: that is to say, to its whiteness' (a topic which he would further explore in other writings: see Section 4 of this Reader).[11]

The second edition of *Only Entertainment* (2002) contained a new concluding chapter, 'The waning of entertainment', in which Dyer argued that the main idea of entertainment, presenting a utopian sensibility to escape the dreariness of everyday life, was no longer necessary, at least not for 'the comfortable overclass of Western society'. While an 'army of the underpaid, still predominantly female and/or non-white, picks up the pieces of drudgery,' for most people in western countries the labour conditions of paid employment and unpaid domestic work have improved to such an extent that there is no need for escape: 'When pleasure is available anywhere, any time and looks like everywhere and everyone, the dynamic of escape, foundational to entertainment, disappears.'[12] And yet the production and consumption of escapist entertainment has persisted, and Dyer has continued to explore its textures, politics, and resonances. In a 2015 essay on *Jurassic World*, he argues that, on the one hand, the Hollywood film is 'fun entertainment, with its thrills always accompanied by an immediate sense that all will be well', while, on the other, the film 'also hints at the real future', a dystopian perspective of life 'without humans at all, not just in a Jurassic World but in the darker,

---

11. Stephen Bourne, 'Lena's triumphs,' *Sight and Sound* 5:12 (December 1995), p. 64; Richard Dyer, 'Lena: a reply,' *Sight and Sound* 6:1 (January 1996), p. 64.

12. Richard Dyer, 'The waning of entertainment,' in *Only Entertainment*, second edition, London and New York: Routledge, 2002, pp. 179, 176, 178.

off-screen world itself.' During the COVID lockdowns, entertainment in the form of streaming services like Netflix provided a utopian escape from such a darker world, rampant with epidemics, warfare and environmental disaster, in addition to persistent racism, sexism and homophobia. How wonderful it would be indeed if life were seen as entertainment.

10 IN DEFENCE OF DISCO (1979)

All my life I've liked the wrong music. I never liked Elvis and rock 'n' roll; I always preferred Rosemary Clooney. And since I became a socialist, I've often felt virtually terrorised by the prestige of rock and folk on the left. How could I admit to two Petula Clark LPs in the face of miners' songs from the North East and the Rolling Stones? I recovered my nerve partially when I came to see showbiz type music as a key part of gay culture, which, whatever its limitations, was a culture to defend. And I thought I'd really made it when turned on to Tamla Motown, sweet soul sounds, disco. Chartbusters already, and I like them! Yet the prestige of folk and rock, and now punk and (rather patronisingly, I think) reggae, still holds sway. It's not just that people whose politics I broadly share don't *like* disco, they manage to imply that it is politically beyond the pale to like it. It's against this attitude that I want to defend disco (which otherwise, of course, hardly needs any defence).

I'm going to talk mainly about disco *music*, but there are two preliminary points I'd like to make. The first is that disco is more than just a form of music, although certainly the music is at the heart of it. Disco is also kinds of dancing, club, fashion, film etc. – in a word, a certain *sensibility*, manifest in music, clubs etc., historically and culturally specific, economically, technologically, ideologically and aesthetically determined – and worth thinking about. Secondly, as a sensibility in music it seems to me to encompass more than what we would perhaps strictly call disco music, to include a lot of soul, Tamla and even the later work of mainstream and jazz artistes like Peggy Lee and Johnny Mathis.

My defence is in two parts. First, a discussion of the arguments against disco in terms of its being 'capitalist' music. Second, an attempt to think through the – ambivalently, ambiguously, contradictorily – positive qualities of disco.

DISCO AND CAPITAL

Much of the hostility to disco stems from the equation of it with capitalism. Both in how it is produced and in what it expresses, disco is held to be irredeemably capitalistic.

Now it is unambiguously the case that disco is produced by capitalist industry, and since capitalism is an irrational and inhuman mode of production, the disco industry is as bad as all the rest. Of course. However, this argument has assumptions behind it that are more problematic. These are of two kinds. One assumption concerns *music as a mode of production*, and has to do with the belief that it is possible in a capitalist society to produce things (e.g. music, e.g. rock and folk) that are outside of the capitalist mode of production. Yet quite apart from the general point that such a position seeks to elevate activity outside of existing structures rather than struggles against them, the two kinds of music most often set against disco as a mode of production are not really convincing.

One is folk music — in this country, people might point to Gaelic songs and industrial ballads — the kind of music often used, or reworked, in left fringe theatre. These, it is argued, are not, like disco (and pop music in general), produced for the people but by them. They are 'authentic' people's music. So they are — or rather, were. The problem is that we don't live in a society of small, technologically simple communities such as produce such art. Preserving such music at best gives us a historical perspective on peasant and working-class struggle, at worst leads to a nostalgia for a simple, harmonious community existence that never even existed. More bluntly, songs in Gaelic or dealing with nineteenth century factory conditions, beautiful as they are, don't mean much to most English-speaking people today.

The other kind of music most often posed against disco and 'pap pop' at the level of how it is produced is rock (including Dylan-type folk and everything from early rock 'n' roll to progressive concept albums). The argument here is that rock is easily produced by non-professionals — all that is needed are a few instruments and somewhere to play — whereas disco music requires the whole panoply of recording studio technology, which makes it impossible for non-professionals (the kid in the streets) to produce. The factual accuracy of this observation needs supplementing with some other observations. Quite apart from the very rapid — but then bemoaned by some purists — move of rock into elaborate recording studios, even when it is simple, produceable by non-professionals, the fact is that rock is still quite expensive, and remains in practice largely the preserve of middle-class people who can afford electric guitars, music lessons etc. (You have only to look at the biographies of those now professional rock musicians who started out in a simple non-professional way — the preponderance of public school and university educated young men in the field is rivalled only by their preponderance in the Labour Party cabinet.) More importantly, this kind of music production is wrongly thought of as being generated from the grass roots (except perhaps at certain key historical moments) — non-professional music making, in rock as elsewhere, bases itself, inevitably, on professional music. Any notion that rock emanates from 'the people' is soon confounded by the recognition that what 'the people' are doing is trying to be as much like professionals as possible.

The second kind of argument based on the fact that disco is produced by capitalism concerns *music as an ideological expression*. Here it is assumed that capitalism as a

IN DEFENCE OF DISCO

Grace Jones, 1979. (Ron Galella Collection via Getty Images)

mode of production necessarily and simply produces 'capitalist' ideology. The theory of the relation between the mode of production and the ideologies of a particular society is too complicated and unresolved to be gone into here, but we can begin by remembering that capitalism is about profit. In the language of classical economics, capitalism produces commodities, and its interest in commodities is their exchange-value (how much profit they can realise) rather than their use-value (their social or human worth). This becomes particularly problematic for capitalism when dealing with an expressive commodity – such as disco – since a major problem for capitalism is that there is no necessary or guaranteed connection between exchange-value and use-value – in other words, capitalism as productive relations can just as well make a profit from something that is ideologically opposed to bourgeois society as something that supports it. As long as a commodity makes a profit, what does it matter? (I should like to acknowledge my debt to Terry Lovell for explaining this aspect of capitalist cultural production to me.) Indeed, it is because of this dangerous, anarchic tendency of capitalism that ideological institutions – the church, the state, education, the family etc. – are necessary. It is their job to make sure that what capitalism produces is in capitalism's longer-term interests. However, since they often don't know that that is their job, they don't always perform it. Cultural production within capitalist society is then founded on two profound contradictions – the first, between production for profit and production for use; the second, within those institutions whose job it is to regulate the first contradiction. What all this boils down to, in terms of disco, is that the fact that disco is produced by capitalism does not mean that it is automatically, necessarily, simply supportive of capitalism. Capitalism constructs the disco experience, but it does not necessarily know what it is doing, apart from making money.

I am not now about to launch into a defence of disco music as some great subversive art form. What the arguments above lead me to is, first, a basic point of departure in the recognition that cultural production under capitalism is necessarily contradictory, and, secondly, that it may well be the case that capitalist cultural products are most likely to be contradictory at just those points – such as disco – where they are most commercial and professional, where the urge to profit is at its strongest. Thirdly, this mode of cultural production has produced a commodity, disco, that has been taken up by gays in ways that may well not have been intended by its producers. The anarchy of capitalism throws up commodities that an oppressed group can take up and use to cobble together its own culture. In this respect, disco is very much like another profoundly ambiguous aspect of male gay culture, camp. It is a 'contrary' use of what the dominant culture provides, it is important in forming a gay identity, and it has subversive potential as well as reactionary implications.

THE CHARACTERISTICS OF DISCO

Let me turn now to what I consider to be the three important characteristics of disco – eroticism, romanticism, and materialism. I'm going to talk about them in terms of what it seems to me they mean within the context of gay culture. These three characteristics are not in themselves good or bad (any more than disco music as a whole is), and they need specifying more precisely. What is interesting is how they take us to qualities that are not only key ambiguities within gay male culture, but have also traditionally proved stumbling blocks to socialists.

Eroticism

It can be argued that all popular music is erotic. What we need to define is the specific way of thinking and feeling erotically in disco. I'd like to call it 'whole body' eroticism, and to define it by comparing it with the eroticism of the two kinds of music to which disco is closest – popular song (i.e., the Gershwin, Cole Porter, Burt Bacharach type of song) and rock.

Popular song's eroticism is 'disembodied': it succeeds in expressing a sense of the erotic which yet denies eroticism's physicality. This can be shown by the nature of tunes in popular songs and the way they are handled.

Popular song's tunes are rounded off, closed, self-contained. They achieve this by adopting a strict musical structure (AABA) in which the opening melodic phrases are returned to and, most importantly, the tonic note of the whole song is also the last note of the tune. (The tonic note is the note that forms the basis for the key in which the song is written; it is therefore the harmonic 'anchor' of the tune and closing on it gives precisely a feeling of 'anchoring', coming to a settled stop.) Thus although popular songs often depart – especially in the middle section (B) – from their melodic and harmonic beginnings, they also always return to them. This gives them – even at their most passionate, say, Porter's 'Night and Day' – a sense of security and containment. The tune is not allowed to invade the whole of one's body. Compare the typical disco tune, which is often little more than an endlessly repeated phrase which drives beyond itself, is not 'closed off'. Even when disco music uses a popular song standard, it often turns it into a simple phrase. Gloria Gaynor's version of Porter's 'I've Got You Under My Skin', for instance, is in large part a chanted repetition of 'I've got you'.

Popular song's lyrics place its tunes within a conceptualisation of love and passion as emanating from 'inside', the heart or the soul. Thus the yearning cadences of popular song express an erotic yearning of the inner person, not the body. Once again, disco refuses this. Not only are the lyrics often more directly physical and the delivery more raunchy (e.g. Grace Jones' 'I Need a Man'), but, most importantly, disco is insistently rhythmic in a way that popular song is not.

Rhythm, in Western music, is traditionally felt as being more physical than other musical elements such as melody, harmony and instrumentation. This is why Western music is traditionally so dull rhythmically – nothing expresses our Puritan heritage more vividly. It is to other cultures that we have had to turn – and above all to Afro-American culture – to learn about rhythm. The history of popular song since the late nineteenth century is largely the history of the white incorporation (or ripping off) of Black music – ragtime, the Charleston, the tango, swing, rock 'n' roll, rock. Now what is interesting about this incorporation/ripping-off is what it meant and means. Typically, Black music was thought of by the white culture as being both more primitive and more 'authentically' erotic. Infusions of Black music were always seen as (and often condemned as) sexual and physical. The use of insistent Black rhythms in disco music, recognisable by the closeness of the style to soul and reinforced by such characteristic features of Black music as the repeated chanted phrase and the use of various African percussion instruments, means that it inescapably signifies (in this white context) physicality.

However, rock is as influenced by Black music as disco is. This then leads me to the second area of comparison between disco's eroticism and rock's. The difference between them lies in what each 'hears' in Black music. Rock's eroticism is thrusting, grinding – it is not whole body, but phallic. Hence it takes from Black music the insistent beat and makes it even more driving; rock's repeated phrases trap you in their relentless push, rather than releasing you in an open-ended succession of repetitions as disco does. Most revealing perhaps is rock's instrumentation. Black music has more percussion instruments than white, but it knows how to use them to create all sorts of effect – light, soft, lively, as well as heavy, hard and grinding. Rock, however, only hears the latter and develops the percussive qualities of essentially non-percussive instruments to increase this, hence the twanging electric guitar and the nasal vocal delivery. One can see how, when rock 'n' roll first came in, this must have been a tremendous liberation from popular song's disembodied eroticism – here was a really physical music, and not just mealy-mouthedly physical, but quite clear what it was about – cock. But rock confines sexuality to cock (and this is why, no matter how progressive the lyrics and even when performed by women, rock remains indelibly phallocentric music). Disco music, on the other hand, hears the physicality in Black music and its range. It achieves this by a number of features including: the sheer amount going on rhythmically in even quite simple disco music (for rhythmic clarity with complexity, listen to the full length version of the Temptations' 'Papa was a Rolling Stone'); the willingness to play with rhythm, delaying it, jumping it, countering it rather than simply driving on and on (examples – Patti Labelle, Isaac Hayes); the range of percussion instruments used and with different affects (e.g. the spiky violins in Quincy Jones/Herbie Hancock's 'Tell Me a Bedtime Story'; the gentle pulsations of

The 'phallic disco' of the Village People, 1979. (Lynn Goldsmith/Corbis/VCG via Getty Images)

George Benson). This never stops being erotic, but it restores eroticism to the whole of the body, and for both sexes, not just confining it to the penis. It leads to the expressive, sinuous movement of disco dancing, not just that mixture of awkwardness and thrust so dismally characteristic of dancing to rock.

Gay men do not intrinsically have any prerogative over whole body eroticism. We are often even more cock-oriented than non-gays of either sex, and it depresses me that such phallic forms of disco as Village People should be so gay-identified. Nonetheless, partly because many of us have traditionally not thought of ourselves as being 'real men' and partly because gay ghetto culture is also a space where alternative definitions, including of sexuality, can be developed, it seems to me that the importance of disco in scene culture indicates an openness to a sexuality that is not defined in terms of cock. Although one cannot easily move from musical values to personal ones, or from personal ones to politically effective ones, it is at any rate suggestive that gay culture should promote a form of music that denies the centrality of the phallus while at the same time refusing the non-physicality which such a denial has hitherto implied.

Romanticism

Not all disco music is romantic. The lyrics of many disco hits are either straightforwardly sexual – not to say sexist – or else broadly social (e.g. Detroit Spinners' 'Ghetto Child', Stevie Wonder's 'Living in the City'), and the hard drive of Village People or Labelle is positively anti-romantic. Yet there is nonetheless a strong strain of romanticism in disco. This can be seen in the lyrics, which often differ little from popular song standards, and indeed often are standards (e.g. 'What a Diff'rence a Day Makes' – Esther Phillips, 'La Vie en Rose' – Grace Jones). More impressively, it is the instrumentation and arrangements of disco music that are so romantic.

The use of massed violins takes us straight back, via Hollywood, to Tchaikovsky, to surging, outpouring emotions. A brilliant example is Gloria Gaynor's 'I've Got You Under My Skin', where in the middle section the violins take a hint from one of Porter's melodic phrases and develop it away from his tune in an ecstatic, soaring movement. This 'escape' from the confines of popular song into ecstasy is very characteristic of disco music, and nowhere more consistently than in such Diana Ross classics as 'Reach Out' and 'Ain't No Mountain High Enough'. This latter, with its lyrics' total surrender to love, its heavenly choir and sweeping violins, is perhaps one of the most extravagant reaches of disco's romanticism. But Ross is also a key figure in the gay appropriation of disco.

What Ross's records do – and I'm thinking basically of her work up to *Greatest Hits* volume 1 and the *Touch Me in the Morning* album – is express the intensity of fleeting emotional contacts. They are all-out expressions of adoration which yet have built into them the recognition of the (inevitably) temporary quality of the experience. This can be a straightforward lament for having been let down by a man, but more often it is both a celebration of a relationship and the almost willing recognition of its passing and the exquisite pain of its passing: 'Remember me/As a sunny day/That you once had/Along the way', 'If I've got to be strong/Don't you know I need to have tonight when you're gone/When you go I'll lie here/And think about/the last time that you/Touch me in the morning'. This last number, with Ross's 'unreally' sweet, porcelain fragile voice and the string backing, concentrates that sense of celebrating the intensity of the passing relationship that haunts so much of her work. No wonder Ross is (was?) so important in gay male scene culture, for she both reflects what that culture takes to be an inevitable reality (that relationships don't last) and at the same time celebrates it, validates it.

Not all disco music works in this vein, yet in both some of the more sweetly melancholy orchestrations (even of lively numbers, like 'You Should Be Dancing' in *Saturday Night Fever*) and some of the lyrics and general tone (e.g. Donna Summer's *Four Seasons of Love* album), there is a carry-over of this emotional timbre. At a minimum, then, disco's romanticism provides an embodiment and validation of an aspect of gay culture.

But romanticism is a particularly paradoxical quality of art to come to terms with. Its passion and intensity embody or create an experience that negates the dreariness of the mundane and everyday. It gives us a glimpse of what it means to live at the height of our emotional and experiential capacities – not dragged down by the banality of organised routine life. Given that everyday banality, work, domesticity, ordinary sexism and racism, are rooted in the structures of class and gender of this society, the flight from that banality can be seen as – is – a flight from capitalism and patriarchy themselves as lived experiences.

What makes this more complicated is the actual situation within which disco occurs. Disco is part of the wider to-and-fro between work and leisure, alienation and escape, boredom and enjoyment that we are so accustomed to (and which *Saturday Night Fever* plugs into so effectively). Now this to-and-fro is partly the mechanism by which we keep going, at work, at home – the respite of leisure gives us the energy for work, and anyway we are still largely brought up to think of leisure as a 'reward' for work. The circle locks us into it. But what happens in that space of leisure can be profoundly significant – it is there that we may learn about an alternative to work and to society as it is. Romanticism is one of the major modes of leisure in which this sense of an alternative is kept alive. Romanticism asserts that the limits of work and domesticity are not the limits of experience.

I don't say that the passion and intensity of romanticism is a political ideal we could strive for – I doubt that it is humanly possible to live permanently at that pitch. What I do believe is that the movement between banality and something 'other' than banality is an essential dialectic of society, a constant keeping open of a gap between what is and what could or should be. Herbert Marcuse in the currently unfashionable *One-Dimensional Man* argues that our society tries to close that gap, to assert that what is is all that there could be, is what should be. For all its commercialism and containment within the work:leisure to-and-fro, I think disco romanticism is one of the things that can keep the gap open, that can allow the *experience of contradiction* to continue. Since I also believe that political struggle is rooted in experience (though utterly doomed if left at it), I find this dimension of disco potentially positive. (A further romantic/utopian aspect of disco is realised in the non-commercial discos organised by gay and women's groups. Here a moment of community can be achieved, often in circle dances or simply in the sense of knowing people as people, not anonymous bodies. Fashion is less important, and sociability correspondingly more so. This can be achieved in smaller clubs, perhaps especially outside the centre of London, which, when not just grotty monuments to self-oppression, can function as supportive expressions of something like a gay community.)

Materialism

Disco is characteristic of advanced capitalist societies simply in terms of the scale of money squandered on it. It is a riot of consumerism, dazzling in its technology (echo chambers, double and more tracking, electric instruments), overwhelming in its scale (banks of violins, massed choirs, the limitless range of percussion instruments), lavishly gaudy in the mirrors and tat of discotheques, the glitter and denim flash of its costumes. Its tacky sumptuousness is well evoked in the film *Thank God It's Friday*. Gone are the restraint of popular song, the sparseness of rock and reggae, the simplicity of folk. How can a socialist, or someone trying to be a feminist, defend it?

In certain respects, it is doubtless not defensible. Yet socialism and feminism are both forms of materialism – why is disco, a celebration of materiality if ever there was one, not therefore the appropriate art form of materialist politics?

Partly, obviously, because materialism in politics is not to be confused with mere matter. Materialism seeks to understand how things are in terms of how they have been produced and constructed in history, and how they can be better produced and constructed. This certainly does not mean immersing oneself in the material world – indeed, it includes deliberately stepping back from the material world to see what makes it the way it is and how to change it. Yes, but, materialism is also based on the profound conviction that politics is about the material world, and indeed that human life and the material world are all there is, no God, no magic forces. One of the dangers of materialist politics is that it is in constant danger of spiritualising itself, partly because of the historical legacy of the religious forms that brought materialism into existence, partly because materialists have to work so hard not to take matter at face value that they often end up not treating it as matter at all. Disco's celebration of materiality is only a celebration of the world we are necessarily and always immersed in, and disco's materiality, in technological modernity, is resolutely historical and cultural – it can never be, as most art claims for itself, an 'emanation' outside of history and of human production.

Disco's combination of romanticism and materialism effectively tell us – lets us experience – that we live in a world of materiality, that we can enjoy materiality but that the experience of materiality is not necessarily what the everyday world assures us it is. Its eroticism allows us to rediscover our bodies as part of this experience of materiality and the possibility of change.

If this sounds over the top, let one thing be clear – disco can't change the world, make the revolution. No art can do that, and it is pointless expecting it to. But partly by opening up experience, partly by changing definitions, art, disco, can be used. To which one might risk adding the refrain – If it feels good, *use* it.

Originally published in *Gay Left* 8 (Summer 1979), pp. 20–23.

11 VIEWS OF *NATIONWIDE* GO WIDE (1980)

Nationwide seems like a series of dribs and drabs that don't add up to much and are all pretty obvious. Yet such an impression is misleading. In a study published two years ago by the British Film Institute (*Everyday Television: 'Nationwide'*), Charlotte Brunsdon and David Morley showed how *Nationwide* constructs a particular image of British society, gathering all its disparate items together in a vision of Britain as composed of ordinary yet unique individuals, with the family as the true social unit. Thus the programme cuts across and denies class, virtually ignores race and keeps intact the view of women as makers of home for men to return to. Their study revealed the complexity of the way the programme produced this 'common-sense' for the viewer.

What David Morley's follow-up study (*The Nationwide Audience*, British Film Institute) shows is that this common-sense promulgated by *Nationwide* is not necessarily taken that way by actual viewers. Beneath its apparent obviousness, *Nationwide*'s messages are so complex that they can be interpreted in a number of different ways. David Morley sets out to explore these, through a series of interviews with groups ranging from bank managers to trade union officials, from white university students to West Indian women in further education.

His approach departs from the traditional ones of audience research. He wants to get away from both the idea that the media simply makes us think what it wants us to, and the assumption that everybody makes sense of the media in an entirely unique way. Rather he shows how our class, sex and race position, *and* how we make sense of it according to the ideas available to us, actually determine how we understand what we see on television.

His findings – with generously quoted and often vivid statements from interviewees – certainly vindicate his approach. He shows how there is a definite overlap between some groups and the world-view of the programme itself, notably groups of apprentices and managers, and to such groups this world-view is simply 'the way things are'. At the opposite end of the spectrum, there are two groups who oppose the programme – the groups of Black women who feel totally excluded by it, and a group of shop stewards who see it as a deeply reactionary show. Particularly interesting is the difference between these shop stewards and a group of trade union officials who are critical of the programme, but in a conciliatory way, lacking the stewards' outright hostility.

One thing that emerges particularly clearly is how very sophisticated people are about the media itself. Many of the groups, whether accepting or rejecting the programme, are fully aware of the way it constructs a particular world-view. To some this construction is merely a representation of common-sense reality, to others it is a put-on, but either way, very few people fall for the idea that the medium is transparent, simply capturing the reality of the world. They differ in the degree to which they are prepared to read past the constructed image to make sense of the information given in terms of how they see the world.

This is an important book, one of very few that really contributes to our understanding of how audiences relate to the mass media. It shows us both the power of the media to propose a view of the world and the possibility, basically from within a distinctive political (the shop stewards) or subcultural (the Black women) context, of grassroots resistance to this. It should be essential reading to any political activist.

But here we come to a problem. Like so much media studies, David Morley's book is caught up in the jargon and internecine theoretical warfare of the academy. I say this as one who has also been corrupted by this, and it is a real problem. The jargon and theory do, in the hands of a Dave Morley, anyway, deliver a great deal of knowledge and understanding that we might well not have come by any other way. But who do they deliver it to? *The Nationwide Audience* is a lot easier to read than most, but it is still a book for academics. I don't know the way out of this crippling dilemma, but to find a way must be a priority right now.

Originally published in *Comment* 18:15 (19 July 1980), p. 240.

12 *CORONATION STREET* (1981)

This set of essays on *Coronation Street* is primarily concerned with wider issues in understanding television than its title might suggest. *Coronation Street* is an example, a point of departure and of reference. It represents one of broadcasting's most typical forms, the continuous serial. Although potentially available as a vehicle for any kind of fictional world, in practice the continuous serial, a form only known on radio and television, has restricted itself to one such world, that usually designated 'everyday life' or 'family drama' and labelled as the province of 'soap-opera'. *Coronation Street* has been one of the two most successful soap operas on British television, the other being *Crossroads*. It is thus both typical of soap opera and a supreme realisation of its popular and/or commercial potential.

However, these essays are not solely concerned with *Coronation Street* as continuous soap opera at the narrow level of broadcasting specificity. They also address issues concerning the nature of popular/mass culture. They examine both what kinds of things *Coronation Street* says and can say – the representational discourse of *Coronation Street*, of soap opera, if you will; and also the kinds of pleasurable experience *Coronation Street* offers its viewers. Before further considering these two themes, at once in opposition and complementary to each other, I should like first to discuss what is perhaps an absence in these writings, namely, the choice of *Coronation Street* as object.

The purposes behind these essays are the wider ones outlined above. But why *Coronation Street*? Why not *Crossroads*, more successful and more continuous? All the essays certainly see *Crossroads*, *The Archers* and other soap operas and series as important points of reference, yet *Coronation Street* remains the focus. To take one series as a focus is a proper intellectual limitation, yet the choice of *Coronation Street* is not 'innocent'. There is quite a lot at stake in its choice.

It would be wrong to ignore altogether what is assuredly a factor in the choice, namely, the widespread feeling among those who write on the media that *Coronation Street* is somehow 'better' than its soap opera peers. This admiration for the series is most clearly conveyed in Marion Jordan's essay, but it certainly informs the other essays as well as the very choice of *Coronation Street* in the first place. Yet the writers refrain from affirming what is in practice very widely maintained, that *Coronation Street* is better written, better acted, better staged and better constructed (as narrative) than, particularly, *Crossroads*. Many of the effects of representation and of pleasure in the series are sustained and even constituted by these factors. I do not raise this in order to sneak in through the back door easy, unproblematised notions as to what constitutes 'good' television, a 'good' performance, a 'good' script. We should rather be asking what is meant by the label 'good' in these contexts. What qualities are so designated, and what social, moral and aesthetic values are inscribed in them? Does the fact that *Coronation Street* has a particular critical following – though the exact nature and extent of this can only be guessed at – merely derive from the particular class and gender positions occupied by the critics, or do we need to get up the nerve to suggest that evaluative work could have some intellectual legitimacy if rigorously pursued? As it is, evaluation is constantly ushered in unrigorously, whether it be in the inexorable pull of classic Hollywood for the many varieties of structuralist analysis or the endless attempt to pin down progressive texts in the case of more political writers.

But let us leave this embarrassing terrain and focus on a more narrow aspect of the choice of *Coronation Street*. The series lays claim to being 'about' working-class culture and is also marked by the presence of strong and positive female characters. It thus supplies social images that are conspicuous for their rarity on British television, and that are necessarily of particular interest to anyone working within broadly Marxist and/or feminist perspectives, as is the case in this book.

It is important to remind ourselves that *Coronation Street* came out of a particular moment in British cultural history, a moment most strikingly and decisively marked by Richard Hoggart's book, *The Uses of Literacy* (1957).[1] This book, together with other sociological works and novels, as well as films and theatre, was concerned to 'discover' and legitimate a tradition of culture that could authentically be termed 'working-class'. *The Uses of Literacy* was a best seller, not comparable to a Harold Robbins or an Agatha Christie, but certainly by academic standards. Its influence at all levels of institutionalised cultural practice was enormous, and its influence on education, especially the teaching of English, has led to generations of people brought up with some version of its reigning notions. Four things are of particular importance in the inflection Hoggart gave to the definition of working-class culture, and we can trace the relation of each to the wider media appropriation of the book, as well as to *Coronation Street* in particular.

First, Hoggart understood culture in an essentially anthropological sense, not as the artistic product of a given group of people but as patterns of interaction, sets of assumptions, ways of getting along together. What he set out to describe was the 'common sense' of 'everyday life' for the working class, in a way that both caught the apparent naturalness, down-to-earth, air-that-you-breathe feeling of such notions and yet acknowledged the specificity of the actual content of common sense. There

---

1. Richard Hoggart, *The Uses of Literacy*, London: Chatto and Windus, 1957.

is enormous difficulty here, since common sense is both 'wise' in its negotiation of the immediate business of living yet 'blinkered' in its inability to see beyond or above the immediate. There has been a renewed interest in this way of understanding common sense in recent years due to the revival of interest in the ideas of Antonio Gramsci. Hoggart's approach is less political, less Marxist, than Gramsci's but his treatment of common sense is none the less extremely nuanced. Yet, like so many aspects of the book, only one side of the coin was taken. The recognition of the strengths and weaknesses of common sense was read as an unqualified celebration of it. Hoggart's listings of salty aphorisms, his references to the 'full, rich life' of charabanc outings, aspidistras and pub singsongs were appropriated as a reconfirmation of a long-standing belief in the ebullient cornucopia of low-life existence. What now looked exaggerated in Dickens and formalised in music-hall was re-read as authentic through Hoggart's beautifully written personal account of working-class life.

It has often been pointed out that the supreme weakness of Hoggart's book, its glaring absence, is the virtual exclusion of all reference to the political and work institutions of the working class (for example, Critcher, 1979[2]). Labour activists of all kinds are marginalised into one paragraph referring to their untypicality and there is no account of any kind of paid working life. Thus although Hoggart focuses on the working class, the very thing that defines that class as a class – their work (in its relation to the means of production of life in capitalist society) – is missing. Class becomes *only* a matter of life-style, value-systems.

It is interesting to remember that Hoggart's book appeared alongside the 'embourgeoisement thesis', which argued that the specific character of the working class, especially in a period of improved wages, strong unions and the widespread availability of consumer durables, was gradually being eroded so that we were all becoming middle class in our attitudes, values and way of life. One riposte to this thesis, with impressive sociological evidence to back it up (Goldthorpe, 1968–9),[3] was that wages, unions and consumerism did not alter the fundamental relation of the working class to capital and the core of values founded upon that relation. Hoggart's book took a different tack. Working-class values stemmed from the particular historical formation of the home and community life of the working class. These were under threat, especially from the mass media and *a fortiori* television, but if there was resistance to embourgeoisement it was not because of the working class' relation to capital but because of its essential character. Hoggart thus upheld the notion of class and the specificity of working-class culture while at the same time depoliticising them.

---

2. Chas Critcher, 'Sociology, Cultural Studies and the Post-War Working Class', in John Clarke et al. (eds.), *Working Class Culture*, London: Hutchinson Educational, 1979, pp. 13–40.
3. John H. Goldthorpe et al., *The Affluent Worker* (3 vols.), Cambridge: Cambridge University Press, 1968-1969.

Thirdly, Hoggart's stress on home and community meant a stress on women. Once again, his account is nuanced. He recognises how very hard the brunt of domestic labour falls on women and their strength and endurance in the face of it; yet he also draws the most glowing portrait of the warmth of the working-class mother, while offering any number of strikingly sentimental moral asides upon the mores of young working-class women. And, once again, the appropriation of the book takes out the nuances, plays down the hardship and the moralism, plays up the strength and warmth. There is in *The Uses of Literacy* no awareness of the economic role of domestic labour, of the effect of patriarchal traditions in the organisation of domesticity and sexuality, themes that have had a much greater centrality in political and intellectual life in the last decade. Given the book's date, their absence is less striking than the absence of labour politics, though one should note that in a comparable, though less successful, book of the period, *Coal is Our Life* (Dennis, 1969), there is a surprisingly acute sense of the operations of gender within and across working-class culture.[4]

Finally, Hoggart's description of working-class culture focuses on his own upbringing in the 1930s and, as has already been mentioned, is partly concerned with conducting a polemic against the erosion of this culture by the mass media. This backwards look, together with finding the past preferable to the present, inevitably makes it hard not the read the book as nostalgic. I say 'hard not to' because in fact Hoggart is careful to say on many occasions that he is not concerned to upgrade the past, that he does recognise the appalling suffering of the working class in the '30s and before. Yet the dominant reading of the book, and the accusation most often levelled against it, is that it is nostalgic.

It is easy to see how these four aspects of *The Uses of Literacy* – the emphasis on common sense, the absence of work and politics, the stress on women and the strength of women, and the perspective of nostalgia – inform *Coronation Street* and indeed come close to defining its fictional world. (There are even more precise connections, with figures and images from *The Uses of Literacy* appearing in early episodes of *Coronation Street* – the scholarship boy [Ken Barlow];[5] watching television and reading particular newspapers as indicators of fecklessness [the Tanners, now the Ogdens]; the ambivalent class position of publicans; the plethora of splendid mums.)

Coronation Street takes as its mode the interactions of everyday life as realised in common-sense speech and philosophy. The narrative may take more un-everyday events as its focus, the multiplicity of marriages, deaths, disappearances and so on for which soap opera is so often derided. Yet in *Coronation Street* at least these are always

---

4. Norman Dennis et al., *Coal is Our Life: Analysis of a Yorkshire Mining Community*, London: Tavistock, 1969.

5. This is also a constant of a certain strain of working-class fiction, e.g. *How Green Is My Valley*, *The Stars Look Down*, etc.

Betty (Betty Driver), Vera (Liz Dawn), and Ivy (Lynne Perrie) in the Rovers Return, 1983. (Victor Blackman/Daily Express/Hulton Archive/Getty Images)

enacted within the mode of common sense, which is to say that they are also understood and contained by common sense. However, the common sense of *Coronation Street* is that of a particular description in a particular moment (*The Uses of Literacy*), whose truth is guaranteed by being based on personal testimony. In this way the peculiarity of the common sense has been naturalised, which gives it a special authority as a solvent of troublesome issues or perspectives.

The other links between *Coronation Street* and *The Uses of Literacy* may be quickly outlined. 'Life' in *Coronation Street* – though here it is important to bear in mind Christine Geraghty's analysis of soap opera conventions at least as much as the *Coronation Street/Uses of Literacy* nexus – is defined as community, interpersonal activity on a day-to-day basis. Work is seldom shown and, when it is, is treated in terms of styles of personal interaction (e.g. the gossip of the women at Mike Baldwin's factory, the joking relationship between staff and customers in the Rovers Return). Women characters have always been consistently emphasised, a point Marion Jordan substantiates in her essay; and the nostalgic cast of the serial is unmistakable. This was most explicit in the period when the credit sequence was based on a camera zoom from a long shot of a high-rise block of flats to a close-up of a back-to-back street, from the impersonality of modern planned architecture to the human scale of the old working-class street.

Coronation Street came out of the moment of *The Uses of Literacy* and is arguably still caught up in it. Thus what is important about it – its central focus on working-class life and on strong female characters – is still held in the particular way of setting up ideas and images of the working class and women that are crystallised and given a new lease of life in *The Uses of Literacy*. The serial has evolved, but – and here we need more sustained analysis to support or disprove what I'm going to say – its way of realising class and gender remains unchanged. Thus even though it does sometimes show paid work, does acknowledge the role of domestic labour and inequalities between the sexes, can be explicit about wider issues, nevertheless these extensions of subject matter have not really altered the content of the series. Common sense, constructed as a sensible and obvious refusal of wider perspectives, is always at hand to be the vehicle for the resolution of problems, however considerable their implications. Class as materially determined in relation to the means of production, and much less as self-realised in political and social action, is still either absent or (often comically) marginalised. Women's strength and endurance is celebrated, but as the inevitable and given lot of women rather than as socially determinant. The nostalgic tone of the serial consigns any lingering effective class consciousness to something that, to all intents and purposes, is in the past.

This is not to deny the very real strengths of the serial, rather it is to characterise its particular mode and to offer some very sketchy account of its historicity. It may be that what is particular to *Coronation Street* is *also* what is valuable about it. The affirmation of common sense must always put a brake on any theory or politics that does not connect at all with the lived texture of everyday life. The concentration on community and interpersonal interaction certainly counters the reduction of class to paid positions in the economic base, and the acknowledgment of female strength and endurance must be welcome in the context of the nincompoops that pass for the representation of women in most television. Even the nostalgia allows for a certain utopianism, which is to say the assertion of a vivid image of how life should be. I do not propose to argue at length here the legitimacy of utopian imagery in art,[6] and certainly the nostalgic cast of *Coronation Street* may undermine its utopian impulse by discounting it as a thing past. None the less, faced with the cynicism of liberal culture and the widespread refusal in contemporary left culture to imagine the future, we would do well to look at the utopian impulse however and wherever it occurs in popular culture.

Excerpt from 'Introduction,' in Richard Dyer, Christine Geraghty, Marion Jordan, Terry Lovell, Richard Paterson, and John Stewart, *Coronation Street*, London: BFI, 1981, pp. 1–8.

---

6. For discussion of the place of utopianism in Marxist theory of art, see Maynard Solomon (ed.), *Marxism and Art*, Hassocks: Harvester Press, 1980.

13 TEA AND COCOA TELE (1982)

Awards shows, those outside broadcasts of the show business equivalent of schools' prize-givings, are compulsive viewing. I used to think that this was a taste unique to me, that I was alone in Britain slumped in front of these shows. But I'm uncovering closet awards show viewers all the time, and I was recently with a group of socialists of various kinds, most of whom had watched all of either the BAFTA or Oscar awards, and many of whom had watched all of both.

What makes them such effective television? – 'effective' meaning here a lot of people watch them, chat about them afterwards, review them. It is interesting to consider the kind of reason that those professionally involved in the media give. There is among media professionals a certain common sense about why such and such a thing 'works', is effective television in the sense I've just defined. This professional common sense is worth attending to – it can alert us to aspects of the television experience we might overlook and, equally, it is often very revealing about the social values that inform those who provide us with the narrow selection of television entertainment we get.

A reason that is often given for the (relative) ratings success of awards shows is the time at which they are put out. After the ten o'clock news is a time when you don't quite want to go to bed, but don't want to concentrate too much either. Even a thriller or a sitcom, leave alone a documentary, needs work: your mind needs to be alert enough to *follow* the developments of a plot, to *get* a gag. Awards shows require no such effort. They have the suspense of a thriller (who is going to win?) without any need to follow a sequence of events through. They have jokes, but they are brief and disconnected (where gags in sitcoms are funny because of what has gone before, which you have to remember). In these ways, awards shows are the ultimate example of what many people think about television as a whole – that it makes you intellectually lazy, you just sit there and let it flow in front of you. I don't think most TV is like that – thrillers and sitcoms, as I've been suggesting, make you *make* connections. But perhaps awards shows really are like that, which is why they are so easy, so watchable, so good with a mug of tea or cocoa.

The attitudes of people on the left to this kind of explanation of a programme's popularity are of two kinds. Either the explanation confirms a general suspicion of the media, that it is *all* like this, all encouraging passivity, all playing upon people's worst tendencies towards laziness and cosiness. This is what is known as the 'manipulation' thesis — that the media manipulate us (or usually it is put as 'them') into a state of passivity so as to feed us capitalistic messages.

Alternatively, people reject altogether an explanation based on the time of day a programme is shown and the kind of pleasurable passivity it offers. Those who take this view usually want to stress the particular values and meanings the show expresses, and argue that the popularity is to do with the appeal of those values and meanings. Thus, in the case of awards shows, one might talk of the appeals of glamour (celebrities, fashions), of spectacle, of competition, of success and so on. All of these appeals are quite clearly socially meaningful, they express the values of a materialistic, competitive society (though I'd want to argue they offer other, more progressive things as well).

This kind of argument, about the shows' ideological dimension, is important. I have no difficulty in believing, and feeling, that the awards ceremonies make these appeals. But we shouldn't therefore dismiss the other kind of explanation. Too often on the left, in wanting television to reproduce different values (as it will in a socialist and feminist society), we don't think enough about the things that media professionals do think about, that is, the conditions of reception of television. The format of the awards shows, their relaxing, bright and cheerful undemandingness may be the bearer of reactionary values, but it seems probable that in any world that it is at all challenging to live in there will be times when we need, and deserve, relaxing, bright and cheerful art. There is no reason why such art should carry reactionary values; and we must avoid the left puritanism that finds easiness and bright-and-cheerfulness in themselves a bad thing.

It is this kind of concern that worries me about some of the things I hear about Channel 4. At times it seems that every left cultural worker ever is going to be doing something for the new channel. But in all the discussion I don't hear much talk about pleasure, fun, entertainment; I don't get a sense that people are taking into account the conditions of reception, the tea-and-cocoa syndrome. Here is a wonderful opportunity to help to build a left, feminist culture, in the fullest sense of the word. But the fullest sense includes awareness of the rhythms of everyday life, of the legitimate desire to relax, of wanting to see things sparkle a bit. If the left workers in Channel 4 do not attend to that dimension, and respect it, they may find many people turning off. Then the powers that be can say, there, we told you so, the people don't want socialist, feminist culture.

I don't expect left workers in Channel 4 to be giving us awards shows. But perhaps they should seriously consider giving us something that is ideologically different but still watchable with tea and cocoa.

Originally published in *Comment* 20:8 (17 April 1982), p. 16.

14 BAD FOR A LAUGH (1982)

It seems the easiest thing in the world to deride is American soap opera. *Dallas*, *Falcon Crest*, *Dynasty* – in certain circles you can be sure of displaying your own seriousness and sophistication by mocking series like this. They are indeed celebrations of capitalism, privilege, the family – but this isn't why they are derided. Habitual dismissal of *Dallas* and the rest springs from various kinds of snobbery, not from socialist indignation.

British soaps are less easy targets. *Coronation Street* was long ago defended (by Jonathan Miller) as today's equivalent of Dickens; and its atmosphere or reputation of working-classness feeds the nostalgia of a generation (and more) formed by Hoggart's *Uses of Literacy* and 'kitchen sink' drama. *Crossroads* used to be an easier target, but even this has survived to something like respectability – perhaps because in a recession we can be nostalgic for its furniture showroom affluence? Or is it because there is every sign of ATV/Central killing it off, and its popular bad taste no longer threatens received opinion? Other British soaps do not even get a mention in the derision stakes – perhaps, because they are screened in the daytime, when only such discountables as housewives and the unemployed can watch them.

Dallas and the rest have the audacity to be screened at peak viewing time; they are also American. Much of the derision they receive centres on their Americanness, implicitly if not explicitly. Not America as the epitome of patriarchal capitalism, mind you; but America as the centre of plastic values. The grooming of the performers ('they look like Barbie dolls'), the lavishness of the sets ('like something out of a glossy magazine'), the expert (= 'slick') editing, the banal script … such are the common dismissive comments the series receive. A double standard operates. Take the banality of the dialogue. In *Coronation Street* the trivia of everyday, common-sense gossip binds the programme together; desultory conversation on a topical topic can take up a whole scene in the Rovers and no-one minds. The ins-and-outs of day-to-day life are the fantasy that sustains our interest in *Coronation Street*. In *Dallas* et al. there is different trivia, American trivia, but no more trivial for that. Yet how we like to dismiss US trivia as clichés and herald our own as common sense.

The extremely attractive and openly gay – yet stereotypically 'troubled' – Steven Carrington (Al Corley) in *Dynasty*, 1981. (BFI National Archive)

Particularly galling about US trivia is its pretentiousness. *Dynasty* even makes references to Freud, to alternative philosophies of the world (notably hedonism versus responsibility, business interests versus ecological ones). American soap trivia is conscious of self – all those 'I'm trying to find out who I am' declarations British people mock as they muddle through in self-ignorance.

The current exemplar of such attitudes is Peter Conrad, author of *Television – the Medium and the Manners*, which pretty well hates TV in general, for the same sort of reasons that F.R. Leavis and his followers hated American popular/mass culture in general – that it was destroying true values, placing plastic ones in their place, the implication being that only the British, or those few of them/us who resisted the blandishments of American culture, still preserved 'real' values (e.g. elitism, privilege, complacency?). Conrad it was that *The Observer* got to review *Dynasty*, not just as part of a regular TV review column, but as a veritable display of neo-Leavisite clever-dickery.

It's always been hard to distinguish right from left in criticism of the mass media; but it is important to do so. *Dynasty* et al. are not bad because they speak with/to 'common sense', because they deal with family issues, because they are nice and glossy to look at, because they are American; they are not bad by the yardstick of some set of mythical, 'obvious' human values. If we want to criticise them, we must not use the weapons of derision that traditional criticism has given us – not because we shouldn't be humorous (heaven forbid that I should want even less humour on the left), but because that habitual derision has built into it attitudes and values that are in no way socialist and feminist.

Dismissal also stops us getting on with understanding why, after all, these series are popular. (The neo-Leavisite position would of course say: what do you expect people as crass as 'the people' to like?) It also prevents us seeing how people may *use* the programmes. *Gay News* dismissed *Dynasty* and its gay character in just the same frightfully witty terms as Peter Conrad and others – without considering the *possible* impact of this character (Steven). He is stereotypically 'troubled' – but he is also liked by the other characters, is extremely attractive (in line with the norms of the series, anyhow), and his concerns are seen as being as legitimate as those of the other characters. Of no other mainstream TV series can this be said. It may not be enough, but we're not going to get completely socialist feminist representations in a non-socialist, sexist society. And maybe such small steps forward hasten the happy day of the good society?

Originally published in *Comment* 20:13 (26 June 1982), p. 16.

15 TAKING POPULAR TELEVISION SERIOUSLY (1985)

Two of the most widespread notions used in the discussion of television are 'entertainment' and 'representation'. Both are powerful terms, with a wealth of connotations. We tend to take them for granted, without examining just what is at stake in them. They tend to be kept apart – we talk about either whether a programme is entertaining or how it represents reality to us. Following that habit of mind, I shall begin by discussing each term separately, before suggesting how each is in fact an aspect of the other.

ENTERTAINMENT

'Entertainment' is a cornerstone of common sense. It is a term we all use, all the time. Like all common sense terms, its meaning is utterly obvious until we come to define exactly what we mean by it. It is only then that we recognise what a difficult concept it is.

The DES [Department of Education and Science] Report [*Popular TV & Schoolchildren* (1983)] offers a good instance. The Report recognises that there is a problem about entertainment but it talks about entertainment in characteristic ways that sidestep the question of what entertainment is. The Report either raises the question of whether 'serious' topics should be dealt with in entertainment programmes or else it backs off from its analyses with apologetic remarks about such-and-such being 'only' or 'just' entertainment. In either case, what entertainment is remains unquestioned and unexamined.

What I mean by taking entertainment seriously is asking why and how programmes are entertaining, why people like them and what children's main experiences of television are. These are serious questions because they take us to the heart of the reasons why most people watch television. What I do *not* mean by taking entertainment seriously is looking at popular television programmes, noting that they are entertaining and then saying they are *also* about something Serious and Important. I am not arguing for a line of reasoning like 'Of course we all really enjoyed *Minder* but we also thought that…' Rather, I want to understand what the enjoyment is about.

The Human League performing on *Top of the Pops*, offering escape into a world clearly defined as 'youth', with an edge of rebelliousness and cussedness in its liveliness, August 1981. (Michael Putland/Getty Images)

It is customary to come to terms with entertainment in either of two ways. The first is by recourse to a notion of 'escapism'. This is the term used as a full stop to the difficult question of trying to say what is meant about a programme's entertainment quality. In defence of liking *Crossroads* or *Magnum* it is said, 'Oh, well, it's just escapism'. What is rarely asked is what it is we are escaping from and what we are escaping to. To begin to ask this, particularly of producers and children, may help us understand the experience of the pleasure of popular television. As a start, asking people what it was about a programme they enjoyed that offered them escape often reveals even by implication what they wanted to escape from.

Let me take an example from the DES Report of how we may learn from listening to what people say about their enjoyment of entertainment. One of the pupils quoted gives as his reasons for liking *Top of the Pops* that it annoys his father and makes him stop thinking about the problems of the world. These remarks already point to qualities of *Top of the Pops* as entertainment; as a way of offering escape into a world clearly defined as 'youth', with an edge of rebelliousness and cussedness in its liveliness.

They suggest a very different experience from that of ageing rockers who moan about *Top of the Pops* being too soft. There are also 'the problems of the world' that *Top of the Pops* implicitly suggests should be escaped from and the busyness, colour, vitality and a certain kind of sexuality that offers an escape from them. By pursuing these lines of reason, then, we can begin to make sense of how *Top of the Pops* and its viewers construct what the problems of the world are and how they can escape from them. Teachers could take these common sense remarks further. Although one might be cautious about exploring the boy's relations with his father, the family scene is clearly crucial to understanding the dynamics of pleasurable escape into television.

It is important not to confine such discussion to programmes that come already labelled as 'entertainment'. *Tomorrow's World*, which comes on just before *Top of the Pops*, should equally be analysed as entertainment. This does not mean looking at the way it 'sugars the pill' in providing information about technological matters but, rather, looking at the way it constructs its own escape route from the problems of the world. What is entertaining about *Tomorrow's World* is the way that it constructs a tomorrow for today's world to escape into via the unproblematic, colourful, jaunty use of technology. The core of *Tomorrow's World*'s appeal is just as much escapism as *Top of the Pops*.

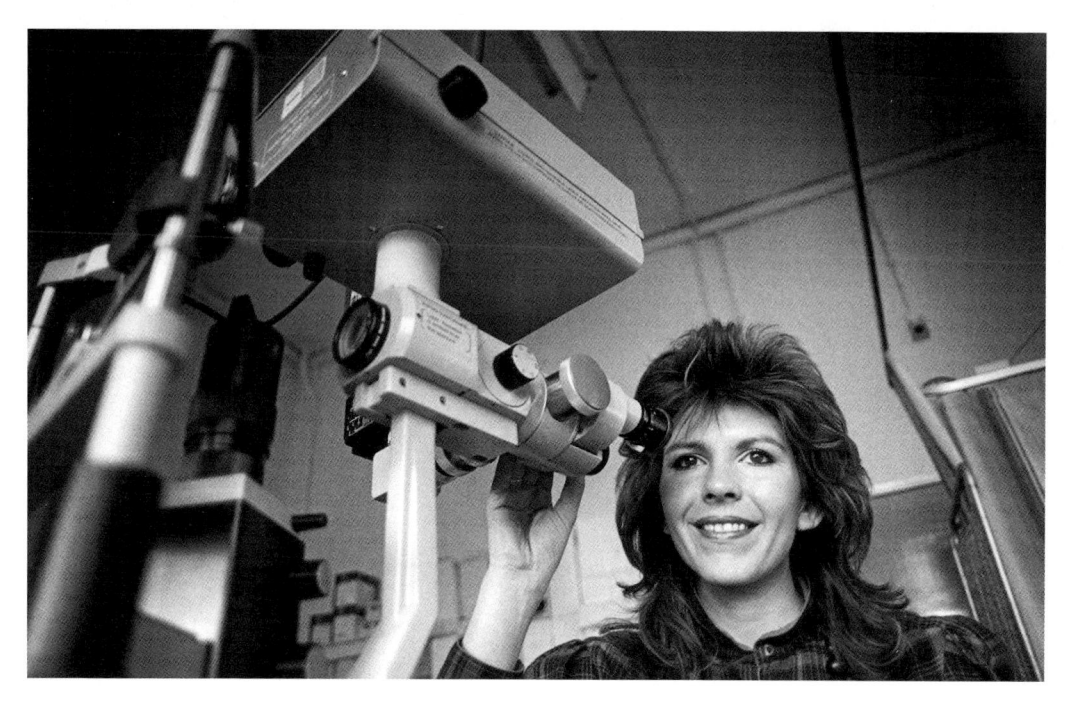

What is entertaining about *Tomorrow's World* is the way that it constructs a tomorrow for today's world to escape into via the unproblematic, colourful, jaunty use of technology; *TW*'s presenter Maggie Philbin trying out a YAG eye laser, 1986. (Jeremy Grayson/Radio Times/Getty Images)

The other way we can approach entertainment is through a notion that is the opposite of escapism. We get much pleasure from escaping into another world, but we also enjoy having our ideas about the world confirmed. Television entertainment gives us the pleasure of seeing that we are not alone in thinking as we do about the world since it appears others think our way, too. There are perhaps two aspects to this pleasure of confirmation. One is the pleasure of feeling we belong to a consensus.

No consensus arises naturally out of what people just happen to think. Television is one of many agencies in society that defines what it thinks is the prevailing consensus and then presents it as if it arises spontaneously from what 'people' think. None the less, we do need to acknowledge that there is something very comfortable about a consensus, a feeling of reconciled differences, common ground between people. When watching television it is very pleasant if you can feel that you belong to the consensus it presents.

The other pleasure of confirmation is the opposite. We all of us also recognise that, in certain aspects of our lives, our thoughts and feelings are not those of the consensus we are presented with. We are thus 'deviants' in those aspects. Every so often television may also throw up images and moments that are not within its consensus, and among them one may find one's own 'deviance' confirmed.

Thus on *Question Time* (knockabout entertainment if anything is), one may hear one's own views being expressed. Usually this does not prove them true – no new evidence is offered, there is no leap forward in reasoning – but it is delightful to hear oneself being spoken, legitimised for a fragile second.

To understand entertainment as both escapism and confirmation is not necessarily to endorse it. Television entertainment identifies the problems to be escaped from, how that escape is to be effected and what the consensus and the deviant positions are. All of these issues are of great political consequence, but we have to get at the issues and their consequence through the experience of entertainment, rather than inferring social implications beneath or despite the entertainment, in the characteristic way exemplified by the DES Report.

REPRESENTATION

Turning now to the concept of *representation*, which needs to be discussed in wider terms than the Report allows. We can distinguish four different connotations of the term, each of considerable importance. First, representation suggests re-presentation, presenting reality over again to us. It is often said that television is a 'window on the world', transparent and unmediated; and it is equally often said that it is nothing of the sort, that it is pure fabrication. The notion of representation can get us out of this empty opposition by focusing on the way television actively makes sense of a world that none the less exists separately from television. 'Representation' insists that there is a real world, but that our perception of it is always mediated by television's selection, emphasis and use of technical/aesthetic means to render that world to us.

Equally there is no perception of the world except one that is mediated through the forms of representation available in the culture, of which television is one of the most powerful. The notion of representation keeps open that tension between television images themselves and the reality that those images *make* sense of. What is politically at stake here is *what* sense they make of the world, not the inescapable fact that they do so.

Secondly, 'representation' suggests the function of 'being representative of'. In other words, it raises the question of *typicality*. To what extent are representations of men and women, whites and Blacks, different classes, etc. typical of how those groups are in society? All communication must deal in the typical. We cannot communicate only through the utterly unique, particular and individuated. It is unhelpful to fall into the position, as the Report often does, that considers stereotypes as *necessarily* derogatory. What matters is not *that* we have typical representations on television, but rather *what* they are, what harm they do to the well-being of the groups that they represent.

Thirdly, there is representation in the sense implied in the Representation of the People Act, that is, in the sense of *speaking for and on behalf of*. This is where the most political heat is generated because, faced with television images, we constantly need to ask not 'What is this image of?' so much as 'Who is speaking here?'. For every image of a woman, it is important to ask who is speaking for women at that point. In the vast majority of cases, the answer would be a man. The same is true of other groups excluded from the mainstream of speech in our society. Television so often speaks on our behalf without letting us speak for ourselves.

Finally, representation should also make us think of the *audience*. In this inflection, we should include ourselves: what does this programme represent to me; what does it mean to other people who watch it? We often leave this stage out of account; especially, I regret to say, in education. Teachers often try to get pupils and students to see what a programme represents 'ideally' (i.e. as *teachers* understand it) without also finding out what it represents to them. We need to learn to listen better – especially to children – to understand what sense they in turn make out of the work represented to them.

Questions that teachers can debate with their pupils stem readily from these different connotations of the term representation. What sense of the world is this programme making? What does it claim is typical of the world and what deviant? Who is really speaking? For whom? What does it represent to us, and why?

ENTERTAINMENT AND REPRESENTATION

'Entertainment' and 'representation' are terms kept by convention apart. They even belong to different registers of speech – *entertainment* is a common sense word, *representation* is far more academic. Along with this goes an assumption that entertainment is not important but trivial, whereas representation is a serious, even heavy issue. Yet we need to look at the way all entertainment necessarily uses representations of the world, just as all representations have, to a greater or a lesser extent, entertainment value. We need to be asking why there is an opposition between entertainment and representation. It is common to think of them as in some sense antagonistic functions of television. Some argue that 'this' is a representation of 'that', but it is 'only entertainment' and therefore of no consequence. Alternatively, more perniciously, entertainment is seen to allow the representation to do its work under cover of the pleasure of the programme. We need to get beyond the assumptions contained in such views, to discuss with students the extent to which they feel that the fact that something is entertainment has written off the way it represents the world, and the extent to which they use the entertainment qualities of the programme to defend themselves against its representational concerns. We need to find out about these things and not start by assuming that we already know them.

Even more importantly, we should ask why certain representations are entertaining. Why is this view of reality enjoyable? Why is that view of what social groups are like a pleasure? It may be that given images are entertaining because they represent how we think life should be. If we take the example of images of women, they may represent fantasies of how women should be which may be nice to escape into. They may reassure people who are anxious about changing roles of women, boys who are anxious in their dealings with girls, and girls who reject the new ideas of womanhood that are currently in society. I don't wish to endorse these pleasures, but I do wish to understand the power of images through what makes them pleasurable.

I have been trying to work here from ideas about entertainment and representation that generate questions. Like all the best educational questions, these must be open-ended questions, not ones to which we already have the answers. On the contrary, we need to learn to listen to the answers to the questions; teachers, especially, need to be in a genuine dialogue with their students and pupils. To take popular television seriously is to get inside the experience of it, to grant a legitimacy to the pleasures it offers and *then* to ask questions of value, social responsibility and politics.

Originally published in David Lusted and Phillip Drummond (eds), *TV and Schooling*, London: BFI, 1985, pp. 41–46.

16 THE COLOUR OF ENTERTAINMENT (1995)

In the middle of *That's Entertainment! III*, the MGM compilation recently released on video, of highlights from its musicals, Lena Horne remarks that it was not always so very jolly working on these paeans to happiness. She says it mildly, ironically, in a tone of probable conciliation, but it comes over like a flash of lightning on a sunny summer's day.

It's not that she's complaining about the work, though she and the film's other hosts, might well do. The *That's Entertainment!* series has never dwelt on it, but making these movies was always more grind than merriment. If common sense did not tell us that you don't get all those elements – music, dance, costume, decor, camerawork – into such perfect condition and so perfectly co-ordinated without labouring at it, plenty of histories and memoirs have reminded us. The time, the heat, the discomfort, to say nothing of Louis B. Mayer's manipulative cruelty and Arthur Freed's womanising and fag-baiting, are well documented. Making *The Wizard of Oz*, that jolly tale of the road to happiness, sounds like misery from end to end.

Nor is Horne saying anything she hasn't said before. In her biographies, in interviews and most memorably in her stage show *Lena Horne: the Lady and Her Music*, she has recounted the racism she encountered at MGM (and throughout her career): the attempts to persuade her to pretend she wasn't Black, the racially coded criticisms of her style (for instance, that she made her mouth too big when she sang), the chronic inability to use her except in self-contained numbers dropped into the films and easily cut out for Southern exhibition, the scandalised reaction when she married a white man. The very fact that someone as magnetic and beautiful as Horne stopped working for MGM in 1950, long before the musical's fortunes started to decline, has always been eloquent testimony to the treatment she received there. And, inadvertently, MGM let us glimpse all this in the first *That's Entertainment!* film, in a sequence showing the stars gathered together at an anniversary dinner. The camera tracks along and reveals the stars being themselves: Judy Garland bubbling, Clark Gable grinning, Greer Garson in period costume, Katharine Hepburn talking, talking – and Horne, silent, staring into middle distance, looking frankly pissed off. Even then, for those who cared to read it, her body language conveyed what her words make explicit in *That's Entertainment! III*.

Publicity shot of Lena Horne, circa 1950. (Gilles Petard/Redferns via Getty Images)

So it's not revelation but context that makes Horne's contribution to *TE3* so startling. All the other hosts in this series (*TE, TE2, That's Dancing!*) have assured us that at MGM life was nothing but fun, respect and fulfilling hard work. Which we don't believe, but the claim is part of the entertainment. As Jane Feuer discusses in her book *The Hollywood Musical*, the show-within-a-show format of so many musicals both reveals the labour and skill involved in putting on an entertainment and yet passes it all off as improvisation, spontaneity, community and having a good time. So it is with the *That's Entertainment!* movies, and it comes as a shock to have someone even suggest anything to the contrary.

What makes Horne's statement more startling still is what comes before and after it. Before, we have a number called 'Pass that Peace Pipe' from *Good News*, brilliantly performed by the forgotten Joan McCracken and a host of people pretending to be college boys and girls. After it, we have Judy Garland, her voice strained, in 'I'm an Indian Too', one of the numbers she shot for *Annie Get Your Gun* before she left it. Both acts are based on the premise that it's fine for whites to do cod versions of Native American dance movements, and that there is something intrinsically hilarious about Native American names – so 'Pass that Peace Pipe' has such merry tongue-twisters as "just like the Choctaws, Chickasaws, Chattanooga Chippewas do". So here's Lena Horne raising the film's racial consciousness, and here's the film carrying on as if she hasn't said a thing.

Horne's contribution puts on to the agenda the whole question of race and musicals of the MGM variety (which were not exclusively made by MGM – *Cover Girl*, *Funny Face* and *Hello, Dolly!* are all 'MGM musicals', even though they were made by Columbia, Paramount and Fox respectively). Horne prompts us to look past the opulence and dynamism to consider the racial character of the entertainment in musicals.

This is not just a question of the way the non-white peoples of the US are represented, though heaven knows there are enough sins of omission and commission here, the former perhaps the more staggering. Let us consider only African Americans, the fount of US popular music, itself one of the greatest glories of twentieth-century culture. Let us also grant that there is too much pain, bitterness and defiance in people like Billie Holiday or Paul Robeson for them to be easily accommodated to the musical's gospel of gaiety. But think what feelgood Black talent was available that was either not used or squandered: Nat King Cole, Billy Eckstein, Ella Fitzgerald, Eartha Kitt, Sarah Vaughan for starters, as well as such dancers as Honi Coles or Katherine Dunham (names less familiar precisely because they were hardly recorded on film). Even when such stars as Louis Armstrong, Pearl Bailey, Cab Calloway, the Nicholas Brothers, Bill Robinson, Hazel Scott, Ethel Waters and Lena Horne were used, it was nearly always in one kind of ghetto or another: the all-Black musical (an outtake from one of the best of which, *Cabin in the Sky*, is included in *TE3*), the number that can be dropped without doing violence to story or editing (such as Horne's intense 'Where or When' in *Words and Music*, also included in *TE3*), or, in the case of the sublime Bill Robinson, kiddies' corner, squiring Shirley Temple. All of these do at least preserve performances on film and, as Donald Bogle argues in his *Toms, Coons, Mulattoes, Mammies, and Bucks*, what these performers achieve in these moments far outstrips the limitations of space and roles allotted them. Something can generally be salvaged from even the most unpromising examples: not only are Robinson's performances with Temple superb examples of his swinging, up-on-the-toes style, but they also provide one of the few images of rapport between an adult male and a female child that is neither smarmy nor sinister. Yet the footage of him elsewhere makes us realise how severely Hollywood restricted his range and thus what magic it passed up.

Except in the few all-Black musicals, Black performers in MGM-style musicals nearly always play characters who are nothing but entertainers. They may be – and often are – slaves, servants, waiters, prostitutes, but all they ever *do* in these roles is entertain. This is how it has been in the movies for a long time: when the white Southerners in *The Birth of a Nation* take their white Northern friends round the plantation, what they show them are Blacks dancing, not cotton-picking. Or else they play professional entertainers, typically club acts seen by the white characters on a night out. Musicals are often about characters who are entertainers, but when the entertainers are white, they usually also have lives – love lives especially, but also careers, vexatious relatives, personal problems of one kind or another. No such wider life is given Black characters (if one can call them characters), depriving them of the emotional resonances that story and characterisation bring to white musical numbers.

Blackness is contained in the musical, ghettoised, stereotyped: 'only entertainment'. Yet containment is the antithesis of the entertainment a musical offers. Bursting from the confines of life by singing your heart out and dancing when you feel like it – this is the joy of the musical. Where the musical most disturbingly constructs a vision of race is in the fact that it is white people's privilege to be able to do this – and what that tells us about the white dream of being in the world.

This is to do with a relation both to physical space and to the cultural spaces of other peoples. This is a given of the fundamental performance elements of the musical: dance and song. Dancing is by definition about bodies in space, about how bodies relate to other bodies, how they move through space, how they make use of or submit to the environment around them. Less obviously, singing too is about space: singing carries differently into space than speech and different kinds of singing, from crooning to belting, impose themselves differently on the world around the singer. Fred Astaire's light voice and deft delivery create an intimacy that envelopes just him and his partner – no one notices when he croons 'Cheek to Cheek' to Ginger Rogers on a crowded dance floor in *Top Hat* before gliding her away to a secluded area. By contrast, at the end of "'S Wonderful' in *An American in Paris*, Gene Kelly and Georges Guetary move further and further away from each other down a Parisian street, yelling alternately to each other the exultation of being in love. They dominate the street and passers-by look fondly on at, no doubt, *les folies de l'amour*.

Musicals typically show us space entirely occupied by white people, dancing wherever they want, singing as loudly or intimately as they need. This is often, as with Black performers, contained within the confines of the space of entertainment: the theatre or cabaret stage. Even so, this was a very elastic space, especially in the hands of a Busby Berkeley in the Warner Bros musicals of the '30s. However, it was one of the distinctions of the MGM tradition to break away from exclusive show-within-a-show presentation, to give us singing in the rain and dancing in the street. This is where it began to be difficult to make better use of Black performers.

One of the loveliest numbers in all the MGM musicals is 'Main Street' in *On the Town*. It is gloriously simple: the setting is a bare rehearsal studio, the performers wear their characters' everyday clothes, the melody is relaxed, the words plain and the dance steps seem little more than choreographed skipping and child's play. In short, 'Main Street' says 'anyone can do this and be so happy'. In the song, Gene Kelly invites Vera-Ellen to imagine they are back in his small town, Meadowville, in middle America, walking down the main street together. As they dance, in their imagination they rejoice in the warmth and freedom of American ordinariness. But down how many main streets in how many small US towns can we imagine a Black couple strolling with such unwary joy? This is not to demand that the musical be realistic, but rather to suggest how even the utopian imagination has its boundaries of plausibility. 'Main Street' works because it feels psychically right to imagine whites – but only whites – so at ease in the heartland of the United States.

This feeling is intensified in numbers which start with a transition from a more confined to a more open space, although it's not always easy to get the impact of this from the *That's Entertainment!* films, which generally only give us the numbers (usually incomplete), not the situations from which they arise. The feeling of fresh air and open spaces, the emphasis on uplift in the dancing in many numbers have their meaning in the way they embody the characters' excitement at transcending constraints on their lives. It is the equivalents of these that makes so many great numbers soar: Gene Kelly, Rita Hayworth and Phil Silvers striding out of their favourite bar into the street in *Cover Girl* to 'Make Way for Tomorrow!'; the coda to 'My Favourite Things' in *The Sound of Music*, cutting from Julie Andrews sitting in her bedroom wondering what to do with these miserable kids to a montage of her leading them on a freewheeling gambol round Salzburg, winding up on a mountaintop ready for the next number, 'Do-Re-Mi'; the bullied underlings who decide to 'Put on [their] Sunday Clothes', strut out of the house, down the street and off to New York in *Hello, Dolly!*. Black people doing the same thing would in the white imagination seem like a terrifying attempt to take over.

Yet what whites do to their environment in these numbers is precisely to take it over. In the examples given, the space they take over is already one they are socially entitled to, but the underlying feeling is of the right to expand out into space, whoever it belongs to. Something of this is evident in another scintillating number from *On the Town*, 'Prehistoric Man', which starts off from Ann Miller telling Jules Munshin in the New York Museum of Natural History that she fancies him far more than the average modern male because he looks like a caveman. Once the dancing gets underway, Miller leads the group (Munshin, Betty Garrett, Gene Kelly and Frank Sinatra) in an unabashed, high-energy exploration of the museum. They use what is to hand to express their libidinal enthusiasm, and the natural history to hand turns out to be the pickings of 'primitive' culture. So there are tom-toms, Arabic instruments, bearskins, wigwams and so on, all grist to white joy. The number – and precisely in its intoxicating exuberance – is the very model of the colonial structure of feeling: expansion into space, control over what's in that space, incorporation of what's there into white agendas. This movement of expansion and incorporation is at the heart of the musical's construction of race.

'Prehistoric Man' romps through the spoils of a space that has already been expanded into: the museum is a repository of white exploration and colonialism. The musical has often been prepared to go further, actually to enter that space (as long as it could recreate it in the studio, of course). The early MGM musicals based on operettas, which tend to get left out of the *That's Entertainment!* films' account of the studio's glories, were sometimes explicitly about colonialism: *Naughty Marietta*, *The Desert Song*, *Rose Marie*, *The Firefly*. In other musicals, the non-white world is oddly free of non-white people: there are no Blacks on the Caribbean island of *The Pirate*, for instance, no Native Americans in *Oklahoma!*. Even a race-sensitive musical like *South Pacific* celebrates the lustiness of white GIs (and, to be fair, one or two Black ones) in 'There Is Nothing like a Dame', performed all over a Polynesian beach devoid of Polynesians save the old woman, Bloody Mary, who caters to their wants (drugs, booze, women).

One of the outtakes featured in *TE3* is 'March of the Hoagies' from *The Harvey Girls*, a Judy Garland musical set in the West. The number shows us the townsfolk striding out into the surrounding country in celebratory mood. With the relentless onward surge of its massed movements and firm editing, plus its torchlight *mise en scène*, it looks like nothing so much as a gathering of the Klans. This is taking possession of the land with a vengeance. No wonder it was dropped. It makes explicit what is masked in an earlier number, 'On the Atchison Topeka and the Santa Fe' (featured in a previous *That's Entertainment!*), which shows the film's heroines arriving on the train of the song's title at the township that is to be their new home. The number – justly prized by aficionados of the genre – has a complex interplay of both featured singers, and choreographed movement and camerawork; it has a great, catchy tune, given rousing but also ruminative and humorous variations; and it is a superb example of a number that expands outwards, as people step down from their long train journey and out into the new township, with the space for song and dance, for release and exhilaration, ever widening as the number proceeds, the interplay of elements evoking an instant (as well as literal) harmony, culminating in a splendid unison dance alongside the train as it pulls out. It has all the brio and spontaneity lacking in 'March of the Hoagies' – yet it too is about possession of the land: the song celebrates one of the main instruments by which this was achieved, the railway, while the number shows white folks in joyous occupancy of the world.

Whites in musicals have a rapturous relationship with their environment. This may be confined to the utopian moments of the numbers, but then they are the reason we go to see musicals. The potentially colonialist nature of this is suggested not only by the way whites stride down streets as if they own them (which in a sense they do) and burst all over other locales (which they don't), but also in the way the cultures of the colonised, as perceived by whites, are incorporated into the fabric of the numbers' music and dance. Not just the ethnographic objects picked out and played with in 'Prehistoric Man', but the gestures, shapes and sounds adopted from 'ethnic' dance: a bit of bottom-wiggling for Ann Miller when she gets hold of some Arab instruments, some bent-over high-stepping and Red Indian hollering for Betty Garrett when she puts on a Native American headdress, and stomps and 'ugh' sounds when they get hold of some African tom-toms.

The musical's propensity to do this sort of thing is sent up in the 'Stereophonic Sound' number in *Silk Stockings* (one of the highlights of *TE3*, in which Fred Astaire and delicious Janis Paige mock the commercial imperatives of the day: more spectacle, hang the plot). At one point they sing of how it is not enough to have dancing any more, you have to have "Russian ballet, or Chinese ballet, or Bali ballet, or any ballet", and with each example they take up, with extraordinary precision and speed, a pose that sums up the national style in question. Numbers that have no overall non-US cultural reference do this all the time – slip into a bit of 'African' here, a bit of 'Irish' there, and so on. We are all familiar with the repertoire: syncopated stomping, with head and shoulders bent forward, is 'Red Indian'; sideways movements of the head, with hands touching above it, is 'Indian' (as in India); fast stamping heels and bent arms circling the body is 'Spanish'; anything that flaunts hips, groin and arse is 'Black'. Singing, and especially orchestrations, can do the same thing. The exactness and rapidity with which it is done are generally breathtaking.

You might see this as eclectic, as a generous recognition of the music and dance riches of other cultures. It could even sound like a postmodern hybridity *avant la lettre*. There is undoubtedly a felt need to refresh and enliven white music and dance

– indeed, white life and spirits – with the vitality, sensuality and sheer difference of other cultures. Yet all these cultures are subsumed into white needs, white goals, white displays. This is, after all, not dancing with the Other, but incorporating it, literally taking the Other into one's own body.

It is even implied that whites are better at Black (and other) music and dance than Blacks themselves. The greatest Southern Black routine in musicals may well be shiningly pink Ann Miller's 'Shaking the Blues Away' in 1948's *Easter Parade* (featured in *TE3*), a *tour de force* of tapping and shimmying. While the Black roots of taps may have been forgotten or never known to white audiences in 1948, shimmies were the 'Black' movement *par excellence* in the white imagination. And, were this not enough, the song, though it never mentions skin colour, is all about what 'they' do 'down South' – as if this kind of cavorting is what Southern ladies and gentlemen get up to.

If Ann Miller does the greatest Southern Black routine, then the greatest exponent of the Black art of tap dance is Fred Astaire (and I'm Cyd Charisse). His case is interesting. In *Swing Time*, he blacks up to pay tribute to his sources, and specifically to Bill Robinson, in the 'Bojangles of Harlem' number. Generously meant, no doubt, but the use of blackface cannot help but be disturbing (even if it is quite far from the grotesqueries of minstrelsy), and wouldn't it have been better if Astaire had used his influence to get Robinson himself on screen? Gerald Mast, in *Can't Help Singing*, commends the several numbers in which Astaire dances with Black men (not women, presumably because this would raise the question of sexuality): 'Slap that Bass' in *Shall We Dance?*, a number with Black and white prisoners in *You'll Never Get Rich* and, perhaps most famously, 'A Shine on Your Shoes' in *The Band Wagon* (featured in *That's Dancing!*). This last takes place in an amusement arcade on 42nd Street; the number starts off from the rhythm of the shoeshine 'boy', Leroy Daniels, doing his job and leads into a *pas de deux* for him and Astaire. It is hardly an equal routine, however. Occasionally both men occupy the screen equally and do the same or equivalent movements, but for most of the time Daniels is choreographically subservient to Astaire. Daniels' happy-go-lucky shoe-shining may give Astaire the inspiration to cheer up in this miserable amusement arcade (which symbolises for him the decline of Broadway entertainment), dancing with a Black dancer may signal recognition of the sources (and masters?) of this tradition, but Daniels is really only there to provide a sunny, rhythmic point of departure for Astaire's brilliance and his character's feelings of release.

Most numbers do not even go so far as Astaire's in acknowledging Black and other ethnic sources. The lively quote, as in 'Prehistoric Man' or 'Stereophonic Sound', is one thing. Ready mastery of exotic dances, especially Latin American ones, is acceptable too. But the degree to which Black and Hispanic music and dance founded US popular music cannot be acknowledged – they are incorporated so far in MGM musicals as to disappear from view.

That's Entertainment! III ends with 'That's Entertainment!' from *The Band Wagon*. It's a list song, laying out all the things that can be called 'entertainment', deliberately including Sophocles and Shakespeare alongside melodrama, comedy, "the lights on the lady in tights" and "the clown with his pants falling down". It takes place on a theatre stage, with odds and ends of scenery on it. In the course of the number, the performers (Fred Astaire, Jack Buchanan, Cyd Charisse, Nanette Fabray and Oscar Levant) move from standing close together to ranging over the whole area of the stage, using flats, hoists and props in a celebration of entertainment's wit, energy and spontaneity. Yet in all the song, there is not one mention of anything that could be called Black, even though the music and dance called upon could not have existed without recourse to Black (and other) cultural forms.

I've always rather balked at the final words of 'That's Entertainment!': "The gag may be waving a flag/That began with a Mr. Cohan/Hip hooray; the American way/The world is a stage/The stage is a world/Of entertainment!' But I've always assumed this was excessive European sensitivity on my part. Now, though, I can't help reflecting on the colour of entertainment in America itself and the way this has been processed so consummately by the MGM musical.

Originally published in *Sight and Sound* 5:11 (November 1995), pp. 28–31.

17 *JURASSIC WORLD* AND PROCREATION ANXIETY (2015)

Jurassic World is anticapitalist, antimanagerialism, and anti-GM; it is also antifeminist, racist, species-ist, and decidedly not queer.[1] It is fun entertainment, with its thrills always accompanied by an immediate sense that all will be well. What underpins all this is the film's anxiety and ultimate reassurance about ideal reproduction, which has to be imagined as white, middle-class, heterosexual, male-led, and human.

It is not necessary to see the film to know that it is about a zoo-cum-theme park featuring prehistoric creatures, some of which get loose and create havoc until they are beaten back. Folded into this basic situation are two stories that offer a way into the wider spectacle: one tracks two brothers, Zach and Gray, who visit, and get lost in, the park; the other tracks two of the park's employees, Claire Dearing (Bryce Dallas Howard) and Owen Grady (Chris Pratt), who by the end of the film become a couple; the two stories are connected because Claire is the brothers' aunt. All of these protagonists play a role in defeating the creatures run amok.

Procreation anxiety runs through both the story of the prehistoric creatures and that of the fraternal and heterosexual couples. The most dangerous creature is not just a pre-historic giant generated from dormant biological material, as are most of the other creatures and as was the case in the *Jurassic Park* films; rather, it is an '*Indominus rex*', a laboratory-produced combination of different genetic elements that have made it not only huge and powerful but also intelligent and predatory. This monstrous product of improper biological procreation is balanced by the two human dangers to the ideal vehicle of reproduction: the divorcing family (Zach tells Gray that most of the families he knows have separating parents) and the independent woman (Claire early on dismisses any idea that she wants children). The defeat of *Indominus rex* is swiftly followed by the arrival of Zach and Gray's mother and father, come to find them at the end of the mayhem, and by Claire and Owen's walking off together, 'to survive' as he puts it, which surely implies their participation in the survival of the species.

---

1. GM is common shorthand for 'genetically modified' foods or, in this case, animals.

This concern with reproduction makes *Jurassic World* progressive in some ways, but decidedly regressive in others. Its anticapitalism is based on a perception of the logic of capitalism being the pursuit of profit at whatever cost. In the *Jurassic Park* films there was a sense of capitalism enabling the pursuit – albeit foolhardy and hubristic – of science and wonder, a notion delivered to the audience through Richard Attenborough's warmly visionary performance as developer John Hammond (perhaps borrowing from his brother David's famed television promotion of the wonders of nature). This figure is reduced in *Jurassic World* to a maverick owner, Simon Masrani, for whom the park is a rich man's plaything, where he is not to be troubled with money matters. In the actual development and running of Jurassic World, however, money is the point, science and wonder merely the means to generate profit. This imperative is presented in the film itself by Claire, in practically Marxist terms: the necessity for profit to continue to expand by stimulating new demand based on ever more singular and spectacular product.

The director of *Jurassic World*, Colin Trevorrow, has couched the critique in more moralistic terms, identifying the *Indominus rex* as a consequence of 'our greed and our desire for profit' which feeds off a constant desire for more 'wonder … bigger, faster, louder, better,' that is, the inherent greed of corporations is matched by the pathological needs of their consumers.[2] Monstrosities like *Indominus rex*, then, are a logical outcome of capitalism, both in their very existence and in the reluctance of capitalist organisations to curb their excesses. For example, Claire runs the park, yet takes quite some time to recognize the need to prioritize immediate human survival over the park's function as a business enterprise.

Of course, the film itself is founded on exactly that same promise of 'bigger, faster, louder, better.' Externally this promise is manifested in its relation not just to the *Jurassic* franchise but to the surrounding Hollywood narrative of ever-improving special effects. Internally, within the film, alongside *Indominus rex*, there's a swarm of pterosaurs breaking out of their aviary, picking off visitors and playing catch with them, as well as the behemoth/leviathan mosasaurus, a humungous sea creature out-mobying Moby Dick. The behemoth's size is made all the more breathtaking by being introduced in the context of a SeaWorld-style attraction, leaping out of the water to snaffle tidbits hung above it, but later grabbing a pterosaur with its human prey in its beak, and later still (spoiler alert) the *Indominus* itself.

---

2. Interview quotations are from: AFP, 'How the Dinosaurs in Jurassic World Came to Life,' *News Corp Australia*, June 10, 2015, at www.news.com.au/technology/innovation/how-the-dinosaurs-in-jurassic-world-came-to-life/story-fnjwucti-1227391097262; and Kabita Maharana, '*Jurassic World*: Synthetic *Indominus Rex* Embodies the Worst Human Tendencies Teases Director Colin Trevorrow,' *International Business Times*, 'IBT Media,' May 26, 2015, at www.ibtimes.co.uk/jurassic-world-synthetic-indominus-rex-embodies-worst-human-tendencies-teases-director-colin-1502955.

Claire's reluctance to close down the park is the culmination of her parroting management-speak throughout the first part of the film. The creatures are 'assets,' security is about 'asset containment,' the park needs 'the wow factor,' Owen is employed to work with velociraptors to 'evaluate patterns of vulnerability,' the creatures' breakout is 'a containment anomaly,' and so on. I often wonder, when faced in life with the implacable mendacity and vacuousness of managerialism, whether I find it more appalling that managers actually believe what they say – or that they don't, and are just deeply cynical. Bryce Dallas Howard's performance suggests something even more disturbing: that questions of belief or cynicism don't even come into it, that the managers are on automatic pilot, perfectly turned-out Stepford people.

Indominus rex is referred to as a 'genetically modified hybrid.' Since the United States does not yet exhibit the anxiety about GM crops that is seen in Europe, where the sobriquet of 'Frankenstein foods' has proved hard to dislodge from public consciousness, perhaps it is a stretch to suggest the film is altogether anti-GM. However, the notion of secretive meddling with nature, with no thought for the consequences, is deeply rooted in US science fiction. Although he is the sole character carried over from the *Jurassic Park* series, the chief geneticist, Dr. Henry Wu, is undeveloped in this film and shows no sign of conscience or remorse. When disaster strikes, he busies himself putting engineered embryos into safe containers, aided by Vic Hoskins, nominally head of security but actually associated with the shadowy InGen organization, the very model of the military-industrial complex, which seeks to use the products of Wu's genetic engineering as weapons of war or other unimaginable forms of sinister social control.

Claire is made to bear the brunt of the film's progressive critiques, even though the actual, dangerously powerful figures are all male: the owner, the scientist, the military man. As the leading lady, she is central to the film and its vestigial romcom elements (she and Owen, ex-lovers, are at first antagonistic, then in each other's arms and finally walking off together to coupledom). She is also pivotal to the film's gender politics. Her immaculately groomed robotic presence furthers the goals of capitalism, managerialism, and genetic engineering and also underlines the distance of the independent career woman from her proper role in reproduction. Not only does she explicitly reject the prospect of motherhood, she is even a lousy aunt, alternately forgetting how much time has passed since she saw her nephews and dispatching them straightaway to her assistant, Zara. The latter is no better: Zara is too busy with her cell phone to keep an eye on the boys, so they sneak off and into danger. It is Zara who becomes the human prey of the pterosaur, snatched by the mosasaurus; she's the genre's usual and useful snotty Brit, there to provide the spectacle of human sacrifice. And being a Brit, she allows the film to avoid the common (though increasingly politically incorrect) trope of offing the minor-character-of-colour.

Claire in turn has to learn to be more like a man. The right kind of man. A joke is made of her becoming a macho action man like Owen, when, in response to his scorn of her not being much use to pursue the *Indominus* 'in those ridiculous shoes,' she adjusts her clothes to make them more practical. He's not convinced that such a cosmetic change will really hack it, but she proves able to handle herself almost as well as he can, even shooting dead a pterosaur pecking away at him. And in those shoes. The first shot of her starts from the shoes and cranes up, and the shoes are repeatedly shown in close-up before and after she becomes an action woman. When he holds his hand out to help her run away from one of the creatures, she bolts past him, high heels or not, and he does a double-take in surprise and admiration. But she has more to learn from him than traditional macho values. She has to learn ethics, to consider the wellbeing of people and animals above the profit motive.

Owen is the right kind of man par excellence. Partly by virtue of cinematography (elevator doors slide open to reveal him lolling centre screen unfeasibly buff beneath the clothes), partly by virtue of the backstory of Chris Pratt's makeover from lovable chubby to stubbled hunk, he is the contemporary beau ideal of masculinity. Like any action hero, he can handle himself in a difficult situation, but he also has the ideal relationship to nature.

Owen lives on the island where the park is situated, but by himself, far from any other human habitation. When Claire goes to fetch him to take a look at the security of the *Indominus rex* enclosure, she finds him mending a motorcycle, that curious American emblem of the natural male's on-the-road freedom. He is at one with nature, rejecting Claire's view that the park's creatures are not real animals. He caresses raptors, gives comfort to dying dinosaurs.

However, he is also in charge of nature. His first scene has him training four velociraptors, later explaining that they have learned to treat him as their alpha male. Toward the end of the film, the raptors are called on to attack the rampaging *Indominus*. When it turns out that they share some DNA with the *Indominus* and begin to side with it against the humans, Owen reasserts his authority so that they turn on the *Indominus*. He may be with the animals, but he is in a commanding relationship to them (like Tarzan) and able to use them against each other in the interests of humanity.

Naturally, Owen and Claire are white, as are Zach and Gray and their parents. The proper whiteness affirmed at the end of the film is perhaps lightly reinforced by an almost daring moment earlier in the film, when adolescent Zach, always eyeing the girls, flirts with a young Black woman, until interrupted by pre-adolescent Gray, who is worrying about the future of their parents' marriage. The Black girl, however, disappears from the film after this moment in typical mainstream-movie fashion. The casting of the secondary parts in *Jurassic World* is nominally racially inclusive but the roles ensure that they remain subordinate. The only really dangerous man, Vic

Hoskins, played by Vincent D'Onofrio, is white. The chief scientist is Chinese-American (B.D. Wong), the park owner Indian (Muslim actor Irrfan Khan). Barry, one of Owen's helpers with the raptors, is played by Black French actor Omar Sy, but if not recognized he could be taken for a native of another island, with almost nothing to do except to be rescued at one point from the *Indominus*. If the casting was not explicitly intended as racist stereotyping, it certainly allows for it: the inscrutable Oriental, the playboy Indian, the good but incapable Black.

Khan and Sy are major stars in their countries of origin.[3] Casting them at once adds to the appeal of *Jurassic World* in the Indian and French (and perhaps, given Sy's parentage, African) markets, while also acknowledging a degree of global and specifically American recognition too. This inclusive but opportunistic casting goes hand in hand with their characters' extreme marginalization, as do the self-inflicted death of Khan's character (by recklessly taking the controls of a helicopter and crashing into the pterosaur aviary) and Sy/Barry's amiable helplessness. Their marginality affirms Hollywood's place at the top of the hierarchy of global cinema (somewhat misleadingly) while also suggesting that the fittest survivors to further the human race are not only white and gender- and sexuality-conformist but also American.

At the end of the film, all creatures quelled, Owen and Claire come together in silhouette against a shaft of light that is shining into a hangar where the survivors are all being attended to. There is a geometrically precise corridor separating the two crowds of wounded and worried victims and customers, as if it is the shaft of light itself that separates them. Then Owen and Claire walk up this corridor of light: they are the future, the white woman conscripted into the couple on the white man's terms.

Also present are Zach and Gray's parents, Karen and Scott, earlier revealed (in Gray's comment to Zach) to be on the verge of divorce. The strong bond finally forged between Owen and Claire stands in stark contrast to the weak one linking Karen and Scott, with him constantly in the background and her emoting in the foreground (and so overwrought when the boys are away that she keeps people waiting at a meeting at her workplace). They endanger proper reproduction, both by failing to provide the security necessary for the boys' growth and by threatening not to stick together. At the end, it's no longer clear that they will divorce: they are together and present for their sons at the end, with Owen and Claire on hand as the very model of what the ideal reproducing couple should be. This finale has already been anticipated in the archetypal grouping of Owen, Claire, and the boys: first, with Owen standing in front

---

3. Hindi cinema is one of the largest in the world and Khan also had international success with the British-made, Hindi-language, Indian-set film *The Warrior* (Asif Kapadia, 2001) and in an impressive secondary role in *Slumdog Millionaire* (Danny Boyle, 2008). Sy is best known as a comedian in France but has also had a considerable international art house presence thanks to the success of a pair of films by Olivier Nakache and Eric Toledano: *The Intouchables* (2011), especially, and *Samba* (2014).

of them, stretching his arms out in symbolic protection, then standing behind them, the reassuring masculine ground for the display of woman and children.

Claire and Owen are pivotal to the film's entertainment value. All films are posited on reassurance: they are after all 'only' films, and entertainment films must guarantee a happy ending. That is their presumed contract with the audience. However, some horror, action, and thrill films take the implicit promise of reassurance as an occasion to give their audience the possibility of safely experiencing and enjoying grimness, terror, pain, and an abandonment of secure coordinates, whereas others – James Bond, buddy franchises – maintain a jaunty, often humorous tone throughout. While *Jurassic World* may occasionally touch on terror for some audience members (one couple with a little girl hurried out before the end of a screening I attended), it mostly maintains a sense of fun, including a thread of verbal and visual jokes: Owen and Claire and the shoes; the boys' mother advising them merely to run from any marauding creatures and Claire similarly suggesting they hold hands for safety; self-reflexive in-jokes such as Gray looking at stills from the 1925 *The Lost World* on a ViewFinder, a guy wearing a *Jurassic Park* T-shirt bought on eBay and the boys escaping in an abandoned Jurassic Park jeep.[4]

The sense of fun is achieved partly through the very setting of the film, which combines two of the major forms of fun-for-a-day attractions, the zoo and the theme park. It is the former that is crucial here, for in many ways it embodies the human image of the animal world and humankind's relationship to it. While it may seem presumptuous, or just a sign of profit-driven escalation, to reclassify this Jurassic park as a world, it is also consonant with the way that people have made of the actual world a zoo, complete with pens, fields, pastures, parks (local, national, safari), reserves, and designated wildernesses, a world that ensures human animals are separate from and in control of all other animals. True, as in *Jurassic World*, the animals may occasionally break out, but an escape only affirms how strong and reliable the system is most of the time. What the image of the world as zoo suppresses, of course, is the slaughter of so many other animals for food, adornment, aphrodisiacs, and sport, and the destruction of habitats that threatens the survival of most animals in the wild. Instead this is a world in which animals are petted, give rides, and above all provide literally spectacular entertainment.

As Owen embodies this ideal of the symbiotic relationship of human to all other animals, caring and at one with them and yet separate and in charge, Claire as his ideal mate learns to be the same. Their relationship, in its lovable rom-com sparring, gags about Claire's clothes, and Owen's almost ridiculous hunkiness, is a major source of the film's sense of fun. Plus, they save the boys. And, looking to the future, they

---

4. The second *Jurassic* film was of course called *The Lost World* in homage to this film, while the ViewMaster was an early stereoscopic device anticipating the immersive thrills of films like *Jurassic World*.

provide an impending model of ideal reproduction to ensure that, even if this particular unnatural, genetically messed-up zoo world fails, Claire and Owen will continue to produce the world as a white, straight, American zoo for the future.

Perhaps there is just a hint of strain in this affirmation. The film's plotting is elliptical, vague about time and space and reliant on implausible coincidences and rushed explanations, no doubt assuming the thrill and threat of the stunningly realized creatures will carry it along. However, although less busy and physiologically impossible than much CGI cinema, *Jurassic World* is still careless about the coordinates of space and time, so that the happy ending is more a product of sleights of hand than resourcefulness or even luck. More to the point, the final shot of Claire and Owen has a quality of excessiveness to it: the forced abstraction of their coming together in silhouette, the unnaturalness of the shaft of light, the portentousness of Owen's manly words 'To survive' and the silhouette-creating walk toward the light.

There is here a shard of uncertainty about whether the world as zoo really has a future, or the world with humans in it at all, and thus whether the underlying reassurance offered by the film really has much substance. The last shot of the film is not actually that of Owen and Claire walking toward the light, but one where the camera skims across the park. It has done so several spectacular times before, to lay out for the viewer the awesome scale of the place and the crowds visiting it. This time, however, the park is empty of humans, and the camera comes to rest on the Tyrannosaurus rex that earlier attacked the *Indominus* and thus saved Owen, Claire, and the boys and in effect most of the visitors to the park too. The Tyrannosaurus was engineered back to life but is not genetically modified, and unlike the *Indominus*, it's a male.

This, then, is a final shot that signifies an end to meddling and a start to leaving the creatures in peace on their island. It also reaffirms the rightful masculine possession of territory. But perhaps it also hints at the real future: not the bright light embracing Claire and Owen as they go forth to multiply, but one without humans at all, not just in a Jurassic World but in the darker, off-screen world itself.

Originally published in *Film Quarterly* 69:2 (2015), pp. 19–24.

SECTION 3
GETTING OVER THE RAINBOW

and other essays on gay liberation

Richard Dyer (right) with Frank Langan in the Birmingham Gay Centre, mid-1980s. (Courtesy of Richard Dyer)

In 1971, Richard Dyer wrote a short un-signed text titled 'Are queers oppressed?' for the first issue of the short-lived *Birmingham Free Press* ('The Paper Which Gets It Straight!'). His contribution appeared alongside pieces on women's liberation, a postal workers' strike, and a Black people's demonstration against prejudice and police brutality, amongst others. In his contribution, Dyer briefly sketched the difficult circumstances under which queer people live: their need to separate sex from work and friendship, for fear of persecution or prejudice; the exploitative nature of the queer scene itself; the risks of promiscuity; and so on. Yet he concluded with a note of political urgency, a recognition of the need to militate:

> Loss of jobs and family and friends if found out, a disjointed anxious double life, the threat of legal and criminal attack (there's still a law even if it is a bit softer) – these are the sort of things to which society's attitude condemns homosexuals. That's why some people are getting together to change things, get a gay liberation going.

As is highlighted in the introduction to this Reader, Dyer was involved in gay activist politics in the 1970s and 1980s, participating in particular in the activities of the Gay Action Group in Birmingham and the Gay Left Collective in London. As a member of the latter, he contributed articles to their journal including 'Gays and class' (1976), and co-authored with Derek Cohen an essay on 'The politics of gay culture' (not included here) for a 1980 book collaboratively edited by the Collective.[1] Beyond this, Dyer's writings on the politics of gay liberation have appeared in a diverse array of publications across the decades, from erotic magazines ('It's being so camp as keeps us going', also absent from this volume, was first published in 1976 in the short-lived British *Playguy*[2]) to commissioned catalogue essays for national art institutions ('The idea of a gay icon', 2009). The essays included in this section of the Reader highlight this diversity; taken as a whole, they reveal the complex ways in which gay liberation is entangled with other forms of activism, and the manner in which its aims and ideals find expression, or are thwarted, in various forms of mass and high culture.

---

1. Derek Cohen and Richard Dyer, 'The politics of gay culture', in Gay Left Collective (ed.), *Homosexuality: Power and Politics*, London: Allison and Busby Limited, 1980, pp. 172–186.
2. Dyer, 'It's being so camp as keeps us going', *Playguy*, 1976; the essay was re-printed the following year in *The Body Politic* 36 (September 1977), pp. 11–13.

First issue of the *Birmingham Free Press*, 1971. (Courtesy of Cadbury Research Library: Special Collections, University of Birmingham, UB/CCCS/B/15)

ARE QUEERS OPPRESSED?

Why do homosexuals deserve consideration among the ranks of the oppressed? Let's not go on about their psychological unhappiness – though that would be enough – but rather about concrete conditions which threaten the real life of a homosexual person.

Two things first. Homosexuals are not all pansy boys and butch girls with nothing better to do with themselves than indulge in perverse sexual pleasures. Survey after survey has shown that homosexuality is no more in one class than another, no more in one type of person than another. Secretly nonetheless, the key point is that, if you prefer sleeping with members of your own sex, you become 'a homosexual', a category of persons. At best you are written off, a fairy, a poof, a dyke; at worst, you are ostracised, even beaten up, queer-bashed. This is why we are forced to hide a whole part of our being.

Living a secret life has oppressive consequences. Sex becomes a compartment of life, kept seperate from work and friendship - something conducted silently in public lavatories or else with strangers picked up in shabby bars. The gay underworld, though it *is* a community, is still very exploitative – the piss-elegant clubs are very expensive and provide nothing more than a dark space; pornography, a real need for a lonely queer, is more expensive if it is destined for homosexuals (and other sexual 'perverts').

Equally, because of keeping things secret, love becomes more difficult. You can't take your boyfriend to meet your parents if you're a boy yourself. Your love is not part of your world: it is seperate, even opposed to it. Love doesn't get too much of a chance when it is not a part of life. Again, the need for anonymity leads to promiscuity, and with it the rapid spread of VD (– which some clinics treat brutally when it is a homosexual that has it).

Loss of jobs and of family and friends if found out, a disjointed anxious double life, the threat of legal and criminal attack (there's still a law even if it is a bit softer) — these are the sort of things to which society's attitude condemns homosexuals. That's why some people are getting together to change things, get a gay liberation going. (If you're interested contact BFP. We'll put you in touch)

'Getting over the rainbow: identity and pleasure in gay cultural politics' was first published in 1981, in the collection *Silver Linings: Some Strategies for the Eighties*, co-edited by George Bridges and Rosalind Brunt. The book was assembled from papers delivered at the twelfth iteration of the Communist University of London, an annual conference devoted to the exploration of Marxist theory and its evolution. As Bridges and Brunt acknowledge in their preface to *Silver Linings*, CUL12 was held a year after Margaret Thatcher had been elected as Prime Minister, a political development which 'had given the left much cause to reflect on setbacks and reconsider strategy.' All of the essays included in *Silver Linings* engage with 'struggles going on – whether on new or existing terrains'; they all also attempt to think through 'the theory and practice of the Broad Democratic Alliance (BDA)', the Communist Party's recognition that the diverse struggles of various groups were politically connected in their desire to disrupt the status quo.[3] Thus Dyer's essay, the third in the volume, comes after Tricia Davis' contribution on 'Feminism and socialism in the eighties' and Stuart Hall's piece on 'Racist ideologies and the media'. It is within the context of ongoing struggle, and the

---

[3]. George Bridges and Rosalind Brunt, 'Preface', in Bridges and Brunt (eds), *Silver Linings: Some Strategies for the Eighties*, London: Lawrence and Wishart, 1981, p. 7.

understanding that gay liberation activism should necessarily take place within the context of a broader coalition of minority or marginalised groups, that Dyer's essay needs to be situated.

'Getting over the rainbow' grounds its arguments in a dictum from Marx: 'people make their own history, but they do not make it just as they please; they do not make it under circumstances chosen by themselves, but under circumstances directly encountered, given and transmitted from the past.' Dyer argues that this can help to account for the evolution of gay culture; it is also 'a dictum that all branches of the left need to integrate into their thinking and their political agenda.' (In a 2016 interview with Catherine Grant and Jaap Kooijman – see Section 7 of this Reader – Dyer emphasised that Marx's position as expressed in this quote 'is absolutely the model of cultural production which informs everything I have done.') Dyer provides an account of the development of gay politics, and acknowledges gains that have been made: 'To have reached a point where a word selected by an oppressed group to describe itself is used almost as normal not only on the left but very generally in the media and in conversation is an extraordinary achievement.' He recognises a particular challenge that gay activism could pose to other forms of political collectivity: the importance it places on pleasure. This, he writes, 'remains a forbidden term of reference, particularly on the left.' ('Pleasure' was also a key term in Dyer's essay co-authored with Derek Cohen, published the previous year: 'We tend to ignore *pleasure* as part of the business of politics – at our peril.'[4]) Dyer raises the concern that the forms of pleasure experienced in gay culture, in which 'discovering and constructing new possibilities for the body' are central, could be seen as bourgeois individualism. However, in 'the long term', he argues, 'denial of the body means that we do not take possession of our bodies politically.' Gay activism's emphasis on pleasure, then, could be a valuable resource for other political groups, a key weapon in their own armory.

In addition to pleasure, gay liberationists were centrally concerned with rejecting the closet, overturning stigma, challenging moral and legal prejudice, and building community. In 'Nice young men who sell antiques: gay men in heritage cinema' (2001) – an essay commissioned by editor Ginette Vincendeau for an anthology almost entirely comprised of essays and reviews previously published in *Sight and Sound* – Dyer highlights how heritage films and gay liberation politics 'developed side by side and some of the former [...] seem pretty clearly inspired by the latter.' Political tactics associated with gay liberation find expression in homosexual heritage films; characters 'come out', for instance, in various permutations (coded, private, overt). These films provide 'the utopian pleasure of a vision of integration even in

---

4. Cohen and Dyer, op. cit., p. 173.

homophobic societies of the past'; they serve the activist impulse to draw awareness to the existence and experiences of diverse peoples throughout history, even if they provide a rose-tinted (or explicitly false) sense of what those groups had to endure. In 'The idea of a gay icon' (2009) – commissioned for a catalogue to accompany an exhibition at the National Portrait Gallery – Dyer notes the brief histories of the contemporary uses of the word 'icon' and 'gay', both of which have only been in wider circulation since the 1970s. Their combination, he writes, 'is not mere coincidence, for the term gay was part of a project about making homosexuality visible and icons are one of the main forms of doing this in contemporary mass media.' He identifies the various limits on who can and cannot be awarded iconic status; he also recognises the extent to which the concept of a gay icon is both Western and 'disproportionately white'. 'Gay icons' he concludes, 'do what gay liberation wanted: they say to straights "We're here" and to gays "You're not alone".'

Individual pieces of writing by Dyer reveal a working through of the politics of gay liberation and its implications for media representation. In 'Pasolini and homosexuality' (1977), which appeared in a short book on the director edited by Paul Willemen, Dyer engages with opinions put forward by the gay critic and academic Robin Wood. Dyer refers to Wood throughout his essay as Robin, following 'the practice in gay liberation writing of calling fellow gays by their first names, regardless of whether one knows them personally or not.' Wood had suggested that some of Pasolini's films could 'be seen as attempting to create a "liberated" world of pure impulse and essential need, beyond ideological determination'; he also claimed that the director's 'uninhibited pleasure in the male body' provides his films with 'a particular significance for the cause of Gay Liberation'. Dyer disputes both points: 'far from being a straightforward expression of gay consciousness', he writes, 'the images of men in Pasolini's work are scarred by an ideology that denies gayness its validity and its subversive implications.' It is notable that Dyer's piece on Pasolini was published in the same year that he organised the 'Images of Homosexuality' season of films at the National Film Theatre, and edited the book *Gays and Film*, both of which were marked by a concern with stereotyping, 'positive images', and the ideological implications of specific representations; despite the historical and geographical sweep of the season, 'Images' did not include any films by Pasolini.

They were also absent from another season programmed by Dyer: 'Directions in Gay Cinema', which took place at the Birmingham Arts Lab from April to June 1982. This season was built around the release of *Taxi zum Klo* (1980) with showings of more than a dozen other films, including double-bill screenings of *Pink Flamingos* and *Glen or Glenda?* (fancy dress optional but encouraged). In his commentary on *Taxi zum Klo* in the Arts Lab's programme, Dyer described the film as 'remarkable' for having a happy ending, and for its even-handed depiction of regular gay existence, including casual sex as well as camp and drag. However, he raised reservations: 'in effectively valorising promiscuity', he wrote, the film 'also valorises masculinity in rather traditional forms.' Because the film is a significant contribution to the history of gay representation, he argued, it is necessary 'to question its assumption'.

The following year, in a review of Vito Russo's 1981 book *The Celluloid Closet: Homosexuality in the Movies*, Dyer registered evolutions in understandings of gay activist politics, and the ways in which these developments complicated Russo's arguments and rendered his thinking murky. (Dyer had previously reviewed Russo's book elsewhere.[5]) Dyer's 1983 'review essay' appeared in the same issue of *Studies in Visual Communication* as his 'Seen to be believed: some problems in the representation of gay people as typical'; his comments in the former on the 'in-betweenism' of homosexuality, on 'homosexuality as a refusal of, and therefore a threat to, traditional gender roles', finds an echo in the latter's exploration of 'in-betweenism' as a regularly deployed stereotype for depicting queers. In the 'review essay', Dyer offers some standard points of praise and criticism, but uses most of his word-count to explore the tension between 'gay liberationist' politics and a newer social materialist approach that is indebted, in part, to Foucault's writings. There are downsides to this newer perspective: 'it does not have one vivid, inspiring focus ("gay is good")'; 'it deals with and on behalf of a category which it itself defines as socially constructed (and thus arbitrary and limiting, and probably to be moved beyond).' However, a social materialist approach to gay politics is

> more positive because it insists on a recognition of social construction, on the fact that most everything in human affairs has been constructed and therefore that most anything can be: it returns to politics the utopian project of what we want to construct rather than what we want to release.

Dyer clearly aligns himself with this perspective. The problem with Russo's book, he argues, is that it seems to be caught between the gay liberationist and social materialist approaches, with a knock-on effect on the clarity of his views. These 'are not problems unique to Russo', Dyer concludes; 'on the contrary, they are the central problems of sexual political debate.' That is, the evolution of gay and queer activist thought and politics always necessarily poses challenges to critical enterprise.

Across the 1980s, HIV/AIDS and the widespread decimation of communities it caused posed urgent challenges to gay activist politics. New tactics and approaches would be needed to combat the transmission of the virus, the inertia of governments and medical bodies regarding treatment, and the widespread demonisation of groups especially susceptible to HIV. The virus was first identified in 1981; in 1985, Rock

---

5. Richard Dyer, review of *The Celluloid Closet*, *Birmingham Arts Lab* film programme (1 April to 30 June 1982), p. 43; Dyer, review of *The Celluloid Closet*, *Gay Information* 9/10 (Autumn/Winter 1982).

Hudson's death from AIDS-related complications provided an extraordinary rupture into the mainstream of visibility for the disease. Dyer's essay on Rock Hudson ('Rock: the last guy you'd have figured?') is notable for being one of the rare occasions on which Dyer has engaged with HIV and AIDS in his writing. The essay appeared in a 1985 issue of the monthly lesbian and gay Canadian magazine *The Body Politic*; an image from the Hudson-starring film *Magnificent Obsession* appeared on the issue's cover. *The Body Politic* – as its title suggested – was an overtly political publication: in the issue featuring 'Rock', several pieces addressed concerns about the HTLV-3 antibody test, which purported to detect exposure to HIV, with the magazine's editorial specifically advising readers not to get tested. Dyer's essay challenges the notion that the revelation of Hudson's homosexuality was surprising, by reading back into Hudson's performances and roles and identifying moments of sexual dissidence in his sex comedies and the melodramas he made with Douglas Sirk. He also draws attention to the way in which press juxtapositions of images of Hudson 'Before AIDS' and 'After AIDS' reiterate a longstanding trope for depicting queerness, one that combines beauty and decay.

Dyer lost many friends and comrades to AIDS in the 1980s and 1990s. In an obituary for Vito Russo written in 1990, Dyer linked Russo's death to that of Jack Babuscio, whose essay on camp appeared in Dyer's *Gays and Film*:

> That both he and Jack Babuscio (and they were good friends) should go in the same year is a blow not just to the narrow world of gay film writers but because of the way both combined so consummately political commitment, love of one's community and a sense of fun and beauty. Now more than ever do we need that spirit.[6]

B. Ruby Rich has drawn attention to the historical importance of Dyer's gay liberationist political writing of the 1970s and 1980s, and its connection to HIV/AIDS. Those 'early writings', she says, were 'hard fought'; they emerged 'out of an era of repression that had left so many angry and, a decade later, so many dead.'[7] In the early 1970s, some people got together 'to change things', to 'get a gay liberation going'. In many ways they were successful, and the reach of gay liberationist ideas became widespread, fundamentally altering manifold forms of culture. The challenges, prejudice, and violence that had to be surmounted by these pioneers should never be underestimated or forgotten.

---

6. Richard Dyer, 'Obituary: Vito Russo', *Capital Gay* 469 (16 November 1990), p. 13.
7. B. Ruby Rich, 'A thousand kindred spirits', *Cinema Journal* 57:2 (2018), p. 156.

18 GETTING OVER THE RAINBOW: IDENTITY AND PLEASURE IN GAY CULTURAL POLITICS (1981)

The 1970s saw the growth of many forms of cultural politics. Not since the years immediately following the Russian Revolution have socialists been so heavily and actively aware of the importance of cultural politics. The gay movement has had a special role to play here, above all in showing how a politics of culture can be rooted in, and grow out of, the already existing culture of an oppressed group. The gay movement activated the political potential of what lesbians and gay men had already achieved in developing against the grain of oppression, a particular way of life, a culture. I want to argue that this relation between a movement and the lived culture of the group that it represents can serve as an object lesson for the left. In addition, I suggest that the particular concerns of identity and pleasure, brought to political flower from the ground of the gay subculture, indicate specific ways of connecting political aims with the way people actually think and feel about their lives.

The development of gay culture is a classic instance of Marx's dictum that 'people make their own history, but they do not make it just as they please; they do not make it under circumstances chosen by themselves, but under circumstances directly encountered, given and transmitted from the past'.[1] This is a dictum that all branches of the left need to integrate into their thinking and their political agenda.

The case of lesbians and gay men is exemplary but it is also extreme, in the sense that culture *is* the situation of gay people. Gays are defined and structurally placed in the sphere of culture – there are the circumstances that are not of our own choosing. Having been so placed, gays have sought to gain control over those conditions and in the process have produced a wealth of new cultural forms, new definitions of identity, new awarenesses of human happiness.

---

1. Karl Marx, 'The Eighteenth Brumaire of Louis Bonaparte', Marx/Engels, *Selected Works in One Volume*, London: Lawrence and Wishart, 1977, p. 96.

To understand this further, we need to consider first the question of the very concept 'homosexual',[2] before going on to the issue of why culture is so privileged an arena of gay movement activity and the significance of some of the forms it takes. It is wrong to think of homosexuality – or almost any aspect of human body activity – as a biological given. Rather, we need to consider how 'the homosexual' has emerged historically as a *social construct*: an idea, and also a way of placing people socially, which has only come about in the last two centuries. There are two main points to stress when making this argument.

First, it is clear that bodily (including genital) contact between persons of the same sex is indeed universal. However, just as with bodily contact between persons of the opposite sex, same sex contact never exists outside a particular social formation. No body contact ever occurs in a social vacuum, and hence is never experienced in a purely 'biological' way. Thus although same sex body contact occurs throughout all history (and incidentally in the animal kingdom) it is never in any given instance ahistorical. What is remarkable about developments since the eighteenth century is the way that body activity has been narrowed down to be also the designation of a certain sort of person. Where once same sex body contact might be recognized as an activity (albeit, in our society, sinful) that people might be involved in, now there is a term, 'the homosexual', for persons who are socially/clinically defined as those who habitually involve themselves in same sex contact. 'Homosexual', a nineteenth-century coinage, designates persons not acts.

Part of the reason for using the laborious mouthful 'same sex body contact' is now I hope evident. It is a problem to use the word 'homosexual' outside the historical period of the word's currency, for you risk blurring the very point that needs to be made, namely that 'homosexuality', as our society calls it and understands it, did not exist outside the actual existence of the word. There is a further reason for avoiding the term – and indeed, now, politically, shunning it – and that is that it focuses so exclusively on the element of genital contact. This leads us to the second stage of the argument about the concept of the homosexual.

The word 'sexual' is notoriously hard to handle, since what one person finds sexual another does not. However, in general usage, the word does imply some degree of genital arousal and activity. There is no reason why we should not have a word that focuses on one particular body organ, but the word, and the history that surrounds it,[3] has the effect of privileging genital functions over all others. Thus bodily relations between persons of the same sex, once they are designated 'homosexual', come to

---

2. For further consideration of these ideas, see Gay Left Collective (ed.), *Homosexuality: Power and Politics*, London: Allison and Busby, 1980.
3. See Michel Foucault, *The History of Sexuality*, translated by Robert Hurley, London: Allen Lane, 1979.

be seen entirely in terms of genitality. This is so even when actual genital activity is felt not to have taken place, as in the common supposed defence of homosexuals (and especially lesbians) that 'it's all right, they don't *do* anything'. This is a doubly offensive, and symptomatic, lie, since it both assumes genital activity would be wrong and at the same time implies that 'doing' and 'screwing' are synonymous, as if the limit of body relations between the same sex is genital. The power of ideas of sexuality is quite extraordinary, for not only do they focus attention on the genitals to the exclusion of all else, but they also have a tendency to reduce other aspects of human life to genital activity. This permeates common sense thought. How often in conversation are a person's motives construed in terms of sexual desire, how often people's problems assumed to be sexual at root. It has become a habit in western society to look to sexuality as the explain-all of life, to see the fulfilment and frustration of genital desire as the key to the truth about what people want in general, what they do and what they are.

That 'the homosexual' is a modern social category, and that sexuality is a word with attendant institutional and social support that privileges the genitals in our understanding of the human body and its relation to being human: these two ideas inform most of what follows. One point must be made clear. The fact that 'the homosexual' and 'sexuality' have just been discussed as ideas does not mean that they exist in a realm of pure spirit. They are ideas by which we live. They are the very means by which we know our place in society and experience our bodies. I live my life in those terms, though in constant struggle within and against them. I do think of myself as a homosexual or, on better days, as gay, and I feel defined as a person by those sexual designations and observe that that is how I am treated too. And I habitually over-privilege genital response and often conflate it with sensual, sensuous and emotional response. What I have just written is a personal way of stating the kinds of issue that I now wish to sketch out about gay cultural politics.

THE CENTRALITY OF CULTURE

Before looking at possible reasons why culture is so central to the gay movement, it would be as well to say something briefly about what I mean the terms 'culture' and 'gay culture' to refer to. I am using 'culture' in the very widest sense to refer not only to the arts but to all those products and practices that both express and constitute the forms, values and emotional structures of social life. The specific references I shall be making to gay culture will hardly touch 'the arts' at all, but will discuss for reasons that will be spelt out later, dress, dancing, forms of relating in public and ways of using and relating to the human body. These are particular instances of the various and manifold forms and activities that constitute gay ways of making sense of the world.

It is important to stress that gay culture does not necessarily know itself as political, much less as politically progressive or socialist. But we cannot afford, anywhere on the left, to be dismissive of the way life is felt, thought and lived by both the people we represent and ourselves. It is within culture that homosexual identities and pleasures are formed. When I use the term 'gay culture', I mean to indicate *any* cultural practice that may be considered significantly homosexual, whether or not it is a radical practice. The term 'gay cultural politics' I restrict to cultural work within the gay movement itself or markedly informed by its perspectives. Again, such activity may well not be radical. It could also be purely reformist or else more centred on individualistic 'revolt' or on the creation of alternative life-styles *within* society as it is.

Reasons why culture is central to the gay movement can be approached through slightly different notions of what the word 'culture' means. Firstly, culture can be used to refer to the ways in which a society thinks and feels about itself. It is the ensemble of ideas, representations and forms that are available to people in a society to make sense of themselves and their society. Culture is not innocent. It is grounded in the interests of the people who produce it and in this sense it is a very similar concept to that of ideology. Like ideology, culture does not operate in a unitary way within a society: it involves contradictions and often antagonisms both within and between social groupings – along lines of class, gender, race and such socially designated factors as sexual orientation. The advantage of the word 'culture' in the present context, rather than ideology, is that it insists on the *material* and *affective* dimension of making sense as well as on the *cognitive*.

Culture in this sense is where and how the very concept and definition of homosexuality are produced. Precisely because, as I have argued, homosexuality is not a biological given, any politics based upon or around it is already a politics of culture, a politics centred on the sense made of particular potentials of the body. Gay politics is always already cultural politics, whether we like it or not.

Secondly the word 'culture' can also designate that sphere of life that is left over when the realm of necessity has been fulfilled. It is the realm of feelings, pleasure, reflection, leisure. It is of course entirely wrong to think that such things do not permeate every aspect of human existence, but a predominant and effective way of thinking about our lives puts necessity in one slot and culture in another. Necessity includes work to *produce* the maintenance of life, and the family and kinship to *reproduce* life. And by very definition gays are seen as being outside these.

But such struggles as the Gay Rights at Work Committee and the campaigns around lesbian mothers brilliantly disrupt the distinction between necessity and culture, between gays and productive/reproductive life. They demonstrate that gays are involved in the labour process and that gays do bear and bring up children. By insisting on gay rights at work, we insist that sexuality and emotion do not evaporate when we clock in but inform every aspect of life. By fighting for the rights of lesbians (and gay men) to the custody and care of children, we refuse the idea that heterosexual intercourse and a concern for life are the same thing.

Much of the 'public' panic surrounding such struggles derives from the way they blur the distinction between sexuality as a private, personal domain, and work and procreation as public and socially responsible. This panic serves to reinforce the idea that gays, by virtue of their sexuality, are to be defined as irrelevant to work and impossible as parents. *As gays* they are to be defined outside production and reproduction. The institutions of the law, social welfare, family organization, and so on, serve to keep us outside productive/reproductive life. Our identity as *gay* is experienced by ourselves and others as in a very different relationship to our identity as worker or parent (or relative). The space we occupy and the space in which we must struggle is therefore primarily the space outside of 'necessity', the space of culture.

IDENTITY

If 'the homosexual' is a social category, then it is evident that actual people who fall into that category are going to be identified with and by it. People grow up to learn that they are homosexual or queer, or gay, and it is with this homosexual identity that gay political culture must necessarily engage.

Gay politics is about transcending the historical category 'homosexual', but it has always been a mistake to imagine that there could be an immediate, magic transcendence, a sudden leap free from the cultural categories within which we think, feel, live and are. Gay politics has necessarily to start from the given category, even if it ultimately wishes to move beyond it. This is not just a question of the political distinction between tactics (accepting and defending the category) and strategy (transcending it). It is only by accepting the category that we can transcend it. This is not idly said. To deny the category is to avoid the actual reality of the situation, namely, that certain people are *placed* in the category 'homosexual', and to ignore a situation is the surest way of ensuring that it remains the same.

What is at stake, to begin with, is who controls the definition of the category. The key significance of the gay movement is that for the first time in living memory, gay people *themselves* determined that they would decide the definition. The major, though by no means wholly secure, victory of this process has been the social acceptance of the word 'gay'. To have reached a point where a word selected by an oppressed group to describe itself is used almost as normal not only on the left but very generally in the media and in conversation is an extraordinary achievement. It signals the first occasion that people designated as homosexual have turned round and determined that they would decide what it means to be so designated.

Struggles over words can often seem trivial. Endlessly correcting people's assumptions that I must be married or have a girlfriend is tiring for me and seems niggling to those I'm correcting. Yet such relentlessness is needed to change ingrained habits of thought, for habits are so hard to change. Word struggles often have a wider resonance. I remember going on a demonstration against the Industrial Relations Bill where people had placards saying 'We're here for the queer', an attack on [Prime Minister] Edward Heath. By asking (successfully) for them to be removed we made a connection between sexism and labour politics, all by objecting to a word. (Similarly, we should object to attacks on Thatcher for being female or on Reagan for being old – there's enough to attack without falling into sexism and ageism.)

Being socially categorized, and determining something of the form of that categorization, also provides the possibility of thinking in terms of collective action. It is by recognizing that one's problems are not unique, that one belongs to a social group, that one is able to think in terms of together changing a general situation rather than accepting a purely personal 'condition'. Gay cultural politics has been particularly important here in exploring new identities, new shared senses of who we are.

An example of what I mean are the debates in the gay movement that surround disco. Disco has been a major development in gay culture in the seventies and the wider disco scene itself grew out of, and is still marked by, gay disco. It is probably the most widespread form of leisure activity that gays are involved in, as both a dance/music form of expression and a space for social and sexual contact. The precise form it takes is important for the gay movement, because that is where so many gays 'are at'. I mean this both literally and figuratively: gays are in discos in vast numbers, and disco culture means a lot to us. Disco is, quantitatively and qualitatively, where we can reach gay people. The discussions at gay movement meetings about disco are often apparently focused on problems of organization – for instance, whether to charge, whether to hold discos in a straight or a gay venue, who will supply the music, etc. But at bottom they are about the business of constructing a gay identity. Thus some people argue that we should take our cue from the existing gay scene saying that there are certain ways of coping, forms of friendship network, the gay bar or club serving as a kind of community, that we could learn from. And they also point out that the kind of music favoured, usually derived from Black music, is in some sense a gay music, and hence already expressive of a gay identity. Others point to the exploitativeness and furtiveness of the gay scene, the predominance of men and masculine modes of behaviour, and want the gay movement to learn from the counter-culture and its lifestyles. The result is alternative discos, at their best a creative fusion or interplay of both of these traditions. The experience of being with gay people is altered, for instance, if the discos are free, if people talk to each other, if they are obviously organized by other gay people, if women and men are equally welcome and made welcome, if people dance in circles instead of either isolated or in couples. Talking about and dancing to different sorts of music can explore or reinforce sexual identities. The wrangling about whether to let Donna Summer or the Rolling Stones predominate is a way of talking through what we want our identity to be. Summer represents disco, an already gay cultural form, at its most sensuous; the Stones represent rock 'n' roll at its most 'alternative' but also its most 'straight' (in sexual terms). They are emblematic of different ways of being. Discussing and dancing to them becomes the very activity of constructing a shared sense of who we are.

Another example which brings out the interplay between pre-political subcultural forms and the construction of new identities is the question of dress. Dress is always a significant aspect of a person, for it reveals class, gender, racial and other subcultural positions whether consciously or unconsciously. Importantly it indicates how the wearer inhabits those positions, how she/he feels about being in that social position. Dress is especially significant for gays since being gay doesn't actually of itself 'show' physically, and it is only through dress that we can make a statement about ourselves that, unlike a verbal pronouncement, is there all the time.

The gay movement could draw on styles of dress that were already developed in the gay subculture, for instance, various forms of drag and prettiness for men, of butch and dyke gear for women. These styles provided a ground for a gay cultural politics of dress. Even before it is self-consciously political, drag and dyke dress is a play with the signs of femininity and masculinity, with what is appropriate dress for 'real' women and men. Gay cultural politics, in its concern with dress, has kept putting these definitions of gender in question. I do not mean to imply that confrontationist drag and dyke gear necessarily makes onlookers think through their own gender identities. Cultural struggle does not work automatically like that, much as many fondly hope it does. But such tactics are part of a wider debate about how and what it is to be a man or a woman, and how the very definitions of femininity and masculinity are posited on heterosexuality. This is to make it sound like an intellectual issue. But the point is rather, that gay cultural politics actually involves dressing, considering how you ad-dress, being sensitive to what you and others wear. And this means bearing a consciousness of the categories of gender and sexuality in the lived texture of appearances.

One could make a similar argument around the current 'masculinization' of the gay male style. Today, gay men are rather more likely to adopt a macho look than drag and prettiness. This too is in a sense a reversal of the signs of masculinity. Gender roles are crucially defined in terms of heterosexuality – 'men', as a social category, are people who screw 'women'. By taking the signs of masculinity and eroticizing them in a blatantly homosexual context, much mischief is done to the security with which 'men' are defined in society, and by which their power is secured. If that bearded, muscular beer-drinker turns out to be a pansy, however are you going to know the 'real' men anymore? From this too stems the play, exaggeration and parody of much contemporary gay masculinization. The most widely known example of this is the disco group Village People, whose dress draws on all the stereotypes of ultra-masculinity in a camped-up flauntingly gay way. There is profound ambivalence in this development. I am not at all clear in my own mind how gay men do actually relate to this masculinization. It can be taken straight – as a worship of the signs of male power, as an attempt to prove 'I may be queer but I'm still a man'. But it *can* be taken ironically and reflexively too, and two things help to encourage this. One is the debate about dress that the gay movement set in motion. People go on talking about the significance of what they wear, and how it does or does not carry and reproduce male power in society. Secondly, there is camp, that characteristically gay repertoire of parody, wit, put-down and send-up. This remains a powerful strain in gay culture, and it has always shown both a great sensitivity to gender roles *as* roles and a refusal to take the trappings of femininity and masculinity too seriously. We have to try to understand the new macho look in relation to all the frames of reference, reactionary and subversive, that can inform it.

PLEASURE

Disco and dress are examples of the way that gay cultural politics is centrally concerned with the contestation of identities. These identities make collective action possible, as the much more confident burgeoning of gay culture with a strong activist current in the USA makes clear. Gay cultural politics is also about pleasure. There is a definite fit between the gay movement's basic concern with sexuality and the centrality of culture to its political practice. Both are to do with pleasure. However, pleasure remains a forbidden term of reference, particularly on the left. Pleasure is something you can *guiltily* have, or have after the important things, or get as a reward for doing other things. As itself a goal, it is still not, to speak paradoxically, taken seriously. And nowhere is this more true than on the left.

It was clear from the start that the gay movement was primarily and perhaps exclusively concerned with sexuality and the consequences of a particular choice of sexuality. The women's movement has also been centrally concerned with sexuality, but women *as* women are not oppressed uniquely or even primarily in terms of their sexual desires but in terms of not being men. Struggles around housework, equal pay, job opportunities and so on do not spring directly from sexual activity. Even those struggles that are essentially concerned with sexuality somehow manage to couch themselves in other terms. Thus, issues of contraception, abortion and nursery facilities tend to run together and to be argued for in terms of what constitutes sane and healthy childcare and how such things free women in relation to paid employment, creativity and so on, rather than in terms of such things making sexuality less attendant with procreative anxiety, more controllable, more *enjoyable*. I know that that argument is there, but none the less that is not, overall, how the debates around the issues developed. None of this could be said of gay movement issues. Queer bashing, police harassment, discrimination in employment, treatment in the media, and all the other areas of gay activism may have the same civil rights flavour, but they all stem from the assertion of the right to a certain form of sexual activity. Nor was the gay movement merely demanding the right and need to love members of the same sex, but to enjoy sex with them. When in 1972 the Birmingham Gay Liberation Front produced the first British gay sex education pamphlet, *Growing Up Homosexual*, pleasure was listed as the first and overriding function of sex, above the expression of love and (a poor third) procreation. Many in the movement pushed further, to insist that promiscuity, one night stands, masturbation, forms of sexuality with minimal, attenuated, or non-existent human relationship elements, were as valid as, or more valid than, monogamy, affairs and love. They were seen as being in some sense more 'direct' and 'honest', less involved in manipulation and hypocrisy.

As Simon Watney points out in his article in *Homosexuality: Power and Politics*, The Gay Liberation Front, which was the most vocal and 'radical' of the gay movement's various forms, saw sexuality as very much more than a particular activity. Sexuality was seen as the key that would unlock the fragmentation and alienation of advanced capitalist patriarchy.

> Gay Liberation attempted to recuperate an illusion. That illusion maintained that our sexuality is the single most determining aspect of our entire existence.[4]

He argues persuasively that a great deal more was felt to be at stake in struggling around sexuality than the pleasure of sexual activity for itself. This is clear too from Aubrey Walter's introduction to *Come Together*, a selection of articles from the GLF newspaper – though he is less critical of GLF's position than is Simon Watney.[5] But GLF was not the whole gay movement, and a far more widespread impulse behind the various gay political activities of the seventies was the assertion of the pleasure of sexuality and the right to that pleasure.

The problem was, again, definition: how to define sexuality. In practice, it meant genital, orgasmic sexuality. In the relation between women and men in the gay movement, this led to some pretty conundrums. On the one hand, in the sexual ideology we inherited, genital sexuality was 'masculine': women were supposed to be: romantic,

---

[4]. Simon Watney, 'The Ideology of GLF', in Gay Left Collective, op. cit., p. 72.
[5]. Aubrey Walter, *Come Together*, London: Gay Men's Press, 1980.

their genital sexuality ineluctably intertwined with love; mysterious, their sexuality not physiologically locatable; or vaginal, a non-starter orgasmically – though not necessarily experienced as such.[6] Male gay culture teetered for a long time on the brink of this inheritance. Some of us wanted to insist on wider notions of sexuality, perhaps feeling there was something to learn from these definitions of female sexuality. Thus there were references to the 'tyranny of the orgasm' and a rejection of the instrumental, goal-oriented approach to coupling. Others wanted to expand the area of genital sexuality, to insist on the validity of more and 'purely' sexual genital activity. Many women were bored by this internal male debate and also put off by the obsession with genitals.[7]

On the other hand... I remember talking to a woman friend of mine about the tyranny of the orgasm and being told, 'Don't knock orgasms – it took some of us a long time to get them.' To move beyond genital sexuality is an achievement for some men; to achieve genital sexuality can be a move beyond for some women.

We have certainly not succeeded in unpicking these contradictions, and this is partly because the whole debate, the very use of the word 'sexual', is still not extricated from the very ideology, discussed above, that separates genital sexuality from the rest of the body. Once this separation happens we are left in a quandary, having to choose between either genitality ('masculine') or emotionality ('feminine'), with no room for anything in between. Like the wider culture of heterosexual permissiveness, much of male gay culture, with its panoply of commercially supported saunas, bars, clubs and cruising places, is always in danger of simply wanting to expand genitality, simply to want more and more of it or to give it the creative power to transcend the present order. A danger however is not the whole story. Much that is happening is also seeking to break down the category 'sexuality', understood as '*genital* sexuality', and replace it with a new understanding and experience of the body in human existence.

BODY POLITICS

Many aspects of gay culture are a body culture, discovering and constructing new possibilities for the body. Disco and dress, already discussed, are in part about, respectively, the pleasure to be gained from using all one's body and the meanings to be constructed in the imaginative use of dress as body decoration. Massage and body awareness groups actively and consciously produce knowledge of what the body is

---

6. See Mary McIntosh, 'Sexuality', *Papers on Patriarchy*, Lewes: Women's Publishing Collective, 1976, pp. 73-75.
7. It is no accident that it is the way men talk about sexuality that becomes the very definition of sexuality in society as a whole, though when women can give it voice they often speak about sexuality very differently.

and can be. More open kissing and hugging between men and men, women and women, are part of the style of the gay movement, both as a public sign that we are gay, but also as a pleasurable experience of friendship and solidarity. Such things begin to create a culture that refuses to refuse the body any more.

Many may well want to label all this bourgeois individualism. Doesn't it smack of California, where the sun always shines and people vote for Reagan? Isn't it the most gross self-indulgence in an age of mass unemployment and economic recession? Certainly it is hard to keep one's eyes on the wider goals of sexual politics when these immediate, hard issues face one. And yet to refuse this explanation of the body is simply to buy back into the cycle of body control that *constitutes* contemporary society.

Society isn't one thing and the human body another. Society is the organization of the human body, how we experience our bodies and what we do to and with them. The human body is a basic unit in any social formation. The paid worker's body, the houseworker's body remain the essential elements of any economy, of any maintenance and reproduction of life. In this society, the use of our bodies is compartmentalized: certain limbs and organs are used for work and nothing else, while pleasure is focused on an ever-narrowing range of 'erogenous' areas. Except when they occur in important activities such as sport and dance, all other body potentials are unknown, unrecognized or marginalized. Such compartmentalization produces body units that are easy to control; it rationalizes the fluidity and range of body potential. It also makes of the body something easier to place in economic exchange relations. It is easier to buy a person's body skill than her/his whole body. It is easier to sell pleasure if you are trying to appeal to one clearly defined region of the body.

This last point has led to the greatest confusion in the development of male gay sexual practices in the past ten years. Because the early gay movement put so much emphasis on genital sexuality, it was easy for capitalism to meet its demands. Bars, saunas, pornography, all the institutions of permissiveness, could seem like an answer to the demand for the liberation of sexuality. As long as sexuality meant genital sexuality, it could be quantified and its 'needs' met – more opportunities to do it more often. (There is a similar ideology in women's magazines like *Cosmopolitan*, though not in lesbian publications.) Our mistake, which we are only just beginning to see, was in demanding the liberation of sexuality, when we need to be demanding liberation *from* sexuality, in the name of the body.

The women's movement has long recognized the political importance of the body. Struggles around contraception, abortion, wife battering and rape are not just 'issues' to form the basis of verbal, moral discussion nor are they only – though this they crucially are – assertions of the individual's right to determine what happens to her body. They also make us see how the very organization of procreation, the family and sexuality in society is done with, through and often to women's *bodies*. Though men find this especially hard to come to terms with and live with, such organization is also done with, through and to their own bodies. Men's physical frustrations and anxieties may have ideological or psychic roots, but where they get expressed is the body.

Ignorance of this on the left constitutes a denial of the body that is fatal for the movement. It means that we neither know our bodies for what they are and can be, nor do we operate effectively in and with them. In an immediate sense, denial of the body may simply make us less efficient in day-to-day political work: more liable to be tired, to be late, to be irritable, to be uncomradely. In the long term, denial of the body means that we do not take possession of our bodies politically.

'Body politics' is not an idle phrase. It points to the way in which society attempts to make over every person into a cog in an efficient system that at the same time fragments any control or knowledge we may have over our bodies. Our bodies are the site of control and power. We are not disembodied economic counters or ideological constructs. Lack of body politics has allowed left theory to lurch from various kinds of idealism to another, though each one calls itself materialist.

On the one hand, Marxism can degenerate into economic determinism. This may *appear* very materialist, because it is dealing with the 'hard' realities of money and work, but it deals with these realities in an abstracted, idealist way. Economic determinism reduces everything to the economic rather than seeing things *in relation to* the economic (and much else besides). It does designate economic categories and chart economic structures, but frequently fails to connect with the realities of factory and office life, the problems of getting and spending money. In other words, it fails to understand how economic structures are *lived and affected* in the skin and bones of people working.

On the other hand, recent Marxist theorists have rightly rejected such economic reductionism. But in their search for an alternative theory, they have come up with one that is equally prone to idealism. Working from theories of language and from psychoanalysis of a certain kind,[8] they have put a valuable stress on the role of ideology in history, and, in particular, on the way people are socially formed into what we understand people to be – what is called 'the construction of the subject'. Yet their theory leads to a position where being 'a person' or 'a subject' is *only* a construction in language and ideology. Granted that society fashions us through words and representations of humanness, but it fashions us out of flesh and blood, not thin air.

None of this means that what the human body is is simply what 'nature' makes it. To go back to the point made at the beginning of this article, the biological activity of

---

8. Namely that deriving from the work of Jacques Lacan and his circle. This should not be confused with the psychoanalytic tradition as a whole. For discussion of this kind of theory, see Terry Lovell, *Pictures of Reality*, London: British Film Institute, 1980.

pleasurable bodily contact between persons of the same sex does not give us the concepts 'sexuality' and 'the homosexual'. It is that those concepts are attempts to make sense (however, in this case, cock-eyed …) out of what are real biological activities. What is at stake is that, first, we are animals and can learn something about our bodies from biology. Secondly, that whatever else may come into play in the organization of our animal bodies to become specifically human bodies, we none the less remain in those bodies and had better learn about them: learn about what is biologically given, what is ideologically fashioned in them, if we want to be effective in history. And being effective in history is a cornerstone of what I take socialism to be about.

Gay culture, even when fully informed by sexual and socialist politics, does not have all the answers. But it does ask some of the questions, it does begin to think through not only gay identities, but *all* sexual and gender identities, and not only to think them through but to live them through the culture of the body. By so doing we make the very stuff of the social formation, our bodies, less amenable to prevailing power structures, more resistant to oppressive definitions and maimed existences. And in the pleasure we get we also get a glimpse of the other end of the rainbow.

Originally published in George Bridges and Rosalind Brunt (eds), *Silver Linings: Some Strategies for the Eighties*, London: Lawrence and Wishart, 1981, pp. 53–67. Courtesy of Lawrence and Wishart (lwbooks.co.uk).

19 NOTES ON GAYS AND CLASS (1976)

One of the good things about the film *Fox and his Friends* is that it has made people talk about the question of gays and class. But is the film's basic point – that gay subculture is a mirror of straight culture, simply reproducing its class divisions and exploitation – really true? I would like to suggest – and it really can only be suggestion, because we simply do not know enough in hard facts about the lives of most gay people – that (i) the class cultures are to a certain extent reproduced in gay subcultures; (ii) *but* the larger part of the gay culture is male bourgeois; (iii) *but* that it is male and bourgeois in a far from simple way. Let me take each of these points in turn.

(i) The gay scene in Birmingham, where I live, can be broken down in social class terms. The four pubs and two clubs can be divided into the posh and the common, the smart and the rough. The small towns of industrial Lancashire (e.g. Blackburn, Preston, Bolton, Wigan) where there is a small bourgeoisie, have distinctively working class gay pubs, as have parts of South London and the East End. Equally, there are gay clubs in London and Manchester almost as exclusive as the gentlemen's clubs of Pall Mall.

How far does this pattern, and its extremes, extend over the country as a whole? I cannot say for sure, but my guess is – not very far. It seems to me that whilst there are different class emphases from pub to pub, club to club, the distinctions are far more blurred than has so far been suggested. The actual class position of the clientele of a particular place may not tally with the vague class tone of that club – you get for instance the middle class gay 'slumming' in 'rough' pubs, and the working class gay escaping the 'masculinity' of his class background amidst the chi-chi of a club.

The ritualised forms of promiscuity – cottaging, baths, trolling are of interest here, for they seem to be further 'outside' of class, participated in fairly equally by all classes (and races). By reducing all interchange to the sexual, promiscuity strips them of class connotations. If class does operate here, it does so not in terms of differentiation of locale (though there are opera-trolling and expensive Turkish baths…), but in terms of the sexual fantasies people from one class (or race) have about people from the other.

(ii) There is then some class differentiation within gay culture – yet I feel the tone that dominates is male and middle class. Of course, gay *activity* is no less widespread in one class than any other (as far as I can make out) – but the way it is socially-culturally *patterned* seems to show a greater influence of male, middle class norms. (Especially where, as in the majority of cases, there is only one pub.)

This becomes more evident if one goes beyond pubs and clubs to include the gay movement (C.H.E., G.L.F., etc.) and gay publications (*Gay News*, *Sappho*, *Playguy*). It is interesting to note how right from the start gay magazines aiming at providing more than just porn (*Timm*, *Spartacus*, *Jeremy*) all just took it for granted that the readership would be interested in high fashion, the arts, cookery and foreign travel. Now obviously there are reasons in addition to class why these magazines (and their successors) should have assumed that these were the things to sandwich between the pix – fashion and cookery are 'feminine' and so fit many gay men's sense of themselves as 'feminine'; the arts are supposedly traditionally tolerant to gayness and besides provide (especially ballet and films) voyeur's bonuses; foreign travel represented a chance to escape prying eyes in the pursuit of love and sex. Yet despite that, fashion, art, cookery (as hobby rather than necessity) and foreign travel (until recently) are indelibly middle class interests. I can't really demonstrate it, but I also feel that the way they were written about, the particular taste that governs the dress and décor concerns, is also essentially middle class. (One way of putting that is to say that gay men have more 'taste' – providing you remember that 'taste' is not an absolute, but rather a set of criteria largely established by the class that dominates a society.)

I do not think all this is because the straight middle class is more 'liberal' or 'tolerant' than the working class. Endless discussions with gay people about their backgrounds suggests that acceptance and tolerance are equally to be found (or not) in both working class and middle class contexts. The explanation has more to do with the fact that gay culture has hitherto always developed in the relatively anonymous setting of city or town centres, away from gay people's immediate neighbourhood and family, away from the group activities of one's peers. Yet neighbourhood and group affiliations are far more typical of working class culture than the individuated, mobile, adaptive lifestyles of the middle class. This means that it was easier for middle class men to establish a gay culture in their own image, into which working class men would make an at times very awkward and difficult entry.

Of course participation in the development of this was even more difficult for gay women, who, brought up as 'women', had to negotiate the isolation of domesticity. It is interesting however to note that the only really working class gay pub that I know in Birmingham is a lesbian pub (it's in West Bromwich actually); and that the lesbian scene in general is far more working class in tone than the gay male scene. It is of course smaller, because most women still have to shake free of the career of being a family-person, but where it does occur it does seem to be more 'working class', perhaps as a combination of (a) the fact that most lesbians have to be working people (that is, going out and doing paid work, not staying in and doing unpaid work); (b) the traditional collectivity of working class women's 'street culture', which establishes the possibility of cultural patterns of interaction more effectively than the double isolation (class and family) of middle class women; (c) *maybe* the identification of 'butchness' with working class style (and the converse identification of the middle class with effeminacy). This being the only available model of not being 'feminine' in the culture as a whole.

(iii) Yet if gay culture is predominantly male and bourgeois, that does not mean that it is *simply* so. Aspects of gay culture can be seen as, implicitly, ambiguously, inflections of the dominant culture that may even run counter to it.

First, the fact that it *is* gay is already counter to the dominant culture, by which it is oppressed (– *Fox* is notably short on the specificity of gay oppression). Second, gay culture does offer the experience of group identity (instead of magnificent individualism), something which the gay movement has been able sometimes to develop into powerful feelings of solidarity and collectivity. Third, camp, however much it can be used against us as stereotype, does also contain elements of send-up, exaggeration of straight roles, awareness of the artifice of social forms that pass for 'natural' in the straight world. Four, many of the forms of gay relationships – the succession of brief affairs, cottaging, the relaxed sexual exchanges at conferences – run directly counter to the compulsive monogamy of straight society (though here again we have to be aware of the ambiguities – promiscuity has always been kind of OK for men; 'permissiveness' is one of the biggest new markets of recent years for an ailing capitalism; the notion of 'responsibility' enshrined in monogamy has a lot to be said for it, but is not always transferred to shorter-term contacts).

It is the contradictoriness of our situation, especially when you try to think it in class terms, that makes it both very difficult to think about, and also encouraging. A contradiction always implies a looser, more open situation, a situation in which struggle is still possible. The success of the gay movement weakens the hold of bourgeois-patriarchal norms on the culture as a whole. At the same time there are enough features of the gay culture which could unite with the more positive features of working class culture. (A major problem in the latter is the importance of the family as a place to live [rather than as 'lineage']; and where I have met husband-and-wife role playing gay couples they have been working class and/or lesbian.) From the outside some such new creation seems to be part of the project of community centres developing not just as centres for gay people but as gay centres inextricably located in specific wider working class communities. The aim of a far closer involvement in the union movement – meaning both raising gay issues through the unions, but also raising gayness in the work place (as heterosexuality is endlessly) – is another such project. Another may be working against fascism in *genuinely* working class, multi-racial organisations. In all cases, sisterhood and brotherhood, camp, responsible promiscuity, have a role to play. That is a difficult practice – about it we need, as someone once said, pessimism of the intellect but – and how – optimism of the will.

Originally published in *Gay Left* 3 (Autumn 1976), pp. 15–16.

20 PASOLINI AND HOMOSEXUALITY (1977)

Editorial note [by Paul Willemen, 1977]:

In *The Times Educational Supplement* of 16 May 1975, Robin Wood published a short article on the work of Pasolini, concentrating on *Arabian Nights*. Robin Wood discussed, amongst other issues, the question of the place and political importance of male homosexuality in Pasolini's films. The article ends with the following statement on the subject:

> Pasolini's recent trilogy (of which *Arabian Nights* is as much the best as *The Canterbury Tales* is the worst) can be seen as attempting to create a 'liberated' world of pure impulse and essential need, beyond ideological determination, a world in which the living, 'magical' identity of things can be perceived. The frank homosexual impulse behind the films is important for several reasons. Certainly anyone unable to respond to Pasolini's celebration of male beauty is missing one of their major delights. One might argue that the uninhibited pleasure in the male body expressed so naturally and unashamedly, never self-conscious or propagandist, seldom even reaching thematic explicitness, gives the film a particular significance for the cause of Gay Liberation; and, unlike the films of certain other homosexual film-makers, they are free from any tendency to degrade women. It is, above all, this aspect of Pasolini's work that facilitates the distancing from bourgeois norms of marriage-and-family, and from the notion of an inevitable association of sexuality with procreation. Liberation has no more persuasive advocate.

The following essay constitutes the response by another Gay Liberation activist arguing that in Pasolini's work, the representation of the male figure is in fact embedded in a tradition of self-oppressive rhetoric.

▲ ▲ ▲

I should like to take up a couple of the points made by Robin Wood in his article. Let me preface this by two remarks. First, the gay movement has always placed considerable emphasis on the political importance of 'coming out', declaring one's gayness openly, and I salute Robin's[1] doing this in this article (– and in *The Times Educational Supplement* too!). Second, what follows are genuinely exploratory notes, suggesting the kinds of problems and materials one would need to look at in order to take Robin's observations further. They are in no way a fully worked out extension of what he says.

The points in Robin's article that I am mainly concerned with are (1) Pasolini's aim of creating a film world 'beyond ideological determination'; and (2) the celebration of the male body in his films.

Robin's view that the trilogy seeks to create 'a "liberated" world of pure impulse and essential need, beyond ideological determination, a world in which the living, "magical" identity of things can be perceived', is very close to the view expressed by Noel Purdon, who sets this project rather more explicitly within Marxist struggle. Pointing to the 'male puritanism' of the 'Stalinist left', Purdon writes:

> [Pasolini's] decision to continue making mass visual fantasies of the great erotic books of historical cultures is an act of mass liberation as well as the purging of personal demons and the airing of personal angels. It is, as he insisted, a political choice to make films such as these, the reverse of the images of television and respectable entertainment.[2]

The problem is, to what extent are the trilogy's images the reverse of mainstream cinema? Indeed, to what extent can they be? The answer to that lies partly in the problem of ideology and partly in the problem of how images work.

Both Robin and Noel Purdon do seem to be operating with a model of ideology that sees ideology on one side and individual human values on the other. It is the men of vision, or good-will, who act as a repository of human values to set against the iniquities of bourgeois and/or Marxist-Stalinist ideology. What seems to have happened here is that the notion of ideology has been taken over from Marxist thought without the attendant notions of structure, class and social being. The absence of these crucial underpinning notions means that ideology can be seen as the very generalised dominant set of values in society as a whole which the great individual adopts, adapts or resists as he (or she?) sees fit. What is lacking is a sense that, on the one hand, the dominant ideology is located in the interests and activities of those

---

1. I follow here the practice in gay liberation writing of calling fellow gays by their first names, regardless of whether one knows them personally or not.
2. Noel Purdon, 'The Erotic Cinema of Pier Paolo Pasolini', *Cinema Papers*, July-August 1975, pp. 113-115, 180.

who dominate in the social structure, and, on the other, that all individuals are placed in the social structure, and it is their place within it that provides them with their ideological point of departure. Thus it is, as Robin suggests, because he was gay that Pasolini was able (in so far as he was) to imagine alternatives to 'bourgeois norms of marriage-and-family'. However, this is not because gay people have any premium on liberated values, but because gay people are that much more structurally dislocated from the norms that dominate, ideologically and structurally, in society. This does give us, potentially, a distance on society and ideology, and certainly helps to account for the radicalism of otherwise extremely privileged artists such as Oscar Wilde, Edward Carpenter, André Gide, Christopher Isherwood and Pier Paolo Pasolini.

Yet this radical potential is counteracted by an equally powerful tendency. For, precisely because dominant ideologies and structures do dominate, gay people have tried to think and feel their gayness in the terms of heterosexual norms which means in terms of guilt, sin, sickness, inadequacy, perversion, decadence... These categories deform the self-images of gay people and are inscribed in our cultural traditions.[3] The work of Pasolini is deeply scarred by them.

Indeed, it cannot help but be scarred by them. Not only because he was isolated (the Italian gay movement Fuori has emerged only in the last couple of years), but because any artist uses a language over which he or she has very little control. Whatever Pasolini may have meant his images to mean, they have built into them meanings that he could not control and that he may very well have been unaware of. Moreover, Pasolini's very commitment to letting images ('the world') speak for themselves reinforces this. Images don't speak for themselves; rather the dominant ideology speaks through them unless subverted in some way or other.[4] The face of Mary at the opening of *The Gospel According to St. Matthew* is dwelt on for some considerable time; we are meant to respond to the meaning inherent in it; but what we actually respond to is the cultural tradition of imaging the Virgin. In this sense then, it does not really matter what Pasolini consciously thought about gay people (though even his recent coming-out in the *Corriere Della Sera* does not seem to be especially affirmative about gayness); inscribed in his images are the dominant ways of thinking about gayness.

Consider two images of male attractiveness: one of Franco Citti in *Accattone*, the other a pin-up by the gay photo studio Per Noi. These could be supplemented by images from other Pasolini films (including Franco Citti elsewhere, Christ's followers, many in the trilogy, and Laurent Terzieff in the early film Pasolini scripted, based on

---

3. For development of the concept of gay self-oppression see Andrew Hodges and David Hutter, *With Downcast Gays*, London: Pomegranate Press, 1974.
4. For the development of this idea, in the context of the depiction of women, see Claire Johnston's article ['Women's Cinema as Counter-Cinema'] in Johnston (ed.), *Notes on Women's Cinema*, London: S.E.F.T., 1973, pp. 24-31.

Pier Paolo Pasolini looking into the camera while shooting *Accattone*, 1961. (Pierluigi Praturlon/Reporters Associati & Archivi/Mondadori Portfolio via Getty Images)

his own novel *La Notte Brava*), as well as other films (for instance, Simone in *Rocco and His Brothers*, the chauffeur and prostitute in *The Conformist*, Adriano in *Anima Nera*, Fiorello in *I Ragazzi del Massacro*). Moreover, they compare with images in post-war Italian fiction – not only Pasolini's own *Ragazzi* and *Una Vita Violenta*, but also Alberto Moravia's 'Agostino' (in *Two Adolescents*), Alberto Arbasino's *The Lost Boy*, Mario Soldati's *The Confession*, and several of Giorgio Bassani's novellas, including *The Gold-Rimmed Spectacles* and *Behind the Door*. Take this description from the Moravia:

> the third was fair, and by his carriage and physical beauty struck Agostino as being better bred than the others. But as he got nearer, his ragged bathing costume, full of holes, and a certain coarseness in his handsome face with beautiful blue eyes, showed that he too belonged to the people.[5]

---

5. Alberto Moravia, *Two Adolescents*, translated by Beryl de Zoete, Harmondsworth: Penguin, 1960, p. 24.

And of course it was at the hands of just such a boy that Pasolini met his death, an irony noted by James Kirkup in an elegy in *Gay News* –

> So Momma Roma got you in the end –
> the bitch goddess and her instrument,
> a bit of teenage rough trade, one of those
> subproletarian ragazzi di vita you immortalised
> in poetry and film – one of your own sorry passions.[6]

What kinds of meaning are condensed in these images? Let's consider the emphasis on adolescence and poverty. Even the pin-up, not benefiting from a surrounding story to anchor its meaning, immediately suggests these qualities – the age of the model, his slightly unshaven face, the broken-down wall and bare wood of the setting, the sullen expression, the quality even of a slight deformity of appearance, a hint of malnourishment. What is implicit in these images is that the person looking at them is older and middle-class. Pasolini himself has spoken of the impact made on him, a *figlio di papa* (a son of the bourgeoisie) of the sub-proletariat life he came to know in the slums of Rome – a life more vital, spontaneous and virile than the repressed, inhibited and anaemic world of respectability above it.

There is, of course, nothing either specifically Italian or specifically gay about this – the interpenetration of class and race with sexuality is widespread in Western culture (e.g., very randomly, *Wuthering Heights*, *Lady Chatterly's Lover*, Valentino, Dietrich, *Emmanuelle*, *Mandingo*). Yet it does seem to be a more insistent feature of how gayness is imaged. It is true that gayness does permit the creation of milieux in which barriers of class and race can be bridged; but this is not what comes across in the images of the adolescent and the older man, or the sub-proletarian *ragazzi* and the bourgeois admirer. Rather what is stressed is *inequality*. It is as if precisely the quality that homosexuality promises, of equality based upon the same social status of the partners (both women or men), has to be denied by insisting on built-in inequalities of class and age. This is partly because the heterosexual norm of inequality between partners exercises its influence over gay consciousness, so that some form of inequality has to be reinvented (– there is a complex interplay in gay fiction between the characters acting out 'masculine' and 'feminine' roles and their class, race and age differences); and partly because an equalisation of differences of status, including differences of gender, would present a far too attractive image of homosexuality to set against the in-built inequalities of heterosexuality (in-built, that is, as long as men and women are socially unequal). Thus, far from being a straightforward expression of gay consciousness, the

---

6. *Gay News*, no. 93, p. 15.

images of men in Pasolini's work are scarred by an ideology that denies gayness its validity and its subversive implications.

This is reproduced in the narratives of the books and films representing gayness. *Death in Venice* as a film becomes a study of the coquettish power of the young (and vital) over the old (and dried-up); novellas like those of Bassani, Soldati and Arbasino all play upon themes of betrayal and humiliation, of old by young (Bassani, Arbasino), of working-class and middle-class (Bassani); and Pasolini's work does not alter this. From *La Notte Brava*, where the poor boys rob the rich boys who have, implicitly, been exploiting them in their turn, to *Arabian Nights* itself, where the selection of boys and girls by a man and woman respectively turns out to be part of a game of heterosexual competition, and where the greatest humiliation threatened in the film is in the final scene where Zumurrud, disguised as a man, threatens to fuck Nuredin. Indeed, the association of gay sex with humiliation – a very common image in gay self-oppression – seems to be something of a feature of Pasolini's work. It is implicit in *Theorem*, and as far back as his second novel, *Una Vita Violenta*. In this, there are three episodes in which the hero, Tommaso, tries to earn money by hustling. He is only successful once. The first attempt, with a teacher, involves his adopting a degrading posture on the school bench, to no avail. In the second, an extended sequence full of easy parodies of queens, he is not degraded by actually having to have sex, and gets the money by beating up an old lady. In the third, he is masturbated by a man in a cinema whom he then intimidates into giving him money (hence reinstating his virility). It is significant that this is Pasolini's most extended treatment of gayness in a direct fashion; that elsewhere, significant in itself, he keeps it marginal; and that where it does surface it bears these marks of association with humiliation and machismo.

To turn now to the second general point; that *Arabian Nights* is a 'celebration of the male body'.

The basis for discussing images of nudity in our culture has been radically altered in recent years by the impact of women's liberation. It is now no longer possible to write innocently of the 'beauty' of a painting, sculpture or photograph of a naked woman, without also taking into account the charge of 'objectification'. The tradition of the nude extolled by Lord Clark can be seen as merely another example of men treating women as sex-objects only this time tarting it up and legitimating it as 'Art'. We are bound I think to pose this question of Pasolini – is it celebration or objectification of, this time, the male body?

The distinction between celebration and objectification is one that is very hard to draw. The 'objectification' position can look very like older puritan proscriptions against looking at naked bodies at all, and a frank enjoyment of nudity is often taken to be a sign of a person's 'liberatedness'. Behind the latter assumption is a belief in certain basic innocent pre-social ways of being human. One can see how Robin's use of 'celebration' in his article is consistent with the implied opposition of ideology and human values, the latter being just such things as a 'natural' sexuality that takes 'innocent' pleasure in looking at the bodies of others. Yet sexuality, no less than any other aspect of human thought, feeling and behaviour, does not exist in a social vacuum. It is always formed and experienced within a specific historical and cultural situation.[7]

What this means with regard to looking as celebration or objectification is that one cannot consider the issue separately from the matrix of power relations, sex roles and moral precepts in which the looking (any looking) at naked bodies occurs. This emerges quite clearly from John Berger's polemic analysis of the nude in Western art in his *Ways of Seeing*. Pointing out that since the Renaissance the nude means the female nude, Berger argues that the nude in art is essentially an expression of the power of men over women – in her stance, her gaze at the spectator, the symbols and settings associated with her, the nude bears witness to the social being of women in this society, existing not in their own right but as objects to be possessed by men.[8]

We have already noted above the way that conceptions of power in sex developed in heterosexual society may infect the thought and feeling of homosexual people. This is both in the sense of recasting the potential social equality of gay relationships in unequal forms, and in the sense of delimiting the norms of attractiveness. This last point needs expanding a little. The insistence on youth, slimness, muscularity in images of male attractiveness in Pasolini as elsewhere, has the effect of narrowing down the range of men it is possible to find attractive. Old men, fat men, effeminate men – such tastes are not respectable, such bodies do not get celebrated. (It should be added that a glance at *Playboy* etc. will show an even more restricted field of attraction).

John Berger stresses that the implication of spectator power in the nude is carried above all by her static quality, for 'in lived sexual experience nakedness is a process rather than a state' and cannot be reduced to a static object. This point is also made and taken further by Laura Mulvey in her article 'Visual Pleasure and Narrative Cinema'.[9] She shows that one of the aesthetic consequences of the objectification of women is a tension in the story film between the woman as spectacle, that the film wishes to stop and contemplate, and the man as protagonist, whose story we wish to pursue.

> The presence of woman is an indispensable element of spectacle in normal narrative film, yet her presence tends to work against the development of a story line, to freeze the flow of action in moments of erotic contemplation. [...] According to the principles of

---

7. For further development of this, see John H. Gagnon and William Simon, *Sexual Conduct: The Social Sources of Human Sexuality*, Chicago, IL: Aldine Press, 1973.
8. John Berger, *Ways of Seeing*, London: Penguin, 1972.
9. *Screen* 16:3 (Autumn 1975), pp. 6–18.

the ruling ideology and the psychical structures that back it up, the male figure cannot bear the burden of sexual objectification. Man is reluctant to gaze at his exhibitionist like. Hence the split between spectacle and narrative supports the man's role as the active one forwarding the story, making things happen.

The assumed male spectator of the film wants both to stop and look at the woman and to know what is going to happen next. It is in juggling these two elements that much of the skill of mainstream cinema lies.

How far does this apply to Pasolini's work, where it is men rather than women who are the spectacle? Looking is a recurrent motif. To take only the trilogy, there are the nuns and the gardener, the women spying on the student lodger taking a bath, the older couple watching the younger couple in *Decameron*, *The Canterbury Tales* and *Arabian Nights* respectively. Yet here the person looked at, the spectacle, is also an agent in the story – and one could say the same of Pasolini's use of Franco Citti, or of Terence Stamp in *Theorem*. In this way then, the two elements that Mulvey notes as in opposition in mainstream cinema, coincide. But of course it is not just a coincidence. In effect, it reinforces the image of male-sexuality-as-activity just as relentlessly as the standard images of women enforce the concept of female-sexuality-as-passivity. That is to say, it reiterates heterosexual norms.

This goes right against the grain of what gay liberation is trying to do, in two senses. First, gay men are brought up to despise themselves, and one form that self-oppression takes is to despise, as a consequence, all other gay men too, so that only 'normal' men are attractive. It is this that seems to be asserted in the indelible heterosexuality and inalienable normalness of Pasolini's 'stud' figures. Second, it is one of the projects of gay liberation to extend the social definitions of what may be thought beautiful or male – passivity, for instance, or gentleness, or camp, as well as activity and muscularity. There is some of this in Pasolini, and it is not his 'fault' there was not more. But it is much harder to bring down the imagery of oppression than we like to think.

Originally published in Paul Willemen (ed.), *Pier Paolo Pasolini*, London: BFI, 1977, pp. 57–63.

21 TAXI ZUM KLO (1982)

Taxi zum Klo has rightly been hailed as something of a breakthrough gay film. It ends happily; it is straightforward and unapologetic; and it tries to think through a central issue within gay culture, that of the conflict between promiscuity and monogamy. It does all this in an easy, accessible manner; it is funny and sexy, with a clear narrative line that nonetheless allows for many moments of lyricism, incidental characterisations and social comments.

The fact that it has a happy ending makes it remarkable. Most of the films in this season ['Directions in Gay Cinema', Birmingham Arts Lab, April-June 1982] have fairly glum endings – often death, or at any rate a sense of the hopelessness of things. *Taxi zum Klo* ends on a high, with its hero's anarchistic coming-out at the school where he works; a title after the end also suggests that his conflict with his lover is later resolved. This alone makes it a remarkable film. But it has also along the way very clearly and cheerfully presented a picture of male gay life. There is no attempt to glamorise gay life, but no attempt to depict it in sordid or depressing ways – the film neither apologises, grovels nor idealises. It simply accepts gay life, not as the same as straight life – far from it – but as ordinary in its own terms as straight life. Casual sex, the ups and downs of domesticity, camp and drag, going to work – the mixture of things that make up everyday life is different from that of the straight world, but they are treated as the normal gay mixture, nothing to be remarked upon, explained or excused. There is even a certain embrace of the inevitable grottiness of life, a stubborn refusal to see life cleaned up, prettified, Hollywoodised. Like most of the New German Cinema, *Taxi zum Klo*'s use of grainy photography, hard-colour stock, location shooting, unfiltered sound and lower middle-class urban settings do not betoken a disgust with life but a recognition of its mucky banality.

The narrative is structured around the tension for the hero between compulsive promiscuity and the attractions of a monogamous relationship. In principle the film offers the viewer these as a difficult choice, with the possibility of finding new forms of relationship which combine the two. In practice, the hero is the hero, the centre of the film. His lover's desire for monogamy is not really given weight within the film, while the hero's promiscuity is the source of much of the humour, excitement and eroticism

GETTING OVER THE RAINBOW

Frank Ripploh in *Taxi zum Klo*, 1980.

in the film – that is, many of its chief pleasures as a film are associated with promiscuity. I find the treatment of the hero, his looks especially, fits rather too comfortably with traditional ideas about rampant male sexuality which has to have its outlet; his monogamous lover is soft and round in looks (not bearded and leathered), he does the cooking, he is 'feminine'. The film, in effectively valorising promiscuity, also valorises masculinity in rather traditional forms. The treatment of sex and of women thus become aspects of the film that I'm uneasy about.

The sex scenes are different according to whether they take place within promiscuity or monogamy. If the former they are very explicit, involving a range of sexual activity; whereas the one sex scene between the hero and his lover is more within the conventions of romantic coupling of the cinema. Actually the simplest way of stating the difference is that in the promiscuity sex scenes we see penises, come, urine; in the monogamy ones we see none of these. It's as if the simplest facts of sexuality – the genital – can only be shown when the sex is real (i.e. promiscuous, masculine, 'hard', 'going all the way'); when it is romantic it somehow stops being fully sexual. The film has no space for something that would break down the distinction between sex and love, for the sexuality of romance, the romance of sexuality.

Women are not central characters in the film, yet they are very important to it. The hero is very friendly with women; in particular, they are able to talk about sex

Cottaging in *Taxi zum Klo*, 1980.

together. Does this reduce women to their sexuality, or does it offer a space in which women can speak the unspoken of their own sexuality? At one point, the hero admits that he is 'traumatised' by the thought of female genitals. Is this just the film's essential misogyny, or a moment when a very widespread feeling (not confined to gay men) is at least, and courageously, acknowledged? Does it tend to feed into the common myth that gay men are gay because they can't stand women? At a seminar on the film at the ICA recently all these views were aired – some of those who defended the film's treatment of women being women themselves. The centrality of the hero's masculine-defined sexuality certainly provokes crucial questions about how women are seen in the film.

There is no doubt that *Taxi zum Klo* is an important and likeable film. It is just because it is so important, because some may take it to be a statement of where gay men are at today, that we need to question its assumption, that we need to argue with it.

Originally published in *Birmingham Arts Lab* film programme (April to June 1982), p. 33.

22 VITO RUSSO, *THE CELLULOID CLOSET: HOMOSEXUALITY IN THE MOVIES* (1983)

Vito Russo's *The Celluloid Closet* is the first book to offer a history of how gays have been portrayed in the cinema. There have been series of articles in gay magazines presenting chronologies of gay characters in films, and two books – Parker Tyler's characteristically elusive, suggestive critical ruminations in *Screening the Sexes* (1972) and the British Film Institute publication *Gays and Film* (Dyer 1977), which raised some of the theoretical problems involved in thinking about homosexuality and film.[1] *The Celluloid Closet* is the first survey/history book on the subject. It is clearly, fluently written, marvellously illustrated, and very informative, a more or less essential book for anyone concerned with the way that our century has constructed and inflected the notions of sexuality and homosexuality and the roles of the heterosexual and the homosexual.

Just because it is such an important book, it deserves more than the rather too easy praise it has generally received. What follows is in two sections: one, a relatively conventional "review," concerned with what the book is about and how it works as a book; the other, an attempt to draw out some of its implicit issues. In the rush to be comprehensive, Russo has never quite pulled out and fully explored many of the controlling ideas of the book. This is a pity – it makes the book look less intelligent and less political than it is. At the same time, many of these ideas seem to me to be caught at a transition point in current developments in theories of sexuality, and of gayness in particular, so that many unresolved problems remain.

The Celluloid Closet shares the problems of some other pioneering works dealing with the representation of social groups, such as those by Molly Haskell (1974) and Marjorie Rosen (1973) on women; Donald Bogle (1973), Thomas Cripps (1977), and Jim Pines (1975) on Blacks; and Ralph and Natasha Friar on Native Americans

---

1. Parker Tyler, *Screening the Sexes*, New York: Holt, Rinehart and Winston, 1972; Richard Dyer (ed.), *Gays and Film*, London: British Film Institute, 1977.

(1972).² It is not easy to write such a book, and one of the major difficulties is organisation. Russo is trying to do three things at once, each important and each necessary. First, he is providing a survey of what have been the main ways in which gays have been represented in films, a catalogue of types and images. Second, this basically synchronic enterprise is crossed with the diachronic aim of providing a history of gay filmic representation, relating the development of the images to changes in both the situation of gay people and the institutions of the cinema. Third, Russo offers a critical perspective on the films, at once aesthetic and political. Partly because of pressures of space and the need to produce something easy to read, he has not entirely satisfactorily worked out a way of combining these three different elements.

To put it simply, I often found it quite hard to work out where the book was going (which is not to deny that it is very easy and pleasant to go along with the book's effortless readability). Thus the first section of the book, 'Who's a Sissy?', focuses on the homosexual man represented as effeminate. Russo has uncovered a mass of unfamiliar material and he presents it well. But then the chapter rather falls apart as he tries to examine both the persistence of the sissy in later periods and what else was going on in the earlier period, and somehow that brings us round by the end of the chapter to a survey of gays in horror films. In between we have a rather thinly informed excursion to German films of the twenties and thirties. None of this deals with the historical specificity of the films except in the vaguest way.

The same sorts of problems plague the other chapters. Each chapter covers a period: Chapter 2 deals with the Hays Code-dominated Hollywood production; Chapter 3 with the gradual emergence of 'adult', 'sexual' themes in the fifties and sixties; and the last chapter with the relationship between cinema and movements for sexual liberation. Admirably, Russo does not want to remain within the somewhat suspect straitjacket of periods; his method of extending outward from a given period to show how a character type produced in one historical moment has a life beyond that particular moment is potentially a very useful one. The problem is that his procedures are not always clear, and the book reads muddled.

Then there are questions of interpretation and evaluation. The book slips between saying what a film means, what its value is from a sexual political standpoint, and whether it says it well. In each case, Russo does not have space to make a full argument and does not always make a very clear one. When one knows something about

2. Molly Haskell, *From Reverence to Rape*, New York: Holt, Rinehart and Winston, 1974; Marjorie Rosen, *Popcorn Venus*, New York: Coward, McCann and Geoghegan, 1973; Donald Bogle, *Toms, Coons, Mulattoes, Mammies and Bucks: An Interpretive History of Blacks in American Films*, New York: Viking, 1973; Thomas Cripps, *Slow Fade to Black: The Negro in American Films, 1900-1942*, London, Oxford, New York: Oxford University Press, 1977; Jim Pines, *Blacks in Films*, London: Studio Vista, 1975; and Ralph E. Friar and Natasha A. Friar, *The Only Good Indian: The Hollywood Gospel*, New York: Drama Book Specialists, 1972.

Vito Russo, 1986. (Craig Golding/Fairfax Media via Getty Images)

the films in question, one finds his remarks sometimes (not often) factually inaccurate, or questionable interpretations, or controversial judgments – and that then begins to make one wonder about the accounts of films with which one is not familiar. European cinema is given a bit too easy a ride; there is a lingering sense of the old critical equations of Hollywood is fun but trash and European cinema is Art. Russo does, moreover, seem to have a category of film 'quality' separable from ideological meaning, and while aesthetic questions cannot be collapsed into ideological ones, equally notions of 'quality' are highly problematic and a well-made film does not make up for reactionary politics. Finally, in terms of coverage the book is really about Hollywood and mostly about male gay representation. There are surprising omissions, and the filmography in particular is oddly selective, without an explanation of the principles of selection. None of this alters the fact that Russo has produced a book of major importance, mapping out the territory of gay representation and uncovering much forgotten material and many hitherto unsuspected titles. The question is what to do with this information, what sense to make of the territory.

One of the difficulties in thinking about anything to do with homosexuality, and sexuality in general, is determining whether the object of one's thought is what society has done with homosexuality at a given point in time or how homosexuality has been socially constructed at a given point. The distinction is crucial, but hard in practice to keep in focus. In the first case, we are talking about something we assume exists before society gets hold of it, whereas in the latter we assume that homosexuality is itself socially produced. It is a question of degree. While there are essentialist positions that see (homo-)sexuality as a given human quality that is the same the world over and throughout human history, most would agree that how any society thinks and feels about (homo-)sexuality, and so lives (homo-)sexuality, is socially constructed. Equally, while many current theories of sexuality emphasizing it as a social construction give the appearance of meaning that it is a category of discourse entirely invented and produced over the past two or three centuries, the theoreticians must posit some kind of raw material, of human physical activity, out of which ideas of sexuality, homosexuality, gayness, friendship, and so on, are fashioned. We need to develop a way of thinking which recognizes the human body and its potentials as theoretically separable and relatively autonomous from the social/cultural/human and yet also encompasses the understanding that we can have very little knowledge or experience of that body except through socially, culturally, humanly specific ways of conceptualising and feeling it. At present the difficulties of thinking through and holding together in one's mind this relationship between the biologically given (always remembering that 'biology' is itself a particular way of making sense of the body) and the ineluctable practices of social construction tend to be too great, and it is hard not to put too great an emphasis on one or another dimension, falling back into essentialist or pure social constructionist conceptualizations. Where one puts the emphasis is crucial, however, and politically so.[3]

Both conceptualizations may issue in forms of radical politics, and I would like to characterize the difference in the gay context as between 'gay liberationist' and some other kind of gay politics that has not yet acquired a name but that I would want to claim is a social materialist politics.[4] 'Gay liberationist' politics was based on a conviction that gayness has certain inherent qualities that straight/bourgeois/patriarchal society had buried away; they needed releasing; and the very act of releasing them was an act of revolution against the society that had repressed them. The other kind of politics starts from the assumption that homosexuality is a social category forming part of a general system of regulating sexuality, whose broad function (and the trouble with this approach is that the function is so broad) is to keep people in their (social) place by assigning them a sexual place – that is, by assigning them a social place (heterosexual, homosexual, bisexual, frigid woman, rapist, masturbator) through the regulation of what appears to be the most intimate and urgent arena of human

---

3. For further consideration of these issues see Michèle Barrett, 1980, *Women's Oppression Today: Problems in Marxist Feminist Analysis*, London: Verso, 1980: Chaps. 2, 3; and Kenneth Plummer (ed.), *The Making of the Modern Homosexual*, London: Hutchinson, 1981, especially the articles by McIntosh and Weeks.

4. See discussion in Simon Watney, 'The Ideology of GLF', in Gay Left Collective (ed.), *Homosexuality: Power and Politics*, London: Allison and Busby, 1980, pp. 64-76.

experience, sexuality.[5] A politics that starts at this point is both more negative and more positive than a gay liberationist one. It is more negative partly because it does not have one vivid, inspiring focus ('gay is good') and because it deals with and on behalf of a category which it itself defines as socially constructed (and thus arbitrary and limiting, and probably to be moved beyond). But it is more positive because it insists on a recognition of social construction, on the fact that most everything in human affairs has been constructed and therefore that most anything can be: it returns to politics the utopian project of what we want to construct rather than what we want to release. (It also, but this is a further argument, frees us from the tyranny of sex, whereas gay liberationism was in danger of reinforcing that tyranny.)

It will be clear where my own convictions lie, but this does not mean that the gay liberation movement was not, and is not, enormously progressive; nor does it mean that gay people have to abandon organizing around a gay identity. Quite apart from the continued need to defend our gay practices from oppression, we can work only within the social categories that exist; we cannot just 'become' something other than 'gay'. But we can be working to establish a society in which the possibilities of the body are radically, differently understood and cherished.

Vito Russo's book seems to be caught between the two perspectives outlined above. This can be seen in his treatment of three key areas – the relationship between sexuality and gender, the nature of male-male friendship, and the question of the gay sensibility.

Russo rightly stresses the role of the sissy image in relation to gay male characters. He points out that the tomboy image is far less a focus of derision and implied homosexuality, since it expresses an aspiration toward things manly and is therefore understandable, whereas the sissy is reaching for womanly attributes. Implicit in this analysis is both the idea that womanliness is regarded as weak or despicable (and therefore demeaning for a 'real' man) and the idea that the male role is particularly narrow and rigidly defined, so that its preservation (and male power along with it) is peculiarly precarious, because it is so unattractive, allowing even less leeway than the female role. (The point here is not that the female role is not also narrow, but rather that it is understood to be properly narrow, and therefore something that a girl might try to get away from even if she should learn restraint eventually – the structure of numerous films centred on spunky heroines; but the narrowness of the male role is not acknowledged, and hence anything which draws attention to it – like sissiness – must at the same time be ridiculed out of court.) Russo has, then, a complex, flexible, and original model of the interplay between gender and sexuality, between how to behave like a man and the imputed sexuality of people who behave like men, and he applies this model sensitively and productively to the films.

---

5. See Michel Foucault, *La volonté de savoir*, Paris: Gallimard, 1976.

The model of a sexuality-gender nexus gives homosexuality a kind of 'in-between' status, homosexuality as a refusal of, and therefore a threat to, traditional gender roles. But is this the case? What clearly is the case is that, at the level of public discourses on sexuality, homosexuality has been understood as in-betweenism, and this is as true of much progressive gay thought (e.g., Edward Carpenter, Magnus Hirschfeld, Charlotte Wolff) as of antigay thought. At this level Russo is describing an indisputable aspect of the social construction of homosexuality. Many of the illustrations in his book clearly show that a play on the signifiers of masculinity and femininity is what allows a figure to be read as gay. The assumption of a gender in-betweenism that is then taken to indicate a specific sexuality was equally made quite explicit in a sequence of photographs produced by the Scientific Humanitarian Committee in 1903 in Germany, illustrating the heterosexual male, the heterosexual female, and the non-male, non-female homosexual in-between.[6]

What is not clear – in current sexual theory no less than in Russo's book – is whether this in-betweenism, even if no longer biologically conceptualized, is true in the sense of homosexuality's being, inherently almost, a refusal of gender roles. While at the macro level of mass-circulation discourses the construction of homosexuality is offered on the model of gender in-betweenism, the actual histories of lesbians and gay men seem as often to involve constructing their sexuality out of, and within, the models of traditional masculine/feminine psychology that are offered them. Why a model of homosexual biography – gay men and lesbians as the most rather than the least masculine and feminine practitioners of sexuality, respectively – has not got into the mass media and the dominant discourse on homosexuality is not a question I know the answer to. But pointing to it does mean that we have to be a bit more careful about our assessment of the sissy.

Russo seems to want to have it both ways with the sissy. He wants to point out its ideological role of shoring up heterosexual gender roles; but he also wants to say it carries within it the seeds of revolution because it does not fit those gender roles. In charting the former, the operations of gender ideology, he is on firm ground, but on the latter he is near to going along with the model of in-betweenism.

If they see themselves as profeminist, gay men can choose to use the sissy as some sort of model of how not to be 'masculine'; this is our historical legacy, as it were, which may help in finding styles of fighting gender roles. But gender roles are not so invariably and rigidly decisive in the construction of homosexuality in the way in-betweenism suggests. Gay struggle against gender roles relates only to homosexuality

---

6. See John Lauritsen and David Thorstad, *The Early Homosexual Rights Movement, 1864-1935*, New York: Times Change Press, 1974 and James D. Steakley, *The Homosexual Emancipation Movement in Germany*, New York: Arno Press, 1975.

itself insofar as, at the level of public representation, the two have been brought together; and this misses many other ways in which homosexuality is constructed (and oppressed) through the categories of male and female sexuality.

A perennial theme in gay (film) criticism has been the question of male-male friendships on screen, the buddy image. Are such images implicitly gay or a denial of gayness? Should we see Butch Cassidy and the Sundance Kid as 'really' a gay relationship or as a relationship in which gayness has been deliberately suppressed? Or is it not gay at all in any sense?

One set of problems in relation to this has to do with procedures of textual criticism. Gay criticism has to deal with the fact that it is not always easy to know with any certainty whether a character is to be read as gay, because gayness is not something that is visible; it does not 'show' as gender or race does. (This is in any case more complex than it appears – gender and race are less hard-and-fast as categories than we are generally led to suppose. Most representation of people of different genders or races involves a mass of signifiers in excess of the very limited and largely ambiguous signifiers of difference given by nature, but with gays, as with class, there are no given signifiers of difference whatsoever.[7]) Russo is very careful in his treatment of this problem. He does not get involved in the kind of reading-in of gayness that many critics go in for. This is partly because he argues from the film texts, clearly showing what the evidence is for reading a given character or sequence as gay/homosexual. Eyebrows may be raised at his inclusion of Laurel and Hardy as a gay couple in several of their films, but the argument is supported by evidence from the films themselves. In addition, Russo is arguing from a definition of gayness as a recognizable cultural form – the signs of gayness are those produced to define gayness, whether by dominant or gay subcultural practices, and it is from these that he is producing his readings. In this way he is very different from those critics, largely psychoanalytic by persuasion and heterosexual by implicit self-definition, who do see homosexuality represented where there are no such signs of it. What this implies is that gayness as subcultural sexual practice and homosexuality as a description of a given human relation are not coterminous – not all people who have same-sex sexual contact are, or identify themselves as, gay. (Let me leave for now the ambiguity over whether one can be gay without identifying oneself as gay, a problem which is yet another road back to the essentialist/social constructionist divide.)

These problems of textual interpretation themselves derive from a second set of problems that are focused on the question of male-male friendships. Critics, gay and otherwise, often make the assumption that intense male-male friendship, in life as in

---

7. See T.E. Perkins, 'Rethinking Stereotypes', in Michèle Barrett, Philip Corrigan, Annette Kuhn and Janet Wolff (eds), *Ideology and Cultural Production*, London: Croom Helm, 1979, pp. 135-59.

movies, is always and necessarily sexual. This is a thorny question, but it would seem that it is at least dangerous to assume a priori that same-sex friendship is by definition sexual. This is the nub of the problem that Michel Foucault's influential work raises in relation to psychoanalysis, which has been the main route through which the idea of the sexuality of human relations hitherto not considered sexual has come to us. Freud's recognition of the crucial role of intense physical relations in childhood (in the child itself, between the child and others) seems like a real gain, a real departure from attempts to deny the body; but securing it, as Freudianism has, so inexorably to notions of sexuality seems part of a tyranny whereby sexuality is the explain-all of life.

Lillian Faderman's *Surpassing the Love of Men* (1981) argues very clearly the difficulty of necessarily assuming that we must call intense female-female relationships in earlier periods, or even our own, lesbian (see also Clark 1982 for a recent discussion of the use of the term lesbian in the women's movement).[8] It would be wrong to make a simple transferral of this female experience to the male one, partly because awareness of sexuality seems more constructed into male experience generally in the periods Faderman covers. Equally, however, we need to resist the temptation, to put it bluntly, of seeing everything in terms of sex. That the intensity of friendship has a bodily dimension is one thing that we need to recognize, but the body cannot be reduced to 'sexuality', which is a very specific concept of genital determination.

Bringing these textual and conceptual sets of problems together, we might argue in analyzing a buddy film that it operates with a concept of male-male friendship as sexual through its deployment of signifiers that indicate this. But it would be a different argument from saying that the film shows, or thinks it shows, an intense but nonsexual friendship between two men but that 'really' the relationship is sexual because 'really' all such relationships are. To call on this 'really' here is to fall back into an essentialist position, which not only takes homosexuality as a given but also prioritizes the sexual in the understanding of human relationships. The problem with doing this is not just an intellectual one: by reinforcing the prioritisation of sexuality we are in danger of acceding to a regime whereby we are controlled through our sexuality.

Russo is clearly caught up in these difficult ideas, and here flatly contradicts himself. He argues that buddiness is always constructed around a denial of homosexuality, but whereas on page 70 he writes that 'gays are the manifestation of what stands between men's complete love of other men and their acceptance of women as friends' so that 'men have never been granted the full emotional potential that they might have had on the screen', on page 148 he writes, 'The appeal of the buddy relationship for heterosexual men has always been that of an escape from the role playing of men

---

8. Lillian Faderman, *Surpassing the Love of Men*, New York: William Morrow, 1981; Wendy Clark, 'The Dyke, The Feminist and the Devil', *Feminist Review* 11 (1982), pp. 30-39.

and women – a safe, neutral emotional zone with no chance for confusion.' In the first case, buddiness is all but sexual, and intense and angst-ridden because of it; in the second it is thankfully not sexual, and a relief because of it. Male-male friendship, in reality or as represented, may be either, and we would do well not to start from the assumption that such a friendship is in some sense or other gay. To say that Butch and Sundance are gay was, at a certain time, outrageous and liberating; to go on saying it may be to reproduce the regime of sexuality.

A third reworking in *The Celluloid Closet* of what I am calling a gay liberationist versus a social materialist theory/politics comes out in the treatment of the idea of the 'gay sensibility'. Here Russo is concerned to show that anything which might constitute a sensibility is rooted in the actual material situation of gay people – ghetto cultures, the experience of passing, the fact of being defined as deviant. So far so good. There is such a phenomenon as a gay sensibility, that is, a characteristic way of feeling about things which has been produced out of the material circumstances of gay people and which gays learn as they come out into any developed gay subculture. The limitations of saying this need to be kept in mind: the situation of gay people did not give off the sensibility; it was the situation within which the sensibility was produced and about which it *made* a sense. And it has to be learned; one would not automatically have it without coming into contact with it somehow. Russo slips from the first, materialist, position to a second, essentialist, position, which sees gays as inevitably having a sensibility of 'difference'.

Russo's desire to hang on to a distinctive gay difference underpins many of his judgments. As a protest against blandness, I feel with him – the gay sensibility is much more fun, much more alive than the straight one. As a basis of action on the basis of a sense of shared feeling, this is good politics. But we should recognize that we have produced this sensibility in history and that we choose to promote it for what is good about it (recognizing, too, that many things about it are sexist, snobbish, and self-oppressive). It seems like freedom to assert the right to express a pregiven gay sensibility, but it is another and perhaps greater kind of freedom to assert the choice of constructing a kind of sensibility and determining the form it takes.

The importance of Vito Russo's book is that it both allows one to see clearly many of these difficult issues and gives one much-needed information and evidence with which to think them through. The problems of the book are not problems unique to Russo; on the contrary, they are the central problems of sexual political debate. In trying to outline some of them, I wish to emphasise the problems I share with him rather than suggest an intellectual distance from him.

Originally published in *Studies in Visual Communication* 9:2 (Spring 1983), pp. 52–56.

23 ROCK: THE LAST GUY YOU'D HAVE FIGURED? (1985)

Near the end of *Lover Come Back*, there's a scene where Rock Hudson goes into his apartment block wearing only a woman's fur coat. Throughout the film he's been observed by two older men – every time they've seen him it's been in some situation where it's looked like he was pursuing or being pursued by every attractive woman around. When the two see him in the fur coat, one turns to the other and says, 'Well – he's the last guy in the world I would have figured'.

The two men in *Lover Come Back* had the same difficulty as much of the world's press when Rock Hudson's gayness became public along with the news of his having AIDS. *People* magazine quoted his aunt Lela saying 'Never would we think that he would be that [i.e. gay]. He was just always such a good person.' The British dailies reached for their usual clichés – 'Legend that Lived a Lie', 'Secret Torment of the Baron of Beefcake', 'Rock Hudson's Jekyll and Hyde Existence' – emphasising the shock it was going to be to the women fans who had so 'thrilled' to his 'husky frame' when they realized that he was 'a homosexual.' There was apparently nothing gay about Rock Hudson's star quality or his appeal. One paper even managed a backhanded compliment by suggesting that, contrary to popular opinion, Rock was a good actor after all – because he had been such a convincing heterosexual.

The reasons why it had been impossible to figure that Rock was 'a homosexual' were revealed by a predictable vocabulary. Rock could not be gay because he was, on the one hand, 'virile', 'muscular', 'square-jawed', 'masculine', and, on the other hand, 'nice', 'good', 'likeable'. The linking term in all this is 'clean-cut', that uniquely US men's style of antiseptic machismo. Difficult for the media to know how to handle this: at best it could mean acknowledging a shift in the perception of gay men – we can be nice *and* butch *and* homosexual, after all. At worst, though, it could be presented as a monstrous deceit practised on the libido of millions of women. Cross either one of these views with the fact of AIDS and you get both the surge of fundraising and sympathy for AIDS 'victims' – because, after all, AIDS sufferers can be nice, and real, men – and the reiteration of the idea that gay men cause AIDS: just

Rock Hudson in *Lover Come Back*, 1961. (John Springer Collection/CORBIS/Corbis via Getty Images)

as Rock deceived women sexually, so gay men have inflicted a deadly disease on the world through their sexuality.

Whether in the benign or malignant version (and many stages of uncertainty in between), what such approaches share is the idea that it is *surprising* to think that Rock Hudson was gay, that there is a contrast between how he seemed on screen and how he was in private, that there was nothing gay about Rock as performer or image. It is this idea, rather than the media coverage of Rock in the light of AIDS, that I want to talk about here.

One can't altogether blame the media for assuming that people would be surprised Rock Hudson was gay. In the most obvious way, there was nothing gay about the Rock we saw.

When it became known that Montgomery Clift, James Dean, Sal Mineo and others of Rock's generation were, to some degree or other, gay, it was not such a surprise, even to those who were not already in the know. Clift and the rest do fit a certain stereotype of the gay man – sad, neurotic, confused. Even their appearance – physically slight, with intense eyes and pretty faces – is of a kind that contrasts with Rock's large frame, slow eyes and classically handsome face. The image of gay men as sad young men, pretty and anguished, was a prevalent one in the popular culture of the '50s and '60s, and Rock did not conform to it.

The difference is very clear when you see James Dean and Rock Hudson together in *Giant*. Dean's Method style looks mannered now – arched torso, hunched shoulders, shifting eyes, staccato speech and a walk so oddly stiff it reminds me of Jack Wrangler (whose walk I used to suppose some bizarre version of butch, though I gather it is in fact arthritic). By comparison Rock is still, straight, unfussy, just *there* in the classic manner of Hollywood stars. Dean's style connotes 'naturalism', an acting convention associated in the period with awkwardness and neurotic emotionality. Rock's style suggests a different sense of the natural – namely normality. His very stillness and settledness as a performer suggests someone at home in the world, securely in his place in society, while Dean's style suggests someone ill at ease in the world, marginal and insecure. Easier, then, to see Rock's performing image as one expressing the security of heterosexuality, and Dean's the insecurity of gay men's position in the world, or their inherent neuroticism. (You'd have to work very hard indeed to see anything in the film of the supposed affair between Rock and James that Britain's shame, *The Sun*, said Elizabeth Taylor said was going on during the filming of *Giant*.)

Neither in looks nor in performance style does Rock conform to the '50s and '60s notion of what gay men are like – but neither does he fit with the images of gay desire that are found in picture magazines and short films of the period (as superbly discussed by Tom Waugh in 'A Heritage of Pornography', *The Body Politic*, January 1983, and in 'Photography, Passion and Power', *The Body Politic*, March 1984). The physique mags

The 'clean-cut' Rock Hudson, 1954. (Hulton Archive/Getty Images)

and soft-core pulp novels centred predominantly on two types of desirable males – the youth and the muscle man – and Rock was neither.

The 'youth' type was identified above all by his crew cut, but also by imagery of jeans, biking gear, campus pennants or other talismans of what's now called youth culture. Tony Curtis, Tab Hunter, Marlon Brando and others fitted this then and belong to the gay iconography of the period, but Rock never did. In the *Saturday Evening Post* spread on him in 1952, he is at home, washing the car, listening to Frank Sinatra albums, eating ham and eggs. It's all very wholesome, unrebellious, normal, even a bit middle-aged – and naked. He's in shorts or an après-shower towel in most all the pictures, and he has a really lovely body. But he is not the other desirable type: he is not a 'muscle man'. He has a large, strong physique, but the contours are soft, the look sleek; he never had much 'definition', was never 'cut', 'ripped' or 'shredded', to use the repellent vocabulary of '80s bodybuilding. Even by the standards of the '50s, Rock was not muscley, not like Steve Reeves or even, say, Jeff Chandler.

THE RICHARD DYER READER

Rock Hudson smoking on the beach, circa 1940. (Bettmann via Getty Images)

I do feel less certain about this than about his not being a sad young man. Rock must in fact have been a pin-up and heart-throb for countless gay men. I well remember seeing *Pillow Talk* when it first came out. There is a scene where Rock and Doris Day, both in (separate) baths spread across a split screen, are talking on the phone. Doris puts her leg up out of the bath and rests her foot against the wall in a typical cheesecake pose; and so does Rock, their feet meeting at the split in the screen. The sight of that sturdy, hairy calf (all in fact you can see) fed the fantasies of this already intensely voyeuristic gay teenager for several months thereafter. Yet Rock never became a source of erotic fantasy for me, and he really doesn't fit the gay pornographic imagination of the time. If many of us did put Rock on our walls (or, more likely, would like to have done), it was because he conformed to more general notions of what an attractive man is. It was not a specifically gay taste, whereas Tony, Tab, Marlon, Steve and Jeff closely fitted the image of '50s gay icons.

If, in relation to '50s and '60s stereotypes of gay men and gay erotic imagery, there is nothing especially gay about Rock Hudson's image, does that mean there is nothing to say about it in gay terms?

We are most used to sensing a star's gayness with someone like Montgomery Clift. Despite the largely unambiguous heterosexuality of his roles, Monty always seemed to be pushing at the boundaries of masculinity, his gayness troubling, inflecting, exploring what it means to be a man (see Tom Waugh's discussion in *Cineaste*, Vol X No 2, Spring 1978). This was not Rock's way. He produced a flawless surface of conventional masculinity. Yet it is a surface strangely lacking in force and intensity. It's a sort of parade of the signs of masculinity without any real assertion of it.

What's fascinating is the way this quality unsettles the apparent complacent heterosexuality of his films. If Monty seems to be trying out new roles for men, Rock – in effect if obviously not in intention – seems to subvert the security with which ideas of masculinity and femininity, normality and heterosexuality, are held. This is especially exploited in the two groups of films that were among his most successful: the sex comedies, and the melodramas he made with director Douglas Sirk.

Rock's sex comedies, from *Pillow Talk* in 1959 to *A Very Special Favor* in 1965, feature not only the kind of gag I opened this article with, but also plots that revolve around sexual ambiguity. What often happens is that, for part of the film, Rock (sometimes deliberately, sometimes not) seems not to be full-bloodedly heterosexual: he is woman-shy, or impotent, or a milquetoast – as a means of getting, usually, Doris Day to drop her defences. *A Very Special Favor*, with Leslie Caron, goes further. Rock actually pretends to have turned homosexual because Leslie has rejected him; she is a psychiatrist, and takes up the challenge to 'cure' him of his 'inversion' in the time-honoured manner.

There is one variation on this pretence motif among the sex comedies. *Man's Favorite Sport?*, directed by Howard Hawks, turns it on its head: Rock is famous for his supposed expertise in what the film avers is a uniquely masculine activity, fishing, but he has never fished in his life. Although the film winds up with him in the arms of Paula Prentiss, he seems throughout rather uninterested in women even though, farcically, he appears to be carrying on with three at once. Here it's macho that's the facade, while in the other comedies it's various notions of unmasculinity.

The pretending-to-be-gay motif even recurs as late in Rock's career as the TV mini-series *The Star Maker*, where he, as Danny Youngblood, allows himself to be discovered by Brenda Vaccaro in bed with another man, so that she will think her daughter Angel is safe with him. He gets to elope with Angel later. (My thanks to my friend Charlotte Brunsdon for drawing my attention to this episode.)

What is all this about? In his book *The Celluloid Sacrifice* (London: Michael Joseph, 1966), Alexander Walker suggests that 'the main aim of the sex comedy's sparring partners … is to make each other neurotically unsure of their gender, their sex appeal and their potency.' Rock pretending *not* to be a wolf in *Pillow Talk* puts Doris Day in a quandary:

> Yes, he *is* the perfect gentleman, but is that really flattering to her as a woman? When he refrains from kissing her, is it just because he respects her or is she really not his type? Of course, he *looks* virile enough, but can one be quite sure? Maybe he dotes on his mother and collects cook-book recipes. And sure enough, Rock's *alter ego* acts as cissily as predicted, and Doris gets panicky. After making men keep their distance for so long, has she now fallen for one with no urge to come hither?

As Alexander Walker sees it, the main effect of this is at Doris's expense, the comedies being at heart misogynistic. He argues that Rock's pretence does not really undermine *his* heterosexual image, even if it does throw her sexual identity into question. After all, we know he's only pretending. And presumably it was assumed that Rock's image was so indelibly heterosexual that he could get away with such stuff.

But the insistent return to this pretending-to-be-a-cissy routine also suggests a more elaborate scenario, now that we know (and can say that we know) Rock was gay. Here is this gay man (Roy Scherer, Jr, Rock's real name) pretending to be this straight man (Rock Hudson) who's pretending to be a straight man (the character in the film) pretending to be a gay man (for the gag in the film). The hysterical pleasures of confusion, so central to comedy and farce, are perhaps even more deliciously delirious here than in, say, *La Cage aux Folles* or *Victor/Victoria*, to which, once you know he's gay, Rock's comedies come so close.

These '60s comedies have a reputation for blandness and safeness, for conventional sexual morality crossed with a complacent view of sex roles. Now they look much more interesting, bristling with sexual hysteria and gender confusion, more aware than they've been given credit for of the instabilities of heterosexuality and normality.

Rock's other great popular success came earlier, in the series of lush, weepy dramas produced by Ross Hunter and directed by Douglas Sirk: *Magnificent Obsession*, 1954; *All That Heaven Allows*, 1955; *Written on the Wind*, 1956; and *The Tarnished Angels*, 1957. Originally dismissed as lachrymose tripe by the critics, these films have generated considerable critical interest in recent years, aided perhaps by Rainer Werner Fassbinder's enthusiasm for them.

One of the characteristics of these films is the extraordinary sense of frustration and dissatisfaction in their central female characters. They move in rich, bland suburban interiors that have all the airless comfort and reassurance of a department store or a mail-order catalogue; they are stifled by the anemic morality and pat emotional texture of their lives. What they need is… well, Rock. In these films Rock figures as the promise of 'life', in his virility and sexual certainty, but also by his association with nature. It is perhaps clearest in *All That Heaven Allows*. Jane Wyman plays a recently widowed suburbanite whose children and neighbours think she should marry a middle-aged, safe, 'undemanding' man. Rock plays the man who comes to prune her trees; he wears lumberjack shirts and reads Thoreau; he is 'natural man.' Jane falls in love with him, and it is clear that what Rock embodies is seen as the answer to her restless, empty life.

Though it is possible to see all this in feminist terms, depicting the inadequacies of life for women in bourgeois society and granting the intensity of female (sexual) desire, still the answer to the woman's problems does seem to be a tall, dark, handsome male – Rock. It is here, though, that the films become really interesting. For although Rock represents the values of natural masculinity, of 'real men', he doesn't really deliver. Marriage is always deferred, his virility is never really put to the test. We never see him 'saving' the woman from her plight, we only have the promise of it. In *Magnificent Obsession*, he will save her by restoring her sight – but the film ends before we know the outcome of his operation on her, finishing on her plaintive cry, 'Tomorrow!' *All That Heaven Allows* ends with Jane, still not married to him, sitting by his bed where he lies, a cripple in a coma. Similarly in *Written on the Wind* and *The Tarnished Angels*, the promise of deliverance he represents for Lauren Bacall and Dorothy Malone can only take place after the film is over, if at all.

Casting Rock adds to the intensity of this endlessly deferred gratification. He looks the part so perfectly – big, strong, good-looking – yet in the end all that he does is *look* the part. Had he the force – the heterosexual commitment – of a Clark Gable or a Steve McQueen, we know that, even if the films had ended in the same way, he'd still be up on his feet 'fulfilling' the woman before we'd left the cinema. With Rock in the part you can't be so sure, and this is what gives the films their terrible sense of desolation. What women want is a real man, but the only real men around are but the promise of fulfilment, endlessly put off, never finally kept.

You could see this as a critique of the very idea of the 'natural man', exposed as a sham that women would do well to turn their backs on. But I think the films do believe in the ideal of, even the need for, virility – it's just that they don't really believe real men exist any more. The films are thus a tragic, rather than a feminist, view of the situation of women.

In both the comedies and the melodramas, Rock's presence throws into question the ideas and the viability of heterosexual masculinity. Perhaps the campy possibilities

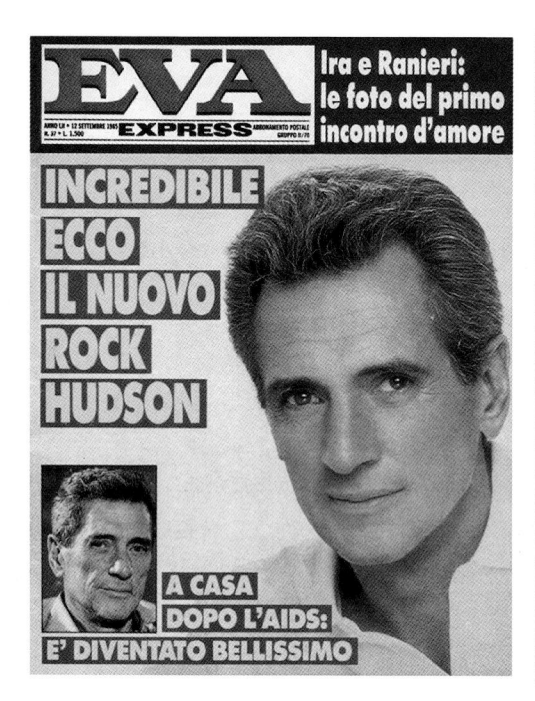

Rock, before and after (or both during?) AIDS, (left) on the cover of *Eva Express*, 12 September 1985; (right) *News of the World*, 18 August 1985.

of this were not lost on the makers of *Dynasty* (who knows what they really think they are doing?) when they cast Rock as a stud farmer and threat to Krystle and Blake's marriage. In that Colorado-Babylon world where there is nothing but image, Rock brought all the weight and authority of a star image which had already given that game away – that there is nothing but images, that the ideals *Dynasty* endlessly gestures towards, of heterosexuality and normality, have always been a sham and a mockery.

Rock shatters the dream of fulfilling heterosexuality, but there is a way that the visual treatment of the news of his illness has also shattered some of the dreams of gay life, California-style.

What dominated the press and television coverage were before and after – Before AIDS and After AIDS – pictures. Rock healthy, strong, gorgeous in stills from films and in early pin-ups, side by side with Rock tired, haggard, tragic. One of the most fascinating examples was the use of a highly touched-up recent photo of him. Some papers (Italy's *Eva Express* for example) said it had been taken after he'd been to Paris for treatment, while others (Britain's *News of the World* for one) said it had been taken 'just a couple of months' before the AIDS story finally broke. Either way, it was put beside a picture of Rock ravaged by AIDS. This mix-up suggests the way the juxtaposition of the 'beautiful' and the 'awful' Rock implies not only chronology (one following another) but also simultaneity, as if the two images were different sides of the same thing, two aspects of the condition of homosexuality.

Such a juxtaposition of beauty and decay is part of a long-standing rhetoric of gayness. It is a way of constructing gay identity as a devotion to an exquisite surface (queens are so good-looking, so fastidious, so stylish, so amusing) masking a depraved reality (unnatural, promiscuous and repulsive sex acts). The rhetoric allows the effects of an illness gotten through sex to be read as a metaphor for that sex itself.

If anything, this way of seeing gayness has become even more prominent with the coming of AIDS, even if the style of the surface has changed. Now as the pecs get bigger, the cadaverous effects of AIDS become even more familiar. The gay glossies set side by side ever more generously proportioned hunks with ever more detailed, alarming and heart-rending accounts of AIDS sufferers. Jeffrey Weeks notes in his new book, *Sexuality and Its Discontents*, the bitter irony of AIDS occurring now, at the end of a period when the prevalent image of gay men as effete was put to rest:

> The cultivation of the body beautiful was a vital part of that [rejection of the effeminate image]. But AIDS is a disease of the body, it wrecks and destroys what was once glorified.

This paradox, this contrast between a bland, even sexless, physical perfection and the raddled awfulness of sexual practices is not, of course, the reality of most gay men's lives. But it is a powerful and deeply rooted image, and is encapsulated in the juxtapositions of Rock Hudson Before AIDS and After AIDS. If Rock's death has brought attention to AIDS, boosted fundraising, made people realize that 'nice people' get AIDS, it has also been used to reinforce venerable myths about gay men.

Originally published in *The Body Politic* 121 (December 1985), pp. 27–29.

24 NICE YOUNG MEN WHO SELL ANTIQUES: GAY MEN IN HERITAGE CINEMA (2001)

In a Las Vegas nightclub in 1955, Noël Coward sang his own version of Cole Porter beginning:

Belgians and Greeks do it
Nice young men who sell antiques do it
Let's do it, let's fall in love.

Quite unintentionally, it's a deliciously neat, if incomplete, summation of gays in heritage cinema: good-looking young men, well turned out in retro clothes amid period objects, fall in love and sell us the pleasures of the past.

Heritage cinema has been notably hospitable to homosexual subject matter (although I'm going to focus on male instances). Early examples include *Olivia* (France 1951), *Loving Couples* (Sweden 1964) and *Young Törless* (Germany 1966), things really taking off in the 1970s with films such as *Death in Venice* (Italy 1971), *Ludwig* (Germany/Italy 1972), *Coup de grâce* (Germany/France 1976), *A Special Day* (Italy 1977), *A Man Called 'Autumn Flower'* (Spain 1977) and *Ernesto* (Italy 1978). Heritage films and gay liberation developed side by side and some of the former – *The Affairs of Love* (Spain 1990), *Another Country* (United Kingdom 1984), *Maurice* (United Kingdom 1987), *Meteor and Shadow* (Greece 1985), *We Were One Man* (France, 1979) – seem pretty clearly inspired by the latter. With possible exceptions (*Colonel Redl* [Hungary 1985], *Death in Venice*, *Ludwig*, *The Music Teacher* [Belgium 1988]), heritage films take a broadly positive view of homosexuality – which is to say that they take such a view while depicting pasts that did not.

To understand what is going on, one may make a distinction between history and heritage. History is a discipline of enquiry into the past; heritage is an attitude towards the legacy of the past. Both have to deal with what comes down to us, what is left over, from the past. However, whereas history uses an examination of the leftovers to try to understand what happened in the past, heritage values them for their own sake, savours the qualities and presence of dwellings, costumes, artworks, objects. Heritage cinema can be used as a vehicle for exploring history, as I'll discuss first, but its main impulse is towards appreciating the things of the past and telling stories of what it was like to live among them. Homosexual heritage cinema is above all about envisaging gay men among the attractions of pastness.

HISTORY

Homosexual heritage films did address issues of gay history. In part, they did what so much early gay history did: they showed that we were there. Just by having gay stories in heritage dress, gay men became part of the wider historical panorama of heritage cinema: we, too, were around in the 1910s and 1920s (*Céleste* [Germany 1981], *Colonel Redl, Coup de grâce, A Man Called 'Autumn Flower', A Month in the Country* [United Kingdom 1987], *Nijinksy* [United Kingdom, 1980], *Young Törless*), there was a gay experience of World War II (*The Dresser* [United Kingdom, 1983], *Europa, Europa* [France/Germany 1991], *For a Lost Soldier* [Netherlands 1992], *The Last Metro* [France 1980], *Mediterraneo* [Italy 1991], *We Were One Man*). Sometimes it's more pointed. *A Special Day* and *The Gold Rimmed Spectacles* (Italy 1988) state that gay men, too, were victims of fascism, explicitly bringing out parallels and differences between their situation and that of, respectively, women and Jews. Other films deal specifically with gay oppression (*Ernesto, Maurice, Meteor and Shadow, A Month in the Country*, the Wilde films); somewhat ambivalently, *The Conformist* (Italy, 1969) relates the rise of fascism to homosexual repression, while *Another Country* links 1930s communism to rebellion against homophobia.

The last example also indicates the way that homosexual heritage cinema might point to antecedents to gay liberation itself. Sometimes this is done by showing characters inspirationally comfortable with themselves despite social attitudes (*The Affairs of Love, Carrington* [United Kingdom 1995], *The Dresser, The Last Metro, Loving Couples, Swann in Love* [France 1986], *Time Regained* [France 1999]). Elsewhere, characters discover and eventually embrace 'who they really are' (*Another Country, For a Lost Soldier, Maurice, We Were One Man, Wilde*), often involving a scene of 'coming out', which may range from the coded and indirect (*De Avonden* [Netherlands 1990]) through the private (*A Man Called 'Autumn Flower'*) to the brazen (*Meteor and Shadow*).

Of all the above, *A Man Called 'Autumn Flower'* is perhaps the most sustained treatment of gay liberation *avant-la-lettre*. Its hero, Lluis, a drag queen (stage name 'Autumn Flower'), is also a political saboteur against the dictatorship of Primo de Rivera in the Barcelona of the 1920s; he fights alongside trade unionists and anarchists, but also explicitly in the name of 'a revolution in which we can be ourselves [that is, gay] twenty-four hours a day'. He and his lover are arrested for trying to blow up de

Rivera's train. Called to his execution, Lluis, with several days' growth of beard, picks up a compact and firmly, carefully applies lipstick, a gesture surely modelled on Marlene Dietrich's at the end of *Dishonored* (United States 1931); then, his arm around his lover, he goes defiantly, unambiguously gay, to his death. Lluis is a hero on the side of anti-dictatorship in a film made (1977) in the first flush of the demise of Franco (1975); he is part of the history of the struggle for democracy in Spain, but the film also insists that he be understood to be so as a homosexual and in the name of homosexuals.

HERITAGE

In such ways, heritage cinema can put gay men into history, but this is not its primary impulse. What is at issue is, rather, heritage, gays belonging in what is handed down as cherishable from the past.

One dimension of this is the importance of queers in the source material of the films, the literary heritage from which most of the films are drawn. Heritage cinema would be extraordinarily diminished without Paul Bowles, Colette, Rudi van Dantzig, Diaghilev, Forster, James, Agnes von Krusenstjerna, Napoleon Lapathiotis, Mann, Proust, Gerard Reve, Rimbaud and Verlaine, Umberto Saba, Sackville-West, Stein, Lytton Strachey, Wilde, Woolf and Yourcenar. More important, though, than this affirmation of the place of queers in cultural patrimony is the look of the films and how gay men fit in, and especially how they are dressed.

Homosexual heritage may use the common perception of European men's clothes since the eighteenth century as highly restricted in terms of shape, texture and, above all, colour. This has often been interpreted as indicating emotional repression, as, in Flügel's influential formulation, a 'great masculine renunciation' in the name of the values effective in the pursuance of business and power: straightforwardness, sobriety and restraint.

Such sartorial restraint can be used in heritage cinema to express homosexual repression and liberation. Redl's many buttoned military jackets are always fully done up, squeezing his slightly podgy frame, suggesting someone ill at ease and anxious about giving himself away; the eponymous hero of *Ernesto* removes his stiff collar when he has sex with the labourer at the start of the film and thereafter, as his sexual confidence flowers, begins to wear light-coloured and, eventually, patterned waistcoats. Quite commonly, films also suggest the danger for queers of trying to draw on colours and fabrics beyond the normal male range. Wilde (in *Wilde*) in cream frock coat and purple or green buttonhole is clearly riding for a fall. *Meteor and Shadow* shows us its poet hero strolling through a public park in tight white trousers and large, loose white shirt with blowsy pink rosette at the neck, obviously queer and soon enough punished for such brazenness.

Things need not go so far as this. *Death in Venice* signals Aschenbach's decline into queerdom through slight but telling departures from the strictest of male attire that he has worn for most of the film. The erotic dimension of his fascination with Tadzio is only borne in on him when he follows Tadzio down a boardwalk and the latter, in a striped, buttock-clinging tank swimsuit, swings round the posts of the boardwalk, looking suggestively at Aschenbach on each turn. Aschenbach, dressed in standard male summer white suit, veers off the boardwalk, confused, sweating. The film cuts at once to a close-up of him looking at Tadzio in the hotel. Aschenbach now, for the first time, wears a dark bow tie with hollow spots. It is rather floppy, unlike the tightly knotted, narrow ties he has worn hitherto, and this floppiness goes along with the white handkerchief flouncing out of his breast pocket, a marked contrast to the handkerchief we have earlier seen him carefully fold and put in his pocket to show only small, sharp peaks. By the time Aschenbach has submitted to the suggestions of the barber and had his hair dyed and his face made up, his clothes have edged much closer to the queer. Furtively following Tadzio through the streets, he now wears a large red band round his beige straw hat and a red tie with a diamond pin; when he skulks in the shadow of a portico, the pin glints in the dark with something approaching vulgarity. He is now in thrall to queer desire; when he dies on the beach gazing at Tadzio, hair dye runs grotesquely down the side of his face. A move into more expressive clothes signals a decline into abject queerness.

Homosexual heritage can express through clothes ideas of the repression and the dangers of the expression of homosexual desire. However, it does not do so so very much. This is perhaps because one of the defining pleasures of the films is looking at men wearing nice clothes. If all that the clothes expressed were restriction and discomfort, they would be a lot less pleasurable to look at, to imagine yourself touching or wearing them. In any case, it is wrong to think of the restraint of male clothing as necessarily repressive and uncomfortable. As Anne Hollander suggests (in *Sex and Suits*), Western male clothing, especially the suit, can also be redolent of ease and grace. The masculine beau ideal of self-control and social conformity is one that, clothes promise, men can be at ease with, be at home in.

To have homosexual characters dressed like this was a declaration that gay men, too, could form part of a graceful, decorous masculinity. Queer masculinity had characteristically been represented as something abnormal, informed by ideas of sickness and effeminacy. In heritage cinema, on the other hand, gay men were shown as indistinguishable from other nicely turned, worth looking at (but not more worth looking at) men.

Good-looking clothes also facilitate the exploration of what men may find attractive in each other. Compare and contrast *Ernesto* and *Maurice*. Both represent relationships between an eponymous middle-class protagonist and a working-class lover – an unnamed labourer in *Ernesto*, Alec in *Maurice*. In both cases, it is the working-class character who knows what he wants, the middle-class one who has to find out. However, and centrally through the use of clothing, *Ernesto* constructs attraction between men overwhelmingly in terms of difference, while *Maurice* moves it towards sameness. In the process, both also suggest different models of gay social integration.

Ernesto opens with a systematic class contrast. As Ernesto selects those to whom he'll give employment that day, his black suit with bowler hat, stiff white collar and pale grey-blue tie stands out against the loose grey trousers and off-white, collarless shirts of the workmen. His youth also stands out, since his pretty, fine features and soft skin contrast markedly with his staid clothes. Class and age differences then take on an erotic charge in the sequences between the labourer and Ernesto. The former's clothes and appearance emphasise a rougher-textured male pulchritude: off-white, lightly stitched shirts or ribbed button-top vests, the buttons undone pulling open across his hairy chest; black hair, short on the sides, but long, wiry and unruly on top. He seems to burst out of his clothes, embodying a fully masculine, wholly unrepressed homosexual desire. Ernesto, by contrast, wears his black suits and stiff white collars; his wavy hair is pomaded into neatness; he is hairless (and we are told has not even started shaving yet) – his is the smooth, neat beauty of the feminine. That the contrast is not only of class and age, but also of gender is made explicit when the labourer refers to himself as the man (and relates this to his role as penetrator in sex).

When Ernesto becomes a man (he shaves, goes with a female prostitute, wants to penetrate the labourer), he meets a boy, Ilio, at a concert. Ilio has longish, fair hair and very soft features, and is not only younger than Ernesto, but also comes from a much wealthier family. As if this isn't enough, the gender equation (higher class plus younger equals more feminine) is reinforced by the fact that he has a twin sister, Rachele; towards the end, Ilio and Rachele swap clothes and the latter, now dressed as a boy, tries to seduce Ernesto, although he remains fixated on Ilio at a dressing table putting on make-up. If Ernesto's sexual preference is not in doubt (he continues to desire the biological male), it is also clear that he now desires the feminine man. What's more, he will probably marry Rachele because that's just what you do: the film ends with him at a party set up for him to announce his engagement to Rachele; he looks about desperately for Ilio and then turns to the camera and shrugs his shoulders. Through the use of always attractive clothes, *Ernesto* retains then an insistence on difference as a structuring principle of male homosexual desire, but implies that it can be maintained alongside conforming to the social organisation of heterosexuality.

The relationship between Maurice and Alec looks at first as if it is of a piece of that between Ernesto and the labourer. Alec's dark ruffled hair, rough-textured collarless shirts, loosely knotted neckerchiefs, heavy, cruddy boots and dirty leggings contrast with Maurice's fair, short-cut hair, stiff white collars, tightly knotted black ties and

Dress and difference in *Maurice*, 1987. (BFI National Archive)

featureless dark shoes. The contrast is most marked when they meet in the garden, Alec in his gamekeeper's gear, Maurice in dinner jacket; that night, Alec climbs into Maurice's bedroom and they make love. Thereafter, however, clothing makes them look more alike: naked in bed together, then both in identical whites for a cricket match and, then, when he comes to visit Maurice in London, Alec wearing a neat blue suit of the same cut as Maurice's. As they lie in bed together in a rented room, the camera tracks over their neatly folded clothes, one man's set indistinguishable from the other's. They are thus integrated with each other and into a conventional masculinity.

Ernesto and *Maurice* both involve adapting (in different ways) to decorous masculinity. Such conformity at the level of costume makes it feel like the men can be integrated at the level of the film's social world. This is characteristic of homosexual heritage. Exceptionally, *A Man Called 'Autumn Flower'* achieves an integration of unmanly queenliness into its *mise-en-scène*, even while depicting a society that deals ruthlessly with homosexual rebellion.

The film begins by underlining the separation of the bright heritage world of assumed heterosexuality and the dark world of queers: Lluis is a successful lawyer living with his mother in a very nice, large bourgeois flat; he goes at night to the dim, tacky nightclub to do his drag act. Part of the trajectory of the film is his insistence on bringing his overtly queer style into the rest of his life, which is also the film bringing it into the *mise-en-scène* of heritage.

In one sequence, Lluis in drag is beaten up and left outside the door of his flat, for his mother to find him, although he runs off before she can open the door. But later, in the full drag of a smart señora (nothing vulgar or showbizzy – in other words, dressing heritage, not camp), he goes to see his mother in her bedroom in the middle of the night to tell her about himself. He insists that she keep the light off and the half-light on him as he speaks is appropriately reminiscent of the confessional. Eventually, however, she insists on putting the light on. He has by this point taken off his (woman's) hat and wig, affirming his homosexual identity as man in woman's clothes. She tells him to come to her and they embrace, the camera tracking back along her bed to where he has left the hat and wig. There has thus been a gradual progress of queer into heritage, from avoiding being seen at all when dumped outside the flat through the half-light of confession to the fully lit embrace of an unequivocally gay self-presentation amidst full, but unflashy and uncluttered, period trappings. Very homosexual, very heritage.

Heritage cinema depicts past worlds in which homosexuality was illegal, mocked, despised and persecuted, in which gay men thought of themselves as queers. Yet it depicts these worlds, including being gay in them, as attractive. Several commentators, notably Andrew Higson and John Hill, have argued that there is a defining contradiction in (British) heritage cinema between ostensible social critique and loving spectacle – the story and dialogue may condemn the worlds depicted, but the look and texture of the films celebrate them. Yet perhaps the films are doing no more than evoking the contradictoriness of the past itself. Against the odds, there were also for queers love and sex and friendship, acceptance and tolerance, and you could still dress well and look good. Beyond this, what I have been trying to show is that, especially through clothes, homosexual heritage cinema does something quite specific with the contradiction between critique and spectacle: it produces the utopian pleasure of a vision of integration even in homophobic societies of the past. In effect, it imagines queers being gay.

Originally published in Ginette Vincendeau (ed.), *Film/Literature/Heritage: A Sight and Sound Reader*, London: BFI, 2001, pp. 43–48.

25 THE IDEA OF A GAY ICON (2009)

In 1882 Oscar Wilde, newly arrived in the USA, had his portrait taken by one of the most important photographers of the day, Napoleon Sarony. He was to use the images to advertise his tour, which is to say himself, but they were also very widely circulated, unauthorised, by the Burrow-Giles Lithographic Company.[1] Wilde was already famous, if not quite yet infamous, but in relatively limited circles. The photographs made him familiar to the masses. Wilde's look in these photos, to which Sarony as well as Wilde himself contributed – the longish hair, velvet jacket and silk stockings, the languid poses, the Turkish carpet and hangings – fixed and spread the idea not only of Wilde but of a type that may not quite have spoken its name yet, but was widely recognised or suspected. Wilde was, literally, the embodiment of a known social category, captured in a photograph. In other words, he was a gay icon.[2]

It may feel heart-sinkingly predictable to introduce an introduction to gay iconography with Oscar Wilde – yet it is precisely that predictability, that excessive familiarity, which makes him so inescapably a gay icon. This is true even if historical investigation should make us worry about just how entirely gay he was (there is no reason to suppose he did not also love, sexually, his wife and other women) and quite how many people knew that his floppy, foppish look meant homosexual (rather than just weird). Wilde to some extent was and certainly has become an icon, a person who is taken to be an embodiment of a wider social category and who is known about through the mass reproduction of, supremely, photographic images of him and her; and in Wilde's case the social category is the homosexual. Before, and even long after, Wilde's trial and disgrace in 1895, when the love that dare not speak its name or shows its face had had that done for it decisively by the law and the press, no one would have actually used the term gay icon. Even thirty years ago it would have

---

1. For a discussion of the Sarony portraits and the Burrow-Giles appropriation of them, and the ensuing court case over copyright, see Jane Gaines, *Contested Culture: The Image, the Voice, and the Law*, Chapel Hill: University of North Carolina Press, 1991, pp. 42–83.
2. In keeping with the terms of the exhibition I am using the term gay to cover both gay men and lesbians, a practice that only some lesbians will feel happy with.

The iconic photograph of Oscar Wilde, 1882. (Napoleon Sarony/Universal History Archive/Getty Images)

meant very little. Icon, if it meant anything, meant an image of Christ or the Virgin Mary or, more arcanely, visual symbolism in art[3] or a kind of sign designated within the fledging discipline of semiotics.[4] Gay as a term designating homosexual was gaining ground, although it would certainly have meant nothing in this regard to the Victorians (or to many people before the 1960s), who had at their disposal venerable

---

3. See, for instance, Erwin Panofsky, *Meaning in the Visual Arts*, New York: Doubleday, 1955.

4. Namely one having meaning by virtue of its resemblance to what it represents. Thus a picture of something is understood to be a picture of that something because it looks like it, rather than because we agree to use an arbitrary sign to designate it or because the something itself causes the sign. Thus a picture of a cow looks like a cow, but the word cow is merely a convention by which English speakers designate the creature, and a cowpat is a sign of a cow because a cow itself created it. In this semiotic distinction, the first is an icon, the second a symbol and the third an index. Photography complicates the issue, as we shall see, because there is a sense in which the object photographed itself, by the virtue of light emanating from it being picked up and fixed on a light-sensitive surface, gives rise to the resultant photograph: outside of fakery and perhaps digitality, there can be no photograph without there having been the object in front of the camera to make it happen. However, we also understand a photograph to look like what it shows and it commonly has conventional associations beyond merely showing. Thus a photographic image is always an index and an icon and very often a symbol. The icon/index/symbol distinction belongs to the nineteenth-century philosopher C. S. Peirce; see James Hoopes (ed.), *Peirce on Signs*, Chapel Hill: University of North Carolina Press, 1991.

terms such as pederast and sodomite, lesbian and sapphic, nelly and molly and tommy, and emergent ones such as invert, uranian and homosexual. The idea of putting any of those terms together with icon would have appeared baffling. Their coming together in the past thirty years is a product of the separate but intertwined establishment of the two terms, gay and icon, in their homosexual and semiotic senses. This though is not mere coincidence, for the term gay was part of a project about making homosexuality visible and icons are one of the main forms of doing this in contemporary mass media. There were images of people relatively widely known to be gay – or lesbians, or queers, or homosexuals – before there was the word gay, but the business of making gay icons is largely a product of recent times. That doesn't mean, however, that it isn't revealing to think about the implications of both halves of the term – icon and gay – in relation to their earlier meanings and connotations.

The religious meaning of the term icon, and the adoption of it for semiotic purposes, is not negligible. The religious icon is part of a fundamental distinctiveness of Christianity, the idea of embodiment. Christ was the embodiment of God and the Virgin bore Him in her body (there is no such embodiment in Judaism, and Mohammed is always referred to as the Prophet or Messenger, not God incarnate). Although Christian icons are only images, they are images of persons who stand for a much wider (in this case the very widest possible) category. What's more they don't just stand for it, they are it; in their very persons, they incarnate it. The idea of embodiment and its image has transmuted into the secular world, and the term icon is now very widely used to mean a person or a thing that at once stands for and is a representative of a wider category. In writing this essay, I have become especially aware of how wholly commonplace a term it has become with, for instance, fashion items, films and cities, as well as people routinely referred to as iconic (sometimes without even an indication as to what they are iconic of). It may include fictional people – in the present context Dorian Gray, Elsie Tanner from *Coronation Street*, Colin in *EastEnders*, Willow in *Buffy the Vampire Slayer*, and Xena in *Xena: Warrior Princess* are examples of iconic fictional gay characters. However, its primary meaning, even in secular use and the one deployed here, still has to do with real people who embody a wider category.

The secularisation of the term is related in part to the challenge to belief in the West during the past centuries and also to the transformation of Christianity into a religion of the here and now rather than of the hereafter (a transformation surfacing in celebrity culture in all those awards ceremonies where no doubt iconic people candidly thank God for their celebrity). It also has to do with the profound effect of two things that are at once wholly comprehensible and yet, at least for a time, seemingly uncanny, like the idea of embodiment itself: the mass circulation of images and photography. The first (in the form of woodblocks, engravings and lithographs in broadsheets, chapbooks and newspapers, long before the advent of photography) made images of people available on a hitherto unimaginably wide scale. A painted portrait – let us say for the sake of the present context of Shakespeare's patron, Henry Wriothesley, widely taken to be homosexual – may have captured the image of someone whose being embodied a certain orientation, and both the person and the portrait may have been well enough known in certain circles to make the person a byword for said orientation. Those circles, however, would be very restricted indeed – really only a few people would ever have seen the portrait of Wriothesley at the time and only with the possibility of reproduction has it become widely known. It is the mass circulation of infinitely reproducible images that made it possible for a private individual's likeness to be known to all and sundry, made icons in the contemporary mass-media sense possible.

The uncanniness of the photographic portrait is that it derives technically from the subject's actual presence in front of the camera.[5] A lithograph of someone – in the case at hand, that of the Ladies of Llangollen (who died just when photography was being invented) is a good example – made the image of the person available to all, but it was still just someone's impression of them and could even have been made up, whereas a photograph can only exist if the person was there to be photographed. But, like a lithograph only more so as the media of mass reproduction developed, a photograph could be seen by thousands and millions. The photograph then is the means for the mass circulation of embodiment and may even make it possible for an individual person to be taken as an embodiment of a wider category, in other words, to be an icon.[6] Mass reproduction and photography are utterly routine now: we don't find them uncanny. And yet something of the extraordinary remains, of a particular person whose appearance can be captured and seen anywhere over and over again; this extraordinariness is part of the process of icon-making, of ordinary people becoming special.

The religious connotation of the word icon does not stop at its semiotic function, but also relates to its lingering extraordinariness. The prime purposes of religious icons are devotion and veneration. In some traditions they are even themselves considered to be endowed with actual godhead, just as the communion wafer commonly is in Catholic tradition. We may not go as far as this with gay icons (although something

---

5. See previous note.
6. In Peircian terms an icon, in this cultural sense, gay or otherwise, is also an index (they are themselves a sign of what they are taken to represent and a photograph of them derives from their physical presence before the camera), a symbol (because much of what makes it possible to read them as anything other than that individual person is purely conventional, e.g. we have come to agree that a limp wrist 'means' queer, a tie on a woman 'suggests' lesbian) and rather more problematically an icon (since any individual lesbian or gay man does not in fact look like the generality of lesbians and gay men, even though they may be taken to do so).

akin to it is possible), but they generally function as something more than a convenient reference point for homosexuality in image communication. On the one hand, while the person concerned may be ordinary, typical, just like you and me, they are also at the same time special. They are special partly just because they are icons, but then they generally become icons because in some way or other they have done or been something special (see below). On the other hand, what these people have done is generally for the most part something admirable or likeable. There are infamous lesbians and gay men (beyond those infamous in their own time just for being gay, such as Wilde or Radclyffe Hall), but can they ever quite be gay icons? Can one imagine Gilles de Rais, Erzsébet Báthory, Ernst Röhm, Roy Cohn, Dennis Nilsen or Jeffrey Dahmer – who have high name and even image recognition – figuring in a gay icons listing or exhibition? In other words, can one have, in the old negative sense of the term, a queer icon? And even less in the more recent radical use of the term queer, which stresses fluidity and destabilisation, whereas icons are fixed as well as positive.

All of which brings me to the significance of the other half of the term under discussion: gay. The word was part of a project that saw the road to rights and equality for people who desired people of the same sex in terms of a visible identity. The gay project was carried vocally in the activities of the Gay Liberation Front and associated movements, but also in the more respectable activity of homosexual rights groups, as well as in the practices of stereotyping in the mass media, which, for their own various purposes – responding, denigrating, taking possession of representation – wanted gays to be recognisable. Informal and vernacular as it is, at once subcultural and mass-media based, the production of gay icons is carrying on the gay liberation project of coming out and becoming visible.

Making gayness visible had to overcome the fact that, apart from actual sexual acts, homosexuality is not something visible, something that can be seen (or of course heard, but we'll stick to the visible for the purposes of this discussion). There had already been a history of queer-spotting – could you tell who was and who wasn't? Were all women wearing ties in the 1920s lesbian? How sure a giveaway were suede shoes for men in the 1960s? But the gay project wanted a more secure visibility, it wanted to make widespread the face, literally, of homosexuality.

The problem is that once you have a recognisable image, you are in the business of fixing an identity, of saying this is what a lesbian or a gay man looks like and this is what they are like. Many gay icons affirm this – you probably didn't need to know that Wilde, Hall, Martina Navratilova or Little Richard were gay to be able to guess as much from their images. Which is to say they affirm stereotypes. The latter are often taken to be simplistic, reductive and derogatory and, in the case of lesbian and gay stereotypes, they tend to reinforce the sense of homosexuality being a form of gender dissonance (we are not real men and women).

Yet these stereotypes do not simply go away. They are a very effective and immediate form of communication, all the more powerfully so for invisible groups (like homosexuals), and they are at least as much a product of lesbian and gay communities as something imposed upon them. Yet the gay project remained uneasy about stereotypes: they were used against us, they did imply that all homosexuals were like this or that, were gender misfits and, if we acted them out, maybe that was a mark of our oppression, of our internalisation of the way we were seen by straights. Gay icons – when they are real gay people taken to be representative of gay people in general – in some measure, if they aren't themselves 'obvious' dykes and poofs, evade this problem. If you didn't know they were gay you couldn't tell just from looking, but such gay icons by definition are proclaimed or proclaim themselves as gay, so that you always do know that this unexceptional looking person signifies that exceptional thing, gay.

There remains though a further ambiguity over gay icons, whether partaking of stereotypicality or not. Something of this ambiguity derives from the nature of the portrait itself. Gay icons do not only exist in portraiture of course; they exist in their publicly recognised activity, in performances, interviews, audio-visual footage and so on. However, it is not just the relevance of portraiture in the present context that makes me raise it here. Albeit not necessarily in posed and/or photographic form, the portrait remains a privileged mode in gay iconography, precisely because it fixes an immediately recognisable and readily reproducible image of its subject. In the process it carries the ambiguity of the social function of portraiture. Before the Renaissance, and really for long after, portraits were of rulers, religious leaders, kings, queens, popes, the nobility, the rich and powerful; while no doubt the portraits of Richard I or Queen Anne – to take once again subjects germane to the topic of gay icons – were of interest because they told viewers what this king and this queen looked like, they were primarily significant because they were The King or The Queen. Only gradually did the portrait become specifically of an individual. With icons, something of the old function remains – the person is significant as themselves but also as lesbian or gay or as being important to the lesbian or gay community, at once themselves as individuals and representative, with the latter always risking sliding over into the vexed question of typicality.

A gay icon then, for the purposes of this discussion, is a widely known and disseminated visual image of a real person who is taken to be representative of the social category homosexual and to be in some way or other valued for it. From this follow the two elements that make a given person come to be considered a gay icon: visibility and representativeness.

A gay icon has to be visible, but this does not absolutely have to be in photographic form: Wilde may well have been visible first in newspaper cartoons and Radclyffe Hall's partner Una Troubridge is iconic in Romaine Brooks's (much reproduced) painting of her. Photography, however, is overwhelmingly the medium of choice in gay icon-making, not least for its affirmation, as discussed above, of the person's existence (and an urgent aim of the gay project was to proclaim the very existence of lesbians and gay men).

Of course if one were to include people who lived before the invention of photography, one would have to resort to pre-photographic sources of imagery. In this essay I have deliberately, for the purposes of historical perspective and resonance, gone beyond the photographic remit of the exhibition it accompanies, but two cautions are in order. The first and simpler of these is that the making of icons is only possible by means of photography, though in the case of people before there was photography, this means photographs of their images in painting and other non-mechanically reproducible media. Gay icons must be represented in images that are widely available and this is only possible by means of photography and its derivatives. Secondly, and more complicatedly, the very idea of making icons belongs overwhelmingly, as I am arguing, to the past twenty-odd years: it is a product of the age of gayness and celebrity. Nominating people as icons from earlier, non-gay times (including those captured in photographs) runs a number of risks. Firstly, it will involve making into icons figures who, with a number of remarkable exceptions (for example, Byron, the Ladies of Llangollen), had no such public position in their own time – it is us now who make them into icons. People with same-sex desires in the past no doubt had their own icons, ambivalently valued for their homosexuality, but these would have only been known in very restricted circles. Now we may rescue queers, or same-sex lovers, of the past from their own ambivalence and opprobrium and see them as gay icons.

Secondly, nominating people from the past as gay icons may be profoundly anachronistic. Not only was the term gay not available, but nor – perhaps, sometimes – was the idea of people being of a specific sexuality or having a particular sexual identity.

Thirdly, even if we are careful to think in terms of 'people who had same-sex loves' rather than of gays *avant la lettre*, we are usually caught up in hints and conjectures, since the hard evidence is rarely to be found. Especially difficult is the language of friendship in previous times, often passionate and physical without necessarily connoting sexuality. This is extraordinarily difficult territory to negotiate. For, just as we should not seek to impose our ideas of gayness onto the past, nor should we assume that because there weren't the words and it was all hints and conjectures that we are not justified in claiming any gay icons at all from the past. There is a tension here between the actual contemporary practice of establishing a pantheon of gay icons and the work of lesbian and gay historians; between, that is, the activity of lesbians and gay men now who appropriate people as gay as they will (and as is their inalienable right) and the historians' quite proper fastidiousness concerning accuracy and the use of today's categories to read back into the past. Sappho, for instance, though widely revered in the ancient world, is almost an invention. Very little of her work survived, and what little we know suggests she had male lovers as well as passionate female friendships. Yet we would not want to renounce her as – now – a lesbian icon, nor could we: her place in the iconographic pantheon is a fact of our cultural life.

Gay icons may have to be made visible. Some may have to be rescued from the obscurity of the past. Alan Turing, widely regarded as the inventor of the computer and thus perhaps one of the most influential people of the past century, was nonetheless in his lifetime hardly known at all outside of the world of mathematics, much less as gay (except to those who attended his court prosecution for being gay, an event that did not receive significant publicity). Some people known at the time for their passionate attachments might have to be rediscovered and, perhaps problematically, redefined as gay and made into gay icons: the bluestockings Elizabeth Carter and Catherine Talbot, for instance, featured in the National Portrait Gallery's recent Brilliant Women exhibition.[7] Others, splendidly notorious in their day, get forgotten, such as the dancer Maud Allan, famous for various Salomé dances and a libel case caused by an article entitled 'The Cult of the Clitoris', which (rightly) insinuated her lesbianism. Some – Lord Kitchener, Marguerite Yourcenar – would almost certainly have been uncomfortable with their private life having the public presence necessary for iconicity. Yet others – A. E. Housman, Daphne Du Maurier, Gerard Manley Hopkins – disliked the fact they were gay and might be horrified to find themselves now yanked into the limelight of iconicity. In some cases, even what they looked like is speculative and tradition-based. The earliest surviving images of the supreme lesbian icon, Sappho, for instance, date from well after her death[8] and the earliest extant portrait of Richard I was made over 400 years after his death.

Others may be famous for what they produced and are well known to be gay but not for their visual image. This is particularly true of writers. If there are some who are iconic in image as well as in name – Wilde, Hall, Gertrude Stein, James Baldwin – many others are not (I'm not sure that I'd recognise with confidence photographs of Paul Verlaine, Langston Hughes or Marguerite Yourcenar). One of the most beloved gay artists, Tom of Finland (Touko Laaksonen), produced some of the most immediately recognisable of all gay erotic imagery, but few would recognise a photograph of

---

7. National Portrait Gallery, London, 13 March to 15 June 2008; see Elizabeth Eger and Lucy Peltz, *Brilliant Women: 18th-Century Bluestockings*, London: National Portrait Gallery, 2008. On Carter and Talbot's relationship, see Lillian Faderman, *Surpassing the Love of Men: Romantic Friendship and Love Between Women from the Renaissance to the Present*, New York: William Morrow, 1981, pp. 125–30.

8. See Dimitrios Yatromanolakis, *Sappho in the Making: The Early Reception*, Boston: Harvard University Press, 2007.

him (in fact the only one in general circulation is by another gay icon many people would probably not recognise from his photograph, Robert Mapplethorpe). It is much easier for someone to be elected a gay icon if they are already visible, hence the predominance of figures from entertainment, sport and politics.

A gay icon has to be taken to represent a wider identity, gay. This does not mean that they have to be lesbian or gay themselves. They do not even need to be of the same sex. There is a long tradition among gay men of enthusiasm for certain kinds of women stars: as one gay icon reportedly said to another – Joe Orton to Kenneth Williams – one could always tell if a man was gay because he had lots of Judy Garland albums. It is possible to see such stars – Garland, Mina, Barbra Streisand, Shirley Bassey, Madonna – as expressing specific aspects of gay culture and existence, and one might trace a shift in the character of these stars from the emotional intensity of a Bette Davis or a Joan Crawford to the upbeat image of a Kylie Minogue, with Princess Diana perhaps occupying a middle position in this trajectory. Such stars may be taken to express aspects of gay existence – and stereotypical terms such as excessive, theatrical and camp often spring to lips when they are mentioned – but in many ways it is the simple fact of the readiness of a group of men to feel that their feelings can be carried in the person of a woman whom they do not desire sexually that is distinctive, and which makes them into gay icons. There is a comparable taste among lesbians for certain kinds of male star, often glamorous transgressors or outsiders, often with ambiguous homosexual associations. Terry Castle has written of the importance of 'Byronic posturing' in the 'self-fashioning' of many lesbians, including many themselves indubitably iconic (Anne Lister, Radclyffe Hall, Vita Sackville-West, Billy Tipton, Marianne Moore, Nancy Spain),[9] while a sort of soft butchness, Elvis Presley or James Dean,[10] for instance, has been linked to the image of stars such as Phranc and k.d. lang. Suggestive in this context is the work of writers such as Mary Renault, Marguerite Yourcenar and Patricia Highsmith whose lesbianism, not itself unknown to contemporaries, might be registered in their taste for often hyper-masculine male gay or homoerotic protagonists (Renault and Alexander the Great, Yourcenar and Hadrian, Highsmith and Tom Ripley). All these examples, from Alexander to Kylie, often have some hint (or more) of homoeroticism in their lives and work and, even when this is not so, they trail the connotations of gay stereotyping vis-à-vis gender: they are in some way misfits in terms of femininity and masculinity, louder and stronger and more libidinous than women are supposed to be (even while dressed up

---

9. See Terry Castle, *The Apparitional Lesbian: Female Homosexuality and Modern Culture*, New York: Columbia University Press, 1993, p. 103.
10. On Dean as a lesbian icon, see Sue Golding, 'James Dean: The Almost-Perfect Lesbian Hermaphrodite', *On Our Backs*, Winter 1988, pp. 18-19; 39-44.

to the nines in frocks or leotards), more soft and sensitive than men are supposed to be (even while glowering and well built).

When the person is of the same sex, to be a gay icon they do not have to be – or be known to be – gay. Here desire usually comes into play. There are, for instance, long traditions of lesbian attachment to opera divas,[11] film stars such as Greta Garbo and Marlene Dietrich[12] and forceful musical theatre stars such as Mary Martin, Ethel Merman, Julie Andrews and Barbra Streisand.[13] There are often rumours about such stars' own lesbianism, but this is not indispensable to their lesbian following. Most often though they are seen – here we go again – as in some sense androgynous or mannish: favoured divas were often those who took on the breeches roles in opera (I think of female passions I know of currently for Sarah Connolly in such parts), donned male clothes (Garbo and Dietrich, Martin as Peter Pan) or were commanding and even loud (vide Merman) in a way associated with masculinity. Similarly, it is the predominant association of sport – and developed muscles – with masculinity that makes many sportswomen likely lesbian icons, whether or not they are in fact lesbian.[14] (There is of course a further history to be written about whether sport is in reality more accommodating to lesbians – or out lesbians – to say nothing of why tennis has been so especially lesbian identified: think Althea Gibson, Billie Jean King, Martina Navratilova, Chris Evert, Ilana Kloss, Amelie Mauresmo.) Such women are thus classic figures of homosexual desire, where the longing to have someone plays complexly with the yearning to be like them or even to be them (albeit not to the point of heterosexuality).

In contrast, gay men's icons of the same sex who are not (or may not be) gay do not, nowadays anyway, play on the borderline of male and female. There may be a felt affinity with the type of soft, troubled, even sad but not androgynous or, in any evident way, homosexual young man: James Dean, Keanu Reeves,[15] Johnny Depp. Just as – maybe even more – common are men who tend towards an excessive, theatricalised masculinity (musclemen, porn stars such as Joe Dallesandro and Jeff Stryker).

---

11. See Terry Castle, 'In Praise of Brigitte Fassbaender (A Musical Emanation)' in Castle, *The Apparitional Lesbian*, op. cit., pp. 200-38.
12. See Andrea Weiss, 'A Queer Feeling When I Look at You' in Christine Gledhill (ed.), *Stardom: Industry of Desire*, London: Routledge, 1991, pp. 283-99.
13. See Stacy Wolf, *A Problem Like Maria: Gender and Sexuality in the American Musical*, Ann Arbor: University of Michigan Press, 2002.
14. On famous lesbian sportswomen - and indeed on lesbian celebrity in general - see Martha Gever, *Entertaining Lesbians: Celebrity, Sexuality, and Self-Invention*, New York: Routledge, 2003.
15. On Dean and Reeves in relation to gay imagery, see Michael DeAngelis, *Gay Fandom and Crossover Stardom: James Dean, Mel Gibson, and Keanu Reeves*, Durham, NC: Duke University Press, 2001, which also discusses Gibson's brief period (that of the *Mad Max* films) of being a gay icon in the excessive, theatricalised masculinity mode before his determined repudiation of it.

With many male stars, and not least the porn stars, the fact that they are not gay, or deny that they are, may even be part of the frisson of excitement.

Beyond such affinities and desires, the assumption or suspicion or just plain hope that someone is gay may be enough to make them a gay icon. People desired by the population as a whole are also going to be desired by lesbians and gay men. Think of the excitement surrounding Richard Gere, Jason Donovan and Tom Cruise, Mariel Hemingway, Catherine Deneuve, Dolly Parton and Madonna. The current Bollywood star Abhishek Bachchan has in recent polls been elevated to the status of gay icon and, in the wake of this, hopeful, or perhaps hopeless, rumours have circulated about his sexuality; in turn he has said how happy he would be to be a gay icon and has starred in what is seen as the first Bollywood gay movie, *Dostana* (*Friendship*), in which he and another major Hindi star, John Abraham, play two friends who pretend to be gay.

There are then many gay icons who are not themselves gay, nor even of the same sex as those for whom they are icons. However, having said all of that, it is probably the case that most gay icons are people who are known or presumed to be gay. This may be so even if they are also quite widely known to be, also, heterosexual: Byron, George Sand, Colette, Virginia Woolf, Bessie Smith, for instance, or, indeed, Sappho and Wilde. Or if they denied it, as Sarah Ponsonby and Eleanor Butler, and Walt Whitman did. Or if in truth we don't really know – as is the case with those I casually recruited above: Richard I, Henry Wriothesley, Queen Anne, Elizabeth Carter and Catherine Talbot, as well as others regularly brought on board without cast-iron justification: Christopher Marlowe, Marie Antoinette, Franz Schubert, Alfred Lord Tennyson, cross-dressing women such as Moll Cutpurse and Mary Anne Talbot, let alone even less secure cases like William Shakespeare or Ethel Merman, for instance.

An especially interesting category of gay icons encompasses people that everyone in their circle knew to be gay, and from whom gossip leaked out to the wider public, and yet who were publicly known as straight. These are the kind of people of whom it is said nowadays that 'everyone knew', but exactly who 'everyone' was in these cases remains uncertain. The list is interestingly long and distinguished, and includes Pyotr Ilyich Tchaikovsky, Selma Lagerlöf, Federico García Lorca, Vita Sackville-West, Ivor Novello, Langston Hughes, Billy Strayhorn, Noël Coward, Cecil Beaton, Benjamin Britten, Luchino Visconti, Dusty Springfield, Patricia Highsmith, John Cage, Rudolph Nureyev, Tove Jansson.

Lesbians and gay men in the 'everyone knew' category were in fact protected by it, since the 'everyone' who knew either didn't mind or weren't going to do anything about it. However, if they were forced out of such circles, they were at once vulnerable to public opprobrium and also on the way to becoming gay martyr-icons. Wilde and Hall are the obvious examples again, but another is furnished by the subject of a recent exhibition, the Victorian painter Simeon Solomon.[16] Everyone in his circle 'knew' and in any case his paintings told the story, but once arrested for importuning his career was finished. Later figures, in times of a greater flux in official public attitudes, have responded with courage, dignity and sense to the fact of exposure – John Gielgud, George Michael – or the threat of it – Sandi Toksvig, Will Young. The last examples take us to what in practice is probably the core of gay iconicity: outness. On the whole, and with some sensitivity to the limitations on outness in previous eras, gay icons are gay people who, true to the gay project, are out as gay.

There are degrees of this and variations on it. The 'everyone knew' category is the half-open closet. Others were widely assumed to be gay because they conformed to a certain type recognised as gay: Herman Bang, Agnes Moorhead, Nancy Spain, Dirk Bogarde, Anthony Perkins, Elton John, Gianni Versace. Some are valued as openly gay even though their work is not – or not mainly – specifically to do with gayness: Ethel Smyth, Alan Turing, Andy Warhol, Angela Davis, Pat Arrowsmith, Waheed Alli, Alan Bennett, Matthew Parris, Miriam Margolyes, Maggi Hambling. Among others in this category are those who were the first openly lesbian or gay person in their field: the first (and in the event last) footballer, Justin Fashanu; the first American footballer, David Kopay; the first army colonel, Margarethe Cammermeyer; the first MPs (Chris Smith and Angela Eagle); the first bishop, Gene Robinson.

Then there are those, in contrast, whose achievement is inextricable from, though not necessarily limited to, their gayness: Jean Cocteau, Noël Coward, W. H. Auden, Quentin Crisp, Joe Orton, Thom Gunn, Audre Lorde, David Hockney, Elton John, Regina Fong (if drag is taken as an unmistakable sign of gay sensibility), Larry Grayson, Rita Mae Brown, Derek Jarman, Alan Hollinghurst, Jackie Kay, Francis Bacon, Julian Clary, Paul O'Grady (even more than Lily Savage), Matthew Bourne, Russell T. Davies, Sarah Waters.

The work of such people is openly coloured by their sexuality, which is not quite the same as those figures for whom proclaiming themselves gay (or whatever term they would have used at the time) was a conscious project: Radclyffe Hall, André Gide, Maureen Duffy, Ellen DeGeneres, Ian McKellen, and those firsts above, Fashanu, Cammermeyer, Chris Smith and Eagle, and then beyond them those who were actually activists, for whom being openly gay was itself a cornerstone of their work, before gay liberation (Edward Carpenter, Magnus Hirschfeld, Del Martin and Phyllis Lyon) and since (Michael Cashman, Peter Tatchell, Angela Mason, Harvey Milk, Ben Summerskill, Simon Nkoli).

---

16. See Colin Cruise et al. (eds), *Love Revealed: Simeon Solomon and the Pre-Raphaelites*, London: Merrell Publishers, 2005.

The idea of gay icons is generous and inclusive, it makes available and celebrates a huge range of people. Yet, finally, one needs to register its limitations. Not everyone who has sex with someone of the same sex – and not even everyone who would consider themselves homosexual (and these two things are not the same – many who have sex with others of the same sex don't see themselves as homosexual) – recognises themselves in gay icons. While their sheer presence in the media may now incite many more people to see themselves in, and even model themselves on, such icons, my bet is that still the majority do not. Moreover, we need to remember how Western this concept is, and within that how disproportionately white, to say nothing of how slippery both I and the exhibition organisers have been about national and geographic scope. And the notion of a gay icon does not in practice centrally embrace all the constituents of sexual politics grouped under the current acronym, LGBT, lesbian, gay, bisexual and transgender.

Categories – such as gay icon – limit what is said, but they are also the means by which things are said and seen at all. The gay icon project values certain kinds of achievement, fixes images, often subtly reinforces stereotypes, makes being out a cardinal virtue, and is unconsciously constrained by being about current perceptions. However, it also makes possible a gay and lesbian public presence, contributes to changing attitudes and laws, and makes gayness familiar and available. Gay icons do what gay liberation wanted: they say to straights 'We're here' and to gays 'You're not alone'. Even ten years ago it was impossible to imagine an exhibition in as august an institution as the National Portrait Gallery on a declaredly lesbian or gay topic – for all the limitations of the very idea of gay icons, it is hard to think the very fact of an exhibition on them anything other than a gain.

Originally published in *Gay Icons*, London: National Portrait Gallery, 2009, pp. 12–23.

SECTION 4
WHITE

and other essays on representation and visibility

The 'white star' Lilian Gish in *The White Sister*, 1923. (Silver Screen Collection/Getty Images)

In the introduction to *The Matter of Images: Essays on Representations* (1993, second edition 2002), Richard Dyer discusses the political significance of cultural representation for social groupings. He unpacks the multiple valences of the word 'representation' – 'How a group is re-presented, presented over again in cultural forms, how an image of a member of a group is taken as representative of that group, how that group is represented in the sense of spoken for and on behalf of (whether they represent, speak for themselves or not)'.[1] The essays in that collection are all instances of 'images of' analysis, and they all engage with these multiple understandings of representation; primarily they focus on depictions of minorities. 'The groupings that have tended not to get addressed in "images of" work', he writes, 'are those with most access to power: men, whites, heterosexuals, the able-bodied.' A 'couple' of the essays in *The Matter of Images*, he concedes, attempt to tackle the powerful, and these seek 'to make normality strange, that is, visible and specific.'[2]

This section of the Reader foregrounds pieces of writing by Dyer in which he pays sustained critical attention to powerful, dominant groups (men, whites, heterosexuals) and the ideological assumptions and instabilities embedded in images of them. Collectively, the essays in this section make visible that which usually remains unmarked and unremarked. They also interrogate the politics of social and cultural visibility, tease at its complexities. Dyer's short essay 'The role of stereotypes' (1979) was first delivered at 'The Representation of Alcoholism in Cinema and Television', a week-long conference held at the National Film Theatre in London in 1978; a related season of films was screened concurrently. Dyer had previously authored an essay on lesbian and gay stereotyping that appeared in his edited volume *Gays and Film* (1977);[3] 'The role of stereotypes' develops points made in that essay and demonstrates their broader resonance and applicability. In the later piece, Dyer identifies – following Walter Lippmann – the value of stereotypes as mental shortcuts, as providing a system of order. Stereotypes can enable a limited level of cultural representation, 'condensing… a host of connotations' into their seemingly simplistic form. Drawing on Orrin E. Klapp's writing, Dyer distinguishes between social types ('those who "belong" to society') and stereotypes ('those who do not'), and relates this to the depiction of alcoholism on screen: 'we surely only have to be told that we

1. Richard Dyer, 'Introduction', in Dyer, *The Matter of Images*, London and New York: Routledge, 1993, p. 1.
2. Ibid., p. 4.
3. Richard Dyer, 'Stereotyping', in Dyer (ed.), *Gays and Film*, London: BFI, 1977, pp. 27–39.

are going to see a film about an alcoholic to know that it will be a tale either of sordid decline or of inspiring redemption.' The distinction between social types and stereotypes, however, is problematic, 'essentially one of degree'; and is of political significance in that it plays a role in the definition of a dominant group's 'others'. Indeed, the function of stereotypes is to 'maintain sharp boundary divisions'; they are deployed 'to make visible the invisible, so that there is no danger of it creeping up on us unawares; and to make fast, firm and separate what is in reality fluid and much closer to the norm than the dominant value system cares to admit.'

Perhaps somewhat unexpectedly, a guiding influence that runs like a subterranean current through Dyer's writings on the workings of dominant power structures and those who wield and benefit from them is Jean-Jacques Rousseau. As an undergraduate student at the University of St Andrews, Dyer read Rousseau's novel *La Nouvelle Heloise* (1761) for a class on pre-romanticism which had a tremendous impact on him. The very first piece of writing he had published – in 1968, whilst still a student – was in a short collection entitled *Helikon* that was put together to mark the International Year of Human Rights. Dyer's piece is concerned with the 'right to love oneself'. It provides an overview of Rousseau's writings and philosophy, focusing in on the Swiss author's rebellion against an 'artificial system of values', a system that is gratuitous, 'not necessary and not absolute'. Dyer identifies Rousseau's bravery in standing apart, forging his own path: 'if an individual has the courage to deny that the system upon which society is built and which dictates or pressurises the actions of that society is necessary, then he is at war with that society. It may after all be that he is all too sane, and that we are but the puppets of the machine'. Dyer has acknowledged Rousseau's influence on him elsewhere; in a short piece for *The Guardian* written in 1998, for instance, he wrote that 'what *La Nouvelle Heloise* seemed to suggest was that there was a connection between how you felt and how the world was organised. And the fact is that much of what I've done subsequently – engaging with popular and lesbian/gay culture, say, and what it means to be a white man – to me stems from that once extraordinary perception.'[4]

The analysis of whiteness is a dominant, radiant thread that can be traced through Dyer's writing, and thus one which is prominently and appropriately acknowledged in this section of the Reader. The ur-text here is 'White', the groundbreaking essay first published in a 1988 issue of *Screen*. It is one of that journal's most cited contributions, and its impact and influence across manifold fields of intellectual and scholarly inquiry persists, decades after its initial publication. 'White' appeared in a themed issue, 'The last "special issue" on race?', that was assembled by Isaac Julien and Kobena Mercer. (As José Esteban Muñoz revealed, *Screen*'s outgoing editor at the

---

4. Richard Dyer, 'Don's delight: Richard Dyer looks back on Rousseau's *La Nouvelle Heloise*', *The Guardian*, 21 April 1998, p. 6.

time, Mandy Merck, proposed an alternative title, 'Dead White', which would have had especial resonance with Dyer's examination of the links between whiteness and death.)[5] In Julien and Mercer's introduction to the issue, 'De Margin and De Centre' – like 'White', a vital contribution to late twentieth-century scholarly and political debates around race and cultural representation – they argue 'that critical theories are just *beginning* to recognise and reckon with the kinds of complexity inherent in the culturally constructed nature of ethnic identities, and the implications this has for the analysis of representational practices.'[6] They draw attention to Stuart Hall's 1988 essay 'New ethnicities'[7] which highlights how, in Julien and Mercer's words, 'the cultural specificity of white ethnicity has been rendered "invisible" by the epistemic violence that has, historically, disavowed difference in western discourses.' Dyer's essay, they state, 'inaugurates a paradigmatic shift by precisely registering the re-orientation of "ethnicity" that Hall's argument calls for.'[8]

'White' was a first, tentative foray into a sizeable topic. The essay draws attention to 'the invisibility of whiteness', the difficulty in seeing it. Dyer attempts to identify consistencies, tropes, in the cinematic representation of whiteness, arguing that if 'we are to see the historical, cultural and political limitations (to put it mildly) of white world domination, it is important to see similarities, typicalities, within the seemingly infinite variety of white representation.' 'White' begins and ends with circumspection: whiteness, Dyer writes, 'seems not to be there as a subject at all'; as the essay only begins to explore its topic, he 'does not even attempt a rounded conclusion'. These hesitancies serve to acknowledge the scale of the larger project it grazes, to recognise the sizeable undertaking ahead. Indeed, 'White' can be seen as a teaser trailer for the widescreen production that is *White* (1997), Dyer's monographic exploration of the field his shorter piece gestures towards. Since the late 1980s, Dyer has published widely on whiteness. Material from *White* has been reformatted and reworked: an essay published in *The Guardian* in 1997, for example, entitled 'Is the camera racist?', skilfully summarised some of the main points from Chapter 3 of the monograph, 'The light of the world', for the newspaper's readership. Other essays – such as a 1993 piece on Lillian Gish (not included here)[9] and a 2013 analysis of *Dirty Dancing* – have expanded Dyer's arguments.

---

5. José Esteban Muñoz, 'Dead White: Notes on the Whiteness of the New Queer Cinema', *GLQ* 4:1 (1998), pp. 127-138.
6. Isaac Julien and Kobena Mercer, 'Introduction: De Margin and De Centre', *Screen* 29:4 (Autumn 1988), p .3.
7. Stuart Hall, 'New ethnicities', in Kobena Mercer (ed.), *Black Film/British Cinema*, ICA Document 7/British Film Institute Production Special, 1988, pp. 27-31.
8. Julien and Mercer, op. cit., p. 6.
9. Richard Dyer, 'A White Star', *Sight and Sound* 3:8 (August 1993), pp. 22-24.

In 2018, in her contribution to the *Cinema Journal* dossier 'Richard Dyer in the House of Cinema', Miriam J. Petty paid tribute to the enduring power of Dyer's writings on whiteness:

> Far from falling out of style, in this moment of American hostilities that are, by turns, racist, xenophobic, homophobic, and sexist, in this long moment of not-at-all postracial but decidedly post-Obama backlash, [Dyer's] eloquent and wide-ranging explications of whiteness remain indispensable in and out of the classroom. *White* alone is deeply relevant for understanding the catastrophe of Donald Trump's election to the US presidency, a disaster in part about white working-class anger and unrealized claims to unearned privilege.[10]

As though taking this as a prompt, Dyer's short essay 'The president's hair' (2018) offers his own perspective on Trump, reading carefully into one of the defining visual characteristics of the former President, teasing at Trump's tresses. He suggests that, rather than laughing at Donald Trump's hair, it should be taken seriously: 'not just weird and noticeable [...] it also literally embodies what fuels his appalling policies.' Dyer identifies the class and gender connotations of Trump's hair, but argues that its 'most sinister aspect' is that 'it shrieks whiteness.' Trump assumes 'the invisibility, inevitability and unspeakability of white ethnicity', with his policies and political decisions prioritising white Americans. His hair embodies this allegiance. 'If nothing else', Dyer argues, 'we can be grateful for Trump having made whiteness visible and spoken again.'

Whereas Dyer takes on POTUS in 'The president's hair', in 'Of rage and despair' (1981), one of several pieces written for the communist magazine *Comment* that are included in this Reader, he confronts and critiques the monarchy. In particular, he chastises the British media for their attempts to normalise Charles and Diana, the Prince and Princess of Wales, to make the couple seem relatable. There is 'an impossible quest', he argues, to identify 'what Charles and Diana "are really like".' The problem with this fruitless endeavour is that 'it inveigles us into being interested in the royals as people rather than in what they stand for.' The couple, he writes, 'no matter how nice [they] may really be, are still reinforcers of class privilege, white supremacy and traditional male/female roles.' In *White*, Dyer briefly returned his critical gaze to Diana, reading her as representative of 'the image of the glowingly pure white woman', arguing that the 'history of Diana [...] could be told through this imagery, until her fall from grace.'[11] *White* was published in the same year that Diana died.

---

10. Miriam J. Petty, 'Just Another Fan of Yours', *Cinema Journal* 57:2 (Winter 2018), p. 171.
11. Richard Dyer, *White*, London and New York: Routledge, 1997, pp. 131–132.

Between the publication of 'Of rage and despair' in 1981 and Dyer's monograph on whiteness, Diana had become an iconic figure for many LGBTQ+ people, especially gay men; indeed, a photograph of her appeared in the National Portrait Gallery's 'Gay Icons' exhibition in 2009, for which Dyer wrote a catalogue essay (which appears in Section 3 of this Reader).

In 'Of rage and despair', Dyer identifies Charles and Diana as representatives of interlocking dominant power vectors, their class status, whiteness and heterosexuality reinforcing each other. Throughout the writings in this section – and, indeed, across his whole writing career – Dyer's politics are always intersectional, even when he is predominantly attending to one particular facet of identity, one specific topic. Class and racial dynamics, for example, are commented on in 'Don't look now' (1982), his sustained analysis of the codes at play in the male pin-up, and of the instabilities in masculinity such images reveal. And towards the end of his essay on 'Heterosexuality' (1997), he identifies the ways in which race and heterosexuality are imbricated:

> Notions of pure race and the importance of preserving racial purity require the control of male-female coitus and reproduction, but they do not require notions of heterosexual desire. Once this is invented, however, all hell is let loose for racial purists. For heterosexual desire foregrounds the erotics of difference and power imbalance, the very things that also underpin notions of race.

An anti-racist politics could emerge from, take power from, a wholesale demolition of heterosexuality: 'Abandonment of heterosexuality (as opposed to man-woman sex) might also be the means of abandoning racialist obsessions.' Through close scrutiny, dominant power formations need to be made strange, made visible, their intersections and interleaving coaxed apart; only then can they be undermined, potentially reduced to rubble. Ultimately, Dyer writes in the introduction to *The Matter of Images*, the aim of 'making normality strange' should be to decentre it, disempower it. 'That may be the point we wish to reach', he writes, 'but we are not there yet.'[12] His writings on whiteness, masculinity, and heterosexuality pave the way and provide useful tools, but there is much work still to be done.

---

12. Dyer, 'Introduction', op. cit., p. 4.

26 WHITE (1988)

This is an article about a subject that, much of the time as I've been writing it, seems not to be there as a subject at all. Trying to think about the representation of whiteness as an ethnic category in mainstream film is difficult, partly because white power secures its dominance by seeming not to be anything in particular, but also because, when whiteness *qua* whiteness does come into focus, it is often revealed as emptiness, absence, denial or even a kind of death.

It is, all the same, important to try to make some headway with grasping whiteness as a culturally constructed category. 'Images of' studies have looked at groups defined as oppressed, marginal or subordinate — women, the working class, ethnic and other minorities (e.g., lesbians and gay men, disabled people, the elderly). The impulse for such work lies in the sense that how such groups are represented is part of the process of their oppression, marginalisation or subordination. The range and fertility of such work has put those groups themselves centre-stage in both analytical and campaigning activity, and highlighted the issue of representation as politics. It has, however, had one serious drawback, long recognised in debates about women's studies. Looking, with such passion and single-mindedness, at non-dominant groups has had the effect of reproducing the sense of the oddness, differentness, exceptionality of these groups, the feeling that they are departures from the norm. Meanwhile the norm has carried on as if it is the natural, inevitable, ordinary way of being human.

Some efforts are now being made to rectify this, to see that the norm too is constructed, although only with masculinity has anything approaching a proliferation of texts begun. Perhaps it is worth signalling here, before proceeding, two of the pitfalls in the path of such work, two convolutions that especially characterise male writing about masculinity — guilt and me too-ism. Let me state that, while writing here as a white person about whiteness, I do not mean either to display the expiation of my guilt about being white, nor to hint that it is also awful to be white (because it is an inadequate, limiting definition of being human, because feeling guilty is such a burden). Studies of dominance by the dominant should not deny the place of the writer in relation to what s/he is writing about it, but nor should they be the green light for self-recrimination or trying to get in on the act.

Power in contemporary society habitually passes itself off as embodied in the normal as opposed to the superior.[1] This is common to all forms of power, but it works in a peculiarly seductive way with whiteness, because of the way it seems rooted, in common-sense thought, in things other than ethnic difference. The very terms we use to describe the major ethnic divide presented by Western society, 'Black' and 'white', are imported from and naturalised by other discourses. Thus it is said (even in liberal text books) that there are inevitable associations of white with light and therefore safety, and black with dark and therefore danger, and that this explains racism (whereas one might well argue about the safety of the cover of darkness and the danger of exposure to the light); again, and with more justice, people point to the Judaeo-Christian use of white and black to symbolise good and evil, as carried still in such expressions as 'a black mark', 'white magic', 'to blacken the character' and so on.[2] I'd like to look at another aspect of commonsensical conflations of black and white as natural and ethnic categories by considering ideas of what colour is.

I was taught the scientific difference between black and white at primary school. It seemed a fascinating paradox. Black, which, because you had to add it to paper to make a picture, I had always thought of as a colour, was, it turned out, nothingness, the absence of all colour; whereas white, which looked just like empty space (or blank paper), was, apparently, all the colours there were put together. No doubt such explanations of colour have long been outmoded; what interests me is how they manage to touch on the construction of the ethnic categories of Black and white in dominant representation. In the realm of categories, black is always marked as a colour (as the term 'coloured' egregiously acknowledges), and is always particularising; whereas white is not anything really, not an identity, not a particularising quality, because it is everything – white is no colour because it is all colours.

This property of whiteness, to be everything and nothing, is the source of its representational power. On the one hand, as one of the people in the video *Being White*[3] observes, white domination is reproduced by the way that white people 'colonise the definition of normal'. Paul Gilroy similarly spells out the political consequences, in the British context, of the way that whiteness both disappears behind and is subsumed into other identities. He discusses the way that the language of 'the nation' aims to be

---

1. Cf: Herbert Marcuse, *One Dimensional Man*, Boston: Beacon Press, 1964.
2. Cf: Winthrop Jordan, *White over Black*, Harmondsworth: Penguin, 1969; Peter Fryer, *Staying Power*, London: Pluto, 1984.
3. Made by Tony Dowmunt, Maris Clark, Rooney Martin and Kobena Mercer for Albany Video, London.

unifying, permitting even socialists an appeal in terms of 'we' and 'our' 'beyond the margins of sectional interest', but goes on to observe that:

> there is a problem in these plural forms: who do they include, or, more precisely for our purposes, do they help to reproduce Blackness and Englishness as mutually exclusive categories? [...] why are contemporary appeals to 'the people' in danger of transmitting themselves as appeals to the white people?[4]

On the other hand, if the invisibility of whiteness colonises the definition of other norms – class, gender, heterosexuality, nationality and so on – it also masks whiteness as itself a category. White domination is then hard to grasp in terms of the characteristics and practices of white people. No one would deny that, at the very least, there are advantages to being white in Western societies, but it is only avowed racists who have a theory which attributes this to inherent qualities of white people. Otherwise, whiteness is presented more as a case of historical accident, rather than a characteristic cultural/historical construction, achieved through white domination.

The colourless multi-colouredness of whiteness secures white power by making it hard, especially for white people and their media, to 'see' whiteness. This, of course, also makes it hard to analyse. It is the way that Black people are marked as Black (are not just 'people') in representation that has made it relatively easy to analyse their representation, whereas white people – not there as a category and everywhere everything as a fact – are difficult, if not impossible, to analyse *qua* white. The subject seems to fall apart in your hands as soon as you begin. Any instance of white representation is always immediately something more specific – *Brief Encounter* is not about white people, it is about English middle-class people; *The Godfather* is not about white people, it is about Italian-American people; but *The Color Purple* is about Black people, before it is about poor, southern US people.

This problem clearly faced the makers of *Being White*, a pioneering attempt to confront the notion of white identity. The opening vox pop sequence vividly illustrates the problem. Asked how they would define themselves, the white interviewees refer easily to gender, age, nationality or looks but never to ethnicity. Asked if they think of themselves as white, most say that they don't, though one or two speak of being 'proud' or 'comfortable' to be white. In an attempt to get some white people to explore what being white means, the video assembles a group to talk about it

---

4. Paul Gilroy, *There Ain't No Black in the Union Jack*, London: Hutchinson, 1987, pp. 55–56. See also the arguments about feminism and ethnicity in Hazel Carby, 'White Woman Listen! Black Feminism and the Boundaries of Sisterhood' in Centre for Contemporary Cultural Studies, *The Empire Strikes Back*, London: Hutchinson, 1982, pp. 212–23.

and it is here that the problem of white people's inability to see whiteness appears intractable. Sub-categories of whiteness (Irishness, Jewishness, Britishness) take over, so that the particularity of whiteness itself begins to disappear; then gradually, it seems almost inexorably, the participants settle in to talking with confidence about what they know: stereotypes of Black people.

Yet perhaps this slide towards talking about Blackness gives us a clue as to where we might begin to see whiteness – where its difference from Blackness is inescapable and at issue. I shall look here at examples of mainstream cinema whose narratives are marked by the fact of ethnic difference. Other approaches likely to yield interesting results include: the study of the characterisation of whites in Third World or diaspora cinema; images of the white race in avowedly racist and fascist cinema; the use of the 'commutation test',[5] the imaginary substitution of Black for white performers in films such as *Brief Encounter*, say, or *Ordinary People* (if these are unimaginable played by Black actors, what does this tell us about the characteristics of whiteness?) or, related to this, consideration of what ideas of whiteness are implied by such widespread observations as that Sidney Poitier or Diana Ross, say, are to all intents and purposes 'white'. What all these approaches share, however, is reference to that which is not white, as if only non-whiteness can give whiteness any substance. The reverse is not the case – studies of images of Blacks, Native Americans, Jews and other ethnic minorities do not need the comparative element that seems at this stage indispensable for the study of whites.

▲ ▲ ▲

The representation of white *qua* white begins to come into focus – in mainstream cinema, for a white spectator – in films in which non-white characters play a significant role. I want to look at three very different examples here – *Jezebel* (USA, Warner Brothers, 1938), *Simba* (GB, Rank Studios, 1955) and *Night of the Living Dead* (USA, 1969). Each is characteristic of the particular genre and period to which it belongs. *Jezebel* is a large-budget Hollywood feature film (said to have been intended to rival *Gone with the Wind*) built around a female star, Bette Davis; its spectacular pleasures are those of costume and decor, of gracious living, and its emotional pleasures those of tears. *Simba* is a film made as part of Rank's bid to produce films that might successfully challenge Hollywood at the box office, built around a male star, Dirk Bogarde; its spectacular pleasures are those of the travelogue, its emotional ones excitement and also the gratification of seeing 'issues' (here, the Mau-Mau in Kenya) being dealt

---

5. John O. Thompson, 'Screen Acting and the Commutation Test', *Screen* 19:2 (Summer 1978), pp. 55–70.

with. *Night of the Living Dead* is a cheap, independently-produced horror film with no stars; its spectacular and emotional pleasures are those of shock, disgust and suspense, along with the evident political or social symbolism that has aided its cult reputation.

The differences between the three films are important and will inform the ways in which they represent whiteness. There is some point in trying to see this continuity across three, nonetheless significantly different, films. There is no doubt that part of the strength and resilience of stereotypes of non-dominant groups resides in their variation and flexibility — stereotypes are seldom found in a pure form and this is part of the process by which they are naturalised, kept alive.[6] Yet the strength of white representation, as I've suggested, is the apparent absence altogether of the typical, the sense that being white is coterminous with the endless plenitude of human diversity. If we are to see the historical, cultural and political limitations (to put it mildly) of white world domination, it is important to see similarities, typicalities, within the seemingly infinite variety of white representation.

All three films share a perspective that associates whiteness with order, rationality, rigidity, qualities brought out by the contrast with Black disorder, irrationality and looseness. It is their take on this which differs. *Simba* operates with a clear black–white binarism, holding out the possibility that Black people can learn white values but fearing that white people will be engulfed by Blackness. *Jezebel* is far more ambivalent, associating Blackness with the defiance of its female protagonist — whom it does not know whether to condemn or adore. *Night* takes the hint of critique of whiteness in *Jezebel* and takes it to its logical conclusion, where whiteness represents not only rigidity but death.

What these films also share, which helps to sharpen further the sense of whiteness in them, is a situation in which white domination is contested, openly in the text of *Simba* and explicitly acknowledged in *Jezebel*. The narrative of *Simba* is set in motion by the Mau-Mau challenge to British occupation, which also occasions set pieces of debate on the issues of white rule and Black responses to it; the imminent decline of slavery is only once or twice referred to directly in *Jezebel*, but the film can assume the audience knows that slavery was soon ostensibly to disappear from the southern states. Both films are suffused with the sense of white rule being at an end, a source of definite sorrow in *Simba*, but in *Jezebel* producing that mixture of disapproval and nostalgia characteristic of the white representation of the antebellum South. *Night* makes no direct reference to the state of ethnic play but, as I shall argue below, it does

---

6. See T.E. Perkins, 'Rethinking Stereotypes' in Michèle Barrett et al. (eds), *Representation and Cultural Practice*, New York: Croom Helm, pp. 135-59; Steve Neale, 'The Same Old Story', *Screen Education* 32/33 (Autumn/Winter 1979/80), pp. 33-8. For a practical example see the British Film Institute study pack, *The Dumb Blonde Stereotype*.

make implicit reference to the Black uprisings that were part of the historical context of its making, and which many believed would alter irrevocably the nature of power relations between Black and white people in the USA.

The presence of Black people in all three films allows one to see whiteness as whiteness, and in this way relates to the existential psychology that is at the origins of the interest in 'otherness' as an explanatory concept in the representation of ethnicity.[7] Existential psychology, principally in the work of Jean-Paul Sartre, had proposed a model of human growth whereby the individual self becomes aware of itself as a self by perceiving its difference from others. It was other writers who suggested that this process, supposedly at once individual and universal, was in fact socially specific – Simone de Beauvoir arguing that it has to do with the construction of the male ego, Frantz Fanon relating it to the colonial encounter of white and Black. What I want to stress here is less this somewhat metaphysical dimension,[8] more the material basis for the shifts and anxieties in the representation of whiteness suggested by *Simba*, *Jezebel* and *Night*.

The three films relate to situations in which whites hold power in society, but are materially dependent upon Black people. All three films suggest an awareness of this dependency – weakly in *Simba*, strongly but still implicitly in *Jezebel*, inescapable in *Night*. It is this actual dependency of white on Black in a context of continued white power and privilege that throws the legitimacy of white domination into question. What is called for is a demonstration of the virtues of whiteness that would justify continued domination, but this is a problem if whiteness is also invisible, everything and nothing. It is from this that the films' fascinations derive. I shall discuss them here in the order in which they most clearly attempt to hang on to some justification of whiteness, starting, then, with *Simba* and ending with *Night*.

SIMBA

Simba is a characteristic product of the British cinema between about 1945 and 1965 – an entertainment film 'dealing with' a serious issue.[9] It is a colonial adventure film, offering the standard narrative pleasures of adventure with a tale of personal growth. The hero, Alan (Bogarde), arrives in Kenya from England to visit his brother on his farm, finds he has been killed by the Mau-Mau and stays to sort things out (keep the

---

7. See Frantz Fanon, *Black Skin, White Masks*, London: Pluto, 1986; Edward Saïd, *Orientalism*, London: Routledge and Kegan Paul, 1978; Homi K. Bhabha, 'The Other Question – the Stereotype and Colonial Discourse', *Screen* 24:6 (November–December 1983), pp. 18–36.
8. See Benita Parry, 'Problems in Current Theories of Colonial Discourse', *Oxford Literary Review* 9:1–2 (1987), pp. 27–58.
9. See John Hill, *Sex, Class and Realism*, London: BFI, 1986, chaps 4 and 5.

farm going, find out who killed his brother, quell the Mau-Mau). Because the Mau-Mau were a real administrative and ideological problem for British imperialism at the time of the film's making, *Simba* also has to construct a serious discursive context for these pleasures (essentially a moral one, to do with the proper way to treat native peoples; toughness versus niceness). It does this partly through debates and discussions, partly through characters clearly representing what the film takes to be the range of possible angles on the subject (the bigoted whites, the liberal whites, the British-educated Black man, the despotic Black chief) but above all through the figure of the hero, whose adventures and personal growth are occasioned, even made possible, through the process of engaging with the late colonial situation. The way this situation is structured by the film and the way Alan/Bogarde rises to the occasion display the qualities of whiteness.

Simba is founded on the 'Manicheism delirium' identified by Frantz Fanon as characteristic of the colonialist sensibility;[10] it takes what Paul Gilroy refers to as an 'absolutist view of Black and white cultures, as fixed, mutually impermeable expressions of racial and national identity, [which] is a ubiquitous theme in racial "common sense"'.[11] The film is organised around a rigid binarism, with white standing for modernity, reason, order, stability, and black standing for backwardness, irrationality, chaos and violence. This binarism is reproduced in every detail of the film's *mise-en-scène*. A sequence of two succeeding scenes illustrates this clearly – a meeting of the white settlers to discuss the emergency, followed by a meeting of the Mau-Mau. The whites' meeting takes place in early evening, in a fully lit room; characters that speak are shot with standard high key lighting so that they are fully visible; everyone sits in rows and although there is disagreement, some of it hot-tempered and emotional, it is expressed in grammatical discourse in a language the British viewer can understand; moreover, the meeting consists of nothing but speech. The Black meeting, on the other hand, takes place at dead of night, out of doors, with all characters in shadow; even the Mau-Mau leader is lit with extreme sub-Expressionist lighting that dramatizes and distorts his face; grouping is in the form of a broken, uneven circle; what speech there is is ritualised, not reasoned, and remains untranslated (and probably in no authentic language anyway), and most vocal sounds are whooping, gabbling and shrieking; the heart of the meeting is in any case not speech, but daubing with blood and entrails and scarring the body. The return to whiteness after this sequence is once again a return to daylight, a dissolve to the straight lines of European fencing and vegetable plots.

---

10. Frantz Fanon, op. cit., p. 183.
11. Paul Gilroy, op. cit., p. 61; see Errol Lawrence, 'In the Abundance of Water the Fool is Thirsty: Sociology and Black Pathology', in Centre for Contemporary Cultural Studies, op. cit., pp. 95–142.

Binarism in *Simba*'s mise-en-scène: white culture (above) and Black culture (below). (BFI National Archive)

The emphasis on the visible and bounded in this *mise-en-scène* (maintained throughout the film) has to do with the importance of fixity in the stereotyping of others – clear boundaries are characteristic of things white (lines, grids, not speaking till someone else has finished and so on), and also what keeps whites clearly distinct from Blacks. The importance of the process of boundary establishment and maintenance has long been recognised in discussions of stereotyping and representation.[12] This process is functional for dominant groups, but through it the capacity to set boundaries becomes a characteristic attribute of such groups, endlessly reproduced in ritual, costume, language and, in cinema, *mise-en-scène*. Thus, whites and men (especially) become characterised by 'boundariness'.[13]

Simba's binarism is in the broadest sense racist, but not in the narrower sense of operating with a notion of intrinsic and unalterable biological bases for differences between peoples.[14] It is informed rather by a kind of evolutionism, the idea of a path of progress already followed by whites, but in principle open to all human beings – hence the elements in the binarism of modernity versus backwardness. Such evolutionism raises the possibility of Blacks becoming like whites, and it is the belief in this possibility that underpins the views of the liberal characters in the film, Mary (Virginia McKenna) and Dr Hughes (Joseph Tomelty), the latter pleading with his fellow settlers at the meeting to 'reason', not with the Mau-Mau but with the other Africans, who are not beyond the reach of rational discussion. The possibility is further embodied in the character of Peter Karanja (Earl Cameron), the son of the local chief (Orlando Martins), who has trained to be a doctor and is now running a surgery in the village. The film is at great pains to establish that Peter is indeed reasonable, rational, humane, liberal. It is always made quite clear to the viewer that this is so and the representatives of liberalism always believe in him; it is the whites who do not trust him, and one of Alan's moral lessons is in learning to respect Peter's worth. It seems then that part of the film is ready to take the liberal evolutionist position. Yet it is also significant that the spokespeople for liberalism (niceness and reason) are socially subordinate; a woman and an Irish doctor (played for comic eccentricity most of the time), and that liberalism fails, with its representatives (Mary, Peter and now won-over Alan) left at the end of the film crouched in the flames of Alan's farm, rescued from the Mau-Mau in the nick of time by the arrival of the white militia, and Peter dying from wounds inflicted on him by the Mau-Mau (represented as a Black mob). Although with its head, as it were, the film endorses the possibility of a Black person becoming 'white', this is in fact deeply disturbing, setting in motion the anxiety attendant on any loosening of the fixed visibility of the colonised other. This anxiety is established from the start of the film and is the foundation of its narrative.

---

12. E.g., Homi Bhabha, op. cit.; Richard Dyer, 'Stereotyping' in Richard Dyer (ed), *Gays and Film*, London: BFI, 1977, pp. 27–39; Sandor L. Gilman, *Difference and Pathology*, Ithaca: Cornell University Press, 1985.
13. Cf: Nancy Chodorow, *The Reproduction of Mothering*, Berkeley: University of California Press, 1978.
14. Michael Banton, *The Idea of Race*, London: Tavistock, 1977; this restrictive definition of racism has been disputed by, inter alia, Stuart Hall, 'Race, Articulation and Societies Structured in Dominance' in UNESCO, *Sociological Theories: Race and Colonialism*, Paris: UNESCO, 1980.

As is customary in colonial adventure films, *Simba* opens with a panoramic shot of the land, accompanied here by birdsong and the sound of an African man singing. While not especially lush or breathtaking, it is peaceful and attractive. A cry of pain interrupts this mood and we see the man who has been singing stop, get off his bicycle and walk towards its source to find a white man lying covered in blood on the ground. The Black man kneels by his side, apparently about to help him, but then, to the sound of a drum-roll on the soundtrack, draws his machete and plunges it (offscreen) into the wounded man. He then walks back to his bike and rides off. Here is encapsulated the fear that ensues if you can't see Black men behaving as Black men should, the deceptiveness of a Black man in Western clothes riding a bike. This theme is then reiterated throughout the film. Which of the servants can be trusted? How can you tell who is Mau-Mau and who not? Why should Alan trust Peter?

This opening sequence is presented in one long take, using panning. As the man rides off, the sound of a plane is heard, the camera pans up and there is the first cut of the film, to a plane flying through the clouds. There follows (with credits over) a series of aerial shots of the African landscape, in one of which a plane's shadow is seen, and ending with shots of white settlement and then the plane coming to land. Here is another aspect of the film's binarism. The credit sequence uses the dynamics of editing following the more settled feel of the pre-credit long take; it uses aerial shots moving through space, rather than pans with their fixed vantage point; it emphasises the view from above, not that from the ground, and the modernity of air travel after the primitivism of the machete. It also brings the hero to Africa (as we realise when we see Bogarde step off in the first post-credit shot), brings the solution to the problems of deceptive, unfixed appearances set up by the pre-credit sequence.

Simba's binarism both establishes the differences between Black and white and creates the conditions for the film's narrative pleasures – the disturbance of the equilibrium of clear-cut binarism, the resultant conflict that the hero has to resolve. His ability to resolve it is part of his whiteness, just as whiteness is identified in the dynamism of the credit sequence (which in turn relates to the generic expectations of adventure) and in the narrative of personal growth that any colonial text with pretensions also has. The Empire provided a narrative space for the realisation of manhood, both as action and maturation.[15] The colonial landscape is expansive, enabling the hero to roam and giving us the entertainment of action; it is unexplored, giving him the task of discovery and us the pleasures of mystery; it is uncivilised, needing taming, providing the spectacle of power; it is difficult and dangerous, testing his machismo,

---

15. Cf: Stuart Hall, 'The Whites of their Eyes: Racist Ideologies and the Media' in George Bridges and Rosalind Brunt (eds), *Silver Linings*, London: Lawrence and Wishart, 1981, pp. 28–52.

providing us with suspense. In other words, the colonial landscape provides the occasion for the realisation of white male virtues, which are not qualities of being but of doing – acting, discovering, taming, conquering. At the same time, colonialism, as a social, political and economic system, even in fictions, also carries with it challenges of responsibility, of the establishment and maintenance of order, of the application of reason and authority to situations. These, too, are qualities of white manhood that are realised in the process of the colonial text, and very explicitly in *Simba*. When Alan arrives at Nairobi, he is met by Mary, a woman to whom he had proposed when she was visiting England; she had turned him down, telling him, as he recalls on the drive to his brother's farm, that he had 'no sense of responsibility'. Now he realises that she was right; in the course of the film he will learn to be responsible in the process of dealing with the Mau-Mau, and this display of growth will win him Mary.

But this is a late colonial text, characterised by a recognition that the Empire is at an end, and not unaware of some kinds of liberal critique of colonialism. So *Simba* takes a turn that is far more fully explored by, say, *Black Narcissus* (1947) or the Granada TV adaptation of *The Jewel in the Crown* (1984). Here, maturity involves the melancholy recognition of failure. This is explicitly stated, by Sister Clodagh in *Black Narcissus*, to be built into the geographical conditions in which the nuns seek to establish their civilising mission ('I couldn't stop the wind from blowing'); it is endlessly repeated by the nice whites in *The Jewel in the Crown* ('There's nothing I can do!') and symbolised in the lace shawl with butterflies 'caught in the net' that keeps being brought out by the characters. I have already suggested the ways in which liberalism is marginalised and shown to fail in *Simba*. More than this, the hero also fails to realise the generically promised adventure experiences: he is unable to keep his late brother's farm going, nor does he succeed in fighting off a man stealing guns from his house; he fails to catch the fleeing leader of the Mau-Mau, and is unable to prevent them from destroying his house and shooting Peter. The film ends with his property in flames and – a touch common to British social conscience films – with a shot of a young Black boy who symbolises the only possible hope for the future.

The repeated failure of narrative achievement goes along with a sense of white helplessness in the face of the Mau-Mau (the true Black threat), most notably in the transition between the two meeting scenes discussed above. Alan has left the meeting in anger because one of the settlers has criticised the way his brother had dealt with the Africans (too soft); Mary joins him, to comfort him. At the end of their conversation, there is a two-shot of them, with Mary saying of the situation, 'it's like a flood, we're caught in it'. This is accompanied by the sound of drums and is immediately followed by a slow dissolve to Black people walking through the night towards the Mau-Mau meeting. The drums and the dissolve enact Mary's words, that the whites are helpless in the face of the forces of Blackness.

Simba is, then, an endorsement of the moral superiority of white values of reason, order and boundedness, yet suggests a loss of belief in their efficacy. This is a familiar trope of conservatism. At moments, though, there are glimpses of something else, achieved inadvertently perhaps through the casting of Dirk Bogarde. It becomes explicit in the scene between Mary and Alan just mentioned, when Alan says to Mary, 'I was suddenly afraid of what I was feeling', referring to the anger and hatred that the whole situation is bringing out in him and, as Mary says, everyone else. The implication is that the situation evokes in whites the kind of irrational violence supposedly specific to Blacks. Of course, being white means being able to repress it and this is what we seem to see in Alan throughout the film. Such repression constitutes the stoic glory of the imperial hero, but there is something about Bogarde in the part that makes it seem less than admirable or desirable. Whether this is suggested by his acting style, still and controlled, yet with fiercely grinding jaws, rigidly clenched hands and very occasional sudden outbursts of shouting, or by the way Rank was grooming him against the grain of his earlier, sexier image (including its gay overtones),[16] it suggests a notion of whiteness as repression that leads us neatly on to *Jezebel*.

JEZEBEL

Like *Simba*, *Jezebel* depicts a white society characterised by order and rigidity, here expressed principally through codes of behaviour and rules of conduct embodied in set-piece receptions, dinner parties and balls. This does contrast with the bare glimpses we get of Black life in the film, but *Jezebel* also explores the ways in which whiteness is related to Blackness, materially and emotionally dependent on it yet still holding sway over it.

Compositionally, *Jezebel* frequently foregrounds Black people – scenes often open with the camera moving from a Black person (a woman selling flowers in New Orleans, a servant carrying juleps, a boy pulling on a rope to operate a ceiling fan) across or towards white characters; Black people often intrude into the frame while white characters talk. This is particularly noticeable during a dinner-table discussion of the future of slavery; when one of the characters, Pres (Henry Fonda), says that the South will be defeated by machines triumphing over 'unskilled slave labour', the chief Black character, Cato (Lou Payton), leans across our field of vision to pour Pres' wine, literally embodying the fact of slave labour. The film's insistence upon the presence of Black people is important in its perception and construction of the white South. As Jim Pines puts it, 'Black characters do not occupy a significant dramatic function in the film, but their social role nevertheless plays an explicit and relevant part in the conflict that arises between the principal white characters.'[17]

---

16. See Andy Medhurst, 'Dirk Bogarde' in Charles Barr (ed.), *All Our Yesterdays*, London: BFI, 1986, pp. 346-54.
17. Jim Pines, *Blacks in Films*, London: Studio Vista, 1975, p .54.

A set piece dinner party in *Jezebel*: whiteness dependent on Blackness, yet holding sway over it. (BFI National Archive)

A Black character intruding in the frame, while white people talk: selling flowers in New Orleans. (BFI National Archive)

Jezebel is distantly related, through the sympathies of its stars, director and production studio, to progressive ideas on race, making it, as Pines says, 'within the plantation movie tradition […] undoubtedly the most liberal-inclined.'[18] These ideas

---

18. Ibid, p. 55. See also Thomas Cripps, *Slow Fade to Black*, New York: Oxford University Press, 1977, pp. 299, 304.

have to do with the belief or suspicion that Black people have in some sense more 'life' than whites. This idea, and its ambivalences, have a very long history which cannot detain us here. It springs from ideas of the closeness of non-European (and even non-metropolitan) peoples to nature, ideas which were endemic to those processes of European expansion variously termed exploration, nation-building and colonialism.[19] Expansion into other lands placed the humans encountered there as part of the fauna of those lands, to be construed either as the forces of nature that had to be subjugated or, for liberals, the model of sweet natural Man uncontaminated by civilisation. At the same time, ideas of nature have become central to Western thought about being human, such that concepts of human life itself have become inextricable from concepts of nature. Thus the idea that non-whites are more natural than whites also comes to suggest that they have more 'life', a logically meaningless but commonsensically powerful notion.

Jezebel relates to a specific liberal variation on this way of thinking, a tradition in which *Uncle Tom's Cabin* and the Harlem Renaissance are key reference points,[20] as is the role of Annie in Sirk's *Imitation of Life*.[21] Ethel Mannin's statement may be taken as emblematic:

> It is of course that feeling for life which is the secret of the Negro people, as surely as it is the lack of it, and slow atrophy of the capacity to live emotionally, which will be the ultimate decadence of the white civilised people.[22]

'Life' here tends to mean the body, the emotions, sensuality and spirituality; it is usually explicitly counterposed to the mind and the intellect, with the implication that white people's over-investment in the cerebral is cutting them off from life and leading them to crush the life out of others and out of nature itself. The implicit counterposition is, of course, 'death', a point to which I shall return in the discussion of *Night of the Living Dead*.

Jezebel is generally, and rightly, understood to be about the taming of a woman who refuses to live by the Old South's restrictive codes of femininity. It is a clear instance of Molly Haskell's characterisation of one of the available models for strong women's roles in classic Hollywood movies, the 'superfemale', who is 'too ambitious and intelligent for the docile role society has decreed she play' but remains

---

19. See Cedric Robinson, *Black Marxism*, London: Zed Books, 1983.
20. See George Frederickson, *The Black Image in the White Mind*, New York: Harper and Row, 1972; David Levering Lewis, *When Harlem Was in Vogue*, New York: Knopf, 1981.
21. I have discussed this in 'Four Films of Lana Turner', *Movie*, No. 25 (1977-8), pp. 30-52.
22. Ethel Mannin, *Confessions and Impressions*, New York: Doubleday, Doran, 1930, p. 157.

'exceedingly "feminine" and flirtatious' and 'within traditional society', turning her energies on those around her, 'with demonic results'.[23] Davis' character, Julie, is strong, defiant of convention (for example, striding into the bank, a place that women do not enter), refusing to behave in the genteel way her fiancé, Pres, requires of her. The trajectory of the narrative is her punishment and moral growth, in two stages. She learns to conceal her defiance and energy beneath an assumption of femininity, but this is still not enough, since it is still there in the malignant form indicated by Haskell; it is only by literally sacrificing herself (accompanying Pres, who has caught yellow jack fever, to Red Island, where fever victims are isolated) that the film is able to reach a satisfactory, transcendantly punishing climax. All of this is entirely understandable within a gender frame of reference; but the film also relates Julie's energies to Blackness, suggesting that her trajectory is a specifically white, as well as female, one.

The most famous scene in the film is the Olympus Ball, at which all the unmarried women wear white. Julie, to embarrass Pres and to cock a snook at out-dated convention ('This is 1852, not the Dark Ages – girls don't have to simper about in white just 'cos they're not married'), decides to wear a red dress. The immediate scandal is not just the refusal to conform and uphold the celebration of virginity that the white dress code represents, but the sexual connotations of the dress itself, satin and red, connotations made explicit in a scene at the dress-maker's ('Saucy, isn't it?', says Julie; 'And vulgar', says her aunt, with which Julie enthusiastically concurs). This is the dress of Julie's that her Black maid Zette (Theresa Harris) most covets, and after the ball, Julie gives it to her. It is precisely its *colourfulness* that, stereotyping informs us, draws Zette – the dress is 'marked' as coloured, a definite, bold colour heightened by a flashy fabric, just as Black representation is. Thus what appears to be symbolism (white for virginity, colour for sex) within a universally applicable communication circuit becomes ethnically specific. The primary association of white with chastity is inextricably tied to not being dark and colourful, not being non-white, and the defiance and vitality narratively associated with Julie's wearing of the dress is associated with the qualities embodied by Black women, qualities that Julie as a white woman must not display, or even have. Of course, the red dress looks merely dark in this black and white film.

Wearing the dress causes a rift between Julie and Pres; shortly after, he leaves for the North on business. By the time he returns, Julie has learned to behave as a white woman should. Once again, the specific whiteness of this is revealed through the figure of Zette. There is, for instance, a scene in which Julie is getting ready for the arrival of Pres at a house party at her aunt's plantation. In her room she moves restlessly about, with Zette hanging on to her as she tries to undo Julie's dress at the back; Zette's

---

23. Molly Haskell, *From Reverence to Rape*, New York: Holt, Rinehart and Winston, 1974, p. 214.

Flouting convention: the red dress at the Olympus Ball. (BFI National Archive)

movements are entirely determined by Julie's but Zette is attending to the basic clothing while Julie is just fussing about. When Julie thinks she hears a carriage coming, she sends Zette to check; Zette runs from the room, and the film cuts to the huge hallway, showing us all of Zette's rapid descent of the stairs and run to the door, before cutting again to show her calling out to the man and boy in livery waiting for carriages at the gate. This apparently unnecessarily elongated sequence not only helps whip up excitement and anticipation at Pres' arrival, but also gives Julie time to take off one dress and put on another, a potentially titillating sight that would not be shown in this kind of film in this period. But using a sequence centred on a Black woman is not only a device to heighten suspense and bypass a taboo image – it works as seamlessly well as it does because it is also appropriate to show a Black woman here.

By this stage in the film, Julie has learned the behaviour appropriate to a white woman in her position. Earlier in the film she openly expressed her passion and defiance; now, awaiting Pres, she has learned to behave as she should. She no longer expresses feeling – she 'lives' through Zette. Zette has to express excited anticipation, not in speech, but in physical action, running the length of a long stair and spacious hallway. It is Zette's excited body in action that we see, instead of Julie's body disrobed and enrobed. When Julie hears the servants at the gate call out, 'Carriage is coming!', she sends Zette to the window to see if it is Pres. The excitement mounts as the carriage draws near. There is a rapid montage of Black people: Zette shot from below at a dynamic angle looking for the carriage, the servants at the gate no longer still but the man moving about, the boy leaping in anticipation, and crowds of hitherto unseen Black children running to the gate, jumping and cavorting. Meanwhile Julie remains perfectly still, only her eyes, in characteristic Davis fashion, darting and dilating with suspense; perfectly, luminously lit, she says nothing, expresses nothing with her body – it is Black people who bodily express her desire.

This use of Black people to express, to 'live', the physical dimension of Julie's life is found throughout the film, most notably after her manipulations have gone awry to the point that one of her old flames, Buck (George Brent), is now about to duel with

Julie with the plantation workers gathered to entertain her guests. (BFI National Archive)

Pres' brother. The Black plantation workers have gathered at the house to entertain the white guests ('a quaint old custom down here', says Julie to Pres' new, and Northern, wife, Amy). As they arrive they sing a song about marrying, heard over shots of Julie, a bitterly ironic counterpoint. She shushes the chorus and tells them to start singing, 'Gonna Raise a Ruckus Tonight', then goes to the edge of the verandah and sits down, beckoning the Black children to gather close round her, before joining in with the singing. The song is a jolly one and the shots of the Black singers show them in happy-go-lucky Sambo style, but the last shot of the sequence closes on Julie, near to tears against the sound of this cheerful singing. The power of the sequence does not come from this ironic counterpoint alone, but also from the way that Julie, by merging as nearly as possible with the singers and joining in the song, is able to express her pent-up feelings of frustration, anger, jealousy and fear, feelings for which there is no white mode of expression, which can only be lived through Blacks.

The point of *Jezebel* is not that whites are different from Blacks, but that whites live by different rules. Unlike the two women with whom she is compared, her aunt and Amy, Julie cannot be 'white'. It is her aunt and Amy who confirm that whites are calm, controlled, rational; Julie transgresses, but in the process reveals white calm as an imposition, a form of repression of life. The film's ambivalence lies in its being a vehicle for Davis. She/Julie is a 'Jezebel', a byword for female wickedness, but nonetheless a star with a huge female following, and who is shot here with the kind of radiance and glow Hollywood reserved for its favoured women stars. There is no doubt that what Julie does is wicked and that her punishment is to be understood as richly deserved; but there is also no doubt that she is to be adored and precisely, as I've tried to argue, because she does not conform to notions of white womanhood.

NIGHT OF THE LIVING DEAD

If Blacks have more 'life' than whites, then it must follow that whites have more 'death' than Blacks. This thought has seldom been explored so devastatingly as in the living dead films directed by George Romero – *Night of the Living Dead* (1969), *Dawn of the Dead* (1978) and *Day of the Dead* (1985).

The *Dead* films are unusual among horror films for the explicitness of their political allegory and unique for having as their heroes 'positive' Black men. In general, the latter have been applauded merely as an instance of affirmative action, casting colour blind a Black man in a part which could equally well have gone to a white actor. As Robin Wood notes, however, 'it is not true that [their] colour is arbitrary and without meaning'; Ben's Blackness in *Night* is used 'to signify his difference from the other

Whiteness and death equated in *Night of the Living Dead*. (BFI National Archive)

characters, to set him apart from their norms',[24] while Peter's in *Dawn* again indicates 'his separation from the norms of white-dominated society and his partial exemption from its constraints'.[25] In all three films, it is significant that the hero is a Black man, and not just because this makes him 'different', but because it makes it possible to see that whites are the living dead. I shall confine detailed discussion here to the first film of the trilogy.

All the dead in *Night* are whites. In a number of places, the film shows that living whites are like, or can be mistaken for, the dead. The radio states that the zombies are 'ordinary looking people', and the first one we see in the film does look in the distance like some ordinary old white guy wandering about the cemetery, somehow menacing, yet not obviously abnormal. John, the brother in the opening sequence, recalls

---

24. Robin Wood, *Hollywood from Vietnam to Reagan*, New York: Columbia University Press, 1986, p. 116.
25. Ibid, p. 120.

pretending to be something scary to frighten Barb when they visited the graveyard as children; he imitates the famous zombie voice of Boris Karloff to scare her now. Halfway through the film, Barb becomes catatonic, like a dead person. The other developed white characters emerge from where they have been hiding, 'buried' in the cellar. Towards the end of the film, there is an aerial shot from the point of view of a helicopter involved in the destruction of the zombies; it looks down on a straggling line of people moving forward uncertainly but inexorably, in exactly the same formation as earlier shots of the zombies. It is only with a cut to a ground level shot that we realise this is a line of vigilantes, not zombies.

Living and dead whites are indistinguishable, and the zombies' sole *raison d'être*, to attack and eat the living, has resonances with the behaviour of the living whites. The vigilantes shoot and destroy the zombies with equanimity ('Beat 'em or burn 'em – they go up pretty good', says their leader, Chief McLelland), finally including the living – the hero, Ben (Duane Jones) – in their single-minded operations. Brother John torments Barb while living, and consumes her when he is dead. Helen and Harry Cooper bicker and snipe constantly, until their dead daughter Carrie first destroys, then eats them. The young couple, Tom and Judy, destined generically to settle down at the end of the film, instead go up in flames through Tom's stupidity and Judy's paralysed response to danger.

If whiteness and death are equated, both are further associated with the USA. That the film can be taken as a metaphor for the United States is established right at the start of the film. It opens on a car driving through apparently unpopulated back roads suggesting the road tradition of 1950s and '60s US culture – the novel *On the Road* (1957), the film *Easy Rider* (1969) with its idea of the 'search for America'. When the car reaches the graveyard (the US?), a Stars and Stripes flag flutters in the foreground. The house in which the characters take shelter is archetypally middle, backwoods North American – a white wooden structure, with lace curtains, cut-glass ornaments, chintz armchairs. It, too, is immediately associated with death, in a series of shock cuts from Barb, exploring the house, to stuffed animal heads hung on the walls. Casting further heightens the all-Americanness of these zombie-like living whites. Barb is ultra-blonde and pale, and her name surely suggests the USA's bestselling doll; John is a preppy type, clean cut with straight fair hair, a white shirt with pens in the pocket, straight out of a Brooks Brothers advertisement. Judy too is dazzlingly blonde, though Tom and the Coopers are more nondescript whites.

What finally forces home the specifically white dimension of these zombie-US links are the ways in which the zombies can be destroyed. The first recalls the liberal critique of whites as ruled by their heads; as the radio announcer says, 'Kill the brain and you kill the ghoul' since, it seems, zombies/whites are nothing but their brains. The film diverges from earlier representations of the black/white, life/death opposition by representing Ben's 'life' quality in terms of practical skill, rather than innate qualities of 'being'. Particularly striking is a scene in which Ben talks about what they need to do as he dismantles a table to make boards for the windows, while Barb takes the lace cloth from it, folds and cradles it, hanging on uselessly to this token of gentility while Ben tries to ensure their survival.

The alternative way of destroying the zombies is burning. Some of the imagery, particularly the molotov cocktails going up around empty cars, seems to recall, in its grainy black-and-white texture, newspaper coverage of the ghetto uprisings of the late '60s, and the 'fire', as an image of Black Power's threat to white people, had wide currency (most notably in the title of James Baldwin's 1963 *The Fire Next Time*). The zombies are scared of light as well as fire, and Ben is associated with both, not only because of his skill in warding off the zombies with torches, but in the way he is introduced into the film. Barb wanders out of the house into the glare of a car's headlights, out of which Ben seems to emerge; a shot of the lights glaring into the camera is followed by another with Ben moving into the frame, his white shirt first, then his Black face filling the frame in front of the light, in a reversal of the good/bad, white/black, light/darkness antinomies of Western culture.

The film ends with the white vigilantes (indistinguishable from the zombies, remember) killing Ben, the representative of life in the film. Much of the imagery of *Night* carries over into *Dawn*, despite their many differences (most notably the latter's strong vein of humour). The opening sequence has white militia gleefully destroying living Blacks and Hispanics who refuse to leave their tenement homes during the zombie emergency; as in *Night*, the Black hero, Peter (Ken Foree), emerges from the light (this time from behind a white sheet with strong, bright light flooded unnaturalistically behind it); it is his practical skills that enable him to survive, skills that only the white woman, Fran (Gaylen Ross), is ultimately able to emulate. Zombieness is still linked with whiteness, even though some of the dead are Black or Hispanic – a Black zombie who attacks a living Black man in the tenement is whited up, the colour contrast between the two emphasised in a shot of the whitened Black zombie biting the living Black man's neck; in the shopping mall, an overt symbol of the US way of life, editing rhymes the zombies with the shop mannequins, all of whom are white.

Day extends the critique of US values to the military-industrial complex, with its underpinnings in masculine supremacy.[26] As Robin Wood argues, the white men and the zombies alike are characterised by 'the conditioned reflex', the application to human affairs of relentless rationality; the scientist, Logan, teaches one of the zombies to be human again, which in practice means killing the military leader, Rhodes,

---

26. Robin Wood, 'The Woman's Nightmare: Masculinity in *The Day of the Dead*', *CineAction!* 6 (August 1986), pp. 45-49.

out of atavistic loyalty to Logan. When Logan earlier tells Rhodes that what he is teaching the zombies is 'civility', to make them like the living, there is a sudden cut to a sequence of the men gleefully, sadistically corralling the zombies to be specimens for Logan's crazed experiments. The whiteness of all this is pointed, as before, by the presence of a Black character, John (Terry Alexander), who is even more dissociated from both zombies and white male values than were Ben and Peter in the earlier films. He is not only Black but West Indian, and he offers the idea of finding an island as the only hope for the two white characters (a WASP woman, Sarah, and an Irish man, Billy) not irrevocably implicated in white male values. He and Billy are not only socially marginal, but also live separately from the soldiers and scientists, having set up a mock home together in the outer reaches of the underground bunker they all share. All the other living characters are redneck males, and although there is a power struggle between them, they are both more like each other and like the zombies than they are like John, Sarah or Billy. At the end of one scene, where Rhodes has established his authority over Logan, there is a final shot of John, who has looked on saying nothing; he rubs the corner of his mouth with his finger ironically, then smiles sweetly at Rhodes, an expression of ineffably insolent refusal of the white boys' games.

The *Dead* films are of course horror movies and there is a danger, as Pete Boss has pointed out, that the kind of political readings that I and others have given them may not be easy 'to integrate […] with the fantasies of physical degradation and vulnerability' characteristic of the contemporary horror film.[27] However, the use of 'body horror' in the *Dead* films to represent whiteness is not simply symbolism, making use of what happens to the genre's current conventions. On the contrary, body horror is the horror of whiteness and the films' gory pleasures are like an inverted reprise of the images of whiteness that are touched on in *Simba* and *Jezebel*.

The point about Ben, Peter and John is that in their different ways they all have control over their bodies, are able to use them to survive, know how to do things with them. The white characters (with the exception of Fran, Sarah and Billy) lose that control while alive, and come back in the monstrously uncontrolled for transgressed m of zombieness. The hysterical boundedness of the white body is grotesquely[28] transgressed as whites/zombies gouge out living white arms, pull out organs, munch at orifices. The spectre of white loss of control is evoked by the way the zombies stumble and dribble in their inexorable quest for blood, often with intestines spilling out or severed limbs dangling. White over-investment in the brain is mercilessly undermined as brains spatter against the wall and zombies flop to the ground. 'The fear of one's own body, of

---

27. Pete Boss, 'Vile Bodies and Bad Medicine', *Screen* 27:1 (January–February 1986), p. 18.
28. Cf. the discussion of the grotesque carnivalesque body in Mikhail Bakhtin, *Rabelais and His World*, Bloomington: Indiana University Press, 1984.

how one controls it and relates to it'[29] and the fear of not being able to control other bodies, those bodies whose exploitation is so fundamental to capitalist economy, are both at the heart of whiteness. Never has this horror been more deliriously evoked than in these films of the *Dead*.

▲ ▲ ▲

Because my aim has been to open up an area of investigation, I shall not even attempt a rounded conclusion. Instead, let me start off again on another tack, suggested by the passing references to light and colour above. I suspect that there is some very interesting work to be done on the invention of photography and the development of lighting codes in relation to the white face, which results in the technicist ideology that one sometimes hears of it being 'more difficult' to photograph Black people. Be that as it may, it is the case that the codes of glamour lighting in Hollywood were developed in relation to white women, to endow them with a glow and radiance that has correspondences with the transcendental rhetoric of popular Christianity.

Of no woman star was this more true than Marilyn Monroe, known by the press at the time as 'the Body'. I've argued elsewhere that her image is an inescapably and necessarily white one;[30] in many of her films this combines with the conventions of glamour lighting to make her disappear as flesh and blood even more thoroughly than is the case with other women stars. Her first appearance in *The Seven Year Itch* (1955), for instance, is a classic instance of woman as spectacle caught in a shot from the male protagonist's point of view. It opens on Richard (Tom Ewell), on his hands and knees on the floor looking for something, bottom sticking up, a milk bottle between his legs – the male body shown, as is routine in sex comedies, as ludicrously grotesque; he hears the doorbell and opens the door to his flat; as the door opens light floods in on him; he looks and there is a cut to the hall doorway, where the curvy shape of a woman is visible through the frosted glass. The woman's shape is placed exactly within the frame of the door window, the doorway is at the end of the hall, exactly in the centre of the frame; a set of enclosing rectangles create a strong sense of perspective, and emphasise the direction of Richard's/our gaze. The colouring of the screen is pinky-white and light emanates from behind the doorway where the woman is. All we see of her is her silhouette, defining her proportions, but she also looks translucent. The film cuts back to Richard, his jaw open in awe, bathed in stellar light. Later in the film, when the Monroe character's tomato plant crashes onto Richard's patio, we

---

29. Philip Brophy, 'Horrality – the Textuality of Contemporary Horror Films', *Screen* 27:1 (January–February 1986), p. 8.
30. Richard Dyer, *Heavenly Bodies*, London: Macmillan, 1986, pp. 42–45.

have another shot of her from Richard's point of view. He looks up, and there is a cut to Monroe looking down from her balcony, apparently nude; the wall behind her is dark, as is the vegetation on the balcony, so her face and shoulders stand out as white. Such moments conflate unreal angel-glow with sexual aura.

The Seven Year Itch is a very smart film. Through innumerable gags and cross-references, it lets on that it knows about male fantasy and its remote relation to reality. Yet it is also part of the Monroe industry, peddling an impossible dream, offering another specifically white ideal as if it embodies all heterosexual male yearning, offering another white image that dissolves in the light of its denial of its own specificity.

White women are constructed as the apotheosis of desirability, all that a man could want, yet nothing that can be had, nor anything that a woman can be. But, as I have argued, white representation *in general* has this everything-and-nothing quality.

Originally published in *Screen* 29:4 (October 1988), pp. 44–64.

27 JEAN-JACQUES ROUSSEAU AND THE RIGHT TO LOVE ONESELF (1968)

One thing of which Jean-Jacques was always convinced was that he loved people. He felt that he was born affectionate, that there was within him an outward-going impulse to love others. And yet when, after a strange and rootless youth, he went to Paris, he found that he just couldn't cope with people, he found that he began to loath people and everything about them.

Although he does not articulate it until near the very end of his life, Jean-Jacques' actions were nearly always guided by self-love. That is, he did by and large what he instinctively felt to be best for him. And what was best for a young man with no knowledge of any but a simple, country community was a subsistence level of income and friendship. To talk of self-love as ambition in the case of Jean-Jacques would be as irrelevant to our discussion as it would have been inconceivable to him. Thus, he wandered about somewhat aimlessly, achieving from time to time magical friendships which he was never to forget. Then he went to Paris.

At Paris, too, he made friends, but none that lasted or that he cherished in his memory. On the whole, he had a miserable time, especially after he had become famous for writing a pamphlet attacking the decadence of the age. He couldn't understand it at first: these were people like himself and those he had loved in the days of his youth. Yet they were mean and sought only to gain an advantage over one another. This, too, was self-love but unlike Jean-Jacques': the self-love of his Parisian contemporaries seemed vicious and destructive. He hated it and wrote a pamphlet against it.

Yet, even in this first pamphlet he has begun to identify the reason for the viciousness of society. And he found precisely that there were forces behind society which set up all sorts of pressures upon the individuals within society. These pressures, whose prime manifestation is ambition, can be traced back to the need men had to co-operate to survive and the bartering and division of labour consequent on such co-operation. It was economic pressures, and particularly trading and mercantile pressures, which allowed wealth to accrue to he who was clever enough to manipulate the system. And as people get richer, so they are inclined to think themselves better, and instead of co-operating for the mutual benefit of all concerned, they start competing, first socially and politically. The machine is set in motion and by the eighteenth century its complexity is considerable. The social pressures created by economic needs have produced civilisation, morality, art – all those embellishments whereby one man may triumph over another, or else, by giving him such lofty names, appease his conscience.

It is magnificent polemic. And as time went on, Jean-Jacques came to see more and more clearly that what was wrong with men, what made them unhappy, was not their nature but their situation.

Situation, however, can be changed. If man is victim of a machine, still, it is only a machine, and it contains within it the instruments by which it may be altered: education and politics.

The trouble with education, as Jean-Jacques saw it, was that its aim was to mould people for society, rather than to teach them to love themselves by doing what is best for themselves. So, at great length and in remarkable detail, he wrote a treatise on education, showing how a child, if left to his own devices except in so far as this might prove dangerous, would teach himself, would see for himself what was best for him and what was worst. And when, in this sense he had grown up, you could introduce him into society.

However, by the time you've educated your first generation, as Jean-Jacques envisaged (i.e., by the time your first generation is of its own endeavours grown up), you would, too, have re-ordered the political machine and thus the society for which a child so educated is destined. This society would be based upon true co-operation among the individuals that made it up, who would all love themselves and do what was best for themselves. And what was best for each must be the health of the society in which they lived, and co-operated, and what is unhealthy is competitiveness and the triumph of one man over another. So that, if there would have to be legal and economic restraints, they would only be to safeguard the health of the relationships between the individuals in society.

What is so unbearable about reading what Jean-Jacques said is that it is not like reading some crazy utopian idealist. If it were, you could bear it that nobody had really taken him to heart, that people had just picked bits out to support their own theories and prejudices, that they had loved themselves in precisely the way that ultimately was to be worst for themselves and for their relationships with others.

And perhaps even as he was writing his great works, which also include a tedious but at times wonderful novel which is really a treatise on love (*Julie, or the New Eloisa*), he realised that no one would really take any notice. His voice, compellingly lyrical as it was, was perhaps not enough on its own to stop the inexorable growth of the machine. Indeed, Jean-Jacques' ideas could even be sucked in with all the other trash, and used as yet another pressure. It is true to say – and yet how unfair – that totalitarianism (fascist or communist or imperialist) and the cheapness of the expression we give to our emotions can be traced back to Jean-Jacques (and of course beyond).

And at another level, Jean-Jacques felt that, dearly as he believed in his ideas, his literary life was a betrayal of all he stood for; he had as it were joined in the game and was little more himself than a fashionable if awkward philosopher on the eighteenth century cultural 'scene'. And so he opted out, because if he were to remain himself, to express and to contribute to others all that was best in and for himself, he would have to do so in a context which did not make the kinds of demands that society imposes.

This was a supreme act of self-love, and if it seems close to selfishness, then this is only because we judge him according to that very artificial system of values which Jean-Jacques rebelled against. A system which is not necessary and not absolute and the gratuitousness of whose existence Jean-Jacques felt with all the more anguish as he understood its power.

He opted out then, but only in order to realise the fullness of his own personality. He would learn truly to love himself, to accept himself. That this decision was motivated in part by a conviction that he was being deliberately persecuted by men is undeniable, but again if we dismiss Jean-Jacques' decision as the weakness of a paranoid, we are merely speaking again for the status quo. It could after all be that it is not him but we who are sick. Of course, few want to harm Jean-Jacques, but that the blind exigencies of society were a threat to his integrity is an insight so overwhelming that Jean-Jacques was bound to conventionalise it into what we call paranoia. Because if an individual has the courage to deny that the system upon which society is built and which dictates or pressurises the actions of that society is necessary, then he is at war with that society. It may after all be that he is all too sane, and that we are but the puppets of the machine when we dismiss Jean-Jacques as a lunatic.

Jean-Jacques then saw that what religious moralists throughout the ages had condemned as iniquitous, the love of oneself, is the most basic impulse of the human mind, but that mere gratifications of immediate whims is the very opposite of self-love. And because gratification was the main value (the most marketable?) offered by society, he opted out, in order to realise the true values that self-love offers.

Nor does Jean-Jacques speak of self-love as a natural right. For Jean-Jacques there are no natural rights: neither absolute God-given precepts nor tyranny are admissible concepts of basic human rights. Rather, his works suggest that we have the right to love ourselves because no one and nothing has the right to forbid our doing so, and because self-love is the only necessary condition for living bearably on earth. From it, all else follows.

A right is usually a moral imperative for which there is no justification. By denying that rights are valid, Jean-Jacques in effect asserts that we have a right to do anything at all really, in so far as we haven't got the right to do anything. And self-love is the most valuable thing to which we can claim, by this argument, a right.

Nor perhaps need it be necessary to opt out as Jean-Jacques felt it was. Perhaps it is not too late to do some of the things he – and others like him – saw needed doing. Perhaps, on a national scale, that is what is happening among the Vietcong, or American Blacks, or even the Scottish Nationalists: they are asserting their right to be themselves, because they deny that any power, however strong, has the right to deny them anything whatsoever.

And perhaps Jean-Jacques did not suffer wholly in vain.

Originally published in *Helikon*, Dundee: John Durham and Son, 1968, pp. 31–32.

28 THE ROLE OF STEREOTYPES (1979)

The word 'stereotype' is today almost always a term of abuse. This stems from the wholly justified objections of various groups – in recent years, Blacks, women and gays, in particular[1] – to the ways in which they find themselves stereotyped in the mass media and in everyday speech. Yet when Walter Lippmann coined the term, he did not intend it to have a wholly and necessarily pejorative connotation. Taking a certain ironic distance on his subject, Lippmann nonetheless lays out very clearly both the absolute necessity for, and the usefulness of, stereotypes, as well as their limitations and ideological implications:

> A pattern of stereotypes is not neutral. It is not merely a way of substituting order for the great blooming, buzzing confusion of reality. It is not merely a short cut. It is all these things and something more. It is the guarantee of our self-respect; it is the projection upon the world of our own sense of our own value, our own position and our own rights. The stereotypes are, therefore, highly charged with the feelings that are attached to them. They are the fortress of our tradition, and behind its defenses we can continue to feel ourselves safe in the position we occupy.[2]

We can begin to understand something of how stereotypes work by following up the ideas raised by Lippmann – in particular his stress on stereotypes as (i) an ordering process, (ii) a 'short cut', (iii) referring to 'the world', and (iv) expressing 'our' values and beliefs. The rest of this essay is structured around these topics, concluding with some tentative remarks on the relevance of what has gone before to the representation of alcoholism. Throughout, I move between the more sociological concern of Lippmann (how stereotypes function in social thought) and the specific aesthetic concerns (how stereotypes function in fictions) that must also be introduced into any consideration of media representations. The position behind all these considerations is that it is not stereotypes, as an aspect of human thought and representation, that are wrong, but who controls and defines them, what interests they serve.

---

1. In relation to film, see Jim Pines, *Blacks and Films*, London: Studio Vista, 1975; Claire Johnston (ed.), *Notes on Women's Cinema*, London: SEFT, 1973; Richard Dyer (ed.), *Gays and Film*, London: BFI, 1977, *inter alia*.
2. Walter Lippmann, *Public Opinion*, New York: Macmillan, 1956, p. 96. (First published 1922.)

(i) Stereotypes as a form of 'ordering' the mass of complex and inchoate data that we receive from the world are only a particular form – to do with the representation and categorisation of persons[3] – of the wider process by which any human society, and individuals within it, make sense of that society through generalities, patternings and 'typifications'. Unless one believes that there is some definitively 'true' order in the world which is transparently revealed to human beings and unproblematically expressed in their culture – a belief that the variety of orders proposed by different societies, as analysed by anthropology and history, makes difficult to sustain – this activity of ordering, including the use of stereotypes, has to be acknowledged as a necessary, indeed inescapable, part of the way societies make sense of themselves, and hence actually make and reproduce themselves. (The fact that all such orderings are, by definition, partial and limited does not mean that they are untrue – partial knowledge is not false knowledge, it is simply not absolute knowledge.)

There are, however, two problems about stereotypes within this perspective. Firstly, the need to order 'the great blooming, buzzing confusion of reality' is liable to be accompanied by a belief in the absoluteness and certainty of any particular order, a refusal to recognise its limitations and partiality, its relativity and changeability, and a corresponding incapacity to deal with the fact and experience of blooming and buzzing.

Secondly, as the work of Peter Berger and Thomas Luckmann, amongst others, on the 'social construction of reality' stresses, not only is any given society's ordering of reality an historical product but it is also necessarily implicated in the power relations in that society – as Berger and Luckmann put it, 'he who has the bigger stick has the better chance of imposing his definitions of reality.'[4] I shall return below to these two problems of Lippmann's formulation – order (stereotypes) perceived as absolute and rigid, order (stereotypes) as grounded in social power.

(ii) Lippmann's notion of stereotypes as a short cut points to the manner in which stereotypes are a very simple, striking, easily-grasped form of representation but are nonetheless capable of condensing a great deal of complex information and a host of connotations. As T.E. Perkins notes in her key article 'Rethinking Stereotypes', the often observed 'simplicity' of stereotypes is deceptive:

> to refer 'correctly' to someone as a 'dumb blonde', and to understand what is meant by that, implies a great deal more than hair colour and intelligence. It refers immediately to

---

[3]. I confine myself here to the discussion of stereotypes as a form of representing persons, although the word itself (especially in adjectival form) is also used to refer to ideas, behaviour, settings, etc.

[4]. Peter Berger and Thomas Luckmann, *The Social Construction of Reality*, Harmondsworth: Penguin, 1967, p. 127. It should be pointed out that Berger and Luckmann do not follow up this question of power as insistently as they might.

her sex, which refers to her status in society, her relationship to men, her inability to behave or think rationally, and so on. In short, it implies knowledge of a complex social structure.[5]

The same point emerges from Arnold S. Linsky's analysis of the representation of the alcoholic in popular magazines between 1900 and 1966, where changing depictions of alcoholics are shown to express complex and contradictory social theories, not merely of alcoholism but of free will and determinism.[6]

(iii) Lippmann refers to stereotypes as a projection on to the 'world'. Although he is not primarily concerned to distinguish stereotypes from modes of representation whose principal concern is not the world, it is important for us to do so, especially as our focus is representations in media *fictions*, which are aesthetic as well as social constructs. In this perspective, stereotypes are a particular sub-category of a broader category of fictional characters, the type. Whereas stereotypes are essentially defined, as in Lippmann, by their social function, types, at this level of generality, are primarily defined by their aesthetic function, namely, as a mode of characterisation in fiction. The type is any character constructed through the use of a few immediately recognizable and defining traits, that do not change or 'develop' through the course of the narrative and which point to general, recurrent features of the human world (whether these features are conceptualised as universal and eternal, the 'archetype', or historically and culturally specific, 'social types' and 'stereotypes' – a distinction discussed below).[7] The opposite of the type is the novelistic character, defined by a multiplicity of traits that are only gradually revealed to us through the course of the narrative, a narrative which is hinged on the growth or development of the character and is thus centred upon the latter in her or his unique individuality, rather than pointing outwards to a world.

In our society, it is the novelistic character that is privileged over the type,[8] for the obvious reason that our society privileges – at any rate, at the level of social rhetoric – the individual over the collective or the mass. For this reason, the majority of fictions

---

5. T.E. Perkins, 'Rethinking Stereotypes' in Michèle Barrett, Phil Corrigan, Annette Kuhn and Janet Wolff (eds), *Ideology and Cultural Production*, New York: Croom Helm, 1979, p. 139.
6. Arnold S. Linsky, 'Theories of behaviour and the image of the alcoholic in popular magazines 1900–1960', *Public Opinion Quarterly* 34 (Winter 1970-71), pp. 573–81.
7. It is important to stress the role of conceptualisation in the distinction between, on the one hand, archetypes, and, on the other, social and stereotypes, since what may be attributed to a type as a universal and eternal trait, hence making it archetypal, may only be a historically and culturally specific trait misunderstood as a universal and eternal trait – it is, after all, the tendency of dominant value systems in societies to pass their values off as universally and eternally valid.
8. See Ian Watt, *The Rise of the Novel*, Harmondsworth: Penguin, 1963, for a discussion of the specificity of such characterisation to the novel form and hence to modern capitalist societies. The distinction between type and novelistic character is discussed in *The Dumb Blonde Stereotype*, BFI Educational Advisory Service, 1979.

that address themselves to general social issues tend nevertheless to end up telling the story of a particular individual, hence returning social issues to purely personal and psychological ones. Once we address ourselves to the representation and definition of social categories – e.g. alcoholics – we have to consider what is at stake in one mode of characterisation rather than another. Where do we want the emphasis of the representation to lie – on the psychological (alcoholism as a personal problem), on the social (alcoholism as an aspect of society) or in some articulation of the two? The choice or advocacy of a more novelistic or a more typical representation implicitly expresses one or other of these emphases.[9]

(iv) It is Lippmann's reference to *our* tradition, and indeed his use of 'our' and 'we' throughout the passage quoted, that takes us into the most important, and most problematic, issue in stereotyping. For we have to ask, who exactly is the 'we' and 'us' invoked by Lippmann? – is it necessarily you and me?

The effectiveness of stereotypes resides in the way they invoke a consensus. Stereotypes proclaim, 'This is what everyone – you, me and us – thinks members of such-and-such a social group are like', as if these concepts of these social groups were spontaneously arrived at by all members of society independently and in isolation. The stereotype is taken to express a general agreement about a social group, as if that agreement arose before, and independently of, the stereotype. Yet for the most part it is *from* stereotypes that we get our ideas about social groups. The consensus invoked by stereotypes is more apparent than real; rather, stereotypes express particular definitions of reality, with concomitant evaluations, which in turn relate to the disposition of power within society. Who proposes the stereotype, who has the power to enforce it, is the crux of the matter – *whose* tradition is Lippmann's 'our tradition'?

Here Orrin E. Klapp's distinction between stereotypes and social types is helpful. In his book *Heroes, Villains and Fools*,[10] Klapp defines social types as representations of those who 'belong' to society. They are the kinds of people that one expects, and is led to expect, to find in one's society, whereas stereotypes are those who do not belong, who are outside of one's society. In Klapp, this distinction is principally geographic – i.e. social types of Americans, stereotypes of non-Americans. We can, however, rework his distinction in terms of the types produced by different social groups according to their sense of who belongs and who doesn't, who is 'in' and who is not. Who does or does not belong to a given society as a whole is then a function of the relative power of groups in that society to define themselves as central and the rest as 'other', peripheral or outcast.

---

9. Among the approaches to this problem that may be signalled here are those of Lukács, Brecht, Eisenstein and Claire Johnston and Pam Cook.
10. Orrin E. Klapp, *Heroes, Villains and Fools*, Englewood Cliffs: Prentice-Hall, 1962.

In fictions, social types and stereotypes can be recognized as distinct by the different ways in which they can be used. Social types, although constructed iconographically similarly to the way stereotypes are constructed (i.e. the way a few verbal and visual traits are used to signal the character), can be used in a much more open and flexible way than can stereotypes. This is most clearly seen in relation to plot. Social types can figure in almost any kind of plot and can have a wide range of roles in that plot (e.g. as hero, as villain, as helper, as light relief, etc.), whereas stereotypes always carry within their very representation an implicit narrative. Jo Spence has argued in the context of the representation of women that despite the superficial variety of images, they all carry within them an implicit narrative pattern:

> visual representations which may appear to deal with diverse ideas but which are all aimed at women tend to act as part of an implicit narrative. This has a 'beginning' and a 'middle' (birth, childhood, marriage, family life) but there is only minimal representation of its 'end', of growing old and dying.[11]

In an article dealing with the stereotyping of gays in films, I tried to show how the use of images of lesbians in a group of French films, no matter what kind of film or of what 'artistic quality', always involved an identical plot function.[12] Similarly, we surely only have to be told that we are going to see a film about an alcoholic to know that it will be a tale either of sordid decline or of inspiring redemption. (This suggests a particularly interesting use of stereotypes, in which the character is constructed, at the level of dress, performance, etc., as a stereotype but is deliberately given a narrative function that is not implicit in the stereotype, thus throwing into question the assumptions signalled by the stereotypical iconography.)

The social type/stereotype distinction is essentially one of degree. It is after all very hard to draw a line between those who are just within and those definitely beyond the pale. This is partly because different social categories overlap – e.g. men 'belong', Blacks do not, but what of Black men? It is also because some of the categories that the social type/stereotype distinction keeps apart cannot logically be kept apart in this way. The obvious examples here are men and women, and it is this that causes T.E. Perkins to reject the distinction.[13] As applied to men and women, the social type/stereotype distinction implies that men have no direct experience of women and that there could be a society composed entirely of men: both of these are virtually impossible. Yet it seems to

---

11. Jo Spence, 'What Do People Do All Day? Class and Gender in Images of Women', *Screen Education* 29 (Winter 1978/1979), pp. 29–45.
12. Richard Dyer, 'Stereotyping', in *Gays and Film*, op. cit., pp. 33–5.
13. See Perkins, op. cit., pp. 140–1.

me that what the distinction points to, as applied to women and men, is a tendency of patriarchal thought[14] to attempt to maintain the impossible, by insisting on the 'otherness' of women and men (or rather the 'otherness' of women, men being in patriarchy the human norm to which women are 'other') in the face of their necessary collaboration in history and society. (The distinction does also refer in part to a real separation in social arrangements, i.e. the fact of male and female 'preserves': the pub, the beauty salon, the study, the kitchen, etc.). What the distinction also maintains is the *absolute* difference between men and women, in the face of their actual relative similarity.[15]

This is the most important function of the stereotype, to maintain sharp boundary definitions, to define clearly where the pale ends and thus who is clearly within and who clearly beyond it. Stereotypes do not only, in concert with social types, map out the boundaries of acceptable and legitimate behaviour, they also insist on boundaries exactly at those points where in reality there are none. Nowhere is this more clear than with stereotypes dealing with social categories that are invisible and/or fluid. Such categories are *invisible*, because you cannot tell just from looking at a person that she or he belongs to the category in question. Unless the person chooses to dress or act in a clearly and culturally defined manner (e.g. the working-class man's cloth cap, the male homosexual's limp wrist) or unless one has a trained eye (as those dealing with alcoholics have?), it is impossible to place the person before one, whereas many social groups – women and men, different races, young and old – are visibly different, and this difference can only be eradicated by disguise. Social categories can be *fluid*, in the sense that it is not possible in reality to draw a line between them and adjacent categories. We make a fuss about – and produce stereotypes about – the difference between women and men, yet biologically this is negligible compared to their similarity. Again, we are led to treat heterosexuality and homosexuality as sharply opposed categories of persons when in reality both heterosexual and homosexual responses and behaviour are to some extent experienced by everybody in their life. Alcohol use is clearly in this category – it is notoriously difficult to draw the line between harm-free and harmful drinking. But stereotypes can.

The role of stereotypes is to make visible the invisible, so that there is no danger of it creeping up on us unawares; and to make fast, firm and separate what is in reality fluid and much closer to the norm than the dominant value system cares to admit.

In the widest sense, these functions of rendering visible and firm can be connected to Lippmann's insistence on stereotypes as ordering concepts, and to the tendency

---

14. By patriarchy I mean the thought system that legitimates the power of men and the subordination of women in society; I do not mean that it is necessarily and simply how all men think of women, although it is an overwhelming determinant on that.

15. See Ann Oakley, *Sex, Gender and Society*, London: Temple Smith, 1972.

towards rigidity that may be implied by this. All societies need to have relatively stable boundaries and categories, but this stability can be achieved within a context that recognizes the relativity and uncertainty of concepts. Such a stability is, however, achieved only in a situation of real, as opposed to imposed, consensus. The degree of rigidity and shrillness of a stereotype indicates the degree to which it is an enforced representation that points to a reality whose invisibility and/or fluidity threatens the received definitions of society promoted by those with the biggest sticks. (E.g. if women are not so very different from men, why are they subordinated?; if alcoholism is not so easily distinguished from social drinking, can we be so comfortable in our acceptance of the latter and condemnation of the former?)

In this perspective, and speaking very tentatively, what is striking about the current media representation of alcoholism is its absence. It seems no longer to be identified as a key social personal problem, to be marked stereotypically as beyond the pale of 'normal' behaviour. Rather it hardly seems to be there at all. This may be related to the development of marijuana use as a focus of media/'public' concern – dope addicts are among the most shrill of today's stereotypes. In this context, all alcohol use seems redolent of old-fashioned values, and especially of 'masculine' values set against the 'effeminacy' of 'hippie' culture. To this one would add the enormous financial involvement of the alcohol industry in the leisure industries, of which the media are a key part, and in particular the reliance of television and cinema on advertising revenue (which, in the current legal situation, cannot come from marijuana promotion but can, and does, from alcohol promotion).

If we look back at the cinema, however, it is fairly clear that the alcoholic did serve *to distinguish clearly* alcohol use from abuse, as if a definite line could be drawn, in order to legitimate the 'social' use of alcohol. This includes the legitimation of excessive consumption, drunkenness and other alcohol-induced anti-social behaviour, since it is possible, by the use of stereotypes, to see this as distinct from 'real' alcoholism. The question that such an analysis poses is, in whose interest was this distinction maintained?[16]

Originally published in Jim Cook and Mike Lewington (eds), *Images of Alcoholism*, London: British Film Institute, 1979, pp. 15–21.

---

16. It is interesting to note that the liquor industry has been anxious to reinforce the view that alcoholism is a special disease suffered by a minority of the population, rather than varieties of harm, which anyone might experience in varying degrees, simply as a result of drinking too much too often. A preventive policy based upon the latter view might well be aimed at reducing levels of consumption (and hence revenue) whereas this would be quite inappropriate in terms of the former view.

29 OF RAGE AND DESPAIR (1981)

In the past few weeks whenever I have tuned in casually and unguardedly to the radio and television, I have been deeply moved. My emotions have lurched from speechless rage to grinding despair.

Take a small item on *Nationwide* the other day. It was about someone going into a small shop in a small country town to have a look around. I have no problem with this kind of item in the ordinary way of things. Unlike many people I know, I'll buy the BBC's presumable definition of early evening as a time for flopping down and letting the little incidents of everyday life pass before the eyes. I'm as happy with going shopping as subject matter at around 6.40 as with any other. But this story of everyday life was told with breathless admiration, because it was a story about Lady Diana Spencer.

My first reaction is rage, ranging all the way from 'How dare they waste my money (my licence fee to the BBC, my taxes to the royals, and my fellows' rates in the small town in the programme) on this trivia?' to 'How dare they try to tell me she's just an interesting person doing a bit of shopping, not the latest in the line of people embodying the worst class, gender and race roles we know?' The parade of upper-class, oh-so-white, very traditionally 'masculine' and 'feminine' images as 'simply' people that 'we all' love seems so outrageous that...

Which is where the rage gives way to despair, because of the absolute absence of any acknowledgement of this outrageousness in the media. The one thing you can't be in today's consensus is a republican. *Nationwide* skilfully handles any whiff of such a thing. Sue Lawley quotes at us the statistic that a third of the British public, according to a poll, aren't much interested (to say the least) in the Royal Wedding. In the face of the barrage from the media constructing the whole of the British public as fawning royalty lovers, this statistic is pretty amazing. But *Nationwide* is not about to allow the consensus it has helped so ardently to build over the years to slip away. So Sue Lawley introduces the statistic in terms of the fact that 2/3 of the public do love the royals. This at once diminishes to the point of deviance the one in three who don't. Then we get a quick series of items about people who are among the one in three, all of whom are shown as just being bored by it. Clearly *Nationwide* couldn't find the people who *object* to it.

Photomontage by Gloria Chalmers. (Courtesy of the artist)

One of the ways that the media make it so difficult to be anti-royalty is by their endless investigation of what Charles and Diana 'are really like'. This is an impossible quest, yet we are kept hanging on – maybe the next documentary, the next interview, the next candid photograph will reveal what has so far proved elusive. What matters about this is not so much that the media is hooking us with a promise it cannot fulfil, but that it inveigles us into being interested in the royals as people rather than in what they stand for.

The royals are constructed as people who are by definition beyond comprehension – and therefore fascinating. Lady Diana – not yet royalty even – is both ordinary and special as she wanders around that small shop – her banal questions are both an indication of how much like you and me she is, and yet the way these questions are trotted out for us signals how touched with specialness she is too.

Thus a BBC documentary tells us that Charles wanted to join the Labour Party when he was at Oxford. At once, we are invited to enter into what his motives were, why he chose the Labour party and so on – we're invited, in other words, to discuss anything other than what Prince Charles actually stands for politically, regardless of what opinions the person who plays the part of Prince Charles may happen to hold. If you show any indifference to what he is really like, this is construed as hostility to his person. But no matter how nice he and Di may really be, they are still living embodiments and reinforcers of class privilege, white supremacy and traditional male/female roles.

In recent years, left criticism of the media has rightly been distrustful of understanding radio and television in terms of either the inherent right wing biases of media practitioners or the media as the direct and inevitable expression of capitalist interests. Such approaches are undoubtedly correct and have been well argued in these pages by Rosalind Brunt and Ian Connell. All the same there have been times in the past weeks when the royalty machine has reduced me to feeling – come back conspiracy theory, come back economic determinism, all is forgiven. Only such ideas seem adequate in their fierce simplicity to the monstrousness of what we've been witnessing while unemployment figures creep to three million.

Originally published in *Comment* 19:16 (8 August 1981), p. 16.

30 DON'T LOOK NOW: THE INSTABILITIES OF THE MALE PIN-UP (1982)

'One of the things I really envy about men,' a friend once said to me, 'is the right to look.' She went on to point out how in public places, on the street, at meetings, men could look freely at women, but that women could only look back surreptitiously, against the grain of their upbringing. It is a point that has been reiterated in many of the personal-political accounts that have emerged from the consciousness-raising of the Women's Movement. And it is a fact that we see endlessly reworked in movies and on television. We have all seen, countless times, that scene of Young Love, where, in the canteen, at school, in church, the Boy and the Girl first see each other. The precise way it is done is very revealing. We have a close-up of him looking off camera, followed by one of her looking downwards (in a pose that has, from time immemorial, suggested maidenliness). Quite often, we move back and forth between these two close-ups, so that it is very definitely established that he looks at her and she is looked at. Then, she may look up and off camera, and we may go back briefly to the boy still looking – but it is only briefly, for no sooner is it established that she sees him than we must be assured that she at once averts her eyes. She has seen him, but she doesn't look at him as he looks at her – having seen him, she quickly resumes being the one who is looked at.

So utterly routine is this kind of scene that we probably don't remark on it, yet it encapsulates, and effectively reinforces, one of the fundamental ways by which power relations between the sexes are maintained. In her book *Body Politics*, Nancy M. Henley examines the very many different non-verbal ways that gender roles and male power are constantly being rebuilt and reaffirmed.[1] She does for gesture, body posture, facial expressions and so on what Dale Spender's *Man Made Language*[2] does for verbal communication, and shows how non-verbal communication is both a register

---

1. Nancy M. Henley, *Body Politics*, Englewood Cliffs, NJ: Prentice-Hall, 1977.
2. Dale Spender, *Man Made Language*, London: Routledge & Kegan Paul, 1980.

Montgomery Clift strikes a pose for a Hollywood publicity photo, circa 1950. (John Kobal Foundation/Getty Images)

of male–female relations and one of the means by which those relations are kept the way they are. Particularly relevant here is her discussion of eye contact.

Henley argues that it is not so much a question of whether women or men look at each other, but how they do. In fact, her evidence suggests that in face-to-face interactions, women look at men more than men do at women – but then this is because women listen more to men, pay more attention to them. In other words, women do not so much look at men as watch them. On the other hand, in crowd situations, men look more at women – men stare at women, whereas women avert their eyes. In both cases, this (re-)establishes male dominance. In the first case (one-to-one), 'superior position [...] is communicated by visually ignoring the other person – *not* looking while listening, but looking into space as if the other isn't there'; whereas in the second case (crowds), 'staring is used to *assert* dominance – to establish, to maintain, and to regain it'.[3]

Images of men aimed at women – whether star portraits, pin-ups, or drawings and paintings of men – are in a particularly interesting relation to these eye contact patterns. A certain instability is produced – the first of several we encounter when looking at images of men that are offered as sexual spectacle. On the one hand, this is a visual medium, these men are there to be looked at by women. On the other hand, this does violence to the codes of who looks and who is looked at (and how), and some attempt is instinctively made to counteract this violation. Much of this centres on the model or star's own 'look' – where and how he is looking in relation to the woman looking at him, in the audience or as she leafs through the fan or women's magazine (not only *Playgirl*, which has male nudes as *Playboy* has female ones, but also the new teenage magazines like *Oh Boy!* and *My Guy*, with their half-dressed pin-ups, and such features as 'Your Daily Male' in the *Sun* and 'She-Male' in *She*).

To repeat, it is not a question of whether or not the model looks at his spectator(s), but how he does or does not. In the case of not looking, where the female model typically averts her eyes, expressing modesty, patience and a lack of interest in anything else, the male model looks either off or up. In the case of the former, his look suggests an interest in something else that the viewer cannot see – it certainly doesn't suggest any interest in the viewer. Indeed, it barely acknowledges the viewer, whereas the woman's averted eyes do just that – they are averted from the viewer. In the cases where the model is looking up, this always suggests a spirituality: he might be there for his face and body to be gazed at, but his mind is on higher things, and it is this upward striving that is most supposed to please. This pose encapsulates the kind of dualism that Paul Hoch analyses in his study of masculinity, *White Hero,*

---

3. Henley, op. cit., p. 166.

Looking through: Paul Newman. (John Springer Collection/CORBIS/Corbis via Getty Images)

Michelangelo's Moses castrates with a glance. (Creative Commons)

Black Beast – higher is better than lower, the head above is better than the genitals below.[4] At the same time, the sense of straining and striving upwards does also suggest analogies with the definition of the very sexuality supposedly relegated to an inferior place – straining and striving are the terms most often used to describe male sexuality in this society.

It may be, as is often said, that male pin-ups more often than not do not look at the viewer, but it is by no means the case that they never do. When they do, what is crucial is the kind of look it is, something very often determined by the set of the mouth that accompanies it. When the female pinup returns the viewer's gaze, it is usually some kind of smile, inviting. The male pin-up, even at his most benign, still stares at the viewer. Even Paul Newman's frank face-on to the camera or the *Oh Boy!* coverboy's yearning gaze at us still seems to reach beyond the boundary

---

4. Paul Hoch, *White Hero, Black Beast*, London: Pluto Press, 1979.

marked, when the photo was taken, by the camera, as if he wants to reach beyond and through and establish himself. The female model's gaze stops at that boundary, the male's looks right through it.

Freud noticed a similar sort of look on Michelangelo's statue of Moses — though Moses is not looking at us but at the Jews' worship of the Golden Calf. Since Freud, it is common to describe such a look as 'castrating' or 'penetrating' — yet to use such words to describe the look of a man at a woman is revealing in ways that Freudians do not always intend. What, after all, have women to fear from the threat of castration? And why, come to that, should the possibility of penetration be *necessarily* fearful to women? It is clear that castration can only be a threat to men, and more probable that it is the taboo of male anal eroticism that causes masculine-defined men to construct penetration as frightening and the concept of male (hetero)sexuality as 'taking' a woman that constructs penetration as an act of violence. In looking at and dealing with these castrating/penetrating looks, women are caught up in a system that does not so much address them as work out aspects of the construction of male sexuality in men's heads.

If the first instability of the male pin-up is the contradiction between the fact of being looked at and the attempt of the model's look to deny it, the second is the apparent address to women's sexuality and the actual working out of male sexuality (and this may be one of the reasons why male pin-ups notoriously don't 'work' for women). What is at stake is not just male and female sexuality, but male and female power. The maintenance of power underpins further instabilities in the image of men as sexual spectacle, in terms of the active/passive nexus of looking, the emphasis on muscularity and the symbolic association of male power and the phallus.

The idea of looking (staring) as power and being looked at as powerlessness overlaps with ideas of activity/passivity. Thus to look is thought of as active; whereas to be looked at is passive. In reality, this is not true. The model prepares her- or himself to be looked at, the artist or photographer constructs the image to be looked at; and, on the other hand, the image that the viewer looks at is not summoned up by his or her act of looking but in collaboration with those who have put the image there. Most of us probably experience looking and being looked at, in life as in art, somewhere among these shifting relations of activity and passivity. Yet it remains the case that images of men must disavow this element of passivity if they are to be kept in line with dominant ideas of masculinity-as-activity.

For this reason images of men are often images of men doing something. When, before the full invention of cinematography, Eadweard Muybridge took an enormous series of photographic sequences, each one in the sequence taken a few seconds after the other, one of his intentions was to study the nature of movement. Muybridge photographed sequences of naked male and female figures. In a study of these sequences, Linda Williams shows how, even in so 'scientific' an undertaking and at such a comparatively 'primitive' stage in the development of photography, Muybridge established a difference between the female subjects, who are just there to be looked at, and the male subjects, who are doing something (carrying a boulder, sawing wood, playing baseball) which we can look in on.[5] This distinction is maintained in the history of the pin-up, where time and again the image of the man is one caught in the middle of an action, or associated, through images in the pictures, with activity.

Even when not actually caught in an act, the male image still promises activity by the way the body is posed. Even in an apparently relaxed, supine pose, the model tightens and tautens his body so that the muscles are emphasised, hence drawing attention to the body's potential for action. More often, the male pin-up is not supine anyhow, but standing taut ready for action.

There is an interesting divergence here in ethnic and class terms, a good example of the way that images of male power are always and necessarily inflected with other aspects of power in society. In relation to ethnicity, it is generally the case that the activity shown or implied in images of white men is clearly related to the split in western society between leisure and work activity, whereas Black men, even though they are in fact American or European, are given a physicality that is inextricably linked to notions of 'the jungle', and hence 'savagery'. This is done either by a natural setting, in which a generalised physical exertion is conflated with the energies of nature (and, doubtless, the beat of drums), or else, more recently, in the striking use of 'Black power' symbolism. This might seem like an acknowledgement of ethnic politics, and perhaps for some viewers it is, but the way the media constructed Black power in fact tended to reproduce the idea of a savage energy rather than a political movement – hence the stress on back-to-Africa (in the white western imagination still an amorphous jungle), or the 'senseless' violence erupting from the jungle of the ghetto.

Such images also put Black men 'outside of' class (though there has been the promotion of specifically middle-class Black images, as with, especially, Sidney Poitier). White men are more likely to be class differentiated, but this does overlap with the work/leisure distinction. Work is in fact almost suppressed from dominant imagery in this society – it is mainly in socialist imagery that its images occur. In nineteenth-century socialist and trade union art and in Soviet socialist realism the notions of the dignity and heroism of labour are expressed through dynamically muscular male bodies. As Eric Hobsbawm has pointed out, what this tradition has done, in effect, is to secure for masculinity the definition of what is finest in the proletarian and socialist traditions – women have been marginalised to the ethereal role of 'inspiration'.[6]

---

5. Linda Williams, 'Film Body: an Implantation of Perversions', *Cinétracts* 3:4 (Winter 1981), pp. 19–35.
6. Eric Hobsbawm, 'Man and Woman in Socialist Iconography', *History Workshop Journal* 6 (1978), pp. 121–38.

Black power as sex appeal: Richard Roundtree in *Shaft*, 1971. (John Springer Collection/CORBIS/Corbis via Getty Images).

The hyper-developed muscularity of Arnold Schwarzenegger, 1976. (Jack Mitchell/Getty Images)

Moreover, it is certainly no *conscious* part of this tradition that these male bodies should be a source of erotic visual pleasure, for men and women.

Sport is the area of life that is the most common contemporary source of male imagery – not only in pin-ups of sportsmen, but in the sports activities of film stars, pop stars and so on. (*She* magazine recently ran a series of pin-ups of wrestlers.)

Although certain sports have very clear class associations (the Prince of Wales plays polo, not football), there is a sense in which sport is a 'leveller'. Running, swimming, ball games are pretty well open to anyone in any class, and so imagery derived from these activities does not have immediate class associations. What all imply, however, is leisure, and the strength and vitality to use it. The celebration of the body in sport is also a celebration of the relative affluence of western society, where people have time to dedicate themselves to the development of the body for its own sake.

Whether the emphasis is on work or sport or any other activity, the body quality that is promoted is muscularity. In the copy accompanying the pin-ups in *Oh Boy!*, for instance, the female readers are called on to 'getta load of his muscles' and other such invitations. Although the hyper-developed muscularity of an Arnold Schwarzenegger is regarded by most people as excessive, and perhaps bordering on the fascist, it is still the case that muscularity is a key term in appraising men's bodies. This again probably comes from men themselves. Muscularity is the *sign* of power – natural, achieved, phallic.

At a minimum, developed muscles indicate a physical strength that women do not generally match (although recent developments in women's sport and physical conditioning suggest that differences between the sexes here may not be so fixed). The potential for muscularity in men is seen as a biological given, and is also the means of dominating both women and other men who are in the competition for the spoils of the earth – and women. The point is that muscles are biological, hence 'natural', and we persist in habits of thought, especially in the area of sexuality and gender, whereby what can be shown to be natural must be accepted as given and inevitable. The 'naturalness' of muscles legitimises male power and domination.

However, developed muscularity – muscles that *show* – is not in truth natural at all, but is rather achieved. The muscle man is the end product of his own activity of muscle-building. As always, the comparison with the female body beautiful is revealing. Rationally, we know that the beauty queen has dieted, exercised, used cleansing creams, solariums and cosmetics – but none of this really shows in her appearance, and is anyway generally construed as something that has been *done* to the woman. Conversely, a man's muscles constantly bespeak this achievement of his beauty/power.

Muscles, as well as being a sign of activity and achievement, are hard. We've already seen how even not overly developed male pin-ups harden their bodies to be looked at. This hardness may then be reinforced by aspects of setting or symbolic references, or by poses that emphasise hard lines and angular shapes (not the soft roundness of the feminine aesthetic). In her book *The Nude Male*, Margaret Walters suggests this hardness is phallic, not in the direct sense of being like an erect penis but rather in being symbolic of all that the phallus represents of 'abstract paternal power'.[7] There is no doubt that the image of the phallus as power is widespread to the point of near-universality, all

---

[7]. Margaret Walters, *The Nude Male*, London: Paddington Press, 1978.

Looking awkward for *Playgirl*, 1980.

the way from tribal and early Greek fertility symbols to the language of pornography, where the penis is endlessly described as a weapon, a tool, a source of terrifying power.

There is a danger of casual thought here. The phallus is not just an arbitrarily chosen symbol of male power; it is crucial that the penis has provided the model for this symbol. Because only men have penises, phallic symbols, even if in some sense possessed by a woman (as may be the case with female rulers, for instance), are always symbols of ultimately male power. The woman who wields 'phallic' power does so in the interests of men.[8]

This leads to the greatest instability of all for the male image. For the fact is that the penis isn't a patch on the phallus. The penis can never live up to the mystique implied by the phallus. Hence the excessive, even hysterical quality of so much male imagery. The clenched fists, the bulging muscles, the hardened jaws, the proliferation

---

8. See, for example, Alison Heisch, 'Queen Elizabeth I and the Persistence of Patriarchy', *Feminist Review* 4 (1980), pp. 45-56.

A hysterically phallic portrait of the young Bogie (Humphrey Bogart) 'at home', circa 1945. (John Kobal Foundation/ Getty Images)

of phallic symbols – they are all straining after what can hardly ever be achieved, the embodiment of the phallic mystique. This is even more the case with the male nude. The limp penis can never match up to the mystique that has kept it hidden from view for the last couple of centuries, and even the erect penis often looks awkward, stuck on to the man's body as if it is not a part of him.

Like so much else about masculinity, images of men, founded on such multiple instabilities, are such a strain. Looked at but pretending not to be, still yet asserting movement, phallic but weedy – there is seldom anything easy about such imagery. And the real trap at the heart of these instabilities is that it is precisely *straining* that is held to be the great good, what makes a man a man. Whether head held high reaching up for an impossible transcendence or penis jerking up in a hopeless assertion of phallic mastery, men and women alike are asked to value the very things that make masculinity such an unsatisfactory definition of being human.

Originally published in *Screen* 23:3–4 (September/October 1982), pp. 61–73.

31 HETEROSEXUALITY (1997)

The study of homosexuality entails the study of heterosexuality. I will begin in a moment by saying why. Yet it has not always seemed so, and I'll discuss this next, before showing how developments in Lesbian and Gay Studies made the study of heterosexuality possible. I then offer a thumbnail sketch of the characteristics of this specific sexuality, hetero, before looking at lesbian and gay work on its politics and history. I end by suggesting ways in which the study of heterosexuality opened up by Lesbian and Gay Studies can lead beyond the study of sexuality alone to that of gender and race as well.

The study of homosexuality entails the study of heterosexuality above all because of the latter's apparent naturalness and rightness. It is this that oppresses us and that we have therefore to refute. If we don't do it, it is not likely anyone else will, because it is not really in the interest of heterosexuals to be dislodged from the comfortable and powerful position of being in the right. And perhaps *only* we can do it. Precisely because we are outside heterosexuality, we can see that it is something specific, something identifiable, something straight and narrow.

There is also a broader sense in which Lesbian and Gay Studies has to study heterosexuality. The very idea of there being categories of sexuality – homo, hetero, bi, for starters – is a culturally and historically specific system of classification. Two things distinguish it. First, there is the very fact of classifying, characteristic of Western society's mania for compartmentalization and discrimination. Second, this system of classification does not classify acts but psychologies and forms of desire – heterosexuality is not man-woman coitus but the desire for it and/or the fact of being identified by the desire for it; thus there are 'heterosexuals' as well as man-woman sex acts. This system of classification limits everyone, but Lesbian and Gay Studies has pioneered the perception of it and (probably) lesbians and gay men can intellectually dismantle it most easily, because we feel so keenly the pressure of its arbitrariness.

That the study of homosexuality entails the study of heterosexuality has however not always been self-evident in Lesbian and Gay Studies.[1] There were at least two

---

1. I take 'Lesbian and Gay Studies' to mean the study of homosexuality by, and openly by, those who identify as homosexual (or by those who study it on our terms). Thus, although homosexuality has long been studied, we can date Lesbian and Gay Studies back to the 1970s - albeit with fabulous precursors.

good reasons why heterosexuality was not immediately on its agenda. Firstly, since homosexuality had been denied, marginalized or denigrated by most scholarship, the prime task for Lesbian and Gay Studies was to discover, promote and celebrate homosexuality. There was far too much to do finding out what gay and lesbian life had been and was like, far too much digging about in archives or under the surface of culture to find lesbian and gay traces, to put any energy into a consideration of heterosexuality. Besides, hadn't it had quite enough attention already? Secondly, it was also hard to imagine how you could study heterosexuality without reproducing a pattern damaging to homosexuality, a pattern reinforcing heterosexual normativity, thus undermining the very project of Lesbian and Gay Studies. The latter was born into a situation where homosexuality had always figured as the thing to be explained, above all in the reigning enigma: why are some people homo? To think of heterosexuality in this context seemed always to mean thinking of a human norm against which to explain the oddity of homosexuality. It was hard to think what the question about heterosexuality could be except: why are some people not hetero?

Two apparently contradictory things had to happen for there to be the possibility of an epistemological shift in the study of heterosexuality. One fulfilled the ambitions of much lesbian and gay activism this century; the second challenged those ambitions. On the one hand, the lesbian and gay movements built a consciousness that although homosexuality may not be the statistical norm, it is entirely normal for us. Once this is accepted, once homosexuality is *a* normality, then it follows that no sexuality can be *the* norm. Consequently, heterosexuality may be a majority practice, it may be in a position to impose itself as if it is the norm, but it is in fact a particular entity that is both open to and in need of describing and explaining.

On the other hand, there has also always been the sense that homosexuality is itself not clear-cut and fixed. From the start of lesbian and gay activism, lesbians and gay men instinctively made common cause with many others who were not wholly or at all homosexual: heterosexual transvestites, transsexuals who have heterosexual relations, bisexuals and three still more unsettling others. The first are transsexuals who have homosexual relations — for is, say, a female-to-male transsexual who has sexual relations with a man therefore homosexual (to themselves they are men having sex with men) or heterosexual (they are 'biologically' women having sex with men)? The second unsettling group is people who change sexuality, who lead long lives as, say, heterosexual and then lead lesbian or gay ones, or of course vice versa (though the latter is probably rarer, given the pressure on people to be straight if they possibly can). Such people's histories can be troubling. For some, it is a case of feeling that they were always really lesbian/gay (or straight) and have now allowed themselves to live and identify thus; such instances reinforce the sense of fixed and definite categories, hetero and homo. Other, though, experience the story of their life differently — that they simply changed, or that they made a decision to change, or that they were really always both but decided to plump for one rather than the other. And they might change again. Here an inner, given identity as hetero, homo or even bi cannot be affirmed, leaving notions of sexual identity fluid and unstable. Thirdly, there is the growing presence of lesbian (and to a lesser extent gay) parents, those who have chosen to parent from within leading a lesbian (or gay) identified life. These unsettle because they definitively unhook procreation from sexuality, undercutting one at least of the definitions of the difference between hetero and homo (in gay chauvinist parlance, between breeders and non-breeders). It should be stressed that all these groups do not prove that everyone is basically anything and everything, but simply that human sexuality is extraordinarily fluid and diverse, not reducible to the hetero, homo, bi formula.

Confidently embracing the normality of homosexuality robs heterosexuality of its claim to be the norm; muddying the hetero, homo, bi distinction unsettles the confidence with which any group sexual identity can be maintained, thus calling hetero into question just as much as homo. In terms of study, these two moves combined with the growing importance of notions of the historical and cultural construction of sexualities touched on above (and mostly developed by lesbians and gay men) to produce the possibility of addressing heterosexuality as something specific, the possibility of making heterosexuality strange.

To those of us libidinally pretty well utterly outside of heterosexuality, seeing its strangeness may seem a pretty easy move to make (though even we needed the political confidence to make it and say we'd made it), but in fact it was and still is rather difficult. Heterosexuality in the sense of man-woman coitus is normative, even if being heterosexual and having heterosexual desire is culturally and historically limited. It is normative in several senses. It is practised by most adults. It is what we have most evidence of being practised throughout history and the known world. The major world religions and systems of law affirm heterosexuality and proscribe homosexuality. Heterosexuality appears to be the means by which human procreation is achieved, thus making it seem an indispensable and natural part of human existence. All of these make of heterosexuality something that is taken for granted, something assumed to be natural; its normality does not need arguing for, it has the force of 'of course'. We do not stop to think about the grammar we use when speaking or the chemical composition of the air we breathe; similarly, we don't stop to think about the most deeply embedded, routinized norms by which we live. Only a major epistemological jolt can achieve this – like, as I have described above, seeing something abnormal as normal and seeing the edges of both normal and abnormal eroded beyond recognition. Then just what constitutes the normal can come into view – and we need to be able to see this, because the normal defines and oppresses what it designates as abnormal.

What then are the particularities of this strange sexuality, hetero? In order of diminishing indisputability, we might note the following five characteristics:

1. Difference is at the heart of sexual object choice

Heterosexuality always involves attraction and intercourse between two persons who, whatever else may be the case, are primarily differentiated by one category: gender. Evidence suggests that in practice, heterosexuals choose partners who in all respects other than gender (e.g. class, race, nationality, age, ability) are more like them than unlike; yet what is privileged in the understanding of the erotics of the choice is gender difference.

2. Difference is conceptualized as oppositeness

Heterosexuality is posited on the gender difference femininity: masculinity. This is widely conceptualized in terms of opposites: male aggression, strength, hardness, roughness and competitiveness as the opposite of female nurture, weakness, softness, smoothness and cooperativeness. This often then defines male and female sexuality within heterosexuality – masculine active, feminine passive (terms in turn often grafted onto homosexual sex, as when gay men used to ask each other whether they were butch or bitch). Such difference as oppositeness is important for a central tenet of heterosexual ideology, namely, that heterosexual partners are complementary to one another, that penises fit vaginas, that masculinity balances femininity, that the combination of the two encompasses the range of human qualities and thus constitutes the proper and perfect form of human (sexual) relationships.

3. Difference is in fact power imbalance

Cliff Gorman, the actor who played the flamboyant queen Emory in both the play and the film of *The Boys in the Band* was interviewed in *The New York Times* in September 1968. Drinking beer from a can, he insistently protested his heterosexuality, and as if to prove his point, he said that he had recently agreed to play a rapist on television and "What could be more heterosexual than that?"[2] Radical feminist theory could not have come up with a better definition of the essence of heterosexuality, of heterosexuality taken to its logical conclusion.

This is the position argued by Sheila Jeffreys, who defines 'heterosexual desire [as] eroticised power difference.'[3] The ideas of difference and complementarity assume a level playing field between women and men; they do not acknowledge or take into

---

2. See Jonathan Ned Katz, *The Invention of Heterosexuality*, New York: Plume, 1996, p. 109.
3. Sheila Jeffreys, *Anticlimax: A Feminist Perspective on the Sexual Revolution*, London: The Women's Press, 1990, p. 299.

account the socially sanctioned power differences between men and women. This notion of the complementarity of difference, as opposed to its power imbalance, is celebrated as pleasurable in innumerable cultural texts. Romance fiction repeatedly returns to the thrill of the more powerful man for the female heroine, just as pornography returns to the image of the delectability of the vulnerable woman. Both romance and pornography are in fact more complex and varied than this, as are real heterosexual relations, but the romance/porn patterns provide something of a base line for the imagination of heterosexuality.

One can think of heterosexuality's vaunted pleasure in difference as a mere mask for its eroticized power imbalance, and no doubt it often is. However, it is probably the case that the promise and sometimes experience of the former co-exists with the latter, as least some of the time. In a study of heterosexual couple dances in the Hollywood musical,[4] I noted a pattern whereby there was a shift within films from numbers early on where partners either do the same thing or else things that complement each other, to later numbers where the woman is dependent on the man, often to the point where she surrenders control over her body to him. Thus in *Top Hat* (1935), the archetypical heterosexual couple, Fred Astaire and Ginger Rogers, do identical tap steps side by side in 'Isn't It A Lovely Day?', their first number together in the film, whereas in the climactic 'Cheek to Cheek' he swings her about, drags her back and finally holds her ever closer to the ground, in all cases making her dependent on him and affirming his power over her body. This shift from complementarity to power difference is if anything still more evident in later dance films like *Saturday Night Fever* (1977) or *Dirty Dancing* (1987). In terms of the films' stories, the shift is from numbers expressing initial desire, flirting and courting, to those expressing the full realization of sexual love. Complementarity of differences seems to need to become male domination and female subordination for a relationship to be consummated. Thus it is not that the imagination of heterosexuality cannot genuinely encompass pleasure in difference but that it has difficulty sustaining it, especially at the moment of the supposed affirmation of heterosexual identity, sex itself.

4. Sexuality has something to do with procreation

Most acts of heterosexual penis-vagina intercourse (which does not account for all heterosexual sex acts) do not lead to procreation – but they might. Heterosexual sex is overwhelmingly the most common means of sexual reproduction; for many religious and moral traditions, sexual reproduction (and therefore heterosexuality) is the purpose of sexuality, in the sense of that being the reason why God gave it to humans or

---

4. Richard Dyer, '"I Seem to Find the Happiness I Seek": Heterosexuality and Dance in the Musical', in Helen Thomas (ed.), *Dance, Gender and Culture*, London: Macmillan, 1993, pp. 49-65.

that nature developed it; for most heterosexuals, avoidance of conception is a tiresome part of the business of leading a heterosexual life.

5. Sexual practice is an affirmation of one's identity as normal

Heterosexuality, in the sense of man-woman coitus, is still statistically the majority sexual practice and is almost certainly regarded by most people as the norm. The desire to be normal and the pressure on people to conform are both very powerful. At the same time, sexuality is especially privileged by Western society as a ground and explanation of who we are. To feel then that one has the normal sexuality is profoundly affirming of personal identity and social belonging.

The fact that heterosexuality is a majority practice, that it most readily appears natural and the norm, that most of what we know about sex in the past or in other cultures is heterosex, all of this makes it hard not to believe that heterosexuality just is the inevitable and proper sexual order of society. It was the political challenge to this that marked the first step in the development of a lesbian (and gay) critique of heterosexuality.

I put 'and gay' in brackets in the previous sentence, because it was lesbian theory that led the way in the intellectual and political project of making heterosexuality strange. This can be traced in the early polemical writings of radical feminism, while in academic spheres the most influential texts have probably been two articles published in 1980: Adrienne Rich's 'Compulsory Heterosexuality and Lesbian Existence' and Monique Wittig's 'The Straight Mind'. Though significantly different in many ways (above all in relation to what they have to say about lesbianism), both these texts see heterosexuality as something imposed on women in the interests of men. Thus Rich speaks of 'compulsory heterosexuality' while Wittig speaks of 'the obligatory social relationships between "man" and "woman"'. Rich lists many of the ways that women are coerced into heterosexuality, the sanctions against those that resist or rebel, the remorseless delivery throughout culture of the message of heterosexual inevitability and rightness. For Rich, all this effort is so huge and elaborate that it gives the lie to the idea that heterosexuality is natural – if it were so, why would it be necessary to sell it so hard, to cajole, threaten and punish so insistently those who don't want to practise it?[5] Wittig focuses more on the assumption of heterosexuality built into the foundations of Western thought, and not least the psychoanalysis still fashionable in cultural theory. She argues that 'the straight mind' is founded on universality and difference: it believes that it alone knows how the world is and thus constitutes all difference as difference from straightness.

---

5. Adrienne Rich, 'Compulsory Heterosexuality and Lesbian Existence', *Signs* 5:4 (1980), pp. 631-60.

> To constitute a difference and to control it is an 'act of power, since it is essentially a normative act. Everybody tries to show the other as different. But not everybody succeeds in doing so. One has to be socially dominant to succeed in it'.[6]

Rich relates compulsory heterosexuality to the situation of women; what the former oppresses is the possibility of relations between women, of which lesbianism is perhaps the exemplary form. Thus although it seems to me that compulsory heterosexuality also oppresses gay men, and that there is just as much hysterical social and cultural investment in making sure that the natural form of sexuality develops in men too, Rich's ideas were not designed to make this point. Wittig on the other hand does include gay and even other kinds of men (non-white, for instance) in those oppressed by the straight mind, because this mind does not just oppress those who are not heterosexual but all those who are different from it. In this perspective, heterosexuality is merely the foundational form of all oppression.

> [...] the straight mind cannot conceive of a culture, a society where heterosexuality would not order not only all human relationships but also its very production of concepts and all the processes which escape consciousness, as well.[7]

Rich, Wittig and others challenged the naturalness of heterosexuality, by showing how culture works to enforce it and arguing that it is in the interests of dominant men to have it thought natural (and therefore presumed to be unchangeable). What they did not point to was any evidence that heterosexuality was not to all intents and purposes natural, in the sense of being universally practised throughout recorded time. This is tackled by Jonathan Ned Katz in his book *The Invention of Heterosexuality*. He draws on the burgeoning work on lesbian and gay history (a field in which his own work has been profoundly influential), for while this did not initially set out to deal with heterosexuality, it has inadvertently shed light on it. Lesbian and gay history has worked predominantly with the model of homosexuality as something experienced in radically different ways in different periods and different societies, a model that can only be explained by conceiving of sexuality, all sexuality, as socially and culturally moulded. In tracing such differences, lesbian and gay historians have inevitably pointed to the changing ways in which sexuality in general, and therefore heterosexuality, has been moulded.

---

6. Monique Wittig, 'The Straight Mind', in *Feminist Issues* 1:1 (1980), p. 108. The quotation is from Claude Faugerton and Philippe Robert, *La Justice et les représentations sociales du système penal*, Paris: Masson, 1978.
7. Wittig, ibid, p. 107.

In *The Invention of Heterosexuality*, Katz shows that, before the mid-nineteenth century, the particular concatenation of assumptions given above that coalesce into heterosexuality did not pertain. Sexual acts between women and men were understood to be the means for human reproduction, and in most societies for most of human existence, survival of the species has been precarious, making it necessary to ensure that such sexual acts were undertaken. Male-female coitus is not however the same thing as heterosexual desire or being heterosexual.

Katz looks at a number of historical moments to demonstrate how very differently (hetero)sexuality has been thought and felt about. The first of these is ancient Greece, for his account of which Katz draws on the work of Michel Foucault (itself corroborated, as Katz notes, by many lesbian and gay classicists). Here the focus is 'free men', and Foucault and Katz argue that, while a distinction was drawn between such men's 'higher', 'spiritual' love and their 'lower', 'earthly' love, these do not correlate neatly with heterosexual and homosexual love (or even vice versa, as a certain gay romanticism about 'Greek love' has sometimes assumed). Rather, high love is focused by free men on other free men, while the baser love is directed at women and boys. The fact that, in the baser love, 'one man's inclinations usually favoured women, another man's, boys' was not significant;[8] whether the higher love involved sexual activity has, however, always been controversial.

Katz's second moment draws on his own pioneering research on the New England colonies between 1607 and 1740. Here the fragility of the new settlements put a premium on sexual reproduction, and thus the crucial distinction was between procreative and non-procreative sex acts. All forms of the latter were an abomination, and in law (if not in practice) the punishment for sodomy and adultery was the same (death). We are worlds away from the validation of heterosexuality as a pleasure in difference and power founded in but not limited to procreation. Katz also discusses the organization of sexuality in nineteenth-century America, from about 1820 to 1850, before the invention of the idea of heterosexuality. Here he stresses the distinction between 'the moral character of passionate love and the immoral character of sensual lust', with the former, expressive of one's affective being, just as likely to be directed towards one's own sex as the so-called opposite one.

It is only towards the end of the nineteenth century that the notion of (and term) heterosexuality comes into being. Katz shows how the influential sexologist Richard von Krafft-Ebing developed a theory of heterosexuality as a form of desire, based upon opposites and especially on the opposition of active (male) and passive (female). This was then elaborated upon by Sigmund Freud to the point that, for him, 'hetero *feeling* defines hetero *being*, whether or not one *acts* heterosexually.'[9] Through the

---

8. Katz, op. cit. p. 35.
9. Ibid, p. 66.

twentieth century the heterosexual emerged more and more clearly as the sexual norm, until challenged by the lesbian and gay movements.

The idea that heterosexuality is an invention, that it is a culturally and historically produced sexuality, does not dispute that there are everywhere and have always been genital acts between women and men. What it does suggest it that there is nothing natural and inevitable about how those acts are thought and felt about, with what feelings they are performed; it suggests that human beings have control over the construction of human sexualities. This control is not exactly individual. As individuals, we do have some degree of control over how we act, but we do so in the context of what we know about acts, what they mean, how they feel, that is to say, what we have in the broadest cultural sense been taught about acts, meanings and feelings. This cultural sense is also humanly constructed, but collectively, without there being any over-riding consciousness in charge of it, and every individual is born into a situation where the cultural sense of things seems just to be there, a given, unproduced. It is this feeling that makes heterosexuality, as invented really so recently in Western history, feel like something natural.

It is striking that it is overwhelmingly lesbians and gay men who have made a start on denaturalizing heterosexuality. Two anthologies on heterosexuality (Hanscombe and Humphries, 1987; Wilkinson and Kitzinger, 1993) were both produced by lesbians and gay men.[10] The second of these caused consternation, distress and outrage among heterosexual women to whom the editors wrote asking them to contribute pieces reflecting on their heterosexuality. Heterosexual women found themselves named for their sexuality in the way lesbians invariably are and often resented it. Carol Nagy Jacklin comes straight out with it: 'Being asked to contribute [...] as a "heterosexual" is offensive, because to say "I am heterosexual" implies that my sexual preference is an unchanging and essential personal attribute and that "I am traditional"'; she goes on to suggest that heterosexual women 'are at greater risk of having inequitable personal relations' and that while the 'disadvantages [of heterosexuality] are clear, the advantages [are] somewhat less so'.[11] Mary Gergen asks 'Why address me so categorically as a heterosexual?' How did Wilkinson and Kitzinger know? 'Because I am married? Or because my husband seems "straight"?'[12] But at least these women replied and started speculating: one dreads to think with what wounded dignity heterosexual men would have reacted.

---

10. Gillian Hanscombe and Martin Humphries (eds), *Heterosexuality*, London: GMP, 1987; Sue Wilkinson and Celia Kitzinger (eds), *Heterosexuality: A Feminism and Psychology Reader*, London: Sage, 1993.
11. Carol Nagy Jacklin, 'How My Heterosexuality Affects My Feminist Politics', in Wilkinson and Kitzinger, op. cit., p. 34.
12. Mary Gergen, 'Unbundling Our Binaries – Genders, Sexualities, Desires', in Wilkinson and Kitzinger, op. cit., p. 62.

Denaturalizing heterosexuality not only unsettles it, it also forms the basis for understanding much else about contemporary culture and society. Many have observed that gender — what we think men and women are and are like — is itself a product of heterosexuality. The latter, as noted, is founded on the notion of the oppositeness of male and female bodies — it requires the notion of gender, or these particular notions of male and female gender, to make sense. Judith Butler speaks of a 'heterosexual matrix', that is

> a hegemonic discursive/epistemic model of gender intelligibility that assumes that *for bodies to make sense* there must be a stable sex expressed through a stable gender (masculine expresses male, feminine expresses female) that is oppositionally and hierarchically *defined through the compulsory practice of heterosexuality*.[13]

A simplification of the stages in Butler's argument would run something like this: bodies do not of themselves 'make sense'; we, that is the culture, *make* sense of them; the only way our culture can make such sense is by imagining that bodies have stable properties and in particular that bodies engaged in reproductive sex have stable properties that can be captured in a simple binarism (male and female); thus the imperative of heterosexuality requires the notion of different genders. Once you knock away the support of nature to both heterosexuality and gender, you are left only with people obliged to do heterosexual sex. Such doing can then be seen as a performance, a key notion in Butler's work. In one of her most dizzying passages, Butler suggest that the very idea of the naturalness of heterosexuality is itself a product of performance: heterosexuality merely imitates what it has learnt heterosexuality is, but as if this is an imitation of something basic, given by nature:

> the *naturalistic effects* of heterosexualised genders are produced by imitative strategies; *what they imitate is a phantasmatic ideal of heterosexual identity* [...] In this sense, the 'reality' of heterosexual identity is performatively constituted through an imitation that sets itself up as the origin and the ground of all imitations.[14]

The implication of Butler's discussion here is not only that heterosexuality is an imitation of something that it takes to be, if you go back far enough, original, natural, something that is not itself an imitation. Because this original never existed, the

---

13. Judith Butler, *Gender Trouble: Feminism and the Subversion of Identity*, New York: Routledge, 1990, p. 151; my emphasis.
14. Judith Butler, 'Imitation and Gender Subordination', in Diana Fuss (ed.), *Inside/Out: Lesbian Theories, Gay Theories*, New York: Routledge, 1991, p. 21; my emphasis.

implication is also that heterosexuality, which is supposed to be the ultimate affirmation of the natural (the normal, the inevitable), constantly fails to achieve this affirmation, because it is only ever an imitation of a fantasy idea of the natural. In short, heterosexuality is a performance that can never pull off what it is supposed to pull off – the fixing of hierarchical gender roles and the suppression of the consciousness of the possibility of all non-heterosexual sexuality. Heterosexuality, and the gender roles it underwrites, in its need to proclaim its own naturalness and normality, can only produce an anxiety at never actually being natural and normal.

This explains much about the images, stories and representations of heterosexuality circulating in our culture: the convoluted stories and relentless repetitions of soap opera, the insane excesses of film melodrama, romance fiction and grand opera, the flight from women as anything but fuck objects in male action fiction and novels of Angst. Cultural representations offer rich pickings for any student of heterosexuality. Why, for example, is there all the running after men in *Pride and Prejudice*, when every instance of actual marriage in the book (or its television adaptation) is absurd and appalling? If cowboys wanted to populate the West, why did they spend so much time galloping away from women? Why is *Sleepless in Seattle* so self-conscious about wanting to present a hetero love story for our times? Why is *Baywatch* so pneumatic? All these perform heterosexuality, but in such remorseless, crazed and alarmed modes that they suggest heterosexuality is indeed on a hiding to nothing in its assertion of its own naturalness and normality.

If denaturalizing heterosexuality casts new light on gender, then it may also do so on race, for the notion of race is profoundly heterosexual. Race is a way of categorizing bodies that reproduce themselves. Notions of pure race and the importance of preserving racial purity require the control of male-female coitus and reproduction, but they do not require notions of heterosexual desire. Once this is invented, however, all hell is let loose for racial purists. For heterosexual desire foregrounds the erotics of difference and power imbalance, the very things that also underpin notions of race. Thus are mobilized the cross-racial desirings that so confuse, alarm and disgust racialist thought. Heterosexuality is in our culture the affective, libidinal means by which people get into man-woman sex, and thus into human/racial reproduction. Abandonment of heterosexuality (as opposed to man-woman sex) might also be the means of abandoning racialist obsessions.

It would be rash to claim that only Lesbian and Gay Studies can (or indeed has) looked at the centrality of heterosexuality to the constitution of sexuality, gender and race. Yet not only have lesbians and gay men been at the forefront of naming heterosexuality as something that requires investigation, it is also central to the logic of Lesbian and Gay Studies to carry those investigations forward. We can, after all, only understand how homosexuality is constructed by understanding it as part of a broader, general system of thinking and feeling about sexuality – and a crucial role in that system is played by particular, limited and limiting ideas of heterosexuality. Equally, we can only understand why homosexuality is denigrated or controversial by understanding the construction of heterosexuality as a norm. To understand lesbian and gay existence, we have to understand heterosexuality; in the process, we produce heterosexuality itself as a bizarre object of study.

Originally published in Andy Medhurst and Sally Munt (eds), *Lesbian and Gay Studies: A Critical Introduction*, London: Cassell, 1997, pp. 261–273.

32 IS THE CAMERA RACIST? (1997)

There is a revealing behind-the-scenes moment in the 1985 film *Handsworth Songs*. A television crew is setting up a studio discussion about that summer's street fighting in Birmingham. The producer is looking at the image of the audience on the monitor in the control room and discussing it with the floor manager in the studio. The producer says something about the number of Black people at the front of the audience. "You're worried there are not too many whites obviously there?" asks the floor manager. No, says the producer, it's nothing like that, a mere technical matter, a question of lighting – "it just looks a bit down".

One might be tempted to think this was some kind of racism, something along the lines of giving Blacks too much of a say. But for the producer it genuinely is a purely aesthetic matter. For him, the image looks 'down': dull, dingy, lacking sparkle. What's more, in the forms of professional common sense, he is right: shoot the scene in the usual way with the usual technology with that audience and it will look 'down'. Equally, if you do it the usual way with a predominantly white audience, it will look 'up', bright, sparkling. The effect is built into the technology and the way we habitually use it.

Photographic images are produced from the effect light has on the chemical make-up of the film in the camera. Objects in the world reflect different amounts of light, and film stock registers this. Skin is no exception. There is something like a 15–20 percent difference in the degree of light reflected by the darkest and fairest skins. It's something that has to be borne in mind when shooting people of different colours. White people need less exposure time, less light, less tightly grained stock than do Black people. The resultant problem is classically evident in multi-racial school photos, with both fair and dark faces together in the frame. Get everything right for the whites and the Black faces look like blobs; get it right for the Blacks, and the white faces are all bleached out.

It is only a matter of adjustment, of paying attention to the many elements involved in photographing people – film, stock, lighting, aperture width, exposure time and development procedures, to say nothing of the subjects of make-up, dress and setting.

One just needs to pay attention to all of this in a flexible way that responds to the variations in human skin colour. In practice, however, the complex process of light and film has taken the white face as the norm, to the disadvantage of Black faces.

There's nothing sinister or deliberately discriminatory about this. It's just that white people are accustomed to taking themselves unthinkingly as the human norm and this operates at the most seemingly objective, technical levels. You can see it in the history of photography and film. Refinements in the chemistry of film stocks, in camera design and development methods, all took the human face as the touchstone for getting things right, and inventors simply took their own white faces and the ones they were working with as the norm.

Later, the invention and introduction of colour was entirely posited on achieving the right pinkness to convey whiteness, with a knock-on effect on everything else, including Black skin. Similarly, manuals on studio lighting from the earliest time give advice on the best way to light a face, a best way that on inspection turns out to be the best way to light a white face.

This has considerable consequences in movies. One is simply that you can generally see white characters on the screen better than Black ones. You really notice the effect of this in films where Black and white characters are of equal importance to the story, but where the faces of the white characters, and therefore their thoughts and feelings, are more fully visible.

In the classic liberal movie *In the Heat of the Night* (1967), Sidney Poitier is more noble and intelligent than fellow cop-cum-antagonist Rod Steiger, but because you can always make out Steiger's features more clearly, he comes over as more complex and nuanced, with Poitier remaining a mere emblem of Black superiority.

▲ ▲ ▲

In common with many recent films (*48 Hours*, *Lethal Weapon*, *Seven*), *Rising Sun* (1993) has two male stars in the lead with equal box-office clout, Sean Connery and Wesley Snipes. They play characters of equal importance in the film, two cops investigating a crime. In separate shots, they are carefully – that is to say differently – lit, so that they look equally beautiful. Yet in scenes together Connery is more fully visible than Snipes, as if he is more decisive in solving the crime and taking the lead. Even when the script may give equal weight to Black and white, lighting may continue to discriminate.

It also gives a glow to white faces on the screen. With men, this is often confined to the temples and back of the head, highlights reminiscent of the spark of genius in classic portraits of Great Men. In *Rising Sun*, you can not only see Connery better, but he is also, literally and figuratively, more enlightened. White women, in contrast, are bathed in light – a complex battery of lights, sophisticated make-up, gauzes, soft focus and much else besides give them an almost angelic glow.

Importantly, they glow rather than shine. Shine is the effect of light bouncing back at the camera, as it does off both dark and sweaty skin. It is corporeal, whereas glow is transcendent. A whole cosmetics industry developed with the aim of eliminating shine, while alongside it popular studio photography and then Hollywood evolved a system of multi-lighting that aimed to minimise the darkness of naturally occurring shadows. The peak moments of all of this are bridal and glamour photography, positively dedicated to achieving glow without shine or shadow.

Film is the art of light. This is not just a suggestive metaphor – film is literally made from light. In itself there is nothing racial about this, but the technology has to be handled flexibly and sensitively in relation to human colour difference. Otherwise, not only does it discriminate against darker peoples, but it also produces a glorifying image of white people that is hard to produce with dark people. It is an image that, when you come to think of it, is not only intoxicating and inspiring, but debilitating and downright peculiar, too.

Originally published in *The Guardian*, 18 July 1997, p. A13.

33 WHITE ENOUGH (2013)

The dirtiness of the dancing in *Dirty Dancing* is most obviously sexual, and fairly obviously class-based;[1] rather more equivocally, it is also racial. As Anahid Kassabian notes, the dirty dancing is 'not-quite-white';[2] I want to argue that, all the same, it is white enough.[3]

DANCE AND SEX

Nearly all the dancing in *Dirty Dancing* is sexual, although only some of it is explicitly so. In the well-lit arena of the public dance floor (at Kellerman's and the Sheldrake), dance has an ostensible role in sexual, and here clearly also racial, reproduction. The dancers are married couples or, more importantly, those who are encouraged to be: the boys who are set up as partners for the Houseman girls are both nice Jewish boys following the paths expected of them, Robbie at Yale and Neil at Cornell, paths that mean they are just the kind of boys Lisa and Baby, respectively, should have sex (that is, dance and have babies) with.

As the dancing is shown, it certainly lacks any sense of overt sexual drive. The occasional shots of couples dancing in the Kellerman ballroom and pavilion make it look sedate and dull, and Neil and Baby's first foray onto the floor is contrasted with a pair of children who, in adopting tango movements, at least go through the motions of erotic abandonment. Later, Billy, one of the staff and Johnny's cousin, remarks to Baby of the first time she has seen the dirty dancing, 'Can you imagine dancing like this on the main floor beside the family fox-trot?'

---

1. For an account of the class dynamics of the film, see David Shumway, 'Rock 'n' Roll Soundtracks and the Production of Nostalgia', *Cinema Journal* 38:2 (Winter 1999), pp. 45-48.
2. Anahid Kassabian, *Hearing Film: Tracking Identifications in Contemporary Hollywood Film Music*, New York: Routledge, 2001, p. 18.
3. I presented an earlier version of this paper in November 2008 at the Leo Baeck Institute in London. I should like to thank Daniel Wildman for inviting me and the audience, especially Michele Aaron, for their comments. I apologise for the several references to my own work in the bibliography.

This clean dancing, despite and because of its respectability and worthy function vis-à-vis reproduction, is certainly not endorsed by the film. Not only is it dull, but it is dishonest and often risible. Robbie turns out to be the least desirable catch in the film, abandoning Penny when she becomes pregnant by him, leading Lisa on, amused when the latter, having decided she's going to sleep with him, finds him in bed with Vivian. The latter is someone Johnny has danced with and also almost certainly slept with: the dancing is part of his job and it is, according to Max Kellerman, supposed to end there ('Teach 'em mambo, cha-cha, anything they pay for, and that's all – keep your hands off'), but it is also clear that such coupling (especially of the female clients with the male staff) goes on. Max has a disparaging term for the women involved – 'bungalow bunnies' – and when Vivian's husband gives Johnny some money to give her 'extra dance lessons' it is pretty likely he knows what he is paying for (Johnny refuses the money, a sign of his moral growth under Baby's influence; sex for pleasure is one thing, for pay, quite another). Neil, the nice Jewish boy proposed for Baby, is viewed critically and mockingly by the film. Once having established that Robbie is at Yale Medical School (high prestige as well as high earning prospects), Max tells the Housemans that his grandson Neil is attending the Cornell School of Hotel Management, and the timing of the line suggests that we are meant to find it amusing. Medical school at Yale trumps Hotel Management, even at Cornell. Later though, the less than prepossessing Neil (another way in which he appears less of a catch than cute Robbie) reminds Baby of what he's got that Johnny doesn't and that all the girls adore: two hotels. This vulgar materialism only serves to lessen him in the film's (and Baby's) eyes.

It is not only that dancing as a conduit to sexual reproduction is discredited by the portrayal of the nice Jewish boys Robbie and Neil but also the way in which sex-for-pleasure is shown to be present in the respectable dancing. On the one hand, this is scorned in the idea of the bungalow bunnies and Johnny's redemption from prostitution (all the more impressive in the context of his telling Baby earlier in the film that he is too poor not to prostitute himself). On the other hand, most attempts at sexiness on the public dance floor are made fun of. A merengue dance class, led by the incandescently sexy Penny (Cynthia Rhodes) to vivid dance music, is introduced by a tracking shot along the dancers' feet that shows they are clad in uncool sandals and socks; Baby steps on the feet of the man beside her and can't keep time; Penny shakes her torso and encourages the other women to do so, to a lot less sexy effect; and when she announces 'When I say stop you're gonna find the man of your dreams,' it is evidently untrue, and in fact Baby pairs with an old woman. In short, sex is very much on the agenda in the merengue class and mocked in the clients' attempts at engaging in it. Later, for the resort's final show, Lisa does a Hawaiian dance stiffly and awkwardly, ironing out any sense of sway and undulation and singing off-key to boot.

All this contrasts with the dancing in the staff quarters, which is at the other end of the spectrum from that on the main floor: groin to groin, and done unequivocally solely for the pleasure of doing it. Its explicit sexual dimension, already evident in the dancing itself from the first time we see it, is spelled out later when Baby and Johnny dancing in his room to 'Cry to Me' leads to actual sex, and then again later when they start to dance in a sexually intimate way to 'Love Is Strange' (though they are interrupted by Neil). Even when not leading to intercourse, its meaning is usually in-your-face sexual: Johnny and Penny are not lovers, but their dancing, both in the staff quarters and in their display routines, signifies sex, notably in Johnny's (Swayze's) pelvic-centered movements, and such movements from Penny as throwing one ankle up on Johnny's shoulder so that her crotch hovers above his.

There are perhaps two exceptions to the sense of dance as sexual, whether overtly or covertly. One is the delicate, easy dancing of Honi Coles, who plays the bandleader, something I shall return to. The other involves the display dances of Johnny and Baby (or, as she becomes through these, Frances). The first, for the Sheldrake show, signifies sexuality in its moves, not least because it is supposed to substitute for Johnny's dance with Penny, although in the performance what is emphasised is the tension around Baby/Frances getting it right. This process, especially the rehearsal sequences,[4] is part of the process leading to their falling in love. Their dance at the end of the film also contains sexual moves, something underlined by the audience whoops and applause, first when he brings his face close up to hers, second (and louder) when he shakes his groin at her. However, there are two other elements here. The biggest audience response comes at the moment that she leaps into the air and he catches her, holding her up on his outstretched arms, and much of the development of the number is the incorporation of everyone, first the staff, then the clients, in a routine closer in spirit to communal celebration than to the spontaneous dance formation achieved in classic musicals or, closer to *Dirty Dancing*, *Saturday Night Fever* (John Badham, 1977). Both the lift and the routine involve sexuality, the former perhaps suggesting the transcendence of orgasm, the latter allowing the audience to let their hair down in the key of sexuality set by Johnny and the staff. And yet, in both cases, sexuality is not what's at stake. But race is.

NOT-QUITE-WHITE

Kassabian glosses her observation of the 'not-quite-white' character of the dirty dancing as 'Irish? Italian? Latina/o?'[5] This is the most explicit, albeit unspoken, racial/ethnic component of the dancing. Johnny was originally conceptualised as Italian-American but with the casting of Patrick Swayze became Irish-American.[6] Latin-American

4. Discussed in detail in Lesley Vize, 'Music and the Body' in Ian Inglis (ed.), *Popular Music and Film*, London: Wallflower, 2003, pp. 27-32.
5. Kassabian, op. cit., p. 18.
6. I've not found any explicit reference to this in the film, but it is a common perception, and Swayze was of part-Irish descent.

The centrality of not-quite-white-but-white-enough re-affirmed: Johnny (Patrick Swayze) and Frances (Jennifer Grey) in *Dirty Dancing*, 1987. (BFI National Archive)

dance features importantly: Penny teaches the merengue and she (and later Baby) dances the mambo with Johnny (at the Sheldrake, their turn is described as 'Mambo Magic'; Neil says to Johnny, 'You always do the mambo'). Even among the clients there is Latin-American dance (albeit awkward, mocked, and nearly safely contained): they learn the merengue and they cha-cha in the pavilion. Neil proposes introducing the Pechanga; also, Lisa dances a Hawaiian dance, yet another non-white form. The dancers in the staff quarters, the real dirty dancers, are very mixed racially, and many might be perceived (probably correctly) as Latina/o. In all these ways, a great deal of the dancing, whether sexually awkward or abandoned, is coded as not-quite-white.

The first time Baby sees the dirty dancing, she asks Billy, 'Where'd they learn to do that?' He shrugs his shoulders: 'I don't know – the kids do it in the basement back home.' 'Home' as in where he himself comes from? 'Basement' as in somewhere low and dark, where such dancing can incubate naturally? The question goes no further, for historically where the dance comes from – albeit mixed with other sources, albeit filtered and exaggerated by white perceptions – is African-American musical culture. This, though, would be 'definitely-not-white.'

Dirty Dancing plays fast and loose with the Black component of dirty dancing. It seems simultaneously to acknowledge it and erase it. African-Americans are among the dirty dancers, not only in the sequences when Baby visits the staff quarters but also in the black-and-white, slow-motion footage behind the first half of the opening and closing credits and in the final communal dance (but blink and you'll miss them). They are in some shots, not in others, with clear errors of continuity, as if the Black performers were only present at some of the shoots. Even when they are present, they are mostly on the edges or in the background. They seem even less present, only glimpsed a couple of times, in the final number, itself a celebration of inclusion which seems nonetheless to have its utopian limits. However, a Black couple are in the centre of the final shot of the film (just behind Johnny and Frances, who are, literally, highlighted), as if at the last moment the film wants to register the source of the film's central pleasure, dirty dancing, only for the film to take this back in the last image of the closing credits (before the fade to black for the remaining credits), a close two-shot on Johnny and Frances – absent from the opening credits, the centrality of not-quite-white-but-white-enough re-affirmed.

The film comes close to acknowledging the connection of Johnny's dancing to Black dance. Toward the end, he tells Neil that he wants to develop an idea he has for the final show combining a Cuban dance with 'this soul dance.' 'Soul' has ineluctable African-American connotations, and even Cuba, as a Caribbean culture, may be thought to be Blacker than continental South America. If this is what we are supposed to think he and Frances do at the final show (and the fact that they have not rehearsed would not preclude this possibility in the utopian drive of the last part of the film), it is not evident in dance terms and not at all musically (a point to which I shall return). Earlier in the film, Johnny and Baby are dancing in his studio; he's more interested in making love and starts to mime the words of the record they're dancing to, 'Love Is Strange,' sung by the Black duo Mickey & Sylvia; Baby joins in. Whites ventriloquising Blacks is the story in little of popular music in the USA. There is more of Johnny miming in the final number, '(I've Had) The Time of My Life,' but this is distinctly white pop; if Johnny's dance and musical roots were showing earlier in the film, they are not by the end.

Acknowledgement and erasure also hold in relation to the Blackest elements of the film: the casting of Honi Coles as the resort's bandleader and the musical soundtrack. Coles was a doyen of classic vaudeville and Broadway tap dance, historically a major form of Black dance.[7] To have him there at all is to register the great tradition of African-American dance; the film may well reckon on a majority of the target audience not knowing who he is, but the way he is introduced, from a long shot of the dull dancing to a mid-shot of him turning round and being revealed to be the bandleader, shows some awareness of just who the film has on board. We only see him dancing twice. There is a brief sequence of his delicate style on his first appearance, followed by a brief duet with Max in front of the band; and, at the end, he sways joyously with the music, encouraging Max to let go and join in like everyone else. His dancing suggests a physical ease and enjoyment that might include sexuality (especially in the context of the final number) but is by no means primarily defined by it. The connection with Max is curious. Jack Weston, who plays Max, is evidently a competent dancer, but in his duet with Coles he hangs his wrist limply, is fussier in his steps than Coles, and has a supercilious grin on his face, as if he can't emulate and must thus slyly mock the subtlety and elegance of Coles' dancing, perhaps because non-Blacks can't (or won't). (I guess there may be a very slight anxiety around gender and queerness with the limp wrist and dancing with a man [albeit not touching], but that doesn't seem to me to be at the forefront of this short moment.) Later, it is Coles, the only Black man remotely foregrounded in the film, who persuades Max to go with the flow of the dirty – or, now, only dirty*ish* – dancing. The film cannot, however, let go even of this casting decision. Coles' character is called Tito Suarez, an unmistakably Latino name, and there is a very curious shot of him at the end of the first sequence in which he appears: a mid-close-up with a halo of blue suffusing his hair. His name and the lighting seem at least to modify the registering of Coles' ethnic belonging and the reminder it constitutes of the roots of dirty dancing.

The music in the opening sequence encapsulates the musical trajectory of the film as a whole. It opens over the black-and-white footage of dancing mentioned above, with 'Be My Baby,' sung by the Black girl group the Ronettes; when the credits cut to the Houseman car on its way to Kellerman's, the music changes to Italian-American Frankie Valli and the Four Seasons' 'Big Girls Don't Cry.' The choices are resonant in narrative terms: the main character is called Baby and she is initially being sung to or for by a female group; the lesson that she must grow up (become a big girl that doesn't cry) comes at her from a male source. But the shift is also aurally one from Black to not-quite-white. The film as a whole takes this shift one stage further.

The soundtrack uses songs of the period, with a high proportion of Black artists: the Ronettes, the Contours ('Do You Love Me?'), Otis Redding ('Love Man,' 'These Arms of Mine'), Maurice Williams and the Zodiacs ('Stay'), the Drifters ('Some Kind of Wonderful'), Solomon Burke ('Cry to Me'), the Shirelles ('Will You Love Me Tomorrow?'),

---

7. Marshall and Jean Stearns, *Jazz Dance: The Story of American Vernacular Dance*, New York: Macmillan, 1968.

Mickey & Sylvia ('Love Is Strange'), Merry Clayton ('Yes'),[8] and the Five Satins ('In the Still of the Night'). This is eleven Black tracks contrasted against another six white ones: Frankie Valli and the Four Seasons, Tom Johnston ('Where Are You Tonight?'), Eric Carmen ('Hungry Eyes'), Zappacosta ('Overload'), Bruce Channel ('Hey! Baby'), and the Blow Monkeys ('You Don't Own Me'). Frankie Valli and Zappacosta are Italian-American, and there is also the Hispanic group Melon providing 'De Todo un Poco' for Johnny and Baby's Sheldrake number, beefing up the not-quite-white quotient.

The Black tracks are especially significant in terms of sexuality. The first dirty dancing Baby sees is done to the Contours, which not only suggests dance as a progression to love ('Do you love me now that I can dance?') but also links this in the lyrics to specific Black, and probably dirty, dances: the Mashed Potato and the Twist (both emphasising the groin area). Baby's first dance with Johnny, which creates a certain sexual frisson (already set up by her interested looks at him), is to Redding's 'Love Man.' Their first love-making is to Solomon Burke's 'Cry to Me'; a later post-coital sequence has the Shirelles' 'Will You Love Me Tomorrow?' playing in the background, and another sexually charged sequence involves, as noted above, Mickey & Sylvia's 'Love Is Strange.' The white artists' tracks have little weight in the sexual narrative, the most important being Eric Carmen and Bruce Channel accompanying Baby learning Penny's part for the Sheldrake show. When sex seems to be rearing its head (Johnny standing behind Baby and making a caressing movement down her arm), she keeps breaking into giggles and he becomes increasingly frustrated; when we may sense that something more than professional is developing between them, when they are practicing lifts in a lake, '(I've Had) The Time of My Life' seeps in unsung on the soundtrack. The latter, along with Swayze's 'She's Like the Wind,' are the culmination of the sexual/romantic narrative: 'She's Like the Wind' is first heard when Johnny and Baby say goodbye, and '(I've Had) The Time of My Life' is the music for their, and eventually everyone's, dance at the final show. '(I've Had) The Time of My Life' is sung by the it-doesn't-get-whiter-than-this duo Bill Medley and Jennifer Warnes. It's a number written for the film and, stylistically, clearly from the period in which the film was made rather than when it was set; it is also perhaps as far from Black influence as it is possible for pop music to get (which is to say, of course, not utterly untouched by it).

It might be that the marginality of Blacks in the film has something to do with realism. Perhaps few African-Americans were employed by upmarket resorts in the early 1960s, or if they were perhaps there was a hierarchy even within the help, so that Blacks did not even fraternise with everyone else when off-duty. *Dirty Dancing* has a liberal impulse. Characters register the particular salience of Blacks in American politics in the period: when Lisa worries that she hasn't brought enough shoes with her, her father

---

8. In fact, written specifically for the film.

points out that this is hardly a tragedy beside 'a police dog used in Birmingham,' indubitably a reference to Southern Black resistance; a little later, Neil seeks to impress Baby (who is set to join the Peace Corps) by telling her that he is going to go to Mississippi later in the summer on the Freedom Ride (connected with Black voter registration). In gender and class terms, the film clearly promotes an ideal of complementary equality within heterosexuality and registers a sharp awareness of class inequality (notably in the intersection of class and gender in Penny's narrative, which also highlights a kind of Ivy League *droit du seigneur* as well as the potential consequences of illegal and thus unregulated abortion). It may be this liberal impulse that accounts for there being any Blacks in the film at all, for the surprising casting of Honi Coles and the dominance of Black music tracks, while realism prevents the film from getting very far with this for fear of falling into improbability.

This argument may account for much of what I have been discussing, and *Dirty Dancing* is in some ways quite surprisingly realist in its delineation of the class and gender politics of its period. But it is also a musical, and one that draws more and more on the genre's utopian impulses as it goes along. The story of the girl plucked from obscurity (whether in the chorus or not) to become a star is a perennial theme of dance-based films: Ruby Keeler in *42nd Street* (Lloyd Bacon, 1933), Maureen O'Hara in *Dance, Girl, Dance* (Dorothy Arzner, 1940), Judy Garland in *Summer Stock* (Charles Walters, 1950), Natalie Portman in *Black Swan* (Darren Aronofsky, 2010). All but Garland share with Jennifer Grey an evidently inferior dancing skill (evident in contrast to others in the films as well as in the eyes of dance snobs) that makes the acclaim their characters achieve all the more magical (at once unbelievable and delightful). Folding everyone into community is also a trope of the musical. The passing along of 'Isn't it Romantic?' at the start of *Love Me Tonight* (Rouben Mamoulian, 1932), the work, family, and religious singing and dancing in *Hallelujah!* (King Vidor, 1929), the Busby Berkeley onstage numbers that show cross-sections of people all engaged in the same, usually amorous, pursuits, the arrival at the station 'On the Atchison, Topeka, and the Santa Fe' in *The Harvey Girls* (George Sidney, 1946), Tony Manero and friends in *Saturday Night Fever*: all impossible, all intoxicating. Both of these tropes, as they are used in *Dirty Dancing*, have little to do with realism. Moreover, as they involve a musical move toward the 1980s of the film's making ('She's Like the Wind' and '[I've Had] The Time of My Life'), it might have been possible to let go of plausibility vis-à-vis the racial divisions of the early 1960s.

WHITE ENOUGH

In fact, what happens is that there is a whitening of the film, both visually and musically. The choreographic climax of Johnny and Frances' final number occurs when she leaps up and is caught and held aloft by him, which represents her achieving what she has hitherto (notably at the Sheldrake) failed to achieve and is also the moment of maximum whooping and clapping from the diegetic audience. Choreography, narrative significance, and applause all suggest this as the climax of the film as a whole. In gender terms, it signifies a shift common in heterosexual couple dances in films[9] from a choreography emphasizing similarity or complementarity between the partners to one emphasising thrilling her-on-him dependency. In racial terms, Frances, spread out above Johnny, dominating the frame, is bathed in a dazzling white light that makes her look blonder, the apotheosis of the traditional affinity between light and white female glamour.[10] The transformation of their number into the final community/production number is initiated and led by Johnny in a move more common in action movies over the past twenty years, where women and non-whites are gathered in but always under the leadership of a white man (Conan, Steven Seagal, Bruce Willis, *The Matrix*, Harry Potter) – in other words, post-1960s utopian inclusion as long as the old hierarchies are still in place and Blacks remain secondary.

This movement toward the white is salient in the context of the film's Jewish setting. It would be possible to see *Dirty Dancing* and not register the fact that it has a Jewish setting. You have to know that Catskills resorts and names like Kellerman, Houseman, Gould (Robbie's name), and Schumacher (the name of the elderly kleptomaniac couple) were usually Jewish, and that the screenplay was based on the personal experience of Jewish Eleanor Bergstein, in order to hear a (rare) Jewish cadence in lines like Jake Houseman's response to Lisa's concern that she has not brought enough shoes, 'This is not a tragedy ... a tragedy is a police dog used in Birmingham,' and to countenance thinking that many of the characters/actors look Jewish, notably Baby/Jennifer Grey (her frizzy hair is reminiscent of Barbra Streisand, the most high-profile and insistently Jewish star of her generation, in a certain period of her career), Jake/Jerry Orbach (though Orbach's mother was not Jewish), and Neil/Lonny Price. Picking up on all this might allow one at once to see the film as 'a sort of Yiddish-inflected Camelot.'[11]

The Jewish setting gives particular resonances to the present-absent African-American elements in at least a couple of ways. One relates to the long history of Jews and Black music in the USA, discussed by Jeffrey Melnick in his *A Right to Sing*

---

9. Richard Dyer, '"I Seem to Find the Happiness I Seek": Heterosexuality and Dance in the Musical', in Dyer, *In the Space of a Song*, London: Routledge, 2011, pp. 89-100. (First published in Helen Thomas (ed.), *Dance, Gender and Society*, London: Macmillan, 1993, pp. 49-65.)
10. Richard Dyer, *White*, London: Routledge, 1997, pp. 122-40.
11. *The New York Times*, August 16, 1987, quoted in http://en.wikipedia.org/wiki/Dirty_Dancing. Accessed on November 20, 2008. 'Camelot' evokes both the optimistic notion of the Kennedy era and the eponymous musical play and film.

the Blues (1999).[12] Many works that defined African-American musical identity for a wider audience were produced by Jews, notably 'Alexander's Ragtime Band' (Irving Berlin, 1911), 'Swanee' (George Gershwin and Irving Caesar, 1919), *Rhapsody in Blue* (George Gershwin, 1924), 'Old Man River' from *Show Boat* (Jerome Kern and Oscar Hammerstein II, 1927, based on the novel by Edna Ferber), and 'Stormy Weather' (Harold Arlen and Ted Koehler, 1932, featured in the eponymous 1943 film celebration of 'the magnificent contribution of the coloured race to the entertainment of the world during the past twenty-five years'). The strong association of Jews with jazz was also present in the figures of Sophie Tucker, billed as 'the Mary Garden of Ragtime'[13] and 'the Queen of Jazz,' and Benny Goodman, known as 'the King of Swing' from the mid-1930s on, and one of whose greatest hits was the Jewish-composed 'Body and Soul' (Johnny Green, 1930). By the time of *Dirty Dancing* this may have been a forgotten history, and it may have been assumed (and perhaps still largely is) that the association of Jews with Black music was never really known to a wider public. However, perhaps the most successful up-front, crossover Jewish entertainment of the last century was *The Jazz Singer*, first a hugely successful play by Samson Raphaelson starring George Jessel on Broadway, then the Warner Bros. film in 1927 with Al Jolson,[14] which led to three remakes: with Danny Thomas (Michael Curtiz, 1952), Jerry Lewis (TV) (Ralph Nelson, 1959), and Neil Diamond (Richard Fleischer, 1980).[15] The facts of choosing this property for the risky, but in the event lucrative and transformative, decision to make the first sound feature film, and of believing in it enough to remake it thrice (providing occasions in the process for leading stars Lewis and Diamond to in some measure come out as Jewish), suggest a knowledge of this story in American culture – and it is all about the relationship between Jewish and Black music. In the most famous version (Jolson's), intercutting suggests an equivalence between Rabbi Rabinowitz's singing in the Synagogue and his son, Jack Robin's, in vaudeville: both

---

12. Jeffrey Melnick, *A Right to Sing the Blues: African Americans, Jews and American Popular Song*, Cambridge, MA: Harvard University Press, 1999. See also Michael Rogin, *Blackface, White Noise: Jewish Immigrants in the Hollywood Melting Pot*, Berkeley/Los Angeles: University of California Press, 1996, and Richard Dyer, *Pastiche*, London: Routledge, 2007, pp. 147-50.
13. Mary Garden was a leading opera singer of the day.
14. J. Hoberman, 'On *The Jazz Singer*' and '*The Jazz Singer*: A Chronology' in J. Hoberman and Jeremy Shandler (eds), *Entertaining America: Jews, Movies and Broadcasting*, New York: The Jewish Museum/Princeton: Princeton University Press, 2003, pp. 77-92.
15. For further discussion of *The Jazz Singer* in a Jewish context, see Hoberman, 'On *The Jazz Singer*', and Vincent Brook, 'The Four Jazz Singers: Mapping the Jewish Assimilation Narrative', *Journal of Modern Jewish Studies* 10:3 (2011), pp. 401-20, the latter a detailed account of all four film versions. See also Corin Willis, 'Meaning and Value' in John Gibbs and Douglas Pye (eds), *Style and Meaning: Studies in the Detailed Analysis of Film*, Manchester: Manchester University Press, 2005, pp. 127-140, for a discussion of the first version's relation to Black culture.

have what we might now call 'soul.' Moreover, Jack sings mostly in blackface, milking a long, non-white but also specifically Jewish tradition of Black impersonation – hugely ambivalent, often racist stereotyping, but also at times an assumption of affinity.[16] In other words, this very high profile property (above all by virtue of the status of the first film version as a decisive turning point in cinema history) insists, however hedged by qualification and appropriation, on the connection between Jews and Blacks. By the time of *Dirty Dancing*, such awareness is erased, undoubtedly reflecting the shift in the perception of Jews in America away from the ghetto and the oppression-sharing status of racial inferiority. The distance between the 1920s *Jazz Singer* and *Dirty Dancing* is that between segregation and a model of assimilation, in which Jewishness all but disappears in the light of whiteness.

This move is also enacted in the narrative. By dancing, sleeping, and siding with Johnny, Frances is making a bid to marry out, having at the start been paired by her parents and the resort with a nice Jewish boy with good prospects. We do not of course know if Johnny and Frances will marry (and we could have a cynical take on the words of the final song to suggest they won't, or at least not happily: 'I've had the time of my life'), but the conventions of romance suggest this is the logical development. Strictly speaking, Frances marrying a Gentile (and, if there is anything to Johnny's Irishness, a Catholic to boot) does not preclude the reproduction of Jewishness, but it certainly muddies the waters, and all the more so when, visually and musically, this means the eradication of the last vestiges of association with racial otherness and elevation to the blonde glow of whiteness.

Since *Dirty Dancing* was made, non-whites (notably Asians and Hispanics) have steadily increased as a percentage of the population of the USA, and a mixed-race President has been elected. The notion of whiteness as a default identity for Americans is being undermined – it is to be hoped irrecoverably. Perhaps the persistence of *Dirty Dancing*'s nostalgia for a time of optimism, liberalism, and emerging sexual freedom is also nostalgia for a time when all of that could still take place under the sign of whiteness.

Originally published in Yannis Tzioumakis and Siân Lincoln (eds), *The Time of Our Lives:* Dirty Dancing *and Popular Culture*, Detroit: Wayne State University Press, 2013, pp. 73–85. Copyright © 2013 Wayne State University Press, with the permission of Wayne State University Press.

---

16. On the dynamics of blackface in a Jewish context, see Rogin, *Blackface*, op. cit.; Melnick, *A Right*, op. cit., pp. 37–42; and Mark Slobin, 'Putting Blackface in Its Place,' in *Entertaining America*, op. cit., pp. 93–99. Brook notes the greater, but complex, acknowledgement of Black music in the later versions of *The Jazz Singer* (Brook, 'The Four Jazz Singers', op. cit.).

34 THE PRESIDENT'S HAIR (2018)

People tend to make fun of Donald Trump's hair. The first joke in *The Telegraph*'s list of the 'The 21 funniest jokes about Donald Trump' (28th April 2017) is Albert Brooks' tweet of 16th March 2015: "Donald Trump announces this morning that he will run for president. His hair will announce on Friday." A trawl of Trump jokes on Twitter reckons 'about 70–80 percent of the entries' are about his hair. The Channel 4 comedy comment show *The Last Leg* pokes fun at Trump so often that it has inaugurated a jar in which to put money every time any of them makes a Trump joke – atop it is a miniature golden toupee in the Trump style.

Laughing at the rich and powerful is good for one's health. Laughing together bonds us in mutual scorn of the enemies of humankind. But we should also be wary of political fun-making. Laughter is an agreeable experience that may make us affectionate for what occasions it; mockery is cruel, which may make us feel sorry for its object; laughter is a safety valve that may relieve us of our horror at a thing like Trump while not actually changing the thing itself. We need to laugh in these terrible times but we also need to think about just what it is we are laughing at. And really Trump is no matter for laughter.

Trump's hair is not just weird and noticeable, the basis of most of the jokes, it also literally embodies what fuels his appalling policies. Most obviously it is a sign of male vanity. Teasing of men's attempts to deal with balding is one of the most venerable of all sources of merriment – it's there in ancient Greek and Roman comedy, in Shakespeare, Molière and Goldoni, in *Carry Ons* and stand-up. Good – great to undercut the pomposity that comes with masculine ageing. The immediate humour in jokes about comb-overs, toupees and implants is that they – the hair-dos – never really work, merely draw attention to the vanity that produced them. But the jokes also tease the anxiety over loss of virility, of both strength and sexual prowess, of power over other men and over women. Trumpian hair jokes might nail the president's misogyny in his "grab a pussy" remark and his prowling of the stage in television debates with Hillary Clinton, and in the near total absence of women in his entourage except for the sprinkling of family members, staring out from faces and bodies lifeless from diet and surgery.

Trump's horrible and ridiculous hair, November 2017. (Jim Watson/AFP via Getty Images)

    But there's also a class dimension to the hair. Cosmopolitan, metropolitan, professional men don't do comb-overs, toupees and implants. They're naff. Honestly balding heads and receding hairlines are cool. Conceivably the biggest single thing that undermined Arthur Scargill's gravitas as a leader in the 1984–1985 miners' strike was his brillo-pad comb-over. Trump's hair is in this lineage. One of the things that is difficult to understand about Trump's victory is the support for this born well-heeled, multiply-bankrupted, mega-rich boss among the chronically poor, deskilled and unemployed, the idea that somehow he can represent them. No doubt misgivings about success and riches are less widespread in the USA than in the UK, but it is also his looks that make him plausible as the champion of those left behind and precisely in his spun-over, planted-atop, lacquer-heavy hair. And the problem is that every time we make some screamingly witty remark about it we confirm the rightness of the hostility and resentment felt by Trump's supporters towards the smart-ass, clever-dick, above-it-all political, professional and cultural classes. From this perspective, our jokes about his hair not only do nothing to undermine him, they even reinforce his position.

Then there's the colour of his hair, some kind of golden. If they have any, all men's hair in later life goes grey and white – in old age, bald or not, different ethnic groups are follically equal. And they can all dye their hair. But to have it blonde (yellow gold) at that age only looks appropriate on white men. This is the most sinister aspect of the 45th president's hair – it shrieks whiteness. Even Trump is politically astute enough not to declare himself white supremacist. When the alt-right announced their joy at his victory, he distanced himself from their statement, in a rather mealy-mouthed way ("it's not a group that I want to energise"). Having said that, alongside his Teutonic surname and Scottish first name, he comes trailing clouds of white heritage. (And historically the Klan claimed a connection to the clans of Scotland.) If the sparse sprinkling of women around him is striking, the sea of whiteness is even more so. This is the whitest administration, not since Obama but since before George Bush Jnr., for chrissakes.

In the 19th century, white people had no compunction about speaking of the superiority of white people. Subsequently, they have been contented to lead the world in the name of a common humanity which they alone have been entitled to embody. Trump leans on this assumption of the invisibility, inevitability and unspeakability of white ethnicity, but when he speaks of putting America first, he really means putting white America first. This is increasingly noted – if nothing else, we can be grateful for Trump having made whiteness visible and spoken again.

The male vanity, class naffness and excessive whiteness of the Trump hair are not incidental to his nastiness and dangerousness as a politician – they fuel it. Commentators often lament that politics now is all about personality instead of policies. But not always was this probably ever so, it is misleading to think either that personality is not political or that it doesn't matter what the personality of a politician is like as long as he or she has the right policies. Politicians have to take decisions, usually under pressure – so their personality matters and suggests which way they will jump. Trump's hair tells us that he has no qualms about limiting women's control over their own bodies by withdrawing funding for birth control and abortion; it boasts of who has the bigger weapons in his risky face-off with Kim Jong-un; it will readily put the men he feels at home with before the future of the planet in his withdrawal from the Paris climate agreement; and it puts white America first by making a start on excluding non-white entry to the country with Mexicans and Muslims.

The president's hair is horrible and ridiculous, but perhaps we should react to it more with horror than ridicule.

Originally published on *The Platform*, 19 March 2018.

SECTION 5
COMING TO TERMS

and other essays on bodies and affect

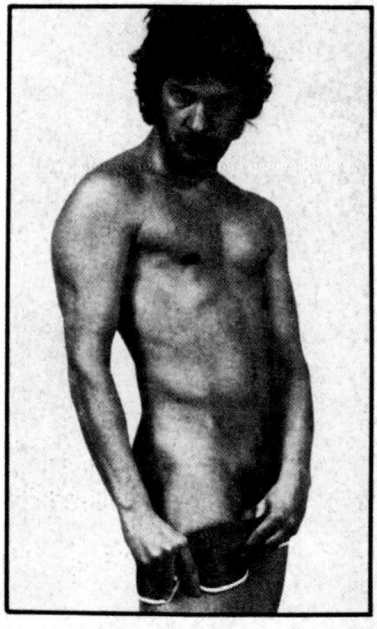

Content page of Montreal-based gay magazine *Attitude + Plus*, 1981. (Courtesy of Thomas Waugh)

The fourth chapter of Richard Dyer's 2015 monograph *Lethal Repetition: Serial Killing in European Cinema*, entitled 'Procuring extraordinary sensations', is not for the squeamish. It includes detailed descriptions of especially revolting sequences in films such as *Antropophagus* and *Lucker the Necrophagous*. In the chapter, Dyer explores 'some of the forms that the aesthetics of nastiness take in serial killer films, that seek to procure us extraordinary sensations';[1] he discusses, in particular, relish, thrill, disgust, and ecstasy. 'Surrendering and wallowing in filth and gore', he argues in his dive into disgust, 'is to obliterate obligations, responsibility, thought, conscience, perspective, civilisation, even nearly consciousness. So it may give one a glimpse of the ecstasy of the sublime.'[2] The depiction of unpleasant acts on the screen in some serial killer films, the sounds and images of bodies torn asunder, may provide a way into understanding or experiencing heightened affective states.

This chapter in *Lethal Repetition* provides just one example of a recurrent topic in Dyer's writing, the focus of this section of the Reader: the relationships between bodies (on screen, in the viewing audience, out in the world) and affect (sensations, emotions, feelings). Collected here are not only essays on forms of cinema that Linda Williams has termed 'body genres'[3] – horror, pornography – but also on types of films which foreground agility, muscularity, physical dexterity (dance films, action cinema); a brief review from 1981 of Kenneth Anger's *Scorpio Rising* ('witty, exhilarating, unpleasant', but also, crucially, 'a deeply *naughty* movie'); a discussion of evolving fashion style and how it reveals shifting attitudes to, and erotics of, the male body ('Old briefs for new', 1989); and a consideration of the historical affiliation between musicality and homosexuality, a connection which pivots on the perceived association of queers with sensitivity and emotionality ('Fond of little tunes', 2023).

The key text in this section, 'Male gay porn: coming to terms' was first published in *Jump Cut* in March 1985, as part of a dossier of contributions on the topic of sexual representation. (The clauses in the essay's title were flipped and slightly altered when the essay was anthologised in *Only Entertainment* in 1992). The dossier, which also featured contributions from Lisa DiCaprio, John Greyson and Thomas Waugh, was preceded by an earlier issue's special section on women and pornography (*Jump Cut* 26, December

---

[1]. Richard Dyer, *Lethal Repetition: Serial Killing in European Cinema*, London: Palgrave/British Film Institute, 2015, p. 60.
[2]. Ibid., p. 73.
[3]. Linda Williams, 'Film Bodies: Gender, Genre, and Excess', *Film Quarterly* 44:4 (Summer 1991), pp. 2-13.

1981), and was followed two issues later by a further dossier on sexual representation (*Jump Cut* 32, April 1987). In his introduction to the 1985 contributions, Chuck Kleinhans highlighted how 'explosive and antagonistic' the debates around pornography were at that time, especially amongst feminists, 'with the participants struggling around definitions and first principles'.[4] Censorship was a central and divisive topic: on one side, anti-porn crusaders such as Andrea Dworkin and Catherine MacKinnon were 'pushing for local censorship ordinances'; on the other, many feminists 'pointed out that police and prosecutors can and probably will use censorship laws against gays, feminists and other progressive people'.[5] Dyer engages with this embattled context in 'Coming to terms', acknowledging some sympathy with Dworkin. He proposes, however, approaching porn as a genre, one defined by the effect it has on the viewer's body. Like 'weepies, thrillers and low comedy', he argues, porn 'is realised in/through the body'; this 'has given it low status in our culture.' However, 'an art rooted in bodily effect can give us a knowledge of the body that other art cannot.'

'Coming to terms' was Dyer's first sustained written engagement with pornography, but had precursors. 'Don't look now' (1982, see Section 4) considered a variety of types of images of men, from anodyne publicity pictures of celebrities through to pornographic photographs. Before this, *Gays and Film* (1977) ended with a filmography that featured a non-partisan array of mainstream, arthouse, underground, exploitation and pornographic films from around the world.[6] In the introduction to the volume, Dyer discussed the decision to include porn, arguing that omitting it 'would have been to capitulate both to the questionable distinction between pornography and non-pornography, and to acknowledge the "superiority" of the latter'; however, its inclusion was not to be understood as an 'easy endorsement of it in terms of some notion of "sexual freedom".'[7] Dyer explored the politics of porn further in 'A conversation about pornography' (1989), a transcription of a discussion with Simon Shepherd and Mick Wallis. Topics opened up for examination by the trio included Dworkin's writings, distinctions between mainstream and amateur porn, the market dominance of American pornography, the relations between porn and the unruliness of desire, porn as a form of (potentially exploitative) labour, and Dyer's arrest for importing 'obscene' materials.

In the conversation with Shepherd and Wallis, Dyer comments on the sophistication of some gay porn, 'for instance in the way films or photos show men looking

---

4. Chuck Kleinhans, 'Opening a forum', *Jump Cut* 30 (1985), p. 23.
5. Ibid.
6. On the politics of this list, see Glyn Davis, 'Filmographies as Archives: On Richard Dyer's List-Making in *Gays and Film*', *Frames Cinema Journal* 19 (Spring 2022), https://framescinemajournal.com/article/filmographies-as-archives-on-richard-dyers-list-making-in-gays-and-film/
7. Richard Dyer, 'Introduction', in Dyer (ed.), *Gays and Film*, London: BFI, p. 2.

at other films and photos, then at each other, then at the camera and so on.'[8] This observation is explored in more detail in 'Idol thoughts: orgasm and self-reflexivity in gay pornography', which was first published in *Critical Quarterly* in 1994. The issue was devoted to queer topics, with contributors including Isaac Julien, Cherry Smyth, and Simon Watney. In his essay, Dyer argues that, although not all gay porn displays an awareness of its own fabrication, the history 'of gay film/video porn has consistently been marked by self-reflexivity, by texts that have wanted to draw attention to themselves as porn'. He focuses in on the porn actor Ryan Idol and discusses the knowing and overt constructedness of some of his films. For Dyer, self-reflexivity has a clear connection with queerness: 'Being meta is rather everyday for queers. Modes like camp, irony, derision, theatricality and flamboyance hold together an awareness of something's style with a readiness to be moved by it.' Gay pornography, that is, can be enjoyed by its consumers through both physical arousal and an arch savvy distance simultaneously.

In his explorations of pornography, Dyer maintains a recognition of porn as capitalist product: 'Pornography is the ultimate in capitalist mass media production', he told Shepherd and Wallis.[9] In 1981, in his essay 'Getting over the rainbow' (see Section 3), Dyer summarised the place of the human body in a capitalist economy and social formation. 'In this society', he wrote, 'the use of our bodies is compartmentalised'; this compartmentalisation 'makes of the body something easier to place in economic exchange relations.' In the same year, Dyer helped to programme a season of dance films at the Birmingham Arts Lab. His introduction to the season ('Why dance?'), which was published in the Lab's cinema programme, articulated a related Marxist critique of the stifling impact on the body of capitalist systems of order. However, Dyer suggested – in line with an argument he would later articulate in relation to pornography – that dance could have political value in provoking an engagement with the body:

> Dance constructs a knowledge of flesh and blood, muscle and tissue, a knowledge of how they can be experienced and used and lived – not a knowledge given by the biology of body, but a knowledge fabricated out of it. This knowledge – felt and sensed more than thought and articulated – can allow us to understand our bodies as they are used and abused and ignored in our society. If we can reconstruct a knowledge of the body, we can place our bodies at the centre of social activity and change.

---

8. Richard Dyer, 'A conversation about pornography', in Simon Shepherd and Mick Wallis (eds), *Coming on Strong: Gay Politics and Culture*, London: Unwin Hyman, 1989, p. 206.

9. Ibid., p. 203.

This knowledge includes an understanding of the relationship between bodies and emotions: 'Dance embodies (literally) attitudes and feelings about the body.' Dyer also authored short texts for the programme about some of the films in the season, several of which highlighted the relationships between bodies and affect. He described the main dance form in *Hello, Dolly!*, for instance, as 'energetic, optimistic, direct', the film suggesting 'the expansiveness of the American ideals of vitality.'

In two essays written for *Sight and Sound* in the 1990s, Dyer discussed in detail the role of the spectator's body in the cinema auditorium. In 'Dracula and desire' (1993), Dyer's critique of Francis Ford Coppola's *Bram Stoker's Dracula*, his own body is pivotal to his analysis. An experience of homophobia in the cinema before the screening leads to an anxious physical awareness of his neighbour: 'throughout the film I kept my body tensed away from him, lest my relaxed knee inadvertently touch his dreary thigh'. Dyer discusses how Coppola's film gestures towards various allegorical readings of vampirism. What is notably absent from it, however, is the queer thrill of a particular strain of vampire fiction, explored elsewhere by Dyer.[10] Recognising that the film is 'not addressed to me', he physically withdraws: 'Just as I held myself off from the man in the seat next to me, so I held myself off from the film.' In his article on *Speed* ('ACTION!', 1994), Dyer grapples with the male viewer's body. He identifies the broad audience desire for speed in popular cinema, but highlights the limits on who can experience such extreme sensations: 'the movies tie them to male characters and male environments, suggesting they are really only appropriate to men.' The dominant masculinity of action movies and that of their putative spectators is fragile, however. The best position for watching such films is at the cinema with one's legs slung over the seat in front, which is also an ideal position for anal sex, cunnilingus, and fellatio: indeed, 'for the male viewer action movies have a lot in common with being fellated.' Thrilled and aroused by the sights and sounds of choreographed bodies in action, the male viewer might be left damp, spent, wanting more, the same again.

Dyer engages at length with the pleasures and horrors of repetition in 'The same over and over', the third chapter of *Lethal Repetition*. (The version of the chapter presented in this Section of the Reader is newly abridged by Dyer himself.) Prior to the publication of *Lethal Repetition*, Dyer had explored the phenomenon of serial killing and its fictional representations in shorter pieces of writing including the essay 'Kill and kill again' (1997) and the second of his contributions to the BFI Classics series,

---

10. Richard Dyer, 'Children of the Night: Vampirism as homosexuality, homosexuality as vampirism', in Susannah Radstone (ed.) *Sweet Dreams: Sexuality, Gender and Popular Fiction*, London: Lawrence and Wishart, 1988, pp. 47-72. This essay was reworked and renamed as 'It's in his kiss!: vampirism as homosexuality, homosexuality as vampirism' for Richard Dyer, *The Culture of Queers*, London and New York: Routledge, 2002, pp. 70-89.

on *Seven* (1999).[11] In 'Kill and kill again', which uses the TV series *Millennium* (1996–1999) as its jumping-off point, Dyer opens up the topic of seriality and its associated affective pleasures: 'We may enjoy the excitement of the threat posed by a serial killer – when will he strike next and whom? When will they get him? – but we can also enjoy discerning the pattern in his acts.'[12] 'The same over and over' explores various permutations of repetition in serial killer films, and the distinct ways in which European examples engage with the theme. Crucially, the depictions of serial murder in these films have an affective charge: they 'show repetition in lethal form and may thus explore or allow the imaginative inhabiting of or surrendering to the experience of it.' In doing so, they provoke a wider recognition of repetition as 'a fundamental aspect of existence', an awareness of both 'its limitations and terrors'. Affective relations to the representation of bodies on screens, that is, can open up wider understandings of the cultural and political positioning and potential of the human subject – however extreme, explicit, arousing, or nauseating those depictions may be.

---

11. Richard Dyer, 'Kill and kill again', *Sight and Sound* 7:9 (September 1997), pp. 14-17; Richard Dyer, *Seven*, London: BFI, 1999. An extract from the latter appears in Section 6 of this Reader.
12. Dyer, 'Kill and kill again', op. cit., p. 16.

35 MALE GAY PORN: COMING TO TERMS (1985)

The main suggestions I'd like to make in this article about gay male pornographic cinema are quite brief and simple. Broadly I'm going to argue that the narrative structure of gay porn[1] is analogous to aspects of the social construction of both male sexuality in general and gay male sexual practice in particular. But before getting on to that, it seems necessary to say a few things by way of introduction. Pornography has recently become a Big Topic in left cultural work,[2] and what I'm going to say needs to be situated in relation to this.

First, a definition – a working definition, the one I'm going to be working with here, rather than a statement of the correct definition of pornography. I want some definition that is as broadly descriptive as possible. Discussion about porn tends to start off by being either for or against all porn and to be caught up in equally dubious libertarian or puritanical ideas. I don't mean to imply that I believe in the myth of objectivity, that I start off utterly neutral. I'm a gay man, who has (unlike women) easy access to porn and can take pleasure in it,[3] but who feels a commitment to the more feminist inflections of gay male politics. I'm also a socialist who sees porn as capitalist production but does not believe all capitalist cultural production always all the time expresses capitalist ideology.[4] I'm constantly looking for moments of contradiction, instability and give in our culture, the points at which change can be effected, and want to start out with the possibility of finding it in porn as anywhere else. So the definition I'm going to use is that a pornographic film is any film that has as its aim sexual arousal in the spectator.

This definition makes porn film a familiar kind of genre, that is, one that is based on the effect that both producers and audiences know the film is supposed to have. It

1. For the rest of the article, gay porn will always refer to gay *male* porn.
2. For a general introduction to this, see Julia Lesage, 'Women and Pornography', *Jump Cut* 26 (1981), pp. 46–47, 60, and the bibliography by Gina Marchetti in the same issue, pp. 56–60.
3. This access is not actually so easy outside of certain major metropolitan centres, and the recent anti-pornography legislation in Great Britain has hit gay porn far more decisively than straight.
4. This argument is developed by Terry Lovell in *Pictures of Reality*, London: BFI, 1981.

is not defined (or I am not asking to define it here), like the Western, gangster film or musical, by such aesthetic, textual elements as iconography, structure, style and so on, but by what it produces in the spectator. It is like genres such as the weepie and the thriller, and also low or vulgar comedy. Like all of these, it is supposed to have an effect that is registered in the spectator's body – s/he weeps, gets goosebumps, rolls about laughing, comes. Like these genres, porn is usually discussed in relation to a similar, but 'higher' genre which doesn't have a bodily effect – weepies (melodramas and soap opera) are compared to tragedy or realist drama, thrillers to mystery/detective stories (based on intellectual, puzzle-solving narratives), low comedy (farce) to high comedy (comedy of manners), and porn to erotica.

I'd like to use porn as a neutral term, describing a particular genre. If one defines porn differently, then the kind of defence of porn as a genre (but emphatically not of most porn that is actually available) that I'm involved with here is not really possible. Current feminist critiques of pornography[5] rightly stress the degradation of women that characterizes so much heterosexual porn, and these critiques in fact define pornography as woman-degrading representations of sexuality. Although feeling closer to some of those feminist articles that take issue with this hard line anti-porn position,[6] I do not feel as out of sympathy with, say, Andrea Dworkin's work as many people, and especially gay men, that I know. Although in relation to gay porn Dworkin is in some respects inaccurate (e.g. in stressing gay porn's use of socially inferior – young, Black – men in 'feminine' positions, whereas similarity between partners is more often the case) or out of date,[7] her rage at what so much of porn consists of is fully justified, and especially so because she effectively defines porn as that which is degrading and out*rage*ous. But I'd like all the same to hang on to a wider notion of sexual representation, and still use the word *pornography* precisely because of its disreputable, carnal associations. (Maybe the feminist debate means that I can't use the word like this – but I don't want to fall for the trap of substituting the word *erotica*.[8])

---

5. For example, Andrea Dworkin, *Pornography: Men Possessing Women*, New York: Putnam's, 1981; Susan Griffin, *Pornography and Silence*, London: The Women's Press, 1981; Laura Lederer (ed.), *Take Back the Night*, New York: William Morrow, 1980.
6. For example, Kathy Myers, 'Towards a Feminist Erotica,' *Camerawork* (March 1982), pp. 14-16, 19, reviews of Dworkin and Griffin by Deborah Allen and Gavin Harris in *Gay Information* 9/10 (1982), pp. 20-27, and by Janice Winship in *Feminist Review* 11:1 (1982), pp. 97-100, and B. Ruby Rich's review of *Not a Love Story* in *Village Voice* (20 July 1982).
7. See Allen and Harris, op. cit., p. 22.
8. 'Because it is less specific, less suggestive of actual sexual activity, "erotica" is regularly used as a euphemism for "classy porn". Pornography expressed in literary language or expensive photography and consumed by the upper middle class is "erotica"; the cheap stuff, which can't pretend to any purpose but getting people off, is smut.' Ellen Willis, quoted by Mick Carter in 'The Re-education of Desire: Some Thoughts on Current Erotic Visual Practices,' *Art and Text* 4 (1981), pp. 20-38.

The fact that porn, like weepies, thrillers and low comedy, is realized in/through the body has given it low status in our culture. Popularity these genres have, but arbiters of cultural status still tend to value 'spiritual' over 'bodily' qualities, and hence relegate porn and the rest to an inferior cultural position.

One of the results of this is that culturally validated knowledge of the body, of the body's involvement in emotion, tends to be intellectual knowledge about the body, uninformed by experiential knowledge of it.[9] Let me try to be clear about this. I'm not saying that there can be a transparent, pure knowledge of the body, untouched by historical and cultural reality. On the contrary, all knowledge is culturally and historically specific, we do not transcend our material circumstances. We learn to feel our bodies in particular ways, not 'naturally'. But an intellectual or spiritual knowledge about the body is different from experiential knowledge of the body — both are socially constructed, but the latter is always in a dynamic material and physical relationship with the body, is always knowledge in and of the body. Intellectual or spiritual knowledge on the other hand divorces social construction from that which it constructs, divorces knowledge about the body from knowing with the body. (Certain types of discourse analysis — but by no means all — clearly fall into the same idealist trap.[10])

Moreover, the effect of the cultural status of intellectual/spiritual accounts of the body is to relegate experiential knowledge of the body to a residual category. Of course idealist discourse accounts do not allow any such category at all.[11] Thus experiential knowledge (except when sanctified by the subjugation of the body in most forms of 'physical education') is allowed to be both inferior and just a given, not socially constructed,[12] to be just 'experience', not socially constructed experiential knowledge. By valuing the spiritual, the bodily is left as something natural, and sexuality as the most natural thing of all. What is in fact also socially constructed (experiential knowledge of the body, and of sexuality) is not recognized as such, and for that reason is not reflected upon, is allowed to go its supposed own way until it meets up with spiritual censors. Even gay and feminist theory have been notoriously reluctant to think through the social construction of the body without lapsing into the Scylla of

---

9. An example of this is the role of the representation of the body in Christian iconography. At one level, the body of Christ could not be a more central motif of Christianity, most notably in the image of Christ on the cross. But the tendency remains to stress what the body means at the expense of what it is, to highlight transcendence over the body. In the Christian story of Christ as the Word made flesh, it is the Word that ultimately matters, not the flesh.
10. The magazine *m/f* is the leading example of this.
11. For a critique of idealism, see Terry Lovell, op. cit.
12. The one area of cultural work that has been concerned with body knowledge is dance, but the leading exponents of Modern Dance such as Isadora Duncan and Ruth St. Denis have been influentially committed to notions of natural movement. See Elizabeth Kendally, *Where She Danced*, New York: Alfred Knopf, 1979.

Lacanian psychoanalysis (where social construction does not construct anything *out of* any material reality) and the Charybdis of both gay liberationist let-it-all-hang-out (where sexuality is a pure impulse awaiting release) and the implicit sexual essentialism of radical feminist ideas of masculine aggression and women's power.[13]

A defence of porn as a genre (which, I repeat, is not at all the same thing as defending most of what porn currently consists of) would be based on the idea that an art rooted in bodily effect can give us a knowledge of the body that other art cannot.

Even now porn does give us knowledge of the body – only it is mainly bad knowledge, reinforcing the worst aspects of the social construction of masculinity that men learn to experience in our bodies. All the same, porn can be a site for 're-educating desire',[14] and in a way that constructs desire in the body, not merely theoretically in relation to, and often against, it.

To do that though means rejecting any notion of 'pure sex', and particularly the defence of porn as expressing or releasing a sexuality 'repressed' by bourgeois (etc.) society. This argument has gained some ground in gay male circles, and with good reason. Homosexual desire has been constructed as perverse and unspeakable; gay porn does speak/show gay sex. Gay porn asserts homosexual desire, it turns the definition of homosexual desire on its head, says bad is good, sick is healthy and so on. It thus defends the universal human practice of same-sex physical contact (which our society constructs as homosexual); it has made life bearable for countless millions of gay men.

But to move from there to suggest that what we have here is a natural sexuality bursting out of the confines of heterosexual artificial repression is much more of a problem.

This is certainly the way that Gregg Blachford's article 'Looking at Pornography'[15] can be read, and seems to be the contention behind David Ehrenstein's article 'Within the Pleasure Principle, or Irresponsible Homosexual Propaganda.'[16] The latter argues that porn movies, unlike mainstream films that imply sexuality but don't show it, give us the pure pleasure of voyeurism which lies unacknowledged behind all cinema.

> The pornographic is obvious, absolute, unmistakable – no lies or omissions or evasions can hold quarter in its sphere.[17]

---

13. See Elizabeth Wilson, *What Is To Be Done About Violence Against Women?* London: Penguin, 1983.
14. See Mick Carter, op. cit..
15. In *Gay Left* 6 (Summer 1978), pp. 16–20.
16. In *Wide Angle* 4:1 (1980), pp. 62–65. I am conscious that because this article, in a manner of speaking, attacks things I have written – and even attacks what it infers from them about my sexual practices – that I may here treat the article rather unfairly.
17. Ibid., p. 65.

Porn is the 'abandon of everything to the pleasure principle' (ibid), conceptualized as pure drive (the more usual appropriation of Freudian ideas than the Lacanian version so influential in academic film studies circles). Porn itself operates with this idea, and the view is clearly expressed in the introduction to *Meat*,[18] a collection of writings from the magazine *Straight to Hell*. The magazine, like the book, consists entirely of personal accounts of gay sexual experience sent in to the magazine by gay men. I have no reason to suppose that the accounts are not genuine both in the sense of having actually been sent in (not ghost written) and describing real experiences. But this 'genuineness' is not to be conflated, as book and magazine do, with the notion of an unconstructed sexuality – raw, pure and so on. A reading of *Meat*, or a look at gay porn, indicates really rather obviously that the sexuality described/represented is socially meaningful. Class, ethnicity and of course concepts of masculinity and gayness/straightness all clearly mark these gay pornographic productions; and indeed the very stress on sexuality as a moment of truth, and its conceptualization as raw, pure etc., is itself historically and culturally produced.[19]

What makes *Meat* and gay movie house porn especially interesting and important is the extent to which they blur the line between representation and practice. *Meat* is based on (I think largely) true encounters that really happened. Watching porn in gay cinemas usually involves having sex as well – not just self-masturbation but sexual activity with others, in a scenario brilliantly evoked by Will Aitken in his article 'Erect in the Dark.'[20] In principle then gay porn is a form of representation that can be the site and occasion for the production of bodily knowledge of the body. In this definition, porn is too important to be ignored, or to be left to the pornographers.

NARRATIVE MANIFESTATION

I'd like now to turn to one of the ways in which the education of desire that porn is involved in is manifested, namely its use of narrative.[21]

It is often said that porn movies as a genre are characterized by their absence of narrative. The typical porn movie, hard core anyway, is held to be an endless series of people fucking, and not even, as Beatrice Faust notes, fucking in the 'normal' physiological order that Masters and Johnson have 'recorded'.[22] Gay porn

---

18. San Francisco: Gay Sunshine Press, 1981.
19. See Michel Foucault, *The History of Sexuality*, New York: Vintage Books, 1980.
20. In *Gay News*, Winter Extra (December 1981/January 1982), pp. 15–20.
21. This is only one element of any full analysis. One of the major elements not discussed here, and that needs work doing on it, is the role of iconography – of dress and setting, and especially performers, the male types that are used, porn stars' images and so on, all drenched in ideological meanings.
22. *Women, Sex and Pornography*, London: Penguin, 1982, p. 16.

(and indeed what hetero porn I have seen), however, is full of narrative. Narrative is its very basis.

Even the simplest pornographic loops have narrative. In those quarter-in-the-slot machines where you just get a bit of a porn loop for your quarter, you are very conscious of what point (roughly) you have come into the loop, you are conscious of where the narrative has got to. Even if all that is involved is a fuck between two men, there are the following narrative elements: the arrival on the scene of the fuck, establishing contact (through greeting and recognition, or through a quickly established eye-contact agreement to fuck), undressing, exploring various parts of the body, coming, parting. The exploration of the body often involves exploring those areas less heavily codified in terms of sexuality, before 'really getting down to/on with' those that are (genitals and anus). Few short porn films don't involve most or all of these narrative elements, and in that order.

Usually too there is some sort of narrative detail – in *Muscle Beach*, one man (Rick Wolfmier) arrives on the scene (a beach) in a truck, the other man (Mike Betts) is already there sunbathing; Wolfmier walks by the sea for a while; there is quite a long sequence of shot:reverse shot cutting as they see each other and establish contact; self-masturbation precedes their actual physical contact with each other; after orgasm, Rickmier drives away again in his truck. Already then minimal character elements are present, of not inconsiderable social interest – the iconography of the truck, the looks of the two men, the culture of the beach and of bodybuilding, and so on.

Even when the film is yet more minimal than this, there is still narrative – and essentially the same narrative, too. Some gay porn loops simply show one man masturbating. A rather stylish version of this is *Roger*, which just has the eponymous star masturbating. The music is a kind of echoing drumbeat; there is no set to speak of; the lighting is red, covering the screen in varieties of pulsating hue; the film cuts between long shots and medium shots in a quite rhythmic way, often dissolving rather than cutting clean. It will be clear that there is something almost abstract or avant-garde-ish about the film, as the cinematic means play visually with its solo subject, Roger masturbating. Yet even here there is a basic narrative – Roger enters, masturbates, comes. (Where you put your quarter in might mean that you start with his orgasm and run on where he comes in; but you'd know and be able to reconstruct the proper narrative order that your quarter has cut across.)

Even in so minimal and abstract a case, there is narrative – *Roger* is a classic goal-directed narrative.[23] The desire that drives the porn narrative forward is the desire to come, to have an orgasm. And it seems to me that male sexuality, homo or hetero, is socially constructed, at the level of representation anyway, in terms of narrative; that, as it were, male sexuality is itself understood narratively.

---

23. See David Bordwell and Kristin Thompson, *Film Art*, Reading, Mass.: Addison-Wesley, 1979.

The goal of the pornographic narrative is coming; in filmic terms, the goal is ejaculation, that is, visible coming. If the goal of the pornographic protagonist (the actor or 'character') is to come, the goal of the spectator is to see him come (and, more often than not, probably, to come at the same time as him). Partly this has to do with 'proof', with the form's 'literalness', as Beatrice Faust puts it, with the idea that if you don't really see semen the performer could have faked it (and so you haven't had value for money). But partly too it has to do with the importance of the visual in the way male sexuality is constructed/conceptualised. It is striking how much pornographic literature, not a visual medium, stresses the visible elements of sex. (Most remarkable perhaps is Walter, the Victorian narrator of *My Secret Life*, with his obsessive desire to see into his partner's vagina, even to the detail of seeing, for instance, what his semen looks like after he has ejaculated it into her vagina.) Men's descriptions of their own erections seldom have to do with how their penises feel, but with how they look. The emphasis on seeing orgasm is then part of the way porn (re)produces the construction of male sexuality.

Could it be otherwise, could sexuality be represented differently? So dominant are masculine-centered definitions of sexuality that it often seems as if all representations of sexuality (pornographic or otherwise) are constructed as driven narrative. But there are alternatives, and one that struck me was the lesbian sequences at the end of *Je tu il elle*, directed by Chantal Akerman. (As Margaret Mead pointed out in her work on sex roles in anthropology, you only need one example of things being different to establish that things can be different in the organization of human existence and hence that things can be changed.) The sequence itself is part of a (minimalist) narrative; but taken by itself it does not have the narrative drive of male porn. It starts *in media res* – there is no arrival in the room, the women are already making love when the sequence starts (though the previous shot has, perhaps ambiguously, established that they are going to make love); there is no sense of a progression to the goal of orgasm; nor is there any attempt to find visual or even (as in hetero porn?) aural equivalents for the visible male ejaculation. In particular, there is no sense of genital activity being the last, and getting-down-to-the-real-thing, stage of the experience. It is done in three long takes – no editing cuts across a sexual narrative (as in gay porn – see below); the harsh white lighting and the women's white bodies on crumpled white sheets in a room painted white, contribute to the effect of representing the sexuality as more dissolving and ebbing than a masculine thrusting narrative. Let me stress that I am not talking about what the women are doing – for much of the time their actions are far more snatching and grabbing than, for instance, the generally smooth, wet action of fellatio in gay porn. My point is the difference in narrative organization, in the cinematic representation of sexuality.[24]

---

24. For further discussion, see Angela Martin, 'Chantal Akerman's films: A Dossier,' *Feminist Review* 3:1 (1979), pp. 24–47.

I am not suggesting that this is a better representation of sexuality, or the correct mode for representing lesbian sexuality. Also I want to bracket the question of whether the difference between the two modes of representation is based on biological differences between female and male sexuality, or on different social constructions of sexuality, or on a combination of the two.[25] All I want to get over is the difference itself, and the fact that male porn, whether homo or hetero, is ineluctably caught in the narrative model. (This is particularly significant in hetero porn in that it is predominantly constructed around a female protagonist,[26] who is attributed with this narrativized sexuality. However, I am not about to get into whether this is a gain – a recognition of female sexuality as desire – or a loss – a construction of female sexuality in male terms.)

The basis of gay porn film is a narrative sexuality, a construction of male sexuality as the desire to achieve the goal of a visual climax. In relation to gay sexual politics, it is worth signaling that this should give pause to those of us who thought/hoped that being a gay man meant that we were breaking with the gender role system. At certain levels this is true, but there seems no evidence that in the predominant form of how we represent our sexuality to ourselves (in gay porn) we in any way break from the norms of male sexuality.

Particularly significant here is the fact that although the pleasure of anal sex (that is, of being anally fucked) is represented, the narrative is never organized around the desire to be fucked, but around the desire to ejaculate (whether or not following on from anal intercourse). Thus although at the level of public representation gay men may be thought of as deviant and disruptive of masculine norms because we assert the pleasures of being fucked and the eroticism of the anus,[27] in our pornography this takes a back seat.

This is why porn is politically important. Gay porn, like much of the gay male ghetto, has developed partly out of the opening up of social spaces achieved by the gay liberation movements; but porn and the ghetto have overwhelmingly developed within the terms of masculinity. The knowledge that gay porn (re)produces must be put together with the fact that gay men (like straight men but unlike women) do have this mode of public sexual expression available to them, however debased it may be. Like male homosexuality itself, gay porn is always in this very ambiguous relationship to male power and privilege, neither fully within it nor fully outside it.[28] But that

---

25. For a discussion of this difficult nature/nurture debate from a socialist feminist perspective that does not discount the contribution of biology altogether, see Janet Sayers, *Biological Politics*, London: Tavistock, 1982.
26. See Dennis Giles, 'Angel on fire: Three texts of desire,' *Velvet Light Trap* 16 (Fall 1976), pp. 41–45.
27. See Guy Hocquenghem, *Homosexual Desire*, London: Allison and Busby, 1978.
28. See Michèle Barrett, *Women's Oppression Today*, London: Verso, 1980, Chapter two, for a discussion of the relationship between male homosexuality and women's subordination.

ambiguity is a contradiction that can be exploited. In so far as porn is part of the experiential education of the body, it has contributed to and legitimized the masculine model of gay sexuality, a model that always implies the subordination of women. But rather than just allowing it to carry on doing so, it should be our concern to work against *this* pornography by working with/within pornography to change it – either by interventions within pornographic filmmaking itself,[29] or by the development of porn within the counter-cinemas (always remembering that the distinction between porn in the usual commercial sense and sexual underground/alternative/independent cinema has always been blurry when you come to look at the films themselves), or by criticism that involves audiences reflecting on their experience of pornography (rather than by closing down on reflection by straight condemnation or celebration of it).

So far all I've been talking about is the most basic, minimal narrative organization of (gay) male pornography. However, gay porn is characterized as much by the elaborations of its narrative method as by its insistence on narrative itself. Though the bare narrative elements may not often go beyond those described above, they are frequently organized into really quite complex narrative wholes. Often there is a central narrative thread – two men who are in love or who want to get off with each other – but this is punctuated by almost all of the devices of narrative elaboration imaginable, most notably flashbacks (to other encounters, or previous encounters of the main characters with each other), fantasies (again, with others or each other, of what might or could be), parallelism (cutting back and forth between two or more different sexual encounters) and so on. All preserve the coming-to-visual-climax underlying narrative organization, but why this fascination with highly wrought narrative patterns? To begin with, of course, it is a way of getting more fucks in, with more people.[30] There is even perhaps an element of humour, as the filmmakers knowingly strain their imagination to think of ways of bringing in yet more sex acts. But it is also a way of teasing the audience sexually, because it is a way of delaying climax, of extending foreplay. In parallel sequences, each fuck is effectively temporally extended, each climax delayed. More generally, the various additional encounters delay the fulfillment of the basic narrative of the two men who are the central characters.

(For example in *L.A. Tool and Die* the underlying narrative is Wylie's journey to Los Angeles to find a job and his lover Hank; Wylie and Hank are played by the stars of the film, Will Seagers and Richard Locke, so we know that their having sex together must be the climax; but there are various encounters along Wylie's way, including

---

29. For some consideration of this, see Paul Alcuin Siebenand, 'The Beginnings of Gay Cinema in Los Angeles: The Industry and the Audience,' doctoral dissertation, University of California, Los Angeles (Department of Communications), 1975.
30. Cf. Sam Mele and Mark Thirkell, 'Pornographic Narrative,' *Gay Information* 6 (1981), pp. 10-13.

memories, observation of other couples, incidental encounters with other men, and even inserted scenes with characters with whom Wylie has no connection, before arrival at Los Angeles and finally making it with Hank.)

There is a third reason for this narrative elaboration. Just as the minimal coming-to-visual-climax structure is a structural analogue for male sexuality, so the effective multiplication of sex acts through elaborate narrativity is an analogue for a (utopian) model of a gay sexual lifestyle that combines a basic romanticism with an easy acceptance of promiscuity. Thus the underlying narrative is often romantic, the ultimate goal is to make love with the man; but along the way a free-ranging, easy-going promiscuity is possible. While not all gay men actually operate with such a model of how they wish to organize their affective lives, it is a very predominant one in gay cultural production, a utopian reconciliation of the desire for romance *and* promiscuity, security *and* freedom, making love *and* having sex.

It is worth stressing how strong the element of romance is, since this is perhaps less expected than the celebration of promiscuity. The plot of *L.A. Tool and Die* outlined above is a good example, as is *Navy Blue* in which two sailors on shore leave seek out other lovers because each doesn't think that the other is gay, yet each is really in love with the other (as fantasy sequences make clear) – only at the end of the film do they realize their love for each other. Or take *Wanted*, a gay porn version of *The Defiant Ones*, in which two convicts, one gay (Al Parker) and one straight (Will Seagers), escape from prison together. Despite Seagers' hostility to Parker's sexuality, they stick together, with Parker having various sexual encounters, including watching Seagers masturbate. The film is a progression from the sadistic prison sexuality at the start (also offered, I know, as pornographic pleasure), through friendly mutual sexual pleasuring between Parker and various other men, to a final encounter, by an idyllic brookside, between Parker and Seagers which is the culmination of their developing friendship. Some men I know who've seen the film find this final sequence too conventionally romantic (which it is – that's why I like it) or else too bound up with the self-oppressive fantasy of the straight man who deigns to have sex with another man. It can certainly be taken that way, but I know when I first saw it I was really moved by what seemed to be Seagers' realization of the sexuality of his feeling for Parker. And what particularly moved me was the moment when Seagers comes in Parker's mouth, and the latter gently licks the semen off Seagers' penis, because here it seemed was an explicit and arousing moment of genital sexuality that itself expressed a tender emotional feeling – through its place in the narrative, through the romanticism of the setting, through the delicacy of Parker's performance. If porn taught us *that* more often…

One of the most interesting ways of making narratives complex in gay porn is the use of films within films. Many gay porn films are about making gay porn films; and many others involve someone showing gay porn films to himself or someone else

The final encounter of Cooper (Al Parker) and Garrett (Will Seagers) in *Wanted*, 1980, as the culmination of their developing friendship.

(with the film-within-the-film then becoming for a while the film we are watching). The process of watching, and also of being watched (in the case of those films about making gay porn) are thus emphasized, not in the interests of foregrounding the means of construction in order to deconstruct them, but because the pleasure of seeing sex is what motivates (gay) male pornography and can be heightened by having attention drawn to it. (There is a whole other topic, to do with the power in play in looking/being looked at, which I won't get into here.) We have in these cases a most complex set of relations between screen and auditorium. On screen someone actually having sex is watched (photographed) by a filmmaker watched (photographed) by another invisible filmmaker (the one who made the film on screen), and all are watched by someone in the audience who is (or generally reckons to be) himself actually having sex. Gay porn here collapses the distinctions between representation and that which it is a representation of, while at the same time showing very clearly the degree to which representation is part of the pleasure to be had in that which it is a representation of. Porn (all porn) is, for good or ill (and currently mainly for ill), part of how we live our sexuality; how we represent sexuality to ourselves is part of how we will live it, and porn has rather cornered the market on the representation of sexuality. Gay porn seems to make that all clearer, because there is greater equality between the participants (performers, filmmakers, audiences)[31] which permits a fuller exploration of the education of desire that is going on. Porn involves us bodily in that education; criticism of porn should be opening up reflection on the education we are receiving in order to change it.

Originally published in *Jump Cut* 30 (March 1985), pp. 27–29.

---

31. This is a question of degree – producers and audiences are not equal in their power of determining the form that representation takes, and especially in a field so fiercely colonised by capitalist exploitation as pornography; and at the psychological level, performers and audience members are not necessarily equal, in that performers are validated as attractive sexual beings to a degree that audience members may not be. But the point is that they are all gay men participating in a gay subculture, a situation that does not hold with heterosexual porn. See Siebenand, op. cit., and also Tom Waugh in the article in this issue of *Jump Cut* ['Men's pornography: gay vs straight', *Jump Cut* 30 (March 1985), pp. 30-36].

36 *SCORPIO RISING* (1981)

Scorpio Rising [US 1963] is a film that is at once dense and immediate, a collage of complex images and overlapping structures which nonetheless make a direct and almost physical impact. It is witty, exhilarating, unpleasant, beautiful, intellectual, sexy… and impossible to pin down. The best way to approach it is to analyse its complex structure. But… a word of warning: the images are so brilliantly and quickly orchestrated in the film, so much happens virtually simultaneously, the visual and musical rhythms are so hypnotic, that no systematic reading can convey its dazzling effect.

The film is structured in several different ways, each superimposed on the others. Most obviously, the film is organised into a series of more or less self-contained sequences, each of which is precisely fitted to a late fifties/early sixties pop song. This series is also ordered in two overall ways: there is first a sort of narrative, though this is only loosely put together. Secondly, the narrative progression is also a ritual enactment, according to the precepts of what Kenneth Anger called 'Magick'.

Anger himself has suggested a division into four parts, which are also four ritual stages: 'Boys and Bolts', preparing for the ritual (assembling machines and getting dressed-up); 'Image Maker', getting physically prepared (freeing the mind with cocaine and 'getting high on heroes' such as Brando); 'Walpurgis Party', the frenzy out of which the ritual acts of Magick emerge (not only urinating on an altar, but also the use of a myriad of Magick talismen); and 'Rebel Rouser – The Gathering of the Dark Legions', ending in death. Finally, these song, narrative and ritual structures are criss-crossed by a number of strands of connected images, drawn most notably from Magick, hero-worship and homosexuality.

The strand of complex Magick imagery – such as a Grim Reaper skeleton, a scorpion preserved in glass, the number 777 – runs through the whole film, and each image weaves some esoteric spell or message. The hero-worship strand has three phases. First of all there are heroes drawn from the mass media, especially James Dean (seen in a pin-up in Scorpio's room) and Marlon Brando, but also the comic book Li'l Abner – a strong but simple fellow who, in the cartoon images shown, seems like a Huck Finn character – that is, another, though less violent, rejector of 'grown-up' society, complete with homo-erotic overtones.

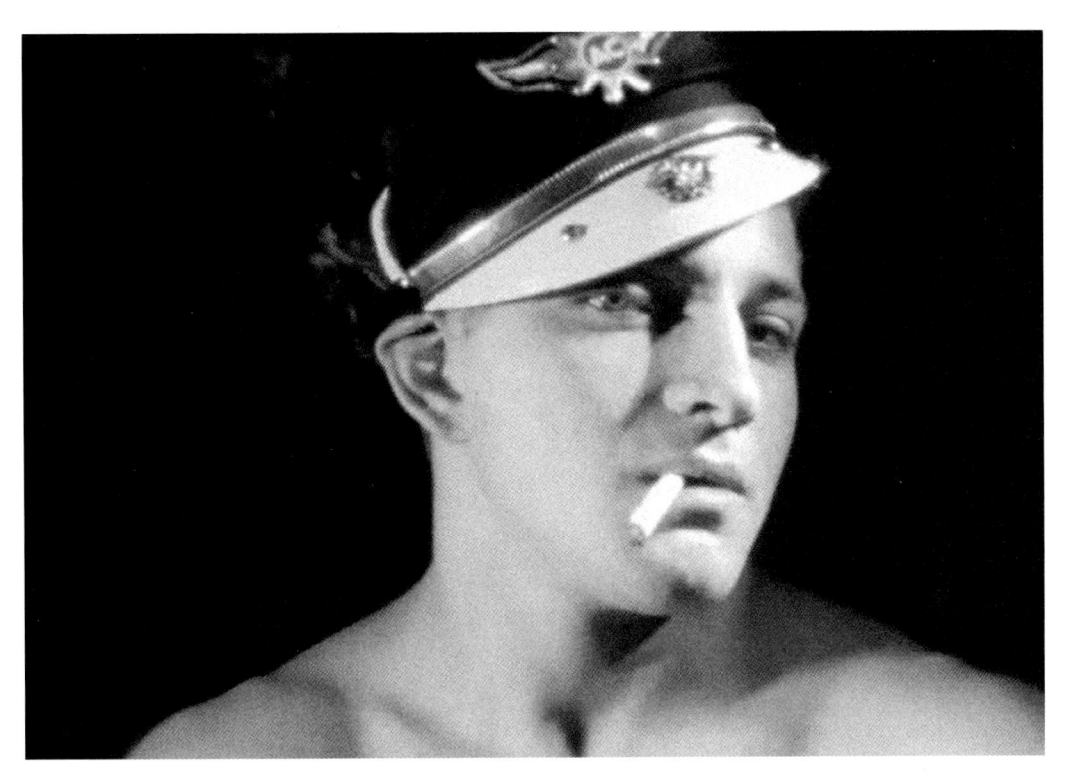

Iconic homo-eroticism in *Scorpio Rising*, 1963.

The next hero is Christ. Scenes from a film supposedly called *The Road to Jerusalem* are cut into the boys going to the party (Christ walking with his disciples), the party itself (Christ looks off screen and the film cuts to a guy having mustard poured on him), and the boys going off on their bikes (Christ rides a donkey into Jerusalem). There is very precise intercutting here. The 'Gentle Jesus'-style Christ of the film touches the blind man's eye, and the film cuts to a man putting a parking ticket on a bike (an image of law and order); the now sighted blind man kneels before Christ, and there is a cut to a close-up of a penis sticking out of a fly. The use of such a milk-and-water image of Christ and these impudent cross-cuttings suggests an anti-Christian message, and that would be appropriate insofar as the film as ritual in part celebrates the new Aquarian age. In Aleister Crowley's Magick philosophy, this displaces the Piscean age of stoicism, self-denial and rigid order of which Christ was the prime embodiment. At the same time – as the accompanying songs make clear – the film does also recognize Christ as a 'Rebel Rouser'.

As the film reaches its climax, a sense of the unleashing of wild forces is conveyed by two more heroes – Adolf Hitler and Puck from Shakespeare's *A Midsummer*

Scorpio (Bruce Byron) in his room with the James Dean pin-up on the wall.

Night's Dream. Hitler is shown in still images, while Puck is shown in a clip from Mickey Rooney's 1935 screen portrayal, urging on events with abandoned glee. All these heroes are enemies of stability: Christ and Hitler in angelic and demonic form, Brando and Puck in social and supernatural form.

What such heroes stand for collectively is a powerful brew of all the forces of disruption.

The homosexual thread consists above all in the insistently erotic way in which the boys are shown, but also in cutting that suggests kissing and fellatio between characters. Anger has said, 'I guess my whole trip is phallic worship', and although the film is only mildly pornographic, it celebrates masculine sex-appeal in terms that are ultimately reducible to ideas of the mythical potency of the phallus – the use of fetish fabrics and objects, the love of symbols of power (bikes, Hitler), the caressing photography of huge back muscles, taughtened abdomens and hard flesh.

All these images and the structures through which they are shot interfuse in an ecstasy of forbidden and dangerous experience… but it is worth mentioning the wit with which this is done. The relations between the songs and the images indicate this most obviously: 'Wind Me Up' to images of putting bikes together and a boy playing with a toy bike; 'My Boyfriend's Back' to shots of both a skull and a completed bike; 'Blue Velvet' to dressing in leather and chains; and so on. There is wit even before the film starts – it is produced by 'Puck Productions', complete with the legend 'What fools these mortals be'. Puck represents mischief, and this is perhaps the heart of the film. Even the Magick, the heroes and the homosexuality are not taken quite straight, but with a literally wicked giggle. *Scorpio Rising* is a deeply *naughty* movie, and the most consummate expression of naughtiness imaginable.

Originally published in *The Movie* 65 (1981), pp. 1284–1285.

37 WHY DANCE? (1981)

Dance is, before it is anything else, body art. It is not the embellishment of the body through clothing, make-up or adornment; nor is it the representation of the body in a medium other than the body. Dance may be used for any manner of purpose – to express character and tell a story as in ballet and theatrical dance; to seduce or be seduced as in ballroom and other social dancing; to perform a function in ritual, as in tribal and religious dance; and so on. But in all these purposes, it is still the human body that is being used.

This is what seems to make it an awkward art in our time. Despite signs of a revival currently, dance remains the most marginalised of all art forms in our society – and this despite the fact that probably more people participate in dance than in any other medium bar speech. Most people have linked hands at midnight on New Year's Eve and moved back and forth to 'Auld Lang Syne', one of the few dance rituals left in our society. Most people will, if perforce under pressure, have a dance at a party. Though dancing is something you have to learn, it is still easier to participate in than the mystique surrounding poetry and painting, or the difficult skills needed for music. Much participation in dance is, it is true, *embarrassed*, an index of how uneasily it fits into our social order, but still there is participation. Yet in the official world of the arts, dance remains marginal. No high critical discourse surrounds it; it is often not reviewed, only taught as an adjunct to sport (see below) and until recently was almost unknown in higher education. Popular dance is dismissed as 'mere' entertainment, and the Modern Dance tradition still tends to be looked on as cranky. Only classical ballet is the form of dance that seeks largely to deny the very basis of dance, the body. Classical ballet is based on an aesthetic of weightlessness, especially surrounding the ballerina, whose hard muscular work all goes to disguise itself as she is, in appearance, borne aloft, like thistle down in her luminous tutu.

Classical ballet and the marginalisation or denigration of dance are symptomatic of how our official, respectable culture discourages us from knowledge of our bodies – that is, from the very ground of our being. This attitude to dance is, though it is a difficult argument to make, of great political significance. All societies are based on the human body – it is their labour that produces the means by which we live, it is their activity that reproduces human life itself. Yet it is difficult to hold on to a real sense of this. Money, machines, management – all in fact produced by flesh and blood – are presented as non-corporeal entities that 'really' make things happen; and the growth of professional medicine has even tended to take our own bodies out of our control. Dance is one of the means by which we can see and experience again the centrality of our bodies not only to our sense of ourselves but to society itself.

In saying this, I am not saying that in tribal societies – or in Modern Dance – the body is known in some 'pure', 'real' way, unmediated by how the surrounding culture thinks and feels about the body. (This is the way that these two forms of dance are often thought about, as being somehow 'natural'.) But such forms – and indeed all dance – do *recognise* the body and see it as an essential human resource, not something that the human spirit or psyche is encumbered with. Dance constructs a knowledge of flesh and blood, muscle and tissue, a knowledge of how they can be experienced and used and lived – not a knowledge given by the biology of body, but a knowledge fabricated out of it. This knowledge – felt and sensed more than thought and articulated – can allow us to understand our bodies as they are used and abused and ignored in our society. If we can reconstruct a knowledge of the body, we can place our bodies at the centre of social activity and change.

Dance's only rival in this respect is sport. Like dance, sport enables the participant to feel the strength, energy and capacity of the human body and enables the spectator to enjoy its power, grace and vitality. Yet although players and spectators do enjoy sport for these aesthetic, sensory reasons, sport is engulfed in a rhetoric of competition and achievement that tends to obscure such aspects. Dance too can be seen in these terms – rivalry over the height of a leap in ballet or the number of taps in a tap routine, the regulation of social dance in competitive ballroom dancing – but they are not central to it. Dance constructs the body as a source of energy to be experienced, and sees the enjoyment of the movement in the control over the body in time and space. Sport constructs the body as the means to win, to achieve. Dance – the weight of the 'discourse' of dance – is experiential; sport – the weight of its discourse – is instrumental.

I have sketched out this position on dance as a preliminary for discussing the various ways that film relates to the discourses of dance in our society. Dance embodies (literally) attitudes and feelings about the body. All bodies are sexed, they are either female or male, so the import of dance is also always sexual-political. It is no accident that the two groups historically most involved with dance in the twentieth century have been women and gay men. The Modern Dance movement was pioneered by women, and although the discourses that they used in this regard centred on notions of natural dance that need very careful handling, they were clearly – if also not fully consciously – in revolt against the way that dance had hitherto placed women's bodies within conceptions that bolstered male outlooks – denying the terrors of the female body in classical ballet; subjecting it to be 'led', seduced, conquered in social dance; turning it into the lifeless parading and positioning of revue and burlesque (and Busby Berkeley). Many of the changes within the forms just mentioned have gained strength from the example of Modern Dance – not least the Royal Ballet's most recent full-length ballet, a tribute to the destroyer of ballet, Isadora Duncan. Gay men too revolted against a construction of the human body that denied the male body could be a source of erotic pleasure. The real history of this remains to be written, since it was necessarily covert, but the construction of a body aesthetic that combined traditional notions of the male body (muscularity, athleticism) with grace and prettiness and expressivity can clearly be seen from the Diaghilev-Nijinsky collaboration to the development of disco dance in gay clubs in the USA in the early '70s.

I'd like to end by turning to the question of the relation of film to dance. Film is in part a record of dance and hence much of the interest of the season [of dance films at Birmingham Arts Lab in 1981] resides in seeing a wide range of dance and in thinking it through in some of the terms outlined above.

But the relation of film to dance is also particularly interesting in two further respects. First, most films are narratives, they tell a story. Moreover, even the most dancey films seldom tell their story only through dancing. What happens is that a surrounding narrative is set up into which danced sections are inserted. In this way, the films often become films *about* dance, about the way dance figures in social life.

Secondly, both dance and film are crucially based on movement, and in examining the interrelation of the way each uses movement we can learn something about the aesthetics of both media. In a discussion with a friend about the films of Yvonne Rainer – whose work I don't really 'get' – we came to realise that whereas I seemed to like dance (and dance films) the more they approximated to the concerns of music with rhythm and melody (in dance, 'line'), she seemed to like dance the more closely its concerns approached those of painting and sculpture with space. The fact of our personal tastes is neither here nor there, but this is an interesting distinction. In thinking about it, it also seemed that, when it came to the methods of filming dance, there was too a rough and ready difference according to whether rhythm, melody/line or space were the predominant element that the filming seems to want to render. Where the musical elements (rhythm and melody/line) predominate, editing is far more elaborated; whereas where space predominates, long takes are more likely to be favoured. Editing tends to fragment space, whereas the long take keeps the spatial coordinates of a scene continuously before our eyes. There seems to be a further distinction within the editing-music connection, which corresponds to the distinction between montage and continuity editing. The former is not concerned with the preservation of space at all, but with the inter-relation of shots; whereas the latter still breaks up a sequence with editing but, by a series of rules developed in the early years of the cinema, seeks to disguise or make invisible this editing. A pronounced use of montage tends to emphasise rhythm since it is itself a rhythmic resource; whereas continuity editing seems closer to melody/line, there a sense of continuous movement is nonetheless subtly underpinned by the rhythm of editing.

There is also a correlation between the type of treatment and the type of dance – montage being especially appropriate for highly rhythmic forms of tap and disco, continuity editing to the emphasis on line in both classical ballet and Modern Dance, the long take to the treatment of movement that is not really quite dance at all as it is traditionally understood but rather 'found' movement (i.e. the use of movement 'found' in life, or at rehearsal). *Brigadoon* and *Swingtime* are both interesting for combining longish takes with continuity editing, especially for the couple dances which are both an evocation of harmony and grace (though 'line') but also an exploration by the couple of the space of their relationship in the world in which it (problematically) exists. *Fame* and *Finian's Rainbow*, on the other hand, betray, in their mixture of montage and continuity editing, a lack of conviction in breaking up the space of the fictional worlds they are evoking – *Fame* due to its cynical opportunism, *Finian's Rainbow* due to its ironical attitude towards the utopian tradition of the musical.

FAME

Fame deals with the life of a dance and drama college in New York over three years. Musically and choreographically it draws on disco, but unlike *Saturday Night Fever* and *Thank God It's Friday*, it does not articulate disco in the context of, respectively, boring jobs and conventional suburban life, and thus disco becomes simply an expression of 'youth'. The young people of the film are located in different social milieux, but the social meaning of disco culture is never expressed because the film is so focused on a group, 'youth', that by definition (so vague a definition as the film's anyway) crosses other social categories. The origins of disco in gay culture never get a look in, and one might even suggest they are actually repressed since the one gay character rather conspicuously does not dance a step, even when practically everyone else does in the number in the college canteen. The connection of disco with Black dance is presented, but in a deformed way, focused entirely on Leroy (Gene Anthony Ray), exuding a Black defiance that the film carefully refuses to endorse, and expressed, in dance, entirely in terms of his sex appeal – a sex appeal founded, as the film sees it in his rehearsal number, on crotch appeal. The film thus buys rather emphatically into the way that white culture distances all its inability to develop a knowledge of the body in dance onto Black people, simultaneously celebrating this while labelling it primitive and genital.

The sex appeal of Leroy (Gene Anthony Ray) as expressed through dance in *Fame*, 1980. (United Artists/Archive Photos/Getty Images)

SWEET CHARITY

Sweet Charity is probably the most extended meditation on the function and meaning of dance that the cinema has produced. Although it focuses on dance as escape, as an aspect of entertainment and leisure, it systematically analyses the variety of dances that occupy those particular social spaces, evokes their pleasures and yet finally finds them wanting. This is done through the choreography itself, through settings and through the cinematic treatment, especially through montage, which not only works rhythmically but also associatively, that is, by editing in images from outside of the scene which set off reverberations of meaning within the scene. This is done most extensively in 'If My Friends Could See Me Now', a number in which the heroine Charity (Shirley MacLaine) seeks to express her happiness at being with the man of her celluloid dreams, film star Vittorio Vitale, and to do so reaches for a plethora of showbiz references, including Groucho Marx, Al Jolson and the hat-and-cane routine of the standard song-and-dance man. Time and again this brilliance is put to the task of undermining the dance form and the pleasure and escape that it seems to offer – 'Big Spender' reveals the emptiness of commercial sex, the Pompeii Club dances the hypocrisy of high life and so on. 'There's Gotta Be Something Better Than This' uses Jerome Robbins style choreography, so redolent of American energy and optimism from *On the Town* and *West Side Story*, for a dance in which Charity and her two women friends express their hopeless hopes of climbing out of their social condition. It is a dazzling film that manages to be both very enjoyable and yet critical about the nature of enjoyment in contemporary society.

DANCE, GIRL, DANCE

Dorothy Arzner was one of only two women (the other was Ida Lupino) directing major Hollywood movies between the end of the silent cinema and the early seventies. It is this, together with an explicitly 'feminist' speech and an interesting treatment of female stereotypes and male dullness, which have interested critics about *Dance, Girl, Dance*, and this has rather left the fact that it is a dance film out of account. The film in fact uses three forms of dance and clearly spells out their social meaning. The first is burlesque, unequivocally shown as the objectification of women for the sexual delectation of men. The second is traditional classical ballet, wholly identified with a transcendent femininity – Judy (Maureen O'Hara) is seen to express her true self in a ballet of her own creation called 'Morning Star', in which she dances the star, a magical spiritual value. The third form of dance is modern ballet, in which movements from everyday life and popular dance forms (including Black dance) have been incorporated into an overall classical vocabulary. This dance – the product of a male manager and male choreographer – is set up by the film as the pinnacle of dance achievement, and one to which by the end of the film Judy must bend her 'natural' talents. The 'feminist' critique of burlesque sits uneasily with this rather snobbish and traditional view of dance, but it is in the juxtaposition of the three dance forms and the clear signalling of their gender meanings that much of the fascination of the film lies.

SWINGTIME

It is time that we stopped being so uncritical of the image of Fred Astaire. He is unquestionably a consummate dancer, with a lightness of touch rare in white tap dancers; he imaginatively developed social dances (foxtrots, waltzes etc.) into extended pas de deux and continually sought to extend these styles into the kind of American Theatre Ballet that Agnes de Mille and Jerome Robbins developed in the 40s. Yet his status as *the* greatest male tap dancer served to mask the fact that this was a Black dance form based on an aesthetic of syncopation and extemporisation similar to that of jazz, and that there were dozens of Black dancers as skilful as Astaire. This may not have been his 'fault' – and his superb 'Bojangles of Harlem' number in *Swingtime*, a *homage* to Bill Robinson, shows that he was aware of tap's heritage – but it was part of the effect of his image. Moreover, the gentlemanly image (encapsulated in his white tie and tails outfit), the soft voice and weedy physique all seem to offer Astaire as the antithesis of the *macho* male image Hollywood has more characteristically peddled. Yet, like another star in this mould, Cary Grant, Astaire's image is consistently articulated through the most implacably male centred narratives, both in the plots of the films and in the narratives of the dance numbers themselves. Nowhere is this more true than in the films with Ginger Rogers. Always she plays a lively, independent woman whom Astaire spends the whole of the film tracking down until he has seduced her out of independence. He uses every trick in the book – subterfuge, pretending to be what he isn't, pestering, or calling on her to take pity on him because she has rejected him... The dances with her begin with her resistance and then show that broken down as she is coaxed into the dance, a dance whose contours and direction he controls. Of course it is part of the dynamic of the film that we want him to succeed – we've come to see the numbers and without Ginger they mostly don't happen; so we too are drawn into willing the breakdown of her autonomy. Occasionally this may lift off into an expression of equality and mutuality, each dancer responding to the other (as, here, in the exhilarating 'Pick Yourself Up'), but mostly it is her capitulating to him. In the face of this, John Wayne's lumbering courtesy towards women or even Clint Eastwood's frank hardness seem almost preferable, if not, alas, nearly so nice.

THE RED DETACHMENT OF WOMEN

The Red Detachment of Women is one of several ballets created during the Cultural Revolution in China. The question of the dance form used is particularly interesting. These new ballets were a deliberate rejection of the forms of classical Chinese dance, since these forms were seen as the preserve of an aristocratic élite. The rejection of these forms was both a rejection of the values of this élite and an attempt to democratise dance by making it accessible and comprehensible to all. Yet what may puzzle us is the degree to which this dance revolution seems to be accomplished by importing dance forms from the West, surely the living embodiment of the capitalism which the Communist state was equally implacably hostile to? However, Mao's approach was never as mechanistic as many forms of Marxist aesthetics. He understood that the meaning and effect of art is inextricably bound up with particular historical situations. The meaning of a kind of movement has perhaps a *very* general meaning across cultures, but its social and political meaning will change according to its more immediate context. The kinds of leaping movement incorporated from the West into Chinese ballet certainly have in both contexts something of the excitement of the defiance of gravity, of the vitality of human exertion, but whereas in the West this was tied, in different phases, to notions of transcending the body or to various forms of humanism, in China the form was most obviously linked to the metaphor of the 'Great Leap Forward' that was the Cultural Revolution. What makes *The Red Detachment of Women* particularly interesting for us in this context is the fact that these movements should be so wholeheartedly given to women. The leap in Western dance is the very heart of *male* dance, whereas in Chinese ballet at this point the ideas of defiance and vigour are constructed as equally appropriate to women and men.

Originally published in *Birmingham Arts Lab* film programme (1 July – 30 September 1981), pp. 4–8.

38 OLD BRIEFS FOR NEW (1989)

Personally I'm pleased that the little chap in the new Levi's ad is wearing sparkling white, generously cut briefs. If it does for them what the launderette version did for boxer shorts, I'll be well content. This, I might add, has nothing to do with personal taste, but does suggest a shift in attitudes towards the male body that are some advance on the usual mix of disdain, derision or misplaced awe.

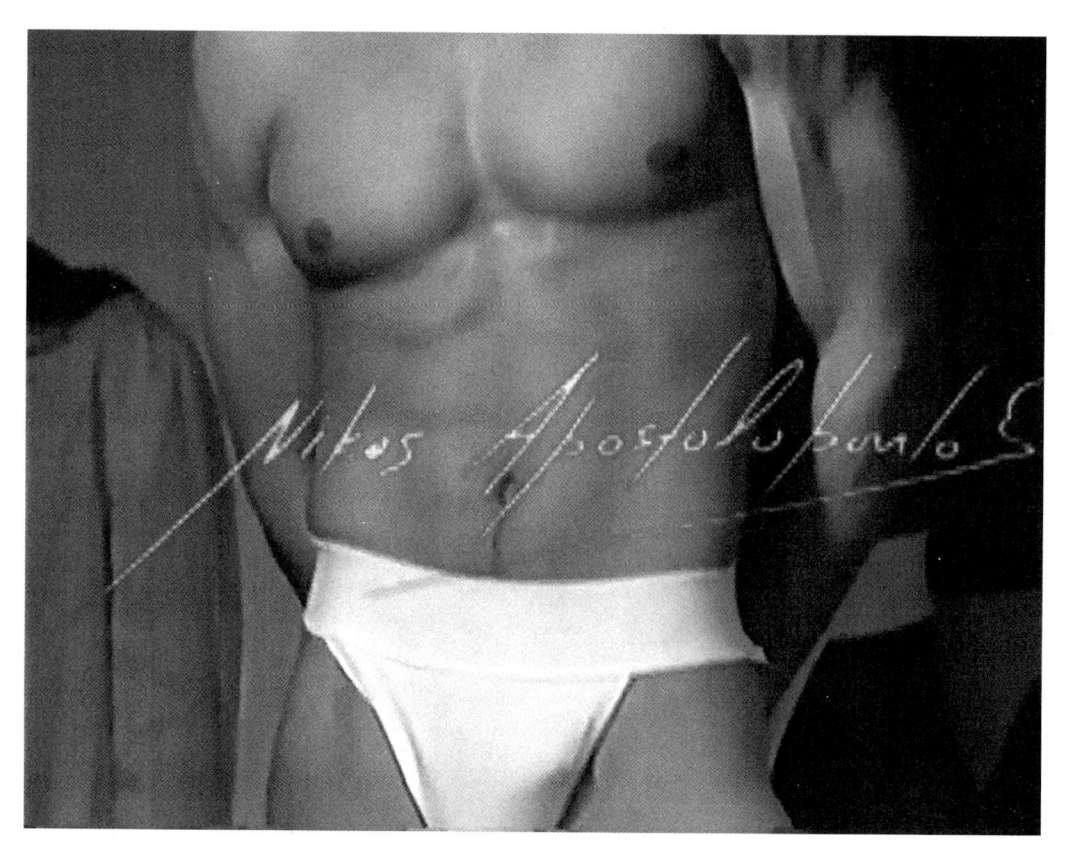

Nikos men's underwear, a postmodern collage of the jockey brief and the jock strap, here shown on a Paris catwalk, 1995.

The Levi's ad is not an isolated event. For some time now, the image of men's underwear has been, so to speak, coming out of the closet. Designer labels – Armani, Cerruti, Calvin Klein – have been bringing out their own lines and there's been a retro cult for Y-fronts and Fruit of the Loom that has made even these labels seem designer orientated.

Nikos – whose new boutique opened in London earlier this year – is only really known for his underwear. In France, Italy and some other European countries, boutiques specialising in underwear, either men's or men's and women's, are now quite common. Nor is this just a phenomenon of haute couture – British Home Stores, Burtons, Top Man, Next and other high street chains now offer a range of underwear clearly emulating Nikos et al. It's all very different from how we used to think and feel about how to cover up what's 'down there'.

Men's knickers have generally been perceived in two modes. One is medical – all those considerations about the healthiness of hanging free versus support – a set of views that, significantly, only ever aroused controversy when it was suggested that tight briefs might lead to impotence. The other is giggling, which is in part, an admirable response to seeing men divested of the dignity of trousers, but which also suggests that there must be something intrinsically silly about what men wear under their trousers.

That point has been further rubbed home by countless wags' *penchants* for ill-cut shorts in polka-dot hearts and cupid designs, or seaside 'gift' shops offering miscoloured nylon briefs with leering snakes or tadpoles adorning the relevant parts. It's the stupidity of male sexual desire that is at stake here, splendidly cut down to size, but correspondingly naturalised as silly.

The revival of boxer shorts was a (hopefully) last ditch attempt to keep those modes in circulation. Though beige and fetchingly buttock hugging on Nick Kamen, and available in the designer labels in plain colours or simple patterns, boxers rapidly became the vehicle of the old silly motifs and slogans in all those tube and rail outlets. Certainly a garment that doesn't cling to the body is likely to be less grubby when it comes to washday and will make less explicit that part of the male body too often associated with boredom, obligation or rape. Is it easier to work up some sexual enthusiasm for men's sexual parts when the latters' association with drudgery, dreariness and violence is played down? As long as women still have a servicing relationship to men's clothes and bodies, other perceptions of men's underwear may seem to fall wide of the mark – however, these perceptions might be worth examining if they could suggest other forms of relationship.

There always was another way of perceiving men's underwear of course, to be found in the pages of gay magazines and scores of mail order catalogues offered, with varying degrees of explicitness, to the gay market. Bikini briefs were the greatest success, mass marketed as 'skants' by the sixties and becoming the staples of men's underwear ever since. They were overtly 'sexy' yet, partly because of their gay association, perhaps slightly overdid it. The emphasis on smallness had an uneasy relation with obsessive concerns about bigness, and their name and style recalled women's underwear; fine for the androgynous sixties but less so for the difference-loving eighties. In short, if there was to be a revision in men's underwear, that was not where it would draw its inspiration.

The new men's underwear, which like practically all male fashion was also pioneered by gay men, draws on two earlier styles, often simultaneously. On the one hand, the new designs often use the wide waist bands and sharply cut away pouch of the jock strap – most obvious in many of Nikos's briefs, which are the ironic culmination of a gay sartorial history. The jock strap, however, was the image of straight masculinity, a purely functional garment associated with the, then, macho world of sport. It became a talisman of desire in much gay pornography, associated with the men you could not, but then just might, have.

Throughout the seventies, however, what had been objects of desire, associated with the status of straightness, were taken over by gay male culture. Gay men increasingly turned themselves into their own objects of desire – hence working out, 501s and jock straps. In Nikos's versions, function is blatantly irrelevant, everything is exaggerated (more cut away, thicker waist bands), sexiness is all.

The other source for the new underwear is the jockey brief aka Y-fronts. Their introduction was a key moment in the history of men's underwear. It is the bra of that history. Like the latter, it moulds the body part concerned into a streamlined form, an attractive and inaccurate bulge.

This bit of the male anatomy allows a little more room for manoeuvre than the female breast, leading to the distinction, immortalised for me in the words of an assistant at Marshall and Snellgrove in Birmingham in the sixties, between men who are 'up-wearers' and those who are 'down-wearers'.

But like the bra, and even more insistently, as befitted a masculine garment in the mid-20th century, it could also be passed off as practical. Jockey briefs offered support (something neither breasts nor testicles knew they needed) but at the same time through the frontal opening made allowance for the male genitals' other principal function. All of this made it look and feel sexy while appearing sensibly, masculinely utilitarian.

The new men's underwear, when it is not a straightforward recycling of jockey briefs, is often a postmodern collage of them and the jock strap, taking bits from one and bits from the other – wide waist bands, but full briefs; 'good' cotton with jock strap elastic; cut-away fronts but generously cut backs; and so on. Most fascinating, and postmodern, of all is the reference to the jockey brief's frontal opening. Y-fronts were always a contraption really. If the opening was cut generously enough to permit ease of use, the penis was likely to flop out of it at any time; but if it was cut small enough to prevent this, it was a bit of a fiddle pulling the penis through and then, inadequately shaken, back. Whether in acknowledgement of this perhaps insurmountable design problem, the new underwear often dispenses with frontal opening but retains the piping and stitching of the old jockey, so that it looks like there's an opening there. What once had a function – physiologically and psychologically, to make men feel alright about wearing so sensuous a garment – is now simply reduced to a decoration, a gesture at the idea of the masculine as the functional.

All of this makes the new men's underwear playfully sexy. It clearly signals sexual difference, creating explicitly erotic underwear without recourse to the feminine or androgynous. It draws on earlier versions of what might be the indelibly male in underwear, but by ingeniously recombining, eroticising and exaggerating them, it undermines the grim authority they were supposed to have. It turns humour and irony into adjuncts to, not deflaters of, sexiness.

Originally published in *New Statesman and Society* (24 March 1989), pp. 43–44.

39 DRACULA AND DESIRE (1993)

The cinema was packed. Tom and I took the first two seats together we could find and I didn't take notice of whom I was sitting next to. We were in any case too engrossed in unguarded conversation to be bothered. It was freezing outside, but hot in the cinema, so we had to take off successive layers of clothing. I was just starting to struggle out of a pullover when the person sitting next to me gave my knee a sharp knock. I turned in surprise and he hissed, 'There's no need to keep rubbing your leg against mine.' I was so startled by this sudden eruption of homophobia that I immediately went into politeness overdrive, I was sorry, I really hadn't realised. And throughout the film I kept my body tensed away from him, lest my relaxed knee inadvertently touch his dreary thigh. Perhaps it was only this that made me feel alienated from the new *Dracula*, but I suspect also that Coppola's Stoker's vampires are not my vampires, not by any means queer.

There is no doubt that Bram Stoker's *Dracula*, which the new film follows so fully, is the literary *locus classicus* of the vampire. Huge though the corpus of vampire tales is, the character of Dracula dominates. His is probably the only vampire's name most people know: it sells holiday tours and images of dictatorship in Romania, it is used in the titles of films in which he does not appear (such as *Dracula's Daughter* and *Brides of Dracula*). Dracula is the vampire *par excellence*. Yet, admirable and fascinating as much of Stoker's novel is, I prefer Sheridan LeFanu's 'Carmilla,' or Richard Matheson's *I Am Legend*, or above all Anne Rice's *Interview with the Vampire* and its sequels. Similarly in films, I prefer non-Draculas like the aforementioned *Daughter*, *Kiss of the Vampire*, *Daughters of Darkness* or *Near Dark*, or those that only take Stoker's *Dracula* as a point of departure (Murnau's *Nosferatu*, Bela Lugosi's incarnations, Peter Sasdy's *Taste the Blood of Dracula*). The new *Dracula* is not of these.

Francis Ford Coppola and scriptwriter James V. Hart have, as the credit that opens the film, 'Bram Stoker's *Dracula*' suggests, indeed gone back to Stoker. In terms of inclusion of incidents and characters, there is more left of the novel here than in any previous film versions with the possible exception of the 1970 Spanish *El Conde Drácula* (Jesús Franco). To the now well-trod lines of Jonathan Harker's visit to Transylvania and Dracula's coming to England to wreak havoc on Harker's friends and relatives are added elements that have only occasionally appeared in previous versions (the character of the Texan, Quincy p. Morris; the pursuit of Dracula back to Transylvania finally to ensnare him). The one substantial new element added to this, a prologue explaining how Vlad the Impaler became Dracula, gives a particular inflection to the story, but remains true to the project: it is well known that Vlad was an inspiration to Stoker.

The manner of telling also owes more than usual to Stoker. The use of multiple narrative strands (Jonathan and Mina, Lucy and her beaux, the asylum, Van Helsing) is sustained, as in the novel, until two-thirds of the way through, when it is ironed out into a linear, much less engrossing stalk-and-kill climax. The film also makes a stab at retaining the novel's multiple points of view, with sequences inaugurated by voice-overs, captions and visuals that link the subsequent events to a particular character's perspective. Care is even taken with the novel's emphasis on different ways of telling, both formal modes (diaries, letters, news-stories) and media (handwriting, typing, cylinder recording). To the latter is added reference to the cinematograph, not as a source of the story we are seeing, but as something that Dracula himself has recourse to in his seduction of Mina.

Coppola's *Dracula* flings itself at all this narrative material, emerging like a music video directed by Dario Argento. As in a video, narrativity comes at you in snatches, more a suggestion of connected incidents across a welter of vivid imagery than a fully presented plot. As in Argento's *Suspiria*, say, or some other post-60s horror movies like Sam Raimi's *The Evil Dead*, narrative, and with it the pleasures of tease and suspense, are unimportant; it's the maelstrom of sensation that matters. This means that the story may be hard to follow if you either haven't read Stoker's *Dracula* or have a less than total recall of it (I remembered who Renfield and Quincy were, but it goes so fast that I had a hard time figuring out how and why at the end Mina gets to Transylvania before her menfolk). With *Suspiria* or *The Evil Dead*, this doesn't matter too much since there's so little plot anyway, and it may not matter with this *Dracula* either. The point, perhaps, was not to do Stoker in full-blooded re-creation, but simply to allude to as much as possible of the book while getting on with the business of creating a particular feeling and exploring the connotations of the Dracula idea.

As to the feeling, Coppola has certainly achieved something distinctive. Always one of cinema's great colourists, he has here come up with a symphony in engulfing red and black. The prologue is shot in near-silhouette, black on red, setting the colour key signature for the film. Early sequences in Victorian England are anaemically coloured, gradually to be swallowed by red and black, vermilion and pitch, blood and the night. I am not the first to have reached for 'engorgement' as a word to describe the film. It's not just the redness of blood swelling the film's climaxes, but the fullness of the image, bursting to the edge of the frame with thick colour and dense visual texture. Most remarkably, it's in the vampires' costuming, most voluminous when they are most needy. They look bloated with lust, and yet move then with greatest speed and ease, gliding not walking, as if motored by the desperate urgency of desire. When Lucy has become a vampire, she is dressed entirely in white, with bridal lace and fold upon fold of silk, and her face too is pale as death; yet her shrouded body rears up turgidly, the lace ruffs round her neck are puffed like a monstrous lizard, even her cheeks seem fuller. Even without the red, she is the embodiment of engorgement.

To this stunning – and wearying – feeling, Coppola adds many of the connotations of vampirism. The vampire motif always has something to do with the idea of a being, or way of being, that literally lives off another. It was born (in the early nineteenth century) of a society increasingly conscious of interdependency, while losing that firm sense of fixed, rightful, social hierarchy that had concealed dependency; in short, it was born of industrial capitalist democracy. The vampire idea deals in the terror of recognising, challenging or being challenged by dependency, and always registers this through the body: the dependencies of its needs and drives, especially, but not exclusively, sexuality. Like all long-lived popular cultural ideas, innumerable variations can be played on this basic concept, its vivid iconography and compelling narrative patterns. Folklorists stress the fear of the living that the dead are not well and truly dead, a fear that may also conceal a hope; Marxists liked to compare capitalists to vampires, feeding off the labour of the working class. In *Ganja and Hess* (1971), Bill Gunn used the vampire idea to explore the dependencies of race and colonialism; the British short *The Mask of Lilith* (1986) similarly explored vampirism as a metaphor for gender, sexual and racial oppression and resistance.

The possibilities are endless, and Coppola and Hart know a good few of them. You want the attraction and terror of sexuality, the attraction of the terror of sexuality? Here it is, in Dracula's metamorphosis from glowering bearded prince to cadaverous old goat to *fin-de-siècle* dandy, and in the wolf/ape thing that takes Lucy in the night. You want, more specifically, male fears of female sexuality? Here is the engorged, uncontrollable libidinous preference of Lucy and Mina for Gary Oldman's dandy Dracula over Keanu Reeves' sensitive but proper Jonathan. Or AIDS is a possibility, flung in here in a few lines ominously connecting sex, blood and disease. There's even a vegetarian reading, in a cut that has the audience groaning as at a bad pun and which is borrowed from *The Hunger*, where Van Helsing's dismemberment of Lucy's head is followed straight on by him carving with relish into a side of rare beef.

Or how about the vampire as the old world, old Europe, Eastern Europe, leeching off modern, industrialising, Western Europe (and North America)? This has in recent years been seen as one of the novel's most interesting themes, stressed not only in the references to modern means of communication (typewriters, cylinders), but in the characters of the Texan (the new rich of the New World) and Jack Seward, the lunatic-asylum director with new, rational and humane ideas about madness and its

Jonathan Harker (Keanu Reeves) faces Count Dracula (Gary Oldman) in *Bram Stoker's Dracula*. (BFI National Archive)

treatment. This is all there in Coppola's *Dracula*, given new inflection by a sequence at the cinematograph and by rendering parts of the final stalk-and-kill to look like a Western, the genre that encapsulates the conquering destiny of ethnically European expansion. The film is even aware of a gendered dimension to modernity, not so much, as in the book, through Mina, associated through typing with the New Woman's skill with technology and the possibility of an independent career, but in the way female nudes are interpolated into the endlessly repeated film shown in the sideshow booth where Dracula seduces Mina, a recognition of the simultaneous historical production of woman and cinema as spectacle.

The film seems to know about all the above; such themes are there not just by virtue of the completeness of its use of the novel's incidents and characters. Yet none of them is really developed or compelling. It's postmodern allusionism, a welter of things to make reference to without any of them mattering much. The most interesting and, surprisingly enough, original is a Christian interpretation. Christianity has, of course, always been part of the vampire tale, but often in a rather perfunctory way. Holy water and a cross held up in the vampire's face might put him or her off for a while, but so did a bunch of garlic; real destruction could only come about by a stake through the heart, vaguely Christian perhaps, but pretty pagan too. The

Christian possibilities seemed not to have survived the riposte of the character in Roman Polanski's *Dance of the Vampires* (1967), who waives aside a proffered crucifix with the information that he's Jewish. There are few vampire films (or pieces of writing) since in which Christianity has any force, yet it is the one theme that gets some development in the new film.

The potential for a fuller Christian reading of the vampire idea is obvious. The central sacrament of Christianity is wine drunk as blood (in the Catholic doctrine of transubstantiation, this is at the spiritual level no mere symbol, it is the actual blood of Christ); the most important icon of Christianity is a dead man who has eternal life. Most writers and filmmakers have failed to exploit this, either because they depict vampires as the enemy of Christianity, or because they are not interested enough in Christianity to bother. In Coppola's *Dracula*, by contrast, Dracula is strongly associated with Christ.

The opening section depicts Vlad as a Defender of the Faith against the Turks (in other words, against Islam, though the film perhaps prudently plays that down); when he discovers that his beloved Princess Elizabeth has killed herself, thinking him dead, he believes God has deserted him (as, on the cross, did Christ); blood gushes from the crucifix on the altar and Vlad, soaking and drinking it up while railing against God, becomes a vampire, Dracula. When Dracula seduces Mina (a reincarnation of Elizabeth), he makes a cut in his breast for her to suck at; such a cut is familiar iconography in medieval and later Christian art, and the connection is insisted on by cross-cutting with Mina marrying Jonathan and taking communion with him, drinking wine/blood as a sign of transcendent union. When Dracula is finally impaled, his face metamorphoses from hideous white slug to long-haired dandy via a bearded incarnation that is Vlad but also looks like countless images of Christ. In short, though the theme disappears from view from time to time, Dracula here is an anti-Christ, not so much in the sense of being an enemy of Christ as in being an inversion of the Christ idea. Drinking Christ's blood while cursing God damns him to eternal life, dependent forever on human blood, having gorged on and rejected divine blood. He offers his eternal life by the same token as Christ offered his, the drinking of his blood.

But what do we feel about all this? Christlike or anti-Christ, what is our relation to him? Worship or identification, pity or revulsion? The long life of the vampire idea resides in just such various possibilities. If the image started out as one seen from the outside, there was always the possibility that it could be seen and felt from within; if the vampire is an Other, he or she was also always a figure in whom one could find oneself. The image allowed that from the start of its appearance in modern western culture (if indeed it had any life before in folk cultures, as many modern western writers like to claim). The narrative devices used ostensibly keep the vampire at a distance: the tale is often presented as one told to the narrator by another narrator who sometimes themselves have only heard it told; even when a direct first-person narrative is used, the vampire is not the narrator. Yet he or she is always the most interesting, memorable and even attractive figure in the tale. If the narrator and all around so easily fall prey to the vampire's magnetism, nay charm, the latter must have something; the narrator often tells us little about him or her self, and other characters, for all the vampire needs their blood, seem anaemic by comparison. The vampire was always a figure to be desired as well as feared, to be identified with as well as distanced from. One of the magical things about *Interview with the Vampire* is the device of presenting the tale as a transcript of a tape-recording of the hero telling his story to a journalist; not only does this give the word to the vampire himself, it also draws attention to the fact of doing so. Jody Scott's polymorphous lesbian science-fiction variant carries this breakthrough triumphantly forward in its very title, *I, Vampire*.

In film, there is no such grammar to tell you with whom you are supposed to identify. Without voiceover or relentless subjective camera, it's much less clear who is 'telling' a film. But like vampires in literature, film sets up distance only to have it converted to identification.

The device of the journey, taken from Stoker, often serves to put the vampire at a distance: there is a strong sense of a movement away from what the western, urban-minded audience would find familiar and towards the strangeness of foreignness. Honeymooners, the next step for the young unmarried heterosexual couples supposedly making up the bulk of the audience, might especially seem ideal identification figures to lead the viewer into the realm of the vampire other. Yet this device is even less insistently (if resistibly) distancing than the narrational devices of written fiction. It is true that few vampire films make the vampire a clear central figure whom we stay with throughout – I can only think of movies such as *Graveyard Shift*, *Nick Knight* or *To Die For*, plus films about real-life 'vampire' Peter Kürten (*Le Vampire de Dusseldorf* and *The Tenderness of Wolves*) and George A. Romero's *Martin*. (The film of *Interview with the Vampire*, supposedly under contract, has not yet seen the light of day.) Yet the journey motif has led in some interesting directions, often inviting involvement more than encouraging distance.

In *Kiss of the Vampire* (Don Sharp, 1965) the lacklustre honeymooning couple cannot hold a candle to the vampires who prey on them. With the wife in their thrall, their leader says to the husband, 'Now that your wife has tasted one of life's rarer pleasures, do you think she will want to return to you?' Who cannot see that he is right? Who would not rather spend time with the sister and brother, she bursting voluptuously out of her gown, he gazing with intense, melancholy eyes at you as he plays intense, melancholy music at the piano? And who would not prefer that delirious costume ball to sitting at home with this stodgy British hubby? Similarly in *Daughters of Darkness* (Harry Kümel, 1970) a pasty pair of newlyweds wind up on a wintry night in a deserted hotel on the Belgian coast. In the circumstances, who would want to keep to the straight and narrow when you could feel queer with the only other guests, Delphine Seyrig and companion? Well, of course, many people would, including the man sitting next to me. There's undoubtedly a queer way of reading vampirism, and my neighbour knew that's what I was hoping for.

I want 'queer' here to carry as many meanings as possible. Certainly I don't just mean lesbian and gay, but any apparently marginalised, sexualised identity (which includes many perceptions of women and non-white, even non-Anglo ethnic groups). But I do mean to include the old as well as the new connotations of queer, the despicable as well as the defiant, the shameful as well as the unashamed, the loathing of oddness as well as pride in it. The vampire has played every variation on such queerness. The 1922 Nosferatu is a hideous outsider, driven on by his lust, eyes falling out of his head at the sight of Thomas' sturdy frame and unable to resist Mina's deadly allure; to identify with him, as one still might, is to identify with loneliness, self-hatred and loathsome desire. To identify with Bela Lugosi's Count is still to identify with isolated outsiderdom, but already with someone more refined and fascinating than the dullards ranged against him. *Taste the Blood of Dracula* (1969) is one of the most enjoyable exposés of Victorian values in all cinema, with respectable bourgeois fathers secretly randy for the sensation that only Dracula can bring their jaded palates and their daughters killing them off with glee under Dracula's tutelage; Christopher Lee's Count is as straight (and English) as can be, but how deliciously he provokes normal society against itself. And with *Kiss of the Vampire*, *Daughters of Darkness* or *Near Dark*, the vampires become the thing to be, infinitely preferable to the world they feed off.

Coppola's Dracula, like Stoker's, like Christopher Lee's, does not belong with these vampires. He's not a pervert. He might occasionally turn to male flesh (between the scenes in the film as between the chapters in the book) and have on hand female vampires mutually pleasuring each other, but there is none of the delighted and sustained homoeroticism of 'Carmilla' and *Interview with the Vampire*, or *Daughters of Darkness*, *The Velvet Vampire*, *The Hunger*, Barbara Steele in *Danza Macabra* and, a rare male example, the Dutch *Blood Relations*. He may in the end be destroyed for his disruptive desire, but it's really business as usual in terms of the representation of heterosexual male sexuality. Dracula — Stoker's, Lee's and Coppola's — is rampant, driven, rearing sexuality, uncontainable by modern, domestic, feminised society. It is ugly — beneath the dandy veneer lurks slug-like, leech-like desire; but it's what women want, even in its ugliness: Lucy is ecstatic beneath the half-ape, half-wolf that takes her in the garden and Mina does not flinch, even when her dandy slits his chest open for her. And like Stoker's dripping prose and Hammer's thickly coloured textures and solid *mise en scène*, only more so, Coppola's film is full of blood, stiff with desire, a hymn to engorgement.

Yet Dracula is an outsider, without being socially marginal. One version of the vampire idea precisely presents normal male sexuality as outside of society. If 'society' resides in moral order, in marriage, in the unemotional, unerotic workplace, then it has no place for driving randiness and uncontrollable priapism, themselves conceived as the nature of male sexuality. Normal male sexuality in this perspective accords straight men too the glamorous badge of outsiderdom. No matter that they also have unequal power over women and children, no matter the vastness of the heterosexual sex industries, no matter the ubiquity of sexual tension at work – at the level of representation, male sexuality is seen as profoundly unsocialised and unsocialisable. Thus Stoker's, Lee's and Coppola's Dracula, thus the dominant image of the vampire, so commandingly virile, so unerringly straight, also expresses the profound contradictoriness of the cultural construction of heterosexual masculinity, at once dominant and disgusting, natural and horrible, mainstream and beyond the pale.

But that's not what *I* want from vampires. For all its incidental pleasures (some of the costumes, the US stars doing English accents, picking up the allusions as a genre aficionado is bound to), the new *Dracula* was not addressed to me. Just as I held myself off from the man in the seat next to me, so I held myself off from the film. Just as he perhaps believed that all gay men are after all straight men, so the only place for me in relation to this *Dracula* would have been as alienated assistant at the spectacle of straight male engorgement. In a way, the man next to me was right: I had no place there. But with so many other vampires to feast with, I can manage without this one.

Originally published in *Sight and Sound* 3:1 (1993), pp. 8–12.

40 IDOL THOUGHTS: ORGASM AND SELF-REFLEXIVITY IN GAY PORNOGRAPHY (1994)

What makes (gay) pornography exciting is the fact that it is pornography. I do not mean this in the sense that it is exciting because it is taboo. The excitement of porn as forbidden fruit may be construed in terms of seeing what we normally do not (people having sex), what is morally and legally iffy (gay sex) or what is both the latter and, in Britain, not that obtainable (pornography itself). All of these may constitute porn's thrill for many users, but they are not what I have in mind here.

Nor do I mean that the category 'pornography' makes pornography exciting because it defines the terms of its own consumption and is moreover a major player in the business of constructing sexual excitement. Pornography does indeed set up the expectation of sexual excitement: the point of porn is to assist the user in coming to orgasm. However, it is also the case that no other genre can be at once so devastatingly unsatisfactory when it fails to deliver (nothing is more boring than porn that doesn't turn you on) and so entirely true to its highly focused promise when it succeeds. In this pragmatic sense, porn cannot make users find exciting that which they do not find so. Yet in a wider sense, pornography does help to define the forms of the exciting and desirable available in a given society at a given time. The history of pornography – the very fact that it has a history, rather than simply being an unvarying constant of human existence – shows that excitement and desire are mutable, constructed, cultural. There can be no doubt at all that porn plays a significant role in this, that it participates in the cultural construction of desire. However, this too is not what directly concerns me here.

When I say that it is the fact that it is porn that makes porn exciting, I mean, for instance, that what makes watching a porn video exciting is the fact that you are watching some people making a porn video, some performers doing it in front of cameras, and you. In this perception, *Powertool* (1986) is not about a character meeting other characters in a prison cell and having sex; it is about well-known professional sex performers (notably, Jeff Stryker) on a set with cameras and crew around them; it's the thought and evidence (the video) of this that is exciting. Now I readily concede that this is not how everyone finds porn exciting. For many it is the willing suspension of disbelief, the happy entering into the fantasy that *Powertool* is all happening in a prison cell. I shall discuss first how a video can facilitate such a way of relating to what's on screen, and it may indeed be the most usual way. Yet I do not believe that I am alone or even especially unusual in being more turned on by the thought of the cameras, crew and me in attendance. I shall look at this phenomenon in the rest of the article, focusing especially on the videos of the current gay porn star, Ryan Idol. I shall end by considering the apparent paradox of such self-reflexive porn – that it is able to indicate that it is 'only' porn and yet still achieve its orgasmic aim.

▲ ▲ ▲

Gay porn videos do not necessarily draw attention to their own making. By way of illustration, let me consider one of the more celebrated scenes in gay porn, the subway sequence which forms the last part of *Inch by Inch* (1985).

A subway draws up at a station; a man (Jeff Quinn) enters a carriage of which the only other occupant is another man (Jim Pulver); after some eye contact, they have sex, that is, in the matchlessly rigorous description of *Al's Male Video Guide* (1986), 'suck, fuck, rim, titplay';[1] at the next station, another man (Tom Brock) enters the carriage but the video ends, with a title informing us that 'the non-stop excitement continues ... in the next Matt Sterling film, coming February 1986'.

This sequence unfolds before us as an event happening somewhere of which we are unobserved observers. In other words, it mobilises the conventions of realism and 'classical cinema'.[2] The first term indicates that what we see we are to treat as something happening in the real world. The second refers to the ways in which a film or video places us in relation to events such that we have access to them from a range of vantage points (the many different shots and the mobile camera that compose a single sequence in such cinema), while not experiencing this range as disruptive or (as it is) impossible; a special feature of this cinema is the way it enables the viewer to take up the position of a character within the events, most obviously through the use of point-of-view shots and the shot/reverse shot pattern. Videos do not really give us unmediated access to reality, nor do viewers think that they do. What I am describing

---

1. *Al's Male Video Guide*, New York: Midway Publications, 1986, p. 132.
2. For a brief account of 'classical cinema', see the entry in Annette Kuhn and Susannah Radstone (eds), *The Women's International Companion to Film*, London: Virago, 1989. For a more exhaustive account, see David Bordwell, Janet Staiger and Kristin Thompson, *The Classical Hollywood Cinema*, New York: Columbia University Press, 1985.

are particular (if commonplace) ways of organising narrative space and time in film and video (between which I make no distinction for the purposes of this discussion).

The realism of the *Inch by Inch* sequence is achieved most securely by the use of location shots taken in a subway. These open the sequence and punctuate the action five times, reminding us of a real life setting that had really to exist in order to be filmable. The interior of the subway carriage could be a set – it looks very clean and the graffiti are too legible and too appropriate ('SUCK', 'REBELS', 'BAD BOYS') to be true – but the accuracy of the seating and fittings, the harsh quality of the lighting and the fact that all four sides of the carriage are seen, suggest either an unusually expensive set or an actual carriage rented for the occasion. The lack of camera or set shake suggests that the lights passing outside are indeed passing rather than being passed, but the care with which this is done is itself naturalistic. The high degree of realism in the setting is complemented by filmic elements associated with realism, such as handheld camera and rough cutting on action. Further, the sound gives the appearance of having been recorded synchronously with the action, so that the grunts, heavy breathing, gagging, blowing and 'dialogue' ("Suck that cock", "That feels good" etc.) don't sound like they've been added later, as is more usual with porn videos.

The performances too suggest a realism of genuine excitement. Both performers have erections most of the time (by no means the rule in porn) and their ejaculations, partly through the skill of the editing but also in some longer takes, seem to arise directly from their encounter. This compares favourably with the worked-for quality betrayed in much porn by the sudden cut to an ejaculation evidently uninspired by what the performer was doing in the immediately preceding shot. To such technical realism we may add a quality of performance, a feeling of abandonment and sexual hunger (especially on the part of Jim Pulver), unsmiling but without the grimly skilled air of many porn performances.

The quality of abandon relates to the idea of the real that all the above help to construct. This is a notion that anonymous sex, spontaneous, uncontrolled sex, sex that is 'just' sex, is more real than sex caught up in the sentiments that knowing one's partner mobilises or sex which deploys the arts of sexuality. As John Rowberry puts it, 'The sensibility of wantonness, already considered anti-social behaviour when this video was released, has never been more eloquently presented.'[3]

The rules of classical cinema are used in the sequence with exactly the degree of flexibility that characterises their use in Hollywood. The first, establishing interior shot of the carriage shows both Jeff and Jim and thus their position in relation to one another. Both sit on the same side of the carriage and the camera is positioned behind Jim's seat pointing along the carriage towards Jeff. The first cut is to a medium close-up

---

3. John Rowberry (ed.), *The Adam Film World Guide* 14:11, Los Angeles: Knight Publishing Corporation, 1993, p. 93.

Inch by Inch, 1985: Jeff Quinn and Jim Pulver.

of Jeff, with the camera at pretty much the same angle towards him as in the establishing shot – thus the spatial dislocation is only one of relative closeness and not one of position; it may be said to resemble the activity of the human eye in choosing to focus on one element out of all those before it; in short, we don't notice the cut but go along with its intensification of the situation, allowing us to see the lust in Jeff's eyes.

The next cut is to Jim. The direction of Jeff's gaze in the previous shot, as well as the continuing effect of the first, establishing shot, do not make this sudden change of angle disturbing. Moreover, although the camera is at 45 degrees to Jim, just as it was to Jeff, and although Jim is looking to his right off-screen and not at the camera, just as Jeff was looking to his left off-screen, nonetheless we treat the shot of Jim as if it is a shot of what Jeff sees, as a point-of-view shot. I think this is true despite one further discrepancy, namely that, although Jeff's gaze is clearly directed at Jim's face (and still is in the next shot of him), nonetheless this shot of Jim is a medium shot from a lowish angle, which has the effect of emphasising his torso (exposed beneath an open waistcoat), the undone top button on his jeans and his crotch; in other words, Jeff, in the shot on either side of this, is signalled as looking at Jim's face (even, it appears, into his eyes), yet this shot, if taken as a point-of-view shot, has him clearly looking at Jim's body. Yet such literal inaccuracy goes unnoticed, because of the shot's libidinal accuracy – it's not Jim's eyes but his chest and crotch that Jeff wants.

These few shots show how very much the sequence is constructed along the lines of classical cinematic norms, how very flexible these norms are, and in particular how they can be used to convey psychological as much as literal spatial relations. Such handling characterises the whole sequence, which it would be too laborious to describe further. However, the sequence, like much porn, does also push the classical conventions much further than is normal in Hollywood, perhaps to a breaking point.

Linda Williams, in her study of (heterosexual) film/video pornography, *Hard Core: Power, Pleasure and the 'Frenzy of the Visible'* (1989), discusses the way that the genre has been propelled by the urgent desire to see as much as possible of sexuality, by what she calls 'the principle of maximum visibility.'[4] Two aspects of this are particularly relevant here.

One is the lengths to which porn goes to show sexual organs and actions. Williams lists some of the ways that this has operated: 'to privilege close-ups of body parts over other shots; to overlight easily obscured genitals; to select sexual positions that show the most of bodies and organs [...] to create generic conventions, such as the variety of sexual "numbers" or the externally ejaculating penis.'[5] These are what a friend of mine calls 'the plumbing shots' and are presumably what made John Waters remark that porn always looks to him 'like open-heart surgery'. The camera is down on the floor between the legs of one man fucking another, looking up into dangling balls and the penis moving back and forth into the arsehole; or it is somehow hovering overhead as a man moves his mouth back and forth over another's penis; and so on. Such spatial lability goes much further than classical norms, where the camera/viewer may, in effect, jump about the scene but will not see what cannot be seen in normal circumstances (even in actual sex one does not normally see the above, because one is doing them). Very often the editing of these sequences betrays gaps in spatial and temporal continuity, ignored, and caused, by the 'frenzied' (to use Williams's suggestive term) will to see. The moment of coming is sometimes shot simultaneously from three different camera positions, which are then edited together, sometimes one or more in slow motion. Such temporal manipulation through editing again breaks the coherence of classicism. Devices like this may work because – as in the 'incorrect' shot of Jim described above – they are in tune with the libidinal drive of the video. But they may also draw attention to the process of video making itself, so that what the viewer

4. Linda Williams, *Hard Core: Power, Pleasure and the 'Frenzy of the Visible'*, Berkeley/Los Angeles: University of California Press, 1989, p. 48.
5. Ibid., p. 49.

is most aware of is the cameraperson down on the floor, the performer's climax shot from several cameras, or the editor poring over the sequence, things that may spoil or may, for some, enhance the excitement of the sequence.

The other aspect of the 'principle of maximum visibility' of interest here, and central to Williams's book, is showing what is not, and possibly cannot be, seen in actual sexual intercourse, most famously the ejaculating penis. Here the difference between straight and gay porn is especially significant. As Williams discusses, much of the 'frenzy' of heterosexual porn is the desire to show and see what cannot be shown and seen, female sexual pleasure, something of no concern to gay (as opposed, of course, to lesbian) porn. Equally, the oddness of showing the man ejaculating outside of his partner's body is less striking in gay porn; withdrawal to display (especially when involving removing a condom, or ignoring the fact that in the fucking shots he is using one) is odd, but much (probably most) actual gay sex in fact involves external ejaculation (and did so even before AIDS).

Yet the insistence on seeing the performers' orgasm is an interesting feature of gay porn too. As in straight porn, it brings the linear narrative drive that structures porn to a clear climax and end, as well as relating to the importance of the visible in male sexuality. Within gay sex, seeing another's orgasm is delightful because it is a sign that the other is excited by one and is even a sort of gift, a giving of a part of oneself. Such feelings are at play in come shots in gay porn. Additionally, one may see come shots as a further dimension of a video's realism. Come shots are rarely, if ever, faked; we really are seeing someone come. This is happening in the story and fictional world of the video, but it's also happening on a set. Its conventionality, its oddness when involving withdrawal, the often disruptive cut that precedes it, all draw attention to it as a performance for camera. This breaks classical norms, but it is the foundation of the excitement of pornography that I want to discuss in the next section.

▲ ▲ ▲

If gay porn, like straight, runs the risk of disrupting its own illusionism, some of it has been happy to capitalise on this. Most gay porn is like the subway sequence in *Inch by Inch* (though less accomplished in its deployment of codes of realism and classicism), but a significant amount is not. In its history (not much shorter, according to Waugh, than that of the straight stuff[6]), gay film/video porn has consistently been marked by self-reflexivity, by texts that have wanted to draw attention to themselves as porn, that is, as constructed presentations of sex.

---

6. Tom Waugh, *Hard to Imagine: Gay Male Eroticism in Photography and Film, from its Origins to Stonewall*, New York: Columbia University Press, 1996.

This may be at the level of narrative: films about making porn films (*Giants*, 1983; *Screenplay*, 1984; *Busted*, 1991; *Loaded*, 1992); about taking porn photographs (*Flashback*, 1980; *Juice*, 1984; *Bicoastal*, 1985; *Make It Hard*, 1985; *Rap'n about 'ricans*, 1992); about auditioning for porn films (*The Interview*, 1981; *Abuse Thyself*, 1985; *Screen Test*, 1985); about being a live show performer (*Le beau mec*, 1978; *Performance*, 1981; *Times Square Strip*, 1982; *The Main Attraction*, 1989); about having sex in porn cinemas – just like the patrons (*The Back Row*, 1973; *Passing Strangers*, 1977; *The Dirty Picture Show*, 1979). It may be at the level of cinematic pastiche or intertextual reference (*The Light from the Second Storey Window*, 1973; *Adam and Yves*, 1974; *The Devil and Mr Jones*, 1974; *Five Hard Pieces*, 1977; *Cruisin' 57*, 1979; *Gayracula*, 1983; *Early Erections*, 1989[7]). It may be a display of a star, someone known for being in porn (*Best of the Superstars*, 1981; the *Frank Vickers Trilogy*, 1986–89; *Deep Inside Jon Vincent*, 1990; *Inside Vladimir Correa*, 1991); or more specifically a film about being a porn star, showing him on the job (*Inside Eric Ryan*, 1983; *That Boy*, 1985). There are even successful films that are histories of gay porn (*Good Hot Stuff*, 1975; *Eroticus*, 1983). Where the film does not refer to film porn as such, it may well refer explicitly to the psychic elements necessary for the production of porn: narcissism (e.g. a man making love to his own mirror image (*Le beau mec*, 1978; *Pumping Oil*, 1983)); exhibitionism (e.g. a bodybuilder fantasising posing nude (*Private Party*, 1984)); voyeurism (*Le voyeur*, 1982; *On the lookout*, 1992); and dreaming and fantasising themselves, two of the commonest motifs in gay porn films, resulting in elaborate narrative structures of flashbacks, inserts, intercutting and stories within stories. All of these elements of content can be supplemented by the form of the film itself. The *Interview* films (1989–) for instance have the subject talking to the off-screen but heard director while stripping, working out and masturbating. *Roger* (1979) cuts back and forth between long shots and close-ups of the action (Roger masturbating), using different shades of red filter, the rhythmic precision of the cutting drawing attention to itself and hence to the film's construction of a celebration of its eponymous subject.

I am far from claiming that this tradition of self-reflexivity is characteristic of most gay porn. If the list I have given (itself very far from complete) is impressive, it constitutes but a drop in the ocean of the massive gay film/video porn business. Yet the tradition is there and encompasses many of the most successful titles. The self-reflexive mode would not be so consistently returned to, did it not sell – and it would not sell if it did not turn people on. Moreover, it is not unreasonable to assume that some people (like me) take pleasure in non-self-reflexive porn by imagining the rehearsals, the camera and crew, by focusing on the performers as performers rather than as characters.

---

7. These films refer respectively to *A Star is Born*, Garbo, Cocteau and Brando movies, *The Devil and Miss Jones*, fifties stag movies (and *Five Easy Pieces* of course), *American Graffiti*, *Dracula*, and educational television documentaries.

Ryan Idol on the cover of *Stallion*, May 1993.

I want to examine gay porno self-reflexivity by focusing on the work of one highly successful contemporary porn star. Ryan Idol is a young man who must have blessed his parents and perhaps God that he was born with so appropriate and serviceable a name. Few stars can have got their own name so often into the title of their videos (*Idol Eyes*, 1990; *Idol Worship*, 1992; *Idol Thoughts*, 1993) or had it used as the basis for so many puns in magazine feature spreads ('Ryan Idol, Yours to Worship' (cover, *Advocate Men*, July 1990); 'Idol Worship' and 'Pinnacle' (cover and feature title, *Advocate Men*, March 1993); 'Richard Gere was My Idol – So to Speak', *The Advocate Classifieds*, 18 May 1993)). Ryan seems to have no existence, no image, other than that of being the subject of sexual adulation. What is exciting about him is that he is a porn star.

There is with all movie stars a potential instability in the relationship between their being a star and the characters they play. When the fit is perfect – Joan Crawford as Mildred Pierce, Sylvester Stallone as Rocky Balboa – we do not, except in a camp appreciation, sit there thinking that we are seeing a movie star baking pies by the score or becoming World Heavyweight Champion; in so far as the discrepancy worries us at all, we resolve it by seeing the role as expressive of personality qualities in the star – in the case of Joan and Sly, for instance, variations on notions of working-class advancement. There is, in other words, a set of cultural categories to which both role and star image refer, beyond that of simply being a very famous performer in movies. Porn stars – like, to some extent, musical stars – cannot mobilise such reference so easily; they are famous for having sex in videos.

There can be an element of wider social reference in porn stars' images. The extremely successful Catalina company has created an image of the California golden boy, with no existence other than working and making out. This is an image that seems to offer itself as stripped of social specificity, a sort of pornographic utopia uncontaminated by class, gender or race, although it is of course highly specifically white, young, US and well fed. Residually, gay porn stars are still generally given social traits. Jeff Stryker, for instance, perhaps the biggest contemporary star, is repeatedly associated with working-class iconography, through roles (a mercenary in *Stryker Force*, 1987, a garage mechanic in *The Look*, 1988, a farm boy in *The Switch is On*, 1987) or accessories in pin-ups (spanners, greasy jeans). This is often reinforced by the idea of him as an innocent who, willingly but almost passively, gets into sexual encounters (as in his gaol videos, *Powertool*, 1986 and *Powerfull II*, 1989, or the farm boy in the city narrative of *The Switch is On*). It would however be hard to say anything even as broadly definite as this with Ryan Idol, even though he has played a lifeguard (*Idol Eyes*, 1990), college quarterback (*Score Ten*, 1991) and naval officer (*Idol Worship*, 1992). Even these roles in fact play upon the one clear role that he has, being a porn star.

The sense of his not offering anything but himself as body is suggested by his readiness to play with different body images in his many porn magazine spreads. In *Advocate Men* in July 1990, he has almost bouffant hair with a still boyish face and body. This look is capitalised on in the spread in the November 1991 issue of the short-lived *Dream*, which seemed to be addressing itself to men and women, straight and gay simultaneously; unusually for an Idol spread, there are no shots with erections, he is posed on black satin sheets and his expression is one of practised but unsullied yearning. Before that (at least in terms of publication, if not actual shoot), in *Mandate*, June 1990, the hair is cut much shorter at the sides, the top more obviously held stiffly in place with spray, he uses a leather jacket as prop, and poses more angularly, which, together with harder directional lighting, makes him look both more muscley and more directly sexual. Something similar is achieved in *Jock*, December 1991, though with more tousled hair and the fullest sense of social reference (a locker-room and football gear, part of the publicity for *Score Ten*). By 1993, however, there was a more radical alteration of the image, and in two, almost simultaneous forms. His hair is long and Keanu Reeves-ishly floppy now and his body less defined. In *Advocate Men*, March

1993, he poses by a pool, more in the 'art' style of a gay photographer like Roy Dean than this magazine's usual house style. In *Mandate*, June 1993, he is sweaty, with grease marks on his body, a much raunchier look, which is picked up in his pictures in *The Advocate Classifieds* for 18 May 1993, which have some residual boxing iconography.

There are continuities in this imagery, but these serve to emphasise him qua porn star. The thong tanline is unchanging, a tanline associated with exotic dancers, that is, sex performers. More significantly, he consistently poses in ways that relate very directly to the viewer. He holds his body open to view, his arms framing rather than concealing it, his posture, especially from the hips, often subtly thrust towards the camera (especially notable in shots lying on his side in *Dream* or seated in *Torso*, December 1991). This sense of very consciously offering the body is reinforced by the fact that he almost invariably looks directly, smilingly, seemingly frankly, into the camera, and has an erection. The only variation in the latter is that it is more often free standing or lightly held in the early photos, more often gripped and pointed in the later ones. There is absolutely no sense here of someone being observed (as if voyeuristically) as they go about their business nor of someone posing reluctantly, embarrassedly, just for the money. That impression is reinforced by interview material: "I'll do maybe one or two adult films, mostly as an outlet for my exhibitionism" (*Advocate Men*, July 1990), 'Ryan reveals that he likes showing off his big body. "I like doing it and I like watching it," he says' (*Prowl*, June 1991). In *Ryan Idol: A Very Special View*, 1990, scripted by Ryan himself, he talks at length about the pleasures of posing for photographs and of being an exotic dancer.

His magazine spreads, a vital component of any porn star's image, construct him as nothing other than a porn star, and this is echoed by the information on his life. Porn stars are seldom given an elaborate biography, but there is usually an implication of something in their lives other than pornography. Though Ryan has not made so many videos, he has done very many photo spreads and personal appearances. Interviews with him give the impression that that is what his life consists of, the more so since the establishment of the Ryan Idol International Fan Club (which includes a 'hot line', a co-star search, a 'Win a Date with Ryan Contest', and a sales catalogue, including posters, T-shirts, pictures, 'paraphernalia' and cologne; in short, 'We're offering [the fans] many, many ways to get closer to Ryan Idol' (*The Advocate Classifieds*, 18 May 1993). *A Very Special View* offers a day in the life of a porn star, but unlike other such videos featuring, for instance, Vladimir Correa or Jon Vincent, Ryan's day does not consist of sexual encounters but a photo shoot, a strip show and doing solos for us. His career even has its own narrative dynamic, to do with the gradual extension of what he does on camera. In all his videos he does solos and in most he is sucked off; in *Idol Eyes*, the penis in the close-ups of him fucking Joey Stefano is in fact David Ashfield's, as subsequent coverage revealed; but in *Score Ten* he did his own stunt work and, with a fanfare of publicity, in *Idol Thoughts* he sucks someone else off. This trajectory, itself following the pattern of many porn narratives, is part tease, keeping something in reserve for later in the career, but also part play with the question of sexual identity – Ryan makes straight porn videos, was 'open' in early interviews ("I share my lovemaking equally with women and men", *Dream*), though much less equivocally gay more recently ('"Do you enjoy sucking dick?" "What do you think? I think it's a turn-on. And I think that question is pretty much answered in *Idol Thoughts*"', *Advocate Classifieds*). Such fascination with the 'real' sexual identity of porn stars in gay videos is a major component of the discourse that surrounds them, but it also contributes to the sense that with Ryan sex is performance rather than identity.

His videos further emphasise his existence as porn star. Only two are actually about him being a porn star (*A Very Special View* and the footage in *Troy Saxon Gallery II*, 1991) but the rest all play with the idea of his having his being in the pleasures of looking. In *Idol Eyes* he spies on others having sex but is first really turned on by looking at himself in the mirror, getting into different outfits in front of it and masturbating at his own image. His voice-over talks about his learning to get off on men through getting off on himself (a casebook statement of one of the Freudian aetiologies of homosexuality). Similarly in *A Very Personal View* he jacks off looking at himself in the bathroom mirror, saying in voice-over: "Nothing wrong with that – I do enjoy being with myself – sometimes it's much more exciting – especially when someone … might be watching" (a rider I'll return to). In *Score Ten* he masturbates in front of a fellow student (as payment for the latter's having written a paper for him), posed on the bonnet of a car with the student inside, so that he, Ryan, is framed and kept distant by the windscreen. *Idol Worship* has him strip off and masturbate in the control room of the ship he commands, all the while telling the crew not to look, to keep their eyes on their instruments, orders which they obey. *Trade Off* (1992) is about Ryan and Alex Garret as neighbours spying on each other through their windows. Thus we have voyeurism (*Idol Eyes*, *Trade Off*), narcissism/self-looking (*Idol Eyes*, *A Very Special View*), display (*Score Ten*), denial of looking (*Idol Worship*), a series of entertaining plays on what is at the heart of porn: looking, showing, being looked at.

The most sustained exploration of this is *A Very Special View*, especially in the opening and closing solo sequences. In the first, Ryan is discovered by the camera when he wakes up and masturbates; this is accompanied by a voice-over in which he says he does this every morning and how he enjoys it. The treatment is for the most part classical; we are invited to imagine that Ryan doesn't know we are there and has added the commentary later. Yet even here Ryan teases us with the knowledge that he does know we are, as it were, there.

The sequence is in two parts, the first on the bed, the second in the bathroom. At the end of the first, Ryan is pumping his penis hard and glances at the camera momentarily and then again on a dissolve to the bathroom sequence. It is in the latter that Ryan makes the remark in voice-over quoted above, that it can be more enjoyable to make love to oneself, "especially if someone might be watching". Earlier in the sequence he has evoked the possibility of another person being present:

> There's no better way to start the day than to stroke my cock and bring myself to a very satisfying orgasm. Come to think about it, there is one better way and that would be to have someone working on my hard cock as I awake and slowly, slowly getting me off.

This comment runs the risk of reminding the viewer of what is not the case, that he is not in bed with Ryan sucking him off. The later comment alludes to what is the case, that someone is watching him – the camera/us. This immediately precedes his orgasm, so that what is in play as he comes is the fact of looking and being looked at.

When we first see him in the bathroom, he is looking at himself in the mirror, and several other mirrors duplicate his image. He masturbates in the shower, but a close-up towards the end makes it clear that he is still appraising himself in the mirror. When he comes, he looks straight ahead, head on to the camera. But is he looking at the mirror or the camera, at himself or us? Either or both, for our pleasure in him is his pleasure in himself.

The last sequence plays much more strongly on the presence of the camera and Ryan as image. He goes into a friend's bedroom to have a rest. He strips to his briefs and gets on the bed, then turns to the camera, saying "Do you want to see?", a rhetorical question in a porn video, and takes off his briefs. The sense of him as a performer is emphasised by the mirrors in the room. Not only do they connote display, narcissism and exhibitionism, they are also the means by which we see the cameraman from time to time. Perhaps this is an accident – 'bad' video-making – but with a star like Ryan it is entirely appropriate. What is he but someone being filmed? At two points we see an image of him which the camera draws back to reveal has been a mirror image; any distinction between the real Ryan and the image of Ryan is confounded.

Most remarkable though is Ryan's constant address to the camera. Once he runs the risk of reminding us of other, unavailable possibilities – "Imagine it anyway you want", he says, but of course should we wish to imagine having sex with him, we have to imagine something other than what we are seeing. But for the rest he talks entirely about the situation we are watching. He speaks of his control over his penis ("I make it do what I want"), an obvious asset in a porn star. He draws attention to the narrative structure of the sequence, its progress towards orgasm, by saying that he is about to come, but won't do it just yet, how he likes to hold off for as long as possible. He even draws attention to the porn viewing situation, by saying twice that he wants the viewer to come with him, something porn viewers generally wish to do. The shouts that accompany his orgasm are punctuated by glances to the camera, still conscious of our intended presence, still reminding us that he is putting on a show for our benefit.

▲ ▲ ▲

In emphasising self-reflexive gay porn, I not only don't want to give the impression that it is the more common form, but also don't want to suggest that it is superior to less or un-self-reflexive examples. Intellectuals tend to be drawn to the meta-discursive in art; since what they themselves do is a meta-activity, they take special comfort from other things that are meta, like self-reflexive art. Yet it interests me that so viscerally demanding a form as pornography (it must make us come) can be, and so often is, self-reflexive.

According to much twentieth-century critical theory, this ought not to be so. It has long been held that work that draws attention to itself – cultural constructs that make apparent their own constructedness – will have the effect of distancing an audience. A film that draws our attention to its processes of turning us on ought not to turn us on; you shouldn't be able to come to what are merely terms. As Linda Williams puts it, pornography has a problem:

> sex as spontaneous *event* enacted for its own sake stands in perpetual opposition [in porn films] to sex as an elaborately engineered and choreographed *show* enacted by professional performers for a camera.[8]

Yet, as I have tried to show, in much gay porn, at any rate, the show *is* the event.

This is of a piece with much gay culture. Being meta is rather everyday for queers. Modes like camp, irony, derision, theatricality and flamboyance hold together an awareness of something's style with a readiness to be moved by it – *La traviata*, *Now Voyager* and 'Could It be Magic' (in Barry Manilow's or Take That's version) are no less emotionally compelling for our revelling in their facticity. The elements of parody and pastiche and the deliberate foregrounding of artifice in much gay porn are within this tradition. Episodic films like *Like a Horse* (1984) and *Inch by Inch* move from one obviously constructed fantasy to another – from a jungle encounter to a no-place, abstracted leather sequence to an Arab tent, from a studio rooftop to a studio beach to a studio street – without for a moment undermining their erotic charge. This is characteristic of the way we inhabit discourse. We are constantly aware of the instability of even our own discourses, their hold on the world still so tenuous, so little shored up by a network of reinforcing and affirming discourses, and yet our stake in them is still

---

8. Williams, op. cit., p. 147; Williams's italics.

so momentous. We see their deliberation but still need their power to move and excite; it's thus so easy for us to see porn as both put-on and turn-on.

This, though, is not mainly what is at play in the Idol oeuvre. For here there is no sense of putting on a fantasy, no sense of performing anything other than performance. The idea of sex as performance is generally associated with male heterosexuality, and the element of working hard to achieve a spectacular orgasm is certainly present in much gay porn. Yet performance in the Ryan Idol case means much more display, presentation, artistry, the commitment to entertainment – literally a good show. It is a construction of sexuality as performance, as something you enact rather than express.

Gay men are as romantic and raunchy, as expressive and essentialist, as anyone else. Yet much facilitates a perception of (gay) sex as performance. Owning to one's gay identity – itself so fragile a construct – is perilous: seeing sexuality as performance rather than being is appealing, since it does not implicate that compelling notion, the self. At the same time, dominant culture does little to naturalise our sexuality, making it harder to see gay sex acts as a product of pure need. We are less likely to think of gay sex in terms of biology than of aesthetics.

Paradoxically, there is a kind of realism in pornographic performance that declares its own performativity. What a porn film really is is a record of people actually having sex; it is only ever the narrative circumstances of porn, the apparent pretext for the sex, that is fictional. A video like *A Very Special View* foregrounds itself as a record of a performance, which heightens its realism. It really is what it appears to be.

This realism in turn has the effect of validating the video, and the genre to which it belongs. By stressing that what we are enjoying is not a fantasy, but porn, it validates porn itself. As Simon Watney has argued, the importance of doing this in the age of AIDS could not be greater.[9] And by specifically celebrating masturbation, videos like Ryan's also validate the very response that porn must elicit to survive, that is, masturbation. The most exciting thing of all about porn is that it affirms the delights of that most common, most unadmitted, at once most vanilla and most politically incorrect of sexual acts, masturbation.

Originally published in *Critical Quarterly* 36:1 (1994), pp. 49–62.

---

9. Simon Watney, *Policing Desire: Pornography, AIDS and the Media*, London: Methuen/Comedia, 1987.

41 ACTION! (1994)

It must have been the way I was saying it. When people have asked me if I've seen any good films lately, I've replied, 'Oh yes, *Speed*', and they've looked startled. It's as if I wasn't saying the title of a film but lapsing into some ill-understood subcultural jargon: 'Yeah, man – speed'. Perhaps I lengthened the vowel or arched my body involuntarily, because they weren't entirely wrong. *Speed* is, like, speed.

In all truth, it isn't as much of a trip as one could imagine it being. There's nothing in it like the camera hanging out of the jeep in *Hatari!*, or skimming over Julie Andrews in *The Sound of Music* or the hand-held prowling in *Wolfen*, none of the magnificent shock cuts and zooms of Hammer horror or the likes of Mario Bava and Dario Argento, let alone the thrillingly torrential cutting of the Odessa steps sequence in *Battleship Potemkin* or the eponymous tempest in *Storm Over Asia*. Nor is there the gross-out factor in *Speed* that might elevate it to late-night and video-cult status, none of the gore of even a mainstream movie such as *Under Siege* (kitchen knives in skulls, fingers in eyeballs), to say nothing of the I-can't-believe-I'm-seeing-this climaxes of films such as *Basket Case* or *The Re-animator* (but don't bother to check this out on the British release videos). Indeed, *Speed* teasingly draws back from delivering such an experience, even when it titillates us with the promise that it's about to show us a white, middle-class mother and baby smashed to smithereens.

Speed gets its rush from a sheer squandering of sensational situations. Keanu Reeves is a cop who has to deal with three desperate predicaments: a plummeting lift, a bus primed to explode if it drops to below 50 mph and an out-of-control subway train. One situation follows straight after the other, set in motion by an obscurely vengeful ex-cop (Dennis Hopper) with a genius for deadly remote-control technology. Any one of these variations on velocity would have been enough for most movies. *Speed* is like Sylvester Stallone dangling over the ravine at the start of *Cliffhanger* plus the office explosion in *Lethal Weapon 3* plus the train crash in *The Fugitive* plus the chase along the sunken canal in *Terminator 2*, all put end to end with no boring bits in between. No dodgy politics. No naff attempts at psychologizing the villain: he's a nutcase. No mushy buddiness: the film barely pauses when Keanu's partner is blown to bits through his (Keanu's) lack of foresight. No elaborate excuses to get the camera to linger on the star's muscles: Keanu's not that kind of boy. And no love interest to send the kids into frenzies of squabbling and going to the loo: there is a girl (Sandra Bullock on fine form) and Keanu does get her, but it's all done on the run with only a quick clinch at the end. This is the movie as rollercoaster: all action and next to no plot.

The cinema has always had the potential to be like this. Whether or not it is true that the first audiences for the Lumière brothers' film of a train entering a station ducked in terror as it advanced towards them, the idea that they did has often seemed to be emblematic of what film is about. The Lumières ushered in a new technology, that has become ever more elaborate, revelling in both showing and creating the sensation of movement. *Train Arriving at a Station* and *Speed* belong to a distinguished lineage. It includes all those celebrations of movement so prized by earlier commentators on film: the simple documentary dwelling on movement, be it vast or tiny, train crashes or water fleas (to take oft-cited early examples); such staged delights as the Keystone Cops, cowboys and Indians, Fred and Ginger, climaxes *à la* Griffith; and all those attempts to make cinema move analogously to music, as in animated abstract ballets or 'symphonies' of the great modern cities. The lineage also includes, however, *This is Cinerama*, Imax cinema presentations and now (in Portrush, Northern Ireland, at Granada Studios in Manchester, at the Trocadero in London's Piccadilly) the Showscan Dynamic Motion Simulator, a 'magic chair' that promises to deliver 'the ultimate fantasy: Reality'. The celebration of sensational movement, that we respond to in some still unclear sense 'as if real', for many people *is* the movies.

I would not want to erect this into an absolute aesthetic principle, as some theorists have done. The stasis of filmmakers such as Ozu, Duras and Akerman is just as authentically cinematic as the movement of Murnau, Minnelli or, indeed, Jan de Bont, the director of *Speed*. Yet stillness and contemplation are rare in popular cinema. The triumph of the word 'movie' over the more static 'pictures' or evocative 'flicks' is not just a product of US cultural imperialism; it also catches something of the sensation we expect when we go to the cinema.

It seems, though, that we seldom want the sense of movement and excitement, the speed, by itself. How many times does one want to visit the Imax or, probably, a Showscan Dynamic Motion Simulator? We generally want the exhilaration and rush embedded in a fiction. Such fictions situate the thrills. They refer us to the world. They do not usually pretend to show us the world as it really is, but they point to that world. They offer us thrills and elations we might seldom have, might think it impossible really to have, but they relate such imaginings of elation to the human coordinates of the real world: the environments we live in, the social categories in which we have our being. In the process, they propose and legitimate kinds of thrills, and who gets them and who pays the price.

In contemporary cinema, it is the action film that most characteristically delivers speed in a story. One has only to think of the stars of such films – Schwarzenegger, Stallone, Bruce Willis, Harrison Ford, Steven Seagal, Jean-Claude Van Damme, and now Keanu Reeves – to have an indication of whose thrills are being legitimated: straight white men. This doesn't mean that no one else can possibly imagine having the thrills alongside Arnie or Keanu, but it does contribute to the reproduction of a masculine structure of feeling. Extreme sensation is represented as experienced not within the body but in the body's contact with the world, its rush, its expansiveness, its physical stress and challenge. There is nothing wrong with such feelings of extreme and, as it were, worldly sensation, but the movies tie them to male characters and male environments, suggesting they are really only appropriate to men. This is not a matter of saying that I want – let alone my wanting women to want – to have quite this kind of sensational experience, but that there is a deeper, underlying pattern of feeling, to do with freedom of movement, confidence in the body, engagement with the material world, that is coded as male (and straight and white, too) but to which all humans need access.

In *Speed*, as in most action films of the past 15 or more years, it is not quite true to say that *only* straight, white men get the thrills. We now have a well-established pattern, whereby the hero is accompanied by white women and men of colour (rarely women of colour) who are also exposed to the dangers that bring the thrills. Though the screaming heroine or cringing Black man do still crop up, women and men of colour are nowadays more likely to be allowed to be tough and brave, to be able to handle themselves and often to have skills the white hero doesn't possess. Even if they don't start out that way, they eventually make the grade. The figure of the Black police chief or crack platoon leader who provides back-up at crucial moments is a staple of the genre, as is the moment when the heroine finally has to kill, deliberately and efficiently, to save the cornered hero.

Speed loses its potential Black helper, the bus driver in the central segment, early on, leaving Keanu and his white helper to save the busload of mainly non-white passengers. The helper, though, is a woman (Sandra Bullock). Unlike her (literally) poor fellow commuters, she's travelling by bus only because she has had her driving licence taken away for speeding (the film is not without a sense of humour). She has to take charge of the bus when the driver is incapacitated and performs brilliantly, managing sharp corners and interweaving across busy traffic lanes, all at top speed, splendid aplomb and verve mixed with terror. She does get the thrills of extreme physical danger and the exultation of mastery of a machine. Yet *Speed* still conforms to the pattern of contemporary action films by constituting her as helper. She's not the main man. Conan (in the Schwarzenegger films) and Indiana Jones are two of the many heroes who now do their thing with women and Black people in tow, but never quite as equals, never with quite the same access to the speed of worldly sensation.

Worldly thrills are seldom bought at no price. In the classic Western and jungle adventure film, to take relatively easy targets, it is the native people who pay the biggest price for the white man's exhilaration. With Rambo or a film like *Under Siege*, it's anyone who gets in the way, which generally means other males – many action films are indeed mainly affairs between men. *Speed* largely avoids giving us time to note death: there are innocent bystanders knocked off and some police, but by and large the film is oddly benign. Old ladies petrified to leap from lifts, babies in prams, poor commuters of colour on the unstoppable bus, such people are safe in *Speed*, not expendable as they might be in many other films. The price is elsewhere, in things. It is the transport system itself that is smashed about: cars, lorries, barriers, planes and even the roadway itself in a final eruption of a subway train from below. It is an orgy of destruction of one of the great frustrations of modern urban living – getting about.

It is not impossible to imagine action movies otherwise. They don't have to be about the destruction of subject peoples and the natural environment, they don't have to centre forever on straight white men. The shifts in gender and race roles I've already suggested indicate the possibility of change. The problem with *Passenger 57* (which in any case was no worse than *Under Siege*, say, or *Die Hard 2*) was not that its hero was a Black man, and certainly not Wesley Snipes' inadequacy as a star, but dull plotting and direction. There are many precedents for the woman as hero of adventure, notably Leni Riefenstahl's mountain films, Fearless Nadia (the Indian star celebrated in the wonderful recent film *Fearless: The Hunterwali Story*), Sigourney Weaver in the *Alien* films, and the 'women warriors' discussed by Yvonne Tasker in her recent book *Spectacular Bodies*.

Yet I would not want to underestimate how difficult it will be to make it normal and unremarkable to have people of colour and women as subjects of worldly sensation. Experience of space has race and gender dimensions which set limits to how plausible or exceptional one may find a representation. Colour ghettoization, for instance, instils assumptions about space that are hard to shake. White people often say they are fearful of going into Black ghettos, but seldom stop to consider that such ghettos are themselves surrounded on all sides by the powerful white ghetto. Entering and being in white space can be profoundly intimidating, however at ease Wesley Snipes or Danny Glover may appear in it on screen. Even more fundamentally, perhaps, much cross-cultural research suggests that we start learning our relation to our environment from the moment of cradling, and that we learn it differently according to gender. To feel that it is OK to be unrestrained, to kick against what surrounds you, to thrust out into the world is what boys learn, not girls. To see women strain against the world may be inspirational, but also at some psychic level unbelievable. Heroes of action who are other than male and white (and straight and able-bodied) are still going to feel exceptional for some time to come.

Action movies as the most common contemporary form of the cinema of sensation ally the speed they offer with white male characters. Women and people of colour may be let in on the action, but either in secondary roles or with a strong sense of their exceptionality. Yet the experience action movies offer is in another way not so traditionally masculine at all.

To go to an action movie is to sink back in the seat and say, 'show me a good time'. Maybe we also cringe, shield our eyes, convulse our bodies — maybe we are often not so much more sophisticated than those putative Lumière audiences — but mentally we abandon ourselves to the illusion. Many have seen this as the essence of nearly all film experience, no matter what the genre; it underlies the notion of 'classical cinema' that has become so entrenched in film studies.

Such surrender to pleasure has greatly worried cultural, and not just film, criticism. Perhaps the image that most famously captures this intellectual worry about movies as sensation is that of the feelies in Aldous Huxley's *Brave New World*: the masses hooked up to a wash of sensations as part of an enforced passivity that keeps them mindlessly turning the cogs of capitalism. There is a point here. Passivity in life, in politics, is problematic: it means acquiescing to a status quo that damages people along class, gender, racial, sexual and other lines; for many women lying back within heterosexual sex has not always meant enjoying it; and there are besides always others who pay the real price for the megabuck sensations of the world's well-to-do minority. Yet it is hard not to see in Huxley's hatred something else: a libidinal fear of passivity itself.

Modern discussion of cultural pleasures tends to take sexuality as the founding form of all enjoyment, as the appetite *par excellence*. (I look forward to a return to theory and criticism which takes eating as its primary metaphor for understanding enjoyment.) Pleasures that are approved or disapproved of get mapped onto ideas of what sex is like. The notions of active and passive have been made to do a great deal of muddled but suggestive work, ineluctably correlated with gender roles within heterosexuality. On the one hand, proper gender identity has seemed to be realized in the performance of active male and passive female coital roles. On the other hand, a phantasm of sex as assault has haunted the minds of heterosexual male intellectuals. As a result, when they have imagined passivity in sex they have imagined something terrifying. Passivity is thus both demeaning for a man, because it makes him like a woman, and frightening too. So it is with all delectation — since sex provides the measure of all pleasures. The worst thing imaginable is to go to the cinema to lie back and enjoy it. Which suggests another terror, lurking beneath the fear of being like, and being treated like, a woman. For what kind of a man is it who lies back and enjoys it? A queer, of course. Queers of every sex know that passivity need not be alarming, but then that's queers for you, not a palatable message for chaps hell-bent on being straight.

In relation to adventure movies, there is a delicious paradox here. Such movies promote an active engagement with the world, going out into it, doing to the environment; yet enjoyment of them means allowing them to come to you, take you over, do you. When Jean-Claude Van Damme kicks his way out of trouble, when Harrison Ford leaps into the torrent in *The Fugitive*, when Keanu lies on his back under the careering bus in *Speed*, we may identify with them, imagine the rush of excitement as we brace ourselves against, and master, the world; but we're also letting ourselves be carried along, going with the flow of the movie, ecstatically manipulated.

The favoured position of hardcore fans for watching action movies in the cinema is slumped in the seat with legs slung over the seat in front. This is an excellent position for anal sex as well as for cunnilingus and fellatio. Come to think of it, for the male viewer action movies have a lot in common with being fellated. At the level of cultural imagery, the fellatee is considered the butch one – perhaps because he supplies the phallus, perhaps because fellatio facilitates a masculine dissociation of mind and body more readily than face-to-face coital positions. Whatever the reason, men cherish the illusion that their masculinity is not compromised by being fellated. Yet it's the other person, male or female, who's doing the work, really being active. So it is with action movies. In imagination, men can be Arnie or Keanu; but in the seat, it's Arnie or Keanu pleasuring them. Now that's what I call speed.

Originally published in *Sight and Sound* 4:10 (October 1994), pp. 6–10.

42 THE SAME OVER AND OVER (2015)

M [Germany 1931] opens with a children's counting game. Children are formed in a circle with one child standing in the middle; she repeats a rhyme and counts round and round, with one child having to drop out at the end of each repetition, until there's none left. The rhyme is one invented for the serial killer Fritz Haarmann,[1] which is why the children's mothers call it horrible; Haarmann's victims become in the game those who are out one by one. The overall narrative structure of *M* does not follow this rigorous repetitiousness,[2] but there is a strong sense of repetition in the killer Hans Beckert's procedures, buying treats for each victim, killing them by strangling, and above all whistling 'In the Hall of the Mountain King'.[3] This is itself a highly repetitious tune, as playfully menacing as the children's bogeyman rhyme, a short refrain repeated over and over, with a prominent, thrice repeated 1–2–3 figure, within it. The rhyme and the whistle are rigorous forms of repetition, in a context of lethality.

The repetition structure of *M*'s rhyme and whistle, clear-cut, self-contained, is the polar opposite of the whole narrative organisation of *Nature Morte* [United Kingdom 2006]. This deals with a killer who paints women as he is killing them. An art dealer, Oliver Davenport, writes a book about artist John Stephenson, who painted women as he killed them, but is now dead, although he had an accomplice, Lec, who is still killing and painting – and who knows who influenced whom? Davenport buys some of Stephenson's paintings, but in the course of doing so has drug and BDSM experiences, nearly becomes a victim himself and by the end of the film seems himself to have started killing. The film immerses us in this web of repetition, so intricate and hallucinatory that it is hard to follow, you're not sure who's been killed and who not, or when events are happening in relation to each other. The effect is evoked (down

---

1. Recorded by Magnus Hirschfeld in his 1931 *Sittengeschichte der Nachkriegszeit*; see Maria Tatar, *Lustmord: Sexual Murder in Weimar Germany*, Princeton, NJ: Princeton University Press, 1995, p. 185.
2. On serial form in *M*, see Anton Kaes, *M*, London: British Film Institute, 2000, pp. 35ff.
3. From Edvard Grieg's incidental music for Henrik Ibsen's *Peer Gynt* (1867).

to an absence of punctuation that embodies the fitful flow of the film) by TdSmith5:[4] 'This movie seems to have no end, it goes on and on and on "one month later" then "six months later" it's the same over and over…'

Where the rhyme and whistle in *M* are self-contained and rigorously repetitive, *Nature Morte* is fluid, confusing, open-ended in its repetitions. The rhyme and whistle of *M* are locked into clear, simple, rigid temporal patterns, while *Nature Morte* is temporally uncertain, bordering on the phenomenological timelessness of the BDSM scenarios and drug experiences it shows. Serial killing narratives fit somewhere along this spectrum, from repetition rigid, countable, closed, to repetition vague, imprecise, open.

▲ ▲ ▲

Multiple murder as the *raison d'être* of a story makes repetition the central organising principle of its narrative structure. The term serial killer, displacing maniac, monster, psychopath, stranger killer and multiple murderer, invokes narrative organisation in its very choice of the word serial. It is quite a labile word. Used in relation to an item of a production line, one with perhaps a serial number, it means repetition of the same; used of cultural production, it means a string of connected episodes making up an overall story, as opposed to the series, in which each episode is a completed variation on a basic situation and set of characters. All of these notions may be in play in the serial killer aesthetic of repetition.

The popularised criminological notion, the *modus operandi* (MO), also evokes repetition, the idea that the killer always kills in the same way. In investigative narratives this is often the basis of their being caught: the killer always uses the same means of killing or targets the same kind of victim, or there is some signature elaboration of the cadavers or the scene of the crime.

Landru [France 1962] makes a joke of repetition: the MO is always the same, picking up the woman, marrying, travelling to his second home in the country, killing (we never see by what means), incinerating; the comedy is registered in the amusement of the ticket girl at the station who sees him taking one woman after another for a trip but assumes he's just a Lothario, in the English neighbours typically fussing about the smoke generated by his incinerating the victims, and in the gradual speeding up, showing each stage in the repetition each time a little more shortly, so that the killings takes on a comic jerkiness.

Landru is funny partly because the exact repetitions push things towards the cartoonish, whereas in reality repetition never is repetition, in the sense of exactly

---

4. See http://www.imdb.com/title/tt0884803/reviews?ref_=tt_urv. My reference to the punctuation should not be read as snotty: TdSmith5 is an impeccable blogger in this regard.

the same over and over. Repetition can never in any circumstances, serial killer or otherwise, actually be the repeating of the same thing, because by virtue of being repeated the thing is not the same, it exists in relation to what has gone before and what come after, it is in a temporal sequence.[5] Moreover, repetition in serial killer narratives, even when doing just the same over and over is evoked, turns out to involve variation and pattern. Repetition's temporality enables in serial killing narratives an exponential play of anticipation and suspense, expectation and shock, as well as promoting particular senses of time, of remorseless onwardness, of regression and even sometimes of timelessness.

There may for instance be a sense of escalation, in the nastiness of the means used by the killer and also in the means used by the film-maker to show it. *Strandvaskaren* (*Drowning Ghost*) [Sweden 2004], a mild film by post-1970s serial killer standards, nonetheless also ups the level of how much nastiness we are shown and for how long. The first killing is very briefly shown (a man's head bashed against the wall), the second is almost out of sight (we just see, in long shot, the victim's shaking legs as he is strangled behind a corner); next a man is slashed with a scythe (we see a figure wielding the scythe but not the head being slashed off, which we only learn about later, when a woman finds the head in a sack on her dining room table); then a woman is impaled on a coat hook (we don't see it being done, but rather the result, the impaled body with blood dripping into a pool of blood below and a mid-close-up showing blood glistening at the neck wound); then a man, drinking milk out of a carton in a school kitchen, finds the door locked behind him and, when he presses his face up to the door's window, is stabbed through the eye, the blood splattering onto the window before being seen running into the milk from the dropped carton seeping out under the door; next a man is stabbed in the leg, and then as he is howling, bleeding, trying to crawl away, the killer takes an axe and finishes him off (the latter is not shown, but this is much the longest drawn out killing sequence, intensified by the victim's howling). After this gradual escalation in nastiness (from out of sight to shock cut but not really seen slashing, to splatter and grim jokiness (the blood in the milk), to stabbing with a knife leading to axing, with drawn out agony in between),

---

5. On notions of repetition, see *inter alia* Bruno Dubourgel, 'Vers un récital des sources', in Dubourgel (ed.), *Figures de la répétition. Recherches en esthétique et sciences humaines*, Saint-Étienne: CIEREC/ Université Jean Monnet, 1992, pp. 7-12, Umberto Eco, 'Interpreting Serials', in *The Limits of Interpretation*, Bloomington: Indiana University Press, 1994, pp. 83-100, Robert Fink, *Repeating Ourselves: American Minimal Music as Cultural Practice*, Berkeley: University of California Press, 2005, Bruce Kawin, *Telling It Again and Again*, Boulder: University of Colorado Press, 1989, and Graziella Pagliano, 'Ripetitività, produzione culturale e letteratura', in Francesco Casetti (ed.), *L'immagine al plural. Serialità e ripetizione nel cinema e nella televisione*, Venice: Marsilio, pp. 85-91; in this literature, Roland Barthes, Gilles Deleuze, Jacques Derrida, Sigmund Freud, Martin Heidegger and Søren Kierkegaard are often called upon.

the film draws back, with a man killed with a quick stab from a pitchfork, shown in black-and-white flashback, and finally the chief protagonist's dispatching of the killer almost by accident (he gets caught up in the blades of the motorboat she is trying to escape in).

Repetition also allows for a complex play with time. Most narrative is driven by enigmas, with especial urgency in crime fictions: who did it? how? why? Serial killer narratives are interested in these questions, but when is even more pressing in terms of their unfolding. When produces here an aesthetic in which the predictable (it will happen) plays off against the unpredictable (you don't know when). Serial killer narratives both guarantee a multiplicity of killings and withhold knowledge of when they will occur. There may be some common temporal patterns – opening with a killing, another soonish to suggest seriality, gradually increasing in frequency towards the end – but these are no more than rule of thumb, not what we can be sure of getting.

In *A Bay of Blood* [Italy 1971], the killings come thick and fast; in *Fritt vilt* (*Cold Prey*) [Norway 2006] you have to wait half the film for the first killing and thereafter are not sure when the next one will come. You know when you go to see these films that there's going to be a killing, and another, and more, but you don't know when. Therein lie the different thrills offered the audience.

A Bay of Blood opens with a woman in a wheelchair killed by a contraption that hangs her, only for the man who set this up to be killed in his turn. This sets the homicidal pace of the film, with the brevity of the screen time (84 minutes) matched by that of story time (the events all take place within about 24 hours). The killings come so hard upon each other's heels and there is so little time to get to know the characters that it is difficult to imagine feeling tense in relation to the film, better to sit back and, as in a variety show, wait for the next turn. This is reinforced by there being several killers, an intricate plot so hard to follow many must give up trying to do so, and the vividness (for the period) of the deaths (graphic special effects and shock cut editing); the use of slow pans across the bay where all this happens, always with beautifully coloured skies and an air of peace, accompanied by dreamy jazz-pop, offsets the violence, perhaps heightening it by virtue of contrast, perhaps taking an ironic or indifferent stance towards it. These temporal qualities – lots of vivid deaths in a short space of both screen and story time, offset by languorous interludes – may encourage a sense of appalled dismay at the carnage or giggling at its too-much-ness, but either way they are a solvent of the kind of engagement at the basis of conventional suspense.

Cold Prey is temporally the opposite of this. The five young people on holiday together in the Norwegian mountains assume that the abandoned hotel they take refuge in after one of them has an accident is a safe haven. We know, because we've chosen to see this film, that it can't be so. The opening is hectic: first a black screen and the sound of panting, then bright flashes of a boy running in snow, the high contrast cuts viscerally suggesting the experience of fear; then a montage about a missing boy (interviews with parents, television and newspaper coverage). Thereafter, and thus in impressive contrast, the film settles down, letting us get to know the characters and enjoy their easygoing, jokey, supportive relationships, all taking place against the white beauty of the mountains to which the film cuts from time to time. It unfolds unhurriedly as if it is just a light drama about a group of friends, as if their interactions are the point – but we know better. The whole tension of the first half and more of the film resides in the characters getting along and coping with the accident, breaking into and exploring the hotel, set against our being on generic tenterhooks waiting for the first killing. Once the killings start, they are sudden even though expected, a common affect in serial killer films, but there is still for a while no great pick up of pace, although now the characters too start to anticipate the next killing. Even at the end, with the tension ratcheted up after all but one have been killed, the suspense is still about waiting: the killer thinks he has killed everyone and takes all the bodies to throw them into a ravine; we see the one survivor waiting for the moment to strike – but when?

In addition to such rhythmic affects, there are two further temporal potentials for the serial killer film. One, very common, is based in the role of developmental explanations for the killer's activities; here the past is felt in the present. The other, much rarer, occurs when the repetitiousness of repetition is allowed to have its head, with the film opening out onto endlessness and timelessness. Most serial killing has no finish in sight. It ends when the killer is caught or dies. Lack of closure – coming to a stop but not a finish – intensifies the sense of remorselessness, of the terror of endlessness; it also creates the possibility of a sense of temporal uncertainty.

And Soon the Darkness [UK 1970] only seems to end with the death of the serial killer. It concerns two young British women, Jane and Cathy, on a biking holiday in France, who fetch up in an area where there has been a killing or killings (even this uncertainty contributes to the film's elusive sense of time). They have a quarrel and separate, and then later Jane finds Cathy's murdered body. Convinced the young man Paul that Cathy fancied is responsible, she clubs him repeatedly with a stone; when the local policeman turns up, she turns to him only to find him violating and trying to strangle her; Paul, who has survived Jane's assault, knocks the policeman out. Throughout there are many other possible suspects, including two oafish male peasants, the policeman's deaf and somewhat demented father, an Englishwoman living alone and a (female) café owner, but in the end the killer is the local policeman. Or is he? It's over – or is it?

The last shot of the film is of a broad country road of a kind seen throughout the film, deserted apart from a police car speeding, presumably, towards the scene of the final confrontation and, cycling in the opposite direction, two young women on bicycles. The police are about to restore order but young women in deserted places are always vulnerable. Moreover, the café owner has said the road has a "bad reputation", suggesting that all may not be resolved. This chink in the closure and reassurance the last shot should provide might give way to more doubts. How reassuring is it that the police are coming to a scene where one of their own is the culprit? And anyway is he? Do we really know he killed all the others or is he just carried away by Jane's vulnerability and hot pants? Has Paul killed the policeman, or put him out of action (it's not altogether clear), because he's a rival for Jane? I think overridingly we're supposed to assume the policeman is the serial killer and now all is well, but there is just this lingering disquiet about whether anything is ever quite fully finished. This gives the title, *And Soon the Darkness*, a resonance: night never comes in this film, which takes place over the course of a long sunny summer's day, but metaphorical darkness always threatens.

The eponymous Schramm's seriality [*Schramm*, Germany 1994] is taken as a given from the start, rather than established cumulatively in the course of the film. It begins with what is in fact his end. An opening title from Carl Panzram,[6] "Today I am dirty but tomorrow I'll just be dirt", provides a keynote not only for the grottiness that follows but also the sense of temporal pointlessness, the endless round of dirt to dirt. It is followed by blurred images and the sound of heavy breathing, suggestive of something homicidally ghostly going on; however, as the images come into focus, we see they are of a marathon race and we can assume that the breathing is of a runner; later we will learn that Schramm runs marathons. This opening, where the ghastly is revealed to be something else and unexceptionable, is followed by a shot of a newspaper with the headline 'Lonely Death of the Lipstick Killer', the camera slowly zooming in on the picture of the killer, and then a track along drops and sprays of white paint on a black ground, gradually joined by red spots until the camera reaches the face that we have just seen on the newspaper, Lothar Schramm. The headline and the shot of Schramm bleeding establish that he is dying;[7] the imagery suggests action painting and porn come shots as well as blood. When (in flashback) Schramm kills a pair of proselytising Christians who call at his door, he creates a spray of blood on the walls, again evoking action painting. However, the camera track that starts the film shows, as we only fully understand at the end, Schramm's blood from a nose bleed, after falling from a ladder whitewashing the wall in order to cover the blood spray from the Christian victims. The tracking shot, with its modernist aesthetic, and the final explanation together suggest an existential sense of the absurd, the momentous imagery of killing and art turning out to be just that of a household accident.

---

6. US serial killer 1891–1930, the quotation taken from a letter written shortly before his death.

7. Mikel J. Koven, *La dolce morte: Vernacular Cinema and the Italian Giallo Film*, Lanham, MD: Scarecrow, 2007, suggests that the rest of the film shows how Schramm, 'alone and bleeding to death, reflects back on his life' (p. 185).

Las horas del día (*The Hours of the Day*) [Spain 2003] is at once more formally rigorous than *Schramm* in terms of beginning and ending and even more immersed in everyday repetition. It opens with classic establishing shots, each one taking us nearer the story's location, that is, initially, the tower block where the protagonist Abel lives; the film ends with a series of shots in the reverse direction. Nothing could more clearly indicate start and finish. There are also significant events in Abel's life: breaking up with his fiancée Tere, going to the wedding of his best friend Marcos (and telling him during it that his bride Carmen once came on to him), his widowed mother taking up with a new man, his deciding to grow a beard. The latter also chimes with the beginning and end: the first shots of Abel are of him shaving, while the last thing we know about him is that he has decided not to shave any more. And then there are the murders, in one case sort of premeditated (he takes a taxi, directs the driver to a deserted field and kills her there), one opportunistic (he follows an old man who has been squabbling with his daughter at a metro station into the gents' toilet and kills him there). Yet these striking temporal elements (the film's own insistent signalling of beginning and ending, important life events, eruptions of homicidal violence) are all treated with the same impassive camera, always at a distance, very often outside buildings, static, compositions emphasising rectangularity, with no non-diegetic music. Everything is on a par: shaving, having breakfast, opening up his shop, hanging out with Marcos, killing someone, eating with Tere, splitting up with Tere, preparing dinner, then chatting up a girl waiting for her boyfriend, and then, and then again. Moreover, there is no clear indication of how much time is passing. Does he kill the taxi driver on the same day that he has a row with his assistant in the shop over her pay? How long is it between the first time we see him chatting with Marcos and the wedding? What time of day is it in the otherwise deserted metro station? The rhythm of the film suggests a rigorously linear sense of time, and yet with unacknowledged ellipses and a vagueness about time of day that flattens everything into a banal repetitivity. The killings may be a reaching for moments of intensity relieving the monotony of Abel's life, but it doesn't feel like they achieve this; they seem more like just more of the same, just another thing to do again, just killing time.

Like *The Hours of the Day*, *Sombre* [France 1998] too has strong indicators of time, the better to foreground the virtual timelessness of Jean's continual driving and killing. One of these indicators is the Tour de France. This occurs at various points in the film and its importance is emphasised by the film ending with a very long series of tracks along the faces of the crowds watching the race. The Tour is a model of temporal and spatial order: it has a beginning and end and temporally defined stages, as well as corresponding spatial co-ordinates. Nothing could be less like Jean's travelling, embodied in long takes of driving along, representing who knows how many days or places.

A different kind of temporal indicator are the stories that people tell: a woman Jean picks up (and later kills) reminisces about the happy day her mother came to collect her from her convent school; a man tells Jean and some others a rather louche story about a lottery winner; a woman tells another about her relation with Jean and the other woman in turn speaks of her marriage and her one great love. These are in important ways different. The man tells a story about someone else, the women about themselves. The woman who speaks about her relationship with Jean is Claire, with whom he seems to be on the verge of having a relationship until he bundles her into the car of the woman to whom she then tells her story, a story we know to be untrue. The telling of the stories also emphasises time. Claire moves from present, to past, to future and conditional perfect in her story: "We always fight, we have for a long time. This time maybe he's going to leave me. He isn't always violent. If he was I would have divorced him." The woman she speaks to recounts her fleeting adolescent romance, nipped in the bud by both sets of parents, and continues: "Life began. It carried on. And now it's almost over", a bleak summary of life's co-ordinates. She also tells of meeting up again with the man many years later for an illicit afternoon together – "And then he died. Eleven days later. At 9.25 pm", startlingly precise temporal co-ordinates in a context of temporally vague story-telling. But whether precise or imprecise, false or true, someone else's story or their own, all this storytelling, with its internal registering of time by virtue of tenses and the idea of memory, contrasts with Jean, who has no stories and whose life, driving and killing, goes on and on with no clear sense of when and where.

There is a brief shot early on of a blindfolded boy walking about with his arms stretched out in a countryside, with the sound of the sea over, and we might treat this as a childhood memory, but it remains unexplained, unrooted, if anything emphasising the sense that Jean has no developmental story, only repetition. Something like a conventional narrative seems to be developing between Jean and Claire and her sister, Christine. He picks up Claire when her car has broken down, meets Christine, has sex with her, seems to be trying to kill her until Claire intervenes, ties Christine up, goes to a disco with Claire, has sex with Claire, forces her into a passing car. The sisters' story holds the vestiges of domestic narrative, a garden party where the dynamics between them and their mother are glimpsed. We also learn that Claire is a virgin, a temporal marker of sexual narrative. After they have had sex, she asks Jean if he noticed that she cried, in a way that suggests being moved by the experience. Almost immediately Jean hails a passing car and forces Claire into it. His rejection of her is a rejection of temporal organisation, of her insistence on the momentousness of this, her first sexual experience. Once in the car we have the longest developmental narration in the film, Claire's false account of her life with Jean, the other woman's reminiscences, culminating in that very precise statement of the time of death of her great love. Jean, and the film, however now revert to their default: driving and killing and driving, duration and flow rather than narrativised and timed time.

The Hours of the Day and *Sombre*, although organised around a sense of repetition that runs counter to conventional narrative time, nonetheless produce opposite senses of repetition. In *The Hours* repetition is monotony, boredom, pointlessness; killing is just another possible item in the never-ending passing of the hours of the day, themselves the relentless repetition of arbitrarily determined chunks of time. *Sombre*, on the other hand, evokes a loss of the sense of time, a surrender to might-be-any-time driving and killing, to a sombreness that obliterates any clear sense of time of day, to a never-beginning, never-ending duration.

▲ ▲ ▲

[Repetition] can lock us into the compulsive insatiability of neurosis or free us into the spontaneity of the present tense; it can strengthen an impression, create a rhythm, flash us back, or start us over; it can take us out of time completely.[8] (Bruce Kawin)

Serial killer films may show the horror of repetition or provide the pleasures of it. They may also, in their common recourse to variation and escalation, betray a sense of the impossibility of true repetition. Even in the serial killer film at its purest, the slasher, something more than just killing and killing holds sway. In as unelaborated an example as *Rovdyr* [Norway 2008], where little attempt is made to establish the characters, either of the young holidaymakers in the Norwegian backwoods, or the barely articulate, hulking, hairy killers, whose faces are rarely shown, where there is no explanation, just remorseless hunting and killing, even here a modicum of variation is introduced in the modes of killing: shooting, knifing, people getting caught in animal and in man traps. However, and with notable exceptions (*The Abominable Dr. Phibes* [UK 1971], *Tras e cristal* (*In a Glass Cage*) [Spain 1987], *The Crimson Rivers* [France 2000], *The Girl with the Dragon Tattoo* [Sweden 2009]), European serial killer films have largely eschewed the more elaborated examples of variation: killings embodying fantastical backstories turn out to have nothing to do with them (*Drowning Ghost*), multiple murders are really only motivated by the killing of a single victim (*The Sleeping Car Murders* [France 1965], *The Oxford Murders* [Spain/UK/France 2008]) or are chimeras (*The Element of Crime* [Denmark 1984], *Death and the Compass* [UK/Spain/USA 1992]). Realist backstories may provide a sense of an explanatory beginning, but, especially when internally repeated or extended (*Peeping Tom* [UK 1960], *Der Dirnenmörder von London* (*Jack the Ripper*) [Switzerland/West Germany 1976], *Aimilia,*

---

8. Kawin, op. cit., p. 5.

the Pervert [Greece 1974], *Cold Light of Day* [United Kingdom 1989], *Last Screening* [France 2011]), may also simply provide the template for repetition of the originatory event in the act of killing itself. Elsewhere – *And Soon the Darkness, The Hours of the Day, Nature Morte, Sombre* – there is just repetition, with no beginning point, no original that is being repeated, no teleological potential end point, just the same over and over.

Repetition has long been considered a bad thing. Philip Jenkins suggests that what is frightening about serial killing is the very idea of being gripped by the childlike compulsion to repeat, what Bruce Kawin calls 'useless repetition ... an unfulfillable compulsive cycle';[9] equally, serial killing may be felt as the horrific logical conclusion of a society based on repetitive work and media organisation. At the level of cultural production, Roland Barthes, for one, writes of the boredom of repetition, as something shameful, weighed down by the past, by a dreary need for consistency and insistence over against the freshness and turbulence of originality.[10] However, as Bruce Kawin's *Telling It Again and Again* argues, there is repetition and repetition.

Serial killer films show repetition in lethal form and may thus explore or allow the imaginative inhabiting of or surrendering to the experience of it. This may be understood as showing the horror of it, the grip of compulsion, the triumph of capitalist and digital organisation, the dread regression to childhood – but it also allows for the thrill of compulsion without the consequence, the embrace of our conditions of subservience, the longed for recapture of childish satisfactions.[11] Serial killer films embody in their forms all of these possibilities and yet more, a confrontation with a fundamental aspect of existence, since forever but with renewed force in contemporary culture, namely repetition itself, its limitations and terrors, and the – troubling – possibility of enjoying these.

Abridged version of Chapter 3 from Richard Dyer, *Lethal Repetition: Serial Killing in European Cinema*, London: BFI/Palgrave, 2015, pp. 35–58. This edit was assembled by Dyer for this Reader in 2021.

---

9. Philip Jenkins, *Using Murder: The Social Construction of Serial Homicide*, New York: Aldine de Gruyter, 1994; Kawin, op. cit., p. 12.

10. Roland Barthes, *Le plaisir du texte*, Paris: Éditions de Seuil, 1973, pp. 66–69.

11. Cf. Matt Hills, *The Pleasures of Horror*, London: Continuum, 2005: 'serial killer fiction can almost be considered as a dramatisation tout court of [the Freudian notion of] repetition-compulsion' (p. 65).

43 FOND OF LITTLE TUNES: THE SISSINESS OF MUSIC IN *ROPE* AND *TEA AND SYMPATHY* (2023)

Phillip plays Poulenc at the piano, Tom listens to Chopin on the phonograph: so both may be queers. They are protagonists in, respectively, *Rope* (1948) and *Tea and Sympathy* (1956). These were among the first high-profile Hollywood films to deal with male homosexuality, that is, they were about it and sought to keep it at bay. The long, equivocal association of classical music with femininity and gay men is crucial to this process and to its lack of complete success.

▲ ▲ ▲

There is a very deep-rooted association of music and homosexuality in men, coalescing, especially in Anglo-Saxon cultures, around classical music towards the end of the nineteenth century and dissipating from the 1960s onwards.[1] Elizabeth Gould summarises the association thus:

> It is difficult to overstate music's long, persistent, and uneasy relationship with homosexuality in Western society. Associated with femininity for centuries, particularly in

---

1. Accounts of this association, trailing back fitfully to ancient Greece, include Leo Treitler, 'Gender and Other Dualities of Music History' in Ruth A. Solie (ed.) *Musicology and Difference: Gender and Sexuality in Music Scholarship*, Berkeley: University of California Press, 1993, pp. 23–45, and James Kennaway, *Bad Vibrations: The History of the Idea of Music as a Cause of Disease*, London: Routledge, 2016. Writing in 1994, in a locus classicus of the emergent queer musicology, Philip Brett could still observe: '*All* musicians, we must remember, are faggots in the parlance of the male locker room' ('Musicality, Essentialism, and the Closet' in Philip Brett, Elizabeth Wood and Gary C. Thomas (eds), *Queering the Pitch: The New Gay and Lesbian Musicology*, New York: Routledge, 1994, p. 18); I don't think one could find that view represented in public cultural production in the past thirty years or so, but its persistence may be greater than I realise in everyday discourse.

North America,[2] participation in music has been believed to emasculate and thus homosexualize men and boys.[3]

In the novel *Despised and Rejected* (1918), all the men who are homosexual are musical, be it composers, performers or enthusiasts. If not all the many texts — novels, plays, films[4] — associating gay men with music go quite this far, the association frequently functions as a default homo trait.

This may well be informed by the common assertion of homosexual men indeed having a special affinity for music, made alike by gay-identified writers (e.g. Xavier Mayne: 'Doubtless music is preeminently the Uranian's art. His emotional nature goes out to it and in it, as in no other'[5]) and those not (e.g. Havelock Ellis: 'As regards music, my cases reveal the aptitude which has been remarked by others as peculiarly common among inverts'[6]).[7] Mayne's reference to 'emotional nature' points to the implications of the association. It is drawn out by Edward Carpenter: 'As to music, this is certainly the art which in its subtlety and tenderness — and perhaps in a certain inclination to indulge in emotion — lies nearest to the Urning nature.'[8] Terms like 'emotional', 'sensitive', 'refined' and 'neurotic' are all used to identify the inherent quality of both music and homosexual men, and thus of the connection between them.

This quality may be viewed negatively. Oswald in *Imre: A Memorandum* (1906) speaks of music as a 'super-neurotic, quintessentially sexual, perniciously homosexual art.'[9] Sensitivity may be linked to weakness and hence decadence. In *Whiteoaks* (1936), having just learnt of his brother Finch's shared love of music with a boy who is in love with him, Renny is equally appalled to learn what Finch spends his spare cash on:

---

2. In the USA, the association seems confirmed by the preponderance of gay men among its composers: Samuel Barber, Leonard Bernstein, Marc Blitzstein, Paul Bowles, John Cage, Aaron Copland, David Diamond, Julius Eastman, Stephen Foster, Lou Harrison, Jerry Herman, Cole Porter, Ned Rorem, Stephen Sondheim, Billy Strayhorn, Virgil Thomson, and lyricist Lorenz Hart.
3. Elizabeth Gould, 'Homosexual Subject(ivitie)s in Music (Education): Deconstructions of the Disappeared', *Philosophy of Music Education Review* 20:1 (2012), pp. 45–6.
4. See appendix.
5. Xavier Mayne, *The Intersexes: A History of Similisexualism as a Problem in Social Life*, Naples or Florence: privately published, 1908, p. 395.
6. Havelock Ellis, *Studies in the Psychology of Sex. Volume II Sexual Inversion*, Philadelphia: F.A. Davis, 1927, p. 283.
7. See Judith Peraino 2006, *Listening to the Sirens: Musical Technologies of Queer Identity from Homer to Hedwig*, Berkeley: University of California Press, 2006, pp. 71–78.
8. Edward Carpenter, *The Intermediate Sex: A Study of Some Transitional Types of Men and Women*, London: George Allen & Unwin, 1908, p. 111.
9. Edward Prime-Stevenson (2003) *Imre: A Memorandum*, Peterborough (Ontario): Broadview Press, 2003 [(As Xavier Mayne) Naples: The English Book-Press, 1906], p. 144.

'Concerts – my God, more music – to make you more spineless';[10] Hanno's queerness and musicality, in *Buddenbrooks* (1901), undermine the eponymous business dynasty; teachers and students in the private academy in *Lucifer with a Book* (1949) foster an atmosphere of dissipation in soirées at once homosexual and musical.

Behind these connections is the notion of femininity and the dangers it poses for men. The idea that music is emotional and therefore feminine, and that too much contact with it is liable to weaken men, goes hand in hand with the association with sexual licence and often therefore homosexuality. This is an attitude traceable throughout Western history,[11] evident in music teacher Barry's recollections, in *Outrageous Fortune* (1943), of being called a sissy, Adam's gag at song composer Kip's expense in *Adam's Rib* (1949)[12] and Tom's fellow students calling him 'sister boy' in *Tea and Sympathy* (1953/1956). One shorthand for it is the appellation 'long-haired music', qualifying an art form with a term denoting the improper disciplining of male appearance. The patriotic march composer John Philip Sousa was quoted in the Houston *Post* in 1903 boasting, 'Longhaired men and shorthaired women you never see in my audience';[13] in 1964 Anna Frankenheimer could still issue a diatribe about the preponderance of homosexuals in classical music titled 'A Much-Needed Upbraiding of Long-Hair Music.'[14]

Yet the association of queers, music, sensitivity, decadence and femininity may be viewed more positively. In his collection of writings on music, Edward Prime-Stevenson (1927) suggests a lineage of 'Uranian' music from the ancient (Western) world, from the lyre player Iopas in the *Aeneid* (who gives his name to the collection) to, especially, Wagner and Richard Strauss.[15] In the quotations above, Xavier Mayne (Prime-Stevenson's pseudonym) and Edward Carpenter see intense emotional responsiveness as a good thing. Decadentist writing embraces perversity: in *The Green Carnation* (1894), Lord Reginald (Reggie) Hastings (based on Lord Alfred Douglas) declares: 'I must have music, and the sins that march to music.'[16] In *Whiteoaks*, sensitivity is triumphant. The exchange quoted above is triggered by Finch's brothers discovering a letter from

---

10. Mazo de la Roche, *Whiteoaks: A Play*, Boston: Little, Brown and Company, 1936, p. 43.
11. See e.g. Treitler, op. cit., 1993; Marcia Citron, *Gender and the Musical Canon*, Cambridge: Cambridge University Press, 1993; Ian Biddle and Kirsten Gibson (eds) *Masculinity and Western Musical Practice*, Burlington VT: Ashgate, 2009; Sam de Boise, *Masculinities, Music, Emotion and Affect*, PhD thesis, University of Leeds, Department of Sociology and Social Policy, 2012; Kennaway, op. cit., 2016.
12. Kip says that he is so convinced by Amanda's arguments for gender equality that he 'may go out and become a woman', to which Adam mutters to Amanda, 'he wouldn't have far to go'.
13. Cited in Patrick Warfield, 'The March as Musical Drama and the Spectacle of John Philip Sousa', *Journal of the American Musicological Society*, 64:2 (2011), p. 312.
14. Anna Frankenheimer, 'A Much-Needed Upbraiding of Long-hair Music', *Fact* 1 (1964), p. 12.
15. Edward Prime-Stevenson, *Long-Haired Iopas: Old Chapters from Twenty-Five Years of Music*, Florence: The Italian Mail, 1927.
16. Robert Hichens, *The Green Carnation*, New York: D. Appleton, 1894 [(Anon.) London: Heinemann, 1894], p. 11.

his music friend Arthur that opens 'Darling Finch'; when Finch realises why his brothers are so appalled, he at first makes to kill himself but then, thinking better of it, he

> sinks with a gasp of relief to the piano seat. There is a pause, then he brings his hands down in a wild tumult of sound, challenging and triumphant.[17]

The play is centrally about who is going to inherit a family fortune when its centenarian matriarch dies; everyone assumes it won't be her 'very sensitive and nervy' grandson Finch,[18] but she recognises his courage in determining to pursue music and leaves everything to him, and the play ends with him playing the piano.

Music may be a bond between homosexual men: Hanno and Kai (*Buddenbrooks*), Bert and Art (*Bertram Cope's Year* 1919), Paul and Kurt (*Anders als die Anderen* 1919),[19] Finch and Arthur (*Whiteoaks*). In *The Picture of Dorian Gray* (1891), we learn of Alan Campbell, an old acquaintance of Dorian's:

> He [Alan] was an excellent musician […] and played both the violin and the piano better than most amateurs. In fact, it was music that had first brought him and Dorian Gray together – music and that indefinable attraction that Dorian seemed to be able to exercise whenever he wished.[20]

The bond is often embodied in the image of two men at the piano: in *The Green Carnation* Reggie plays and Esmé Amarinth (i.e. Oscar Wilde) 'lean[s] largely upon the piano, in an attitude of rapt attention';[21] at a soirée in a small college town, Bertram Cope 'would lay his hand on' Arthur's when the latter was at the piano, which betrays them to some of the fellow guests;[22] Dulcimer (*The Green Bay Tree* (1933)) says 'Some of my happiest hours are spent embroidering while Julian plays the piano'; the way the brutish bouncer Erik gazes lovingly at Fingers as he plays piano in the club where they work contributes to the queer overtones of *Nocturne* (1946).[23]

The homosexuality may also be in the music itself. It is the 'fervor and intensity'[24] with which, in *The Christmas Tree* (1948), Pierre plays Beethoven's 'Moonlight Sonata'

---

17. De la Roche, op. cit., p. 44.
18. Ibid., p. 1.
19. Striking that in the first unequivocally gay film, the main characters are musicians.
20. Oscar Wilde, *The Picture of Dorian Gray*, London: Penguin, 2000 [London: Ward, Lock and Co., 1891], pp. 158-9.
21. Hichens, op. cit., p. 72.
22. Henry Blake Fuller, *Bertram Cope's Year*, Middleton, DE: Okitoks Press, 2017 [Chicago: Alderbrink Press, 1919], p. 82.
23. For more discussion of this intriguing film see Mark Osteen, *Nightmare Alley: Film Noir and the American Dream*, Baltimore: Johns Hopkins University Press, 2012, pp. 163-5.
24. Isabel Bolton, 'The Christmas Tree' in Bolton, *New York Mosaic*, London: Virago, 1998 [New York: Charles Scribner's, 1948], p. 184.

that reveals to Larry, and Larry's mother, the nature of their relationship. There is no suggestion that there is anything specifically homosexual about Pierre's playing, but this is implied in other cases. In *Teleny* (1893) Des Grieux hears in the eponymous pianist's 'soft music' 'things hitherto so strange, the love the mighty monarch felt for his fair Grecian slave, Antinoüs' and then, as the music changes, he sees

> the gorgeous towns of Sodom and Gomorrah, weird, beautiful and grand; the pianist's notes just seemed murmuring in my ear with the panting of an eager lust, the sound of thrilling kisses.[25]

When in *Buddenbrooks* Hanno tells Kai that he spends every evening improvising at the piano, Kai says he knows what Hanno is thinking about as he plays (i.e. their feelings for each other) and turns 'beet-red' while Hanno looks 'pale and very serious'.[26] Bertram Cope's Arthur plays with 'elaborate expressiveness', Ferdy in 'The Alien Corn' (1931) with 'discreet flamboyance',[27] both consonant with the way Liberace (whose concert career took off in the 1940s) was written about. In *Lucifer with a Book*, Puccini brings out the queer in the straightest boy:

> The sinuous fragrant music […] had a disintegrating effect on [him]. His last pose as a young American executive went out the window. He lolled wantonly on his ottoman, his mouth open to convey that he was in dire physical transport.[28]

John Sharp, the narrator of *Serenade* (1937), describes the threateningly seductive conductor Winston Hawes as an outstanding musician, but

> don't get the idea he was ever one of the boys. There was something wrong about the way he thought about music, something unhealthy, like the crowds you always saw at his concerts, and what it was I can only half tell you.[29]

John is an opera singer, whose voice changes in quality when he comes under Winston's spell. His girlfriend Juana explains to him, 'these men who love other man, they can do very much, very clever. But no can sing. Have no *toro* in high voice […] Sound like old

---

25. Oscar Wilde and Others, *Teleny*, London: Gay Men's Press, 1986 [(Anon.) *Teleny, or the Reverse of the Medal. A Physiological Romance of To-day*, London: Cosmopoli, 1893. In fact privately circulated; no publisher Cosmopoli existed], p. 30.
26. Thomas Mann, *Buddenbrooks*, New York: Vintage, trans: John E. Woods, 1994, p. 716.
27. W. Somerset Maugham, 'The Alien Corn', in Maugham, *The Complete Short Stories*, New York: Doubleday and Company, 1953, p. 532.
28. John Horne Burns, *Lucifer with a Book*, New York: Harper, 1949, p. 232.
29. James M. Cain, *Serenade*, New York: Vintage, 1978 [New York: Knopf, 1937], p. 118.

woman, like cow, like priest.'[30] Something similar is suggested by the contrast between straight-acting Bertram Cope and queeny Arthur when they sing together, Bertram's voice 'a resonant baritone' but Arthur's 'a high, ringing tenor […] almost too sweet.'[31]

Particular kinds of music may also betray homosexuality. Some composers are especially congenial. Tchaikovsky, not least because knowledge of his homosexuality began to circulate from the turn of the century, was a key reference point, especially the Sixth Symphony, the 'Pathétique'. It figures complexly in the eponymous Maurice's relationships with both the platonic Clive and the queeny Lord Risley;[32] Klaus Mann's biographical novel about Tchaikovsky, *Pathetic Symphony*, was published in German in 1935 and English in 1948;[33] the pull of the work is still felt in *Stranger in the Land* (1949) as the protagonist Raymond listens to it on the radio:

> The desolation of the composer's obsessed spirit, the unspeakable longings for forbidden rapture, rose spirally on wave after writhing wave to a shattering climax of anguish as dreadful to hear as the harsh sobbing of a grown man. This music was easy for the sexually twisted to understand.[34]

Wagner was also a key composer,[35] and the homosexual prison officer Captain Munsey chooses the Venusberg music from *Tannhäuser* to accompany his torture of prisoners in *Brute Force* (1947), reinforcing the postwar association of Wagner with Nazism and the latter with perverse sexuality. In *Ecstasy* (1892), 14-year-old Jules, so adoring the adult 'energetic and sturdy' Quaerts that the latter has to tell him 'You ought not to be so fond of me,'[36] plays obsessively at the piano Anton Rubinstein's Romance in E-flat. However, it is Chopin who is most pervasive.

Chopin, with his flowing locks, his relationship with a cross-dressing woman and probable homosexual liaisons[37] as well as the inimitable tenderness of his playing

---

30. Ibid., p. 133.
31. Fuller, op. cit., p. 82.
32. Cf. Bret L. Keeling, '"No Trace of Presence": Tchaikovsky and the Sixth in Forster's *Maurice*', *Mosaic: An Interdisciplinary Critical Journal* 36:1, 2003, pp. 85-101.
33. The 1948 *Pathetic Symphony* is a revision of the 1935 *Symphonie Pathétique*, in its formal organisation and its increased homoerotic content. Klaus Mann, *Symphonie Pathétique. Ein Tschaikowsky-Roman*, Amsterdam: Querido, 1935; Klaus Mann, *Pathetic Symphony: A Biographical Novel about Tchaikovsky*, New York: Allen Towne & Heath, 1948.
34. Thomas Ward, *Stranger in the Land*, Boston: Houghton Mifflin, 1949, p. 167.
35. Cf. Mitchell Morris, 'Tristan's Wounds: On Homosexual Wagnerians at the Fin de Siècle' in Sophie Fuller and Lloyd Whitesell (eds) *Queer Episodes in Music and Modern Identity*, Urbana: University of Illinois Press, 2002, pp. 271-292.
36. Louis Couperus, *Ecstasy*, London: Pushkin Press, trans.: A. Teixteira and John Gray, pp. 24, 101.
37. See Moritz Weber, 'Chopin war schwul – und niemand sollte davon erfahren' ('Chopin Was Gay – and No-one

and composition (notably the nocturnes which appear frequently in these fictions[38]), had long been perceived in terms of effeminacy and its implicit worse. Dorian Gray, Mr Fisher (one of Fay's affaires in *A Scarlet Pansy* (1933)), Dulcimer (*The Green Bay Tree*), Kurt (*Better Angel* (1933)), Pierre (*The Christmas Tree*), Michael (*The Divided Path* 1949) and Andy (*The Night Air* 1950) all play Chopin. A Prelude charts Dorian Gray's decline into depravity in the film version.[39] George, whose upper-class family are scornful of his desire to become a professional pianist, plays, in the film of 'The Alien Corn', bright, sparkling Chopin polonaises and waltzes for other people, but at one point is heard playing alone in his flat and now it is the slow first theme from the first Ballade, suggesting an altogether more tender privacy.

Chopin is known supremely as a composer for the piano as well as being himself a pianist and this is the instrument of choice in much gay representation. Even the violinist Paul in *Anders als die Anderen* is shown at one point playing the piano, wearing some flowing, Orientalist garment, rather like the decadent Dr Sour in *Lucifer with a Book*, playing the piano at his louche, all-male soirées 'in a silk mandarin lounging robe'.[40] The piano has strong domestic and thus feminine associations and there is thus also a long tradition of worry about 'men at the keyboard'.[41] Piano playing also emphasises touch. All instruments involve some degree of holding, but discourse and imagery about the piano especially focus on the quality of the tactile pressure and the movement of the hands. Des Grieux highlights the potential erotic frisson of this on his first meeting with Teleny, whom he has already seen and heard playing so compellingly:

The pianist stretched forth his ungloved hand. [...] I now put my bare hand into his. [...] Who has not been sentient of the manifold feelings produced by the touch of a hand?[42]

Vladimir Horowitz (1903–1989) is widely quoted as observing 'There are three kinds of pianists: Jewish pianists, homosexual pianists, and bad pianists.'[43] Definitely the first,

---

Should Know about It') (radio programme, SRF Schweizer Radio und Fernsehen, 16 November 2020, https://www.srf.ch/kultur/musik/spaetes-outing-chopin-war-schwul-und-niemand-sollte-davon-erfahren).

38. On the gendered reputation of the nocturnes, see Jeffrey Kallberg, 'The Harmony of the Tea Table: Gender and Ideology in the Piano Nocturne', *Representations* 39, 1992, pp. 102-133. *Nocturne* is not only the title of a film but also of a piece of music that a sexually ambiguous character is seen composing in its opening sequence.

39. For a discussion of the use of Chopin in the film, see Michael Long, *Beautiful Monsters: Imagining the Classic in Musical Media*, Oakland: University of California Press, 2008, pp. 216–221.

40. Burns, op. cit., p. 158.

41. Cf. Gary C. Thomas, 'Men at the Keyboard: Liminal Spaces and the Heterotopian Function of Music' in Daniel Goldmark, Lawrence Kramer and Richard Leppert (eds), *Beyond the Soundtrack: Representing Music in Cinema*, Berkeley: University of California Press, 2007, pp. 277-291.

42. Wilde, *Teleny*, op. cit., p. 33.

43. I have not been able to find the source of this quotation.

Paul (Conrad Veidt) at the piano in *Anders als die Anderen*, 1919.

he was widely rumoured to be the second of these; some might unkindly observe that Liberace was all three. His was also probably the highest profile image of the effeminate and supposed gay pianist in America even by the end of the 1940s, when he was still mainly known through hugely successful concert performances. As the cafe pianist in *South Sea Sinner* (1950), he plays the same Chopin Ballade that George plays alone in 'The Alien Corn'. As he plays, he describes to a customer its special quality: 'See how beautifully each phrase blends with the other', adding that 'Always I included Chopin in my concerts'. His use of the word 'blends' is evocative, for throughout the texts associating gay men and music, there recurs a notion of the particular kind of music that such men are especially drawn to.

In *The Tenth Moon* (1932), for instance, Blaine Decker, the young music teacher marooned in Dell River, Ohio, yearning for Europe and his lover Starr in Paris, tells his one soul mate Connie of his thoughts on accepting his job:

I said to myself, 'My dear fellow, this is the end for you – you are going into the wilderness. No one will have heard of Debussy or Ravel. They will think Brahms is a disease and Mussorgsky – a mineral water!'[44]

This is a suggestive list. Only Brahms remains from what was the standard concert repertoire of the time – no Haydn, Mozart, Beethoven, Mendelssohn, Dvořák or Tchaikovsky (although the last's 'Pathétique' symphony does crop up later in an evening of listening to the gramophone); and while one cannot be sure what rumours Blaine (or Dawn Powell) may have heard, of the composers in his list only Debussy married. More to the point still is the predominance of composers who moved beyond the established tonal system to harmonies that seemed more fluid and uncertain and who valued passing colours and textures over an impressive overall organisation. As James Kennaway puts it, by the end of the nineteenth century (and into the twentieth), music

> that seemed to focus on the sensual pleasures of sound, relating to timbre and instrumentation, which had already been seen as feminine earlier in the century, began to be linked to effeminacy and homosexuality.[45]

Nadine Hubbs[46] notes the special affinity felt by gay US composers for French music in this tradition: Debussy, Ravel, Satie, Poulenc, 'blurry, effeminized, other'.[47]

Des Grieux evokes just such a quality when he hears Teleny playing a gavotte 'that seems to smell of *lavande ambrée*'.[48] Oswald writes of the Gypsy music that accompanies the realisation of his love for the eponymous Imre: 'those melting chromatics, poignant cadences – those harmonies eternally oriental, minor-keyed, insidious, nerve-thrilling'[49]: 'melting' recalling Liberace's blending, and it was common to associate 'Oriental' musical qualities with a sensuousness felt to be more in tune with queer sensibilities. Jules in *Ecstasy* improvises, lighting on a phrase 'of plaintive minor melancholy' which he pursues 'higher and higher […] following the curve of crystal rainbows lightly spanned on high';[50] Reggie in *The Green Carnation* plays 'a plaintive,

---

44. Dawn Powell, *Come Back to Sorrento*, South Royston, VT: Steerforth Press, 1997 [As *The Tenth Moon*, New York: Farrar & Rinehart, 1932], p. 28.
45. Kennaway, op. cit., pp. 87–8.
46. Nadine Hubbs, *The Queer Composition of America's Sound: Gay Modernists, American Music, and National Identity*, Berkeley: University of California Press, 2018, p. 141.
47. Adam in *Adam's Rib* observes, disapprovingly, of Kip's florid playing of his own song 'Farewell Amanda', which Amanda finds 'very pretty', that it is 'pretty French'. The song is in fact by Cole Porter.
48. Wilde, *Teleny*, op. cit., p. 27.
49. Prime-Stevenson, *Imre*, op. cit., p. 127.
50. Couperus, *Ecstasy*, op. cit., pp. 118–9.

fleeting air – an air that was like a wandering moonbeam, the veritable phantom of a melody';[51] the violin playing of the angel in *The Wonderful Visit* (1895) is now like a flame, now like 'two flirting butterflies of sound [...] swift, abrupt, uncertain';[52] Kurt (*Better Angel*) improvises 'tinkling sounds, pulsing off into silence.'[53]

In *Despised and Rejected*, Dennis is disconsolately playing a nursery tune, but then 'without realising what I was doing, I was finding chords that began to release, bit by bit, some of the music that was imprisoned in my head'.[54] In *The Gay Year* (1949), at a party, Wally plays some chords, then begins 'weaving a minor melody out of the threads of his earlier chords'; Joe, the straight protagonist who has the eponymous year of being gay before deciding he's really not, listens on: 'From minor to major [they] progressed through the afternoon, Wally's music becoming stronger, yet never attaining what Joe hoped for when brought to fulfilment in the "major"'.[55] Both Dennis and Wally are departing from the conventional and solid, happily, but to the exclusion of the straight sensibility.

▲ ▲ ▲

Rope and *Tea and Sympathy* have this rich fund of imagery, discourse and sounds to draw on in their approach to homosexual characterisation. For the former, the music hints not just at the fact that the two central protagonists are homosexual but at this homosexuality's affective character; in *Tea and Sympathy* the music-femininity-effeminacy-homosexuality nexus is what is under interrogation.

These were high profile postwar Hollywood films. Both were based on successful plays, conferring prestige as well as title recognition, *Rope* staged in London and New York in 1929, *Tea and Sympathy* on Broadway in 1953. Both films had star names above the title, *Rope* Alfred Hitchcock and James Stewart, *Tea and Sympathy* Deborah Kerr. *Rope* was moderately successful, *Tea and Sympathy* less so. *Rope* for many years suffered from a focus on Hitchcock's creation of the illusion of the film being shot in one continuous take, but has gradually risen in critical esteem, Amy Lawrence even observing that of 'all Hitchcock's American films, the one that has benefitted the most from the shifting tides of theory is *Rope*'.[56] However, while Vincente Minnelli's critical

---

51. Hichens, op. cit., p. 154.

52. H. G. Wells, *The Wonderful Visit*, London: Macmillan, 1895, p. 102; cf. Yoonjoung Choi, '*The Wonderful Visit* and the Wilde Trial', *The Wellsian: The Journal of the H. G. Wells Society* 31, 2008, pp. 43-55.

53. Richard Meeker, *Better Angel*, Boston: Alyson, 1987 [New York: Greenberg, 1933], p. 275.

54. Rose Allatini, *Despised and Rejected*, London: Persephone, 2018 [(As A. T. Fitzroy) London: C. W. Daniel, 1918], p. 75.

55. Michael De Forrest, *The Gay Year*, New York: Castle Books, 1949, p. 37.

56. Amy Lawrence, 'Jimmy Stewart is Being Beaten: *Rope* and the Postwar Crisis in American Masculinity', *Quarterly Review of Film & Video* 16:1 (1997), p. 41.

reputation has grown considerably in recent years, *Tea and Sympathy* has by and large not benefitted from it. Both films have enjoyed notable queer analyses, D. A. Miller on *Rope* and David Gerstner on *Tea and Sympathy*,[57] Miller's article in turn stimulating several other contributions.[58] Both use music by sissy French composers.

▲ ▲ ▲

In *Rope*, two young men, Phillip (Farley Granger) and Brandon (John Dall), strangle an ex-schoolmate, David, and conceal the body in a large chest. They then hold a small party, laying out a buffet on the chest. The guests are Mr Kentley (David's father), Mrs Atwater (his aunt), Kenneth (a friend of David's), Janet (David's ex-fiancée and Kenneth's current one) and Rupert Cadell (James Stewart), who was housemaster to all the young men. In the course of the evening, Rupert realises what Phillip and Brandon have done and calls the police.

Phillip is a pianist. He plays the piano in the play, once at the beginning, a show tune, but in the film he is preparing for a first recital at the Town Hall. This embeds him further in the web of connotations by which he may be read as gay,[59] connotations that are rooted in, as David Greven puts it, 'the foundational cultural stereotype of [...] the gay male as signal arbiter of aesthetic standards'.[60]

Mrs Atwater asks Phillip if he wants to know whether his concert will be a success. Taking his hands to read the palms, she says 'These hands will bring you great fame'. It is of course a macabre gag: we know that the fame that will come to him from his hands will be for murder rather than music. However, reinforced by the camera moving close in on his hands, it is only the most underlined of moments associating Phillip's hands with music, murder and homosexuality. She observes of his hands: 'Good fingers – strong – artistic', exactly the combination needed for piano playing and strangling, and sex. While she discusses other characters in terms of their star signs, it is only Phillip's hands that she tries to read.

---

57. D. A. Miller, 'Anal Rope' in Diana Fuss (ed.) *Inside/Out: Lesbian Theories, Gay Theories*, New York: Routledge, 1991, pp. 119–141; David Gerstner, 'The Production and Display of the Closet: Making Minnelli's *Tea and Sympathy*', *Film Quarterly* 50:3 (Spring 1997), pp. 13–26.

58. E.g. Scott D. Paulin, 'Unheard Sexualities? Queer Theory and the Soundtrack', *Spectator* 17:2 (1997), pp. 37–49; Patricia White, 'Hitchcock And Hom(m)osexuality' in Richard Allen and Sam Ishii-Gonzalès (eds), *Hitchcock Past And Future*, London: Routledge, 2004, pp. 211–229; David Greven, 'Making a Meal of Manhood: Revisiting *Rope* and the Question of Hitchcock's Homophobia', *Genders* 56 (2012), https://www.colorado.edu/gendersarchive1998-2013/2012/12/01/making-meal-manhood-revisiting-rope-and-question-hitchcocks-homophobia

59. Cf. Miller, op. cit.

60. Greven, op. cit., p. 11.

Emphasis on the hands of Phillip (Farley Granger) in *Rope*, 1948.

D. A. Miller and David Greven argue for the centrality of, respectively, the anus and the mouth in *Rope*'s evocation of gay sex, but one might make a similar case for the hands, at any rate as far as Phillip is concerned. Commonly in the film, when Brandon and Philip are both in shot, the former has his hands tucked into folded arms or else in his pockets, while Phillip's are in view, sometimes looking elegant in the way they hold a glass, other times, when his anxiety is less under control, clenched around one. As well as playing the piano, Phillip's hands are emphasised throughout the film. It is he that strangles David and that pulls off the champagne cork that Brandon has been fiddling with (in a sequence widely read as in effect post-coital). When Mrs Atwater sees Kenneth, she mistakes him for David, and Phillip breaks the glass he is holding, cutting his hand. At one point, Brandon recounts an incident when they were visiting his mother in the country; it was a lovely day,

> the church bells were ringing and in the yard Phillip was doing likewise to the necks of two or three chickens. It was a task he usually performed very competently, but on this particular morning his touch was perhaps a trifle too delicate, because one of the subjects for our dinner table suddenly rebelled, like Lazarus he rose and—

Phillip interrupts him, vehemently, with 'that's a lie!', and this film with supposedly only concealed cuts suddenly cuts blatantly to Rupert looking quizzically towards Phillip. The anecdote unnerves Phillip because of what he has so recently done to David, but Brandon's telling not only draws attention to the delicacy of Phillip's 'touch' in the context of strangling, it also links sound, the church bells, to the act of killing. As he tells the story, the camera moves across from him to Phillip, foregrounding his hand gripping his glass.

In the play text, Phillip[61] plays 'with a rather unpleasant brilliance'[62] 'Dance Little Lady', in 1929 a recent hit from the show *This Year of Grace* by Noël Coward, resonantly gay perhaps but also very mainstream at the time. In the film, Phillip plays the first of the three *Mouvements perpétuels* by Francis Poulenc, composed in 1918, a somewhat obscure example of moderate modernism. Given Hitchcock and scriptwriter Arthur Laurents's cosmopolitanism and the latter's gay subcultural connections, it is perfectly possible that they knew Poulenc was gay, but more to the point is the way this piece fits with notions of a queer tradition of music, French, 'blurry, effeminized, other' (to quote Hubbs again). Several scholars have given precise musicological characterisation to the piece in terms of its tonal uncertainty, including Paulin, Thomas, and Clifton.[63] Here is Paulin:

> Over a moderately paced ostinato bass [...] Poulenc writes a series of brief, unrelated melodies, some of which are highly chromatic and clash rather dissonantly with the unchanging bass. [...] Not connoting homosexuality in any simple or precise way, Poulenc's composition [...] provides a space where non-goal oriented, non-teleological, non-(re)productive fantasies (all implying a distance from rigid heterosexual norms) can be projected and pleasure can be found.[64]

Paulin's observation that 'the pleasures of the work are those of momentary harmonic colours and shifts'[65] is similar to James Kennaway's above, of music 'that seemed to focus on the sensual pleasures of sound, relating to timbre and instrumentation [and culturally] linked to effeminacy and homosexuality'.

The composer Ned Rorem, a friend of Laurents, characterised Poulenc's work in ways consonant with Paulin, Thomas and Clifton and in the process evoked a decidedly queer lineage:

---

61. Named Granillo there.
62. Patrick Hamilton, *Rope*, London: Samuel French, 1929, p. 13.
63. Paulin op. cit., Thomas op. cit., Kevin Clifton, 'Unravelling Music in Hitchcock's *Rope*', *Horror Studies* 4:1 (2013), pp. 63-74.
64. Paulin, op. cit., p. 38.
65. Ibid.

> Take Chopin's dominant sevenths, Ravel's major sevenths, Fauré's plain triads, Debussy's minor ninths, Mussorgsky's augmented fourths. Filter these through Satie by way of the added sixth chords of vaudeville [...] blend in a pint of Couperin to a quart of Stravinsky, and you get the harmony of Poulenc.[66]

In *Music Ho!*, the conductor and composer Constant Lambert, on the heterosexual wing of the mid-twentieth century ballet world, considered Poulenc 'the most "amusing" of the many minor composers who were called on to vamp up the music for Diaghileff's fashionable dinners'.[67]

Phillip plays this amusing, tonally equivocal piece three times in the film, but never gets to the end of it.[68] The first time he is interrupted by the arrival of Rupert, who remarks 'your touch has improved, Phillip' (note 'touch' again). Amy Lawrence suggests that in the period, James Stewart is 'cast as the character who upholds the written word, the law, ideas';[69] here his interruption, despite his positive judgement on Phillip's playing, nonetheless stops it. The second time, the sound of a police siren momentarily draws Phillip's eyes to the window. Rupert, observing how much Phillip likes 'that little tune', keeps goading him about 'what's going on' and also sets a metronome going. Phillip falters, returning repeatedly to the beginning of the piece; he keeps going, breaks off, starts again, finally gives up. The siren and Rupert represent the law in the most obvious sense, but the metronome is an attempted imposition of the rigidly regular tempi of the straight (and white) musical tradition on the wandering and complex rhythms of the *mouvement*. The last time Phillip sets out to play is after Rupert has worked out what the boys have done, looked in the chest and called for the police. Sirens are heard and get louder. Phillip picks out just the little tune on the piano, barely audible against the siren. The tune is finally defeated, and as if to rub in the point, when he gets to the end of it there is a non-diegetic orchestral crash and an entirely different treatment of Poulenc's music over the end credits. As Gary C. Thomas puts it:

> the music's harmonies are straightened out and its deviant tune is corrected and brought to a 'rightful', hetero-lawful, tonic conclusion.[70]

This 'straightening' of Poulenc is already established over the credits at the beginning of the film, 'a fully orchestrated Hollywood bloating', the little tune's 'cool insouciance [...] slowed down and drenched in syrup.'[71]

---

66. Ned Rorem, 'Poulenc', in *An Absolute Gift: A New Diary*, New York: Simon and Schuster, 1977, p. 235.
67. Constant Lambert, *Music Ho! A Study of Music in Decline*, New York: Charles Scribner's Sons, 1934, p. 76.
68. For more detailed accounts see Paulin op. cit., Jack Sullivan, *Hitchcock's Music*, New Haven: Yale University Press, 2006, Thomas op. cit., and Clifton op. cit.
69. Lawrence, op. cit., p. 43.
70. Thomas, op. cit., p. 284.
71. Sullivan, op. cit., p. 145.

There is other music in the film, which comes from the straight world. When Brandon contrives to leave Janet and Kenneth alone together, he suggests they turn the radio on, which they do. Behind their conversation is heard the song 'At the Candlelight Café', a hit love song by Mack Gordon covered by Dick Haymes, Gordon MacRae and Dinah Shore, among others, crooners at the heart of heterosexual pop song production. The version heard here, very quietly, is by The Three Suns, a popular guitar, accordion and electric organ easy listening combo: it provides an unintrusive, highly conventional, sexually untroubled background to Janet and Kenneth's slightly troubled conversation, going over their break-up and then working out that Brandon is trying to sow discord between them and David. The music changes to 'I'm Looking Over a Four Leaf Clover', a hit song from 1927 (by Mort Dixon and Harry M. Woods) that had been a hit again in 1948 in various versions, including for The Three Suns who reached number ten in the hit parade. A cheerful song, it accompanies Rupert and the boys' housekeeper Mrs Wilson discussing the oddities of the party.

The music from the wireless comes literally from outside the world of the apartment, temporally (recent hits) as well as spatially. The Three Suns sing of sunshine in 'Four Leaf Clover' and come from the sunny street outside the apartment shown in the opening of the film. Their music both connects heterosexuality (Janet and Kenneth) and authority (Rupert) to the reassuring outside world and underlines the fact that both are at present in an altogether more sexually and musically unsettling one.

It is against this bland straightness and the credits' bloating that Phillip plays Poulenc's little tune. The fact that it is repeatedly interrupted, invaded by other sounds, never allowed to finish, suggests both the threat of gay charm and its vulnerability. But Phillip does keep trying.

▲ ▲ ▲

Tom Lee in *Tea and Sympathy* is bullied by his fellow college students because he prefers sewing, music and the company of women to sports, girls and the company of men. Laura Reynolds, the wife of the teacher in whose house he boards, takes pity on him and has sex with him to help him realise that he is a real man. The story is framed by Tom going to a reunion ten years later and remembering the events, in the course of which we learn that Laura left her husband, Bill, and that Tom has married.

It is explicit in the play that the problem with Tom is his presumed homosexuality. The word is used of him, as well as fairy and queer. Other elements, in addition to his feminine interests, point in the same direction. He is seen nude bathing in the dunes with an evidently gay teacher, Mr Harris (who encourages his interest in music), and he keeps physique photos in a drawer; he is also a huge fan of the opera singer movie star Grace Moore, and her major hit film *One Night of Love* (already by 1953 twenty years old), so much so that the boys call him Grace. The play is at pains to keep these at bay: Tom doesn't understand why there is anything wrong in going swimming with Mr Harris, the photos were sent to him by his father as part of a course on muscle building, and the apparent opera diva queen propensity could just be part of his interest in music. However, although the play ends with Laura unbuttoning her blouse and bringing Tom's hand towards her breasts, we don't know how successful the sex is, then or in the long term. Although the play text's synopsis insists that Tom 'is wrongly suspected of homosexual tendencies',[72] the play itself leaves room for doubt.

None of the queer hints are in the film, no skinny dipping, no physique photos, no Grace Moore, and not only does Tom wear a wedding ring in the frame story (which catches the light as he sits in the shade at the end of the film), he also has a letter from Laura referring to his marriage (although, unlike several other attendees, he doesn't have a wife in tow). While the director of the play, Elia Kazan, told Warner Brothers that 'the whole thing is about homosexuality',[73] Dore Schary for MGM thought the film could be understood as just being about a young man who doesn't fit in because he likes 'long-hair music.'[74] However, by eliminating even the suspicion of homosexuality the film risks incoherence: if the solution to effeminacy is heterosexuality, then the problem with effeminacy must be homosexuality.

The flashback in the film, like the play itself, opens with Tom singing 'The Joys of Love' to a guitar. Later in the film Tom's father expresses his horror that Tom wants to be a folk singer. In the period folk singing was seen as an overwhelmingly left-wing practice and folk singers were in the sights of the McCarthyite anti-communist drive; communism and homosexuality were both often seen as subversive and unAmerican, so that Mr Lee's dismay is, in its own terms, understandable.[75] However, while the image of a young man singing to an acoustic guitar may well suggest folk song, 'The Joys of Love' is from an altogether more genteel tradition. An eighteenth-century French song,[76] it may have been around so long that it feels 'traditional' but it had

---

72. Robert Anderson, *Tea and Sympathy*, New York: Random House, p. 4.
73. Cited in Jerrold Simmons, 'The Production Code Under New Management: Geoffrey Shurlock, *The Bad Seed* and *Tea and Sympathy*', *Journal of Popular Film and Television* 22:1 (1994), p. 5.
74. Cited in ibid., p. 6.; cf. George Custen, 'Strange Brew: Hollywood and the Fabrication of Homosexuality in *Tea and Sympathy*' in Martin Duberman (ed.), *Queer Representations: Reading Lives, Reading Cultures*, New York: New York University Press, pp. 116-138.
75. Cf. Richard A. Reuss, 'American Folksongs and Left-Wing Politics: 1935-56', *Journal of the Folklore Institute* 12:2-3 (1975), pp. 89-111; Naoko Shibusawa, 'The Lavender Scare and Empire: Rethinking Cold War Antigay Politics', *Diplomatic History* 36:4 (2012), pp. 723-752; Gerald Porter, 'Mythmaking in the Media: The Appropriation of the Traditional Ballad in the British Folk Revivals', *Indian Folklife* 4:1 (2005), p. 10.
76. 'Plaisir d'amour', Jean-Paul-Égide Martini and Jean-Pierre Claris de Florian, 1784.

Tom (John Kerr), Al (Darryl Hickman), and Beethoven in *Tea and Sympathy*, 1956.

been used quite recently in a clear parlour ballad setting in both *Love Affair* (1939, sung by the high, sweet voiced Irene Dunne) and *The Heiress* (1949, the basis for the score by Aaron Copland and sung by Montgomery Clift, who could clearly have played Tom).

Although in the play Tom is several times seen lying in bed listening to (unspecified) music, the only other music directly, diegetically, connected to him in the film is Chopin: the slow movement of the second piano concerto.[77] This is heard when his room mate Al, at Laura's instigation, goes to the school music room to advise Tom on

---

77. Chopin wrote in a letter to his friend and, it is now widely thought, lover, Tytus Woyciechowski, 'I say to the piano what I would have said to you many a time', and this slow movement was likely created thinking of him. See note 35.

how to behave in a more manly manner. Tom is sitting (as when he sings 'The Joys of Love') by a window; there is a bas-relief of a young man in eighteenth-century clothing over the phonograph, presumably a composer, perhaps Mozart. The music, the youthfulness, the pose are drenched in melancholy. When he realises Al has come in, he immediately turns the music off, saying he wasn't really listening anyway; in the previous scene Al, a kind man, has spoken to Laura about the fact that Tom never talks about 'the same things the other guys talk about' but 'long-hair music, all the time, long-hair music'. Tom clearly knows enough to turn off the archetypally long-haired Chopin when Al comes in. Prominently in shot in this sequence is a bust of Beethoven on a table; Al even drapes his arm around it at one point. While there is much that is plangent in Beethoven and in recent years there has been consideration of his possible homosexual feelings, his music has mainly been construed as the epitome of masculinity in music (famously in Robert Schumann's comparison of him with Schubert[78]). Beethoven (and Al) sit in opposition to Tom, who has just turned off Chopin.

Tom's nemesis is Laura's husband, Bill. He is pretty clearly constructed as someone who has repressed his homosexuality, probably hoping in marrying Laura to rid himself of it. At one point, explaining to her his tough attitude towards Tom, he says:

> When I was a kid here in this school I had my problems too. I used to sit in my room and listen to phonograph records hour after hour. I had a place where I used to go and cry my eyes out. [...] But I got over it, Laura, I learnt how to take it.

In the frame story, Tom calls on Bill and finds him in a darkened room listening to music, the slow movement of Mozart's fourth Violin Concerto, which he turns off the moment he realises Tom is there. Mozart does not carry the sissy connotations of Chopin, yet this movement is pretty much as plaintive and limpid as the Chopin Tom was listening to. It may even illustrate Susan McClary's argument about the emergent elements of Romantic sensibility within the Enlightenment framework of Mozart's work,[79] just as here it evokes Bill's emotional sensitivity within the framework of his hard man exterior.

In the non-diegetic music too there is a sense of queer emotionality nestling within something straighter. The score is by the professional Adolph Deutsch, whose generically diverse credits include many Westerns and films noirs as well as *Little Women*

---

[78]. See Robert Schumann, 'Franz Schubert: Four Impromptus for the Pianoforte, Opus 142' in Schumann, *Music and Musicians. Essays and Criticisms* (trans., ed. Fanny Raymond Ritter), London: W. Reeves, 1877, pp. 291-299. [*Neue Zeitschrift für Musik* 9 (1838), pp. 192-93] and also the discussion in Susan McClary, 'Constructions of Subjectivity in Schubert's Music' in Brett et al (eds), op. cit., pp. 205-233.

[79]. Susan McClary, 'A Musical Dialectic from the Enlightenment: Mozart's "Piano Concerto in G Major, K. 453", Movement 2', *Cultural Critique* 4 (1986), p. 161.

(1949) and *Some Like It Hot* (1960). Its overall flavour is the lush popular romanticism of the period, at MGM in general, in the Hollywood melodrama and the string backed arrangements for albums by artists such as Billie Holiday and Frank Sinatra. It incorporates the tune of 'The Joys of Love' and other original material, and notably a theme strongly echoing the 'Pavane pour une infante défunte' by Maurice Ravel.[80] This was dedicated to the (lesbian) Princesse de Polignac, married to the (gay) Prince de Polignac, who was also a composer; at their notably queer salon, Ravel could mix with Wilde, Proust and Diaghilev as well as the gay composers Manuel de Falla and Reynaldo Hahn, and Francis Poulenc. The work was first performed publicly by Ricardo Viñes, Poulenc's teacher and close friend and possibly Ravel's lover.[81] It is plausible that Deutsch and Minnelli knew some of this, but in any case the work fits securely into the tradition of effeminate French musical modernism. Like *Rope*'s *Mouvement perpétuel*, it keeps returning to a same 'little tune', albeit more grave and melancholy than Poulenc's throwaway melody, at once sensual, subtle and refined. Ravel was an important reference point (and often teacher and/or friend) of gay American composers David Diamond, Ned Rorem and Virgil Thomson;[82] he is a touchstone of musical sensibility for Blaine in *The Tenth Moon,* provides the music for the decadent soirées in *Lucifer with a Book* and is the basis for the music that Rae writes for his own dance in *The Divided Path*.

The Pavane motif, heard in the credits, is heard on and off throughout the film in association with Laura as well as Tom. It accompanies her perception of his gender problems, as well as in scenes addressing the lack of sexual tenderness between her and Bill and her making her way to Tom to give herself to him sexually. Although the film's story is told through his flashback and I am focusing on him because of the concerns of this essay, the film is also about Laura, who is as oppressed by machismo as is Tom, he because he fails to be it, she because she has to put up with it and with the stress of women's role in shoring up men's sexual uncertainties. The motif evokes the femininity-homosexuality nexus itself.

At the end of the film Tom reads Laura's letter, seated in what was her garden. It

---

80. I can find no reference to this being a conscious decision, but given the popularity of this piece in the concert repertoire and the fact that it was the acknowledged basis for the hit song 'The Lamp is Low' (1939, Peter DeRose and Bert Shefter (music), Mitchell Parish (lyrics)), it seems unlikely that neither Deutsch nor Minnelli registered the resemblance. I have run it past the Ravel expert Lloyd Whitesell who confirmed the closeness, while my highly musically literate partner declared it pure theft. In one of the few comments on the film's music, the blogger Roadshowfan on the Film Score website wrote: 'It's been a long time since I saw this film but I do remember enjoying Mr. Deutsch's score (even though I seem to recall it sounded a little like Ravel's *Pavane*)' (https://www.filmscoremonthly.com/board/posts.cfm?threadID=114715&forumID=1&archive=0).
81. On Ravel's sexuality, see Lloyd Whitesell, 'Ravel's Way' in Fuller and Whitesell, op. cit., pp. 49–78.
82. Cf. Hubbs, op. cit., pp. 117-151.

tells him (in Laura's voice-over) that she left Bill and that that 'ruined his life'. On these words, Tom looks towards the house and the film cuts to Bill seen through the window, attendant on some college business, Mozart still turned off. The Pavane motif comes in as the camera then pans quite slowly back from Bill to Tom, accompanied by Laura's words comparing the two men and how 'Both of you were crying out to be saved from what you thought you wanted'. A pan can suggest the distance that separates two people and that could be the case here, Bill trapped in his queerness, Tom saved from it. However, a pan can also suggest connection, and this possibility is reinforced not just by Laura's words but by the reoccurrence of the motif. Throughout the film this has always linked Laura and queer men, but it also here links the men themselves, allowing for a recognition of connection, even a bond, between them.

Earlier in the film, when Tom rushes out of the room when he thinks that Laura too thinks he's a queer, the motif comes in as Laura reflects on the situation. The image and the music fade, but then a brass band loudly playing the school anthem bursts in, a brutal incursion of rousing straightness. Heterosexual music is also elsewhere uncongenial. Tom makes a date with the local waitress Ellie, intending to prove his heterosexuality to himself. Laura is appalled at this and, as he leaves to see Ellie, calls him into her living room, hoping to keep him with her. She turns the record player on very low, relaxed tempo dance music in easy listening harmonies, bland, smooth. This cannot keep him, however. Ellie tunes the radio to New Orleans jazz, smoochy, dragging, raw, music which gets brassier as the scene becomes more hysterical, Ellie remembering that the other students call Tom 'sister boy', Tom taking out a knife, perhaps to kill himself. Neither Laura's easy listening nor Ellie's sexy jazz catch Tom's sensibility like 'The Joys of Love' or Chopin, Mozart or Ravel.

▲ ▲ ▲

The association of gay men and music, in practice and in representation, and its trammelled surfacing in *Rope* and *Tea and Sympathy*, is a case study of gay sensibility. This notion, once widely used, suggests that gay men both have a heightened aesthetic sensitivity and responsiveness to the arts and also are drawn to modes of art suffused with off-beat sensuousness, femininity and eroticism. Such modes are at variance not only with the regularity and resolution of the mainstream but also with the principled disruptiveness of the avant-garde and the ascetic rigour of modernism, neither of which favoured the sensual and endearing in artistic production. The notion of gay sensibility has fallen into desuetude, partly because it implied that aesthetic sensitivity was inborn alongside male attraction to men, partly because it was only ever true of predominantly elite white men (and by no means most of them), partly because it did not even account for most art made or enjoyed by gay men. Nonetheless, once understood as socially and ethnically (which is to say, also and therefore, culturally and historically) particular, the notion of gay sensibility does point to a shared affective culture, one that played its part in shaping a gay identity and making a gay world (to use the suggestive subtitle of George Chauncey's *Gay New York*[83]). Shared feelings, that have to be promulgated and learnt, inspire and bond as well as opening up new ways of apprehending oneself and the world. *Rope* and *Tea and Sympathy* gave a glimpse of gay sensibility in a broader cultural platform, and, with Phillip never let to finish Poulenc, and Tom turning off Chopin, and Bill Mozart, suggest how alluring and thus disturbing even little tunes could be.

APPENDIX: MUSICAL HOMOSEXUALS IN FICTION

1891   *The Picture of Dorian Gray* (novel)
1892   *Ecstasy* (novel)
1893   *Teleny* (novel)
1894   *The Green Carnation* (novel)
1895   *The Wonderful Visit* (novel)
1901   *Buddenbrooks* (novel)
1903   'Paul's Case' (short story)
1906   *Imre: A Memorandum* (novel)
1913   *Maurice* (novel)[84]
1916   *The Romance of a Choir-Boy* (novel)
1918   *Despised and Rejected* (novel)
1919   *Bertram Cope's Year* (novel)
1919   *Anders als die Anderen* (film)
1923   *The Vortex* (play)
1929   *Whiteoaks of Jalna* (novel)
1930   *Borderline* (film)
1931   'The Alien Corn' (short story)
1932   *The Tenth Moon* (novel)[85]
1933   *Better Angel* (novel)
1933   *The Green Bay Tree* (play)
1933   *A Scarlet Pansy* (novel)

---

83. George Chauncey, *Gay New York: Gender, Urban Culture, and the Making of the Gay Male World, 1890-1940*, New York: Basic Books, 1995.
84. Begun in 1913, published posthumously in 1971.
85. Republished as *Come Back to Sorrento* in 1997.

1933	*Gentlemen, I Address You Privately* (novel)	
1935	*Symphonie Pathétique* (novel)	
1936	*Whiteoaks* (play)	
1937	*Serenade* (novel)	
1938	*Concert Pitch* (novel)	
1944	*Outrageous Fortune* (play)	
1945	*The Picture of Dorian Gray* (film)	
1946	*Nocturne* (film)	
1947	*Brute Force* (film)	
1948	'The Alien Corn' in *Quartet* (film)	
1948	*Lucifer with a Book* (novel)	
1948	*The Christmas Tree* (novel)	
1948	*Pathetic Symphony*[86]	
1948	*Rope* (film)	
1949	*The Gay Year* (novel)	
1949	*Stranger in the Land* (novel)	
1949	*Adam's Rib* (film)	
1949	*The Divided Path* (novel)	
1950	*South Sea Sinner* (film)	
1950	*The Night Air* (novel)	
1951	*Walk on the Water* (novel)	
1952	*The Liberace Show* (TV)	
1953	*Tea and Sympathy* (play)	
1955	*Sincerely Yours* (film)	
1956	*Serenade* (film)	
1956	*Tea and Sympathy* (film)	

86. See note 33.

SECTION 6
THE PERSISTENCE OF TEXTUAL ANALYSIS

and other essays on form and meaning

La dolce vita, 1960. (BFI National Archive)

Looking and listening – paying close attention to the details of an audio-visual object – are the basic principles of textual analysis in media studies. In recent years, Richard Dyer has reminded us of the importance of this essential practice, most notably in his lecture 'The persistence of textual analysis', which he presented on several occasions between 2013 and 2016. Too often, the audiovisual object tends to be reduced to a mere illustration of a theoretical argument, or is left unexamined in the study of its production or reception, rather than being rigorously analysed. In 'The persistence of textual analysis', Dyer practises what he preaches by bookending his essay with two close readings, opening with the closing sequence of the 1960 Italian neorealist film *Rocco e i suoi fratelli* (*Rocco and His Brothers*) and closing with the opening sequence of the 1972 US Blaxploitation film *Trouble Man*. In each case, Dyer shows how a sequence can be scrutinised through looking and listening, focusing on camera movement, mise-en-scène, sound, and on-screen text, and thus highlighting details that are easily overlooked. Here we present his lecture for the first time in written form, as the key essay of this section.

'The persistence of textual analysis' is not simply a nostalgic plea from a senior scholar lamenting a lost practice. Dyer's 'Notes on textual analysis' (1981), which he presented in 1979 at a conference on film and media studies in higher education organised by Christine Gledhill, shows that Dyer's concern about the status of textual analysis in media studies has been consistent for more than four decades. At the time, he distinguished between a 'theoretical tendency' and a 'sociological tendency', both of which often seemed to take textual analysis for granted: the former through a 'slap happy' analysis of the text in which the object was there merely to support the theory, and the latter by focusing primarily on the producer's intent or the audience's responses. Dyer argued not only for a closer attention to the details of the text, but also for an active engagement with it: 'I want to retain an "openness" to the text, to allow it to "resist" me, so that I do not make it into more than it is or could be, and so that I better understand the problems of the concepts I am interested in.'

In his 'Introduction to Film Studies' (1998, not included here), Dyer recognises another distinction relevant to the practice of textual analysis: a) the formal-aesthetic approach, which sees film as an autonomous object of artistic expression, and b) the social-ideological approach, which sees film as part of larger cultural processes. He argues that both approaches complement and need each other, and that both should involve textual analysis:

[T]he aesthetic and the cultural cannot stand in opposition. The aesthetic dimension of a film never exists apart from how it is conceptualised, how it is socially practised, how it is received; it never exists floating free of historical and cultural particularity. Equally, the cultural study of film must always understand that it is studying film, which has its own specificity, its own pleasures, its own way of doing things that cannot be reduced to ideological formulations or what people (producers, audiences) think and feel about it.[1]

Dyer's own work on film and other forms of mass and high culture clearly combines both approaches, ignoring neither the ideological implications of the object nor its textual qualities. Concerned about the rise of what he calls 'film studies without film', Dyer told Barbara Klinger in a 2015 interview that he might be 'to blame' for such a development, since his books on stardom suggested that one should 'not only look at films' but also at 'everything surrounding' them.[2] Yet his theoretical engagement with stars and stardom (see Section 1 of this Reader) was never a move away from the on-screen performance but rather an expansion of it to include the paratextual and extratextual – elements such as promotion, publicity, critical and fan reception – as part of the 'total star text'.

In addition to his critical take on 'film studies without film', Dyer has outlined the problems with adopting nationality as a key conceptual frame for the analysis of media texts. In his essay 'Going Italian' (2011), he criticises the 'endless' iterations of 'the national cinema problematic that has often tended to dominate studies of European cinemas'. He acknowledges that films produced in particular locations may have local or national characteristics, but argues that recognising these 'is very different from considering that they are in any primary or even perhaps important way about national identity'. He goes on to outline something like a manifesto for textual analysis, one that thickens and enriches the positions taken in the essays already discussed. Most films, he writes, 'are made to make money, to entertain, to create beauty, to have fun.' These impulses should be the starting point for analysis:

Not everything makes money nor entertains: analysis is about unpicking what does and does not, what forms, values and pleasures work and what don't, all themselves culturally and historically distinct issues as well as formal, aesthetic ones. Films (like all forms of art) are an unusual commodity because, despite the stress on generic recognition, they are not identical to one another; their differences too are what have to be

---

1. Richard Dyer, 'Introduction to film studies', in John Hill and Pamela Church Gibson (eds), *Film Studies: Critical Approaches*, Oxford: Oxford University Press, 2000, pp. 7–8.
2. Barbara Klinger, SCMS Fieldnotes interview with Richard Dyer, 13 April 2015, available online at https://vimeo.com/145394630.

analysed. Above all, films are formally organised and affectively addressed and experienced: these are the first social, cultural and historical facts about them, not to be lost sight of in pressing them into the service of meaning and identity.

The emphasis placed on affect here appears elsewhere in Dyer's writings that argue for the value of textual analysis and propose models of best practice. In the final paragraph of 'Notes on textual analysis', for instance, he identifies that 'what we are concerned with in textual analysis is not purely cognitive meaning, but also emotional meaning'; he reasons that 'the media is inextricably involved in phatic, sensuous, sentimental, erotic and experiential signification, and, since it is, this too must be understood and analysed.'

Dyer argues, then, for paying attention to the particularities of each individual media text or object, as well as the ways in which it is 'addressed and experienced'. This includes a nuanced awareness of the distinct forms and affordances of different media, as well as their complex formal and genealogical relationships to each other. Clearly stating these specificities can help to historically situate individual pieces of analysis, and invite reflection on how much the media landscape has evolved and altered. Thus, in 'The television situation' (1973), the second chapter of his monograph on *Light Entertainment*, Dyer discusses the specific characteristics of television in the early 1970s, which, in comparison to film, 'is small, for most people black and white, usually pretty imperfect in reproductive qualities, and can be turned off at will.' Television entertainment, he writes, is indebted to music hall, variety shows, circus, and so on; these other forms, however, are encountered in very different ways to television, meaning that television has to find ways 'to recreate or remodel them'. At one point in his discussion, Dyer compares two 1971 broadcasts of circus shows, highlighting how the choices of television producers over what to depict and how to show it has the ability to shape the material into a 'performance' or 'a cosy family event'. Although domestic television screens are now considerably more developed – with large, colour, high-definition image and sound screens widely available – television light entertainment remains reliant on tried and tested formats (singing and dancing competitions, stand-up comedy, and so on) drawn from variety and the end of the pier.

The attention Dyer proposes in textual analysis to address and experience necessarily includes a sensitivity to personal factors shaping our own engagements with the texts. At one point in his 1972 PhD thesis, Dyer suggests that an objective method for analysing individual media texts might be possible:

Obviously my own response was considerably affected by the circumstances under which I saw the film (circumstances which also include the weather, what I had to eat, my personal life and so on), but this is to some extent controlled by the use of a definite method intended to come to terms with the film itself rather than my own feelings about it.[3]

And yet one of the hallmarks of Dyer's writing is its inclusion of autobiographical content, and the deft moves that are made from the personal to the theoretical, from subjective observation to broader cultural perception. Take, for instance, this extract from his 1993 BFI Classic on *Brief Encounter*:

> It is a truth universally acknowledged that all gay men love their mothers. Yet I sometimes feel that I betray mine with *Brief Encounter*. I recall one Christmas showing it on tape to a group of Australian and Canadian gay men, whose education in the foundations of gay sensibility had revealed a troubling gap. My mother watched it with us and I could see that she was uncomfortable with my doing Laura's lines over Celia Johnson, because it was mocking a lovely film. It was also mocking, or at any rate pastiching, a woman. Yet, like many gay men, I ardently identify with women characters in 'women's films', I prefer the company of women to that of men and I think of myself as pro-feminist. Do I betray this as much as my mother when I camp about with *Brief Encounter*?[4]

This account sets up some of the main arguments explored in the book: the agency and voice of the film's central female character; the queer camp reception of and relationship to *Brief Encounter*; the film's 'quality' and its generic status.

Dyer has gone on to author further contributions to the BFI Classics series on *Seven* (in 1999) and on *La dolce vita* (in 2018). To date, he is the only scholar to have authored three books in the series. Each entry in the series offers up an attempt at sustained textual analysis, combining close reading of the content of the film under scrutiny with observations on the broader social, cultural and political context of its production and reception. For Dyer, his three contributions to the BFI Classics offer an opportunity to model best practice in textual analysis. In a letter addressed to Dyer published in a 2018 *Cinema Journal* dossier, Jackie Stacey praises his 'textual intimacy': 'you find the context in the text and then pursue its implications beyond the text (showing how they are intimately intertwined)'; she selects an extract from Dyer's book on *Brief Encounter* to demonstrate this in operation. Stacey suggests that Dyer's writing challenges Eve Sedgwick's distinction between paranoid and reparative reading, the former concerned with mastery of the text, the latter with affective connection: 'I think that your approach to close reading, your textual intimacy, is a

---

3. Richard Dyer, 'Social Values of Entertainment and Show Business,' PhD dissertation, Centre for Contemporary Cultural Studies, University of Birmingham, October 1972, p. 117.

4. Richard Dyer, *Brief Encounter*, London: BFI, 1993, pp. 11–12.

mode of analysis that combines the best of these two approaches, and demonstrates the importance of not holding them apart.'[5]

What the essays in this section have in common is their combination of text and context, careful close reading with the cultural and political resonances of a scrutinised object. Attention is drawn to the presence, character, and wider implication of details: from Paul Newman and Steve McQueen's 'pairs of dauntless, piercing blue eyes' that 'constitute a central motif' in *The Towering Inferno* (1975) to the significance of Peter Greenaway depicting Eisenstein's penis as uncircumcised (and 'never erect') in *Eisenstein in Guanajuato* (2015), from the ticking of the metronome that Somerset (Morgan Freeman) uses to create 'an oasis of controlled, orderly sound' amidst the 'soft cacophony' of the city in *Seven* (1995) to the noise of Ann Miller's tap shoes ('clean and hard [...] and very fast') in *On the Town* (1949). In relation to each example, larger questions are asked: why might a contemporary audience be moved by Todd Haynes' *Far from Heaven*, despite the distancing effects of its overtly stylised form and blatant borrowings from classic instances of film melodrama? What does the derivative nature of Nino Rota's film scores reveal about the processes of soundtrack production? And always, through example, Dyer argues for the value of looking and listening, and looking and listening again.

---

5. Jackie Stacey, 'Textual Intimacy', *Cinema Journal* 57:2 (2018), pp. 166–167.

44 THE PERSISTENCE OF TEXTUAL ANALYSIS (2023)

I start, on principle, with an example[1]: the last shot of *Rocco e i suoi fratelli* (*Rocco and His Brothers* 1960 Italy). The film has told of the experiences of five brothers and their widowed mother who have migrated from Southern Italy to Milan. Two of the brothers settle in, one (Antonio) taking a job in construction, the other (Ciro) in car manufacture (Alfa Romeo), both marrying Milanese women. A third, Simone, drifts into womanising, hustling, theft, rape and murder; the fourth, Rocco, becomes a successful boxer, even though he hates it, to earn money to pay off Simone's debts. The fifth brother, Luca, is still a child. Just before the final shot, he has been seen inviting Ciro, who is estranged from the family, to come home tonight, which Ciro says he will. The final shot starts as Luca walks past billboards announcing Rocco's success ①; he touches the photo of Rocco ②. The camera follows him as he walks along the billboards and out to the dual carriageway but then stops as Luca carries on up the road ③. The road leads off screen right, the vanishing point obscured by vehicles, a barrier, buildings and trees (all very hard to make out); to the left on the horizon stretch a number of blocks of flats, with a building crane visible behind one. Luca mainly walks, occasionally runs or skips; a small group of factory workers walk past him off right ④, a car drives off left on the other side of the dividing strip ⑤. When he is nearing the end of the road, the word 'Fine' (End) appears ⑥. The shot is accompanied by a song, 'Paese mio', introduced after the sound of the siren calling the Alfa Romeo workers back to work has faded. A male voice to a guitar accompaniment sings about the beauty of the place he comes from (his 'paese'), how he has left his heart there. When the song ends, there is a crescendo orchestral chord.

The image of a figure or figures moving away from the camera into the distance is an extremely common cinematic trope. It suggests at once that life for the characters

---

1. This essay is based on a talk given in Frankfurt-am-Main, London, Stockholm and Vienna. The Frankfurt version is available online at https://www.kracauer-lectures.de/en/winter-2015-2016/richard-dyer/. The essay here is not a transcript of the talk, but it does adhere to the contours of the lecture and should be read in that light (including the absence of footnotes beyond this one).

THE PERSISTENCE OF TEXTUAL ANALYSIS

Rocco e i suoi fratelli (*Rocco and His Brothers*), 1960.

goes on but that the story, and thus the film, is over. This is reinforced here by the orchestral chord, which effects an harmonic closure to the film's non-diegetic score.

The fact that the figure here is a child relates to the importance of the child in post-war cinema, where he, she or they are most commonly seen as suggesting hope, because less implicated in or damaged by the experience of war and genocide. Behind this is a very wide cultural history of childhood innocence and discourses of futurity. While there are countervailing tendencies, be it the mutilated or traumatised children of Robert Rossellini's 'war trilogy' (*Roma città aperta* 1945, *Paisà* 1946, *Germania anna zero* 1948) or Catholic and Victorian ideas of innate childhood evil, here the more positive (and in the period more common) perception is reinforced by Luca's generous invitation to Ciro, his affectionate touching of Rocco's photograph, his lively gait and his generally cheerful disposition throughout the film. The blocks of flats in the distance, with building still going on, reference Antonio's work, which together with Ciro in Alfa Romeo signifies both the successful integration of the two brothers into their new environment and also the booming economy of the period, often seen as Italy's 'economic miracle'. All of this suggests something like a happy end. However, there are other, less positive notes. If the director Luchino Visconti's Communist party membership would suggest that ending with reference to Antonio and Ciro affirms the triumph of the proletariat, in the rest of the film his roots in *melodramma* (that is, both opera and melodrama) show in the greater attention to the tragic characters of Simone and Rocco. The buildings in the last shot may represent the future, but they and a barrier block the horizon, and the road, with rubbish in the gutters, could be seen as going through a wasteland. Most significantly, the song emphasises what is lost, not only in its words but in its mournful 'oh oh' refrain, melancholy tempo and archaic folk mode. In short, the ending pulls both towards a bright modern future and a sense of what is lost in the process. Where one senses the emphasis lies and what one feels about it are where judgement and subjectivity come more fully into play.

The above is a schematic account of the process of textual analysis (rather than how one would necessarily present the results of such a process in another context). I have first described the shot (in rather more detail than one would when one can run the shot, in a lecture, say, or a video essay, although in massively less detail than there are details in even this simple shot). Description is often undervalued or even dismissed. Its challenges are unaddressed: the limitations of language (e.g. what exactly is Luca's gait or the grain of the singer's voice?), notably in rendering formal and affective qualities, and selectivity (in my description, I didn't even consider what Luca is wearing or the exact angle of the dividing strip in relation to the frame of the camera). The methodological value of describing is overlooked: it concentrates attention, works to ensure interpretation is more (or at least as much) rooted in the material as in the interpretive framework or the analyst's predilections, and deploys language's ability to abstract, generalise and categorise.

After the description, I set elements of the shot in context. The latter is first the rest of the film, since any one shot or detail perforce works in relation to everything else in a film (just as a film exists only by virtue of its shots and details). Context is also the wider cultural (including filmic and musical) conventions and habits that are drawn on. I try to be led by what is in the shot (rather than trying to find something I know about beforehand, be it Italian history or the work of Luchino Visconti) and thus to avoid swamping the text with context. Finally, I have suggested an interpretation (one as much to do with affect as meaning) of the shot. In practice one oscillates between description, contextualisation and interpretation (just as one does between part and whole, text and context) and one always brings assumptions to bear. Here my overall interpretive assumption (and I didn't articulate this to myself until I came to write this essay) is that the shot must be seen as ending the film, providing some kind of closure or final statement and feeling about what has come before, and that this has to do with a view of the historical direction of contemporary society. These are hardly unreasonable assumptions, but they mean that I have not considered the shot in its more purely plastic dimensions (its composition and texture) for instance, nor yet considered it just as a story about some people (rather than being representative of something more general) or of course in relation to issues it has not even occurred to me could be raised.

The process I have just given an account of persists despite critiques of it. It persists partly because it is an elaborated and self-aware version of what we do all the time. I lived for many years with a radiologist and we had many enjoyable conversations comparing the way he had to describe the shapes, shadows and light of an x-ray image, relate them to the patterns that medical conditions produce and the particularities of the patient and interpret their implications for therapeutic intervention; not the least interesting aspect of our conversations was that while a radiograph has immediate, practical use, it is still subject to ambiguity and rival interpretation and even to commentary on its beauty. Radiographs, and maps, charts and spreadsheets, and natural phenomena, landscapes, clouds, the stars, entrails, the everyday business of making sense of the world, each other, ourselves, all entail description, contextualisation, interpretation and appreciation. Academic textual analysis is in drawn-out and deliberated form what we all (and by 'we' I mean human beings and all sentient creatures) do all the time, in condensed, habitual, seemingly instantaneous form.

Henceforth however I will talk about textual analysis in Film Studies. It persists here in teaching, where it is the basis of instruction and discussion, whether the text be a film or an advertisement or production spreadsheets or recorded audience interviews, and whether the focus be aesthetic, historical or theoretical; it persists in teaching partly because it is cheap compared to participant observation on film sets, conducting audience interviews or surveys or visiting archives, partly because it is pedagogically focused and provides a shared object of study. It persists in academic production, where even Film Studies work whose focus is, say, social representation or philosophical propositions, has recourse to the analysis of instances. It persists in practices cognate to academic study, in journalistic criticism, fandom, blogging, where accounts, recommendations, enthusiasms and repudiations all are based in and make observations about texts, be that a new release or a star or a niche obsession; even the thumbnail accounts of a film or series in a listings magazine or site or on Netflix, MUBI and so on offer an analysis: a decision to indicate the story situation, for instance, is an analytical decision about the nature of the text and what is important about it, an act of textual analysis. It persists in everyday conversation, in saying what a film is about, or that you like a particular sound, or that a documentary is biased. In short academic textual analysis is an extrapolation from and disciplining of common sense discourse, it is what Alfred Schütz called a 'second-order common sense construct'.

Alongside its persistence, textual analysis has been widely critiqued. The very term 'text' is seen as problematic. It privileges literary forms of cultural production, something reinforced by speaking of 'reading' say a film, poster or series ('Stop Reading Films!' cries John Champagne in the title of an article on the 'absurdity and perhaps even perniciousness of submitting gay porno films in particular to close textual analysis'); text implies language as a semiotic model, one which is at variance to so much audio-visual expression; the literary associations of text tend to point towards meaning, to the dreaded desire to work out what a text is 'about', and away from form and affect. For these reasons, I wish there was another term to use, although we may be able to rescue it by remembering that its roots are in textiles, something tactile and woven. However, even if we don't succeed in ridding the word 'text' of its linguistic and semantic burden in general usage, our practice in approaching media texts can seek to combat it.

The term 'analysis' too has its unhappy connotations, suggesting dismantling a work, destroying it as well as the possibility of pleasure in it. 'Analysis' can seem to propose breaking a work down into elements and ignoring the whole, and indeed if it does this it is doing analysis badly, since (as already noted) all elements only have meaning in relation to each other and the whole, just as the whole only consists of all the tiny elements that constitute it (remembering that 'whole' does not necessarily imply something unified). It is precisely the constant movement between the particular and the overall that counteracts the danger that analysis will merely pick to bits.

It is also often felt that textual analysis wants to fix interpretation, to identify *the* meaning and *the* affect of a film. Faced with the multiplicity of audience (including students') responses, textual analysis may seem to say that only one, or a handful, of these are legitimate, to want to settle the matter, to work out what the film 'really' means, what feeling the film is 'really' trying to convey. This is then intensified when textual analysis seems especially concerned to suggest that the real meaning or affect of a film is at odds with what it most evidently is doing. Thus we may be told that, while we may feel a film is a Western and thus delivering the excitement of adventure and violence, it is really about imperialism, really about masculinity. Westerns are indeed complexly rooted in and dependent on imperialism and masculinity as the ground for their adventure and violence, but what it means to say they are 'about' these things needs some unpicking, an unpicking that makes sense in relation to the visceral experiences they offer.

Yet another critique of textual analysis suggests that it is just subjective and/or culture-bound. Thus textual analyses, for all their dignified and detailed presentation, may nonetheless be held to be 'just' what the proposer of the analysis thinks, 'merely' how they have responded. Here we find that 'everyone sees a different film', 'well that's just how I see it' defensiveness familiar from discussions and seminars. (Only a few years of teaching make very evident that very little is how only one person sees something.) Related to this is a more culturally informed argument, that sees textual analyses as 'only' what someone in a given cultural and historical context could or would think. Notably, the work of earlier scholars may be dismissed as just that of straight white middle-class cis able-bodied men (SWMCAM). It probably is the case that much writing in the field is not willing to acknowledge the situation in which it is written, SWMCAM being notably reluctant to speak from the position of SWMCAM-ness and preferring to take up the unexamined position of the universal historical subject. This is to be critiqued, but it does not mean that there cannot be textual analysis informed by this critique rather than rubbished by it. All forms of knowledge production, including textual analysis, are always situated, by virtue of historical, cultural and individual circumstances – this limits what they can see and hear, but it does not mean that what they see and hear is made up: limitation is not blindness and deafness, a chair seen from several different angles is still a chair seen.

Textual analysis is also often thought to be untheorized. Perhaps it is not as much reflected upon, its procedures methodologised, the status of it as knowledge examined as much as should be the case, although a particular notion of what constitutes theory may also blind us to the degree to which textual analysis is argued for and abstractly elaborated in Film Studies.

Finally, and perhaps most substantially, textual analysis is often thought to operate with a notion of 'the text in itself'. Whether in work rooted in the 'explication de texte' of French literary study or the school of what scholars like Robin Wood and V.F. Perkins insisted was (proper, rigorous) film *criticism*, textual analysis is held to treat the text in isolation, frequently barely even taking context into account. While an inaccurate characterisation of much of this work, the perception of textual analysis's isolationism has led to developments in Film Studies that have sought to rescue Film Studies from the aforesaid problems of textual analysis, developments that often lead to a kind of Film Studies without films. There has often been a call for more studies of production. Certainly this is under-developed (including under-theorised, overly empiricist) in Film Studies, although it either has nothing to say about what is produced or else makes easy, intentionalist or technicist connections between process and product. More prominent in recent time has been work on the audience, a feeling that what one needs to do is to go and ask people for their responses to and understandings of a film. This too is sometimes treated as something easy both at the level of collecting evidence and in terms of the status of what you get (which at best is people's memories of what they thought and felt) and what you do with what you get, how you interpret and use comments. Production and audience work seem to offer a way out of the limitations of textual analysis, by anchoring interpretation unproblematically in the reality of production and audience. A rather different kind of anchor is offered by Theory and perhaps the recent growth of Film and Philosophy, where sorting out fundamentals of both film as a medium and wider notions of medium, communication, meaning and so on can then be illustrated or proven by a filmic example (at worst with little regard for whether the film is representative or for all the other things it is doing). I have unhappy experiences of teaching a theoretical text, in which a clever re-arrangement of a number of theoretical precepts is followed by a textual analysis in which the most elementary errors of description, interpretation and tonal deafness are displayed; this is not inevitable nor invariable, but starting from theory, rather than moving back and forth between theory and instance, permits carelessness and indifference. A last kind of anchoring – and one much closer to my own practice – is placing a film in cultural and historical context. While one needs to draw on such context to understand the film's meaning and affect, it is by no means straightforward either to establish context (not least because one is straying into territory where one's competence, or just time and energy, falters) or to use it in a responsible way in attending to the film: yet another notion we need to unpick is the 'con' (that is, the 'with') of context.

The critiques of textual analysis all alert us to the kinds of epistemological and methodological reflections that need to be made of the practice; all scholarly practices need this but perhaps textual analysis is more backward in developing such reflections than some other areas. Yet there are also good reasons to persist. One is the very fact of its persistence, and the roots of that in everyday discourse. We should always be alert to and connected with common sense, that is, listening to, learning from, reflecting on the senses we hold in common. We should persist in it because we should be grounded in and relevant to the wider culture of filmgoing. It is also the case that we are involved in *Film* Studies. On the one hand, we (people in Film Studies) have chosen to be in Film Studies so it seems odd not to look at and listen to films; and on the other hand, film is not prima facie important enough to warrant a discipline all its own, except in so far as films themselves are deemed to be socially, aesthetically and culturally important and therefore worth really looking at and listening to.

Moreover, there is in fact no such thing as not doing textual analysis. I once attended a lecture about a particular cycle of films in which the speaker said that he never bothered with textual analysis, and indeed never showed or studied actual films but only taught and wrote about the publicity for them, as these were part of the constitution of the cycle. There is no problem with this in itself: what one means by a text may be something more multiplicitous and multi-medial than just a single film. However this does not mean he didn't do textual analysis, it means that he textually analysed posters, advertisements and publicity copy. To give another example: I once heard a scholarly and fascinating paper about audiences in the silent period, drawing especially on diaries of the period. Again the speaker said that he was trying to get away from textual analysis, but to do this he in fact needed to textually analyse the diaries. Moreover he maintained that not textually analysing the films the diarists saw was warranted in part because the diaries showed that people didn't really care about films in the way textual analysis of film implies, they just went to the movies, it was the going to the cinema that mattered. Yet the diary extracts he supplied to illustrate the point told a different story: the writers would say they had been to see a comedy and hadn't found it funny, or that they had wept buckets at some particular film or scene – clearly they did choose what they saw, did have responses and discriminations, were doing first order textual analysis.

Whether focusing on what people (producers, audiences) say, or production spreadsheets or advertising campaigns or a Theoretical essay or an economic history, you are doing textual analysis. There are differences between all these kinds of text and a basic principle of textual analysis is that you should take those differences, material, semiotic, intentional, into account, but that does not mean that you are only doing textual analysis with some kinds of text.

Having said that, it should also be said that there is no such thing as not doing theory. Or rather, not doing theory means not reflecting upon one's practice, not considering what warrant there is for taking this approach and applying it thus, for understanding how one point follows or doesn't from another, for discriminating between kinds of evidence and judging their force and weight. All of this and more constitute theoretical reflection. One can't always think about all of this all of the time; some may choose to focus more on elaborating and deepening such thought, and everyone should have gone through and should return to such reflection to ensure that textual analysis is a rigorous practice. Theory however is no excuse for intimidating obfuscation.

Textual analysis is grounded somewhere between habit and skill. The more you do it, the more you do it; the more you look and listen, the more you see and hear. But it is principled looking and listening. Taking our cue from the root of the word in textiles, we can consider films as woven, of made up of huge numbers of different, inter-relating strands, produced by multiple hands, marshalled with varying degrees of insistence and success towards an overall pattern, but always making available a multiplicity of meanings and affects (the latter widely understood, including nameable feelings and emotions but also encompassing the hard-to-put-into-words qualities of colour, shape, sound and so on). Despite the increased interest in affect in the humanities in recent years, it is still easy for it to slip from view as a central concern, hung up as we academic word users are on meaning.

Textual analysis should also be open, not seeking to fix meaning and affect, inevitably foregrounding some more than others but allowing for the subsequent discovery or emphasising of yet others. It should lay out its argument and evidence with clarity to allow disagreement and counter or supplementary evidence (and with regard to this principle, 'it's just how I see it', 'this is my take on it' are blocking moves, closing down on openness). It should situate itself, the writer upfront about where he, she or they is coming from, the theoretical frameworks brought to bear and the guiding questions made clear (and where not explicated and elaborated, at least evidently implicit). It should be rigorous and systematic. Needless to say few of us manage to live up to all of these principles all of the time.

I end with another example, this time a beginning: *Trouble Man* (USA, 1972). A man called Mr T leaves his girlfriend, saying he can't tell her when he'll see her again; he drives from her villa to his apartment, sending packing a man at the door telling him that someone wants to see him; he changes clothes and drives to a pool room. Most of the sequence shows the driving, with over it both the credits and Marvin Gaye singing the film's theme song, whose words include 'I come up hard, baby, but now I'm cool / I didn't make it sugar, playin' by the rules / I'm checkin' trouble, sugar, movin' down the line'.

I chose this sequence primarily to insist that textual analysis is not something only to be applied to canonical film, or films that one wishes to make canonical. *Trouble Man* not only has little cultural capital within or without Film Studies, it is also not especially prized by aficionados of the Blaxploitation cycle within which it was produced. If it has any reputation to speak of, it is down to the fact that it has a score by Marvin Gaye, and even this does not figure particularly high in celebrations of his work. None of this means that *Trouble Man* cannot or should not be textually analysed.

The account of this sequence that follows also illustrates the role of framing questions in textual analysis. Virtually no textual analysis is done truly randomly (although this might be a useful pedagogic or scholarly exercise to undertake). Much is indeed done to argue why such-and-such is considered canonical or should be, but one can equally ask focused aesthetic and cultural questions. I had *Trouble Man* to hand as an example because it had figured for me in two other contexts, both concerned with the location of music in a film, that is, whether it may be considered 'in' the fictional world of the film or part of the apparatus constructing a perception of or relation to that world, whether it is on the side of the told or the telling, diegetic or non-diegetic. Two questions interested me within this broad context. One had to do with music in Blaxploitation cinema in general and the way, unlike white-centred thriller movies, the music within and without the fictional world of the films was the same. The other was to do with the notion of subjective music, the idea that music may express what a character is feeling, and what difference it makes whether or not the character is or could be aware of this music. Because these are the focus of my analysis, I do not here discuss the relation of the sequence to the rest of the film and in particular how it sets up what follows (just as the ending of *Rocco e i suoi fratelli* closes what has gone before).

THE PERSISTENCE OF TEXTUAL ANALYSIS

It is common in discussion of films to claim that the music is indicating what a character is feeling. Rachmaninov in *Brief Encounter* conveys Laura's melancholic romanticism, Jerome Moross in *The Big Country* tells us how exhilarating it is to ride through wide open spaces. Similarly one might say that in *Trouble Man* Marvin Gaye allows us to feel how great it is to drive along freeways in a smooth car to the sound of funk, especially if you've 'come up hard' but now are 'cool'. Textual analysis does not contradict this but does refine and complicate the formulation.

When Mr T comes out of his girlfriend's villa at the start of the sequence, music kicks in (drums, with cymbals setting up a rhythm) and when he gets into the car and puts on his dark glasses ①, the voice says 'Huh – look at him'. Thereafter the singing is in the first person (as in the lines quoted above) and the voice moreover is the familiar and beloved one of Marvin Gaye (and the film was made at a high point in his career). The stretches of driving alternate between shots from inside the car looking through the windscreen (slightly to the right of Mr T, but within the convention of an

Trouble Man (USA, 1972).

off-the-shoulder shot being a subjective point-of-view ②) and aerial shots of the car moving along the highway ③; at one point, Mr T looks to his right ④ and there is a cut to a moving camera shot of what he sees, the ocean ⑤, and the camera turns back to take up the off-the-shoulder POV shot position ⑥. Once the music starts it is continuous, although at a lower level behind the conversation with the messenger; when Mr T goes into the apartment, he turns on a tape recorder but there is no change in the flow of the music.

First person to third person, an 'I' that could be Mr T and is definitely the singer Marvin Gaye (although not necessarily singing about his actual life), inside and outside the car, point of view and aerial shots, music coming from maybe the car radio, the tape recorder and nowhere, indeterminately diegetic and non-diegetic... Described thus the sequence appears fragmented and disjunctive, but much of this is covered by conventions deriving from classic Hollywood scoring, the musical and music video (a form just developing in 1972). They are however suggestive in relation to the issues of Blaxploitation and subjective music.

The lack of firm distinction between where the music is coming from and Mr T's relation to it is significant in relation to other sequences like this in Blaxploitation films: the (always male) protagonist moving through a metropolitan landscape (be it the Manhattan of *Shaft*, *Superfly*, *Black Caesar* and *Willie Dynamite* or the more open urban spaces of the West coast of *Sweet Sweetback's Baadasssss Song*, *Truck Turner*, *The Mack* and *Trouble Man*). Mr T and co belong in these spaces, and not least because there is no distinction between their music and that of their community and between their music and that of the film's narration. In white-centred thrillers there is a disjunction between the kind of music heard within the world of the film and that used to narrate it, whereas in Blaxploitation it is dissolved, especially in these exhilarating sequences of the confident Black occupation of urban space.

The movement between I and he, Mr T and Marvin Gaye, interior POV shots and exterior aerial ones might be experienced as oscillation or else, especially as bound together by the music, simultaneity. It suggests a subjectivity that encompasses enclosed interiority and awareness of how one looks, of perceiver and perceived, looker and looked at, private listener and participant in a community sound, none of which is especially unusual in the constitution of subjectivity. It also offers audience members possibilities of identification with and admiration and envy of a character (and quite probably all these at once), as well as, especially for the presumed African-American audience, especially watched in a cinema, a sense of all of that as shared rather than only individual.

In short, textual analysis offers an understanding of this nonetheless fairly ordinary piece of film as complex and variegated in a way that neither a production history nor an audience survey could really get at. It pays to look and listen.

FURTHER READING

Champagne, John, '"Stop Reading Films!": Film Studies, Close Analysis, and Gay Pornography', *Cinema Journal* 36:4 (1997), pp. 76–97.

Haraway, Donna, 'Situated Knowledges: The Science Question in Feminism and the Privilege of Partial Perspectives', *Feminist Studies* 14 (1988), pp. 575–599.

Klevan, Andrew, 'Ordinary Language Film Studies' *Aesthetic Investigations* 3:2 (2020), pp. 387–406.

Koivunen, Anu, 'An Affective Turn? Reimagining the Subject of Feminist Theory', in Marianne Liljeström and Susanna Paasonen (eds), *Working with Affect in Feminist Readings: Disturbing Differences*, London: Routledge, 2010, pp. 8–28.

Schütz, Alfred (1953) 'Common-sense and Scientific Interpretation in Human Action', *Philosophy and Phenomenological Research* 14 (1953), pp. 1–38.

Wildfeuer, Janina, and John A. Bateman (eds), *Film Text Analysis: New Perspectives on the Analysis of Filmic Meaning*, New York: Routledge, 2017.

45 THE TELEVISION SITUATION (1973)

The characteristic forms of television entertainment – the performer and audience, the string of acts, the interpolation of drama and song, etc. – derive from music-hall, variety, musical comedy and the musical film. Yet these forms are based in an entirely different situation from that of television, which is hence called upon to recreate or remodel them.

Let us start with some obvious, even banal differences. Previous live entertainments (and much television entertainment is still live, actually or in the sense of appearing to have been recorded as a continuous whole) have been seen in special places – theatres, bars, and so on, with an audience. What was going on was going on in the same place as the audience – the stage, the platform were there in the room with you. Television in contrast is watched at home, with a few people, even alone, and what is going on is going on somewhere else, is merely being transmitted to you. It is this last point that is important in any consideration of television, for producers[1] seem seldom able to make up their minds whether television is simply a means of broadcasting other material or is an artistic medium in its own right.

A further consequence of this gap between show and reception is that the performer and audience are no longer in an interaction situation. Since he cannot see the audience reaction, the performer cannot legitimately respond to it and this seriously affects the nature of what he is doing. His way out of this may be simply to use the audience in the studio, so that the viewer enjoys the relayed interaction. This is the kind of by-play that gives Kenneth Williams' compering for instance (*Meanwhile on BBC2...*) its high points of humour. Alternatively, the performer may try to play on the response that his image is assumed to evoke and thus address himself to an idealised viewer – a strategy employed for instance by Val Doonican and Cilla Black, which will be examined more closely below.

---

1. Throughout this study I use the term producer or director loosely, recognising the complexities of decision making in institutional structures such as television companies and in collective artistic practice such as television production. I mean to indicate simply the person or persons who make the decision under discussion. The term itself, producer or director, I choose following the particular programme's credits.

THE PERSISTENCE OF TEXTUAL ANALYSIS

However, not all television entertainment passes for live. The analogy then is more with film, the finished art object rather than the interaction situation (however vicarious or illusory). The problem here is that television is small, for most people black and white, usually pretty imperfect in reproductive qualities, and can be turned off at will. The musical film (and the odd film revue) depend greatly on spectacle, colour, space (for more imaginative movement), detail and climax, all of which are hard to provide with any impact on television. New ideas of what constitutes spectacle are called for.

Producers seem to conceive the situation in which they are working in three ways, as follows:

(1) television is seen principally as relaying another show and the producer's concern is to find a means of reproducing it. This may be called *the outside broadcast situation*;
(2) the programme can be oriented towards the home viewer, recognising that the communication is one-way but attempting to use this, possibly to convey the illusion of reciprocity. It is always recognised that the television camera and transmission are amongst the givens of the situation. This may be called *the home-oriented situation*;
(3) the show may be self-sufficient, independent of all forms of interaction, in the way that a film, painting or piece of music is. Of course, like them, it intends a response, but this response is not part of the situation at the moment of creation. It is a response to a created object. This may be called *the object situation*.

THE OUTSIDE BROADCAST SITUATION

We must include here both outside broadcasts as they are traditionally thought of, from places outside the television studio – clubs, circuses, theatres – and also those from inside the studio, where a specially organised show is nonetheless relayed as *something going on in the studio*. The camera is not addressed, or only seldom, and the audience is part of the show.

The outside broadcast situation has so far been defined as being (in the way that the producers envisage the situation) simply relays of events, but, of course, the idea of television as an impersonal recording machine is utopian. Television cannot help but be a medium. Where you set up the cameras, which shots you select, their order and rhythm, these things are choices made by the producer (limited by technical considerations and budget only) which determine the interpretation of the show.

This may best be illustrated by comparing two circuses, both transmitted on Easter Monday 1971 – the Robert Brothers' Circus directed by Geoff Hall for Yorkshire Television, and Billy Smart's Circus, produced by Mary David for BBC1.[2] Both opened

---

2. Both programmes were probably recordings, although only the BBC show was so acknowledged.

with a horse act – horses moving round and round the ring, turning at the crack of a whip or a change of music, rolling over and so on. For the Robert Brothers' circus there were cameras at various points round the ring, offering both long and medium shots. One shot followed another with little apparent need other than that of variety, except for close-ups of the horses' heads when they sat up and again when they lay down. For Billy Smart's the cameras were more mobile, and panning and travelling shots were frequent. The camera seemed to move in and out of the ring, at times to be in amongst the animals. At the end a camera inside the artistes' entrance showed the horses trotting off.

Before suggesting the difference of meaning in these two treatments, it may be well to consider them in the context of some differences of overall format. During the Robert Brothers' circus the audience was frequently seen, often in quite thoughtfully composed shots – travelling shots of children (envious? identifying? excited?) watching a tumbling act involving child members of the audience; family groups, father and mother with children in front or on their knees; a little boy being fed ice cream; and some longer shots of sections of the audience. Their reactions were frequently shown, although mostly only after a particular trick or feat – one saw mostly applause and admiration rather than fear or excitement. During Billy Smart's the audience was seldom shown, except in long shots where it formed a backdrop to the act in progress. The audience was, however, involved in the clowns' act, being required to shout 'yes' and 'no' with the clowns and being at one point the location for their act. Where the audience was shown, it looked better-off than at the Robert Brothers'. The linking in both shows was also different. The Robert Brothers' had a commentator, Keith Macklin, who was usually shown between the acts and tended to stress certain 'traditional' qualities of the circus: its internationality, the preponderance of family acts, the passing on of secrets from one generation to another. Billy Smart's had no commentator and link material was provided by Francesco, a white-faced clown in traditional glitter knickerbockers and pointed hat. His introductions, addressed to the camera, were interrupted and complicated by two other clowns, Enrico and Ernesto.

It becomes clear that we have here two remarkably different programmes. It is true that the circuses themselves differed – the Robert Brothers' was a much smaller, cheaper affair then Billy Smart's. But the acts differed remarkably little in what they were – trampolinists here, tumblers there; sealions and elephants here, chimpanzees and tigers there; and Sebastian 'with his unique swinging trapeze act' in both. What really differed was the producer's *interpretation*. The Robert Brothers' circus came across as a routine Bank Holiday outside broadcast. It was the same thing all over again, validated by the notion of tradition. It was a family occasion. Billy Smart's on the other hand was presented as interesting in its own right, and as it were from the performers' point of view. With the shots inside the artistes' entrance, the close-ups (so that we saw reactions that we could not have seen had we been there), the presentation by a member of the company, and the camera's apparent involvement with the acts, the television show presented the circus itself as a *performance* rather than as a cosy family *event*.

The result of this difference of perspective was a completely different sense of what the acts were like. The two major animal acts in each circus – elephants in the Robert Brothers', tigers at Billy Smart's – came across differently over and above the associative qualities of the different animals – sentimentality with the former, danger with the latter. The elephants, shot as was everything else from several static camera positions, were seen dressed up as women. Neither the complexity or shape of the performance nor the reaction of the audience was shown, and it was possible to be distanced enough to find the spectacle pathetic – poor dumb animals dressed up as poor dumb chorus girls. The tigers on the other hand were shot in such a way that the bars of the cage were not visible, so that the picture was always close in on the act, and we could see the interplay of trainer and animal. This interplay was pinpointed as the central quality of the act rather than, say, wildlife spectacle or audience fear.

The most interesting comparison of all is the treatment of the same act, Sebastian. This act takes place on a single trapeze and consists of hand-standing on blocks on the swinging trapeze and building these blocks up one by one. It is not spectacular and graceful in the way that flying trapeze acts are, but it is obviously both difficult and dangerous. The first difference between the two presentations was simply that at Billy Smart's, Sebastian had more time and could therefore build his act up more before starting on the brick-building, which was its climax. More important, however, were differences in the television production. At Billy Smart's, cameras were placed high in the big top and low in the ring: shots of Sebastian from above and below showed the degree of swing of the trapeze, and so revealed the exciting and dangerous quality of what he was doing. There were no cameras so placed for the Robert Brothers, although there were cameras more or less on a level with him (if anything, slightly below). Shots were therefore medium distance and mostly with Sebastian swinging towards and away from the camera. This diminished in appearance the degree of swing, and thus diminished for the viewer the sense of awe and fear which the act seemed to inspire in the audience. It just looked like building bricks, whereas at Billy Smart's it looked like defying death.

It is important to stress that the simplicity or banality of the Yorkshire production does not mean that this was a more 'straight' presentation, less 'interpreted'. It means that the show itself was interpreted as being a routine, banal affair. Boredom is itself an attitude. Either because the circus called forth a less exciting response in the producer or because Hall is simply less sensitive to circuses than David, the Robert Brothers' circus, as a television show, came across as a routine *occasion*, whereas Billy Smart's came across as a (fairly exciting) *series of acts*. For all I know, Hall may have been more true to the event than David, but both were in any case taking opposite approaches to the material: one after (albeit dull) atmosphere, the other after performances.

It is this distinction that divides outside broadcasts. Let us take examples at each end of the scale (many programmes being attempts to do both).

The Good Old Days is a series directed for BBC1 by Barnie Colehan and consisting of a string of variety acts, linked by a chairman and performed in a music hall setting. Shots of the act alone are usually from slightly below stage level: we see them as it were from the audience's viewpoint. More often static shots show both audience and act. The show opens with the camera tracking over the audience to the stage, approaching the show via the audience. Long shots from high up on the side of the house show performer and audience. The runway between orchestra pit and audience allows the performer to get closer to the audience, and by putting the camera behind the performer we are taken close in on the interaction. We see the buxom lady singer cooing at the bewhiskered gentlemen; we see the comic out to shock the ladies. In addition, the frame often contains only members of the audience, who are all dressed in careful and deliberate period fashion. It is performer and audience – and particularly chairman – who are the show, not just performers.

Another example of an 'atmospheric' transmission is *Christmas Eve at the Golden Garter*, directed by Eric Prytherch for Granada from a Manchester night club. The acts here were performed on a small raised level, with audience close in on three sides, a small band backing. The audience was nearly always in the picture; groups at tables, longshots over the audience to the performer, artistes entering between the tables, waiters serving, often crossing right in front of the cameras, a constant coming and going. Close-ups of the performers were, in fact, rare. The light source for the acts was usually a single spot or flood, and the composition showed it stabbing through the smoky atmosphere to the performer. The sound reproduction was the same as the club's – raucous, too loud, harsh. The audience were not so clearly delineated as in *The Good Old Days* but it was nonetheless the acts in that setting that mattered most: the whole hot steamy vulgar brassy atmosphere of the affluent working-class Northern club. At one point the programme went even further than this, recognising itself as a television broadcast. Johnny Hackett's patter act, full of Mancunian references, was played basically at the audience present, but also referred to the presence of the camera. Of course to the people at the club the camera was part of the situation. By referring to it he brought together all the dynamics of the situation.

At the other end of the scale, with the emphasis on the performance itself, is Mary David's *Red Army Ensemble* broadcast for BBC2. For this show the cameras' focus was mostly the edge of the stage and further on to the stage. The audience was very seldom seen: one or two random shots. One seldom saw all the stage, except occasionally from far back in the theatre when it was surrounded by darkness (the audience remains fully lit in *The Good Old Days*). More often one saw groups of performers or even only limbs, movements, one or two figures wholly with others going off the side of the frame. Thus in the fast tumbling Chumaky, what was emphasised was the speed, the dynamism, the ensemble interaction of the dancers. What was not evident was any overall choreographic pattern, but David probably rightly chose to recognise dynamism as one of the essential characteristics of the show and one which would certainly televise better than complex patterns which the size of the television screen could not convey adequately. The presentation could also emphasise certain aspects of individual performances: a kind of hand choreography of the drummer's in a number entitled 'Caucasian Rhythms', the fact that a soloist was on point during the closing 'Friendship Dance'. Again, the interaction of a soloist and chorus in a Russian folk song, 'The Mosquito' could also be shown by cutting from one to the other. The song was sung in Russian, but the close-ups showed the response of one section to another and so conveyed the ponderous humour of it. This kind of production implies a familiarity with the material and a sense of what is important about it artistically. I think David is probably right to pick out what she does, but I want to stress that her agency enters inevitably into the presentation and that she is, in fact, representing the Ensemble to us, in such a way that what she senses as its essential qualities are expressed in television terms. We are not seeing it as the audience sees it: strictly speaking that is impossible. We are seeing it as David sees it.

The outside broadcast situation then tends through the manner in which it is produced to stress either the atmosphere, the good time, of the whole occasion or else the actual qualities and spectacle of the performance. In this way, two different conceptions as to what constitutes entertainment are expressed. One emphasises the warmth and spirit of coming together for a show as the essential delight of the experience; the other presents the amazing and dazzling splendour and skill as the heart of the pleasure. Different meanings within the aesthetics of entertainment are opened out.

THE HOME-ORIENTED SITUATION

There are few programmes in which performers, particularly in introductions and greetings, do not address the camera and therefore attempt to address the domestic audience. But few performers address the camera in the actual performance of their act: they either address no-one or else the unseen studio audience, which since it is unseen is for the domestic viewer only a kind of enlargement of her or himself. This is not surprising, since so very few entertainers are products of television itself: nearly all come from the variety stage and cabaret, or else from the recording studio. They come, that is, from situations where the live audience or else its absence provide primary definitions of the situation. This, together with the fact that most entertainment programmes are recorded, partially accounts for the small number of programmes which exploit the fact that, like radio, television is a live communication medium, rather like a one-way (video-) telephone.

It falls, with important exceptions, to performers whose career has been predominantly in professional broadcasting, often radio, to exploit this, and these are the announcers and linkmen whose presence is crucial to many programmes: Bob Monkhouse (*The Golden Shot*), Pete Murray (*The Melodies Linger On*), Hughie Green (*Opportunity Knocks*) and David Nixon (*Magic Box*).[3] Their ability to do this derives in part from the fact that their whole role consists of introductions and greetings, of link material, and that this role is one that has been developed in broadcasting until it is now a widely accepted convention. It rests upon a sense of addressing a mass individual. That is, it conceives of the audience as an undifferentiated mass, but also recognises that this mass is broken down in terms of reception into units the size of an individual or family group. It addresses the mike or the camera as if it were addressing one person (or group), but the tone does not (cannot) take into account the great range of attitudes that addressing different individuals actually occasions. The tone settled on is a kind of pally, blokeish, 'when you get down to it we're all the same' cheerfulness, well described by Richard Hoggart in *The Uses of Literacy*.[4] It's a cross between a kind of verbal elbow nudging and a cosy, cooing interest and concern for the mass individual addressed.

But it is possible even as a performer to begin to make contact with the home audience, and certain performers – Cilla Black, Val Doonican, Rolf Harris – have developed ways of doing this, making a distinctive use of television.

Cilla Black's show (*Cilla*, directed by Michael Hurll for BBC1), contains much that is not home oriented: the self-addressed solo numbers (as if in a recording studio), the production numbers, the oddly grand ending, with the star standing in silhouette, arms half-outstretched. But in two particulars, the show is very aware that it is television. First, Cilla Black herself, in between songs and often during sketches, constantly stresses her nerves at being in the show, her excitement at being with these big stars, her loud uninhibited laughter – delight or nervousness? – her self-mockery. All this is addressed to the camera, so that we are invited to share the joke, the situation with her. The show also contains sequences in which Cilla tries to realise the system as a two-way communication: using a closed circuit television with a camera unit nearby, she addresses directly people watching in a shop window and then brings them into the

---

3. The particular appeal of David Nixon has been well caught by James Towler: 'There is something rather cosy about David Nixon. He has the approach of everyone's favourite uncle. His friendly informal manner gave [the show] a degree of modesty that was in itself something of a tonic', *The Stage and Television To-day*, 7 October 1971.
4. Richard Hoggart, *The Uses of Literacy*, Harmondsworth: Penguin, 1958, pp. 169–205.

Cilla Black and comedian Jerry Lewis perform on the television show *Cilla*, 1970. (Don Smith/Radio Times via Getty Images)

studio, or else carries on a conversation with a group of schoolboys and then appears from the next room. Here is realised vicariously the possibility of actually being able to make contact with the television star who addresses herself to you.

Val Doonican draws heavily on the assumption that people like the Irish, children and romance; he is also one of the few people who actually sings his songs to the camera. His relaxed singing style involves no sense of theatrical production, the rocking chair gives the song a domestic setting, the songs themselves are arranged in the same easy way, slow enough to allow 'natural' phrasing. The style and the subject matter of the songs go together to create an ideally domestic lyricism. Val Doonican's shows (at least those for BBC1) are also unusual in that they go out live, which is often brought out (perhaps deliberately) by mix-ups over props, crashes off stage and, of course, the absence of edited sequences. By making the studio situation fully apparent, Val Doonican can effectively play upon the notion that the show is one half of an ongoing conversation. *This* is where I am, and I'm *now* at this moment singing to *you*.

Rolf Harris, too, constantly refers to the situation, to what he is doing – exhausted after a dance routine, het-up doing a painting. He is used by the BBC in many capacities other than his own show, which gives him a fund of matey acceptance to draw on. He also gathers together many of the strands of the men-as-buffoons imagery of the advertisements on ITV – in which he also appears from time to time. In a sense, of the three under discussion he is the most identified with television itself.

(To whatever extent a performer may orientate himself towards the domestic audience, as long as there is an audience in the studio he will to a certain extent inevitably respond to it and this will imperceptibly affect his act, especially if humour is involved. There is often a pull between the two audiences, which can be disconcerting.)

All these performers are popular with audiences and so perhaps their friendliness and generosity are responded to with something like the feeling that we reserve for people we know and like. At the same time, it does seem that the fact that you can't answer back, that you know that your response is never really registered by the performer, that you are just a mass individual, in the end undermines the fullness and warmth promised by the home-oriented situation.

THE OBJECT SITUATION

In perhaps the majority of cases there is no direct referral in the shows to a present or a domestic audience. The show is a self-contained product.

The paradigm of this show (if we leave aside the comedy interludes) is *The Black and White Minstrel Show* (BBC1). The songs are all recorded in advance, which means that the dancing and miming have to be exact, unspontaneous and slickly professional. They are usually all three. There seems to be a limited repertoire of songs that recur again and again – the old minstrel numbers, the ballad standards, the cleaner music-hall songs and so on – and the texture of the harmonisation varies little from one number to the next. Indeed, there is as little variation of tempi as possible too, even the distance between a waltz and a march, or a slow and a fast number, being kept minimal. One song flows easily and imperceptibly into the next. The familiarity of the songs is complemented by the simplicity of the production. The overall quality is clean and smooth – costumes just pressed, dance floor just polished. Settings and costumes are of three types – (i) rudimentary iconographic referents to stock show business locales – Paris (a cut-out Eiffel Tower, café tables, advertisement pillars), Cockney London (market barrows, Pearly King costumes), Vienna (chandeliers, ballroom clothes), hillbilly country (check shirts, log cabins, straw hats); (ii) the anonymous showbiz glitter set, diamanté leotards, steps which light up, the rococo of the show girls' headgear, the cyclorama with coloured lighting; and (iii), occasionally, the casual wear which became fashionable in the fifties and acceptable in the sixties – sweaters and slacks for the men, bright, simple patterned dresses for the women. There is minimal differentiation between performers. The girls either wear the same costumes or else different but arbitrarily assigned period or 'character' costumes; their make-up all shows the same conspicuous expertise associated with professional entertainers; the approach to their appearance is basically that of the conventional glamour syndrome of leotards, legs and permanent waves. The men all wear the same clothes and blackface make-up – (although this has been modified to allow some differentiation) – the producer George Inns says: 'apart from their singing, they (the men) are just a background for the pretty girls and costumes.'[5] The dancing is simple, effortless, in unison, deriving in style from both ballroom dancing and the chorus routine in the musical comedy, although both in an attenuated form. The camera work is unobtrusive, shots are from many angles so that there is little sense of the show being performed in one direction (i.e. as to an unseen audience – although one is heard). It is a self-enclosed world. The camera may emphasise choreographic shapes or create effects of perspective and pattern. The whole show is anonymous and highly organized, comparable stylistically (though less lavish or outrageous) with the dance numbers of Busby Berkeley. It fulfils the intentions of its producer – 'It's pure entertainment… It is a show you can watch without having to make any efforts.'[6]

Few shows have achieved quite the same close-knit self-enclosed objectiveness of *The Black and White Minstrel Show*, and shows like *The Golddiggers of London* and the Younger Generation in their various appearances do attempt minimally to project to the camera something like personality and expression. Objectiveness is easier to realise in dance routines; song numbers, especially solos, are more problematic.

It is still the case that the majority of songs are performed on an abstract set with no visible audience and no appeal to the camera. Here come all those inserts of guest singers in comedy and other shows. In theory, we are watching the singer wrapped up in his or her song and its emotions, but, in practice, they are projecting somewhere, probably to the unseen studio audience. They perform outward in one direction, a fact that is emphasised by the camera work. In nearly every case, the studio appears to be set up as a stage – a three sided square which can be seen only through the fourth invisible side. The cameras are placed directly in front of or at an angle towards the performer, but always in a frontal or 'audience' position. This fact is overlaid by camera movements (which tend to be more fluid and changing in the BBC than

---

[5]. Interview with Ann Purser, *The Stage and Television To-day*, 11 December 1969.
[6]. Ibid.

in the ITV companies), but does not disguise the fact that although the singer has no visible audience, studio or domestic, he is in fact performing out to an audience (albeit only of technicians). Thus precisely what the situation is becomes problematic – apparently a mere presentation of a song, inconsistencies in production remind one of both the situation in the studio and of the fact of it being relayed into the home. The song becomes neither a statement (of personality or emotion), cut off from the flux of interaction, nor on the other hand in any clear sense an instance of interaction.

In this chapter we have been brought up repeatedly against contradictions, against situations in which what is being done has not been thought through but rather is allowed to fall between different stools. The first contradiction is between the fact that the camera is a recording instrument and the fact that it is none the less not the equivalent of the human eye, able, in fact, to record only a very limited part of anything, with the consequence that the use of television always involves interpretation by the producer (even when he is not aware of it). Thus although television may bring experiences to the people, it never does so in an unmediated form – television is never the people's medium, but always the producers'. Secondly, the transmission is one-way, where it often wants to be two-way, in interaction – a limitation not imposed by technology but by institutions and history.[7] Thirdly, the transmission and the show itself are live, although at different times from each other – thus the vitality and spontaneity of the show and the immediacy of the transmission are not synchronised (with exceptions, of course). These contradictions within the medium itself, *as it is at present set up*, inevitably affect the success of television entertainment in realising its aims.

Originally published in Richard Dyer, *Light Entertainment*, London: BFI, 1973, pp. 13–22.

---

7. See Hans Magnus Enzensberger: 'Constituents of a Theory of the Media' in *New Left Review* 1:64 (November–December 1970), pp. 13-36.

46 *THE TOWERING INFERNO* (1975)

The very first shot of *The Towering Inferno* is an extreme close-up of a helicopter's rotors. You can't, for a moment, tell what it is you are seeing – it's just a flurry, a virtually abstract impression of chaotic but urgent movement, the urgency underlined by the poundingly impressive, swirling music. Beginning the film like this sweeps us into action, adventure, excitement – not these things as incidents or feelings experienced by characters, but the thrust and form of them recreated in the visual patterns, the flurry, on the screen. The first image is a visual analogue of the feeling the film (we know, because it's a disaster movie) is aiming at.

This continues through the credits. The music, with its constantly moving violins and sonorous timpani beat, is strong and immediate. The visuals – cutting from overhead shots, to camera moving in counterpoint to the 'copter, to bursting through clouds to get a bird's eye view of the Golden Gate Bridge – are a bit like Martini commercials, in which sudden changes of perspective and an immaculate control of the interplay of camera movement and movement in camera create the intended feeling in the texture of the film itself.

Extreme close-up of a helicopter's rotors in *The Towering Inferno*, 1974.

The credit sequence of *The Towering Inferno* promises us a film in which the sensuous experience of technique will embody directly (and allow us to feel directly) what the events and characters on screen tell us is happening. (That would not be particularly original – it is how, to take a couple of random examples, *noir* lighting or Minnellian camera movements characteristically work). We would feel the peril and tension and thrill of the big building on fire, and we might also feel the more complex emotions, swallowed up or brought to a head by the conflagration. But that is not what we get; instead, *The Towering Inferno* is characterised, outside the credits sequence, by an almost classical refusal of sensuous or emotive devices.

The Towering Inferno uses camera movement and wide screen to present actions and characters in the most stable manner possible. A favourite technique is to have a smooth, fairly short piece of camera movement which ends up with what is taken to be the important acts or characters in the scene dead square in the centre. For instance, when Paul Newman, the building's architect, goes to visit Richard Chamberlain, the electrician, at his home, to berate him for faulty, penny-pinching wiring, he gets out of the car and walks screen right into Chamberlain's house (the door is open); the camera has moved across with him, but stops when the house is dead centre, with the open door and passageway dead centre of the house, and with Newman dead centre of the lot. This is not a major scene (although it is the longest confrontation between Newman, the idealist, and the building's rather more commercially minded builders), but is typical of the film's method.

What this method means is that the extraordinary and terrifying things that happen before us on the screen are perceived from a point of view that emphasises stability. It is a disaster movie, but the disaster need not trouble us too much.

In this respect, *The Towering Inferno* can be seen as a retreat to stability from *The Poseidon Adventure* and *Earthquake*. The first of these was closer in time to those moments in the commercial cinema when underground experiments with 'dislocation of perception' surfaced, e.g. *Easy Rider, 2001,* Roger Corman, *Midnight Cowboy*, etc. With its fascinating overturned interiors and its journey upwards into ever more labyrinthine depths, it played around with our perceptions of the normal world, and it cast the whole thing in a mock heroic mode, including a ranting priest, brave Jewish momma, and an escape up a Christmas tree. *Earthquake* encased its title event in a series of banal dramas, but it did try, naively, to simulate, with juddering camera and trembling seats, the experience of being in a 'quake. There is nothing like this in *The Towering Inferno.*

All the same, *The Towering Inferno* is very exciting. Indeed, most people I know found it more exciting than either of the others, and it seems to be doing better business. The main source of excitement, I suggest, is simply that being trapped in a tower block on fire is the sort of thing that could happen easily to any of us but a second is the film's use of stars. Its success could be to do with the way its stable overall perception is underpinned by key reassuring motifs, and with its relevance to the world at large as presented in the media today.

There are a lot of stars in *The Towering Inferno* and they are an exceptionally charismatic lot. This is not an opinion of Newman, McQueen, Dunaway and the rest, but merely factual – they are major stars and it is part of the phenomenon of stars that people identify with them. If these identification figures are in peril, you feel the peril too. Part of the excitement of *The Towering Inferno* must have something to do with this, and the film uses them more purposefully than, for instance, Heston and Gardner are used in *Earthquake*. The choice of two ageing but very considerable stars, Jennifer Jones and Fred Astaire, to play a couple who manage in the first years of old age to come lovingly together, gives a particular poignancy and stress. Faye Dunaway brings from her roles in *Bonnie and Clyde* and *The Thomas Crown Affair* a sensuality and a strength which counteracts both the general sexlessness and the impression that men alone can rescue us in a disaster. (In *Earthquake*, Ava Gardner's neuroticism and Geneviève Bujold's wetness are merely shown to depend on, and ultimately destroy, Charlton Heston's manifest capability in emergency.) She only succeeds in counteracting the latter impression, but at least she is shown being useful. And casting both Paul Newman and Steve McQueen is a masterstroke. Throughout the film we see pairs of dauntless, piercing blue eyes. They come to constitute a central motif in the film.

Those eyes are a feature of Newman and McQueen's images, but meaningfully exchanged looks between men are an important element in the narrative of *The Towering Inferno*. Several of the incidents (for the narrative is composed of incidents, usually overlapping and often concurrent) end with two men looking hard and trustingly at each other – they've come through something perilous together and survived through mutual dependence. Looking square and silent at each other is a model of transparency and trust between males (it is a mode deriving from Westerns, and particularly dwelt on in Spaghetti Westerns). So when at the end of the film Newman and McQueen also look at each other, with those blue eyes, and say they are going to co-operate on new buildings (i.e. Newman will design them so that McQueen can protect them from fire), it is the culmination of a pattern that affirms both that something can be done and that men, in their strong silent way, can do it.

This ending bids for the mythic power of the Western. It re-affirms that it is men who shape the world – but although this is a hark back to an old principle, the film manages to present it as a new way forward. In the film, Newman and McQueen are new men (but still Men) – Newman may even let Dunaway pursue her own career (it is she who has doubts), and McQueen is a fire chief with knowledge as well as guts. They are kept separate from the rest of the cast, who are grouped in the party room,

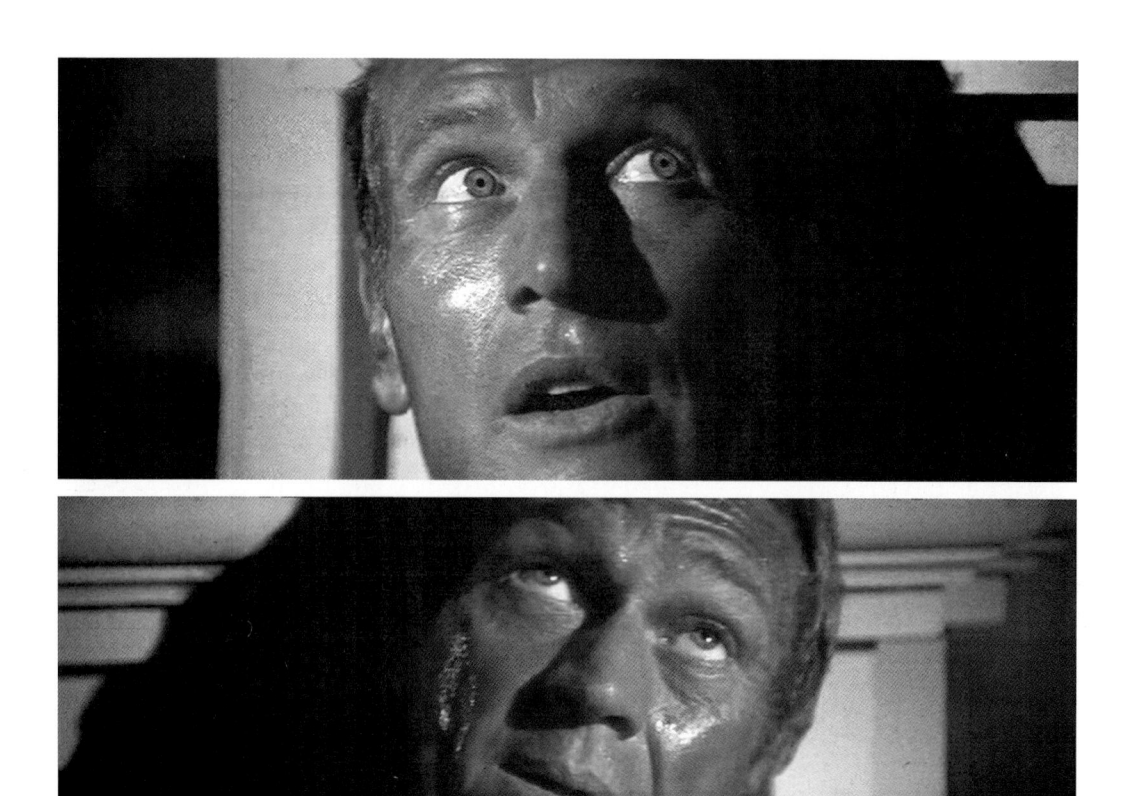

Close-up of Paul Newman; close-up of Steve McQueen.

where Newman and McQueen are seldom seen – their domain is corridors, stairways, air shafts, roofs, and helicopters.

Newman especially is dissociated from all the others responsible for the building. This is particularly suggested by decor in the scene when he goes to visit Richard Chamberlain. Apart from the credits and a couple of sequences of fire engines pounding through the streets, this is the only scene which does not take place in or around the tower. The house is decorated with all the insignia of the old-fashioned home – heavy oak sideboard, horse brasses, copper mugs, tartan coverings – all very different from the smooth, plain, ultra-modern look of the tower. Chamberlain is the film's main villain, and this decor seems to go with an older way of approaching matters (from the viewpoint of profitability), whereas Newman and McQueen suggest at the end a way forward via 'responsible cooperation between men'.

Yet this also *contradicts* what we have been told earlier. The building catches fire because of faulty wiring, itself a product of both wilful negligence and commercial cutting of corners. This is explicitly not Newman's fault — much of the conflict centres on his anger with electrician and builder — yet at the end it is he who is going to do better (without reference to capitalism). McQueen's first line is that fires cannot really be fought above seven storeys; yet at the end, he is proposing collaborating on future buildings with Newman.

This shift can occur without too much violence to the audience's sense of things by the metaphor structure which underpins the film's pile-up of incidents. This structure is registered especially in the use of colour in the film. Apart from some rather garish orange in the lobby shown near the beginning, nearly all the furnishings and clothing in the building are cool and dark, with much use of dark blue, cream and white in the party room, dimly lit green in the PRO's room, sombre brown in the corridors. This of course contrasts very markedly with the leaping yellows and reds of the flames that fill the screen from time to time, and occasionally burst in on the cool colour schema. Thus there is the 'shocking' intrusion of a man on fire, a stumbling black shape with red and yellow flames down its back, across the pale blue carpet near the lift in the party room.

This kind of effect increases as the film goes on (partly, of course, for perfectly acceptable narrative reasons), and points to a shift from a social to a metaphysical explanation of disaster. The causes of the fire, the chat tells us, are capitalistic, social; but as we *see* the film, this element disappears behind the far more powerful image of the twentieth century 'advanced' world, all modern cool, threatened by the elemental force of fire. As the adventure heightens, so this image takes over — and in the end, the fire is only beaten by people (men) taking control of the elements themselves. Newman and McQueen release the water from the huge tanks at the top of the building, unleashing a torrent on the flames. Only after this domination of the elements does a social message re-appear (collaboration on future buildings), but in the process the real social conflicts (profitability versus human well-being) have been eclipsed by the primaeval enormity of the metaphysical metaphor (fire versus water).

It is not, I think, too fanciful to connect *The Towering Inferno* (like other disaster movies, only more so) with that sense of living in an as-never-before disaster-filled world which TV, especially, puts forward. Wars, famines, urban revolt, rising crime — like them, the fire in *The Towering Inferno* is both created by human beings and yet beyond human control. Disasters (in life and in movies) are beyond politicians and the powers that be to bring to an end, and yet are also pursued and caused by them. Moreover, although we know that we — and especially 'they' — are actively implicated, disasters seem so beyond our control as to assume the proportions of a 'natural' event. In the cinema, this feeling becomes the water/earthquake/fire of disaster movies.

The Towering Inferno touches this complex of feelings about the way the world is in particularly suggestive ways, but it also reassures us, partly in the relief of blaming 'nature', not 'society', and of re-relying on blue-eyed male ability, but also in the contrast with disasters on TV. There the jerky camera and half-glimpsed events are part of the message that we can neither do anything nor even really comprehend. *The Towering Inferno* shows men doing something about disaster, and makes all that happens comprehensible, graspable, for the camera has everything in frame, in control, in the centre. Allowing us to perceive it stably, the film allows us to experience, for once, a disaster as not being beyond us.

Originally published in *Movie* 21 (August 1975), pp. 30–33. Reprinted by permission of Cameron & Hollis, Moffat, Dumfriesshire, Scotland; cameronandhollis.uk.

47 NOTES ON TEXTUAL ANALYSIS (1981)

I am aware that many of the points I am going to make are those that any teacher would make about their practice. I apologise then for being obvious. Still, many of the points do not seem to get into print and there is even a certain disjuncture between this pedagogic practice and the tone of much of the writing we use to teach with. (For example, if I say that, when a student declares that *Vent d'Est* is boring, we should talk this through with her or him, I'm sure that is what most of us would do; yet it is interesting that Peter Wollen's discussion of the unpleasure of *Vent d'Est* is the one aspect of his influential paper on the film that has not become a taken-for-granted part of the debate surrounding counter-cinema.)

THE PLACE OF TEXTUAL ANALYSIS

Most media courses involve the analysis of media texts at some point. Some however, and this is probably particularly true of specifically film courses, make the texts the centre of the course, its *raison d'être*.

Against this tendency, two others can be identified that I shall, purely for convenience, term theoretical and sociological tendencies. The first of these sees the text merely as an instance in a more general set of conceptual problems – e.g. you're interested in ideology, or positionality, or narrativity, not the specificities of media texts, any and all of which can be considered in the light of the theoretical issues addressed. The sociological tendency resists the notion that the text 'contains' all its meanings, and emphasises the need to understand its place in the relations of production and consumption that give rise to it. (This includes the sociology of institutions and audience research etc., although I have deliberately posed this tendency in terms that relate it more directly to a notion of meaning production.)

How one constructs and teaches a course clearly depends on what you think is important. All three tendencies – textual, theoretical, sociological – have their appeal and their pitfalls.

To subordinate the theoretical and sociological tendencies to textual analysis in virtual isolation implies either that there is a body of 'great' works that students will necessarily benefit from studying or that a student's relation to media texts is of an especially profound and meaningful kind that it is the job of the teacher to explore and deepen. (Although I don't hold either of these views, they are not so lightly to be dismissed – some evaluative notions do always enter into our selection of media texts to teach with; we *are* teaching *people*, many of whom come to us because the media means a lot to them in various ways.) Textual analysis in isolation – 'pure' practical criticism – is moreover much weakened by its lack of theoretical and sociological dimensions: it acts as if one does not always approach a text with a set of (albeit unauthorised) concepts, and it never defines the material reality of what a text is (i.e. it leaves the definition of a text as 'images on a screen', which is rather like saying a factory is a building with machines in it – of course, there is a sense in which both are true, but both omit the real relations which also define the objects, specifically in terms of what they are for, who controls them, how they are organised etc.)

The limitations of 'pure' textual analysis are clear (and I should say that it is something of a straw man, since I don't know of anyone who actually teaches like that). But there are also problems with theoretical and empirical tendencies which marginalise textual analysis too greatly.

At worst, the theoretical tendency treats the text as an 'illustration' of the theory. This can lead to a cavalier attitude to texts, where all sorts of complexities – and especially those that run counter to the theory – are ignored and the text almost becomes a visual aid. (In other words, it is treated as, in its own terms, unproblematic, just as we habitually complain about the use of film and TV in non-media courses.) In this view, the text has *no* autonomous existence – you can make it mean whatever you (or the theory in question) want it to mean (a view oddly close to the subjectivism we always have to face in students, 'we all see things differently' etc.). I see the relation between theory and text as more dynamic, the text as in some sense a 'test' of the theory, complexifying, qualifying, sometimes contradicting the theory. I *don't* mean disproving it – the fact that a given media text does not fit a given theory, does not prove the theory wrong, qualifies its applicability, and hence makes us understand the theory better. Within this relation, I consider the theory more important – I am more interested in the concepts at stake than the films that I am relating them to; but equally I want to retain an 'openness' to the text, to allow it to 'resist' me, so that I do not make it into more than it is or could be, and so that I better understand the problems of the concepts I am interested in.

The empirical tendency, when it ignores textual analysis, dissolves the text into structures of production (and/or producers' intentions) and audience perceptions, without granting the text any degree of determinacy in what meanings are produced and made possible. Yet each element – producers, text, audience – is mutually determined and determining, and this is the model I like to work from. (I leave open here the question of the *relative* determinacy of each element.) At the same time, in practice, I do over-privilege the text in teaching, partly for kinds of reasons that have their own legitimacy (texts are *there*; they are usually the reason why students have come on the course; I am not a sociologist, etc.). There are two justifications for this – firstly, one can acknowledge that the analyses are provisional, that they need to be inserted into the particular relations of production and consumption of the text in question; secondly, if one stresses the polysemy of the text (i.e. its multiple but *finite* meanings and affects), then one is analysing what meanings and affects the text makes possible, without thereby claiming any meaning as the correct one, or the one most prevalently held by producers or audiences. (I think one can identify which meanings and affects the text itself signals as the correct or prevalent one.) In self-defence, I had better add that if I confess to privileging textual analysis in relation to work on production and consumption this does not mean either that I do not do any work on them or that I assume they can be read off from the text.

Textual analysis is then a key and determinant moment in Media Studies, one that must know its place but must have its place. Partly because of factors in the situation in which we work (e.g. why students come, the time at one's disposal, the limits of one's competence, etc.), partly to make sure the crucial theoretical issues actually bite on the reality they address, and partly because the text is a real determinant in the production of meaning and affect in the media.

TEXTUAL ANALYSIS – WHAT IS INVOLVED

In doing textual analysis, the following factors come into play – the text itself, you and your students, why you are studying it, its situation.

The text itself

Texts do not speak for themselves, or 'contain' meaning and affect. They exist, as print on paper or marks on celluloid, apart from their production and consumption, but their meaning and affect is only activated at the moments of production and consumption (both of which are more properly conceived of as moments of production of meaning and affect).

However, there is a base line of 'fact' about the text that must be respected. E.g. either a programme is made in a two-camera set-up or it is not; either Dorothy Malone wears red throughout *Written on the Wind* or she does not. It is important to get such 'facts' right – one cannot afford to be slap-happy about them. (Many an interesting and important theoretical article becomes hard to teach because the writer has not been careful about this simple level – it is often hard to persuade students of the merit of a theory, if the writer is so clearly textually incompetent.)

This level, though so rudimentary, gives us many problems, which can be ranged under two headings – recall, and media specificity.

Recall is a well-known problem – unless we are studying printed material, we do not have the text right there in front of us to check on. Extracts and slides help, and a Prevost and a VTR are fairly basic demands of any developing Media Studies programme. I also favour reading synopses before viewing (unless repeat viewings are possible) and taking notes during, although I know some people feel this destroys the spontaneity of response and takes people's eyes away from the image.

By media specificity, I simply mean 'facts' about a text such as camera movement and (especially difficult) editing. The problem is to get students to see that those facts are *there* (especially as so often they are not meant to be noticed), and to give them a vocabulary to describe them. This does involve a certain amount of work along the Debrix and Stephenson *Cinema as Art* lines (while eschewing their assumptions), and I favour getting students to write a 'factual' description of a brief media text (or part thereof – it has to be very brief), just so that they get into the habit of looking closely and precisely at what is on the screen, in the text. (This is also quite a good exercise in helping them see how soon a 'fact' becomes a 'meaning', i.e. an interpretation of a fact.)

You and your students

In any analytic activity, persons are always present, doing the analysing. While the analysis does not have its source inside these persons, but is to be understood within the codes and traditions of analysis in play, nevertheless, these persons are involved, with their particular life-histories and circumstances, their thoughts and feelings (which, if not, as they often feel, unique to them, are nonetheless special, insistent and besides inescapable for them).

At a minimum, how one responds to a programme or a film, whether one likes it or not, cries, laughs or is bored, has to be registered as something that may colour one's analytic procedures. More positively, one can use these responses in various ways. Firstly, one can use them as a way into the text ('what was it about the text that made you cry?'). Secondly, one can explore them in their own right – I mean genuinely explore, not celebrate as in certain modes of literary education. Thus one might ask – what knowledge did you have access to that made you respond to, or read, the programme in that way? how has class/gender/race/age/sexual orientation, affected your reading? (This opens us up to wider questions for this conference as to the relative mix in our teaching of student-centred and subject-centred approaches.) Thirdly, these reactions/responses/readings are a useful 'control' to set against the analytical readings. (E.g. most students dislike deconstruction movies, yet are sympathetic to the latters' political claims and often interested by the films in discussion; this does not mean that the films *become* likeable through discussion, since, back in front of the films, the students are still not enjoying them; rather, it becomes part of our understanding of the films that they are for most people unpleasurable to watch and interesting to discuss, an understanding that then leads to a discussion of the nature of those films in relation to others and of their political effectivity. Another interesting example is the relationship between Sirk as a 'distancing' director and students who either giggle at his films or view them through floods of tears.)

Why the text is being studied
Texts do not speak for themselves; nor can they be made to say whatever you want them to say; rather they are articulated in relation to the questions posed of them. It is here that it is crucial to be clear about what I called the 'theoretical' dimension. Students need to know clearly why they are looking at such and such a text.

The reason may be evident from the reference to the media text in some theoretical or critical text being used; or it may be clear from the overall shape of the course (though students often do not perceive the shape that is so obvious to us in the courses we devise). Equally, it may be necessary to spell out the reasons before a screening, at the end of a lecture or wherever. I even favour giving students quite specific things to look for – precise questions to pose of the text – while viewing.

Such a procedure clearly interferes with any 'direct' response to the text by the student. In an ideal world, one would give such a first 'innocent' viewing, for the kinds of reason outlined in the previous section (and also through discussion to demystify the notion of direct or innocent readings and responses), but where such leisure (time and money) is not possible, a screening whose purpose is not first explained is falsely innocent (there are always reasons for selecting a given text to show) and a waste of time (students find it hard to answer the questions you want to pose of the text, if they only know the questions after the viewing).

Let me add three riders to this.

i) The questions must be genuine questions; i.e. the students are to pose theoretical issues in relation to the text, not impose an (the teacher's) interpretation.
ii) This work takes one beyond unpremeditated media viewing – for instance, great importance may be attached to a signifying element that students might well not have noticed had you not asked them a question about it. This often understandably worries students – what is the status of the analysis, if it is so different from how they view a text ordinarily? (and, we slip into assuming, how ordinary people see it, on television or at the pictures?). Studying a text clearly is different from ordinary viewing, but if we hold on to a notion of the text's polysemy, we should be able to include or come to terms with what we take to be unpremeditated readings.

iii) The questions posed will be determined by the theoretical issues one wishes to address, or which one finds addressed in the critical or theoretical tradition in which one is working. These questions and these traditions need, like the text itself, to be historicised. This resolves itself into the question, is one analysing the text for what it means now or for what it meant when it was first produced (or, as a certain academic possibility, at various points in between)? There is no easy or quick answer to this. My own bias is towards the former, since I am primarily interested in texts in relation to the society in which they occur. However, one must always recognise that one cannot travel in time, wholly recover the meanings and affects current in a given moment in the past – rather one engages with a text's historicity through the perspective of the present. (I am not sure what knowledge is produced by an analysis that ignores the text's historicity altogether, merely making it a reflection of contemporary concerns.)

The situation of the text

As suggested above, work on the relations of production and consumption of a text gives one a definition of the object of textual study – the text not as a purely formal or 'material' (i.e. made of stuff) entity but also as having certain 'materialist' (i.e. socially and historically determined and determining, functions, values and effects).

One should not lose sight of the purely formal and material level – it is important to understand the internal rules of harmony or the technical limitations of a camera. (One can show how these are in turn socially and historically determinate, but at a much broader level than need concern us every time we want to discuss why a particular chord occurs on the soundtrack or a particular camera movement is used, which may often be because no other way was 'conceivable'.) Equally, one must not, as formalist critics and media practitioners tend to, mystify them to the extent of being the sole determinants of meaning and affect. They need to be articulated with the materialist understanding of what a text is.

This means understanding the specific determinant contexts of the text and how the text works within them. In other words, not just the background of the text, but its *situation*, how the text is *in* its background. Here we cover familiar enough ground – close to the media: the industry (the particular production companies, etc.), filmic conventions (i.e. 180 degree rule, etc.), authors, genres, and further away, dress and gesture codes, the other media and arts, political debate, economic structures, patriarchy, etc. (I leave unresolved here the question of distinctions between structural and ideological levels.) Clearly, one is in danger of taking the whole world on board here, turning Media Studies into the meaning of life. I tend to favour a slower and more limited approach, working outwards from the text to its immediate contexts and only pointing in the most general way to the wider horizons of capitalism and patriarchy (they are, after all, pretty soon present in microcosm in the immediate contexts of the particular studio, the particular authorial and generic code). This is partly to do with timidity, but also because I don't want to fall into the trap of making sweeping connections between Text and Society, which a) tend to treat the text as somehow not a part of society and b) fail to ground the analysis in the concrete mediations between textual practices and other levels of the social formation.

This work is, as well as, to me, the most interesting, also the most difficult. The student is grasping ever more information that s/he is to bring to bear on the text that is the point of departure. (E.g. the classic chicken-and-egg of author, genre and star study – you need to see a lot of films to understand the code, but you can only grasp the code through specific instances of it – the answer is to jump into the hermeneutic circle and get on with the work, not hoping for a point of initial *or* final knowledge.) Moreover, it involves you and the students in accepting words like 'probable', 'likely' and 'possible', which our positivistic heritage finds peculiarly unsatisfactory. Thus if the context involved is authorial or generic (the two most common in Film Studies), one has to acknowledge that, though they may determine a text, they do not do so absolutely or certainly. (E.g. if it is true that Minnelli's films play on a notion of 'the reality of the imagination', then it seems likely that this is how we are to read Daisy's 'reliving' of previous experiences in *On a Clear Day You Can See Forever*. However, 'Minnelli' may not think that any more; *and* the film goes into a world where belief in the actuality of the possibility of such 'reliving' has some currency; *and* there is the generic context (the numbers, set in the past, as utopian escapes from the present), the star context (Barbra Streisand as the embodiment of will-power, making things happen)).

Textual analysis orchestrates these four elements in a *process* of understanding and interpretation. It produces knowledge, but knowledge that is neither absolute (it is from a perspective), nor final (it is always a process that is going on), nor certain. But in these regards, it is no different from any other form of knowledge.

I'd like to tack on here a point that does not seem to fit anywhere else. Throughout the above I have used the term 'meaning', to refer to what we are after, and only added occasionally 'and affect'. This was to save time and space. However, I think it is important to retain some word like 'affect', to remind us that what we are concerned with in textual analysis is not purely cognitive meaning, but also emotional meaning. I do not mean to suggest that Media Studies return to the throbbing declarations of certain forms of criticism, or to deny altogether the 'intellectual' potentialities of the media, but rather to say that the media is inextricably involved in phatic, sensuous, sentimental, erotic and experiential signification, and, since it is, this too must be understood and analysed.

Originally published in Christine Gledhill (ed.), *Film + Media Studies in Higher Education*, London: BFI, 1981, pp. 145–151.

48 THE SPACE OF HAPPINESS IN THE MUSICAL (1998)

Musicals are discourses of happiness. A narrative sets up problems or tensions to which the numbers offer solutions or, at any rate, respite: the numbers constitute definitions of happiness.[1] These happinesses can readily be categorised – love, yearning, fun and so on – but such terms do not catch the forms of the feelings of happiness, constructed from the rhythms, colours, shapes, movements and harmonies of music, body movement and film itself. Such feelings may touch on constants of human experience but they are also culturally and historically specific. The rise and decline of the musical may itself be taken as an indication of changing conceptions of happiness in Western culture. Such conceptions, and the actual feeling of them, are not socially innocent. Some modes of feeling may, at a minimum, be a privilege of some social groups, and may even express the values and sense of identity of members of those groups. One example of this, which I want to focus on here, is the motif of expansion in the musical, the way a number develops outwards from its moment in the narrative, opening up spatially and temporally. This feeling of expansion is utterly blissful; it is also the feeling form of geographical expansion, of male going out into the world, of imperialism and ecological depredation.

---

1. There are exceptions to this, numbers that do not express happiness in some form, but these are rarer than one might think. Even a 'serious' musical like *West Side Story* has really only one number ('A Boy Like That') that is not in fact about happiness (and that is swiftly eclipsed into a duet with 'I Have a Love') – even 'The Rumble', though it ends in death, is about the exhilaration of violence. This is an unusual pleasure for the musical to deal with, but it is still a form of pleasure. Much more aberrant in a musical – and never major numbers – are songs with very little pleasurable content, such as 'You've Got to be Taught' in *South Pacific* (about racism as indoctrination) and 'Is This What Feeling Gets?' in *The Wiz* (about the pain of learning to feel). Even these, by virtue of being sung in a musical, probably have a high element of happiness in their narrative function: the fierceness of 'You've Got to Be Taught' gives a pleasurable release to the character's anger, while 'Is This What Feeling Gets?' is also a soaring moment of revelation and self-knowledge. There are other examples, but they take some digging out – virtually all numbers in musicals are about happiness in one form or another.

THE PERSISTENCE OF TEXTUAL ANALYSIS

The 'Prehistoric Man' sequence from *On the Town* (1949) Top left ①: [back row] Ozzie (Jules Munshin) and Claire (Anne Miller); [front row] Gabey (Gene Kelly), Chip (Frank Sinatra) and Hildy (Betty Garrett).

437

In this article I will expand on this argument, by focusing on a single number, looking first at how music, dance and film interact to create an exhilarating sense of expansion, before considering the way this relates to both gender and imperialism in the number. My example is 'Prehistoric Man' from *On the Town* (MGM 1949), directed and choreographed by Stanley Donen and Gene Kelly.[2] The number is a classic one from a classic film from the classic period of the musical. It is a superb example of the co-ordination of music, body movement, camerawork and editing, making already wonderfully skilled, energetic and joyous dancing seem even more dynamic to the point that space expands to hold or express the energy.

THE NOTION OF THE PRIMITIVE

Before turning to this, we need briefly to consider the notion of the primitive that the number deploys. The lyrics and initial setting (a dinosaur skeleton, the 'pithecanthropus erectus') signal the prehistoric, but, as indicated in the following sections, the number moves to the primitive, most explicitly through museum artefacts but also in dance and moments of instrumentation. Notions of the prehistoric refers to forms of natural, including anthropoid, existence, whereas the primitive, at any rate in this context, refers to forms of human but 'uncivilised' existence (a judgement performed on other societies by those that consider themselves paradigmatic of civilisation).[3] Moreover in 'Prehistoric Man', primitivism is located not only in non-Western cultures but also in the Native and African peoples of the USA. The primitive is a negative white colonialist construct, but it is not simply that. Paradoxically perhaps, the primitive was also a badge of aesthetic and even political modernism. This can be found in non-white as well as white art, notably within the Harlem Renaissance and figures such as Duke Ellington and Katherine Dunham. In this context, the primitive could be seen as a critique of modernity, of the soullessness of industrialisation, of the repressive anti-body ideology of bourgeois (and white) society, of the emptiness of capitalism as an organising principle for society. Thus, if celebration of the primitive does indeed demean those it designates as primitive, it may also simultaneously envy or desire them.[4]

---

2. Betty Garrett said that Ann Miller did contribute her own steps to the number and that Kelly choreographed it but 'in the Ann Miller style' (Jerome Delamater, *Dance in the American Musical*, Ann Arbor MI: UMI Research Press, 1981, p. 200).
3. Cf. Marianna Torgovnick, *Gone Primitive: Savage Intellects, Modern Lives*, Chicago: University of Chicago Press, 1990; Susan Hiller (ed.), *The Myth of Primitivism: Perspectives on Art*, London: Routledge, 1991.
4. Editorial note: In a later version of this essay, Richard Dyer adds the line 'and may also be turned back upon the designators in the form of critique.' See Richard Dyer, *In the Space of a Song: The Uses of Song in Film*, London and New York: Routledge, 2012, p. 106.

NARRATIVE FUNCTION

In *On the Town*, three sailors, Gene Kelly (Gabey), Frank Sinatra (Chip) and Jules Munshin (Ozzie), have a day on shore leave in New York. They begin by seeing the sights, then start looking for girls, enlisting the help of taxi driver Betty Garrett (Hildy), who falls for Chip/Sinatra. On a visit to the Natural History Museum, they meet Ann Miller (Claire). When she sees Ozzie/Munshin standing next to an effigy of a 'pithecanthropus erectus', she screams but then takes out her camera to snap him and the effigy together, because, she explains, they look exactly alike. She then goes on to explain to the whole group that she much prefers men like Ozzie/Munshin, for 'there are all too few modern males who can measure up to the prehistoric', leading into 'Prehistoric Man'.

The number functions first to express Claire/Miller's personality and desires. At the same time, it achieves a number of utopian escape functions. The contextually immediate narrative drive is the search for Gabey/Kelly's dream girl, 'Miss Turnstiles' (Vera-Ellen); this number is a pleasurable distraction from the frustrations of the search. More broadly, the narrative is about the boys' search for girls: this number celebrates a reciprocal female eagerness and the heterosexual delight that ensues. A lightly expressed motif in the film is the relation between the group and the individuals that compose it, and especially the threat posed to the male group by individual members developing heterosexual interests: here the number welds everyone temporarily into a cohesive, exhilarating group and on the basis of the expression of heterosexual desire. Finally, the number is set in a museum, a place of quiet and stillness: the number, in its noise and dash, joyously breaks free from this epitome of stuffiness; what's more, it does so without apparently disrupting the museum or getting the group into trouble.

MUSIC

The song's basic structure is the standard AABA of popular show tunes, but with some degree of looseness. The last A expands the melodic line and brings it to a close on an exultant high. This A is, however, only used twice; for much of the number, the melody is not resolved, and this contributes to the tremendous sense of momentum, an onward rush seeking resolution. This is aided by the tempo, a lively 4:4 throughout, which picks up sudden and terrific speed when the band comes back in after a longish drumming interlude. Ann Miller's belting delivery is accompanied by a dance band, initially quite unobtrusive with lightly jazzy woodwind embellishments but gradually becoming more raucously intrusive. The instrumentation takes on big band sounds, now 'elephant' calls à la Ellington, now brassy blare à la Basie, especially in the final, melody-only sections of the number. All this non-diegetic sound is supplemented diegetically by, on the one hand, Ann Miller's taps, rhythmically and musically interrelated with the orchestration, and, on the other, hollers, grunts, Tarzan yells and 'Indian' calls as well as the instruments in the museum's display that the group pick up: mainly drums, but also for Miller a brief go at 'Oriental' pipes, drums and gong ⑦.[5]

We may take it that in some sense the music constructs the feelings of the characters for us. This is a general rule of Hollywood music and even more in the musical, but here reinforced by the interaction of diegetic and non-diegetic music. The handling of melodic structure, the quickening tempo and the increasingly improvisational instrumentation make this feeling one of drive, energy and abandon – but abandon within the limits of a still coherent musical structure. The music also contributes to the construction of the feeling of release embodied lyrically in the notion of the primitive. This relates to notions of letting go of the restrictions of civilised life – rhythmically regular, melodically rounded off – with the aid of the instrumental and vocal sounds of 'primitive' cultures (grunts, drums, etc.). The latter include African-American music. 'Prehistoric Man' is the jazziest part of the score of *On the Town*. Lyrically, the song rejects jazz – prehistoric man was blessed because he 'didn't have bebop' – but musically it gives itself up to it, above all in the ever mounting band improvisation, but also in the Ellington and Basie references. In context, and perhaps still potentially in 'Prehistoric Man', such jazz is dangerous and disruptive (and was a focus of moral panic comparable to that greeting rock 'n' roll and punk in later generations). However, this 'Cotton Club' primitivism was already a fairly safe frisson by the end of the thirties, and a certain kind of jamming had become routine for white session musicians by the late forties. In other words, musically 'Prehistoric Man' elaborates the idea of primitive abandon as something recoverable, by whites, without threat to their investment in (rhythmic and melodic) orderliness: in short, you can have abandon without abandoning anything.

DANCE

There are three kinds of dance in the number.[6] The first is the danced walk widely used in musicals, familiar from vaudeville routines in movies and used as the foundation for the number 'Main Street' later in *On the Town*. There, in a number about the simple delights of strolling in an American heartland – the main street of a small town – this style's 'Americanness' is made explicit: dancing that can be done by anyone, a mere introduction of rhythm and bounce into walking, democratic and ordinary, cheerful

---

5. Numbers refer to frame enlargements above.
6. Plus one or two other movements, such as the jokey swaying on the words 'Bebop! Bebop!', Munshin's equally jokey bump and grind with the prehistoric man and some standard, high energy, chorus framing of the principal dancer towards the end.

and unstrenuously energetic. Though there must be examples of non-white US dancers dancing in this style, its associations are overwhelmingly middle-American, that is, white. For all the importance of the primitive in the number, it is also important that the group get choreographically into the dancing through so indelibly all-American a style – this is a number about white Americans indulging in 'the primitive' rather than non-white cultures taking over white Americans on their own non-white terms. The second form of dance is a range of movements referring to the idea of the primitive: ape-like gambolling, 'Hawaiian' swaying, 'Native American' and 'African' stomping, slinky 'Arab' movements ⑦ and two forms of African-American references, the jitterbug ⑥ and hand shaking suggestive of 'holy roller' Black Christianity ①. These are all larkily adopted, speedy and witty improvisations that always signal the fact that the dancers are not themselves primitives.

The third, and most important kind of dance is tap. Miller uses taps that are clean and hard (no shuffles, brushes, scuffs, etc.) and very fast (in the forties, she held the record for the number of taps per minute). The combination was referred to as a 'machine gun' style.[7] She uses more ball taps than any other, some heel and almost no toe. This keeps her high, but not as light and high as, say, up-on-the-toes Bill Robinson, and it produces the strong, staccato sound. All of this, combined with her trademark twirling-while-tapping, billowing skirt and big, happy smile, creates a splendid sense of drive, energy and enthusiasm, less refined than Robinson or Fred Astaire, less virtuoso than Eleanor Powell, less easy-does-it than Gene Kelly, less athletic than the Nicholas Brothers. In one test of her speed (in 1950), Miller was shown to be able to outpace with taps the fingers of a champion typist on a keyboard.[8] The contest is an apt one. In African-American and minstrel tradition, tap was improvisatory and expressive,[9] but in much of white vaudeville it could be aligned to the latter's investment in performance as feat or skill, and in particular in the notion of human activity as motor or machine like.[10] Tap in this form – and especially 'machine gun' tap – is thus allied with the modern and industrial, not with the primitive. Yet the number centres on Miller and her character's lust for the latter. Particularly intriguing are the sections of the number where the 'primitive' drumming by the others is played off against Miller's tapping. This could be taken as a delightful utopian reconciliation of modernity and the primitive, or else as asserting the mastery of the modern (in the foregrounded machine gun taps of the dancer who leads the number) in the context of

---

7. Rusty E. Frank, *Tap! The Greatest Tap Dance Stars and Their Stories 1900-1950*, New York: Da Capo, 1990, pp. 241-249.
8. Ibid., p. 246.
9. Cf. Marshall Stearns and Jean Stearns, *Jazz Dance: The Story of American Vernacular Dance*, New York: Macmillan, 1968; Jerry Ames and Jim Siegelman, *The Book of Tap*, New York: David McKay, 1977.
10. Cf. Albert F. McLean, *American Vaudeville as Ritual*, Lexington KY: University of Kentucky Press, 1965.

THE RICHARD DYER READER

an indulgence in a primitivism of which the dancer is nonetheless not actually a part. Either way, the play of modernity and primitivism, in the sound of the dance itself, is at the heart of the number.

SPACE

The space occupied by the number is two adjacent rooms in the Natural History Museum, one (the prehistory room) containing dinosaur skeletons and the effigy of the prehistoric man, the other (the anthropology room)[11] a range of artefacts. The latter include a totem pole, a reproduction of the Lascaux cave paintings, a display case of African statuettes, a human-sized African idol in a coloured straw 'temple' ⑧ and displays of African or Native American drums, spears and skins and Arab musical instruments. This is a nature museum and the song is about 'prehistoric' man, yet the anthropology room provides, in exact contradiction, cultural and historical, even contemporaneous artefacts. Such casting of contemporary non-Western cultures into the mould of the primitive, which can then be elided with the prehistoric, was entirely conventionalised in museum display until really very recently. The number capitalises on this, with the display providing motifs for the number. The group pick up and play drums and musical instruments, dress up in costumes and use clubs and spears as part of the routine, and Miller dances to and around the African idol ⑧. The artefacts also seem to suggest the cod dance movements taken up by the group and detailed above. It is in part through the appropriation of the display's construction of the primitive that the number develops its élan, realising Miller's sung utopia of the prehistoric/primitive.

The anthropology room also provides space. Both rooms give on to each other, with no doorways or marked entrances. In the course of the number, the group moves from the prehistory to the anthropology room and then back. However, we don't see the anthropology room until the group moves into it, and there is never an establishing shot of it. We glimpse it behind Miller and Munshin, when she moves him away from the group during the second verse, but it is only with the lateral tracking shot (4–5) of the whole group stepping into the anthropology room that we begin to have any fuller sense of it, and we never see it in more than a long shot in which the performers dominate the frame. The anthropology room is then the glimpsed space that can be expanded into, the promised land for the dancing.

The movement into that space and how that space is handled cinematically construct the elation of expansion. In the broadest terms, the film moves from a static mid-shot grouping to dancing that travels throughout two large (museum exhibition

---

11. These are my designations.

THE PERSISTENCE OF TEXTUAL ANALYSIS

room) spaces. The need to dance, to give bodily form to the excitement of desire, finds, miraculously, in a museum of all places, the space it needs. This is underscored by the use of moving camera and editing.

There is a fair amount of unobtrusive small camera movements reframing the movement of the group and especially Miller. There are also more spectacular camera movements, notably a number of lateral tracking shots:

- right to left with Miller and Munshin, marking a return of the couple to the group;
- left to right with the whole group, marking the whole transition from the prehistory to the anthropology room (④–⑤);
- right to left with Miller, marking the start of the return to the prehistory room;
- immediately following this, right to left with Miller and the rest, marking the arrival back in the prehistory room.

Much the longest and most (probably literally) remarkable of these is the second: it is so much longer than any previous camera movement, it takes us into a space we have only barely glimpsed, it accompanies the first dancing in the sequence. Just as this dancing is an enthusiastic stride, looking as if it knows exactly where it's going, so the unimpeded lateral track conveys a sure-footed, unimpeded velocity. As in a Busby Berkeley number, it opens up from the 'stage' of the prehistory room to another room that a theatre spectator could never see, but within the framework of a 'real space', a museum: in other words, the magic of cinema realised in a putatively everyday life space. The sense of magic is heightened by the camera gliding past a museum display case ⑤, not actually passing through a wall, but perhaps giving the sensation of doing so.

The shot's élan is further enhanced by the way it is formally kicked off. At the end of the immediately preceding shot, Miller throws her head and shoulders back as she moves away from the effigy, the slight backward movement emphasising the sense of propelling the rest of the body forward ②; the film cuts immediately to a little further back, with Miller continuing her forward movement ③. This is a match on action, that is at once therefore unobtrusive but also dynamic – the film's small spatial jump reinforces Miller's thrust forward. The shot continues with Miller dance-walking towards screen left and then as it were leaning slightly back towards the left of the frame while starting to move forward; at the same time, the rest of the group walk-dance in from the left of the frame behind her, moving in the same direction as her. It is only as she starts to move left to right, backed by them, that the camera starts its long lateral left to right track. Miller's two backward movements emphasising forward propulsion, the reinforcement of the sense of direction from the group as a whole, her leaning back into the frame signalling the frame itself, making palpable the camera's fast, smooth movement in concert with the dancers – all of this is the most breathtaking co-ordination of three types of movement (performer, camera and editing) to create a glorious sense of the surge of expansion.

Less spectacularly, the first track listed above starts its right to left movement only at the point that Miller links an arm with Munshin and steps off right to left with him, while the third is, as it were, cued by an orchestral blare and Miller going into a twirling tapping right to left travelling movement. This track comes to a halt when Miller puts her foot down, throws her arms in the air and looks at the camera, but there is then an immediate cut to a slightly different angle, Miller turning her head towards the camera and going straight on with more twirling tapping and the rest of the group coming in from the right as the camera tracks with them. The co-ordination of movements is again consummate. Miller's momentary taking up of a position before the cut sutures it but also emphasises movement by the very fact of momentarily interrupting it; her turning of the head immediately after the cut underscores the dynamic shift of position. Yet, pleasurable as these returns to the starting point are, they are less sweepingly exhilarating than the move out into new (anthropological) territory.

The cut described above that leads into the latter also has the effect of opening up space for Miller to move into, from the relative confinement of the space around the effigy to a bigger space in which to step out. This kind of cut, both dynamic but also another way of suggesting the joy of expanding out into space, is used elsewhere in the number. Miller moves away right from the effigy and the film cuts to a shot further back. Miller dances with the group, then taps towards the camera and at a moment when she has both arms raised to the level of her head, there is a cut of breathtaking precision to a point further back, at which point she once again throws her head and shoulders back while moving forward into the newly re-opened space. The spatial dislocation of the editing recreates the dynamic of expansion into space but entirely within classically coherent co-ordinates.

Before the cut between tracking shots just discussed, Miller gives a 'come here!' whistle in the direction of the off-screen group; when they join her, it is from a space we have been reminded of by the whistle. The latter is not really necessary – it is an additional suturing of the cut that constitutes a rather emphatic assertion of coherent space. However, there is in the middle of the number a departure from such spatial coherence. When the group starts to use the anthropological artefacts of the museum, spatial coherence is carefully signalled. The group is dancing round Miller; Munshin leaves them going off right and the film cuts to his arriving at the drum display that was in the background of the previous shot. This is entirely classical. However, a little later, after Miller's first real solo tap display, there are a series of cuts to the group (in various combinations) dressed up in and/or playing with anthropological artefacts (6–7). Quite apart from the rapidity of the cuts (making getting into and out of costume temporally impossible), it ceases to be clear where the space of each shot is in relation to those before and after it. Particularly noticeable is the cut between Kelly, Sinatra and Garrett in a Native American boat and Munshin dancing with the effigy; at the end of the first of these, Garrett points off to the *right*, presumably at Munshin; but we know where the effigy is, to the *left* of the anthropological room as it has been presented to us. This may also be the most delirious shot in the number, positively polymorphous perverse, that is, regressively primitive: Munshin is dancing with his effigy (playing with himself), dressed in a grass skirt, which is androgynous, potentially redolent of homo, hetero and trans sexuality, and doing the rude Black dance, the jitterbug ⑥. It's unlikely that one notices this regressive incoherence in any troubling way, but it does suggest a momentary abandon of cultural and spatial sense, a kind of surrendering to an inchoate, in this sense truly primitive state. This occurs at the point of maximum visual reference to and mixing up of non-white cultures. Such a pleasurable abandon of Western spatial reason cannot be maintained. At the end of the sequence, we have a series of longish takes centred on Miller and then the two lateral tracks taking us back to the prehistory room, the cut between which is, as we have seen, insistently sutured visually and aurally.

CULTURAL CONSTRUCTION: GENDER

'Prehistoric Man' is a woman-centred number not only in the evident sense that a woman, Ann Miller, initiates it in the narrative and sings it solo, such that the number may be said to express her feelings and the way she communicates this to the others and engages them in it. She also leads the dance, initiating the very act of dancing as well as leading, first, Munshin to the rest of the group, and then the whole group from one room to the other and back. The choreography foregrounds her, both in the sense that she has all the elaborated dance movement and in that the others group round her as she dances. Most importantly, the cinematic opening up of space detailed above always coincides with a decisive, forward movement by Miller. The camera only moves for the first time left to right when Miller links an arm with Munshin and steps forward with him, and it only starts its long left-to-right track from one room to the other when she leans back into the frame as she thrusts herself forward ④. Similarly, most cuts (apart from the dressing-up montage in the middle of the number) are on her action – as she moves away from or thrusts off from ((②–③) the effigy, as she takes up a split-second position before moving on back into the prehistory room, as she thrusts off from the group. In short, the number constructs her as the focus and source of its dazzling energy and oomph.

One might argue that all of this is put to the service of showcasing Miller as sexual spectacle. Centring on Miller is centring on a woman showing her legs, with a button front skirt that is progressively unbuttoned (between cuts) so that by the end it is parted up to her crotch. Some of her movements are slinky and suggestive with echoes of the bump and grind of burlesque. However, the number is above all concerned with expressing her (or Clare's) desire – if she is 'showing', it is because she takes a libidinal pleasure in attracting the male. Given the force of her dancing and the sense that it is she (Ann Miller)[12] that is making up the steps, improvising and inspiring improvisation, it would seem on balance that the number (albeit directed and master choreographed by men) is at least as much about female desire as about female desirability – and indeed, delightfully, that it constructs the latter as a response to active female desire: a woman is heterosexually desirable because she fiercely desires.

The other woman in the number, Betty Garrett, does exactly what the men in the group do. She is not differentiated from them as they circle and showcase Miller, even having the same expression of rapt admiration of her dancing. Group cohesiveness is thus embodied in the shared inspiration of one group member's libido.

One would be hard put to it to assign gender to the dance movements. Though women are often marginalised in accounts of tap, no claim has ever been made that it is an inevitably masculine tradition, or that there are masculine and feminine forms of tap, or that Miller dances in a notably feminine, or come to that masculine way. Similarly, the dance movements of the rest of the group cannot really be gendered. In short, the whole thing is a distinctly heterosexual utopia yet, unusually, one not founded on insistent difference or power imbalance[13] and fully at ease with a woman taking centre stage.

CULTURAL CONSTRUCTION: IMPERIALISM

The movement from the space of prehistory to anthropology is one from an irretrievably past space to one demonstrably attainable: anthropological museum artefacts are signs of people having been to the 'primitive' world and brought back trophies. Though I don't want to reduce anthropology to imperialism, it did develop and exist in relation to it. The readiness with which this white group takes up, plays with and makes fun of these artefacts is of a piece with the insensitivity that has led to them being transported from their origins and placed in a museum in the first place. The very mixing up of them, in a montage that puts them all on a primitive par,[14] suggests the processes of the popular colonial imagination, in which colonised peoples become a vast, undifferentiated other.

---

12. See note 2 above.
13. Cf. Richard Dyer, '"I Seem to Find the Happiness I Seek": Heterosexuality and Dance in the Musical', in Helen Thomas (ed.), *Dance, Gender and Culture*, London: Macmillan, 1993, pp. 49-65.
14. As opposed to the painstaking distinctions canvassed by anthropology proper.

In this context, the exciting treatment of space, the exhilaration of expansion, reproduces the feeling form of imperialism. In a variation on the surging cowboy movement and pounding music of the Western, or the vast panoramas and searing excitement of the jungle adventure film, 'Prehistoric Man' constructs for us the feeling of colonial expansion, conveying a sense of its appeal and dynamic allure. That this is at some remove from the explicit imperialism of the Western or jungle adventure, and that it centres on a woman, does not diminish its affinity with the spirit of white masculine imperialism.

This does not mean that we should regard the pleasures of outward and expansive movement as inherently morally wrong. It is gorgeous to throw one's arms in the air, to rush out into the space around one – such feelings do not spring from an intrinsic desire to conquer and destroy. However, we need to ask, who has the right to such feelings and who, and what, pays the price for them? In 'Prehistoric Man', the right is given to white women as well as men, but the price is still paid by non-white peoples. Moreover, though the number does not reference this, the price is also paid by the environment: the thrill of human expansion can be the depredation of nature. A number like 'Prehistoric Man', the epitome of the Hollywood musical's affirmative energy and optimism, is an embodiment of the terrible philosophical dilemma of reconciling increases in human happiness with the moral and practical limitations on it.

Originally published in *Aura: Film Studies Journal* IV:1 (1998), pp. 31–45. Courtesy of Aura Publishing.
The original version of the essay includes an appendix featuring the song's lyrics and thirty screenshots. Here, we have only included the eight screenshots that are featured in the slightly altered reprint, published in Richard Dyer, *In the Space of a Song: The Uses of Song in Film*, London and New York: Routledge, 2012, pp. 101–113.

49 SOUND IN *SEVEN* (1999)

'I saw *Seven* recently at a cinema in the West End of London, and I was extremely disappointed to discover that this outstanding film was accompanied by sound of appalling quality. [...] I realise that the mood of the film is particularly dark, moody and that clarity of image and sound was not the director's main aim. However, the extent to which the sound was obscured goes beyond the concept of artistic licence.'

(Letter in *Screen International*[1] from Hugo Ruiz)

"Would you please be quiet?"

(Somerset to Mills at the Gluttony murder scene)

You hear *Seven* before you see it. Briefly over darkness there is the sound of traffic, of horns sounding at different registers, and of television talk programmes, probably news, the sound quality recognisable even while you cannot quite make out what is being said. Then the image fades up on Somerset in his kitchen. Similarly, the film ends with a fade to black with the sound of helicopter blades continuing over.

Such sound montage runs throughout the film, a soft cacophony of cars (motors, horns, brakes), voices (people in the next apartment or on the street, television, domestic and police radio, walkie talkies), footsteps down the hall, snatches of music (radio, records, muzak), dogs, water pipes (knocks, hiss), squeaks (kids, rats, floorboards), bottles falling over, planes, helicopters, subway trains and all the other aural detritus of city life, and rain. This is all elaborately crafted, albeit based upon actually occurring sounds. It is not really naturalism. On the one hand, just pointing a microphone out of the window would not produce such an effect. On the other, we do not in life choose to hear all this sound around us, we do not attend to the patina of noise around us,

---

1. *Screen International*, 1041 (9 January 1996), p. 8.

Somerset's metronome.

and most films minimise it down to a vague 'ambient sound'. In *Seven*, it is not minimised, it is insistently and remorselessly present.

There is no decipherable speech during the first forty seconds of the film, showing Somerset getting ready to go out, just sounds. Inside, any sound Somerset makes is clearly related to what we see him doing (putting a mug in the sink, pouring leftover coffee down the drain, walking across the kitchen, pulling his tie up to his neck) and is also very quiet: the sounds he makes are deliberate and minimal. Outside the apartment, the dominant sound over the cars and voices is a siren. Given that *Seven* is a thriller, we are most likely to assign the siren to a police car and it might even be the one going to the scene of the crime to which the film cuts almost immediately. However, as with Somerset's quiet precision, the siren also relates to the wider sense of sound in the film.

Just before the opening credits, after he and Mills have met at a domestic murder scene, Somerset lies in bed. There is as ever the muffled racket of the city, notably of voices raised in conflict. Somerset puts out his hand and sets a metronome going, and the clamour outside becomes louder and more echoey as he none the less falls asleep. The metronome is an oasis of controlled, orderly sound that enables him to sleep. Later, when the police captain brings Somerset news of the second murder, he (Somerset) stops typing on the word 'Greed', a cessation of deliberate noise (emphasised by an overhead shot of his hands freezing at the keyboard) that underscores his pricking his ears up. He then asks a man scraping his name off the door to stop doing so, putting an end to a tiny but needlessly intrusive noise. He cannot halt the sounds of the city and the rain, but he can take responsibility for the sounds he is able to control.

Throughout the film, Somerset's speech is also spare, quiet, to the point. This is in part a function of Morgan Freeman's expressively minimalist acting style – much of Somerset's script was cut because of it,[2] just as Mills's was elaborated for Brad Pitt. The difference in acting style also articulates the symbolically significant difference between the characters. Where Somerset speaks when he needs to or remains silent, and only makes quiet, purposeful or unavoidable sounds, Mills is constant hubbub. There is a scene of him getting up immediately after the credits; after he's put on a tie, he stubs his foot against a metal object on the floor, exactly the unnecessary, careless noise absent from the scene with Somerset minutes before. At the Gluttony scene, he chatters, talks about another case, jokes, says "Woops!" when he sees the victim's feet tied together, until Somerset asks him to be quiet and eventually to leave. Subsequently in the car, he keeps clicking at a ball-point pen. And so on throughout the film. If Somerset seeks to keep the noise of the world at bay and to add only what is strictly necessary to it, Mills adds to it unthinkingly all the time.

Mills's early morning scene, like Somerset's, fades up on the sound of a police siren. Throughout the film, sound reminds us that crime and violence are ever present: police cars, television reports, squabbling and screams, children watching a cavorting cartoon in the apartment through which Mills chases Doe. It is the habitual background of life. At the pre-credits murder scene, the duty cop reports, "The neighbours heard them screaming at each other like for two hours, there was nothing new, then they heard the gun go off, both barrels." The sound of aggression, conflict, hysteria, is something we have learnt to become indifferent to, because, as Doe says of sin, "it's common, it's trivial, [and so] we tolerate it morning, noon and night," or at any rate until it's too late.

When Somerset sets his metronome going, the camera tracks slowly in on it to close-up. There is a crash of thunder, which eclipses the sound of the metronome and then segues into a synthesised crash and the beginnings of the rhythms of the credit sequence soundtrack. This can be described in musical terms: a repeated, rather throbbing bass figure, later overlaid with a faster, blurred, more metallic beat in a higher register; the piece organised as a fugue brought to a close with a single, sung phrase and a loud, very reverberative single deep drum beat; the whole recorded with a strong echo quality. However, the sounds themselves combine those recognisably produced by what are conventionally deemed musical instruments – drum, cymbal, bass, synthesiser, voice – with others that would not be – the squeak of plastic, scratching with chalk, a match's flair, doors opening on creaky hinges and sounds familiar from space movies ('weird' electronic descending notes, the burps and beeps of interplanetary

---

2. Fincher: 'We trimmed stuff for Morgan. Morgan is one of those guys who'll come up to you and go, "I can just look at the guy and do all this, you can cut this stuff."' (Judy Sloane, 'Killer Movie', *Film Review*, February 1996, p. 34).

radio). In other words, music and 'noise' are fused, indistinguishable one from the other. The remorseless hubbub of the city bleeds into the music of the credits.

This is entirely appropriate. First, the music accompanies close-up shots of John Doe about his work, not killing but preparing and recording – the credit sequence takes us into the mind of the killer. This is the special appropriateness of the sung phrase, 'You get me closer to God', cried out of the tumult of sound, salvation plucked from sin. Secondly, the track is performed by Nine Inch Nails, making reference to the track 'Closer' on the album *The Downward Spiral* (1994). In fact it bears little specific relation to the track, beyond taking the sung phrase from it; the significance is much more the recognisable sound of a group notoriously fascinated with Charles Manson and the controversial fact that the album was recorded in his house. Thus this soundtrack blurs the distinction between music and noise, and relates both to sin.

The closing credits sequence, David Bowie's 'The Hearts [sic] Filthy Lesson', works to some extent in a similar way, aurally and allusively. Though instrumentally more conventional, there is an overlay of industrial sounds. It is taken from the album *1. Outside* (1995), subtitle *The Nathan Adler Diaries: a hyper cycle*. The album booklet presents parts of said diary, written by a detective specialising in 'art-murder', real killings (as of the horrifically described 'art-ritual murder of Baby Grace Blue. […] It was definitely murder – but was it art?') and 'concept-muggings', all placed historically in relation to such figures as 'the Viennese castrationists', Guy Bourdin and Damien Hirst, to which we might add Helmut Newton and *The Eyes of Laura Mars*, Bret Easton Ellis's *American Psycho* and Doe himself as performance artist. 'The Hearts Filthy Lesson' is signalled on the album 'To be sung by Detective Nathan Adler'; *Alfred* Adler was a psychoanalytic theorist most popularly understood to deal with the violence of the human psyche; the images accompanying the track in *Seven* resemble Doe's obsessive collages but also the chalk writing on the board in the police headquarters – in other words, authority and the law are folded into the song's bleak vision alongside cruelty and vice.

'Closer' and 'The Hearts Filthy Lesson' take us into the heart of darkness, and this is also true of the music score by Howard Shore (whose previous credits include killer movies such as *The Silence of the Lambs* 1991, *Single White Female* 1992 and *Sliver* 1993). It is characterised by: a use of what are widely perceived as dark musical elements (low registers; brass, basses, cellos), sometimes set off by very high, 'sinister' string notes; for much of the time de-emphasised rhythm, the music insinuating and spreading its darkness; strongly marked rhythms for action sequences (the descent on Victor's apartment, Mills's pursuit of Doe) and the climax; and tonal progression that endlessly promises melody and completion but never really delivers it, drawing one endlessly onwards through the darkness. In its first introduction, outside the Gluttony murder scene, it emerges imperceptibly within the sound of heavy rain and a truck passing – if, unlike Nine Inch Nails, it is more traditionally 'musical', its introduction none the less connects it to the city's sodden clamour. Once inside the house, the music eclipses outside sound, with only the sounds of human movement (footfalls, clothes rustling) and speech heard against it. The deeper the detectives enter into the house, the more menacing and dominant the music score seems to become.

Throughout the film, the introduction of the score is triggered by the encounter with Doe and his work: Mills standing over Greed written in blood on the floor; Somerset turning to look at the plastic strips found in the Fat Boy's stomach that the chief leaves for him and paying a return visit to the victim's apartment; Mills and Somerset returning to Gould's apartment to look at a wrongly hung painting;[3] moving in on Victor's corpse; the investigation of Doe's and Pride's apartments; the ride to the last two bodies. Only the music for the entry to the sex club, site of the Lust murder, is not Shore's sombre brass and strings; this is heavy rock, reminiscent of Nine Inch Nails, but in fact by the film's sound designer Ren Klyce and Steve Boedekker. Hence it retains the associations of 'Closer', while also being unsurprisingly close to the film's relentless aural montage.

The score may be monotonal, but it is not monotonous. The repeated introduction of this restricted musical palette in relation to Doe's work establishes it as redolent of sin. Variations enable it to express aspects of sin such as energy, insinuation and intensity. The first is apparent in the action sequences.

For the descent on Victor's apartment the variations on Shore's dark colours include: driving and melodic spiralling for the cops leaving the briefing and the cars speeding out of the precinct garage; urgent, staccato chords for the arrival at the apartment block and the cops dressed like militia storming the stairs; mysterious and tense held chords for moving along the corridor to the apartment door, climaxing musically on a track in on the door; a crash for breaking and entering. The music is overlaid with the louder sounds of the police chief's echoing briefing, doors opening and slamming, feet clattering, cars hitting the ground and tyres screeching in the rush. Despite the differences in tempo, much the same music is being used for cops as is elsewhere used for the killer, with here the music subordinated to the noise. This is appropriate. The glee with which Victor is pursued is comparable with Doe's mania. As Somerset remarks of the cops, "They love this."

In another action sequence, when Mills chases Doe, the music provides a remorseless underlying pounding, sometimes eclipsed by the sound of shooting, rain and human movement. At two moments, when Mills first bursts outside onto a fire escape into the deluge and when he is felled to the ground and crawls through the water and rainfall, an unexpected falling phrase in the higher strings gives the sequence an astonishing sense of agony in the Christian sense, suffering of cosmic significance.

---

3. Identified as such by Gould's widow; behind it are the words 'Help me' written by Victor's hand.

The insinuation of sin is suggested musically throughout the film, where the music is not 'mickey-moused' in a one-to-one way to character, camera movement or editing, but rather seeps in, sometimes hidden in the ambient sound, spreading itself out alongside the image. There is a more symbolic effect of insinuation in the score when Mills cuddles up to Tracy in bed, the last time we see her in the film. The music is tender and intimate, yet with enough of the brooding, menacing qualities to hint at Tracy's destiny without drawing attention to it. Even when Mills is being most caring, in contact with an embodiment of goodness in the film, sin will not let the soundtrack alone.

Intensity is expressed in the final sequence, with the recognition of sin in Mills. This is one of the few sections of the film where the music is to a certain extent 'mickey-moused' (though the cheeriness of the term hardly does justice to the grimness of the effect). Throughout the final twenty minutes or so of the film, the music seems to be ever rising, the melodic line going higher, the harmonic progression approaching climactic resolution, getting louder. Yet it never really gets higher, does not resolve nor even really get much louder. As Christa Lykke Christensen at the University of Copenhagen said to me, the music seems like it's about to burst but never does. Then, when the van driver delivers the box, there is a very long, slow fade on a sustained note. There is no music as Somerset looks, opens, investigates the box. The music comes back with a deep, staccato, jabbing chord on an alarmingly swift pan to Somerset turning sharply to look at Mills and Doe in the distance; each subsequent cut (between Somerset, Mills with Doe, and the box) is accompanied by this chord, with an overlay of high, sinister sounds. This pattern, subtly varied and with interspersed passages of the slower, dark, spreading music of the rest of the film, continues for the remainder of the sequence, eventually getting louder, ending on long sustained, mounting notes as Mills shoots Doe, as he is drawn inexorably – or what the music makes feel is inexorably – into his sin. The music only ends with the slamming of the police car door on the psychologically and morally destroyed Mills.

There are in the diegetic music exceptions to the association of music with sin. Tracy and Somerset are characters who bond together and are not implicated in white male seriality; both play classic African-American music – Tracy has 'Trouble Man' by Marvin Gaye and 'Straight No Chaser' by Thelonious Monk on at the dinner party. Somerset is listening to 'Now's the Time' by Charlie Parker on the radio when she phones him. In the library scene, where Somerset investigates the literature on the deadly sins, the cops put on Bach's 'Air on a G String'. Though emanating from a portable radio, the sound quality has the clarity and amplitude of the film's own score. The film cuts between Somerset and Mills, pursuing their rather different sets of evidence, Somerset literature and theology, Mills photos of the crimes; yet the Bach carries over both. Only occasionally are ambient sounds heard over it – the cops laughing, Somerset's light footfalls, the television when Mills gives up for the night. The calm and rationality of Bach embrace them both, an oasis of literally and metaphorically uncontaminated sound that only draws attention to the unremitting sense of aural defilement in the rest of the film.

Extract from Richard Dyer, *Seven*, London: BFI, 1999, pp. 50–57.

50　THE TALENTED MR ROTA (2004)

In 1972 the Academy of Motion Picture Awards refused the nomination of Nino Rota for Best Original Music Oscar for *The Godfather*: he had incorporated music from an earlier film and therefore the score was not deemed original. To us now the decision seems astonishing – *The Godfather* score is widely recognised as one of the great soundtracks. Besides, the recycled music was just a single melody, the love theme that occurs two thirds of the way through, musically transformed from its appearance in *Fortunella* (1957), which in any case had been a huge flop in Italy and virtually unseen outside it; and moreover it was Rota's own music. Nonetheless, the Academy had a technical point: the love theme was not strictly speaking original to the film.

You could say that the most original things about Nino Rota's film music spring from his lack of originality. And that he is unoriginal in several ways. First, he endlessly recycled himself. *The Godfather Part II* (1974), for which he did get an Oscar, contains far more of the music from *The Godfather* than the latter does from *Fortunella*, plus new themes (for young Vito and Kay) taken from earlier stage and television works. The main theme from the Italian melodrama *The Mountain Woman* (1943) was reworked for the British middlebrow hit *The Glass Mountain* (1949) as well as serving as the first movement of Rota's *Symphony on a Love Song* (1947), whose second and third movements provided the music for Visconti's *The Leopard* (1963); this in turn contains a waltz already used by Rota in the neorealist *An American on Holiday* (1945) and the costume drama *Appassionatemente* (1954). Rota's whole output is crossed by these chains of recyclings, though when one considers the scale of that output (more than 150 film scores) it is surprising there are not more, that he in fact produced a continuous stream of fresh melodies.

Rota was also widely considered to be unoriginal in his basic musical style. Born in 1911, he could musically speaking have been born 40 years earlier. His work is untouched by concert music's move towards atonality or seldom even displays the lush late romanticism of Rózsa or Korngold which served Hollywood so well. His music was unfashionably direct, melodic, ironic and unassuming.

Then too, his music is full of references to other music – quotations, echoes, parodies, pastiches. The neorealist melodrama *Without Pity* (1948), about Italian women and African-American GIs, incorporates Black spirituals into the soundtrack; the storm

Nino Rota at the piano, circa 1972. (Keystone/Hulton Archive/Getty Images)

sequences for René Clément's *Barrage sur le Pacifique* (1957) draw on Stravinsky's *The Rite of Spring*; a folk song invented by Rota for the Mascagni biopic *Immortal Melodies* (1953) becomes the motif of longing for home running through *Rocco and His Brothers* (1960); one of the main themes of *La dolce vita* (1960) is shamelessly and appropriately based on 'Mack the Knife' from *The Threepenny Opera*, with just one note – brilliantly – changed.

This is endlessly inventive but derivative. So flexible is Rota, so responsive to genre and director, he is at times a chameleon, producing effective scores that could have been written by many others. The music for *Waterloo* (1970), for instance, was good enough to have Kubrick approach him to do the music for *Barry Lyndon* (1975), but you'd be hard put to recognise it instantly as 'Rota'.

He was especially adept at scoring for comedy, a gift probably best known outside Italy from the music for the sequence in *The Godfather Part II* where Clemenza takes the young Vito along to steal a carpet. Yet Rota composed for 40 comedies, the biggest single category in his oeuvre, working for such beloved post-war comics as Totò and Alberto Sordi. There seems to be a special affinity between Rota and Turinese comic Macario, a childlike, moonfaced figure reminiscent of Harry Langdon; here the sweetness of the music is in tune with Macario's guileless, good-natured, sentimental character. His *L'eroe della strada* (1948) also displays the rich potential of Rota's unoriginality. Macario's character, demobbed and unemployed, takes on whatever jobs turn up, each new direction wittily echoed by lightly parodied music. At one point he gets a job painting wall slogans for a political party; different people pass by and Macario nervously alters the slogan to fit what he takes to be their affiliation, each alteration accompanied by a squawky, perky version of, among others, the 'Internationale', 'Deutschland über Alles', a Sousa march or an operetta tune. No one does such quick, glancing comic commentary better.

It is just this flexibility, this ability to draw on a huge range of musical styles, that makes Rota such a great film composer. He also worked exceptionally hard: in addition to the film scores, he wrote 74 concert works and 28 works for theatre, opera, ballet and television, and had a full-time post as director of the Bari Conservatory of Music. He did his film work in a hurry, often on the train, usually without seeing the film or reading the script.

This means the music often has an unusually disengaged quality. Unlike the work of Max Steiner and others within the Hollywood studio system, Rota's music does not underline every detail, movement and gesture, but neither does it impose itself, seeming to lead the images, as with Prokofiev's music for *Alexander Nevsky* or Morricone's for *Once Upon a Time in the West*. Rota's music carries on alongside the story and characters, to often fascinating effect. In the lovely, sad comedy *A Dog's Life* (1950) a young couple, Franca and Carlo, go to visit the flat they are to live in when they marry; he chatters on eagerly about his work as a garage mechanic, but she looks round at the dirty, drab apartment, seeing her dull future. The scene is accompanied by an exquisite little waltz, all delicately spiralling strings, that seems anachronistic in relation to the setting and characters and is not specifically synchronised with their movements and exchanges. It appears to express something like the gap between Franca's aspirations and the dreary reality of her life, but it is not 'what Franca is thinking' nor is it there to get you to identify with her. Rather it recognises her feelings and sympathises, yet sees how flimsy and outdated are her aspirations.

The same disengagement works differently in René Clément's *Plein soleil* (1960), the first film adaptation of Patricia Highsmith's *The Talented Mr Ripley*. The film opens in Rome and then moves to the southern seaside village of Mongibello. For each location Rota wrote a cod-regional theme – a bit *dolce vita*-ish for Rome, all mandolins and swooping cadences for Mongibello – and these carry on cheerfully beside the cynical, deceitful and finally murderous goings-on, catching the amoral, amused tone of Highsmith's work that makes it so fascinating.

Such disengagement allows Rota to play fast and loose with where the music is coming from – that is, whether from inside the world of the film or outside it; from what the characters can hear or from what only we, the audience, hear. *The Godfather* opens with a trumpet blowsily playing a nostalgic waltz; this is the main theme of the film and it's in the background on and off throughout the trilogy. It also crops up in the music the characters hear, notably music they dance to. In *The Godfather* it is the waltz Don Corleone and his daughter Connie dance to at her wedding, with mandolins to the fore ensuring it retains its Sicilian feeling, reinforcing the film's concern with cultural continuity. It is also danced to at the party for young Anthony's First Communion at the start of *The Godfather Part II*. Here Michael and Kay are dancing to another tune while Kay gently reproaches him with still being mixed up in criminal activity despite his promises to the contrary; "I'm trying," he assures her, and as the camera tracks away the dance band gives way to the *Godfather* waltz, initially with the characteristic brushed cymbals and solo clarinet of end-of-the-evening arrangements, then with mandolins and strings seeping in.

The first two *Godfather* films are both in part about becoming American: how the old Mafia values can be reconciled with the new American way and how it is the latter that becomes corrupted by the former. The waltz expresses something of this; in the first film still the solid old world, in the second insidiously infiltrating mainstream American values. And it's such a lovely tune, its lilt lulling or entrancing, just like the sentimental appeal of Mafia notions of family and honour. The ability to create such complex and ironic effects and at the same time be emotionally touching, so we understand the feelings that draw people into terrible actions, is at the core of Coppola's best work. It is surely this which made him hold out for Rota for *The Godfather* against Rota's indifference and Paramount's preference for Henry Mancini.

Something technically similar happens near the beginning of Fellini's *Amarcord* (1973). A barber and his friends are discussing the bonfire celebrations to be held later that evening, with a bubbling, bustling woodwind tune accompanying them on the soundtrack. "What are you going to play tonight?" asks one of the friends. "A new tune I've composed," says the barber, who then takes out a clarinet and in perfect time with the soundtrack he can't hear starts to play Rota's jolly tune. *Amarcord*, a film that might seem just a series of warm, nostalgic vignettes, is full of such complexities, throwing into doubt any notion that we should treat it straightforwardly as someone's memories (despite the title, 'I remember'). And the way Rota's score crosses back and forth between on-screen and background music, often to the point where we're not sure which it is, is part of the film's dreamy complexity. A boy sneaks up on Gradisca, the local woman of his dreams, as she gazes oblivious at Gary Cooper on the screen of a deserted cinema; the music is themes we've already heard in the film yet played as if they are coming from the screen. Where is this music coming from? From Rota and Fellini, as composer and director? From Fellini as the film-maker 'remembering' this? From inside the boy's mind? From the cinema screen itself? As in all classic art movies, the paradoxes are never resolved, but seldom are they so enchanting or easygoing.

The Fellini-Rota partnership is, of course, one of film history's benchmark director-composer collaborations. Yet on paper they ought not to have been so well suited. Rota came from a well-to-do family in the northern capital of Milan and then lived in Rome from the age of 14; Fellini's father was a comfortably-off commercial representative in the provincial seaside town of Rimini. Rota had an artistically well-connected background and a classic high-cultural education; Fellini's cultural formation was the circus, cartoons and revue. Rota was apparently asexual and if anything discretely gay; Fellini was very publicly married (to Giulietta Masina), a notorious womaniser and, if the films are anything to go by, fascinated by homosexuality. Above all, Rota was steeped in and lived for music whereas Fellini had little developed interest in it – he went to concerts only out of friendship to hear Nino's premieres.

Yet theirs was a famously productive relationship over the course of 15 features and two shorts, ending only with Rota's death in 1979. Fellini pushed Rota. The score for *8½* (1963) is an astonishing set of variations on what might seem the unpropitious ground of circus music. For *Satyricon* (1969) Fellini had Rota invent a music out of electronics, African, Asian and distorted European instruments, and modes from Ancient Rome to produce a sound both dimly recognisable yet strange and opaque, just like the film itself. For *Casanova* (1976) Rota, at Fellini's request, took a movement from his preludes for piano and transformed it into a manic leitmotif that sounds at once utterly 18th and utterly 20th century, as well as composing an extraordinary and sinister homosexual mini-opera.

In return Rota gave Fellini's vision a delicate warmth and irony. Fellini's first film *Lights of Variety* (1951, co-directed with Alberto Lattuada and with music by Felice Lattuada) is raucous and cruel beside the treatment of similar material in *A Dog's Life*, and it is tempting to put much of the unpleasant taste of *The City of Women* (1980) down to Fellini goading Luis Bacalov into writing a Rota-like score that has everything of Nino except the wry heart. Nino often softens Federico. The other main musical theme of *La dolce vita* (the one not based on 'Mack the Knife'), for instance, is sparkling and threatening behind the credits. It goes through several variations including one much slower, with a telling shift in the stress of the melody and with clarinet and piano to the fore. The first time this occurs is when Marcello Mastroianni and his occasional lover, rich girl Anouk Aimée, chat with some prostitutes in the Piazza del Popolo; there is no reason in the dialogue or action for what has been a blowsy, jazzy tune to give way unobtrusively to this version of the theme, but it lends the sequence a wry sadness. The artistic temptations of *La dolce vita* are heartless cynicism and portentousness; here Rota alters the tone, offering a melancholy that does not take itself too seriously.

For all their (productive) differences, Rota and Fellini had two things in common. One was an interest in magic: Rota and his friend Vinci Verginelli amassed a huge collection of esoteric writings; Fellini came always to consult magicians before embarking on a project (famously abandoning one as a result); the elements of magic in his and Rota's work were seriously meant by both. They also shared a particular kind of outsider position. Fellini had nothing of the privileged or politically committed background of such peers as Rossellini, Visconti and Antonioni, but nor did he work straightforwardly in popular genre and star cinema. Rota, not taken seriously in the classical-music world, came to popular music and movies from the outside. Fellini was formed by popular culture, yet the kind of fame he had as a film-maker put him at a distance from it; Rota, playing Mozart at four and conducting his own oratorio at 12, nonetheless found in popular music the tunefulness, humour and sentiment that had become out of bounds in classical music. Both film-maker and composer responded to popular culture, recognising and feeling its appeal, and yet were not quite inside it, not unselfconsciously producing and consuming it.

This creates extraordinary effects in their work. In *La strada* (1954) the heroine Gelsomina (Masina) runs away from the brutish man to whom she has been sold; she sits by the road, not knowing what to do, when suddenly four clown-musicians appear, tootling the bustling, circusy music so identifiable as 'Rota-Fellini'. She follows them into a small town where a religious procession is taking place to the sound of a brass band with leaden orchestration, then there is a tightrope walker accompanied by a tinkling tune on a music-box. The melody for the clowns, the procession and the high-wire act is in fact the same, but in different arrangements.

Having the same theme for clowns, religion and acrobatics suggests an affinity between them. On the one hand, religion is recognised to have something of the absurd and of showbiz about it, as is clear from Fellini's *Le notti di Cabiria* (1957), *La dolce vita* and *Roma* (1972), for the last of which Rota wrote a particularly naughty comic tune for the ecclesiastical fashion show. Yet Rota also composed much devout Catholic music (not least for the sentimental religious drama about a boy, a donkey and St Francis *Never Take No for an Answer*, 1951). And neither Fellini nor Rota would ever have considered anything to be absurd and therefore trivial or to be 'merely' showbiz. The sudden appearance of the clowns 'saves' the lost Gelsomina, and the tightrope walker, who wears angels' wings, will turn out to be the person who gives her self-esteem. If religion is showbiz, then showbiz in its turn is revelatory, spiritual, magic in the most serious sense of the word. That is why all can share the same tune.

Rota's work came out of his specific circumstances as a highbrow composer working in a popular medium, out of gay discretion and, by all accounts, an other-worldly disposition. But it touches us far beyond these particularities. It expresses the sense that we are all outsiders, and that this is no big deal. When we speak we use a language that is not our own; all self-expression is caught in the contradiction that the only means of expression available are shared with others and are not of our own making. Rota's music, with its echoes and repetitions and the way it is emotionally within and without the scene it accompanies, embodies a central paradox of being human: that we are only ever ourselves and yet are never original. This is one of the shock-horror discoveries of poststructuralist thought, yet here it is in the music of Nino Rota, with neither shock nor horror, but wry, melancholy, funny and charming – really rather original in its unoriginality.

Originally published in *Sight and Sound* 14:9 (September 2004), pp. 42–45.

51 FAR FROM HEAVEN (2007)

With Julianne Moore blazing at its centre in red and gold, like a bouquet of autumnal foliage in a fine china vase, Todd Haynes' *Far from Heaven* is an explosion of synthetic delights. Which is not to say it lacks emotional impact – far from it. *Far from Heaven* is a movie for hardcore film geeks and regular folk alike, a stunning, and stunningly improbable, fusion of postmodern pastiche and old-school Hollywood melodrama. It's both a marvellous technical accomplishment and a tragic love story that sweeps you off your feet.

Andrew O'Hehir[1]

The first time I saw *Far from Heaven* (USA Todd Haynes 2002), there were moments when I could not see the screen for crying. On the other hand, I was fully conscious of the way the film was doing 1950s Hollywood melodrama, was pastiche. Obviously it could be the case that my response was aberrant, but the film was successful (relatively speaking) at the box office, and most critics registered something like the same response[2] as did most people I know. This does not mean that crying as you get the pastiche is the only possible response – for some people, the pastiche may indeed interfere with the possibility of responding emotionally – but there are enough of us about to indicate that this is a possible and legitimate one. At

---

1   Available online at: http://www.salon.com/ent/movies/review/2002/11/08/far_from_heaven/
2   Cf. the views collected online at: http://www.rottentomatoes.com/m/far_from_heaven/. For more extensive critiques see Amy Taubin, 'In Every Dream Home', *Film Comment*, September-October 2002, pp. 22-26; Lucas Hilderbrand, 'All That Haynes Allows', 2002, available online at: www.popmatters.com/film/reviews/f/far-from-heaven.shtml; Gabrielle Murray, 'The Last Place in the World... A Review of *Far from Heaven*', 2003, available online at: www.sensesofcinema.com/contents/03/25/far_from_heaven.html; Laura Mulvey, '*Far from Heaven*', *Sight and Sound* 13:3 (2003), pp. 40-41; Sharon Willis, 'The Politics of Disappointment: Todd Haynes Rewrites Douglas Sirk', *Camera Obscura* 54, 18:1 (2003), pp. 131-174; Pam Cook, *Screening the Past: Memory and Nostalgia in Cinema*, London: Routledge, 2004, pp. 11-15; Lynne Joyrich, 'Written on the Screen: Mediation and Immersion in *Far from Heaven*', *Camera Obscura* 57, 19:3 (2004), pp. 187-218.

a minimum, *Far from Heaven* is an especially strong vindication of the proposition that pastiche and emotion are not incompatible.

In the film, set in a suburb of Hartford, Connecticut in the 1950s, middle-class white couple Cathy and Frank Whitaker (Julianne Moore and Dennis Quaid) are regarded as the perfect couple, 'Mr and Mrs Magnatech' (the name of the company he works for). In the course of the film, however, Cathy discovers that Frank is homosexual; as they drift apart, she finds that the only person she feels at ease with is Raymond, their Black gardener (Dennis Haysbert). The two strike up a friendship, but the town is scandalised: her friends are appalled, her daughter's friends and their mothers shun her, his daughter is attacked by white boys and his Black neighbours throw stones at his house. The couple realise that they must stop seeing each other. Frank leaves home to live with another man; Raymond goes to Baltimore, a city with a larger Black community; Cathy is left alone with the two young children and her reliable and selfless Black maid Sybil (Viola Davis).

Far from Heaven is highly palimpsestic, layered over at least three previous films, each of which shows through: *The Reckless Moment* (USA Max Ophüls 1949), *All That Heaven Allows* (USA Douglas Sirk 1955), *Fear Eats the Soul* (*Angst essen Seele auf* Germany Rainer Werner Fassbinder 1974), the last itself a conscious reworking of *All That Heaven Allows*. Each echoes while altering a basic narrative situation: a middle-class white married woman without a husband[3] forms a relationship with a socially inferior man (Irish immigrant petty criminal (*The Reckless Moment*), labourer (*All That Heaven Allows*), Arab migrant worker (*Fear Eats the Soul*), African-American (*Far from Heaven*)), which does not work out due to social attitudes.[4] *Far from Heaven* also makes specific visual and verbal references to its antecedents: for instance, to the shot of the main character weeping on her bed in *The Reckless Moment*, to the symbol of a branch of autumnal foliage in *All That Heaven Allows*, to Emmy's bald statement to Ali in *Fear Eats the Soul*, "You are beautiful" (which Cathy says to Raymond). There are also more pervasive stylistic links, above all the use of colour in Sirk's work, splitting the screen into warm and cold areas (something that also characterises the Fassbinder film).[5]

Given the looseness of the word, it would mean something to refer to all of the above as pastiche, but in relation to the concept of pastiche canvassed in this book, they are more usefully considered echoes, references, quotations and remakings. What makes *Far from Heaven* also, and primarily, pastiche is its thoroughgoing imitation of the attitude, *mise en scène* and look of the films made by Douglas Sirk for Ross Hunter in

---

3   Two are widows; in *The Reckless Moment*, the husband is away on business throughout the film; in *Far from Heaven*, Frank leaves Cathy in the course of the film.
4   *All That Heaven Allows* and *Fear Eats the Soul* have endings that do suggest the couple may have a future together.
5   On the use of colour in the film, see Willis, op. cit., pp. 148-153, as well as Todd Haynes' DVD commentary.

the 1950s, including *All That Heaven Allows* as well as *Magnificent Obsession* 1954, *Written on the Wind* 1957 and *Imitation of Life* 1959. There are all sorts of ways in which *Far from Heaven* differs from these, including the contemporary cast, different aspect ratio, the explicit treatment of homosexuality and inter-racial desire, the cutting ratio[6] and the music,[7] and perhaps Cathy's skirts are slightly fuller and the silences between people more achingly awkward.[8] Yet in many more ways the film is very close: the painstakingly recreated style of settings and costumes (not based, as in heritage cinema, on study of the interior design and couture of the period but these as they appear in the movies), the use of lighting, the predominance of two-shots over close-ups, the held-in style of performance, the use of overt symbols (Cathy's mauve scarf that flies off in the wind and leads her to Raymond, the branch of glowingly autumnal foliage that reminds her of him), the concern with the interface between inner feeling and social attitudes. In short, between *Far from Heaven* and the Ross Hunter Sirks there is extreme closeness with elements of discrepancy and slight distortion, very like but not quite.

Far from Heaven could hardly work as a mainstream film if it depended on so precise a knowledge of Sirk. His films are major points of reference within academic film studies and they have had a camp following,[9] but most people are not film studies students and by the 2000s Sirk melodramas were not even shown so very much on television, making both a camp take-up and a very widespread awareness of them much less strong. Yet enough people clearly did get *Far from Heaven* for it to have adequate box office success. There is almost certainly a hierarchy of knowledge in play. At a minimum, anyone would recognise that the film does not work in the ways other recent films do that deal with domestic dramas, not glossy late women's films (*The Mirror Has Two Faces* 1994, *Waiting to Exhale* 1995), not understated semi-independents (*You Can Count On Me* 2000, *In the Bedroom* 2001, *The Shipping News* 2001), not heritage style (*The End of the Affair* 1999, *The Hours* 2002), not problem-of-the-week made-for-TV movies, not soap opera. Yet one might not be able to place it beyond this,[10] and one

---

6   Much quicker than in Sirk (editor James Lyons in 'Anatomy of a Scene' on DVD of *Far from Heaven*).

7   The composer for the Sirk films was Frank Skinner, who produced pasticcios of classical music melodies (*All That Heaven Allows*, for instance, combines inter alia 'Warum?' from Schumann's *Fantasiestücke*, Liszt's 'Consolation' and Brahms' First Symphony); Elmer Bernstein's score for *Far from Heaven* is in this sense wholly original, and more chromatically lush.

8   James Zborowski's 2005 MA dissertation discussed at length the way that similar devices in Sirk and *Far from Heaven* are often put to different aesthetic ends. See also Willis, op. cit., notably her discussion of stammering, pp. 153-158.

9   Barbara Klinger, *Melodrama and Meaning: History, Culture and the Films of Douglas Sirk*, Bloomington: Indiana University Press, 1994.

10 Seen in more of an art cinema context, it might be easier to relate *Far from Heaven* to Fassbinder, Almodóvar, François Ozon and of course Haynes' earlier films (*Superstar: The Karen Carpenter Story* 1987, *Poison* 1991, *(Safe)* 1995, *Velvet Goldmine* 1998).

friend of mine just said she found it 'peculiar'. Equally even many 'hardcore film geeks' will not pick up on every detail of the pastiche: when I first saw *Far from Heaven*, I did not make the connection to *The Reckless Moment*, nor did I think about the resonance from *Imitation of Life* of the nurturing relationship between the white woman and her Black maid, nor did I know about the relative difference in the editing speed. I suspect responses to the film operate mostly somewhere between bafflement at its difference and geekish noting of every Sirkian nuance, in a general recognition of 1950s clothes and settings, of colour that no longer accords with our ideas of realism, of unironic emotional intensity, of the idea of weepies and women's pictures, in short, a broad sense of the way they made movies then about things like this.

What is the effect of doing this story this way? I want to suggest a number of answers that cover some of the responses that the film makes possible.

IT ENABLES THE FILM TO TELL THE STORY IN THE PARTICULARLY INTENSE AND MOVING WAY CHARACTERISTIC OF THIS KIND OF MELODRAMA.

In itself, this is to say nothing of it as pastiche. It simply means that the film uses the genre's generative powers to create a certain kind of world and feeling. However, the fact of the hard-to-ignore elements of distortion and discrepancy already noted, and, even more, the fact that this kind of story has not been told in this kind of way for over thirty years, bring even this most direct function of using the style into the orbit of pastiche.

IT ENABLES THE FILM TO TELL A STORY OF THE 1950S IN A STYLE OF THE 1950S.

Hollywood melodramas of the 1950s did not tell stories of homosexuality and mutual inter-racial desire,[11] yet *Far from Heaven* tells such a story, respecting 1950s social norms, in that very mode. The sense of period mode is also reinforced by drawing

---

11 Homosexuality was implicit and/or marginal in films, including melodramas, through most of Hollywood's history, and it is the unspoken but quite evident focus of *Tea and Sympathy* 1956. However, explicit, and still quite restricted, treatments only really begin with, for instance, *Suddenly Last Summer* 1959, *Advise and Consent* 1961, *A Walk on the Wild Side* 1962 and *The Children's Hour* 1962. Mutual inter-racial desire (as distinct from Black-on-white rape scenarios) is treated in two films at the end of the 1950s that, however, remove it from, respectively, the USA and the present: *Island in the Sun* 1959, set on a Caribbean island, and *The World, the Flesh and the Devil* 1958, set in a world almost entirely annihilated by germ warfare. Such desire did not become a fit subject for sympathetic or central characters in Hollywood movies until *Guess Who's Coming to Dinner?* 1967.

Cathy Whitaker (Julianne Moore) in *Far from Heaven*, 2002. (BFI National Archive)

upon aspects of the way such stories were about to be told in cinema. It borrows its imagery for the gay bar from *Advise and Consent* 1961,[12] thus a film made only a few years later than when *All That Heaven Allows* was made and when *Far from Heaven* itself is set, 1957; its colouring also reminds me of the covers of US gay pulp novels of the period. The held-off quality of the performances in the scenes between both Quaid (Frank) and Nicholas Joy (Frank's unnamed live-in lover) and Moore (Cathy) and Haysbert (Raymond) also recall those in progressive and studiedly unraunchy treatments of both kinds of relationship, notably in the films of Sidney Poitier (including *Guess Who's Coming to Dinner?*). The violence of the racist response to Cathy and Raymond's friendship has some echo of that depicted in Sirk's *Imitation of Life*, when Frankie (Troy Donahue), the white boyfriend of Sarah Jane (Susan Kohler), beats her up on learning that she is a Black woman passing for white.

Yet we know that *Far from Heaven* was not made in the 1950s and probably could not have been made then using this mode. This is not just a question of censorship but of the mode itself. What is not imagined in a mode of representation may also have

---

12 Haynes refers to this in his DVD commentary (chapter 6).

been unimaginable, may have been framed precisely as that which cannot be seen or heard, nor evidently thought and felt. The contours of a structure of feeling are delineated by what is excluded, the emotional pressures at work feel like they do precisely because some of them are implicit. The moment fifties melodrama started including homosexual and inter-racial desire and rendering them explicit, it would no longer have been 1950s melodrama as it actually was.

Far from Heaven is then inescapably poised between a sense of telling a 1950s story in a 1950s way and a recognition that a 1950s way could not tell that story and remain a 1950s way. This can then set in train the question of how the film mediates our relationship to the 1950s. On the one hand, it may bring us in imagination closer to the people of the 1950s. Done without parody or irony, we may feel encouraged to feel the feelings of the 1950s through the expressive modes available then, to feel what it was possible to feel. On the other hand, the very fact of pastiche – that it is not quite like an actual film of the period – ought also to alert us to the limitations of this historical imagining. *Far from Heaven*'s pastiche thus simultaneously in its likeness enables us in imagination to feel with the 1950s in the terms of the 1950s while in its not-quite-likeness conveying the epistemological difficulty of such imagining. To put it the other way round, pastiche reminds us that a framework is a framework, and also that this is enabling as well as limiting – enabling and setting limits to the exercise of transhistorical sympathy.

IT REMINDS US, HOWEVER, THAT THEY DON'T MAKE FILMS LIKE THIS ANYMORE.

The feeling of the dialectic of sameness and difference vis-à-vis the past that the pastiche enables is almost bound also to remind us that the classic Hollywood melodrama's way of doing emotion is not contemporary cinema's, that there are not films like *All That Heaven Allows* or *The Reckless Moment* anymore. Moreover, *Far from Heaven*, though it is so much like them, none the less in its exceptionality and its pastiche distortions and discrepancies actually affirms that such films are not made anymore. Some of the intensity of the emotional response to the film feels like a longing for there to be such films and a gratitude for having given us one now in which some of the elements we may stumble over in them (because of changing attitudes and tastes) have been dealt with, but then, just because of the differences, an intensification of regret that such films are not made. What happens in the film is sad but we may also be sad for there not being films that do sadness like this anymore. In particular, the desire for unaffected, unalloyed, unironic emotional intensity in the depiction of interpersonal relationships seems harder to come by now, pushed to the margins of action films or else rendered too directly, easily and vacuously in close-ups of people saying

"I love you". There is something about the difficulty of emotion in 1950s melodrama, not least in its interface with social expectation, that gives it a special intensity, and it seems a cultural loss no longer to have this at one's disposal. The pastiche of *Far from Heaven* reminds us experientially of what we have lost even while confirming that it is lost, which only makes it all the more poignant as well as being, perhaps, critical of today's emotional economy.

IT SETS IN PLAY OUR RELATIONSHIP TO THE PAST.

The mixture described above specifically in relation to the 1950s – of sympathetic imagining and registering of difference – also embodies the dialectic of our relationship to the past more generally. It suggests that we can enter into the feelings of our forebears through immersion in their art but also reminds us that this is a highly limited and circumscribed activity. This itself is a variation at the level of affect on the perennial ambiguity of our relationship to the past, in that irresolvable tension between a sense that people in the past were people like ourselves, with desires, dreams, hopes and fears like us, and yet that we cannot know that for sure, and moreover that much of what they felt seems strange, opaque, other. Pastiche can embody that tension at the level of how we feel about people in the past.

At the same time, a pastiche like *Far from Heaven* may also serve as a reminder that what we know of the past, above all of the feelings of the past, we know through the art that is left behind. We can't read off the 1950s from its melodramas, but not only did the latter none the less constitute one of the major frameworks of feeling available in the period, they are also one of the things we have got that enable us to make some move toward connection with the past, our past. (Obviously the extent to which we feel it is our past depends on who we are, and the intensity and poignancy of the relationship to a past is in turn affected by what investments we have in it.)

IT SUGGESTS THE WAY IN WHICH FEELING IS SHAPED BY CULTURE.

Recognising that what we know about how things felt in the 1950s comes – problematically but only – from cultural artefacts (and in this case films) may also enable us to reflect on the fact that how we feel right now is itself framed by the traditions of feeling we inherit, mobilise and hand on. In other words, the pastiche of *Far from Heaven* not only makes the historicity of its affect evident but can also allow us to realise the historicity of our own feelings. It is hard to experience our feelings historically: they seem – and, in terms of the exercise of our conscious will, largely are – unbidden, unconscious, visceral, unruly. Yet just as *Far from Heaven* suggests a way of feeling intensely that is at once recognisable and other, so it also allows us to extrapolate from that to the historical shaping of our feelings. If in the 1950s frameworks of feelings structured how people felt, then it must be so now. To know this is also to be able to reflect upon it.

Extract from Richard Dyer, *Pastiche*, London and New York: Routledge, 2007, pp. 174–179.

52 GOING ITALIAN (2011)

I am a latecomer to Italian Film Studies and I come to it from Film rather than Italian Studies. This is not to say that Italian cinema has not always been important to me. *La dolce vita* (Federico Fellini, 1959) and *La maschera del demonio* (as *Black Sunday*; Mario Bava, 1960) were formative films of my adolescence, the former seen in the sybaritic surroundings of the Curzon Cinema, Mayfair, the latter no less appropriately in a past-its-best picture palace on the Old Kent Road, both films and venues equally thrilling to a boy from the suburbs. Meanwhile the monthly *Films and Filming* gave enticing coverage to films that I didn't see at the time, such as *La notte brava* (Mauro Bolognini, 1959) and *La battaglia di Maratona* (Jacques Tourneur, 1959). I pretended to admire *L'avventura* (Michelangelo Antonioni, 1960) when it first came out in Britain, then decided it was an exemplar of that elitist bad object, the art film, and decided to show it accordingly in an introduction to film class, only to discover it was as wonderful as I had first wanted it to be. *Rocco e i suoi fratelli* (Luchino Visconti, 1960), *C'era una volta il West* (Sergio Leone, 1968), *Prima della rivoluzione* (Bernardo Bertolucci, 1964), *Suspiria* (Dario Argento, 1977) all suggested the riches to be found in Italian cinema, though in fact gave little sense of just how rich a cinema it is: the silent epics were footnotes in general film histories, while the comedies and, especially, the melodramas were largely ignored and undistributed. I also taught Italian cinema pretty well as soon as I started teaching, though usually following the approved paths of neorealism (taught as 'a movement') and the already canonical *autori*. But I didn't quite know what to do intellectually with my enthusiasm.

Perhaps decisive in finding a way to do Italian film that also accorded with my postgraduate intellectual formation was working in the Anglistica department of the Istituto Universitario Orientale in Naples in 1987. This department was greatly influenced by the Birmingham school of Cultural Studies (where I had studied), reorienting the study of literature and introducing new objects of study under the rubric of English (in fact I taught a course on British cinema there, which would raise eyebrows among many scholars of British cinema). It was not just the intellectual stimulation of the Naples department that was decisive but two consequences of being in Italy. One was discovering, mainly on afternoon TV, classic Italian cinema's rich vein of comedy and melodrama, films like *Romanticismo* (Clemente Fracassi, 1958) and *Anna* (Alberto Lattuada, 1951), stars like Totò and Amedeo Nazzari, and international figures like Anna Magnani, Sophia Loren, Alida Valli and Raf Vallone in a wholly new context. They gave me a much broader sense of Italian popular cinema, suggesting a field of investigation that might benefit from some of the approaches to culture, and popular culture, that my Birmingham and Naples colleagues were pursuing. The other important factor was the serendipitous discovery in a bookshop of Vittorio Spinazzola's *Cinema e pubblico* (Bompiani, 1974). His study of post-war Italian cinema is organized around the paradox of the popular, its different meanings (and not least the different stresses of meaning between *il popolare* and the popular) and especially the contrast between a kind of film (neorealism) made in the name of the people and the kinds of films (American movies, or else Italian comedies, melodramas, pepla and *gialli*) the people actually chose to go and see. This suggested a way to teach Italian cinema (within the limits of subtitled availability in the UK), a way that did not neglect the canonical moment of neorealism, but also interrogated it through the notion of the popular, partly by tracing its continued influence (notably in the *commedia all'italiana*), partly by contrasting it to the rest of Italian film output (including the peplum and *giallo*).

Looking back it surprises me to realise that, for someone as little interested in an auteur approach to film as me, Fellini figured especially all along. But then I did experience *La dolce vita* as life changing and, even though I knew no Italian and therefore understood practically nothing of what was going on, I was intoxicated by *8½* (1963) when I sneaked away from a school trip to Italy to see it in a cinema in Rome. Early results of the latter were a film-and-context case study on the film taught in an evening class in Burton-on-Trent and a short article on it for the weekly part work *The Movie*. Fellini proved fascinatingly decisive for teaching the popular in Italian cinema, for his apparent distance from but actual continuity with many of the supposed precepts of neorealism in films such as *Le notti di Cabiria* (1957) and *La dolce vita* and also for the take on the peplum offered by *Satyricon* (1969). It was then perhaps an inevitable step that, for the only time in my life, I taught a whole course on a director, to wit, Fellini. He is a by-word internationally for art cinema who nonetheless worked within the commercial film industry, had many huge box office hits and always drew his imagery and soundscape from popular culture (notably circus, variety, music and the cinema).

One of the advantages of the popularity problematic is that it got me away from the national cinema problematic that has often tended to dominate studies of European cinemas (within and without Film Studies departments). The need for me to do this in part stemmed from teaching in a Film Studies context. While the issue of national cinema is one of the standard ones in the discipline, there is no need endlessly to rehearse it and its difficulties with every specific national cinema studied. Besides, there is after all no reason why students who have signed on to study film should be required to be interested in Italian national identity; if what is important about a film is said to be its contribution to Italian identity, why should that particularly interest people interested in film?

There is also an intellectual need to get away from the focus on national cinema and, a fortiori, national identity. That there are specificities to Italian, British, Swedish, or Hindi or Hollywood, cinemas is not in doubt and much of the study of, say, Italian films has to be concerned with understanding those specificities – but in order to understand the films better rather than because those films are 'about' national identity. Films are indeed sometimes made to say something about national identity: Rossellini in one interview said that that, rather than realism, had always been the primary aim of neorealism, and films like *La dolce vita*, *Ladro di bambini* (Gianni Amelio, 1992) and *Gomorra* (Matteo Garrone, 2008) are clearly in some measure 'state-of-the-nation' films. Even with such examples, what is most interesting – and wonderful – about them is not necessarily what they 'say': even a film as politically driven as *Gomorra* may be better understood in terms of, for instance, its extraordinary uncentred narrative structure and its attractive use of colour in the context of bleak events. Besides, most films are not made to say things, they are made to make money, to entertain, to create beauty, to have fun. What makes money in a given culture, what constitutes fun or beauty, these may in part be nationally specific, and that is worth registering, but that is very different from considering that they are in any primary or even perhaps important way about national identity.

Reference to making money or entertaining is often used in discussion of film in a way that seems to suggest an end point. In case I should be misunderstood as implying this, I should stress that acknowledging the impulses towards money, beauty, fun, is the beginning. Not everything makes money nor entertains: analysis is about unpicking what does and does not, what forms, values and pleasures work and what don't, all themselves culturally and historically distinct issues as well as formal, aesthetic ones. Films (like all forms of art) are an unusual commodity because, despite the stress on generic recognition, they are not identical to one another; their differences too are what have to be analysed. Above all, films are formally organized and affectively addressed and experienced: these are the first social, cultural and historical facts about them, not to be lost sight of in pressing them into the service of meaning and identity. Cultural and historical specificity is a primary methodological principle (though not one that should make it impossible to see both continuities and influences beyond the cultural-historical moment), and this ineluctably (although not necessarily strongly) entails national specificity, but as something that helps us to give a better, particularized account of any given instance of filmic beauty and fun.

Although I brought the issue and complexities of the popular from (British-originated) cultural studies to bear on Italian cinema, I have not especially wanted to explore more specific issues from my own past in this, for me, newer context. I am for instance very aware of stars in Italian cinema and have much enjoyed getting to know all sorts that I knew either not at all or hardly, and I have explored aspects of this – in the use of stars in neorealist cinema (much more widespread than the classic thumbnail sketch of the 'movement' would suggest), in Fellini's approach to casting. However, I have not personally wanted to test the model of stars developed in relation to Hollywood cinema against the Italian instance. The 2003 Stockholm 'Popular European Cinema' conference focusing on stars convinced me that much of the Hollywood-derived methodology for studying stars was, *mutatis mutandis*, perfectly viable for Italian (or other non-Hollywood) stars: one of the main planks of the method is respect for cultural and historical difference, some of the differences between Hollywood and Italian cinema are matters of degree (for instance, the latter industry less securely vertically integrated than the former), others of kind that have to be taken into account but do not overturn the basic analytic method (e.g. the different development of genre in Italian cinema, not just what genres are prevalent but both the stronger sense of generic overlaps and the importance of film cycles). You'd have to take all that into account in understanding both stardom in general and specific stars in Italian cinema, but taking such things into account was always a principle of star studies. However, I myself do not want to do that work.

On the other hand, my growing academic interest in Italian cinema coincided with an increasing interest in music in film. I have always been interested in musicals and am currently doing some work on songs in Italian cinema, extraordinarily pervasive in a cinema that reckons it doesn't do musicals. I've also become interested more generally in how music works in film (and in this am very much riding on the back of wonderful work on the topic in the past fifteen years or so in Film Studies). I put this together with my turn to Italian cinema recently with a study of the work of the composer Nino Rota. There was intellectual logic to this, not least given his complex relationship to the popular, something that accounts for the remarkable affinity between his approach and that of Fellini. It was also though a labour of love. Partly it was an embrace of formal celebration, a piece of writing with rather little cultural-political agenda. I also realised, after I had started, that Rota had been a significant figure in my life. His theme from *The Glass Mountain* (Edoardo Anton and Henry Cass, 1949), a British film half set in Italy, was in the British top ten for a year when I was about five and although I didn't especially like it, my mother did and I heard it interminably. *Never Take No for an Answer* (Maurice Cloche, 1953), a film that I and those around me wept through repeatedly in Catholic church halls, was the English language version of *Peppino e Violetta*, with music by Nino Rota. *La dolce vita*, *Rocco e i suoi fratelli*, the Godfather films, *Satyricon*, *Anna* and many other films that had marked my life turned out to have – wonderful – scores by Nino Rota. What I didn't know until I got started was just how many scores (more than 150) there were, nor how lovable and at the same time elusive. Pursuing this suggested a very different conception of music-and-film than that proposed by Hollywood-based accounts, one that ran counter to assumptions about identification as the central mechanism of attending to film. This makes me think that, while there are basic methods of study that need only inflection and modification in being applied to different cinemas, it may also be the case that studying different cinemas (Italian or otherwise) may in turn be able to inflect and even challenge the hegemony of the Hollywood instance.

The main drawbacks to coming late to Italian cinema and from Film Studies are language and context. I speak Italian and have even taught and lectured in it in Italy, but it is only in the last fifteen years that I have spent a great deal of time there. I have had very little formal instruction in Italian, which means that I don't feel an inwardness with the way the language works (in the way I once did with French, which I studied at University), and I have only had the immersion in Italian that comes from being in Italy and almost exclusively with Italians too late in my life ever to be able to acquire the subtlety and range of linguistic knowledge that I observe in my Italianist colleagues. Films most often involve colloquial dialogue, always harder to understand than more formal (and academic) discourse, and I am aware of how much I miss, even now.

I was watching *La ragazza con la valigia* (Valerio Zurlini, 1961) on (Italian) television a couple of weeks back and was aware that Claudia Cardinale was not forming the words that one heard coming from her character. An (Italian) friend came in and just in passing expressed surprise and delight that the voice belonged to Adriana Asti and in a manner 'più Milanese di così…'. I can tell if someone is not speaking formal Italian, and can even hear, for instance, the weak 'r' in some Northern speakers or the dropped final vowels of Roman and Neapolitan speech, but I don't think I'll ever be able to make such quick and felt identification of a dialect, which means that I am condemned to miss the full resonance of a given regional accent, in a culture in which regionality is so important, even obsessive; I miss this affective dimension.

Along with this recognition (hardly one I had never had before) came several other reflections. One is just how difficult it is to acquire the detail of cultural knowledge that a native or long time resident has. This puts limits on the richness and inwardness of one's account, and one will always have need of 'native informants'. However, it is important not to think that only an insider knows about their culture. To see something from the outside is not the same as seeing it from the inside, but it is not necessarily less insightful. Secondly, there is the problem of the scope of contextual knowledge, all there is potentially to know (for everything, even human biology and the history of the world, is context) and the under-theorised notion of pertinence that must guide which contexts we in fact choose to bring into play.

Thirdly, there is the fascinating field of voice and body in Italian cinema, the significance of such widespread post synchronisation, how it relates to other aspects of sound, the significance of dubbers' voices being familiar in their own right. This relates to the biggest issue of all: language in film (signalled by Ginette Vincendeau at the NECS conference in Lund in 2009). It is odd to realise how very little work has been done on this. There is work on the voice in film and a little bit on dialogue as an aspect of script and performance, but I can't help feeling that there must be a great deal more to be said. Linguistics and translation theory ought to be able to work in conjunction with film theory and analytic methodology to produce a rich account of how any given language – say, Italian – works in film. I feel one ought to be able to marry consideration of the way Italian constructs meaning and affect, its mode of reference, the relation of spoken and written language with questions of how language works in film in relation to image and other sounds (including non-verbal human ones), accounts of how Italian is performed linguistically and paralinguistically with how performance works in film, and so on. In short, we ought to be able to find a way of speaking about the linguistic specificity of film and of Italian film. Sounds like an ideal, genuinely interdisciplinary project for Italian Film Studies.

Originally published in *The Italianist* 31 (2011), pp. 287–292.

53 EISENSTEIN'S PENIS (2023)

In Peter Greenaway's exuberantly intellectual and often gorgeous film *Eisenstein in Guanajuato* (2015), Sergei Eisenstein speaks of and to his penis and the film shows it quite frequently, sometimes in close-up. It is notable in an early scene, when Eisenstein has just arrived in Guanajuato during his sojourn in Mexico in 1931 researching and part-shooting his never finished film *¡Que viva México!*. He takes a shower, something he says is unknown in Russia, and delights in the sensuous experience of it, waggling his penis with glee and noting that it is responding in evident appreciation of his guide, Palomino Cañedo's attractiveness. Yet, while he refers several other times to his Jewishness, his penis is not circumcised, and while both he and Cañedo speak of it involuntarily registering his sexual excitement, it is never erect.

It is not certain whether, or to what extent, Eisenstein thought of himself as Jewish. According to Ronald Bergan, Eisenstein considered himself only an eighth Jewish, although the website 'Jew or Not Jew', while suggesting that he is in the category 'barely a Jew', nonetheless claims that he 'was definitely proud of his Jewish roots, and used Yiddish slang and humour'. His father was part-Jewish, his mother not at all: it's probable that he was not circumcised. At a Jewish wartime rally in Moscow in 1941, Eisenstein reportedly asked the writer Ilya Ehrenberg 'Does it hurt to be circumcised when you're forty years old?', perhaps indicating that he was not himself so but, conceivably, if he was not just being jokey, that he was contemplating becoming so. In a war effort film made a year later, *An Appeal to the Jews of the World*, Eisenstein, according to Marie Seton, for 'the first time in his life, spoke as a representative of his father's people' (by which she clearly means the Jews). Given that there had been a campaign against him in Hollywood, ostensibly anti-communist but also often anti-Semitic, it is not implausible that in Mexico he was on his way to taking on a greater identification with his Jewish roots which eventually led to him raising the matter of adult circumcision.

In *Eisenstein in Guanajuato*, Eisenstein twice refers to himself as a Jew. He speaks of the campaign against him, concluding 'So, exit Eisenstein: Jew, Red, Troublemaker, Communist', putting Jew first, before other labels that he would certainly have embraced. Later, Hunter Kimbrough, a businessman in charge of production, irritated

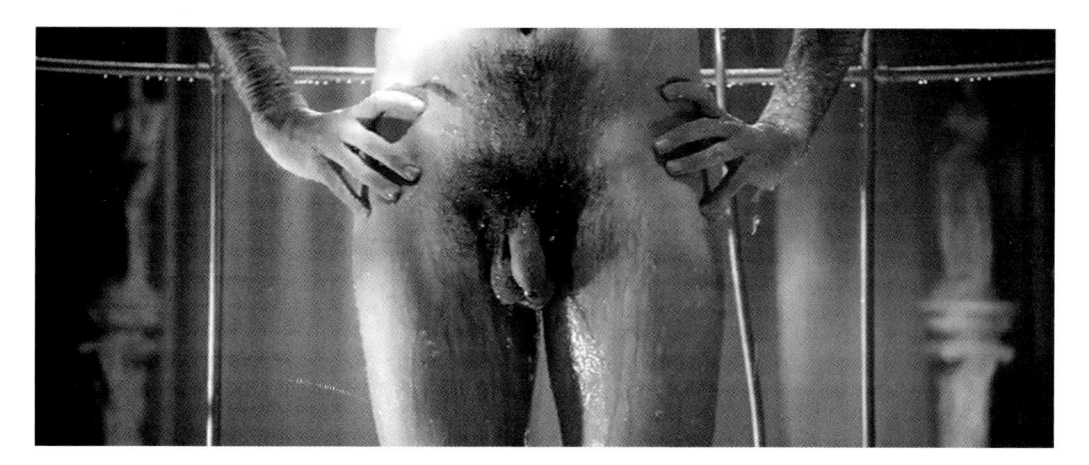

Eisenstein's uncircumcised, and even rather generously caparisoned, penis.

with Eisenstein's lack of productivity and respect, says 'You're like a Negro – kind words and consideration are not enough'. Eisenstein chuckles and replies, 'I thought I was a Red. Now I'm also a Black? And, you also forgot, a Jew'. He also twice draws attention to Jewishness, once amused by meeting one of America's biggest stars, Al Jolson, 'the blacked-up singing son of a Russian rabbi', another time commenting on Joseph Schenck looking lost in Russia, adding 'All Jews look lost in Russia, but there is never a better home for them.'[1]

This apparent embrace of his Jewishness is accompanied with close-ups of his uncircumcised, and even rather generously caparisoned, penis. We don't need to see a man's penis in order to accept that he is Jewish (and, when we don't know this about him, it is not of itself a reliable sign that he is: Muslims, some Orthodox Christian churches and, still, about 75% of US men are circumcised). However, if it is shown, it becomes meaningful. Circumcision is not just a sign of Jewish belonging, but also of the covenant between the Jewish people and God: circumcision is the practice God required of the Jews as a token of His special relationship with the Jewish people. Circumcision is also a marker of a stigmatised identity, evoking a history of anti-Semitism stretching back to even before the advent of Christianity. In short, to show a Jewish circumcised penis is no little thing, and to show Eisenstein uncircumcised, without any gloss on the complexity of his position vis-à-vis Judaism, risks looking like gentile carelessness.

---

1. Schenck emigrated to the US from Russia in 1892, when he was 16; he visited Moscow in 1928 to discuss with Eisenstein his coming to Hollywood.

It is now conventional wisdom to consider Eisenstein gay, to trace various possible longings, encounters and relationships in his life as well as queer, erotic and camp imagery in his films. Gregory Woods provides a clear and circumspect account of the former, Al LaValley and Tom Waugh among others have uncovered the queerness of his work and he has ben important for gay filmmakers such as John Greyson and Derek Jarman.[2] In fact Eisenstein denied having gay feelings (leave alone doing gay things), telling his biographer Marie Seton: 'A lot of people say I'm a homosexual. I never have been, and I'd tell you if it were true. I've never felt any such desire'; Seton later comments that he 'could not tolerate the idea of homosexuality in himself'. In 1934 he married Pera Atasheva (to whom he speaks by phone in *Eisenstein in Guanajuato*), shortly after the introduction of anti-homosexual legislation in the USSR. All of this may constitute the denials and masks of closetry, or it may be the case that he did have the desire but did not act upon it. However, while there is no indisputable evidence that he had a sexual relationship with Jorge Palomino y Cañedo in Mexico, Eduardo de la Vega Alfaro makes a strong case for it, based especially on the erotic drawings made by Sergei as a present for Palomino and on some (understandably) circumspect comments in his letters.

In *Eisenstein in Guanajuato*, the relationship with Palomino is entirely explicit, with Palomino buggering Sergei and the latter looking very contented after the initial pain, and then Palomino masturbating Sergei to orgasm. Sergei makes it clear that this is his first homosexual experience (and, it feels, his first sexual experience of any kind with another person). It is also implied that it is a romance, Sergei begging Palomino to come back to Moscow with him and Palomino looking sad that he can't (including because he is married with children). Before giving in to Palomino, Sergei says that he has always resisted such desires before, but this, together with the photographs of paintings of naked men that Sergei has with him and his own homoerotic drawings, indicate an awareness of himself as gay.

We don't need to see sexual organs to know that sex is taking or has taken place. Elmer Bäck's performance when Palomino masturbates him to orgasm is a masterpiece: he wriggles and writhes, grabs and sinks back, clutches the sheets, yelps and yells, all in ways far from the heaving and arching, grunts and cries of delight of sex scenes in mainstream cinema or the practised vocabulary and controlled abandon of pornography. Throughout one long take he is covered with a sheet up to his waist, and we don't need to see him erect, or being rubbed, or coming in order to have a sense of how he is feeling these. Indeed, to show these things would not of themselves have conveyed the shifts and complexities of excitement, tension, thrill and joy that Bäck conveys in his performance.

---

2. For example, *Imagining October* (UK, 1984, Derek Jarman), *Pissoir* (aka *Urinal*) (Canada, 1988, John Greyson).

Palomino (Luis Alberti) masturbating Sergei (Elmer Bäck) to orgasm.

Yet *Eisenstein in Guanajuato* insists on us contemplating the penis in gay sex, and specifically erection. Already in the early scene in the hotel shower, when Sergei notes that his penis is responding to Palomino, he reprimands it, saying, 'Signor prick, behave!', but it clearly is not doing so, not even a little tumescent. Later, sharing a bed with Palomino, Sergei gets undressed but says he has an unattractive body and 'I have a prick only fit for peeing'; he covers his penis with his hands. But Palomino says he is attractive, and instructs him to uncover his penis and 'make it rise'; Sergei takes his hands away and Palomino says, 'You see, it takes on a brand new life' but we can see that it hasn't. Palomino on the other hand (that is, Luis Alberti playing the role) clearly does have an erection, albeit in long shot, albeit perhaps a bit droopy. Yet, as described above, when Palomino masturbates Sergei, the latter's penis is covered with a sheet, which, in the context of all this penis display, looks like coyness.

The erect penis in gay sex is not just an instrument of penetration and a vector of ejaculation, it is a thing of visual and tactile delight in its own right. It has its own erotics and aesthetics. Once we see the penis in a gay sex scene in a film, it matters whether it is erect, not because of the kind of guarantee of actorly excitement demanded of gay pornography (although that may come into it), but because of what it conveys of eroticism and affect.

When Sergei says it hurts when Palomino penetrates him, the latter says, 'that's what every virgin must say', and when Sergei says he's bleeding, Palomino says virgins are supposed to bleed. While gay men too have sex for the first time and before that may be considered virgins, and while people may bleed when anally penetrated, this discourse of virginity and bleeding does feel very heterosexual, a fortiori in the absence of Sergei's erection and ejaculation in this highly explicit scene and film.

It wouldn't matter if we didn't see the penis at all in *Eisenstein in Guanajuato*. The boyish glee of showering or of romping naked round his luxurious hotel room could be conveyed without showing the full body and certainly without repeated close-ups of his penis, nor do we need to see Bäck's penis to accept Sergei as Jewish and homosexually responsive. Yet seeing the penis is important to the film.

Ronald Bergan comments in his biography that 'Eisenstein was "out" as a phallic obsessive' and many have followed him in affirming this. On Bergan's gloss, this includes but is not confined to gay sexual desire: it is also a delight in verticality in design, the celebration of phallic shapes wherever they may be found (notably in a famous photo of Eisenstein astride a giant cactus) and, in a speech delivered by Eisenstein in 1930 to the Technicians Branch of the Academy of Motion Picture Arts and Sciences in Hollywood in 1930, an affirmation of strength and virility as the roots of civilisation. Peter Greenaway too has spoken of the phallus as a symbol of 'aggressive sexuality, the male principle, penis-worship, the male ego'. Showing the penis in *Eisenstein in Guanajuato* could resonate with this perception of the penis as phallus, with all the grandeur this implies.

However, quite apart from the mismatch between the awesome phallus and the humble penis, there is a particular difficulty in showing the penis in the context of Jewishness and gay sex. Of course Jewish and homosexual men partake of patriarchy, invest in it, are privileged within it (albeit not straightforwardly). There are things to be said about the fact that it is the male Jew who is the bearer of the sign of God's covenant, and what that has to do with Jewish belonging usually being understood to be passed down matrilineally. Much too has been said about gay male fascination with hypermasculinity, including in its toxic forms. But just as Jewish and gay men experience vicissitudes in their encounters with patriarchy, so the penis in Jewish and gay imagery and sensibility is a religious, erotic and aesthetic signifier in a complex relationship to ideas of virility, ego and the phallus. Palomino says to Sergei, when the latter is disparaging his penis, 'Respect it': in a film this means attention to what it looks like and what that signifies.

READINGS AND REFERENCES

Anon, 'Sergei Eisenstein', *Jew or Not Jew*, 2008, http://www.jewornotjew.com/profile.jsp?ID=321.

Bergan, Ronald, *Eisenstein: A Life in Conflict*, London: Little, Brown 1997.

Bergan, Ronald, '*The Battleship Potemkin* Comes Out of the Closet', *The Arts Desk*, 23 April 2011, https://theartsdesk.com/film/battleship-potemkin-comes-out-closet.

Christie, Ian and Richard Taylor (eds), *Eisenstein Rediscovered*, London: Routledge, 1993.

Gillespie, David, 'Sergei Eisenstein and the Articulation of Masculinity', *New Zealand Slavonic Journal* 42 (2008), pp. 1–53.

Hoyle, Brian, 'When Peter Met Sergei: Art Cinema Past, Present and Future in *Eisenstein in Guanajuato*', *Journal of British Cinema and Television* 13:2 (2016), pp. 312–330.

Keesey, Douglas, *The Films of Peter Greenaway: Sex, Death and Provocation*, Jefferson, NC: McFarland, 2006.

LaValley, Al, 'Maintaining, Blurring and Transcending Gender Lines' in Barry P. Scherr and Albert J. LaValley (eds), *Eisenstein at 100*, New Brunswick: Rutgers University Press, 2001, pp. 65–76.

Rubenstein, Joshua, and Vladimir Pavlovich Naumov (eds), *Stalin's Secret Pogrom: The Postwar Inquisition of the Jewish Anti-Fascist Committee* (trans. Laura Esther Wolfson), New Haven: Yale University Press, 2001.

Seton, Marie, *Sergei M. Eisenstein: A Biography*, New York: Grove Press, 1960.

Vega Alfaro, Eduardo de la, 'Breves notas sobre los amores "ilícitos" de Eisenstein en México', *Corre Camara* (2017), http://www.correcamara.com.mx/inicio/int.php?mod=noticias_detalle&id_noticia=6530.

Waugh Thomas, 'A Fag-Spotter's Guide to Eisenstein', *The Body Politic* 35 (1977), pp. 15–17; reprinted in Waugh, *The Fruit Machine: Twenty Years of Writings on Queer Cinema*, Durham NC: Duke University Press, 2000, pp. 59–68.

Woods, Gregory, *Homintern: How Gay Culture Liberated the Modern World*, New Haven: Yale University Press, 2016.

SECTION 7
MASCULINITY IS SO *BORING*

and other conversations with Richard Dyer

COMMENT & ANALYSIS

Why Richard's got stars in his eyes

"I'm very fond of British films but I often feel I'm being indulgent"
— Richard Dyer

PETER WALTERS meets the new professor of film studies at the University of Warwick

GIVEN a multi-million pound budget and the chance to indulge his movie fantasies, Richard Dyer knows exactly which sort of film he would make.

It would be a musical and it would be huge, an all-singing, all-dancing extravaganza, set in Birmingham's Bull Ring.

Britain's first professor of film studies smiles at the thought. He admits he has a weakness for the big spectaculars that Hollywood has always done so well.

As a professional observer of cinema, his favourite movie of all time is one of those larger-than-life productions, the 1944 Judy Garland romance Meet Me In St Louis. And Garland herself has a special place in his own personal hall of fame.

It will be October before Richard Dyer, chairman of Warwick University's film and literature department for the past five years, can call himself professor. But already he's getting a taste of the mystique that goes with his new title.

One radio station has already sought his professorial views on the films of today's biggest movie star, Arnold Schwarzenegger. And he's expecting further demand for his opinions.

The department he heads is one of only half a dozen round the country specialising in the study of film, the only genuinely new art form to come out of the 20th century.

Its work is academic rather than vocational. Practical experience of film-making is not part of the course and Richard Dyer and his colleagues are not in the business of turning out fledgling directors and cameramen for the film industry.

Nevertheless, Warwick can boast one direct link with the industry that's in the news just now.

Vadim Jean, co-director of the acclaimed low-budget British film Leon the Pig Farmer, was a Warwick graduate, as were three other members of his production team.

None, as it happens, took a degree in film studies at Warwick, but Richard Dyer doesn't hold that against them. He says he has a soft spot for British films, although he has few illusions about the state of the home-grown industry.

Even The Crying Game, regarded as the most financially successful British film of recent times, will not directly benefit the industry. Most of the money for it was raised abroad and that's where the profits will go.

Part of the problem, in Richard Dyer's view, is that film in Britain has never carried quite the artistic prestige that it has had in other European countries, notably France and Italy.

"The pinnacle of our culture in this country," he says, "is literature, which includes theatre but not the visual arts. We have never taken film all that seriously."

He does see some sort of future for the British industry as a producer of so-called 'heritage' films like Howard's End, the celluloid equivalent of the National Trust, and of movies like the recently released Orlando, which will find a niche in the international art cinema market.

What it should not do is attempt to rival Hollywood.

"What I like about Hollywood films is the finish that they have. I'm very fond of British films but I often feel I'm being indulgent. There's something a bit creaky about a lot of them."

He wouldn't include the widely-admired My Beautiful Launderette in that, nor the classic British hit of the '40s that still ranks high in his top ten – Brief Encounter.

He's just completed a study of Brief Encounter for the British Film Institute, exploring the film's social roots and its enduring appeal for audiences.

It's something of a new venture. Much of his published work up till now has concentrated on Hollywood stars, a major study element in the degree course he teaches.

He's 'taught' Greta Garbo, an actress he considers another of his all-time greats for her self-mocking quality, Fred Astaire, still regarded by modern students as the epitome of a lost world of elegance, and Sidney Poitier, the first major black star and an actor whose reputation has risen in recent years.

Of British film actors, only perhaps Michael Caine, he thinks, has that key ability, shared by so many Hollywood stars, to look as though he's not acting.

Britain's true strength in the world of the moving image, he feels, lies in its television industry. If there is a defensive battle to be fought, he thinks it should be fought over our public television, which is still streets ahead of anybody else's.

It may sound like heresy for somebody up to his eyes in film. But Richard Dyer believes that not even Hollywood is making anything quite as watchable as Casualty.

Personal favourites: Judy Garland and (below) the British classic Brief Encounter, starring Celia Johnson and Trevor Howard

▶ **RICHARD'S TOP TEN**
☐ Meet Me in St Louis
☐ Brief Encounter
☐ Maciste in Hell (Italian muscleman epic).
☐ India Song (France).
☐ Pakeezah (Indian musical).
☐ Day of the Dead (US horror).
☐ Storm over Asia (Soviet silent film).
☐ Seduced and Abandoned (Italy)
☐ Tokyo Story (Japan).
☐ Girls in Uniform (Germany).

Evening Telegraph
Founded by W. I. Iliffe, February 9, 1891

Wasting time

WARWICKSHIRE'S assistant chief constable puts his finger on an important issue when he produces figures showing how much police time is being wasted attending trials that do not in the end take place.

He blames criminals who maintain their not-guilty plea right through the court process, knowing full well that when the crunch comes they will admit the offence.

Delaying tactics and the pressure put on witnesses has become more widespread. And it is clearly unacceptable that of 428 Warwickshire officers detailed to give evidence in trials, only 204 did so.

Tackling this abuse will not be easy, without compromising defendants' rights. It may be worth taking a closer look at the American system of plea-bargaining, but the risk is always there that you are *encouraging somebody to admit to a crime they did not commit*, simply for a quieter life.

More effective would be accelerated court procedures which cut out delay and brought cases to a conclusion more quickly. That way, all sides would benefit.

A question of . . .

COVENTRY'S track record for preserving its heritage has not been of the best.

There are numerous examples of symbols of the city's past being scrapped with little thought for their value, either as a legacy to the citizens or their marketable importance as a tourist attraction.

It is refreshing, therefore, to learn that the relatively new sculptured panels in the Upper Precinct — a mere 40 years old — are to be preserved when the major facelift of the city centre takes place.

. . . preservation

AND while on the subject of preservation, it is pleasing to see Coventry City Council admit a blunder was committed when thousands of flowers grown specially for the Mayor-making were dumped.

The lesson to be learned is simple. If you are going to throw away people's money, tell them first or don't do it.

Head Office: Corporation Street, Coventry CV1 1FP
Newsdesk: 633633

Editor .... Neil Benson
News Editor .... Peter Mitchell
Features Editor .... Diane Chalmers
Sports Editor .... Roger Draper

Coventry Evening Telegraph, 5 June 1993.

In June 1993, Richard Dyer gave an interview to the *Coventry Evening Telegraph*, which appeared under the pleasingly tacky headline 'Why Richard's got stars in his eyes'. The hook of the piece was Dyer's forthcoming promotion to professor at the University of Warwick. Written in a tabloid tone and style, the article offers a valuable insight into its moment – in particular, of the slow-but-steady enshrining of film studies as a viable subject of study within higher education. As with all interviews with Dyer, there are surprises and provocations: given the budget and resources, he claims he would like to make an enormous musical, 'an all-singing, all-dancing extravaganza, set in Birmingham's Bull Ring'; he praises Michael Caine for his 'ability, shared by so many Hollywood stars, to look as though he's not acting'; he criticises British cinema but praises its television ('not even Hollywood is making anything quite as watchable as *Casualty*'). A sidebar lists Dyer's ten favourite films, choices that register predictable long-standing passions (*Meet Me in St. Louis*, *Brief Encounter*) and an investment in queer viewing pleasures (*Mädchen in Uniform*, *Maciste in Hell*), but also a generous and capacious cinephilia (*India Song*, *Pakeezah*, *Seduced and Abandoned*, *Storm Over Asia*).[1]

Interviews with Dyer – and he has given many, the published number markedly increasing in the last decade – are often marked by their generosity, what Patricia White has identified as 'the unique combination of the scholarly and the sociable that characterises Richard Dyer's contribution' to film, media and cultural studies.[2] This final section of this Reader attempts to capture and convey this 'unique combination' through a selection of some of the interviews Dyer has given. He has been involved in a number of 'career overview' interviews, such as the SCMS Fieldnotes conversation with Barbara Klinger conducted in 2015, The Cinematologists' exploration of the ongoing salience of Dyer's ideas and themes, or José Arroyo's 2019 dialogue with Dyer in front of an audience at the Flatpack Film Festival;[3] in these, the writing and reception of key publications are foregrounded, and anecdotes are rehearsed and reworked. Distinctive

---

1. Peter Walters, 'Why Richard's got stars in his eyes,' *Coventry Evening Telegraph*, 5 June 1993, p. 8.
2. Patricia White, 'I Know Where I'm Going!', *Cinema Journal* 57:2 (2018), p. 172.
3. Barbara Klinger, 'Fieldnotes: Richard Dyer interviewed by Barbara Klinger', Society for Cinema and Media Studies, 13 April 2015, https://vimeo.com/145394630; Dario Llinares and Neil Fox, The Cinematologists podcast, 'Episode 43: Professor Richard Dyer', 6 April 2017, http://www.cinematologists.com/podcastarchive/2017/4/6/episode-43-professor-richard-dyer; José Arroyo, 'In conversation with Richard Dyer at Flatpack', *First Impressions: Notes on Films and Culture*, 4 May 2019, https://notesonfilm1.com/2019/05/04/in-conversation-with-richard-dyer-at-flatpack/

perspectives and fresh material have a tendency to surface in these overviews, however. An interview with Erec Gellautz and Anna Schober published in 2020, for instance, revisits a number of Dyer's formative moments and writings, before heading off in more dynamic directions. Notably, in response to a question about *RuPaul's Drag Race*, Dyer provides a detailed account of his relationship with drag and its politics:

> I have several times been asked to write about drag, but I need to say I do not understand it. I do not get it. I still feel it is making fun of women and I often find drag queens so masculine. I feel they have all the masculinity that I felt oppressed by as a child being kind of channelled through all these sequins and all these feathers. I find it very often alien. [...] The people I admire are people like butch lesbians and sissy boys, people who do not fit. They are neither denying biology – and I think biology is here, even if very little, I don't think it's nothing, but nor does it give you very much – nor are they claiming some sort of essential gender identity [...] They are not claiming either of those things, but finding a way of pushing the boundaries of sex and gender and denying the sharp distinction.[4]

The political potential of 'inbetweenism' – explored at length in Dyer's essay on queer stereotypes 'Seen to be believed' (1983)[5] – is here revisited, the categorical challenge posed by those who 'do not fit' set against the drag queen's reification of binarisms.

Similarly, at one point in The Cinematologists' podcast interview with Dyer, he is asked to reflect on the 1961 film *Victim* and his own essay about it.[6] Dyer suggests he could have been more generous 'about what it could do' in its historical context, 'and what it had managed to do'. The interviewer compares *Victim* – with its infamous overt declaration of homosexuality, "I wanted him", delivered with anguish and passion by Dirk Bogarde's blackmailed barrister – to *Moonlight*, and asks Dyer whether he thinks that the representation of queer sexuality onscreen remains somewhat chaste:

> I think it's extraordinarily explicit. [...] The two moments in *Victim* and *Moonlight* – in *Victim* it's the photograph of them in the car, and in *Moonlight*, it's the two on the beach. But [...] on the beach, what's going on there, is masturbation. It is true it's in a context

---

4. Anna Schober and Erec Gellautz, 'Trying to Find Out What Is Really Going on with Common Sense: Interview with Richard Dyer', in Anna Schober and Brigitte Hipfl (eds), *Wir und die Anderen: Visuelle Kultur zwischen Aneignung und Ausgrenzung*, Köln: Herbert von Halem Verlag, 2021, pp. 40-41.
5. Richard Dyer, 'Seen to be believed: Some problems in the representation of gay people as typical', *Studies in Visual Communication* 9:2 (1983), pp. 2-19.
6. Richard Dyer, '*Victim*: hermeneutic project', *Film Form* 1:2 (1977), pp. 3-22, reprinted as '*Victim*: hegemonic project' in Richard Dyer, *The Matter of Images: Essays on Representation*, London and New York: Routledge, 1993, pp. 93-110.

of affection, but nonetheless… What I quite like, being such a sentimentalist, is it's all about the love in their eyes, and I actually found that much more positive, actually, than the "I wanted him" [in *Victim*] – that seems to me [to be about] the awfulness of lust. And I just quite like the fact that there's a sadness around it, because I love sadness as a notion.

Dyer goes on to mention examples of explicit queer sexuality in film and television, such as *Weekend*; this section of the interview, however, is marked by the delicate unpacking of the ongoing historical significance of *Victim*, and by the use of nuanced comparison to highlight tonal distinctions and continuities across decades of queer cinema.

In addition to career overview discussions, Dyer has also given more focused interviews on specific texts or themes. These include a 'conversation about pornography' with Simon Shepherd and Mick Wallis (1989), the honest and direct tone of which ensures that the text is peppered throughout with salty, memorable quotes ('I like glossy, hi-tech, well-photographed, well-nautilized bodies. I know this is all a construction, but the urgency of the desire it sets in motion is so great that I then find real life, real men, wanting'; 'I find people in SM gear silly – but then I also find my own fantasies stupid, when I'm not being turned on by them').[7] This particular discussion serves as a useful marker in the evolution of Dyer's thoughts about pornography, its publication date falling between the essays 'Coming to terms' (1985) and 'Idol thoughts' (1994) (see Section 5 of this Reader for both of these texts). In contrast, Dyer's contribution to the 'Fantasy/Animation' podcast provides his only extended consideration of children's media: the conversation with Chris Holliday and Alex Sergeant (2019) focuses on the animated series *Peppa Pig*. Although Dyer concedes his lack of interest in programmes for children, the series is teased apart at length with wit and invention, Dyer suggesting that it provides a fantasy of banality, making out that life is more straightforward and boring than it truly is. 'Everyday life isn't that straightforward', he says, 'even for children.'[8]

The interviews chosen for this section of the Reader are all wide-ranging in the topics they explore, privileging a thematic over a chronological approach. Joe McElhaney's interview, 'Masculinity is so *boring*', first appeared in 1985, just prior to the publication of *Heavenly Bodies*. It was published in *Three or Four Things*, the newsletter

---

7. Richard Dyer, 'A conversation about pornography', in Simon Shepherd and Mick Wallis (eds), *Coming on strong: gay politics and culture*, London: Unwin Hyman, 1989, pp. 204, 208.
8. Christopher Holliday and Alexander Sergeant, 'Peppa Pig', episode 20 of the Fantasy/Animation podcast (May 2019): https://www.fantasy-animation.org/all-episodes/2019/5/3/episode-20-peppa-pig-neville-astley-and-mark-baker-2004-

of the Department of Cinema Studies at Tisch School of the Arts, New York. The same issue also included Robert Stam writing about new Latin American cinema, a piece on Hollis Frampton, and various 'ramblings and gossip'; the cover featured a still of Kirk Douglas and Lana Turner from *The Bad and the Beautiful*. McElhaney's conversation with Dyer explores gay and lesbian viewers' relationship with stars, campness, authorship, masculinity, ethnicity, and the status and influence of key theorists including Bellour and Lacan. Thoughtful dissections of the views of other writers – such as Andrew Britton on camp – are supplemented by pointed comments on individual films, stars, and directors. There are significant revelations: even at this early juncture, Dyer was planning on writing a book about ethnicity. Two of the three examples explored in 'White' (1988, see Section 4 of this Reader) – *Jezebel* and *Night of the Living Dead* – are mentioned as potentially worthy of scrutiny. A response to a question about authorship – 'I think one should marginalise the importance of the author. I think [that] work on [gay directors such as Murnau or Cukor] needs to be done with a reconstructed notion of authorship' – prefigures the argument about strategic essentialism that Dyer would go on to elaborate at length in the essay 'Believing in fairies' (1991).[9]

The April 1997 issue of gay porn magazine *Torso* featured 'To be reel', an interview with Dyer by Matthew Rettenmund, the author of the 1995 novel *Boy Culture*. The cover model was 'video stud' Matt Bradshaw; in a separate feature inside, readers were promised, 'Lorenzo outgrows his jockstrap'. Dyer's name, disappointingly, did not feature on the cover. Obviously, Rettenmund asks Dyer about nudity on screen and about pornography but also addresses other concerns. Perhaps because the interview appears in a non-academic publication, basic questions are raised: 'Why do people have a hard time taking popular culture seriously?', 'Is there such a thing as a "gay movie"?', 'Do you ever shrug your shoulders and say, "It's just a movie"?' These prods lead to insightful observations even though, as Dyer self-reflexively acknowledges in relation to one of his answers, 'I don't know if that's the kind of answer you want. I can't imagine it in *Torso*!' Catherine Grant and Jaap Kooijman's 2016 interview with Dyer for *NECSUS*, the journal of the European Network for Cinema and Media Studies, explores the ways in which three particular themes – pleasure, the obvious, queerness – permeate various aspects of Dyer's writing. Like Rettenmund's, their questions can be seen as provocations. Thinking and talking across his output, Dyer outs himself as a Marxist (again), discusses the value of using plain language, and addresses the limited attention he has given to AIDS in his work.

---

9. Richard Dyer, 'Believing in fairies: the author and the homosexual', in Diana Fuss (ed.), *Inside/Out: Lesbian Theories, Gay Theories*, London and New York: Routledge, 1991, pp. 185–202.

This section (and the Reader as a whole) closes with a new interview with Dyer, 'Writing out of love or politics', conducted by us in July 2021 over Skype. Questions were assembled to specifically address gaps in previous interviews, and to explore topics that had emerged in the assembly of this book. The conversation lasted for well over two hours, sliding easily between reminiscence, theoretical reflections, and overt gossip. In 1985, Joe McElhaney wrote that 'the flexibility and openness which distinguish [Dyer's] writing are so consistent with Richard as a person that it is difficult to separate the two'; the scholarly and the sociable merge. Decades later, as all of those who have interviewed Dyer can attest, this remains true.

54 MASCULINITY IS SO *BORING* (1985)
with Joe McElhaney

For virtually anyone writing during the last eight years on gay cinema, the star system, or popular culture in general, the contributions of Richard Dyer have clearly been seminal. His approach has been characterized by its attention to both cultural and historical specificity as well as a certain tentative or exploratory attitude towards his object of study. Dyer almost never approaches a text in order to clearly and definitively place it in relation to the culture that produced it or in the ways in which it may be read by that culture or appropriated by various subcultures. Rather, the work itself and the ways in which it may be read are subject to many historical and cultural determinants which render them ambiguous and fluctuating. This at least partly explains his aversion to Lacanian feminism and its tendency to lock in and neatly categorize responses, a tendency he regards (in the accompanying interview) as 'a reactionary dead end.'

This interview came about as a result of Dyer presenting a colloquia in the Department [of Cinema Studies at Tisch School of the Arts, New York University] on May 3 on 'Lesbian and Gay Cinema in Weimar Germany.' The colloquia itself (accompanied by a slide presentation) was easily the most popular of the 1984–85 academic year, with over sixty people in attendance. Ultimately, however, the colloquia for me was little more than a pretext for meeting and interviewing Dyer. It would be an understatement to say that Dyer's work has been important to me and I sometimes feel that my own writing has been little more than a very dim echo of Dyer's.

I would like to thank Richard for not only agreeing to be interviewed but also for his friendship. It is probably not all that important as far as appreciating his writing to know that he is also an extremely nice person. But the flexibility and openness which distinguish his writing are as consistent with Richard as a person that it is difficult to separate the two.

▲ ▲ ▲

JM: *Since much of your writing has been concerned with both the star system and with gays in film, I thought we might begin by talking about the function of stars in gay male culture, in particular female stars. In the past you have written about such stars as Lana Turner, Diana Ross, Barbra Streisand, and Rita Hayworth, all of them major icons in gay male culture. But you generally only touched on their importance to gay men in the essays, if at all. (I don't mean this as a criticism. The essays generally took on broader concerns than gay reception.) In your forthcoming book,* Heavenly Bodies, *there are chapters on Marilyn Monroe and Judy Garland, both of them stars with substantial gay male followings. Do you deal with the ways in which these stars function in gay culture in the book?*

RD: In the Garland chapter, yes. In fact, that chapter is entirely about how gay men would read Judy Garland and I tried to introduce the notion of a gay reading of a particular star. I did it partly through analyzing what gay men said about Judy Garland, both in the gay press and in letters sent to me through advertizing I did in the gay press. Then I tried to see if there was any kind of fit between the specifics of her image and performance style and the specifics of gay male subculture. I also wanted to bring in a wide range of ways that Judy Garland could be made sense of to a gay community and also to get historically specific. The chapter is very much about the post-1950 Judy Garland but it also includes ways in which you read back into the forties movies. I don't think there's any evidence to suggest that she was crucial to gay men prior to 1950.

JM: *Did you get very many letters from gay men who may have been fans during the fifties?*

RD: Yes, but they're disappointing in a way. I got fewer responses than I expected to and I only got five from people who actually remembered her from the fifties. What was interesting was that people were much younger than I expected. I can remember a period when Judy Garland was very important to me and when you said you were a Judy Garland fan [it] was almost like saying you were gay. The person who initiated me into gay culture (not sexually, but into gay culture) was a Garland fan and I remember his view of her had a very negative element to it. He would say, 'Oh, she's awful and dreadful and that's just like us.' He didn't say it quite that explicitly but it was the idea that we were poor old things like her. But I didn't actually find much evidence in the writing or in the letters about that negative self-identification with Judy Garland. The trouble is all the evidence I've got is remembrances or things written since Gay Liberation. There's very little evidence of what people actually thought during the fifties. Actually, no evidence at all apart from this wonderful British film magazine called *Films and Filming*. It's a kind of closeted gay magazine which makes it fascinating, in a way. They were very interested in Judy in a positive way as well, though the idea that we all loved her because we hated ourselves was what I personally remember being brought up to think although I have no evidence for it.

JM: *If you look at the pre-1950 films, there are all these elements of camp and androgyny to her performances which have historically appealed to gay audiences so even without all the publicity about what a terrible life she had, it's not inconceivable that she would have developed a gay following anyway.*

RD: But I think that Garland is perhaps *the* gay female star. That's why all those extra-textual readings are so important. It's not so much that we're all obsessed with self-pity and self-loathing (although that may be part of it) as that it allows us a way of seeing a kind of homology between Garland, girl next door (but with all these problems) and gay men, brought up to [be] 'ordinary' but who actually turn out to be 'different.' I think it fits in with a very essentialist view of homosexuality that we are somehow born different and I probably don't agree with it. But I think it's a major defining discourse.

JM: *So many of the female stars popular with gay men have had well-publicized problems with men, with drugs and alcohol, and various other scandals – Lana Turner, Ava Gardner, Rita Hayworth, Marilyn Monroe, and so on.*

RD: Yes, that's right. But I wonder if that's what's important about them. One thing that would be interesting to do would be to make an argument for a kind of straight construction of homosexual men during the forties, fifties and sixties as essentially tragic, self-pitying characters. And therefore that straight discourse constructs our interest in the Ava Gardners of this world as being about self-pity and self-loathing. I wouldn't say that this straight discourse is not accurate at all. But I think what's equally important is our admiration for the strength of these women and for their going against norms, and so on.

JM: *In the case of Gardner, there's really no self-pity at all in her stage image or the ways in which I've understood gay men to appreciate her.*

RD: Yes, that's right, and the same is true of Lana as well. All the letters I received on Garland (and the youngest person who wrote was 17) said that what they liked about her was that she was very good and left it at that. (Most people's actual experience of a star is not that they represent blah blah blah but that they are wonderful and 'of course' you like them.) But beyond that, nearly all of the letters said that she had a tough life but she kept going. It was always that combination. So they *were* interested in the suicide attempts and all of that but not in a ghoulish way. Yet it *was* important for them, even the 17-year-old.

JM: *And that aspect of Garland may appeal to heterosexuals as well.*

RD: Oh, sure! She *was* popular with heterosexuals. (Laughs) I've got a wonderful cutting from an *Evening News* from when she was alive called 'Pat Learns to Walk from Singer's Inspiration.' It's about a spastic who was so inspired by Judy's overcoming of her troubles that she thought that if Judy could overcome her troubles so could she. And she learned to walk as a result of it. An inspiring human interest story. (Laughs) Of course she might have been a lesbian but the story didn't say anything about that.

LESBIAN ICONOGRAPHY / LESBIAN PORNOGRAPHY

JM: *There has probably been even less writing on lesbian urban subcultures and their fascination with female stars than gay male.*

RD: One of the things that I think is important for gay men as well as lesbians is to be aware of the danger of being essentialist. One needs to talk about materially, historically, and specifically located lesbian or gay subcultures. I do think that's crucial. In

The iconic Marlene Dietrich, 1930. (Eugene Robert Richee/John Kobal Foundation/Getty Images)

relation to lesbians, there has been a much smaller development of an urban lesbian subculture. The only work I know has been done in Germany which has been quite interested in relating the iconography of Dietrich and Garbo and some of the German stars we are not all that familiar with (like Asta Nielsen and Elisabeth Bergner) to a distinct lesbian iconography of the twenties.

JM: *Like gay men, lesbians are often attracted to androgynous female stars.*

RD: Yes, that's right. But in this German work it is related to the Radclyffe Hall/Gertrude Stein *garçonne* tradition of the twenties. There was a whole tradition of films in Germany about women dressing as men with all kinds of fascinating ambiguities. The first *Victor/Victoria* was a German film (although it's not very interesting in those terms). But when it comes to more contemporary figures, I don't know of anyone who's really done the work about the correspondences. Until the last few years the dominant lesbian formation was into ideas of alternative women's culture, revaluing women's mythology, relating lesbianism to the ultimate in womanhood, and really getting into the mythic and natural. They were terribly hostile to the mass media and would have no truck at all with anything in movies. Now you've got an emergent sense of a dyke tradition which didn't just go away. There's an attempt to rediscover that and begin to define what it consists of. But so far I haven't read anything which gets beyond something like the Chris Straayer piece on *Personal Best*. I think that's a terrific piece but in that he just talks about the women enjoying the more lesbian-identified character, and about them enjoying her body and her looks and so on. But he doesn't get into talking about whether there is a particular construction of a look that lesbians will go for.

JM: *Do you think it is just very difficult to contextualize and historicize the moment you're living in?*

RD: That could be the reason, yes. One of the emphases of feminism is to be very wary of talking about attractiveness. That immediately involves hierarchies of discrimination. And also to be wary of saying that lesbians are going to be attracted to the androgynous, that is to say, more masculine woman. Both of those are kind of forbidden views within feminism. I imagine it is quite hard for a more dyke-identified culture to find a voice worth speaking given the kind of moral force of feminism. Of course, now there are new lesbian pornography magazines, *On Our Backs* and *Bad Attitude*, and so on. They're quite interesting. *On Our Backs* is almost like what a dyke magazine in the fifties would have been like if you could have had such a thing. The iconography is very aggressive: cropped hair, tough expressions, male clothes. There is even a pin-up. The magazine seems willing to go back into all this butch and femme.

But *Bad Attitude* is much more glossy. I saw one two-page spread of a woman lying on her back with her legs open and wearing this frilly blouse and no bra and it's quite like an image I use in my pornography lectures which is right out of straight men's magazines. But l haven't had time to actually put it all together. To say: Now what is that image in lesbian culture? Is that formally different or is it simply different because it's aimed for a different audience? What real difference does the production and consumption context make? Who is actually buying this magazine – heterosexual men?

CAMP

JM: *I was wondering if we could talk about Andrew Britton's article, 'For Interpretation: Notes Against Camp.' It attacked both your piece, 'It's Being So Camp As Keeps Us Going,' and Jack Babuscio's chapter on camp in* Gays and Film. *I suppose we could just begin by asking if you have any immediate response to Britton.*

RD: My response to Andrew Britton's piece (which is a sort of mean response) is: Yes, I agree with all of those criticisms and it's what I said in my article to begin with. My piece was a typical on the one hand/on the other hand academic article (although it was actually published in a gay porn magazine and then reproduced in *The Body Politic*). It was saying that there are both good things and bad things about camp. What Andrew Britton did was simply deny all the good ones and repeat all the bad ones.

JM: *Britton argues that camp always trivializes.*

RD: I said that as well, but I also think that's one of its strengths because it's often trivializing things that merit trivialization.

JM: *Britton writes primarily about camp response rather than self-consciously camp works. I think he's quite right in arguing against, for instance, the sort of camp response of someone like Jack Babuscio towards Jennifer Jones in* Duel in the Sun *or Bette Davis in* Beyond the Forest. *It's quite problematic in cases like those in which the desires, the frustrations, the angers of the female characters are very precisely articulated and I think cases could be made* for *the films along feminist lines. So for someone to be laughing at all of this is pretty appalling.*

RD: I say in my piece that the problem with camp is that it is *so* relentlessly trivializing and I get quite fed up with it, too. It is completely unable to distinguish between what merits trivialization and what doesn't. And it is also quite misogynistic at times. But again, I think we're back to ambiguity arguments. Is it laughing at the social construction of femininity or is it laughing at women? And that's how ambiguous it is, really. You can't push one without pushing the other. I feel that Andrew Britton's piece is just too morally against camp. He's a very nice person but he will write in this bombastic way and it sometimes defeats the things he wants to do. At the point he was writing his camp piece he was very into Hollywood as Great Art. I think he feels that camp is not impressed by arguments about Great Art which is probably one of the good points about camp, that it's not going to bow down just because it's John Ford.

JM: *But didn't you argue in your piece that John Wayne is camp?*

RD: Yes, but I don't think anything *is* camp. I just think that anything can be *read* as camp.

JM: *Still, I don't know of anyone who reads John Wayne as camp.*

RD: I think I put John Wayne in my article slightly to be provocative. There's certainly no camp following for Wayne. But when some people watch Wayne they shriek with laughter at the excessive masculinity and I think that's a camp response.

JM: *A* gay *camp response?*

RD: Well, no…

JM: *The first step would be to get substantial numbers of gay men into a theatre to actually see a John Wayne movie.*

RD: I can understand Andrew Britton's anxiety about calling John Wayne camp because I love *Red River* and *Rio Bravo* and *The Man Who Shot Liberty Valance* and *The Searchers*. I do think that John Wayne embodies something very serious and those films have dealt with it very seriously. So to simply shriek with laughter is to not see what those films are doing. But on the other hand, that's a very privileged film studies kind of discourse. Outside of that, those movies are just westerns and there are a lot of things about westerns that are very ideologically oppressive. And one not unhealthy response is to laugh. You're right that one is unlikely to ever see *The Searchers* with a camp group. More problematic are some of the Bette Davis films where you feel that what's being missed is a kind of statement about women and what's being laughed at is women.

JM: *I felt that acutely in New York a couple of years ago when I sat through a double bill of* Stella Dallas *and* Mildred Pierce *with a largely gay audience which laughed hysterically for four hours.*

RD: I'm sure I would find it very disturbing. But isn't that because we're all caught up in this film studies ideological discourse? And at the same time, we don't know exactly what these people are laughing at.

JM: *The problem is that we're talking about a level of response which is very difficult to theorize or be precise about in any way.*

RD: What you can't do is say what *a* response is. You can maybe talk about what a range of responses might be about. That's one of the problems about doing audience work. When I say I'm doing work on Judy Garland's gay following, people often say, 'What is the reason?' As if there could only be one reason why it's so. Obviously, you can delineate a range of responses (not all but some of them) so that they can begin to make sense.

JM: *What about explicitly camp works like John Waters? Do you see any value in that aggressive form of camp?*

RD: I don't particularly like the films, but I like the argument that they assert deviancy very positively in the way that people like to talk about Genet and that whole tradition. I can see all that argument. But when I actually watch the films, I've very troubled. For instance, what *really* is funny about Divine? Is she funny in the ways that she is able to run rings around people? Or is it that she's this fat woman we can all shriek with laughter at? I know Divine is a man but I think drag is always problematic and I don't think Divine is any less so.

JM: *I don't know that I ever laugh at Divine. I think her performances are much too self-consciously outrageous and 'knowing' to even allow for that kind of response. Also, I think that the films themselves are [too] complex in the various levels at which they operate to argue that we're all just laughing at a fat drag queen.*

RD: Another response I have (and this is my Marxism creeping back in) is: Aren't these films utterly cynical and nihilistic and disconnected with anything that's wrong with society? I know that's a terribly moralistic reaction but I tire of Waters very quickly and I feel that the films aren't really all that outrageous. It's just the usual 'let's get at the middle classes and shock them and feel like we're doing something.' There's nothing important about that. They've always been shocked. But I'm quite attracted to the way that people who do like the films argue for them. It's just that when I see the films I'm not very responsive.

Divine in John Waters' *Female Trouble*, 1974. (John Springer Collection/CORBIS/Corbis via Getty Images)

JM: *It's very interesting to see a film like* Female Trouble *with a mixed straight and gay crowd and to listen to the responses. For instance, when Edith Massey tells her straight hairdresser nephew in the film, 'The world of the heterosexual is a sick and boring life,' all of the gay people in the audience cheer and the straights just have to sit there and take it.*

RD: Well, that's a good moment. The thing about camp, like all humour, is that it's completely unruly. You can't guarantee it politically and ideologically. So when people want to claim some form of humour is inherently subversive or inherently reactionary, I think it's usually neither. And the way we've talked about the Waters films shows that. I suppose one could say that those films are available to be used in ways that are progressive and ways that are reactionary. But the films themselves are neither. They make available a series of images which at certain moments can be used quite shockingly to assert a kind of anti-heterosexism (which we should assert). But at the same time we may be laughing at misogynistic images of women.

GAY AUTHORS / GAY AUDIENCES

JM: *You have written about openly gay directors like Pasolini and Fassbinder and have expressed major reservations about their work and their status as gay directors. How do you feel about work being done on more closeted gay directors or on gay directors working within more oppressive systems than Pasolini or Fassbinder?*

RD: I think a lot more work needs to be done on gay authors and a lot more work needs to be done on gay audiences. My students often say to me, 'Of course you're anti-auteurist unless the director happens to be a woman or gay.' Which is true, in a way. I really couldn't care less who directs it. I don't want to put forward a position that there are no authors. I think that's a silly position. But I think one should marginalize the importance of the author. Yet, clearly if I say we should do work on Murnau or Cukor in terms of their being gay it's a way of privileging the director again. I think this work needs to be done with a reconstructed notion of authorship and until that notion is reconstructed, people will still be locked between old-fashioned auteurism or else a complete anti-auteurism. I'm much more interested in seeing people like Cukor or Murnau placed clearly within a definable gay discourse. If we can't do that, I don't know how much mileage there is in it. I think Murnau is wonderful but I'm not much interested in Murnau as this special person. I'm interested in how a gay discourse could and couldn't be articulated at a certain point in time. Yes, Murnau was the person that 'did it,' but what interests me is the discourse rather than the particularity of Murnau. I do think this work can and should be done. But I really want people to spend a bit more time thinking more carefully where figures like Murnau are placed. I don't want to do a Peter Wollen and put it in inverted commas and shelve the problem. At the same time, I don't want to do the classic Sarris position of all these wonderful people expressing themselves. I think Janet Wolff is the only person I see who has formulated a position on authorship which both acknowledges that there are specific, discreet individuals who produce works of art while at the same time says those authors are not to be given the centrality that the authorship theory gives them. They have to be marginalized or seen as only one element in relation to production.

JM: *Al LaValley recently published an article in* American Film *outlining the various ways in which gay men have historically responded to certain films, genres, directors, stars, etc. What did you think of that piece?*

RD: I think it's essentialist to say that gay people like this, that or the other and I do think Al LaValley gets into that problem. I happen to know that that is half the length of the original piece he wrote so one doesn't know how much more careful that longer piece is. It's easily read as saying that gay men just *do* have these feelings without really seeing how it's related to any specific social situations of gay men and how in the face of that social situation and in particular places (mainly urban areas) a subculture developed defence mechanisms for dealing with their situation and part of that defence mechanism is a way of reading movies.

JM: *Don't you think it's time to stop writing these very general pieces on camp and gay subcultures and begin to deal with very specific works, very specific stars, very specific kinds of responses?*

RD: Absolutely, yes. And begin to uncover real evidence for it.

JM: *But when you talk about uncovering evidence for subcultural responses, where is that evidence?*

RD: Well, it is difficult. There are gay novels, there are people's memories, there are biographies. All historical work has this problem. It's just slightly worse for gay history.

JM: *The most problematic section of LaValley's piece is the one dealing with 'the natural man.'*

RD: I couldn't quite figure out why he called it that.

JM: *He begins with a definition of it, cites the Michael Ontkean character in* Making Love, *and then he starts talking about all of those stud figures from Tennessee Williams and William Inge. I couldn't see any relation between the two.*

RD: Yes, I know. It was odd.

JM: *He also never seems to question the extremely problematic place these stud figures have as gay icons.*

RD: I think the formulations earlier in the piece are quite good and better than Jack Babuscio's. But the natural man section does seem very unsatisfactory. Somebody really does need to grasp that nettle and the recurrence of these macho images in gay culture. To what extent are these images linked up with notions of straightness, naturalness, and also to even a camp kind of masculinity – Tom of Finland, or Jeff Chandler, or the fashion for muscles? I just think someone really needs to think through this macho image, where it comes from, how it's constructed, what it has to do with questions of our self-esteem. What *was* interesting was when LaValley talked about *Splendor in the Grass* in which the men are more closely identified with nature. You might be able to work up quite an interesting line with things like *Song of the Loon* and Whitman and a whole gay tradition which does have something to do with men in nature.

JM: *But LaValley makes all these connections between Inge and the Natalie Wood character, with Wood somehow representing Inge and Warren Beatty as the object of Inge's desire.*

RD: Yes, that's the worst kind of unreconstructed authorship approach, that the characters represent the author. What LaValley really wants to talk about is masculine-identified men and their relation to gay sexuality. But that section of his article is too compressed and unthought through. Also, I just think masculinity is so *boring*. I've just written a piece about the representation of male sexuality in the general media and it's one of the pieces I most hated writing because partly I find the way the media constructs male sexuality is rather repulsive. On the whole, I don't really like writing about something that I don't, in some sense, enjoy. I don't think one should write pieces celebrating one's own responses. But I think it's important that one's responses inform what one writes. If you don't like the stuff, your writing can become rather lifeless. That's why I found that piece difficult to write. There's something so boring about straight male sexuality, the image of it.

JM: *What do you think of the increased use of the male body and male sexuality in advertising – the Calvin Klein ads, and so on?*

RD: At the level of: Do I like it? Yes, I do. The only way I like masculinity is as a spectacle. I don't want anything else to do with masculinity. I feel that they have begun to find ways of making men spectacle in a way that doesn't impugn their masculinity. One of the things that seems to be happening now is the increase in women having muscles. That sleek, hard look is in a lot of advertising now. You could take the line that there's nothing inherently wrong with muscle tone and that it's good that it's both available to men and women. But I'm not really sure that you can free it of its cultural baggage like that. Muscles always connote masculinity. You cannot suddenly not connote it. What doesn't seem to become influential is Boy George and Prince and that kind of look.

JM: *Boy George was picked up predominantly by teenage girls.*

RD: Yes, you don't see many men walking around looking like Prince or Michael Jackson. It's not as if there aren't images in popular culture of feminized men, but they seem rather isolated. They're not influential. It's Wham! that's influential.

JM: *They recently gave a press conference announcing that they are not gay. It seems people have been talking.*

RD: Oh, really? I think one of them, the one who doesn't do anything, isn't gay.

DISCO / GAY ROCK

JM: *You wrote a piece for* Gay Left *in 1979 called 'In defence of disco'…*

RD: My most controversial piece. (Laughs)

JM: *You wrote, among other things, about its appeal to gay men in that it was non-phallocentric (as opposed to rock 'n' roll) emphasizing instead a kind of whole body sexuality and that its lyrics could often be read as somehow 'speaking' to gay men (in a coded or indirect way) about their sexuality and their lifestyle. Since that time, disco has changed enormously and we have had (coming out of England, primarily) some openly gay rock groups – The Smiths, Bronski Beat, Culture Club, Frankie Goes to Hollywood, etc. What do you think of these changes?*

RD: When I wrote that piece, disco was just on the point of changing. I think the whole masculinization of gay culture is what has happened to disco, where now we have this driving beat, all that high energy stuff. So I don't like what's happened to disco. But in terms of groups, I think Bronski Beat is particularly interesting. Aside from the fact that I quite like the records and their 'doing' Donna Summer (a nice appropriation of what was an old gay culture and wresting it away from what unfortunately happened to poor Donna) what is especially interesting is their working classness. I don't know how much that's understood in the States.

JM: *In the States, they have often been taken to have a conventional clone look – the shaved heads, the Levi's, the plaid flannel shirts, and so on.*

RD: In Britain, that's more of a skinhead look. It's not *that* much of a gay look. It's certainly not a clone look. It absolutely connotes working classness and they are definitely working class. That's a real departure within gay iconography. Also, their decision to not continue working as a group is rather like when they said Rimbaud's greatest act of poetry was to stop writing. When they started, Bronski Beat always kept saying that they were not interested in success and making a lot of money and that they would quit if it just got too much for them. And most people's reactions were, 'Oh, yeah. I'll bet.' So their breaking up is really kind of hopeful, in a way.

ETHNICITY

JM: *I understand you've been working on ethnicity in film and are planning to do a book on it.*

RD: The book is very far in the future, although I do teach a course on it. One of the important things about the ethnicity project is to look at whiteness as an ethnic identity as well as Blackness, and try to deconstruct and denaturalize Blackness. I am interested in the way the films construct Blacks and we get into stereotyping and all that through films like *Car Wash* and *St. Louis Blues*. But I'm also interested in the construction of whiteness. We look at *Jezebel*, for instance, in the way that the Blacks function to highlight the emotional repressedness of the white characters. Very often the Bette Davis character is unable to express her emotions in certain ways and it is her servants and plantation workers who express, physically and emotionally, what she cannot. Which tells us something about the construction of Blackness and whiteness in relation to emotion. We also look at *Night of the Living Dead* and *Dawn of the Dead*, particularly *Night of the Living Dead*. It may seem incidental that the main character is Black and progressive somehow because the film doesn't make any big deal out of his being Black. But I think his being Black is significant because I think the zombies are white and in all sorts of ways the zombies represent the dead hand of white culture.

JM: *And the Black character has to deal with that hysterical, incapacitated blonde woman.*

RD: Exactly. Even the ones who aren't zombies either become zombies (like her) or else they are part of that family devouring itself. And the house has a lot of things about it that are coded as being part of a genteel white society. Of course, at the end the white rednecks shoot the Black man. It's almost as though whites represent death and the one man who represents life is Black. That's an idea that can be traced back to the Harlem Renaissance and certain ideas that Blacks represent life and whites represent a kind of sterility or death.

JM: *Imitation of Life, The Cotton Club.*

RD: Yes. But I certainly don't want to get into a line that whites are oppressed, too. Sometimes when masculinity was put into the melting pot there were people who went around saying, 'Oh, poor men. They suffer, too.' I'm not into *that*. (Laughs) Anyway, I'm extending the course next semester. We look at Marilyn Monroe as a white woman and her image of whiteness and why that was important and how that linked up with images of desirable sexuality during the fifties. We also plan to look at *Son of the Sheik*, *The Searchers*, *The Birth of a Nation*, *The Godfather* films to look at questions of variations within white ethnicity, *Marked Woman* and Bette Davis as a white star.

JM: *James Baldwin has written about Bette Davis…*

RD: Yes, I know. Isn't it wonderful? He thought he was ugly until he saw Bette Davis and saw that she had the same eyes as his.

BEGINNINGS & ENDINGS

JM: *What is your academic background? How did you begin teaching and writing about film?*

RD: My undergraduate degree was in French. I guess I've always been interested in the movies and liked the movies. But I actually worked in the theatre after I graduated and then I went to the Centre for Contemporary Cultural Studies at the University of Birmingham. I was originally going to study homosexuality in fiction but I decided I couldn't face reading all those books. (Laughs) So I decided that what interested me was showbiz and the idea of entertainment. I decided that the easiest material to use would be musical films rather than theatre. (Of course, now I think there are problems in the fact that one sees a film over and over again and how that transforms it into a different object of study.) Film studies was just beginning to develop in Britain and somebody asked Stuart Hall, who was the director of the Centre, whether there was anyone who could teach film. I was at the university and he said, 'Could you?' I said, 'Yes, of course I can.' (Laughs) And I gradually taught myself about film in the course of teaching evening classes. Even now, though, I would rather be teaching cultural studies with film as a particular object of study rather than in any way that wants to valorize films as Great Art.

JM: *Do textual analyses interest you at all?*

RD: They interest me and of course I do it. I'm actually even interested in formalistic textual analysis. It fascinates me. I don't think you can analyze movies without being textually sensitive. I'm very against sociological reductionism. It's a constant danger in cultural studies. So I'm all for the specificities of the medium. But I don't want to isolate it from production or consumption. I'm more interested in putting textual analysis together with various modes of reading. I'm very interested in film and dance, for instance, and the ways in which different formal strategies build and construct a different perception of dance. Those things fascinate me. But they don't have much principal urgency. It feels like an indulgence to do it. Most formalism is kind of arid. It doesn't seem to ask very interesting questions.

JM: *What about Bellour on Hitchcock?*

RD: I'm absolutely fascinated that Bellour should be taken up by Anglo-Saxon film studies. It seems to me that Bellour is essentially an old-fashioned French classicist and what he's saying is, 'Aren't these films beautiful?' I was taught to do that because the education of French I had included being taught French critical method and what you did was celebrate the perfection of Racine or whatever. And I think Bellour just celebrates the perfection of Hitchcock.

JM: *I think Bellour's approach is a bit more complex than that. He often speaks of the classical cinema as being both pleasurable and alienating.*

RD: Perhaps you're right. I've just never made it through in Bellour's writing to where he made that final move to finding it alienating... Then there's that whole psychoanalytic formalistic school.

JM: *Does it interest you at all?*

RD: I can't say it doesn't interest me. You can't be in film studies and not know about it. I certainly don't want to do it. I think Freud is very interesting and psychoanalysis is very interesting. You can't be in this culture and not be affected by it. It's a culturally and historically specific thing you need to know about. But I think Lacan has been the really bad influence. In twenty years' time, someone may want to write about this strange little twist in film studies in the seventies when this very obscure figure, who by chance happened to be Althusser's analyst, should somehow be introduced into film studies and then be constituted as the mainstream of psychoanalysis, when he's so marginal in France and in the whole psychoanalytic tradition. And what is even more bizarre, this homophobic, misogynistic theorist is then taken up by feminists. It's difficult to get one's head around why all that happened. I can understand why male feminists would want to use it because I think there's a way in which the kind of systemization and ritualization of what we take for Lacanianism is a way of distancing yourself from emotion. It's a very characteristic male strategy to even name feelings, to think that by systematizing them you've got a grip on them. I can understand why *that* happened and why a lot of the people who said this is great feminist theory were, of course, men in *Screen*. But why then also feminists would pick it up I don't know since it leads to a position that feminism is a waste of time. We're all inevitably caught up in these structures of discontent and anxiety and there's nothing you can do about it. It excuses heterosexual relations not changing.

JM: *Some of the more recent and more interesting work has been concerned with both straight women and lesbians rediscovering pleasure in cinema.*

RD: That kind of work is very good and very significant, particularly the lesbian work that is beginning to emerge as a counter to all of that moralistic and psychoanalytic tradition in feminism. I think that's fantastic. It's the most positive thing that's happening. But it seems to me there may be desire on the part of the psychoanalytic school to rush in to that position and appropriate it. I don't know how you can twist Lacanian psychoanalysis around to somehow have a theory that makes it possible to read it any other way than the phallically anxious way that Lacanian theory suggests. It just seems to me a dead end and a very reactionary dead end. But the new work being done on the spectator is very encouraging as long as it doesn't fall into the grip of psychoanalysis. Unfortunately, I think that's likely to happen since semiotic psychoanalysis is so hegemonic within American film studies. But I hope not.

Originally published in *Three or Four Things*, a newsletter of the Department of Cinema Studies, Tisch School of the Arts, New York University, 2:2 (Spring 1985), pp. 10–18.

55 TO BE REEL (1997)
with Matthew Rettenmund

Movie buffs have made Richard Dyer their patron saint. The charming British professor was a trailblazer in film studies, one of the first to write about homosexuality in film as an openly gay man. Along with his insights, his popularity is due to his writing style, which is extremely accessible, peppered with one-liners. His book-length works are the seminal studies *Gays and Film*, *Stars*, *Heavenly Bodies*, *Brief Encounter* and *Now You See It*, and he has written on topics as diverse as Paul Robeson's crossover appeal, why gay men *looove* Judy Garland and Ryan Idol's cult of celebrity.

Dyer gave a rare Stateside presentation as part of The Eighth Annual New York Lesbian & Gay Festival, a sold-out lecture entitled 'Nice Young Men Who Sell Antiques Do It' that explored representations of gay men in period pieces like *Maurice* (1987). He was well-received, with a capacity crowd hanging on his every word. An insight into Dyer's mass appeal was how he good-naturedly dealt with a faulty mike by exclaiming, 'It's all right – I have a classically trained voice!' He did the rest of his speech unaided by electronic enhancements, giving the evening the air of a one-man show. Noël Coward would've been bitterly envious.

We turned the spotlight on Dyer during his stay in the country that gave him so much to analyze, including Marilyn Monroe, Hollywood excess, Kenneth Anger and the best porn on the planet.

▲ ▲ ▲

MR: *When did you come out in your private life?*

RD: Oh, dear. I think I'm one of those people that was always out. I was a queeny little boy, really. Although I didn't make a decision to come out, when I was about 17 or so, I thought, 'Well, this is obviously not going to change, I'm going to go on… wanting men.' (Both laugh) I thought what you had to do was be very outrageous. I thought that was how you had to live in order to be gay, so I was very queeny, before Gay Liberation. That was the way I came out – not by telling people that I was gay, but just by *being*.

MR: *You're also openly gay professionally.*

RD: Again, there was never a moment of decision. When I went to do graduate work, I was accepted to do work on 'gays in fiction' – I never did it, I changed the topic, but that's what I was accepted to do. I never said, 'I'm gay,' but they had no doubt. (Both laugh) Some of the earliest things I published were gay things, so it was pretty clear.

Also, to the first job I got, I wore women's jumpers at that stage (both laugh), pretty little women's jumpers. I remember one of the heads of departments saying that he thought I should dress less like a student. I thought it was amazing because none of my students dressed like that, so it was pretty obvious what he was saying.

MR: *Do you encounter people who are shocked that your career is in studying, writing about and teaching film and television theory?*

RD: Yes, certainly. Once they know that, they're not surprised that I do gay things, as well. (Laughs) Yes, I think people still think, 'Wow, you make a living just looking at movies and talking about them?' I think perhaps a *little* bit less now than 20 years ago.

MR: *Why do people have a hard time taking pop culture seriously?*

RD: Because what's established as what's to be taken seriously is high culture, and that's thought to be something that's difficult, something that takes itself seriously, that has to *be* taken seriously and is not concerned with commerce. I think people think of popular culture as being something which is above all about entertainment and always is commercial. I don't know if people still really quite believe that, but certainly for many, many years art's claim to its own superiority lay precisely in saying, 'Well, we're doing it because we believe in it, not just for money, not just to please you,' whereas obviously popular culture *is* about pleasing.

I mean, I think, actually, all art is about pleasing. The idea that it's about something not to do with pleasure is a 19th-century idea. But for a certain period, that's how art established its particular value in society.

MR: *It was always about pleasing someone, whether it was the masses or some rich patron.*

RD: Exactly, exactly.

MR: *What did you think of the film* Stonewall *(1996)?*

RD: I think it's very enjoyable, and I don't have an opinion about whether it's accurate. I wasn't *excited* by it. I felt rather bad about that because I thought, 'Here I am with the apparently typical English response of not being really carried away.' For some reason, it didn't elate me.

MR: *What's your opinion of* Philadelphia *(1993), and how do you think it's affected gay representations onscreen since? If it has?*

RD: I wonder if it has at all, really. I feel very awkward about it, because that was another film that I just found quite boring. I do appreciate the argument – and the same is true of *Stonewall*, that was shown on primetime television in Britain – that *Philadelphia* was shown in shopping malls across the States. I saw it on an airplane when I was flying to San Francisco. This is extraordinarily mainstream for something that is so unambiguously gay and pro-gay. It's very important, but there's something bland about it. My feeling is that the industry thinks, 'We've done that. We don't need to do it again.' What *is* successful is drag queens, like *The Adventures of Priscilla, Queen of the Desert* (1994) and *The Birdcage* (1996). That seems to be more influential, that embrace of lovable drag queens; you could say *Stonewall* – in that sense – is not particularly different from those films.

MR: *You were in the film version of the late Vito Russo's* The Celluloid Closet *(1996). Were you happy with the way it turned out?*

RD: I was very happy and sort of conceited with it! (Laughs) I imagined they wouldn't use me. I think it's moving; I didn't expect it to be. I expected it to be useful and interesting, but it's very powerful, the way it's edited. I'm very happy for Vito. I think he would've been pleased.

MR: *Is there such a thing as a 'gay movie'?*

RD: Hmmm. It depends on how academic an answer you would like! You could say that 'gay' doesn't mean people who love people of the same sex. It's a very specific historical thing that lasted about 20 years, from 1970 to 1990 and was very much about saying, 'I am homosexual, I feel positive about it,' and that was what Gay Liberation was all about, and it was really important for that to happen at that time.

You could say any film – even a film made by a man about lesbians like *Lianna* (John Sayles, 1982), which I know a lot of lesbians prefer to *Desert Hearts* (1985), for instance

Richard Dyer in *The Celluloid Closet*, 1996.

— you could say that's as much a lesbian film as *Desert Hearts*, because it's got this affirmative quality to it, and because it's about identifying as gay and owning that identity.

Now, in the '90s – I'm not opposed to it, but there is a kind of shift among people in the big urban centres to be much less invested in that, and to be much more interested in exploring diversity and not saying, 'Being gay is the most important thing to me.' There is a more fluid, open-minded – or open-*ended*, I might say – attitude.

It's like people now looking at *The Killing of Sister George* (1968), which from a Gay Liberation perspective is one of the worst films ever made. You can now look at it from a queer perspective and say, 'This is fine, we can see that it reflects certain aspects of how lesbians lived at the time and why shouldn't we get into being butch and femme.' There's no such one thing as a gay or even a queer film anymore – it's elastic. I don't know if that's the kind of answer you want. I can't imagine it in *Torso*!

MR: *We'll see. Directors of films that could be seen as homophobic because they villainize gayness – Demme, Verhoeven – what do you think when they say, 'Well, someone* has to be the villain*'?*

RD: That's increased in recent years, in a lot of very good films – like *Seven* (1995), which I think is one of the best films made in the last 10 years, or *The Last Seduction* (1994), which I think is pretty terrific, or *The Silence of the Lambs* (1991), which I don't think is so wonderful, but even so it's a good film. This villainizing was not just at the time of *Cruising* (1980) or *The Detective* (1968).

If we'd had many representations in cinema, a few killers wouldn't matter; we can hardly, post-Dahmer, say, 'There are *no* gay serial killers.' Gay people are capable of everything, and that includes bad things. But I think there is something about those films I mentioned in which it isn't just *incidental* that the killers are homosexual, it's an *explanation* of the killing, and that's not acceptable. You also have all these lesbian killer films like *Butterfly Kiss* (1994, 1996 in US), *Sister, My Sister* (1995)... *Basic Instinct (1992)*.

Yes, and *Heavenly Creatures* (1994) – it's amazing how many there are, and it runs right through from Hollywood to art cinema. What's interesting is that there's ambivalence among lesbian friends of mine about those films. I don't think those art films do explain the killing as being due to lesbianism, but they do *associate* lesbianism with killing. There is a certain way in which you can read them as being about killing *men*, and there's a glee in that. I don't know any lesbians who actually think men *should* be killed, but there's the level of fantasy. I actually found *Thelma & Louise* (1991) interesting in that context.

MR: *Do you ever shrug your shoulders and say, 'It's just a movie'?*

RD: Well, I'm very interested in that question, actually. I remember when I went to see *Fatal Attraction* (1987). At the time, everyone was saying, 'This is a dreadful anti-woman film,' and some people also saw it as a kind of AIDS horror film. It was, if one may say such things, an ordinary audience in the suburbs. And I wondered if most of those people thought it was necessarily anti-woman, leave alone about AIDS, or if they just thought it was about *this* woman, who happens to become obsessed with *this* man. Why is it we are so convinced people always interpret things? That's what *academics* do, is make generalizations on the basis of particular cases. One has to be careful.

I *do* think it's still the case that we get our ideas of who we are and who other people are from the mass media, and it does matter. If you listen to people's conversations, they constantly use images and ideas and references to the movies to argue about what they think reality is.

MR: *Who's your favorite star to analyze?*

RD: I've rather stopped writing about stars. Judy is my favourite star, I'm loyal to Judy. I loved writing about her, partly because I almost learned to be gay through learning to love Judy. I remember one of the first gay men I ever met more or less said, 'Well, if you're going to be gay, you've got to love Judy.' (Both laugh)

MR: *Speaking of female stars, what do you think of Camille Paglia?*

RD: I think I've been influenced by the prejudice against her. (Both laugh) I've often thought of something small she'd written, 'Well, *that* sounds quite interesting!' and then people have told me she's so kind of unacceptable and stupid and disgraceful and so on, egotistical, and since I'm lazy I didn't read *Sexual Personae*. I'm very instrumental in what I read — I read what I need to for what I'm working on at the moment; I've just finished a book called *White*, about whiteness in culture, not only in film, coming out in the spring. Next, I'm going to work on 'music in film.'

About Camille Paglia, I'm struck by the fact that my lover, who I've been with more than a year, thinks she's wonderful, and he's very sensitive, intelligent, pro-woman, not a reactionary idiot. Because he isn't an academic, he's outside a particular investment against her, so that almost makes me feel that at some point I have to read her.

MR: *Why are so many of the biggest film icons female?*

RD: For gay men, there's a simple answer: Female stars often express love for men, so you identify with them because they're the only characters going around expressing what if feels like to love men.

There's also this thing of identifying because you're interested in femininity and in what your relationship to it is. I actually think that gay men's relationship to femininity and to women is terribly complicated and there's a lot of misogyny in it, and I think there's a way in which the cults around women are ways of not really seeing them as women, but as seeing them as these almost like *monsters* of femininity. I do think that's a problem at times in gay men's interaction with, as it were, 'real' women. And that comes out of our own ambivalence about our own femininity. There's the Gay Liberation rhetoric of embracing our femininity and refusing straightness and masculine role models, yet at another level there's an incredible investment in masculinity — you only have to think of gym culture, gay porn to see it.

I know a gay man who I'm old enough to be his father — I'm well and truly old enough — and he's absolutely obsessed with Barbra Streisand to a degree I never was with Judy. That surprises me because I would've thought what I think of as '*The Advocate* model of homosexuality' — that we're regular guys — I thought that really had sort of become established. I don't particularly want it to be, but I thought it had been. I'm surprised that young gay men do still have that fascination with women.

MR: *I guess we still have older gay men saying, 'Well, if you're going to be gay, you've got to love...' fill in the blank.*

RD: I don't know who the younger ones would – Madonna, I suppose, but even she now is a bit passé for teenagers.

MR: *If audiences are so taken with movie stars onscreen, why do they care so much about details of stars' private lives?*

RD: I know... People aren't interested in the lives of someone like Rosemary Harris, someone who's famous as an actor or actress, for interpreting a role. It's the role that matters. With *stars*, the role is almost an excuse just to see them.

MR: *Marilyn survived a nude photo scandal (1952) by saying she'd had to pose to survive and wasn't ashamed, and Madonna survived hers (1985) by defiantly saying she wasn't ashamed. Both careers seemed to be enhanced. What would a similar scandal do to a career today?*

RD: I think if Tom Cruise did a pinup in *Playgirl* – or even more if he did a pinup in *Torso* – it would be a scandal.

MR: *There was a flap (1996) over a video that has that veejay Simon Rex in it from before his MTV days. He isn't with another guy, but he masturbates, and yet the flap was very minor.*

RD: It depends on what sort of star we're talking about. If they're a mainstream Hollywood star, it might still be a problem. But there's something about contemporary youth culture that it's sort of funky to be gay or associated with gayness. It depends on what sort of market we're talking about. I think male nudity is still a problem. Although there's an *extraordinary* amount of near-nudity, I still think 'penis' is a problem. (Both laugh)

MR: *When a star like Madonna mimics another star, like Marilyn Monroe, in a video or photo layout, do you think most of the audience that responds positively does so because they like Marilyn, so they get what Madonna's doing, or do they like it because they're fooled into thinking they're seeing something really incredible and new?*

RD: I really don't know, and I'm very interested in it. I was at the party at the New York Lesbian and Gay Film Festival and it was suggested, 'Why don't you have a Shirley Temple?' and then I spoke to someone and they said, 'What is that you're drinking?' and I told them and it was obvious they'd never heard of Shirley Temple. I'm not sure that she's so important that one *should* have heard of her, but I was surprised that someone in film hadn't. There are stars like Marilyn who everyone does know, but I don't know how much sense of 20th century popular cultural history is known. I was talking to someone who told me how many of her graduate students hadn't seen *Now, Voyager* (1942).

MR: *In the '90s? In the '60s, you'd have had to catch classic films at revival houses or occasionally on TV, but now everything is on video.*

RD: There's so *much* on video it's not clear what is – maybe *that's* what it is, not that people are ignorant, it's just that there isn't a clear shared culture anymore.

MR: *I haven't read your writings on porn, but can you analyze porn flicks in the same way as art films or Hollywood blockbusters?*

RD: I think you can. There's a problem about porn, which is that it isn't very interesting. Of course, it's *utterly compelling* if it turns you on. I like porn, but there's a way in which it's so single-minded; it's not rich like some other movie texts are, so there are limits to what you can say. But I think you can talk about narrative structure, camera angles. There's a book by Linda Williams about heterosexual porn which talks about porn being like musicals in that it has stories which are interrupted by long 'numbers.' If you think of the French films of Cadinot compared to the California Catalina films, they are clearly coming from very different worlds. Whether you could distinguish between the different California movies, I don't know.

MR: *It'd be hard enough to tell the actors apart. (Both laugh) When do you think we'll have a major star who is openly gay?*

RD: I think it could still be a long way away, partly because Hollywood is slow and cautious. The real challenge is whether homosexuality becomes seen as normal. There is greater tolerance of homosexuality and even a fascination, there's still a perception of it as queer, and some gay and lesbian activists are pushing that. As long as it's queer, there is a problem with straight people identifying with it. They might approve it, or love it, or get off on it – but they won't identify with it. Identification is a major part of why people go to the movies. I as a gay man can go see *Sleepless in Seattle* (1992) and identify with either character in the sense of imagining being lonely and in that situation. I can treat it as being just about love, not necessarily heterosexual love. I'm not sure very many heterosexuals can make the same step.

Until that happens, it is hard to see that there would be a really, really major, openly gay star.

Originally published in *Torso* 14:9 (April 1997), pp. 71–74.

56 PLEASURE | OBVIOUS | QUEER (2016)
with Catherine Grant and Jaap Kooijman

This conversation was held at King's College London on 13 April 2016 in front of a live audience. It has been edited for publication. The original interview (in live and published forms) included three short audiovisual essays created by the interviewers, which were used as spurs to explore thematic concerns that run through Dyer's work.

PLEASURE

JK: *In 1982 you wrote: 'I don't say listening to Diana Ross and reaching out and touching at her shows would make anyone join a movement to change the world; but at least it vividly expresses the pleasures of a better world.'[1] This is very much in line with the argument you have made in 'Entertainment and utopia' as well as in the 'In defence of disco' essay: the significance of feeling and experiencing the pleasure of a better alternative that can be imagined or even realised. You made this argument at a time when entertainment was frowned upon from both the conservative right as well as the progressive left. You explicitly address the latter: disco cannot make the revolution but it definitely feels good; do not simply dismiss it as capitalist culture, but use it. Now almost four decades later, do you believe the attitudes towards entertainment have changed? To put it simply, is disco – or entertainment – still in need of defending today?*

RD: In some ways no, although that does depend on where you are. In some parts of the world, for instance among intellectuals in Italy, you do still feel the need to defend entertainment – where there is still a commitment to a certain traditional left realist project, or the ideas of Brecht or Godard and so on. But in Great Britain and North America and many parts of Europe, no, I don't think there is a need. The question

---

1. Richard Dyer, 'Diana Ross', *Marxism Today*, June 1982, p. 37 (also included in Section 1 of this Reader).

is: is there such a thing as entertainment anymore? That's what I am not sure about. Entertainment is very much posited upon an idea of escape. When I started thinking about entertainment people would say things like 'It takes you out of yourself', or 'It takes your mind off things'. And of course people still have problems, but there was very much the sense then that most of life was hard but you had entertainment to take you away from it for a bit. While now, because of all sorts of changes, you can listen to music anywhere you go all the time — and even choose the music, not just accept the music that is there. That sense of a gap between a bad life and something to escape into has disappeared or is greatly diminished. I don't know whether that is a good or a bad thing but it changes the nature of entertainment. In that sense I would no longer know what I would then be defending. That despising of the popular, that despising of what is enjoyable, may still be there, but it is not a discourse that has so much weight anymore.

JK: *'In defence of disco' was not written in defence of scholarly attention, although I am sure disco was frowned upon in academia at that time as well. I would like to turn to the notion of the pleasure academic scholars have in their objects of study. There seems to be a discrepancy between film studies, in which cinephilia is widely respected, and the study of other forms of popular culture, such as television and pop music, in which 'fandom' — note the difference in vocabulary — is very much contested. Both the benefits as well as the pitfalls of being invested in the object of study have been recognised — the distinction between being extremely knowledgeable of the object on the one hand and the danger of not having a critical distance on the other. What is missing in the debate is a point that you made regarding the choice of objects in* White. *In the SCMS Fieldnotes interview [with Barbara Klinger, 2015] you explain that you did not want to write about the whiteness of objects that you despise, such as Nazi propaganda, as that would enable a position of moral superiority. Instead, selecting objects you liked forced you to be more rather than less critical.*

RD: What I understood cultural studies to be was a critical engagement with popular culture, which meant you took it seriously, but did not mean you therefore said it is all wonderful or all bad. The point was that you were critically engaged and that included the political as well as the aesthetic. My dream was always to do things that showed that the aesthetic and political were not different. The article I wrote about Blaxploitation came the nearest to saying 'actually the politics is in the aesthetic, not in the films' overt politics'.[2] What is driving a project for me is always politics and pleasure, but sometimes it is more pleasure and sometimes it is more politics. So when it was about the pleasure, I had to think of the politics; when it was about the politics, I

---

[2]. 'Music and presence in Blaxploitation cinema' in Richard Dyer, *In the Space of a Song: The Uses of Song in Film*, London and New York: Routledge, 2012, pp. 156-174.

had to think about the pleasure. *White* was very much a political project. Most of what I wrote about in that was not what I particularly liked or disliked, but I thought I must do some case studies on things that I do really like. However, there is a difference between the two case studies. In the case of the white man's muscles the fact is that I do not like those films – action films, pepla, Tarzan, Rambo – most of them bore me to tears. I just like muscle men. I feel there is something of the pleasure in the bodies that I do not really talk about in the essay. It is almost like the ideology still wins in that case. I loved *The Jewel in the Crown* (1984), although I was aware of the critique. That case study was more successful partly because it sees the politics in the form – the delaying, the pleasures of the sadness that is in that series – but also because it tries to identify what the pleasure is that is being offered about a certain spectacle of whiteness – its ideological implications, but also the pleasure of it.

I think it is really important when you write critical work to realise that you are not superior, you are no better than what you are writing about. It is important to maintain that. That goes back to what is an endemic problem with the classic left – and what is left of that – that sense of 'we know better' and 'we are not contaminated by all those pleasures'. Yet, pleasure is available and we should engage with it – we must not be separated out from it. I am not trying to justify my pleasures. I am trying to use the pleasure I have as a way into understanding the hold of certain works, both the aesthetic and political hold, and sometimes that is the same thing. This is essential to a book I am most attached to, which is in some ways my most personal book, and which is probably the least read: *Nino Rota* (2010). The book's central idea of ironic attachment is precisely about being attached – delighted, moved – but nonetheless with a kind of self-awareness and self-reflexivity. So you do not distance yourself but at the same time you are not so much inside of it that you do not have some sense of all the political, aesthetic, and formal organisations going on.

AUDIENCE: *In your talk at the recent SCMS event ['Richard Dyer in the House of Cinema', Atlanta, 30 March 2016] you said almost in a kind of throwaway line that you remain a Marxist. That is not a statement you make all the time, even though it is implicit in your work.*

RD: I suppose I don't say I'm a Marxist very often – most Marxists wouldn't think I was, probably. What does that mean? An early Marx quote has been like a mantra for me. It is usually translated as 'people make their own history, but not in circumstances of their own choosing'. That to me is absolutely the model of cultural production which informs everything I have done. This means that people are active and that there is agency. People do things, and it is not inevitable what will be done. Also, it is about the importance of realising the circumstances, not just the particular technology that is at our disposal but also the language that we speak, the ideas we are brought up with, and the frames of understanding that are available to us. These circumstances limit what we can see but also make it possible for us to see anything at all. Rigid Marxists perhaps used to say the circumstances are the economy, but my understanding of the circumstances not of our own choosing is quite broad. I feel the need to keep the dialectic between agency and circumstances in play always.

OBVIOUS

CG: *We picked 'obvious' as a theme because of something I witnessed you saying in a Q&A session at a packed public event back in 1997 to mark the publication of* White. *You presented brilliantly on the central ideas of the book and afterwards a brave soul asked you, 'Isn't it all rather obvious?' I cannot remember your exact reply but you affirmed the importance of the obvious. Looking back at your work, an engagement with obviousness is something that I see throughout. How important has the obvious been for you?*

RD: I think, probably, you're absolutely right. It is the most important. Most of my bigger projects have been about taking an obvious idea, or something that's endlessly said and therefore is thought to be obvious. Rather than taking the usual academic route, which is to say, 'well, it appears to be this, but really it's that', I ask, 'well, what are the implications of this obviousness?' With entertainment what does it mean that people keep saying 'it's only entertainment'? What's that 'only'? What is the implication of thinking of it in terms of escape? From what, to what, how? Let's follow through on the obviousness rather than thinking it responds to some psychoanalytically-discovered thing that we cannot prove is even there, or whatever particular other paradigm it might be. Similarly with whiteness: why is it white? Why do you say white people? Why a colour and why that colour? And with serial killing: what's the seriality? Even with pastiche, which is not such an obvious word in everyday circulation but is very commonly used in the writing of people with a lot of cultural capital. Again, what does it mean to use that word? For me, in the context of cultural studies the idea expressed by the Austrian philosopher Alfred Schütz was very formative, namely that theory builds upon what is common-sense but also involves thinking about the common-sense, not to disprove or prove it but to think about its implications. Schütz called theory a second-order, common-sense construct. That was also very similar to what Richard Hoggart was doing in his work. So yes, I think obviousness is absolutely central.

I suppose another side of that has to do with Gay Liberation, in the sense that if you are gay heterosexuality is no longer obvious. Being gay makes you think about the non-inevitable, the non-natural, the non-unquestionable-ness of things, be it whiteness or heterosexuality, and so on. There is something very particular about the fact that it is perfectly possible to use all the languages of normality at the very point at which you know they are not your languages, and that does give a particular way into thinking about the construction of the obvious. It works in both directions – respecting the obvious and thinking it through, but also thinking that the obvious is not a given of nature but something that is culturally produced.

CG: *When you mentioned the obvious at the recent SCMS event someone in the audience backed this up by saying that there is no 'Richard Dyer way', no Richard Dyer paradigm. This surprised me, as the specificity of your work has spread so far and wide. For example, the set of paradigms in 'Entertainment and utopia' has been portable and shareable. Maybe some people do not recognise them as the 'Richard Dyer way' because they are not mystifying. They don't try to make themselves sound complicated. Would you say that this has been a conscious part of your ethos?*

RD: Absolutely. I think that one should use plain language – as plain as possible. One should get one's ideas across by example, through one's practice. Often the way to be successful in academia is to have authority, and I think you have authority partly through a demeanour, but also through a rather terrifying language. That's certainly how I experienced being on the edge of *Screen* in the 1970s – this terrifying language of authority. I didn't do that, and of course it was a political choice not to do that. Just imagine how the queens in Gay Liberation would have responded to me. I've always had a life outside of academia and I think that is a very good thing. It gives you a reality check, to use a phrase that was often used back then.

CG: *Throughout your work you combine close attention to the film text and the historical context, with a philosophical grounding and an understanding of sociological structures. In recent years you have been privileging the role of textual analysis in everything that you do. Why did you feel a need to defend textual analysis?*

RD: Partly just because I feel there is a drift within film studies, and even more in television studies, to what I think of as 'film studies without films' – always looking at fans, at production (although perhaps people don't do that enough), at all sorts of discourses around the film, while actually not looking at the film itself. Obviously when you study film stars you do look beyond just the films, but why bother to look at fans if you don't look at the films at all? The films are why the fandom is there in the first place. I do slightly regret what I said at the SCMS event in Atlanta, that I think textual analysis is just looking and listening. That is at the heart of it, but of course there is no such thing as unexamined looking and listening which does not already bring to bear frameworks of understanding, and one should reflect upon them. When you do that you are into epistemology and into theory and so on. Also you have to do the contextual work in order to be a kind of corrective to any idiosyncratic subjective point of view. But when the reason we study a phenomenon is because of the films, then we must study the films.

JK: *In your essay on stereotypes you write, 'The role of stereotypes is to make visible the invisible so that there is no danger of it creeping up on us unawares; and to make fast, firm and separate what is in reality fluid and much closer to the norm than the dominant value system cares to admit.'*[3] *Could we say then that stereotyping is used to make things obvious?*

RD: A particular function of stereotyping is to make things simple. So in a way it makes something obvious that might not be true. To call something a stereotype is to be critical of it, thus we tend to only be critical of stereotypes that we see as stereotypes. In the case of gay and lesbian stereotypes we all know that there is a huge range of ways of inhabiting sexuality and degrees of feeling impulses towards the same sex and towards the opposite sex. It is messy and complicated. Stereotypes make it seem like there's this or there's that, and that's part of their function. But stereotypes are also quite hard to get away from. I have tried to make a distinction between stereotypes and the more positive social type, the latter being a social category that could be seen to belong to society. This was linked to Gay Liberation, which was about advocacy on behalf of gay and lesbian people. First of all you have to constitute gay and lesbian people as a category who could be represented. Many of the critiques of this said that gayness was an invention. Yes, but if we hadn't said there was a category of people called gay we couldn't have fought on their/our behalf. What case could we have made, on what grounds? That was the form it had to take, as we were invisible and some kind of typification is actually useful. I won't say I defended stereotypes but I did worry about the question how one can speak on behalf of a social group which is in fact not visible. There is a famous early feminist book called *Hidden from History* – which does not mean that no one could see women but that they were hidden from accounts.[4] Yet gays and lesbians were not only hidden but literally invisible. Even when they were in full view you would not necessarily know that they were there. So there was a very particular concern with how do you represent a group that is not immediately obvious, except in the case of those who are 'obvious' in a stereotypical way.

---

3. Richard Dyer, 'The role of stereotypes', in Jim Cook and Mike Lewington (eds), *Images of Alcoholism*, London: BFI, 1979, p. 19 (also included in Section 4 of this Reader).
4. Sheila Rowbotham, *Hidden from History: 300 Years of Women's Oppression and the Fight Against It*, London: Pluto Press, 1973.

QUEER

JK: *When one reads your line – 'I remember being a queer and have never been entirely convinced that I ever became gay' – out of context, one might interpret it as a form of nostalgia, in the sense that with gay and lesbian visibility and even acceptance in mainstream culture something was 'lost' in the process. However, the line appears in your introduction to* The Culture of Queers *(2002), in which you explicitly argue against romanticising oppression and celebrating negativity. You do not deny that there was 'subversion, play, passion or irony', but as you write 'they may either mask the reality of the oppressiveness of the category queer or accept too high a price in the name of intensity of feeling and refinement of expression.'[5] I would like you to reflect on this double-sidedness, on the 'secret' pleasure of queer culture in times of oppression.*

RD: One of the chapters in *The Culture of Queers* is about representations of gay men in heritage cinema.[6] Those films are paradoxical, because they are nostalgic films, but they are nostalgic for a time in which you could be murdered or certainly sent to prison for being gay. But I love those kinds of films. Even in the periods they depict you could wear nice clothes, even then there was *something*. It is never just something to be nostalgic about, because there was a price to pay. But there never was just a price to pay either. For about a hundred years up until the beginning of Gay Liberation queer obviously was a very negative thing to be called and there were anti-gays laws and such. Gay was an affirmative turn and Gay Liberation has been a very successful movement, but there has always been a looking back at that period. Oscar Wilde is a good example. People say, 'Look at Oscar Wilde. How brilliant. How witty. Maybe he could not have had the insights about paradoxes of pastiche, and such… he could not have done that if he had not been gay'. Yes, but look what happened to him. There is a price to be paid. You need to always keep those two sides in play. I did grow up to cherish the sad young man – 'Isn't he gorgeous? I wish I could be like him!' – but at the same time he is a *sad* young man. It is ambivalent, though that's a funny word to use in a way. Yes, we survived it and we did all sorts of things that need to be cherished, but it was at a cost and for probably most gay men the cost was too high. The cost was suicide, the cost was loveless marriages. Most men weren't Oscar Wilde or even queens screaming in nightclubs on King's Road in Chelsea, where I had my first gay experience – that was not the experience of most gay men, leaving aside the question of the experience of lesbians.

I tried to capture this in the context of two kinds of discourse. One was the idea 'Oh, what a pity we had Gay Liberation, as it has taken away all the indirection, that wonderful source of wit, brilliance, nuance, innuendo and all of that'. You couldn't

---

[5]. Richard Dyer, 'Introduction', in Dyer, *The Culture of Queers*, London and New York: Routledge, 2002, p. 7.
[6]. Richard Dyer, 'Homosexuality and heritage' in Dyer, *The Culture of Queers*, ibid., pp. 204-228.

have had Julian and Sandy, this outrageous comic duo on the radio in the 1960s, as that was nothing but innuendo. And there is an interesting argument to say that Gay Liberation, by making us visible, made us targets for oppression. I believe nonetheless that we achieved a good moment for many, and things have changed. Second, *The Culture of Queers* was also a reaction to – not a reaction against but a recognition that it was different than – Queer with a capital Q, which is all about 'it is playful', 'it is complex', 'it is brilliant'. All of those imply having established gayness. Once you accept gayness as something positive and unquestionable then you can start being witty. Queer in the old sense meant you had to be witty in the need to survive. Queer in the new sense is posited on the assumption that things are basically much better. On a more personal level, until I was twenty-one or twenty-two, I didn't think I was evil, but I thought I was an emotionally and sexually inadequate person, yet I would just do the best I could do. I don't think I ever got rid of that. In a way that is good, as it made me never forget the price to be paid.

JK: *The Culture of Queers also includes a chapter on Rock Hudson, which is one of the few essays in which you explicitly write about AIDS. Obviously, AIDS has had a devastating impact on real lives, but also a major impact on the representation of homosexuality, giving Gay Liberation an even stronger political urgency. Referring to your earlier work on the representation of homosexuality the negative stereotypes that were oppressive in the 1970s became fatal with the coming of the AIDS epidemic. As you conclude in the Rock Hudson essay, 'If Rock's death brought attention to AIDS, boosted fundraising, made people realise that "nice people" get AIDS, it has also been used to reinforce venerable myths about gay men.'[7] Therefore, the relative absence of AIDS in your work is surprising, as it would seem a logical continuation of your earlier discussion of these 'myths' as part of the representation of homosexuality and its stereotypes. I hesitate to ask this question, as I prefer to focus on what you have written about, but in this particular case I genuinely wonder why.*

RD: I'm glad you ask this question, although I don't really know what the answer is. A partial answer is that a lot of other people already were doing great work on that, Simon Watney in particular. I got interested in history and on questions of representation before that, and also on things other than just explicit queer representations. But at the same time, yes, you are right. Even in that Rock Hudson article it is actually the smaller part of the article. I guess it was almost opportunistic of me to attach it to that, as Hudson had just died. In a way I was more interested in the question of now that everyone knew he was gay, how then to look back on the films, what difference

---

7. Richard Dyer, 'Rock: the last guy you'd have figured?' in *The Body Politic* 121 (December 1985), p. 29 (also included in Section 3 of this Reader).

would that make? Somehow it was an interesting exercise, although one with all sorts of problems. Also, I knew lots of people who died. For example, Jack Babuscio and Dave Sargent, who were two of my peers in terms of writing about queer cinema. Then eventually Vito Russo, although that was a bit later. Also closer to home, friends and so on.

I think there is something about it that evoked disgust in me. I remember a long time ago at a meeting in this group Gay Left, of which I was briefly a member, one of the people in that group had been arrested for what was called cottaging – I don't know if that term is still used, but anyway, picking up a man in a public toilet. At the meeting he said, 'None of you contacted me. We are supposed to be in this group and you weren't supportive.' We went around the room, in the way you did in those days to deal with such things. I don't remember what the other people said but I remember saying that cottaging disgusted me. Going to the toilet doesn't exactly thrill me. I hate public toilets. In a way cottaging appalled me as an activity, so something inhibited me. I think there is some deep disgust in me around sex and around bodily functions. I don't know where that comes from. I had sweet, relaxed parents, and I don't think I should feel it, but I *do*. There was probably something about AIDS, even though we shouldn't think of it as a price of sin or a price of having sex. But the fact is that at that time it so completely reinforced that feeling of a connection between sex and illness and disgust that I guess I just couldn't bring myself to face it.

CG: *This begs a question about the role of disgust in your work, including your recent book* Lethal Repetition *(2015). When I attended one of your talks on this topic I was really shocked, as this was not the Richard Dyer I thought I knew. But then there always seems to have been an interest in disgust in your work.*

RD: Maybe that is true. I always have liked that kind of stuff. *Lethal Repetition* deals with disgust most explicitly, as does the vampire article, in which I see vampirism as a kind of metaphor for queerness – although I really pushed that towards the melancholic, romantic version of the sad young man.[8] Yet even part of Bram Stoker's *Dracula* is actually about the thrilling disgustingness of the act of vampirism. In *Lethal Repetition* I did a whole section on the pleasure of disgust, including a discussion of one of the most disgusting films, *Lucker the Necrophagous* (Johan Vandewoestijne, 1986), which is about someone who likes to have sex with dead bodies. He leaves them to putrefy for days and days and then licks them all over. Why would you enjoy being disgusted? It did take me back to potty training. I had a brief relationship when I was a student

---

8. Richard Dyer, 'It's in his kiss!: Vampirism as homosexuality, homosexuality as vampirism' in Dyer, *The Culture of Queers*, op. cit., pp. 70-89.

in France with someone who was a psychoanalyst and he always used to reprimand me when I took a book with me when I went to have a shit. He would say, 'You are trying to deny yourself one of the pleasures of life.' I thought that was nonsense, but actually he was right. That's what potty training does – all those fascinating smells, the relief of it, the warmth of it, the funny shapes, how fascinating shit is, and then, 'Stop! You mustn't look at it. Naughty boy!' Such a combination is very much what goes on in the pleasure that is offered in films that really foreground disgust. This is all very personal, but it does come down to the ambivalent and even conflicting relation between disgust and pleasure. Actually, now I want to write a book about niceness, as I really want the world to be nice. Even though I'm fully aware that it is a problematic concept. Niceness has been such an important guiding principle for me in my life.

AUDIENCE: *Your work clearly is informed by your experience as a gay man, but you have also written about lesbian cinema. I wonder whether and how lesbian women have influenced your work.*

RD: I always thought, 'Who am I to write about lesbians?' At the time of Gay Liberation I was very committed to equal consideration. In *Gays and Film* (1977) not only did we manage, with quite some difficulty actually, to find someone to write a section on lesbians and film, Caroline Sheldon, but also I made sure that my chapter (there were only three chapters) was half about lesbian film.[9] And similarly, with the season at the National Film Theatre we absolutely made sure it was half-and-half. But your question is more interesting than that, relating to gender. I do think it is different to be brought up a man or to be brought up a woman. There is an alliance between lesbians and gays, as well as bisexuals and transsexuals, because we are all brought up at odds with conventional definitions of gender, but all the same differently. I certainly think lesbian writing made me aware of that, such as Jackie Stacey's 'Desperately Seeking Difference' (1987), which also loosened up the idea that you are either gay or you are not.[10] The push to recognise, intellectually, that there is a wide range rather than a strict boundary between gay and straight came very much from lesbian writing. It is thinking about gender. Mary McIntosh, who was involved in Gay Liberation as well as the Women's Movement, wrote a brilliant article in a time when the focus was on sexuality rather than gender, and she said no, there is no sexuality separate from gender.[11] You cannot separate the two. Femininity is often being dumped on, even within

---

9. Richard Dyer (ed.), *Gays and Film*, London: BFI, 1977. It was in fact Angela Martin who discovered Sheldon. *Gays and Film* contains three essays: 'Lesbians and Film: Some Thoughts' by Caroline Sheldon, 'Stereotyping' by Richard Dyer, and 'Camp and the Gay Sensibility' by Jack Babuscio.
10. Jackie Stacey, 'Desperately Seeking Difference', *Screen* 28:1 (1987), pp. 48-61.
11. Mary McIntosh, 'Queer Theory and the War of the Sexes', in Joseph Bristow and Angela Wilson (eds), *Activating Theory: Lesbian, Gay, Bisexual Politics*, London: Lawrence and Wishart, 1993, pp. 30-52.

a certain kind of lesbian style, such as the rights of the femme to be recognised as lesbian, which is an interesting struggle. And equally, if you look at objects of desire in male culture they are not on the whole sissies. They are hunks. Not in the 19th century but in the 20th century it is masculinity all over the place that has been valued at the price of femininity. Of course femininity is a construct and there is very much to say against it, but there is also a lot to be lost when we no longer cherish femininity.

Originally published in *NECSUS: European Journal of Media Studies* 5:1 (2016), pp. 95–110.

57 WRITING OUT OF LOVE OR POLITICS (2023)
with Glyn Davis and Jaap Kooijman

GD: *Let's start with your time at the Centre for Contemporary Cultural Studies (CCCS) in Birmingham where you were a student from 1969 to 1972. Did you feel part of that group? Was it a kind of home for you at the time that you were studying there?*

RD: It certainly was at the time, very much so. In some ways, the way cultural studies developed *afterwards* – which I had nothing against but it was not really the way I developed, as it became so much more anthropological and media studies and so on. I wrote this introduction to [the 2018 edition of Stuart Hall and Paddy Whannel's] *The Popular Arts* and when I looked back at [the original 1964 edition], I thought, 'That's what I thought I went to the Cultural Studies Centre to do.' And I felt I was closer to that, and in a way to Richard Hoggart, even than to Stuart, even though he was my supervisor. But at the time, I felt very much at home there, yes. In every way: personally, as well as intellectually and politically.

JK: *In 2014, the fiftieth anniversary of the centre was celebrated with the* Back in the CCCS *exhibition and a conference, even though the CCCS was forced to close in 2002.*

RD: I didn't ever see the exhibition. The organiser asked everyone to write something about CCCS and I couldn't think what to write. In a way, what I wanted to write was something like, 'I'm not sure I have thought anything new since I was there.' You know, that everything I think now is just a variation on what I learned then. It felt wrong, it felt too sort of lovey, it felt too, 'Oh, it was all so wonderful!' So, I didn't say anything and I was the only person that didn't say anything.[1]

---

1. The exhibition consisted of contemporary portraits of some CCCS alumni, including Dyer, shot by photographer Mahasiddhi (Roy Peters). The requested text was used to caption the portraits. Dyer's read: '*How did your time at the Centre shape who you are/what you became? (Brevity being the soul of wit here!)*: can't answer.' The concision of Dyer's answer might explain why his portrait was not included in Mahasiddhi's 'Back in the CCCS: a photo essay', published in Julian Henriques and David Morley, with Vana Goblot (eds), *Stuart Hall: Conversations, Projects and Legacies*, London: Goldsmiths, 2017, pp. 275-303.

GD: *One of the pieces that we're including in this collection is your 1971 essay on Tom Jones that was written for the first issue of* Working Papers in Cultural Studies. *Can you tell us how that piece of writing came about?*

RD: Well, I originally went to Birmingham to write about homosexuality and fiction, that is what I got the grant for. But then I decided I didn't want to do that and decided I would do showbiz and ideas of entertainment. I was not sure, initially, what way to go. I think two of the things I did quite early on after the PhD were to write about *The Sound of Music* and also to write about different stars. I didn't think of it as 'star studies' but it's just that they were forms of entertainment like the Tom Jones show [*This Is Tom Jones*], the Cilla Black show [*Cilla*], whatever. And so, I decided to do Tom Jones. I mean, I enjoyed the Tom Jones show, one of the most popular shows at the time on TV. He was a very, very big star.

There was also a feeling it was important to do television. Even film was already starting to be an old medium. And I did want to write about something that really was very, very popular in a popular mass medium and to write about it seriously. I think I even thought of doing Vera Lynn, that was another possibility. But in the end, it was Tom Jones.

GD: *When you were going to write about gay fiction, what books were you thinking of writing about?*

RD: I think it was mainly going to be English language. *Maurice* by E.M. Forster had not yet been published, so it wouldn't have been that. It would have been, like, Isherwood, Baldwin, Angus Wilson. And I also collected a lot of lesser-known novels, some of which were quite middlebrow. But also, pulp fiction with titles like *Maybe Tomorrow* and *Summer in Sodom*. *Summer in Sodom* was one of my favourites! Many of these, like *Maybe Tomorrow*, ended up in the 'Sad Young Man' [essay]. So, it was going to be right across the board. There was a book that came out more or less the year I went to Cultural Studies, which was about Victorian gay writing. And I think *Teleny* had been rediscovered and reprinted.

And then I might have also looked at titles such as *The Sling and the Arrow* and *The Leather Boys*, which were quite serious books, actually. That was the kind of range of things but it would have included some pulp, quasi-porn fiction.

GD: *And you set those aside for Tom Jones instead?*

RD: Well, yes, for musicals really, that was the PhD. I think I thought, 'Do I want to plough through all these books?' I mean, I enjoyed reading them but did I really want to study them? I was very dedicated. Along the lines of *The Popular Arts*, and Richard Hoggart, you really had to study these things fully and properly, and really look at them. And I thought, 'These books are pretty dreary.'

I mean, I don't think that now, funnily enough. I think if I look at them now, I actually rather like reading some of those books now. But at the time, it just felt, 'Oh dear!' Not because of the negative images… because it was pre-gay liberation – well it was the time of gay liberation in the States – but it was pre-my being in gay liberation. They just seemed like dreary books, really, so I thought, 'Do I really want to do this?' And I liked the idea of doing showbiz, which had been very important to me growing up. That was my culture growing up, really.

JK: *If I understand it correctly, you really got into the American genre of the musical because it was entertainment. So, your PhD could also have been about another form of entertainment?*

RD: It could have been, yes. I thought that musicals were a good thing to do. I thought films were a good thing to do, because you could see them more than once. Although actually then, it was very hard to see a film more than once. If it was a current film I could go to the cinema several times, of course, but you couldn't stop and start it. There wasn't even video recording then. So, in a way, it wasn't true that you could see them over and over again in the way that I might think you should. But nonetheless, they seemed more 'pinnable-down' than live musicals, or pantomime, or a number of the other things I might have considered looking at, though I did look at those in passing.

I got the idea that a lot of them are about the idea of entertainment, often because they are literally about putting on a show. But even when they weren't that, they are sort of about happiness; how to be happy, how to achieve happiness. It seemed like it chimed in with ideas of what is entertainment, what is happiness? So that is why it seemed to just fit very well with wanting to think about the notion of entertainment.

JK: *In one of the reports of the CCCS it says that there was a 'firm contract' to publish a Fontana paperback entitled* That's Entertainment!*, based on your PhD. Do you remember why that didn't happen?*

RD: Yes, I do and I remember it with great… not bitterness exactly, not resentment, but something along those lines. They said, 'We don't want an ordinary academic book, we want something that is much more user-friendly.' I was all in favour of that and all in favour of writing something that would be widely accessible, that would not be narrowly academic.

So, I wrote this book, and some people have seen the version of it. And I haven't ever gone back to it. But I thought it was in some ways quite well written, and written with a love of writing. I love writing anyway, but often I have written things and I've felt that I've got to get them out, get them done, and so on. And then I look at them and I think, 'Oh, you really should have loved the writing more.' Whereas that one, I really did spend a lot of time on it. And then they said, 'Oh, it's too popular, it's not academic enough.' I don't think I offered to try and write it differently. And then I never tried to get it published. I should have tried somewhere else, but I didn't. So, that's the story.

But actually, this thing about writing… *Light Entertainment* was the first longer thing I ever wrote. I thought that I was someone that wrote in a way that anyone who could read could read. And friends of my mother's were very 'Oh my goodness!', they had never met anyone who had written a book – which was not really a book, but anyway – they bought it and their daughter, who was sort of my age, she read it. She was an educated person, but I don't think she had been through tertiary education. And she said to me, 'Oh, no, it was too clever for me.' It has obviously stuck with me, that.

I don't know how interesting this is but there are three things. One is that slight thing – which I have, too – about, implicitly, 'Oh, it's clever,' meaning, 'I don't trust it.' Who do you think you are? I mean, probably she didn't mean that, but I think there is a way in which English people, British people, say 'clever' that is actually quite problematic. And I do it too, actually.

[Secondly,] I was thinking, 'How could she say it was clever if she didn't understand it?' And how often people say this about high theory. 'Well, it's really brilliant, I don't understand it but it's really brilliant.' Well, how can you say that if you don't understand it?

But the third thing was that I was downcast to think I had written something that an intelligent woman couldn't understand. Reading it now, I can see there is more jargon in it and more assumptions about intellectual life than I realised at the time. Still, compared to [writing by] many other people, it is pretty straightforward. But it was quite disturbing, in a way, to think of wanting to be someone that wrote for 'general readers' and realising that that readership is nonetheless still quite… maybe not narrow, but a very particular band of the population. It was a bit of an upsetting lesson in a way, which has obviously stayed with me.

GD: *Reading about CCCS, there is a thread which comes through which is about engaging with the public beyond the academy, about ensuring that the politics that is threaded through the CCCS' intellectual work also has relevance to a real-world context. And I wonder whether that was feeding into you trying to find your voice, if you like, in the 1970s.*

RD: Well, I think it was. I think probably at a certain level, I want to be 'a writer.' And in fact, one of my favourite-ever gigs was when I was invited to the Melbourne Writers Festival. Admittedly, it was as a writer about film, and it came through the Film Institute there, they were involved in the festival. But still I really liked the fact that I was invited as a writer. When I was very young –12, 13, 14, 15 – I used to say, 'I want to be a writer.' And I would write these different things and rewrite them and rewrite them, and I just loved that! But being what I thought was 'a good writer,' was probably even more important than who was going to read it. But yes, secondly, that was very important.

You're not going to be writing to just everybody and everybody is not going to read it. But nonetheless, I did think it was important to try and get into some kinds of journalism and explore what other cultures might call being a public intellectual. That was very important. And yes, to reach out, and try all sorts of different kinds of levels of writing too, from *Screen* through to popular radical journalism.

JK: *Talking about* Screen, *in his book* British Cultural Studies: An Introduction *(1990), Graeme Turner writes the following about you: 'Dyer's work does not belong to the same tradition as that of the Birmingham CCCS. While not typical of it, his interests in cinema are part of that branch of screen studies, most closely identified with the British Film Institute in London and the major film journal in Britain,* Screen.' *I was struck by this explicit disconnection of you from CCCS, and the connecting of you to* Screen.

RD: I think that is really interesting. In relation to the CCCS, at the time I felt I was dead centre in what the Centre for Cultural Studies was about. It was really only after I left that I felt it developed in different ways that, you know, perhaps were in embryo there then.

What I am more surprised about, in relation to what Graeme Turner said, is to align me with *Screen*. Because I think it is absolutely right with the BFI. The BFI was absolutely crucial in my development. I became very involved with the education department there in all sorts of ways. That department was always intimidated by *Screen*, and used *Screen*, particularly in teaching and in these summer schools it did, but it was very much not working like *Screen*. *Screen* was very hostile and very dismissive and condemning of a lot of the work of the British Film Institute and of the CCCS. The British Film Institute's journal was *Sight and Sound*, which at the time was of course quite conservative and traditional, and I certainly didn't see myself identified with that. Perhaps because of what was happening with Cultural Studies, and because I got a job teaching film, I found myself more at home with the British Film Institute and its education department, which was also developing study materials for schools. *Stars* came out of that actually, and I did a thing on 'The Dumb Blonde.' There was also the possibility of doing film programming. There was a whole way in which that seemed to offer a way of doing what I thought I was doing in the PhD anyway, in a way that neither *Screen* nor what Cultural Studies was becoming, offered.

JK: *And your first article in* Screen *was not about film, but on the male pin-up.*

RD: And that of course, is after Mandy Merck had taken over. Even though she has a commitment to that kind of high theory, she also was a journalist and also knew a lot about the industry. So, she really changed the character of *Screen*, very importantly.

GD: *It would be interesting to hear you reflect on the connection between scholarship, adult education, and the BFI at that point in the 1970s.*

RD: Yes, I suppose the crucial person there really is Christine Gledhill. There were other people like Christopher Williams. It was Christopher who was beginning to develop television work of the same sort of level of seriousness as the film work. And it was he that asked me to write the *Light Entertainment* book on television. But Christine was very taken with the idea of stars and of course she then went on to edit this wonderful anthology [*Stardom: Industry of Desire*, 1991]. I remember, I was writing or thinking about writing a piece about Lana Turner when I was working in Reading, but at the same time I was also involved in discussing what we were going to do and organising the teaching and some of these summer schools. And I said, 'Well, why don't we do something on stars and why don't we do Lana Turner?' And she said, 'What would that be?' And I said, 'Well, I think we can take these four films, *Ziegfeld Girl*, *The Postman Always Rings Twice*, *Imitation of Life*, and *The Bad and the Beautiful*.' And she said, 'Oh God, wouldn't that be wonderful!?' She was so excited by the films that we would show. She came from a much more literary background; she had been doing a PhD on Thomas Hardy, for instance.

But she, with of course other people, was developing this work with schools and feeling they wanted some written material, and that's what [led to the development of] 'The Dumb Blonde' [study pack]. Then that led to there being a pack specifically on Marilyn Monroe. And that idea led to the idea of there being packs about different stars. I don't think I did any others, but there was a Robert Redford one. I think there may have been a Jane Fonda one.

But even before all of that there was the musical and Colin MacArthur who knew I was working on the musical said, 'Why don't you do…' because they had already done the Western and the gangster film and others. There was a feeling that to write about popular cinema, you had to have different sorts of models, other than using the great authors. It wasn't that they were against authorship – or 'auteurism'

– but nonetheless, you had to have other models. And that's why both genre and stars seemed like manageable, conceptually distinct things you could develop which were also characteristic of popular culture. And genre was very important to them, so that's why they wanted the musical, that is why they encouraged me to write that study. What the teachers got was a whole film, which was actually *Sweet Charity* – which was partly because we couldn't get an MGM film because MGM wouldn't let them have it – and then extracts from various other musicals. And then this study guide, which had a little history and 'how would you teach it?'

JK: *When putting together this collection, we were surprised by how much television you have covered in your writing, particularly in the 1970s and early 1980s. Many people now see you as a film scholar rather than a television studies scholar. Could you reflect on that?*

RD: Yes. Within the Film and Television Studies department at Warwick, I felt other people were doing television. I don't really think television is aesthetically all that interesting if I am honest. When it was the Tom Jones show or when it was *Coronation Street*, although there were aesthetic arguments there, the impulse was very strongly around the defence of the popular and the defence of this new medium and taking popular television seriously. It wasn't driven by a kind of awe at how rich and incredible and fantastic television is.

But I am also slightly doubtful. I had a resistance to the kind of television that people that don't like television like. I actually like the television that people that don't like television like. I suppose now, things like *Line of Duty* have become sort of 'everybody's television.' But there was a period in which things like *Inspector Morse*, or certainly *The Jewel in the Crown*, were sort of respectable. I was wary of writing about the television I really liked. I didn't want to be championing a kind of television which is already 'this is what television should be.' On the other hand, I don't actually like a lot of the other television, so I didn't feel inclined.

I remember Jason Jacobs presenting a textual analysis of a beginning of a quiz show, and it was extremely good, and he is extremely good. But I thought, 'is it really worth doing? Is it a text that's worth the trouble?' So, although my position is, you can textually analyse anything, there is a question about what is really worth textually analysing. You can textually analyse it and he proved it to me, and he was very interesting. But I still thought, is it really worth all this energy? Maybe I just drifted apart from television in a way. I do watch television, but it's very upmarket what I watch now if I'm honest. I don't watch *The Masked Singer* or *Strictly*. I don't watch what is perhaps 'real' television. I don't watch reality TV. I don't watch soap operas. So, in a way, I have kind of lost touch with 'real television culture'.

JK: *We have not included 'Entertainment and utopia', which will raise some eyebrows, as it is arguably your most influential article. Why do you think it had such an impact?*

RD: Well, whatever its limitations or strengths in itself, I think it offered a way of talking about the enjoyment of popular culture in a way that was nonetheless politically informed or concerned. I found a way for people who wanted to have a critical political engagement with the media to nonetheless see it in terms of the pleasures it offers, the enjoyments it offers.

More generally, it offered a model that could take account of the fact that people enjoyed entertainment, that you didn't have to look down upon people for enjoying these things, but there is something socially, politically at stake in the enjoyment. And I think that was perhaps something that people wanted because I think people recognised how a lot of writing about the popular is either just sentimental... or just empirical; just saying, 'There was this and there was this,' and so on. Or else is kind of awful.

I find it very difficult to believe that people would teach that article and a piece of Adorno as a kind of comparison! But Adorno is only the most austere version of a kind of general left distrust of pleasure, distrust of enjoyment. I think maybe also there was a feeling about the joylessness of the Soviet Union and the evident failure of socialism. It was hard not to feel that was connected to a kind of disconnect from the needs of people for pleasure, for enjoyment, for happiness and so on, and maybe that article suggested there might be a way through that.

JK: *I think it resonates now so much, because it moves beyond the representational and it is really about what utopia feels like and not what it represents.*

RD: Yes.

GD: *Do you feel that there is a 'Richard Dyer's Greatest Hits'?*

RD: Well, yes in the sense that the things that get taken up, like 'Entertainment and utopia', the pin-ups [essay], the disco [essay], the article 'White'... I don't think they are necessarily the best things I have written, which is quite a different issue, but I do see that they somehow hit a spot that helped people or offered something.

GD: *That is an interesting distinction. So, what do you think are the best things that you've written?*

RD: *Heavenly Bodies* and *Pastiche*, I think are probably the two best. I think they are the two with the least flaws. Particularly some of the later ones, like *Nino Rota*, and the book on serial killers [*Lethal Repetition*], are REF [Research Excellence Framework] books, you know what I'm talking about? I think I felt the pressure to get things out and I now look at them and think, 'If you had spent more time, you could have honed them, you could have cut things, you could have made the argument clearer, there would not be so many stodgy passages.'

Heavenly Bodies and *Pastiche*, I really feel the whole thing works, it all hangs together. Lots of people said that the case studies in *White* are sort of problematic and that the photography chapter is interminable. There are too many examples in the Nino Rota book, but I felt I must show that I've seen all these films. And the central chapter in the Nino Rota book, which is, to me, the most important chapter, is the one that most suffers from that. If I could just have had the time to think, cut that, keep the argument clearer.

GD: *Your book* Now You See It *stands out among your other work, as it explores experimental as well as narrative cinema.*

RD: What is in *Now You See It*, was what there was to be in it. In other words, there wasn't a selection in a way, there was what there was, because it is a narrow thing: that the films had to be made by, about, and in some sense for lesbians and gay men. I mean, it's a bit stretched, of course, in relation to the Swedish and the German chapters. But nonetheless, that was what there was. There were other things I didn't know about at the time, but that's what I found out then. I like some [experimental cinema] but I probably dislike more than I like. I do try with avant garde film and I sort of see the argument and I see the point, but a lot of the time perhaps I just don't get it in some sort of way. I am not really at ease with it, I think, in all truth. So, it is there [in *Now You See It*] because it is historically important. That is very much a book that is not written out of love, that is a completely politically committed book, you know, like *White*. I think there were the books that I wrote out of love, and the books that I wrote out of the political [urge], and they tend not to be the same ones. Which may be, again, why *Heavenly Bodies* works, even *Pastiche*. There is both a reason for writing about them — let's really get to grips with what stars do, let's really clarify what this big term everyone uses is. But at the same time, I loved writing them and I loved the material, and I felt very engaged and fascinated.

I used to teach avant garde film when I was starting out, and underground film, not just lesbian and gay stuff, but Brakhage and Warhol and so on. I taught all of that stuff, and it wasn't just a gay issue there. There was also a feeling, which in a way came from *Screen*, that it was important to write about independent film, that is the term they would use. There was that notion that everything was so contaminated: Hollywood and European art cinema were basically contaminated by capitalist values — and patriarchal values, of course! So that was why it was important to look at films made by the grass roots or some such notion.

JK: *Can we make a jump to gay liberation? In the book* Silver Linings, *which includes your 'Getting over the rainbow' essay, you are described as follows in the notes on contributors: 'Richard Dyer has been active in the gay movement in Britain since it started.' Were you there?*

RD: Well, I think so. I mean, you'd have to ask Jeffrey Weeks, he could 'book, chapter and verse'. I didn't call the first ever Gay Liberation meeting. And of course, before gay liberation, there was the Campaign for Homosexual Equality, which actually went back into the 1950s, in relation to the Wolfenden Report, and I was in my early teens then. So, obviously it depends on what you call 'the homosexual movement.' But if it's Gay Liberation, specifically, I didn't call the first meeting, which was at the LSE in London. I was in the Campaign for Homosexual Equality group in Birmingham, but that felt problematic: it was too reformist, in a way it was too closeted. I hate saying that, because I completely understand why people needed to be closeted. Nonetheless, that's what seemed to be the problem with it. And so that's why I suggested that we form in Birmingham something we called the Gay Action Group, because we thought Gay Liberation was too American, and also too London, and we were very much wanting to be something local. But I was one of the people that set it up and arranged where the first meeting was.

JK: *The statement 'active since it started' also highlights that you always have been an openly gay scholar, something which we now tend to take for granted.*

RD: I was kind of an openly gay student. That was before gay liberation, and before there was any rhetoric about it. It was almost like, well, I couldn't be anything else. I don't know, I always wonder how I appear to other people now, but certainly, I was obvious when I was at St Andrews University. St Andrews University! Of all universities to be obvious in! And then when I went to Cultural Studies, they must have assumed I was gay because of what I was supposedly going to write about, and anyway, I made no secret of it. I remember, one of the first gay magazines in Britain was called *Jeremy*. *Jeremy* sold itself as bisexual, it did have pictures of women, but it had far more pictures of men, and it was obviously gay, really. We had a study room in the Cultural Studies Centre, which had various journals, and I would just slip a couple of copies of *Jeremy* in, implying that alongside *Culture and Society* and *The New Statesman*, there would be *Jeremy* as just another journal to be there. And actually, I was going to be in a photo spread in *Jeremy*. But it folded before that issue was published. Whether I would have put that issue into the Cultural Studies reading room, I do not know. Of course, I could have done the Marilyn Monroe line, and say, 'Well, I needed the money.' When in all honesty it wasn't done for the money. It was paid, but that's not why I did it.

GD: *You were able to balance an activist life, an Adult Education life, and an academic life simultaneously. How do you think the activist life fits with an academic career, and has it become less possible to combine them?*

RD: I do think there was a feeling that academics should not be in an ivory tower, they should not be only talking to each other. It was a very general cultural assumption that you were paid by the state, you had a duty to try to contribute to society. Of course, that has become transformed into the notion of 'impact'; that is now managerialised into this codified notion. But in many ways, it was the same idea as working in the British Film Institute or organising film screenings at the Birmingham Arts Lab of gay films and discussions. It all just seemed part of the same remit of being an academic. I look back and I think it would be more difficult now because it was much more explicitly tied to a political project than 'impact.' Of course, impact is exactly a way of drawing the teeth from all of that kind of activity. There was a time in which if you wrote for something like *The New Statesman* or *Marxism Today*, that could be counted as part of your intellectual activity, whereas now, of course, it would not be because it has all been codified. It would be if it was in *Screen*, but it wouldn't be if it was in *Marxism Today*. I was told the first time I didn't get promoted, that they did think I had written too many things in places like *Gay Left* and *Marxism Today*, and so on. And I never really knew whether that was really saying, 'all this political stuff,' or 'all this queer stuff.'

JK: *Coming back to all the different journals that you have published in: how did you select the venues for your work?*

RD: I did propose pieces to *Gay Left*. I had a relationship with *Marxism Today*; they suggested topics to me. They said, 'Would you like to go to the Diana Ross concert…' so they obviously had a sense that I could write for them. The same with *Sight and Sound*, they had a very good editor for a period. He had the great gift of knowing what his writers would be good to write about. The *Speed* piece ['ACTION!'], actually, was my idea, but a lot of the pieces were him saying, 'Oh, wouldn't you like to write about x?' Very, very seldom have I proposed things. Even the three film classics for the BFI: it wasn't my idea to do them, they always asked. Even *Heavenly Bodies* was a commission, *Stars* was a commission.

GD: *We've asked you to re-read Paul Gilroy's review, published in the* Times Literary Supplement *(1997), of your book* White. *While the review is positive overall, Gilroy does criticise you for seeming 'more or less content that the idea of "race" remains secure as a way of making sense of the world.'*

RD: I take on board a lot of his comments. I am interested in him saying I am better on men than on women. I did think, 'Well, maybe that's true,' although in terms of the amount of space the treatment of women and men is equal and the awareness of gender difference in white representation is also consistent. One of the things I think about *White*, the book, is that it is actually a book of queer theory, because central to it is the problem of heterosexual reproduction. And I don't know whether he picked up on that. Where he says that one should abandon the notion of race and that really, I hold on to the notion of race, that is a really difficult problem in Cultural Studies, cultural analysis.

I gave a paper quite recently, and I read a book which I hadn't read before by Nell Painter, *The History of White People*. She's got this very nice formulation at the end, which is actually about skin colour. But she is saying really, all people are the same colour, it's just that some of them are a bit pinker and some are a bit browner, but it is basically the same colour. And then one of the papers at this conference came from somebody who knew about evolution and was very much sort of supporting that view. So yes, in a way, we should abandon the notion of race, but if you are doing Cultural Studies, you are actually describing the ideas that are in circulation, you are not [solely] talking about biology and science.

I remember Paul Willemen accused me of a similar thing in relation to *Gays and Film*. He said, 'Well everyone is really bisexual, so writing about gays in film is limited,' and lots of queer theory would say the same; that writing about 'gay' or 'lesbian' is sort of narrowing, and you should abandon that notion. And I think [also in relation to race], well, maybe that's where we want to get to, but what I am talking about is where we are and trying to describe how it is we are. So, I don't know what the way out of that is. I think there is a way in which the problem with all Cultural Studies work is that it is describing what is and there is the danger somehow that that then fixes that what *is* is what it must be, and it doesn't really show a way forward to how we could live without a notion of race.

GD: *Could you say a little bit about your shifting relationship to European cinema and how you feel that has altered?*

RD: Well, I think when I started, I was kind of an Americanist effectively, even though I was never interested in film as a way of understanding America. When I worked in the American Studies department [at Keele], I did read some of the American classics that they were teaching and I tried to become more knowledgeable about American history and so on, but that was not my background. I think going to America was, as much as anything, the key experience. Every time I have been to America, I have had a really nice time and yet I have felt like a foreigner. It is not in any way a criticism of America. I just feel more European. After all my first degree was in French, I had also studied German; of course, I was then living in the European Union. I felt that is where my home was, and every time I went anywhere in Europe, whether I spoke the language or not, I felt at home.

What really amazes me is how incredibly un-European British culture is. I looked just this morning, to see what was on at my local art cinema: almost entirely English language films. The people that go to such cinemas are almost certainly absolutely against Brexit, but they are actually not really European in orientation. I suppose I felt that it was important to be European in orientation, not because Europe is any better but it is where I felt at home, and it seemed to me was being undervalued within film studies. Meeting Ginette Vincendeau was a turning point for me, because I realised the whole idea of the popular European was really very important.[2] One of the reasons why Europe was often not really engaged with, in certain quarters anyway, is because it was seen as elitist. It was seen as all kinds of classical music and Ingmar Bergman, all of which I also like. Let's not have an a priori position that only the popular is good, that is just as stupid as that only the elite is good. That is partly why the serial killers book is about European cinema, because it is taking a popular notion – one that's assumed to be about American culture – and saying let's look at it.

I suppose also, it would be wrong of me not to admit that my partner is Italian. But the interest in European cinema and European culture does pre-date that. Obviously, the fact that I now spend half the year in Italy reinforces that sense of European connection. Teaching all over Europe was also very important to me. Though I am at home in the English language in a way I am not in Italian, actually. I think where you are at home is important.

This is an abridged and edited transcription of a Skype conversation held on 1 July 2021.

2. See, on this topic, Richard Dyer and Ginette Vincendeau (eds), *Popular European Cinema*, London and New York: Routledge, 1992.

INDEX

2001, 424
42nd Street, 123, 289
48 Hours, 280
8½, 459, 471
Aashiqui 2, 72, 74–8
Abraham, John, 206
Accattone, 160–1
Adorno, Theodor, 534
Adventures of Priscilla, Queen of the Desert, The, 510
Advise and Consent, 465–6
AIDS, 139–40, 178, 180, 186–7, 334, 345, 353, 488, 512, 523–4
Aimée, Anouk, 460
Aitken, Will, 308
Akerman, Chantal, 310, 355
Alberti, Luis, 479
Alexander Nevsky, 457
All That Heaven Allows, 184–5, 463–4, 466–7
Allan, Maud, 203
Alli, Waheed, 207
Amarcord, 458
Amelio, Gianni, 472
American in Paris, An, 47, 49, 120
American on Holiday, An, 455
Amsterdam International Gay and Lesbian Film Festival, 1
And Soon the Darkness, 364–5, 369
Anders als die Anderen, 373, 376–7, 390
Anderson, Moira, 58
Andrews, Julie, 19, 120, 205, 354
Anger, Kenneth, 299, 316, 318, 508

Anna, 471, 473
Annie Get Your Gun, 118
Another Country, 188–9
Antonioni, Michelangelo, 460, 470
Antropophagus, 299
Appassionatemente, 455
Appeal to the Jews of the World, An, 476
Arabian Nights, 158, 163, 165
Archers, The, 99
Argento, Dario, 333, 354, 470
Arlen, Harold, 291
Armstrong, Louis, 118
Arrowsmith, Pat, 207
Arroyo, José, 485
Arzner, Dorothy, 289, 325
Astaire, Fred, 19, 49–50, 55, 62, 119, 122–4, 271, 325–6, 355, 425, 441
Asti, Adriana, 474
Atasheva, Pera, 478
Attenborough, David, 7
Attenborough, Richard, 126
Attitude, 6, 23
Attitude + Plus, 6–7, 298
Auden, W.H., 207
Audry, Jacqueline, 5

Babuscio, Jack, 140, 496, 501, 524
Bacall, Lauren, 185
Bacalov, Luis, 459
Bach, Johann Sebastian, 453–4
Bacharach, Burt, 38, 43, 91
Bachchan, Abhishek, 206

Bäck, Elmer, 478–80
Bacon, Francis, 207
Bad and the Beautiful, The, 488, 532
Badham, John, 284
Bailey, Pearl, 118
Baldwin, James, 203, 236, 505, 528
Band Wagon, The, 123–4
Bang, Herman, 207
Barbarella, 52, 54
Bardot, Brigitte, 52
Barrage sur le Pacifique, 456
Barry Lyndon, 456
Barthes, Roland, 362, 369
Bassey, Shirley, 33, 204
Báthory, Erzsébet, 200
Battleship Potemkin, 354, 480
Bay of Blood, A, 363
Baywatch, 277
BBC, 7, 39, 62, 251, 253, 412–13, 416, 418–21
Beaton, Cecil, 206
Beauvoir, Simone de, 52, 221
Beavers, Louise, 76
Beethoven, Ludwig van, 373, 378, 386–7
Being White, 217–18
Bellour, Raymond, 488, 506
Bennett, Alan, 207
Benson, George, 93
Bergan, Ronald, 476, 480
Berger, John, 164
Berger, Peter, 245
Bergner, Elisabeth, 495
Bergstein, Eleanor, 290

INDEX

Berkeley, Busby, 120, 289, 322, 421, 443
Betts, Mike, 309
BFI (British Film Institute), 4–6, 9, 302, 398, 531–2, 537
Billy Smart's Circus, 413–15
Birmingham Arts Lab, 9, 12, 21, 53–4, 138–9, 166, 168, 301, 322, 327, 537
Birmingham Free Press, 135–6
Birth of a Nation, The, 119, 504
Blachford, Gregg, 307
Black and White Minstrel Show, The, 420–1
Black Caesar, 410
Black Narcissus, 226
Black Swan, 289
Black, Cilla, 412, 418–19, 528
Blaxploitation, 395, 408, 410, 517
Blow Monkeys, The, 288
Bluebell in Fairyland, 66
Body Politic, The, 6, 14, 140, 180, 496
Bogarde, Dirk, 207, 219, 221–2, 225, 227, 486
Bogart, Humphrey, 63, 265
Bogle, Donald, 119, 169–70
Bollywood, 206
Bonnie and Clyde, 425
Bont, Jan de, 355
Born Yesterday, 23
Bourdin, Guy, 451
Bourne, Matthew, 207
Bourne, Stephen, 85
Bowie, David, 24, 72, 451
Bowles, Paul, 190, 371
Boy George, 502
Boys in the Band, The, 270
Bradshaw, Matt, 488
Brakhage, Stan, 535
Bram Stoker's Dracula, 302, 332–9
Brando, Marlon, 181, 316, 318
Breakfast at Tiffany's, 62, 64
Brecht, Bertolt, 247, 516
Brent, George, 232
Bridges, George, 136, 153, 225
Brief Encounter, 13, 218–19, 398, 409, 485, 508

Brigadoon, 323
Britten, Benjamin, 206
Britton, Andrew, 488, 496–7
Broadway, 48, 51, 64, 123, 286, 291, 379
Brock, Tom, 341
Bronski Beat, 503
Brooks, Romaine, 201
Brown, Rita Mae, 207
Brunsdon, Charlotte, 97, 184
Brunt, Rosalind, 3, 84, 136, 253
Brute Force, 375, 391
Buffy the Vampire Slayer, 198
Bujold, Geneviève, 425
Bullock, Sandra, 355–6
Burke, Solomon, 287–8
Burrows, Elaine, 5
Bush Jnr., George, 295
Butler, Eleanor, 206
Butler, Judith, 23, 72, 276
Byron, Bruce, 318
Byron, Lord, 202, 206

Cabin in the Sky, 118
Caesar, Irving, 291
Cage, John, 206, 371
Cagney, James, 29, 57
Caine, Michael, 485
Calloway, Cab, 118
Calvin Klein, 329, 502
Cameron, Earl, 224
Cammermeyer, Margarethe, 207
Camp, 25–6, 35–6, 67, 71, 90, 135, 139–40, 148, 156–7, 165–6, 194, 204, 301, 347, 352, 398, 464, 478, 488, 492, 496–9, 501
Canterbury Tales, The, 158, 165
Car Wash, 504
Cardinale, Claudia, 474
Carmen, Eric, 288
Caron, Leslie, 183
Carpenter, Edward, 160, 174, 207, 371–2
Carry On Camping, 67
Carry On Cleo, 65
Carry On Constable, 65, 68, 70–1

Carry On Cowboy, 65–6
Carry On Henry, 51, 68
Carry On Nurse, 68–9
Carry On Regardless, 67–8
Carry On Screaming, 65, 67
Carry On Sergeant, 65, 68
Carry On Spying, 65, 67
Carry On Teacher, 68
Carry On Up the Jungle, 65
Carry On Up the Khyber, 65
Carry Ons (film series), 65–6, 70, 293
Carter, Elizabeth, 203, 206
Casanova, 459
Cashman, Michael, 207
Castle, Terry, 204, 205
CCCS (Centre for Contemporary Cultural Studies), 3–6, 8–9, 11, 19, 136, 470, 505, 527–31, 536
Celluloid Closet, The (book), 139, 169–77
Celluloid Closet, The (documentary), 510–11
Cervulle, Maxime, 9
Chalmers, Gloria, 252
Champagne, John, 404, 411
Chandler, Jeff, 181, 501
Channel 4 (four), 84, 106, 293
Channel, Bruce, 288
Chapman Report, The, 51, 52
Charles, Prince, 11, 214–15, 251–3, 263
China Syndrome, The, 53–4
Chopin, Frédéric, 370, 375–7, 382, 386–90
Christensen, Christa Lykke, 453
Christianity, 198, 238, 306, 335–6, 441, 477
Christie, Agatha, 100
Cinema Journal, 13–14, 214, 300, 398–9
Cinematologists, The, 485–6
Citti, Franco, 160, 165
City of Women, The, 459
Clark, Petula, 74, 87
Clary, Julian, 207

542

INDEX

Clayton, Merry, 288
Clément, René, 456–7
Cliffhanger, 354
Clift, Montgomery, 24, 180, 183, 255, 385
Clinton, Hillary, 294
Clooney, Rosemary, 87
Cocteau, Jean, 207, 346
Cohen, Derek, 135, 137
Cohn, Roy, 200
Cole, Nat King, 118
Coles, Honi, 118, 284, 286–7, 289
Colette, 190, 206
Coming Home, 53–4
Connell, Ian, 84, 253
Connery, Sean, 280
Connor, Kenneth, 65, 68
Conrad, Peter, 108–9
Contours, The, 287–8
Cook, Pam, 21–2, 247, 462
Cooper, Gary, 459
Copland, Aaron, 371, 385
Coppola, Francis Ford, 302, 332–9
Corbett, Harry, 67
Corley, Al, 108
Corman, Roger, 424
Coronation Street (book), 6, 83, 99
Coronation Street (television series), 99–104, 107, 198, 533
Cottaging, 67, 154, 156, 168, 524
Coventry Evening Telegraph, 484–5
COVID-19, 12, 14, 86
Coward, Noël, 3, 170, 188, 206–7, 382, 508
Crawford, Joan, 28, 33, 35, 57, 204, 347
Cripps, Thomas, 169–70, 229
Crisp, Quentin, 207
Crosby, Bing, 45, 49
Crossroads, 99–100, 107, 111
Crowley, Aleister, 317
Cruise, Tom, 206, 514
Cukor, George, 30, 488, 500
Culture of Queers, The, 9, 14, 522–4
Curtis, Tony, 181
Cutpurse, Moll, 206

Dahmer, Jeffrey, 200, 512
Dale, Jim, 67
Dall, John, 380
Dallas, 107
Dallesandro, Joe, 205
Dance, 3, 48, 123, 271, 284, 287, 290, 301, 302, 306, 320–7, 438, 446
Dance of the Vampires, 336
Dance, Girl, Dance, 289, 325
Dantzig, Rudi van, 190
Danza Macabra, 338
Daughters of Darkness, 332, 337–8
Davies, Russell T., 207
Davis, Angela, 207
Davis, Bette, 23, 33, 57, 204, 219, 230, 232–3, 496–7, 504–5
Davis, Tricia, 136
Davis, Viola, 463
Day, Doris, 19, 182–4
De Mille, Agnes, 325
De Rais, Gilles, 200
Dean, James, 180, 204–5, 316, 318
Dean, Roy, 348
Death in Venice, 163, 188, 191
Decameron, 165
Defiant Ones, The, 313
DeGeneres, Ellen, 207
Deneuve, Catherine, 206
Depp, Johnny, 205
DES (Department of Education and Skills), 84, 110–11, 113
Desert Hearts, 510–11
Diaghilev, Sergei, 190, 322, 388
Diamond, David, 388
Diamond, Neil, 291, 371
Diana, Princess, 11, 204, 214–15, 251–3
DiCaprio, Lisa, 299
Dickel, Simon, 12
Dickens, Charles, 101, 107
Didion, Joan, 75
Dietrich, Marlene, 162, 190, 205, 494–5
Dirty Dancing, 213, 271, 282–92
Disco, 8, 12, 20, 55, 59, 81–3, 87–96, 146–8, 322–3, 503, 516–17, 534

Dishonored, 190
Divine, 498–9
Dodd, Ken, 38, 42
Dog's Life, A, 457, 459
D'Onofrio, Vincent, 129
Don't Lose Your Head, 65–6
Donahue, Troy, 466
Donovan, Jason, 206
Doonican, Val, 412, 418–20
Dostana, 206
Douglas, Kirk, 488
Dracula, 302, 332–9, 524
Drifters, The, 287
Du Maurier, Daphne, 203
Duffy, Maureen, 207
Dumb Blonde Stereotype, The, 6, 20, 220, 246, 531–2
Dunaway, Faye, 425
Dunham, Katherine, 118, 438
Durbin, Deanna, 58
Dworkin, Andrea, 300, 305
Dynasty, 107–9, 186

Eagle, Angela, 207
Earthquake, 424–5
EastEnders, 198
Eastwood, Clint, 326
Easy Rider, 235, 424
Ebsen, Buddy, 62
Eckstein, Billy, 118
Ehrenberg, Ilya, 476
Ehrenstein, David, 307
El Conde Dracula, 332
Eisenstein in Guanajuato, 399, 476–81
Eisenstein, Sergei, 12, 247, 399, 476–81
Ellington, Duke, 438–40
Ellis, Bret Easton, 451
Ellis, Havelock, 371
Ellis, John, 20, 22
'Entertainment and utopia', 10, 12, 81, 83, 516, 520, 534
Ernesto, 188–94
Evert, Chris, 205
Evil Dead, The, 333
Ewell, Tom, 238

INDEX

Faderman, Lillian, 176, 203
Falcon Crest, 107
Fame, 323–4
Fanon, Frantz, 221–2
Far from Heaven, 399, 462–9
Fashanu, Justin, 207
Fassbinder, Rainer Werner, 184, 463–4, 500
Fatal Attraction, 512
Faust, Beatrice, 308, 310
Fear Eats the Soul, 463
Fellini, Federico, 458–60, 470–1, 473
Femininity, 23, 57, 59, 61, 147–8, 174, 183, 204, 229–30, 270, 325, 370, 372, 379, 388–9, 497, 513, 526
Feminism, 6, 53–4, 57, 96, 218, 272, 491, 495, 506–7
Finian's Rainbow, 323
Fitzgerald, Ella, 55, 60, 118
Five Satins, The, 288
Fonda, Henry, 51, 57, 227
Fonda, Jane, 12, 14, 21, 51–4, 57, 532
Fong, Regina, 207
Ford, Harrison, 356, 359
Ford, John, 497
Foree, Ken, 236
Forster, E.M., 190, 375, 528
Fortunella, 455
Foucault, Michel, 139, 142, 173, 176, 274, 308
Fox, 118
Fox and his Friends, 2, 154–7
Fracassi, Clemente, 471
Frankie Valli and the Four Seasons, 287–8
Franklin, Aretha, 58
Freeman, Morgan, 399, 450
Freud, Sigmund, 108, 176, 259, 274, 308, 350, 362, 369, 506
Friar, Ralph and Natasha, 169–70
Fugitive, The, 354, 359
Funny Girl, 55–7
Funny Lady, 56

Gable, Clark, 74, 116, 185
Ganja and Hess, 334
Garbo, Greta, 74, 205, 346, 495
García Lorca, Federico, 206
Gardner, Ava, 425, 492–3
Garland, Judy, 1, 18–19, 22–4, 25–36, 75, 78, 116, 118, 121, 204, 289, 491–3, 498, 508, 512–13
Garrett, Betty, 121–2, 314, 437–9, 445–6
Garrone, Matteo, 472
Garson, Greer, 116
Gay Action Group, 6, 135, 536
Gay icon, 68, 135, 138, 181, 183, 196–208, 215, 501, 503
Gay Left, 5–7, 11, 82, 135, 503, 537
Gay Left Collective, The, 6–7, 135, 524
Gay Liberation, 6, 68, 138, 149, 158, 172, 200, 492, 509–11, 513, 519–23, 525, 536
Gay Liberation Front, 6, 149, 155, 200
Gay News, 109, 155, 162
Gaye, Marvin, 408–10, 453
Gaynor, Gloria, 91, 94
Gays and Film, 5, 138, 140, 169, 211, 300, 496, 508, 525, 538
Gellautz, Erec, 486
Genet, Jean, 12, 498
Geraghty, Christine, 103–4
Gere, Richard, 206, 347
Gergen, Mary, 275
Gershwin, George, 91, 291
Gerstner, David, 379
Giant, 180
Gibson, Althea, 205
Gide, André, 160, 207
Gielgud, John, 207
Gilbert, Jeremy, 11–12, 83
Gilroy, Paul, 217–18, 222, 537–8
Girl with the Dragon Tattoo, The, 368
Gish, Lillian, 210, 213
Gladrag, 6
Glass Mountain, The, 455, 473
Gledhill, Christine, 22, 395, 532

Glen or Glenda?, 138
Glover, Danny, 357
Godard, Jean-Luc, 516
Godfather, The, 14, 218, 455, 458, 473, 504
Godfather Part II, The, 455, 457–8, 473
Golddiggers of London, The, 421
Gomorra, 472
Gone with the Wind, 219
Good Old Days, The, 416–17
Goodman, Benny, 291
Gordon, Mack, 383
Gorman, Cliff, 270
Gospel According to St. Matthew, The, 160
Gould, Elizabeth, 370–1
Grable, Betty, 40
Granger, Farley, 380–1
Grant, Cary, 326
Grant, Catherine, 137, 488, 516–26
Grayson, Larry, 112, 207
Green, Hughie, 418
Greenaway, Peter, 399, 476, 480–1
Greven, David, 380
Grey, Jennifer, 285, 289–90
Greyson, John, 299, 478
Growing Up Homosexual, 6, 149
Guess Who's Coming to Dinner?, 466
Guetary, Georges, 120
Gunn, Thom, 207

Hall, Radclyffe, 200–1, 204, 207, 495
Hall, Stuart, 3–4, 19, 84, 136, 213, 224–5, 505, 527
Hallam, Paul, 5
Hallelujah!, 289
Hambling, Maggi, 207
Hammerstein II, Oscar, 291
Hancock, Herbie, 92
Handsworth Songs, 279
Hardy, Thomas, 532
Harlem Renaissance, 229, 438, 504
Harris, Rolf, 418, 420
Harris, Theresa, 230

INDEX

Harvey Girls, The, 121, 289
Haskell, Molly, 169–70, 229–30
Hatch, Tony, 38
Hawks, Howard, 183
Hawtrey, Charles, 23, 65–71
Hayes, Isaac, 92
Haymes, Dick, 383
Haynes, Todd, 399, 462–9
Haysbert, Dennis, 463, 466
Hayworth, Rita, 120, 491, 492
Heath, Edward, 146
Heavenly Bodies, 6, 9, 19–20, 22–3, 487, 491, 508, 534–5, 537
Hello, Dolly!, 118, 120, 302
Hemingway, Mariel, 206
Henderson, Lisa, 13–14
Henley, Nancy M., 254, 256
Henry, Lenny, 8
Hepburn, Audrey, 23, 62–3
Hepburn, Katharine, 57, 116
Heston, Charlton, 425
Heterosexuality, 8, 147, 157, 162, 165, 180, 183–6, 192, 194, 205, 215, 218, 249, 267–78, 289, 353, 358, 384–5, 389, 519
Highsmith, Patricia, 204, 206, 457–8
Higson, Andrew, 194
Hill, John, 194, 396
Hirschfeld, Magnus, 174, 207, 360
Hirst, Damien, 451
Hitchcock, Alfred, 379–80, 382–3, 506
Hitler, Adolf, 317–18
Hobsbawm, Eric, 260
Hockney, David, 207
Hoggart, Richard, 4, 9, 84, 100–2, 107, 418, 519, 527, 529
Holiday, Billie, 58, 60, 118, 387
Hollander, Anne, 191
Holliday, Chris, 487
Holliday, Judy, 23
Hollinghurst, Alan, 207
Hollywood, 2, 19, 23, 29, 32, 47, 52, 62–4, 75–7, 81, 85, 94, 100, 118–19, 126, 129, 170–1, 180, 219, 229, 233–4, 238, 255, 271, 281, 291, 326, 342, 344, 370, 379,

Hollywood *cont.*
383, 385, 387, 410, 440, 447, 455, 457, 462, 465, 467, 472–4, 476–7, 480, 485, 497, 508, 512, 515, 535
Homosexuality, 14, 33–6, 138–40, 142, 144, 158, 162, 169–76, 187–8, 194, 200, 202, 249, 267–9, 273, 277–8, 299, 302, 311, 316, 319, 350, 370, 372–3, 375, 378–8, 459, 464–5, 478, 486, 492, 505, 508, 513, 515, 523–4, 528
Hopkins, Gerard Manley, 203, 373
Hopper, Dennis, 354
Horne, Lena, 23, 60, 85, 116–19
Horowitz, Vladimir, 376
Hours of the Day, The, 366, 368–9
Housman, A.E., 203
Howard, Bryce Dallas, 125, 127
Hubbs, Nadine, 378, 382
Hudson, Rock, 1, 14, 139–40, 178–87, 523
Hughes, Langston, 203, 206
Human League, The, 111
Humperdinck, Engelbert, 42
Hunger, The, 334, 338
Hunter, Ross, 184, 463–4
Hunter, Tab, 181
Huxley, Aldous, 358

I Could Go On Singing, 29, 36
Idol Eyes, 347–50
Idol Thoughts, 347, 349–50
Idol Worship, 347–8, 350
Idol, Ryan, 301, 340, 346–9, 353, 508
Imitation of Life, 76, 229, 464–6, 504, 532
Immortal Melodies, 456
In the Heat of the Night, 280
In the Space of a Song, 9
Inch by Inch, 341–3, 345, 352
Interview with the Vampire, 332, 337–8
Isherwood, Christopher, 160, 528

Jacklin, Carol Nagy, 275
Jackson, Michael, 502

Jackson, Millie, 58
Jacobs, Jason, 533
Jacques, Hattie, 65
Jagger, Mick, 39
James, Henry, 190
James, Sidney, 68
Jansson, Tove, 206
Jarman, Derek, 207, 478
Jazz Singer, The, 291–2
Je tu il elle, 310
Jeffreys, Sheila, 270
Jennings, Wade, 30
Jeremy, 6, 155, 536
Jessel, George, 291
Jesus Christ, 160, 197–8, 306, 317–18, 336
Jewel in the Crown, The, 226, 518, 533
Jezebel, 219–21, 227–33, 237, 488, 504
John, Elton, 207
Johnson, Celia, 398
Johnston, Tom, 288
Jolson, Al, 57, 291, 324, 477
Jones, Duane, 235
Jones, Grace, 33, 74, 89, 91, 94
Jones, Jennifer, 425, 496
Jones, Quincy, 92
Jones, Tom, 3, 19, 37–46, 528, 533
Joy, Nicholas, 466
Judy Garland Show, The, 18
Julien, Isaac, 212–13, 301
Jump Cut, 299–300
Jurassic World, 85, 125–31

Kamen, Nick, 329
Karloff, Boris, 235
Kassabian, Anahid, 282, 284
Katz, Jonathan Ned, 270, 273–4
Kawin, Bruce, 362, 368–9
Kay, Jackie, 207
Kazan, Elia, 385
Keele University, 5–6, 8–9, 538
Kelly, Gene, 19, 47–50, 120, 121, 437–41, 445
Kennaway, James, 370, 372, 378, 382

545

INDEX

Kern, Jerome, 38, 291
Kerr, Deborah, 379
Kerr, John, 386
Killing of Sister George, The, 6, 511
Kim Jong-un, 295
King Richard I, 201, 203, 206
King, Barry, 9, 21
King, Billie Jean, 205
King, Carole, 77
King's College London, 9, 516
Kiss of the Vampire, 332, 337–8
Kitchener, Lord (Herbert), 203
Kitt, Eartha, 118
Kitzinger, Celia, 275
Klapp, Orrin E., 19, 211, 247
Kleinhans, Chuck, 300
Klinger, Barbara, 9, 396, 485, 517
Kloss, Ilana, 205
Klute, 53–4
Knight, Gladys, 58
Koehler, Ted, 291
Kohler, Susan, 466
Koivunen, Anu, 83, 411
Kopay, David, 207
Korngold, Erich Wolfgang, 455
Krafft-Ebbing, Richard von, 274
Kristofferson, Kris, 56
Krusenstjerna, Agnes von, 190
Kubrick, Stanley, 456

L.A. Tool and Die, 312–13
L'eroe della strada, 457
La Cage aux Folles, 184
La dolce vita, 9, 12, 394, 398, 456, 459–60, 470–3
La maschera del demonio, 470
La ragazza con la valigia, 474
La strada, 460
Labelle, Patti, 92, 94
Lacan, Jacques, 152, 307–8, 488, 491, 506–7
Ladro di bambini, 472
Lady Gaga, 24, 72–4, 77–8
Lagerlöf, Selma, 206
Lambert, Constant, 383
Landru, 361–2

lang, k.d., 204
Lapathiotis, Napoleon, 190
Lasén, Amparo, 12
Lattuada, Alberto, 459, 471
Lattuada, Felice, 459
Laurents, Arthur, 382
LaValley, Al, 478, 481, 500–2
Lawley, Sue, 251
Lawrence, Amy, 379, 383
Lawrence, Tim, 8, 11–12
Le notti di Cabiria, 460, 471
Leavis, F.R., 108
Lee, Christopher, 338–9
Lee, Peggy, 87
Leinfellner, Stefanie, 6
Leone, Sergio, 470
Leopard, The, 455
Lethal Repetition, 6, 9, 12, 299, 302, 524, 534
Lethal Weapon, 280
Lethal Weapon 3, 354
Levi's, 328, 329, 503
Lewis, Jerry, 291, 419
Liberace, 374, 376, 378
Life on Earth, 7
Light Entertainment, 4, 6, 81, 83, 397, 530, 532
Light from the Second Story Window, The, 72
Lights of Variety, 459
Linsky, Arnold S., 246
Lippmann, Walter, 211, 244–7, 249
Little Richard, 200
Little Women, 387
Llinares, Dario, 2
Locke, Richard, 312
Looking, 13
Lorde, Audre, 207
Loren, Sophia, 471
Love Me Tonight, 289
Lovell, Terry, 83, 90, 152, 304, 306
Lover Come Back, 178–9
Lucker the Necrophagous, 299, 524
Luckmann, Thomas, 245
Lugosi, Bela, 332, 338
Lupino, Ida, 325

Lynn, Vera, 93, 528
Lyon, Phyllis, 207

M, 360–1
MacArthur, Colin, 532
Mack, The, 410
MacKinnon, Catherine, 300
MacLaine, Shirley, 324
MacRae, Gordon, 384
Mädchen in Uniform, 485
Madonna, 24, 72, 204, 206, 514
Magnani, Anna, 471
Magnum, 111
Magnificent Obsession, 140, 184–5, 464
Malone, Dorothy, 185, 431
Man Called 'Autumn Flower', A, 188–9, 194
Mancini, Henry, 458
Manilow, Barry, 352
Mann, Thomas, 190
Mannin, Ethel, 229
Mao Zedong, 45, 326
Mapplethorpe, Robert, 204
Marcuse, Herbert, 95, 217
Margolyes, Miriam, 207
Marie Antoinette, 206
Marlowe, Christopher, 206
Martin, Del, 207
Martini, 4, 385, 423
Martins, Orlando, 224
Marx, Groucho, 324
Marx, Karl, 3, 137, 141, 518
Marxism, 6–8, 11, 27, 29, 100–1, 104, 126, 136, 152, 159, 172, 301, 326, 488–98, 516, 518
Marxism Today, 7–8, 22, 537
Masculinity, 19, 23, 33, 35, 39, 45, 47–8, 68, 74, 128, 139, 147–8, 154, 167, 174, 183, 185, 191, 194, 204–5, 215–16, 256, 259–60, 266, 270, 302, 307–8, 311, 330, 339, 359, 404, 486, 488, 497, 501–4, 526
Masina, Giulietta, 459–60
Mask of Lilith, The, 334

INDEX

Mason, Angela, 207
Mast, Gerald, 123
Mastroianni, Marcello, 459
Mathis, Johnny, 87
Matrix, The, 290
Matter of Images, The, 9–10, 211, 215
Mauresmo, Amelie, 205
Maurice, 188–95, 390, 508
Maurice Williams and the Zodiacs, 287
Mayer, Louis B., 116
McClary, Susan, 387
McCracken, Joan, 118
McCrindle, Jean, 83
McDonald, Paul, 9, 22
McElhaney, Joe, 487–9, 490–507
McIntosh, Mary, 150, 172, 525
McKellen, Ian, 207
McKenna, Virginia, 224
McQueen, Steve, 185, 399, 425–7
Mead, Margaret, 310
Medhurst, Andy, 2
Medley, Bill, 288
Meet Me in St. Louis, 35, 485
Melnick, Jeffrey, 290–2
Melon, 288
Mercer, Kobena, 212–13, 217
Merck, Mandy, 213, 532
Merman, Ethel, 205–6
Meteor and Shadow, 188–90
Meyer, Laverne, 3
MGM, 30, 35, 49, 75, 116, 118–21, 123–4, 385, 387, 438, 533
Michael, George, 207
Michelangelo, 258–9
Mickey & Sylvia, 286, 288
Midnight Cowboy, 424
Milk, Harvey, 207
Miller, Ann, 121–3, 399, 436–47
Miller, D.A., 379–80
Miller, Jonathan, 107
Mina (Anna Maria Mazzini), 204
Mineo, Sal, 180
Minnelli, Liza, 57
Minnelli, Vincente, 57, 355, 379, 388, 424, 435

Minogue, Kylie, 204
Monkhouse, Bob, 68, 418
Monroe, Marilyn, 20–1, 23–4, 238–9, 491–2, 504, 508, 514–15, 532, 536
Moonlight, 486
Moore, Grace, 384–5
Moore, Julianne, 462–3, 466
Moore, Marianne, 204
Moorhead, Agnes, 207
Morin, Edgar, 19
Morley, David, 97, 98, 527
Moross, Jerome, 409
Morricone, Ennio, 457
Motown, 3–4, 58, 87
Mozart, Wolfgang Amadeus, 378, 386–90, 460
Mrs Dale's Diary, 69–70
Mulvey, Laura, 164–5, 462
Muñoz, José Esteban, 212–13
Munshin, Jules, 121, 437, 439–40, 442–5
Murnau, Friedrich Wilhelm, 332, 355, 488, 500
Murray, Pete, 418
Muscle Beach, 309
My Fair Lady, 62, 64

Napoleon, 44
National Portrait Gallery, 23, 138, 203, 208, 215
Nationwide, 97–8, 251
Nature Morte, 360–1, 369
Navratilova, Martina, 200, 205
Navy Blue, 313
Nazzari, Amedeo, 471
NECS (European Network for Cinema and Media Studies), 475, 488
Nee Jathaga Nenundali, 72
Netflix, 86, 403
Never Take No for an Answer, 460, 473
Newman, Paul, 257–8, 399, 424–7
NFT (National Film Theatre), 4–5, 138, 211, 525
Nicholas Brothers, The, 118, 441

Nielsen, Asta, 495
Night of the Living Dead, 219–20, 229, 233–8, 488, 504
Nighthawks, 6
Nijinksy, Vaslav, 189, 322
Nikos underwear, 328–30
Nilsen, Dennis, 200
Nine Inch Nails, 451, 452
Nino Rota, 6, 9, 473, 518, 534–5
Nixon, David, 418
Nkoli, Simon, 207
Nosferatu, 332, 338
Novello, Ivor, 206
Now You See It, 9, 12, 508, 535
Nureyev, Rudolph, 206

O'Grady, Paul, 207
O'Hara, Maureen, 289, 325
Obama, Barack, 214, 295
Oh Boy!, 256, 258, 263
Oklahoma!, 121
Oldfield, Julian, 3
Oldman, Gary, 334, 335
Olivia, 188
On A Clear Day You Can See Forever, 435
On the Town, 47–9, 85, 120–1, 325, 399, 436–47
Once Upon a Time in the West, 3, 457, 470
One Night of Love, 384
Only Entertainment, 9, 11, 81, 85, 299
Orbach, Jerry, 290
Ordinary People, 219
Orton, Joe, 204, 207

Paglia, Camille, 513
Painter, Nell, 538
Paradise Garage, 8
Paramount, 62, 64, 118, 458
Parker, Al, 169, 313–14
Parker, Charlie, 453
Parker, Dorothy, 75
Parris, Matthew, 207
Parton, Dolly, 206
Pasolini, Pier Paolo, 138, 158–65, 500

547

INDEX

Pastiche, 9, 534–5
Pastiche, 346, 352, 455, 462–3, 465, 467–9, 519, 522
Paulin, Scott D., 380, 382–3
Payton, Lou, 227
Peck, Ron, 5, 6
Penis/phallus, 12, 19, 41–3, 92, 93, 259, 263–6, 271, 313, 317–18, 331, 344–5, 349–51, 359, 399, 476–80, 514
Pepla, 471, 518
Peppa Pig, 487
Peppino e Violetta, 473
Perkins, Anthony, 207
Perkins, T.E., 245–6, 248
Perkins, V.F., 248, 405
Petty, Miriam J., 214
Philadelphia, 510
Philbin, Maggie, 112
Phranc, 204
Piaf, Édith, 74
Pidduck, Julianne, 9
Pillow Talk, 182–4
Pines, Jim, 169–70, 227–8, 244
Pink Flamingos, 138
Pirate, The, 36, 48–9, 121
Pitt, Brad, 450
Playboy, 54, 164, 256
Playguy, 6, 135, 155
Plein soleil, 457
Poitier, Sidney, 219, 260, 280, 466
Polanski, Roman, 336
Ponsonby, Sarah, 206
Popular Arts, The, 84, 527, 529
Pornography, 1, 72, 151, 264, 271, 299–301, 304–15, 318, 330, 340–53, 404, 478–9, 487–8, 493, 495–6, 515
Porter, Cole, 38, 91, 94, 188, 371, 378, 385
Portman, Natalie, 289
Postman Always Rings Twice, The, 532
Poulenc, Francis, 370, 378, 382–3, 388, 390
Powell, Eleanor, 441
Powell, Rachel, 4

Powertool, 340–1, 348
Pratt, Chris, 125, 128
Prentiss, Paula, 183
Presley, Elvis, 40, 87, 204
Price, Lonny, 290
Prince, 502
Prokofiev, Sergei, 457
Proust, Marcel, 190, 388
Pulver, Jim, 341, 342, 343
Purdon, Noel, 159

Quaid, Dennis, 463, 466
Queen Anne, 201, 206
Question Time, 113
¡Que viva México!, 476
Quinn, Jeff, 341, 343

Rainer, Yvonne, 322
Raphaelson, Samson, 291
Ravel, Maurice, 377–8, 382, 388–9
Ray, Gene Anthony, 323–4
Reagan, Ronald, 146, 151, 234
Reckless Moment, The, 463, 465, 467
Red Detachment of Women, The, 326–7
Redding, Otis, 287–8
Redford, Robert, 55, 532
Redgrave, Michael, 57
Redgrave, Vanessa, 57
Reeves, Keanu, 205, 334–5, 348, 354–9, 387
Reeves, Steve, 181
Renault, Mary, 204
Resonancias, 12
Rettenmund, Matthew, 8, 23, 488, 508–15
Reve, Gerard, 190
Rhapsody in Blue, 291
Rhodes, Cynthia, 283
Rice, Anne, 332
Rich, Adrienne, 272–3
Rich, B. Ruby, 140
Richard, Cliff, 39
Riefenstahl, Leni, 357
Rimbaud, Arthur, 190, 503
Ripploh, Frank, 167
Rising Sun, 280

Riviere, Joan, 72
Robbins, Jerome, 325
Robert Brothers' Circus, The, 413–15
Robeson, Paul, 23, 118, 508
Robinson, Bill, 118–19, 123, 326, 441
Robinson, Gene, 207
Rocco and His Brothers, 161, 395, 400–2, 408, 456, 470, 473
Roger, 309, 346
Rogers, Ginger, 119, 271, 326, 355
Röhm, Ernst, 200
Rolling Stones, The, 87, 147
Roma, 162, 401, 460
Romanticismo, 471
Romero, George, 233, 337
Ronettes, The, 287
Rooney, Mickey, 318
Rope, 370, 379–82, 388–91
Rorem, Ned, 371, 382, 388
Rosen, Marjorie, 169–No170
Ross, Diana, 14, 22–3, 33, 58–61, 94, 219, 491, 516, 537
Ross, Gaylen, 236
Rossellini, Robert, 401, 460, 472
Rota, Nino, 399, 455–61, 473
Roundtree, Richard, 261
Rousseau, Jean-Jacques, 3, 212, 240–3
Rowberry, John, 342
Rózsa, Miklós, 455
RuPaul's Drag Race, 486
Russo, Vito, 139–40, 169–77, 510, 524

Saba, Umberto, 190
Sabrina Fair, 62, 63, 64
Sackville-West, Vita, 190, 204, 206
Sade, Marquis de, 66
Sand, George, 206
Sappho, 155, 203, 206
Sargent, Dave, 524
Sarony, Napoleon, 196, 197
Sartre, Jean-Paul, 3, 221
Saturday Night Fever, 94–5, 271, 284, 289, 323

548

INDEX

Satyricon, 459, 471, 473
Scargill, Arthur, 294
Schober, Anna, 486
Schubert, Franz, 206, 387
Schütz, Alfred, 404, 411, 519
Schwarzenegger, Arnold, 262–3, 356, 359
SCMS (Society for Cinema and Media Studies), 13, 485, 517–18, 520
Scorpio Rising, 12, 299, 316–19
Scott, Hazel, 118
Screen, 2, 212–13, 506, 520, 531–2, 535, 537
Screen Education Notes, 19
Seagal, Steven, 290, 356
Seagers, Will, 312–14
Searchers, The, 497, 504
Sedgwick, Eve, 398
Sennett, Richard, 26
Sergeant, Alex, 487
Seton, Marie, 476, 478, 481
Seven, 9, 280, 303, 398–9, 448–54, 512
Seven Year Itch, The, 20, 238, 239
Seyrig, Delphine, 338
Shaft, 261, 410
Shakespeare, William, 124, 199, 206, 293, 317
Sharif, Omar, 55
Sheldon, Caroline, 525
Shepherd, Simon, 1, 300–1, 487
Shirelles, The, 287, 288
Shore, Dinah, 384
Shore, Howard, 451
Show Boat, 291
Sight and Sound, 23, 137, 302, 531, 537
Silence of the Lambs, The, 451, 512
Silk Stockings, 122
Silvers, Phil, 120
Simba, 219–27, 237
Sims, Joan, 68
Sinatra, Frank, 40, 60, 75, 121, 181, 387, 437, 439, 445
Singin' in the Rain, 48

Single White Female, 451
Sirk, Douglas, 140, 183–4, 229, 433, 462–6
Sleepless in Seattle, 277, 515
Sliver, 451
Smith, Bessie, 206
Smith, Chris, 207
Smyth, Cherry, 301
Smyth, Ethel, 207
Snipes, Wesley, 280, 357
Soap, 7
Soap opera, 55, 83, 99, 102–3, 107, 277, 305, 464
'Social Values of Entertainment and Show Business' (PhD dissertation), 3–4, 19, 22, 81, 397–8, 528–9, 532
Solomon, Simeon, 207
Sombre, 366, 368–9
Some Like It Hot, 387
Sound of Music, The, 120, 354, 528
South Sea Sinner, 376, 391
Spain, Nancy, 204, 207
Speed, 302, 354–9, 537
Spender, Dale, 254
Spinazzola, Vittorio, 471
Springfield, Dusty, 39, 206
St. Johns, Adela Rogers, 75
Stacey, Jackie, 398–9, 525
Stallone, Sylvester, 347, 354, 356
Stam, Robert, 488
Stamp, Terence, 165
Stanwyck, Barbara, 57
Star Dossier One: Marilyn Monroe, 20–1, 532
Star Is Born, A (1937), 72, 74–7
Star Is Born, A (1954), 22, 24, 25, 28, 30, 34–6, 72, 75–8
Star Is Born, A (1976), 24, 56, 72, 75–7
Star Is Born, A (2018), 24, 72–8
Star Maker, The, 183
Stars, 6, 9–10, 19–22, 24, 508, 531, 537
Steele, Barbara, 338
Steiger, Rod, 280

Stein, Gertrude, 190, 203, 495
Stereotypes, 175, 211, 220, 244–6, 249, 521
Stewart, James, 104, 379–80, 383
Stonewall, 510
Straayer, Chris, 495
Strachey, Lytton, 190
Stranger in the Land, 375
Strauss, Richard, 372
Strayhorn, Billy, 206, 371
Streisand, Barbra, 18–20, 22, 24, 33, 55–7, 60, 75–7, 204–5, 290, 435, 491, 513
Stryker, Jeff, 205, 341, 348
Summer Stock, 35, 289
Summer, Donna, 20–1, 55, 58, 60, 80, 94, 147, 503
Summerskill, Ben, 207
Sunday, Bloody Sunday, 6
Superfly, 410
Suspiria, 333, 470
Swayze, Patrick, 284–5, 288
Sweet Charity, 324, 533
Sweet Sweetback's Baadasssss Song, 410
Swingtime, 323, 325–6
Symphony on a Love Song, 455

Take That, 352
Talbot, Catherine, 203, 206
Talbot, Mary Anne, 206
Talented Mr. Ripley, The, 457
Tall Story, 51–2
Tarnished Angels, The, 184–5
Tasker, Yvonne, 357
Taste the Blood of Dracula, 332, 338
Tatchell, Peter, 207
Taxi zum Klo, 138, 166–8
Taylor, Elizabeth, 23, 180
Tchaikovsky, Pyotr Ilyich, 94, 206, 375, 378
Tea and Sympathy, 370, 372, 379, 384–6, 389–91, 465
Temple, Shirley, 119, 514
Temptations, The, 92
Tennyson, Alfred, 206
Tenth Moon, The, 377, 388

549

INDEX

Terzieff, Laurent, 160
Thank God It's Friday, 96, 323
That's Entertainment! (unpublished monograph), 4, 529
That's Entertainment!, 116, 118, 120, 121, 124
That's Entertainment! III, 118–19, 121–4
Thatcher, Margaret, 136, 146
Thelma & Louise, 512
Theorem, 163, 165
This Is Tom Jones, 19, 37–40, 528
Thomas Crown Affair, The, 425
Thomas, Danny, 291
Thomas, Gary C., 370, 376, 383
Thomson, Virgil, 371, 388
Tipton, Billy, 204
Toksvig, Sandi, 207
Tom of Finland, 203, 501
Tomelty, Joseph, 224
Tomorrow's World, 112
Top Hat, 119, 271
Top of the Pops, 111–12
Torso, 349, 488, 508–15
Total star text, 20, 29, 396
Totò, 457, 471
Tout Va Bien, 54
Towering Inferno, The, 12, 399, 423–8
Trevorrow, Colin, 126
Trouble Man, 395, 408–10, 453
Troubridge, Una, 201
Truck Turner, 410
Trump, Donald, 214, 293–5
Tucker, Sophie, 291
Turing, Alan, 203, 207
Turner, Graeme, 531
Turner, Lana, 2, 12, 229, 488, 491–3, 532
Tyler, Parker, 169

Un Chant d'Amour, 12
Underground cinema, 1, 300, 312, 424, 535
Under Siege, 354, 357
University of St Andrews, 3, 6, 9, 212, 536

University of Warwick, 5–6, 8–9, 485, 533
Up the Sandbox, 55
Uses of Literacy, The, 84, 100, 102–4, 107, 418

Vaccaro, Brenda, 184
Vadim, Roger, 51, 52, 53, 54
Valli, Alida, 287–8, 471
Vallone, Raf, 471
Van Damme, Jean-Claude, 356, 359
Vaughan, Sarah, 49, 118
Verginelli, Vinci, 460
Verlaine, Paul, 190, 203
Versace, Gianni, 207
Very Special Favor, A, 183
Very Special View, A, 349–50, 353
Victim, 486, 487
Victor/Victoria, 184, 495
Village People, 93–4, 148
Villarejo, Amy, 2, 6, 12
Vincendeau, Ginette, 137, 475, 539
Visconti, Luchino, 206, 402, 455, 460, 470

Wagner, Richard, 372, 375
Walk on the Wild Side, 9, 51–2
Walker, Alexander, 184
Wallis, Mick, 1, 300–1, 487
Walter, Aubrey, 149
Walters, Margaret, 263, 485
Wanted, 313–14
Warhol, Andy, 207, 535
Warner Bros., 219, 291, 385
Warnes, Jennifer, 288
Waterloo, 456
Waters, Ethel, 118
Waters, Sarah, 207
Watney, Simon, 23, 149, 301, 353, 523
Waugh, Thomas, 180, 183, 299, 345, 478, 481
Way We Were, The, 55–7
Wayne, John, 28, 35, 292, 326, 497
Weaver, Sigourney, 357
Weekend, 487

Weeks, Jeffrey, 172, 187, 536
Wells, Mary, 58
West Side Story, 325, 436
West, Mae, 33
Wham!, 502
Whannel, Paddy, 84, 527
What Price Hollywood?, 72–6
What's Up Doc?, 57
White, 9–10, 210, 214, 513, 517–19, 535, 537–8
White, Patricia, 485
Whiteness, 2, 8, 10, 23, 85, 128, 212–30, 235–8, 280, 292, 295, 504, 513, 517–19
Whitfield, June, 68
Whitman, Walt, 206, 501
Wilde, 189–90
Wilde, Oscar, 160, 190, 196–7, 200–1, 203, 206, 373, 376, 388, 522
Wilder, Billy, 62
Wilkinson, Sue, 275
Willemen, Paul, 138, 158, 538
Williams, Christopher, 532
Williams, Kenneth, 65, 68, 70, 71, 204, 412
Williams, Linda, 259–60, 299, 344–5, 352, 501, 515
Williams, Raymond, 2
Willie Dynamite, 410
Willis, Bruce, 290, 356
Wilson, Angus, 528
Windsor, Barbara, 68
Without Pity, 455
Wittig, Monique, 272, 273
Wizard of Oz, The, 116
Wolff, Charlotte, 174
Wolff, Janet, 500
Wolfmier, Rick, 309
Wollen, Peter, 5, 429, 500
Wonder, Stevie, 94
Wong, B.D., 129
Wood, Robin, 5, 21, 138, 158–60, 163, 233–4, 236, 405
Woods, Gregory, 478
Woolf, Virginia, 190, 206

Working Papers in Cultural Studies, 3, 19, 528
Wriothesley, Henry, 199, 206
Written on the Wind, 184, 185, 431, 464
Wyman, Jane, 185

Xena: Warrior Princess, 198

Young, Will, 207
Yourcenar, Marguerite, 190, 203–4

Zappacosta, 288
Zurlini, Valerio, 47